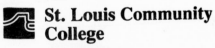

DIFFUSION OF INNOVATIONS

Fourth Edition

DIFFUSION OF INNOVATIONS

Fourth Edition

EVERETT M. ROGERS

THE FREE PRESS
New York   London   Toronto   Sydney   Tokyo   Singapore

The Free Press
A Division of Simon & Schuster Inc.
866 Third Avenue, New York, N.Y. 10022

Printed in the United States of America

printing number

1 2 3 4 5 6 7 8 9 10

Library of Congress Cataloging-in-Publication Data

Rogers, Everett M.
    Diffusion of innovations / Everett M. Rogers—4th ed.
       p.   cm.
    Includes bibliographical references and indexes.
    ISBN 0-02-874074-2 (cloth).—ISBN 0-02-926671-8 (paper)
    1. Diffusion of innovations.   2. Diffusion of innovations—Study and teaching—History.
I. Title.
HM101.R57   1995   94-24947
303.48′4—dc20   CIP

The first edition of this book, by Everett M. Rogers, was published as *Diffusion of Innovations*; the second edition, by Everett M. Rogers with F. Floyd Shoemaker, was published as *Communication of Innovations: A Cross-Cultural Approach*; the third edition, by Everett M. Rogers, was published as *Diffusion of Innovations*.

CONTENTS

PREFACE

The first edition of this book, *Diffusion of Innovations*, was published in 1962. At the time, there were 405 publications about this topic. The second edition (and revision), *Communication of Innovations: A Cross-Cultural Approach* (co-authored with F. Floyd Shoemaker), was published in 1971, nine years later. By then the number of diffusion publications had quadrupled to about 1,500. Twelve years later, when the third edition, *Diffusion of Innovations*, appeared, the total number of diffusion publications more than doubled again, to 3,085. Today, another dozen years later, the total number of diffusion publications approaches 4,000. No other field of behavior science research represents more effort by more scholars in more disciplines in more nations. The present book is based on a broader foundation of diffusion research than the three earlier editions.

This book is both (1) a revision of the theoretical framework and the research evidence supporting this updated model of diffusion, and (2) a new intellectual venture, in that new concepts and new theoretical viewpoints are introduced. The stream of diffusion scholarship over the past fifty years or so represents both similarities and differences, continuities and discontinuities, and so must my four books, each published a decade or so apart. By no means, however, do I seek only to synthesize the important findings from past research; I also strive herein to criticize this work (including my own), and to lay out directions for the future that are different from the past. I titled the present book *Diffusion of Innovations* to identify it with the fifty-year sequential tradition of diffusion studies marked by my 1962 book of the same title.

Most diffusion studies prior to 1962 were conducted in the United States and Europe. In the period between the first and second editions of my diffusion book, during the 1960s, an explosion occurred in the number of diffusion investigations conducted in the developing countries of Latin America, Africa, and Asia. The classical diffusion model was usefully applied to the process of development that was a priority for these nations. In fact, the diffusion approach was a natural framework in which to evaluate the impact of development programs in agriculture, family planning, public health, and nutrition. In studying the diffusion of innovations in developing nations, I gradually realized that certain limitations existed in the diffusion framework. In some cases, development programs outran the diffusion model on which they were originally based. Certain modifications thus were made in the classical diffusion model.

The present book also differs from its predecessors in that it reflects a much more critical stance. During the past thirty years or so, diffusion research has grown to be widely recognized, applied, and admired, but it has also been subjected to constructive and destructive criticism. This criticism is in large part a result of the stereotyped and limited ways in which many diffusion scholars have defined the scope and method of their field of study. Once diffusion researchers became an "invisible college," ° they began to limit unnecessarily the ways in which they went about studying the diffusion of innovations. Such standardization of approaches, especially in recent decades, has begun to constrain the intellectual progress of diffusion research.

Most past diffusion studies have been based on a linear model of communication, the process by which messages are transferred from a source to a receiver. Such a one-way view of human communication accurately describes certain types of communication; many kinds of diffusion do indeed consist of one individual, such as a change agent, informing a potential adopter about a new idea. But other types of diffusion are more accurately described by a convergence model, in which communication is defined as a process in which the participants create and share information with one another to reach a mutual understanding (Rogers and Kincaid, 1981). In the present book we seek to show the improved understanding that can be achieved by conceptualizing certain kinds of diffusion in light of this convergence model. This emphasis on diffusion as information-exchange among participants in a communication process is found particularly in Chapter 8 on diffusion networks.

°*An invisible college* is an informal network of researchers who form around an intellectual paradigm to study a common topic.

The present book makes use of the important concepts of uncertainty and information. *Uncertainty* is the degree to which a number of alternatives are perceived with respect to the occurrence of an event and the relative probabilities of these alternatives. Uncertainty motivates an individual to seek information. *Information* is a difference in matter-energy that affects uncertainty in a situation where a choice exists among a set of alternatives (Rogers and Kincaid).

One kind of uncertainty is generated by an *innovation*, defined as an idea, practice, or object that is perceived as new by an individual or another unit of adoption. An innovation presents an individual or an organization with a new alternative or alternatives, with new means of solving problems. But the probabilities of the new alternatives being superior to previous practice are not exactly known by the individual problem solvers. Thus, they are motivated to seek further information about the innovation to cope with the uncertainty that it creates.

Information about an innovation is often sought from near-peers, especially information about their subjective evaluations of the innovation. This information exchange about a new idea occurs through a convergence process involving interpersonal networks. The diffusion of innovations is essentially a social process in which subjectively perceived information about a new idea is communicated. The meaning of an innovation is thus gradually worked out through a process of social construction.

My thinking and writing about the diffusion of innovations has benefitted a great deal in recent years from my collaboration with three hot young diffusion scholars: James W. Dearing of the Department of Communication at Michigan State University, Arvind Singhal of the School of Interpersonal Communication at Ohio University, and Thomas W. Valente of the Center for Communication Programs, School of Hygiene and Public Health, Johns Hopkins University. Professors Dearing, Singhal, and Valente read and critiqued a penultimate draft of this book, a review process from which it emerged improved.

Throughout the present book we seek to represent a healthily critical stance. We do not need "more of the same" diffusion research. The challenge for diffusion scholars of the future is to move beyond the proven methods and models of the past, to recognize their shortcomings and limitations, and to broaden their conceptions of the diffusion of innovations. We offer this fourth edition as one step toward this important goal.

Everett M. Rogers
Albuquerque, New Mexico

DIFFUSION OF INNOVATIONS

Fourth Edition

1

ELEMENTS OF DIFFUSION

> There is nothing more difficult to plan, more doubtful of success,
> nor more dangerous to manage than the creation of a new order
> of things. . . . Whenever his enemies have the ability to attack the
> innovator they do so with the passion of partisans, while the oth-
> ers defend him sluggishly, so that the innovator and his party alike
> are vulnerable.
>
> —Niccolò Machiavelli, *The Prince*

Getting a new idea adopted, even when it has obvious advantages, is often very difficult. Many innovations require a lengthy period, often of
many years, from the time they become available to the time they are
widely adopted. Therefore, a common problem for many individuals and
organizations is how to speed up the rate of diffusion of an innovation.

The following case illustration provides insight into some common difficulties facing diffusion campaigns.

Water Boiling in a Peruvian Village:
Diffusion That Failed

The public health service in Peru attempts to introduce innovations to villagers to improve their health and lengthen their lives. This change agency
encourages people to install latrines, to burn garbage daily, to control house
flies, to report cases of infectious diseases, and to boil drinking water. These
innovations involve major changes in thinking and behavior for Peruvian villagers, who do not understand the relationship of sanitation to illness. Wa-

---

ter boiling is an especially important health practice for villagers in Peru. Unless they boil their drinking water, patients who are cured of infectious diseases in village medical clinics often return within a month to be treated again for the same disease.

A two-year water boiling campaign conducted in Los Molinas, a peasant village of 200 families in the coastal region of Peru, persuaded only eleven housewives to boil water. From the viewpoint of the public health agency, the local health worker, Nelida, had a simple task: to persuade the house-wives of Los Molinas to add water boiling to their pattern of daily behavior. Even with the aid of a medical doctor, who gave public talks on water boil-ing, and fifteen village housewives who were already boiling water before the campaign, Nelida's diffusion campaign failed. To understand why, we need to take a closer look at the culture, the local environment, and the in-dividuals in Los Molinas.

Most residents of Los Molinas are peasants who work as field hands on local plantations. Water is carried by can, pail, gourd, or cask. The three sources of water in Los Molinas include a seasonal irrigation ditch close to the village, a spring more than a mile away from the village, and a public well whose water most villagers dislike. All three sources are subject to pollution at all times and show contamination whenever tested. Of the three sources, the irrigation ditch is the most commonly used. It is closer to most homes, and the villagers like its taste.

Although it is not feasible for the village to install a sanitary water system, the incidence of typhoid and other water-borne diseases could be greatly re-duced by boiling the water before it is consumed. During her two-year cam-paign in Los Molinas, Nelida made several visits to every home in the village but devoted especially intensive efforts to twenty-one families. She visited each of these selected families between fifteen and twenty-five times; eleven of these families now boil their water regularly.

What kinds of persons do these numbers represent? We describe three village housewives—one who boils water to obey custom, one who was per-suaded to boil water by the health worker, and one of the many who rejected the innovation—in order to add further insight into the process of diffusion.

Mrs. A: Custom-Oriented Adopter. Mrs. A is about forty and suffers from a sinus infection. The Los Molinas villagers call her a "sickly one." Each morning, Mrs. A boils a potful of water and uses it throughout the day. She has no understanding of germ theory, as explained by Nelida; her motiva-tion for water boiling is a complex local custom of "hot" and "cold" distinctions. The basic principle of this belief system is that all foods, liquids, medicines, and other objects are inherently hot or cold, quite apart from their actual temperature. In essence, hot-cold distinctions serve as a series of avoidances and approaches in such behavior as pregnancy, child-rearing, and the health-illness system.

Boiled water and illness are closely linked in the norms of Los Molinas; by custom, only the ill use cooked, or "hot" water. Once an individual becomes ill, it is unthinkable to eat pork (very cold) or drink brandy (very hot). Extremes of hot and cold must be avoided by the sick; therefore, raw water, which is perceived to be very cold, must be boiled to make it appropriate to consume.

Villagers learn from early childhood to dislike boiled water. Most can tolerate cooked water only if a flavoring, such as sugar, cinnamon, lemon, or herbs, is added. Mrs. A likes a dash of cinnamon in her drinking water. The village belief system involves no notion of bacteriorological contamination of water. By tradition, boiling is aimed at eliminating the "cold" quality of unboiled water, not the harmful bacteria. Mrs. A drinks boiled water in obedience to local norms, because she perceives herself as ill.

Mrs. B: Persuaded Adopter. The B family came to Los Molinas a generation ago, but they are still strongly oriented toward their birthplace in the Andes Mountains. Mrs. B worries about lowland diseases that she feels infest the village. It is partly because of this anxiety that the change agent, Nelida, was able to convince Mrs. B to boil water.

Nelida is a friendly authority to Mrs. B (rather than a "dirt inspector" as she is seen by other housewives), who imparts useful knowledge and brings protection. Mrs. B not only boils water but also has installed a latrine and has sent her youngest child to the health center for a checkup.

Mrs. B is marked as an outsider in the community of Los Molinas by her highland hairdo and stumbling Spanish. She will never achieve more than marginal social acceptance in the village. Because the community is not an important reference group to her, Mrs. B deviates from village norms on health innovations. With nothing to lose socially, Mrs. B gains in personal security by heeding Nelida's advice. Mrs. B's practice of boiling water has no effect on her marginal status. She is grateful to Nelida for teaching her how to neutralize the danger of contaminated water, which she perceives as a lowland peril.

Mrs. C: Rejector. This housewife represents the majority of Los Molinas families who were not persuaded by the efforts of the change agents during their two-year water-boiling campaign. In spite of Nelida's repeated explanations, Mrs. C does not understand germ theory. How, she argues, can microbes survive in water that would drown people? Are they fish? If germs are so small that they cannot be seen or felt, how can they hurt a grown person? There are enough real threats in the world to worry about—poverty and hunger—without bothering about tiny animals one cannot see, hear, touch, or smell. Mrs. C's allegiance to traditional village norms is at odds with the boiling of water. A firm believer in the hot-cold superstition, she feels that only the sick must drink boiled water.

Why Did the Diffusion of Water Boiling Fail?

This intensive two-year campaign by a public health worker in a Peruvian village of 200 families, aimed at persuading housewives to boil drinking water, was largely unsuccessful. Nelida was able to encourage only about 5 percent of the population, eleven families, to adopt the innovation. The diffusion campaign in Los Molinas failed because of the cultural beliefs of the villagers. Local tradition links hot foods with illness. Boiling water makes water less "cold" and hence, appropriate only for the sick. But if a person is not ill, the individual is prohibited by village norms from drinking boiled water. Only individuals who are unintegrated into local networks risk defying community norms on water boiling. An important factor regarding the adoption rate of an innovation is its compatibility with the values, beliefs, and past experiences of individuals in the social system. Nelida and her superiors in the public health agency should have understood the hot-cold belief system, as it is found throughout Peru (and in most nations of Latin America, Africa, and Asia). Here is an example of an indigenous knowledge system that caused the failure of a development program.

Nelida's failure demonstrates the importance of interpersonal networks in the adoption and rejection of an innovation. Socially an outsider, Mrs. B was marginal to the Los Molinas community, although she had lived there for several years. Nelida was a more important referent for Mrs. B than were her neighbors, who shunned her. Anxious to secure social prestige from the higher-status Nelida, Mrs. B adopted water boiling, not because she understood the correct health reasons, but because she wanted to obtain Nelida's approval. Thus we see that the diffusion of innovations is a social process, as well as a technical matter.

Nelida worked with the wrong housewives if she wanted to launch a self-generating diffusion process in Los Molinas. She concentrated her efforts on village women like Mrs. A and Mrs. B. Unfortunately, they were perceived as a sickly one and a social outsider, and were not respected as social models of appropriate water-boiling behavior by the other women. The village opinion leaders, who could have activated local networks to spread the innovation, were ignored by Nelida.

How potential adopters view the change agent affects their willingness to adopt new ideas. In Los Molinas, Nelida was perceived differently by lower- and middle-status housewives. Most poor families saw the health worker as a "snooper" sent to Los Molinas to pry for dirt and to press already harassed housewives into keeping cleaner homes. Because the lower-status housewives had less free time, they were unlikely to talk with Nelida about water boiling. Their contacts outside the community were limited, and as a result, they saw the technically proficient Nelida with eyes bound by the social horizons and traditional beliefs of Los Molinas. They distrusted this outsider, whom they perceived as a social stranger. Nelida, who was middle class by Los Molinas standards, was able to secure more positive results from housewives whose socioeconomic level and cultural background were more similar to hers. This tendency for more effective communication to occur with those who are more similar to a change agent occurs in most diffusion campaigns.

Nelida was too "innovation-oriented" and not "client-oriented" enough. Unable to put herself in the role of the village housewives, her attempts at persuasion failed to reach her clients because the message was not suited to their needs. Nelida did not begin where the villagers were; instead she talked to them about germ theory, which they could not (and probably did not need to) understand. These are only some of the factors that produced the diffusion failure in Los Molinas. Once the remainder of the book has been read, it will be easier to understand the water-boiling case.

This case illustration is based on Wellin (1955).

What Is Diffusion?

Diffusion is the process by which an innovation is communicated through certain channels over time among the members of a social system. It is a special type of communication, in that the messages are concerned with new ideas. *Communication* is a process in which participants create and share information with one another in order to reach a mutual understanding. This definition implies that communication is a process of convergence (or divergence) as two or more individuals exchange information in order to move toward each other (or apart) in the meanings that they give to certain events. We think of communication as a two-way process of convergence, rather than as a one-way, linear act in which one individual seeks to transfer a message to another in order to achieve certain effects (Rogers and Kincaid, 1981). A linear conception of human communication may accurately describe certain communication acts or events involved in diffusion, such as when a change agent seeks to persuade a client to adopt an innovation. But when we look at what came before such an event, and at what follows, we often realize that the event is only one part of a total process in which information is exchanged between the two individuals. For example, the client may come to the change agent with a problem, and the innovation is recommended as a possible solution to this need. The change agent–client interaction may continue through several cycles, as a process of information exchange.

So diffusion is a special type of communication, in which the messages are about a new idea. This newness of the idea in the message content gives diffusion its special character. The newness means that some degree of uncertainty is involved in diffusion.

Uncertainty is the degree to which a number of alternatives are perceived with respect to the occurrence of an event and the relative probability of these alternatives. Uncertainty implies a lack of predictability, of structure, of information. In fact, information is a means of reducing uncertainty. *Information* is a difference in matter-energy that affects uncertainty in a situation where a choice exists among a set of alternatives (Rogers and Kincaid, 1981, p. 64). By differences in matter-energy we mean inked letters on paper, sound waves traveling through the air, or an electrical current in a copper wire. Information can thus take many forms, as matter or energy. A technological innovation embodies information and thus reduces uncertainty about cause-effect relationships in problem-solving. For instance, adoption of residential solar panels for water heating reduces uncertainty about future increases in the cost of fuel.

Diffusion is a kind of *social change*, defined as the process by which alteration occurs in the structure and function of a social system. When new ideas are invented, diffused, and are adopted or rejected, leading to certain consequences, social change occurs. Of course, such change can happen in other ways, too, for example, through a political revolution, through a natural event like a drought or an earthquake, or by means of a government regulation.

Some authors restrict the term "diffusion" to the spontaneous, unplanned spread of new ideas, and use the concept of "dissemination" for diffusion that is directed and managed. In this book we use the word "diffusion" to include both the planned and the spontaneous spread of new ideas.

Controlling Scurvy in the British Navy: Innovations Do Not Sell Themselves

Many technologists believe that advantageous innovations will sell themselves, that the obvious benefits of a new idea will be widely realized by potential adopters, and that the innovation will therefore diffuse rapidly. Seldom is this the case. Most innovations, in fact, diffuse at a disappointingly slow rate.

Scurvy control illustrates how slowly an obviously beneficial innovation spreads (Mosteller, 1981). In the early days of long sea voyages, scurvy was a worse killer of sailors than warfare, accidents, and all other causes of death. For instance, of Vasco de Gama's crew of 160 men who sailed with him around the Cape of Good Hope in 1497, 100 died of scurvy. In 1601, an English sea captain, James Lancaster, conducted an experiment to evaluate the effectiveness of lemon juice in preventing scurvy. Captain Lancaster commanded four ships that sailed from England on a voyage to India; he served three teaspoonfuls of lemon juice every day to the sailors in one of his four ships. Most of these men stayed healthy. But on the other three ships, by the halfway point in the journey, 110 out of 278 sailors had died from scurvy. The three ships constituted Lancaster's "control group"; they were not given any lemon juice. So many of these sailors became sick that Lancaster had to transfer men from his "treatment" ship in order to staff the three other ships.

The results were so clear that one would expect the British Navy to adopt citrus juice for scurvy prevention on all its ships. But it was not until 1747, *about 150 years later*, that James Lind, a British Navy physician who knew of Lancaster's results, carried out another experiment on the *HMS Salisbury*. To each scurvy patient on this ship, Lind prescribed either two oranges and one lemon, or one of five other diets: A half-pint of sea water, six spoonfuls of vinegar, a quart of cider, nutmeg, or seventy-five drops of vitriol elixir. The scurvy patients who got the citrus fruits were cured in a few days, and were able to help Dr. Lind care for the other patients. Unfortunately, the supply of oranges and lemons was exhausted in six days.

Certainly, with this further solid evidence of the ability of citrus fruits to combat scurvy, one would expect the British Navy to adopt this technological innovation for all ship's crews on long sea voyages, and in fact, it did so. *But not until 1795, forty-eight years later.* Scurvy was immediately wiped out. And after only *seventy more years*, in 1865, the British Board of Trade adopted a similar policy, and eradicated scurvy in the merchant marine.

Why were the authorities so slow to adopt the idea of citrus for scurvy prevention? A clear explanation is not available, but other, competing remedies for scurvy were also being proposed, and each such cure had its champions. For example, Captain Cook's reports from his voyages in the Pacific did not provide support for curing scurvy with citrus fruits. Further, Dr. Lind was not a prominent figure in the field of naval medicine, and so his experimental findings did not get much attention in the British Navy. While scurvy prevention was generally resisted for years by the British Navy, other innovations like new ships and new guns were accepted readily. So the Admiralty did not resist all innovations.

This case illustration is based on Mosteller (1981).

Obviously more than just a beneficial innovation is necessary for its diffusion and adoption to occur. The reader may think that such slow diffusion could happen only in the distant past, before a scientific and experimental approach to evaluating innovations. We answer by calling the reader's attention to the contemporary case of the nondiffusion of the Dvorak typewriter keyboard.

Nondiffusion of the Dvorak Keyboard

Most of us who use a typewriter or who do word processing on a computer do not realize that our fingers tap out words on a keyboard that is called "QWERTY," named after the first six keys on the upper row of letters. The QWERTY keyboard is inefficient and awkward. This typewriter keyboard takes twice as long to learn as it should, and makes us work about twenty times harder than is necessary. But QWERTY has persisted since 1873, and today unsuspecting individuals are being taught to use the QWERTY keyboard, unaware that a much more efficient typewriter keyboard is available.

Where did QWERTY come from? Why does it continue to be used, instead of much more efficient alternative keyboard designs? QWERTY was invented by Christopher Latham Sholes, who designed this keyboard to slow down typists. In that day, the type-bars on a typewriter hung down in a sort of basket, and pivoted up to strike the paper; then they fell back in place by gravity. When two adjoining keys were struck rapidly in succession, they jammed. Sholes rearranged the keys on a typewriter keyboard to minimize such jamming; he "anti-engineered" the arrangement to make the most commonly used letter sequences awkward. By thus making it difficult for a typist to operate the machine, and slowing down typing speed, Sholes' QWERTY keyboard allowed these early typewriters to operate satisfactorily. His design was used in the manufacture of all typewriters. Early typewriter salesmen could impress customers by pecking out "TYPEWRITER" as all of the letters necessary to spell this word were found in one row of the QWERTYUIOP machine.

Prior to about 1900, most typists used the two-finger, hunt-and-peck system. Later, as touch typing became popular, dissatisfaction with the QWERTY typewriter began to grow. Typewriters became mechanically more efficient, and the QWERTY keyboard design was no longer necessary to prevent key jamming. The search for an improved design was led by Professor August Dvorak at the University of Washington, who in 1932 used time-and-motion studies to create a much more efficient keyboard arrangement. The Dvorak keyboard has the letters A,O,E,U,I,D,H,T,N, and S across the home row of the typewriter. Less frequently used letters were placed on the upper and lower rows of keys. About 70 percent of typing is done on the home row, 22 percent on the upper row, and 8 percent on the lower row. On the Dvorak keyboard, the amount of work assigned to each finger is proportionate to its skill and strength. Further, Professor Dvorak engineered his keyboard so that successive keystrokes fell on alternative hands; thus, while a finger on one hand is stroking a key, a finger on the other hand can be moving into position to hit the next key. Typing rhythm is thus facilitated; this hand alternation was achieved by putting the vowels (which represent 40 percent of all letters typed) on the left-hand side, and placing the major consonants that usually accompany these vowels on the right-hand side of the keyboard.

Professor Dvorak was thus able to avoid the typing inefficiencies of the QWERTY keyboard. For instance, QWERTY overloads the left hand, which must type 57 percent of ordinary copy. The Dvorak keyboard shifts this emphasis to 56 percent on the stronger right hand and 44 percent on the weaker left hand. Only 32 percent of typing is done on the home row with the QWERTY system, compared to 70 percent with the Dvorak keyboard. The newer arrangement requires less jumping back and forth from row to row; with the QWERTY keyboard, a good typists' fingertips travel more than twelve miles a day, jumping from row to row. These unnecessary intricate movements cause mental tension, typist fatigue, and lead to more typographical errors.

One might expect, on the basis of its overwhelming advantages, that the Dvorak keyboard would have completely replaced the inferior QWERTY keyboard. On the contrary, after more than 50 years, almost all typists are still using the inefficient QWERTY keyboard. Even though the American National Standards Institute and the Equipment Manufacturers Association have approved the Dvorak keyboard as an alternate design, it is still almost impossible to find a typewriter or a computer keyboard that is arranged in the more efficient layout. Vested interests are involved in hewing to the old design: Manufacturers, sales outlets, typing teachers, and typists themselves.

No, technological innovations are not always diffused and adopted rapidly. Even when the innovation has obvious, proven advantages.

As the reader may have guessed by now, the present pages were typed on a QWERTY keyboard.

Details on resistance to the Dvorak keyboard may be found in Dvorak and others (1936), Parkinson (1972), Lessley (1980), and David (1986a).

Four Main Elements in the Diffusion of Innovations

Previously we defined *diffusion* as the process by which an *innovation* is *communicated* through certain *channels* over *time* among the members of a *social system*. The four main elements are the innovation, communication channels, time, and the social system (Figure 1–1). These elements are identifiable in every diffusion research study, and in every diffusion campaign or program (like the diffusion of water-boiling in a Peruvian village).

Figure 1–1. Diffusion Is the Process by Which (1) an *Innovation* (2) Is *Communicated* Through Certain *Channels* (3) Over *Time* (4) Among the Members of a *Social System*

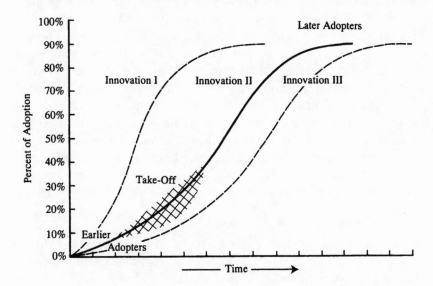

The following description of these four elements in diffusion constitutes an overview of the main concepts that will be detailed in Chapters 2 through 11.

1. The Innovation

An *innovation* is an idea, practice, or object that is perceived as new by an individual or other unit of adoption. It matters little, so far as human behavior is concerned, whether or not an idea is objectively new as measured by the lapse of time since its first use or discovery. The perceived newness of the idea for the individual determines his or her reaction to it. If the idea seems new to the individual, it is an innovation.

Newness in an innovation need not just involve new knowledge. Someone may have known about an innovation for some time but not yet developed a favorable or unfavorable attitude toward it, nor have adopted or rejected it. "Newness" of an innovation may be expressed in terms of knowledge, persuasion, or a decision to adopt.

Among the important research questions addressed by diffusion scholars are (1) how the earlier adopters differ from the later adopters of an innovation (Chapter 7), (2) how the perceived attributes of an innovation, such as its relative advantage or compatibility affect its rate of adoption, whether relatively rapidly (as for Innovation I in Figure 1–1) or more slowly (Innovation III), as is detailed in Chapter 6, and (3) why the S-shaped diffusion curve "takes off" at about 10- to 25-percent adoption, when interpersonal networks become activated so that a critical mass of adopters begins using an innovation (Chapter 8). It should not be assumed that the diffusion and adoption of all innovations are necessarily desirable. Some harmful and uneconomical innovations are not desirable for either the individual or the social system. Further, the same innovation may be desirable for one adopter in one situation, but undesirable for another potential adopter in a different situation. For example, mechanical tomato-pickers have been adopted rapidly by large commercial farmers in California, but these machines were too expensive for small tomato growers, and thousands of farmers have thus been forced out of tomato production.

TECHNOLOGICAL INNOVATIONS, INFORMATION, AND UNCERTAINTY. Most of the new ideas analyzed in this book are technological innovations, and we often use the word "innovation" and "technology" as synonyms. A *technology* is a design for instrumental action that reduces the uncertainty in the cause-effect relationships involved in achieving a desired outcome.* A technology usually has two components: (1) a *hardware* aspect, consisting of the tool that embodies the technology as a material or physical object, and (2) a *software* aspect, consisting of the information base for the tool. For example, we often speak of (1) "computer hardware" consisting of semiconductors, transistors, electrical connections, and the metal frame to protect these electronic components, and (2) "computer software" consisting of the coded commands, instructions, and other information aspects of this tool that allow us to use it to extend human capabilities in solving certain problems. Here we see an illustration of the close relationship between a tool and the way it is used.

---

* This definition of technology as information is based upon Thompson (1967) and Eveland (1986), who stress the uncertainty-reduction aspect of technology, and thus the important role of information, a view of technology that has not been widely recognized. Technology is information and transfer is a communication process, and so technology transfer is the communication of information (Eveland, 1986).

The social embedding of the hardware aspects of a technology is usually less visible than its machinery or equipment, and so we often think of technology mainly in hardware terms. Indeed, sometimes the hardware side of a technology is dominant. But in other cases, a technology may be almost entirely composed of information; examples are a political philosophy like Marxism, a religious idea, a news event, a rumor, assembly-line production, and quality circles. The diffusion of such software innovations has been investigated, although a methodological problem in such studies is that their adoption cannot be so easily traced or observed in a physical sense.

A number of new products involve a hardware component and a software component, with the hardware purchased first so that the software component can then be utilized. Examples are VCRs and videotapes, cameras and film, and compact disc players and CDs. Often a company will sell the hardware product at a relatively low price in order to capture market share, and then sell the software at a relatively high price in order to recover profits (Bayus, 1987). An example is the Nintendo game-player, which is sold at a fairly low price (about $100), but with each Nintendo video game sold at a relatively high price (about $60). This is sometimes called a shaver-and-blades strategy.

Some innovations only have a software component, which means they have a relatively lower degree of observability and thus a slower rate of innovation. Such idea-only innovations have seldom been studied by diffusion scholars, perhaps because their spread is relatively difficult to trace.

Even though the software component of a technology is often not so easy to observe, we should not forget that technology almost always represents a mixture of hardware and software aspects. According to our definition, technology is a means of uncertainty reduction that is made possible by information about the cause-effect relationships on which the technology is based. This information often results from scientific R&D activities when the technology is being developed. A technological innovation usually has at least some degree of benefit for its potential adopters. This advantage is not always very clear-cut, at least not to the intended adopters. They are seldom certain that an innovation represents a superior alternative to the previous practice that it might replace.

So a technological innovation creates one kind of uncertainty (about its expected consequences) in the mind of potential adopters, as well as representing an opportunity for reduced uncertainty in another sense (reduced by the information base of the technology). The latter type of potential uncertainty reduction (from the information embodied in the technological innovation itself) represents the possible efficacy of the innovation in solving an individual's perceived problem; this advantage provides the motivation that impels an individual to exert effort in order to learn about the innovation. Once such information-seeking activities have reduced the uncertainty about the innovation's expected consequences to a tolerable level for the individual, a decision concerning adoption or rejection will be made. If a new idea is used by an individual, further evaluative information about its effects is obtained. Thus, the innovation-decision process is essentially an information-seeking and information-processing activity in which the individual is motivated to reduce uncertainty about the advantages and disadvantages of the innovation (see Chapter 5).

We distinguish two kinds of information in respect to a technological innovation.

1. *Software information*, which is embodied in a technology and serves to reduce uncertainty about the cause-effect relationships in achieving a desired outcome.
2. *Innovation-evaluation information*, which is the reduction in uncertainty about an innovation's expected consequences.

The main questions that an individual typically asks in regard to software information are, "What is the innovation?" "How does it work?" and "Why does it work?" In contrast, an individual usually wants to know such innovation-evaluation information as, "What are an innovation's consequences?" and "What will its advantages and disadvantages be in my situation?"

TECHNOLOGY CLUSTERS. An important conceptual and methodological issue is to determine the boundaries around a technological innovation. The practical problem is how to determine where one innovation stops and another begins. If an innovation is an idea that is perceived as new, this boundary between innovations ought to be determined by the potential adopters who do the perceiving. In fact, this approach is used by diffusion scholars and by market researchers in positioning studies (described in Chapter 6). For example, a California study of the diffusion of recycling found that households that recycled paper were also likely to recycle bottles and cans, although many families only recycled paper

(Leonard-Barton and Rogers, 1980); presumably the two recycling behaviors represented two innovations that were part of an interrelated cluster of recycling ideas. A *technology cluster* consists of one or more distinguishable elements of technology that are perceived as being closely interrelated. Some change agencies promote a package of innovations because they find that the innovations are thus adopted more rapidly. An example of a technology cluster was the package of rice- or wheat-growing innovations that led to the Green Revolution in the Third World countries of Latin America, Africa, and Asia. In addition to the so-called miracle varieties of rice or wheat, the cluster included chemical fertilizers, pesticides, and thicker planting of the seeds.

Past diffusion research has generally investigated each innovation as if it were independent from other innovations. This is a dubious assumption, in that an adopter's experience with one innovation obviously influences that individual's perception of the next innovation to diffuse through the individual's system. In reality, a set of innovations diffusing at about the same time in a system are interdependent. It is much simpler for diffusion scholars to investigate the spread of each innovation as an independent event, but this is a distortion of reality.

CHARACTERISTICS OF INNOVATIONS. It should not be assumed, as it sometimes has in the past, that all innovations are equivalent units of analysis. This assumption is a gross oversimplification. While consumer innovations like mobile telephones or VCRs may require only a few years to reach widespread adoption in the United States, other new ideas such as the metric system or using seat belts in cars require decades to reach complete use. The characteristics of innovations, as perceived by individuals, help to explain their different rate of adoption.

1. *Relative advantage* is the degree to which an innovation is perceived as better than the idea it supersedes. The degree of relative advantage may be measured in economic terms, but social prestige, convenience, and satisfaction are also important factors. It does not matter so much if an innovation has a great deal of objective advantage. What does matter is whether an individual perceives the innovation as advantageous. The greater the perceived relative advantage of an innovation, the more rapid its rate of adoption will be.

2. *Compatibility* is the degree to which an innovation is perceived as being consistent with the existing values, past experiences, and needs of potential adopters. An idea that is incompatible with the values and norms

of a social system will not be adopted as rapidly as an innovation that is compatible. The adoption of an incompatible innovation often requires the prior adoption of a new value system which is a relatively slow process. An example of an incompatible innovation is the use of contraceptive methods in countries where religious beliefs discourage use of family planning, as in Moslem and Catholic nations. Previously in this chapter we saw how the innovation of water boiling was incompatible with the hot-cold complex in the Peruvian village of Los Molinas.

3. *Complexity* is the degree to which an innovation is perceived as difficult to understand and use. Some innovations are readily understood by most members of a social system; others are more complicated and will be adopted more slowly. For example, the villagers in Los Molinas did not understand germ theory, which the health worker tried to explain to them as a reason for boiling their drinking water. New ideas that are simpler to understand are adopted more rapidly than innovations that require the adopter to develop new skills and understandings.

4. *Trialability* is the degree to which an innovation may be experimented with on a limited basis. New ideas that can be tried on the installment plan will generally be adopted more quickly than innovations that are not divisible. Ryan and Gross (1943) found that every one of their Iowa farmer respondents adopted hybrid seed corn by first trying it on a partial basis. If the new seed could not have been sampled experimentally, its rate of adoption would have been much slower. An innovation that is trialable represents less uncertainty to the individual who is considering it for adoption, as it is possible to learn by doing.

5. *Observability* is the degree to which the results of an innovation are visible to others. The easier it is for individuals to see the results of an innovation, the more likely they are to adopt it. Such visibility stimulates peer discussion of a new idea, as friends and neighbors of an adopter often request innovation-evaluation information about it. Solar adopters often are found in neighborhood clusters in California, with three or four adopters located on the same block. Other consumer innovations like home computers are relatively less observable, and thus diffuse more slowly.

Innovations that are perceived by individuals as having greater relative advantage, compatibility, trialability, observability, and less complexity will be adopted more rapidly than other innovations. Past research indicates that these five qualities are the most important characteristics of innovations in explaining the rate of adoption.

RE-INVENTION. or the first several decades of diffusion research, it was assumed that an innovation was an invariant quality that did not change as it diffused. I remember interviewing an Iowa farmer years ago about his adoption of 2,4-D weed spray. In answer to my question about whether or not he had adopted this innovation, the farmer described in some detail the particular and unusual ways in which he used the weed spray on his farm. At the end of his remarks, I simply checked "adopter" on my questionnaire. The concept of re-invention was not yet in my theoretical repertoire, so I condensed the farmer's experience into one of my existing categories.

In the 1970s, diffusion scholars began to study the concept of *re-invention*, defined as the degree to which an innovation is changed or modified by a user in the process of its adoption and implementation. Some researchers measure re-invention as the degree to which an individual's use of a new idea departs from the mainline version of the innovation that was originally promoted by a change agency (Eveland and others, 1977). Once scholars became aware of the concept of re-invention and began to measure it, they began to find that a considerable degree of re-invention occurred for many innovations. Some innovations are difficult or impossible to re-invent; for example, hybrid seed corn does not allow a farmer much freedom to re-invent, as the hybrid vigor is genetically locked into the seed for the first generation in ways that are too complicated for a farmer to change. Certain other innovations are more flexible in nature, and they are re-invented by many adopters who implement them in a wide variety of different ways. An innovation is not necessarily invariant during the process of its diffusion. And adopting an innovation is not necessarily the passive role of just implementing a standard template of the new idea.

Given that an innovation exists, communication must take place if the innovation is to spread. Now we turn our attention to this second element in the diffusion process.

2. Communication Channels

Previously we defined *communication* as the process by which participants create and share information with one another in order to reach a mutual understanding. Diffusion is a particular type of communication in which the message content that is exchanged is concerned with a new idea. The essence of the diffusion process is the information exchange through which one individual communicates a new idea to one or several others. At its most elementary form, the process involves (1) an innovation, (2) an individual or other unit of adoption that has knowledge of the innovation or experience with using it, (3) another individual or other unit that does not yet have experience with the innovation, and (4) a communication channel connecting the two units. A *communication channel* is the means by which messages get from one individual to another. The nature of the information-exchange relationship between a pair of individuals determines the conditions under which a source will or will not transmit the innovation to the receiver, and the effect of the transfer.

Mass media channels are often the most rapid and efficient means to inform an audience of potential adopters about the existence of an innovation, that is, to create awareness-knowledge. *Mass media channels* are all those means of transmitting messages that involve a mass medium, such as radio, television, newspapers, and so on, which enable a source of one or a few individuals to reach an audience of many. On the other hand, interpersonal channels are more effective in persuading an individual to accept a new idea, especially if the interpersonal channel links two or more individuals who are similar in socioeconomic status, education, or other important ways. *Interpersonal channels* involve a face-to-face exchange between two or more individuals.

Diffusion investigations show that most individuals do not evaluate an innovation on the basis of scientific studies of its consequences, although such objective evaluations are not entirely irrelevant, especially to the very first individuals who adopt. Instead, most people depend mainly upon a subjective evaluation of an innovation that is conveyed to them from other individuals like themselves who have previously adopted the innovation. This dependence on the experience of near peers suggests that the heart of the diffusion process consists of the modeling and imitation by potential adopters of their network partners who have adopted previously. So diffusion is a very social process (see Chapter 8).

HETEROPHILY AND DIFFUSION. An obvious principle of human communication is that the transfer of ideas occurs most frequently between two individuals who are similar, or homophilous. *Homophily** is the degree

---

* This concept and its opposite, heterophily, were first called to scientific attention by Lazarsfeld and Merton (1964). *Heterophily*, the opposite of homophily, is defined as the degree to which two or more individuals who interact are different in certain attributes.

to which two or more individuals who interact are similar in certain attributes, such as beliefs, education, social status, and the like. In a free-choice situation, when an individual can interact with any one of a number of other individuals, there is a strong tendency to select someone who is very similar.

Homophily occurs because similar individuals belong to the same groups, live or work near each other, and share the same interests. This physical and social propinquity makes homophilous communication more likely. Such communication is also more likely to be effective, and thus to be rewarding. *More effective communication occurs when two or more individuals are homophilous.** When they share common meanings, a mutual subcultural language, and are alike in personal and social characteristics, the communication of new ideas is likely to have greater effects in terms of knowledge gain, attitude formation and change, and overt behavior change. When homophily is present, communication is therefore likely to be rewarding to both participants in the process.

One of the most distinctive problems in the diffusion of innovations is that the participants are usually quite heterophilous. A change agent, for instance, is more technically competent than his or her clients. This difference frequently leads to ineffective communication as the participants do not talk the same language. In fact, when two individuals are identical regarding their technical grasp of an innovation, no diffusion can occur as there is no new information to exchange. The very nature of diffusion demands that at least some degree of heterophily be present between the two participants. Ideally, they would be homophilous on all other variables (education and social status, for example) even though they are heterophilous regarding the innovation. Usually, however, the two individuals are heterophilous on all of these variables because knowledge and experience with an innovation are highly related to social status, education, and the like.

---

*A further refinement of this proposition includes the concept of *empathy*, defined as the ability of an individual to project into the role of another. *More effective communication occurs when two individuals are homophilous, unless they have high empathy.* Heterophilous individuals who have a high degree of empathy are, in a socio-psychological sense, really homophilous. The proposition about effective communication and homophily can also be reversed: *Effective communication between two individuals leads to greater homophily in knowledge, beliefs, and overt behavior.*

3. Time

Time is a third element in the diffusion process. Much other behavioral science research is timeless in the sense that the time dimension is simply ignored. The inclusion of time as a variable in diffusion research is one of its strengths, but the measurement of the time dimension (often by means of the respondents' recall) can be criticized (Chapter 3). The time dimension is involved in diffusion (1) in the innovation-decision process by which an individual passes from first knowledge of an innovation through its adoption or rejection, (2) in the innovativeness of an individual or other unit of adoption—that is, the relative earliness/lateness with which an innovation is adopted—compared with other members of a system, and (3) in an innovation's rate of adoption in a system, usually measured as the number of members of the system that adopt the innovation in a given time period.

THE INNOVATION-DECISION PROCESS. The *innovation-decision process* is the process through which an individual (or other decision-making unit) passes from first knowledge of an innovation to forming an attitude toward the innovation, to a decision to adopt or reject, to implementation and use of the new idea, and to confirmation of this decision. We conceptualize five main steps in the innovation-decision process: (1) knowledge, (2) persuasion, (3) decision, (4) implementation, and (5) confirmation. *Knowledge* occurs when an individual (or other decision-making unit) learns of the innovation's existence and gains some understanding of how it functions. *Persuasion* occurs when an individual (or other decision-making unit) forms a favorable or unfavorable attitude toward the innovation. *Decision* occurs when an individual (or other decision-making unit) engages in activities that lead to a choice to adopt or reject the innovation. *Implementation* occurs when an individual (or other decision-making unit) puts an innovation into use. Re-invention is especially likely to occur at the implementation stage. *Confirmation* occurs when an individual (or other decision-making unit) seeks reinforcement of an innovation-decision that has already been made, but the individual may reverse this previous decision if exposed to conflicting messages about the innovation.

Previously we stated that the innovation-decision process is an information-seeking and information-processing activity in which an individual obtains information in order to decrease uncertainty about the innovation. At the knowledge stage, an individual mainly seeks software information that is embodied in the technological innovation, information that reduces uncertainty about the cause-effect relationships involved in the innovation's capacity to solve an individual's problem. At this stage the individual wants to know what the innovation is and how and why it works. Mass media channels can effectively transmit such software information.

But increasingly at the persuasion stage, and especially at the decision stage, an individual seeks innovation-evaluation information in order to reduce uncertainty about an innovation's expected consequences. Here an individual wants to know the innovation's advantages and disadvantages in his or her own situation. Interpersonal networks with near-peers are particularly likely to convey such evaluative information about an innovation. Subjective evaluations of a new idea from other individuals are especially likely to influence an individual at the decision stage, and perhaps at the confirmation stage.

The innovation-decision process can lead to either *adoption*, a decision to make full use of an innovation as the best course of action available, or to *rejection*, a decision not to adopt an innovation. Such decisions can be reversed at a later point; for example, *discontinuance* is a decision to reject an innovation after it has previously been adopted. Discontinuance may occur because an individual becomes dissatisfied with an innovation, or because the innovation is replaced with an improved idea. It is also possible for an individual to adopt an innovation after a previous decision to reject it. Such later adoption and discontinuance occur during the confirmation stage of the innovation-decision process.

The innovation-decision process involved time in the sense that the five steps usually occur in a time-ordered sequence of knowledge, persuasion, decision, implementation, and confirmation. Exceptions to the usual sequence of the five stages may occur, such as when the decision stage precedes the persuasion stage. The *innovation-decision period* is the length of time required to pass through the innovation-decision process.

The present discussion of the innovation-decision process is mainly at the level of a single individual, and thus to the case of individual-optional innovation-decisions. But many innovation-decisions are made by organizations or other types of adopting units, rather than by individuals. For example, an organization may decide to implement an electronic mail system on the basis of a staff decision or an official's authority decision; the individual office worker in the organization may have little or no say in the innovation-decision. When an innovation-decision is made by a system, rather than by an individual, the decision process is more complicated because a number of individuals are involved (see Chapter 10).

So time is an important dimension in the innovation-decision process.

INNOVATIVENESS AND ADOPTER CATEGORIES. *Innovativeness* is the degree to which an individual or other unit of adoption is relatively earlier in adopting new ideas than the other members of a system. Rather than de-scribing an individual as "less innovative than the average member of a social system," it is handier and more efficient to refer to the individual as being in the "late majority" or in some other adopter category. This short-hand notation saves words and contributes to clearer understanding. Diffusion research shows that members of each of the adopter categories have a good deal in common. If the individual is like most others in the late majority category, he or she is of low social status, makes little use of mass media channels, and learns about most new ideas from peers via interpersonal channels. In a similar manner, we shall present a concise word picture of each of the other four adopter categories (in Chapter 7). *Adopter categories*, the classifications of members of a social system on the basis of innovativeness, include: (1) innovators, (2) early adopters, (3) early majority, (4) late majority, and (5) laggards.

Innovators are active information-seekers about new ideas. They have a high degree of mass media exposure and their interpersonal networks extend over a wide area, reaching outside of their local system. Innovators are able to cope with higher levels of uncertainty about an innovation than are other adopter categories. As the first to adopt a new idea in their system, they cannot depend upon the subjective evaluations of the innovation from other members of their system.

The measure of innovativeness and the classification of a system's members into adopter categories are based upon the relative time at which an innovation is adopted.

RATE OF ADOPTION. There is a third specific way in which the time dimension is involved in the diffusion of innovations. The *rate of adoption* is the relative speed with which an innovation is adopted by members of a social system. When the number of individuals adopting a new idea is plotted on a cumulative frequency basis over time, the resulting distribution is an S-shaped curve. At first, only a few individuals adopt the innovation in each time period (such as a year or a month, for example); these are the innovators. But soon the diffusion curve begins to climb, as more and more individuals adopt in each succeeding time period. Eventually, the trajectory of adoption begins to level off, as fewer and fewer individuals remain who have not yet adopted the innovation. Finally, the S-shaped curve reaches its asymptote, and the diffusion process is finished.

Most innovations have an S-shaped rate of adoption. But there is variation in the slope of the "S" from innovation to innovation; some new ideas diffuse relatively rapidly and the S-curve is quite steep. Other innovations have a slower rate of adoption, and the S-curve is more gradual, with a slope that is relatively lazy. One issue addressed by diffusion research is why some innovations have a rapid rate of adoption, while others are adopted more slowly (see Figure 1–1).

The rate of adoption is usually measured by the length of time required for a certain percentage of the members of a system to adopt an innovation. Therefore, we see that the rate of adoption is measured using an innovation in a system, rather than an individual, as the unit of analysis. Innovations that are perceived by individuals as possessing greater relative advantage, compatibility, and the like, have a more rapid rate of adoption (as discussed previously).

There are also differences in the rate of adoption for the same innovation in different social systems. Many aspects of diffusion cannot be explained by just individual behavior. The system has a direct effect on diffusion through its norms and other system-level qualities, and also has an indirect influence through its individual members.

4. A Social System

A *social system* is defined as a set of interrelated units that are engaged in joint problem-solving to accomplish a common goal. The members or units of a social system may be individuals, informal groups, organizations, and/or subsystems. The system analyzed in a diffusion study may consist of all the peasant families in a Peruvian village, medical doctors in a hospital, or all the consumers in the United States. Each unit in a social system can be distinguished from other units. All members cooperate at least to the extent of seeking to solve a common problem in order to reach a mutual goal. This sharing of a common objective binds the system together.

Diffusion occurs within a social system. The social structure of the system affects the innovation's diffusion in several ways. The social system constitutes a boundary within which an innovation diffuses. Here we deal with how the system's social structure affects diffusion, the effect of norms on diffusion, the roles of opinion leaders and change agents, types of innovation-decisions, and the consequences of innovation. These issues involve relationships between the social system and the diffusion process that occurs within it.

SOCIAL STRUCTURE AND DIFFUSION. To the extent that the units in a social system are not all identical in their behavior, structure exists in the system. We define *structure* as the patterned arrangements of the units in a system. This structure gives regularity and stability to human behavior in a system; it allows one to predict behavior with some degree of accuracy. Thus, structure represents one type of information, in that it decreases uncertainty. An illustration of this predictability is provided by structure in a bureaucratic organization like a government agency; there is a well-developed social structure in such a system, consisting of hierarchical positions, giving officials in higher-ranked positions the right to issue orders to individuals of lower rank. They expect their orders to be carried out. Such patterned social relationships among the members of a system constitute *social structure*, one type of structure.

In addition to this formal structure among the units in a social system, an informal type of structure also exists in the interpersonal networks linking a system's members, determining who interacts with whom and under what circumstances. We define such *communication structure* as the differentiated elements that can be recognized in the patterned communication flows in a system. Previously we defined homophily as the degree to which two or more individuals in a system talk with others who are similar to themselves. A communication structure is thus often created in a system in which homophilous sets of individuals are grouped together in cliques. A complete lack of communication structure in a system would be represented by a situation in which each individual talked with equal probability to each other member of the system. Such a situation might occur when a set of complete strangers first come together. However, regularized patterns soon begin to occur in the communication network of the system. These aspects of communication structure predict, in part, the behavior of individual members of the social system, including when they adopt an innovation.

The structure of a social system can facilitate or impede the diffusion of innovations in a system. The impact of the social structure on diffusion is of special interest to sociologists and social psychologists, and the way in which the communication structure of a system affects diffusion is a particularly interesting topic for communication scholars. Katz (1961) remarked, "It is as unthinkable to study diffusion without some knowledge of the social structures in which potential adopters are located as it is to study blood circulation without adequate knowledge of the veins and arteries."

Compared with other aspects of diffusion research, however, there have been relatively few studies of how the social or communication structure affects the diffusion and adoption of innovations in a system. It is a rather tricky business to untangle the effects of a system's structure on diffusion, independent from the effects of the characteristics of individuals that make up the system. Consider an illustration of *system effects*, the influences of the structure and/or composition of a system on the behavior of the members of the system. An example is provided by a study of the diffusion of family planning in Korea (Rogers and Kincaid, 1981). Two Korean women are both illiterate, married, have two children, and are twenty-nine years of age. The husbands of both women are high school graduates, with farms of five acres. One might expect that both women would be about equally likely, or unlikely, to adopt a contraceptive method.

But the women are different in one crucial respect: They live in different villages, one in Village A and one in Village B. The rate of adoption of family planning methods is 57 percent in Village A, and only 26 percent in Village B. The social and communication structures of these two villages are quite different regarding the diffusion of contraceptives, even though these innovations had been promoted equally in both villages by the national family planning program in Korea. We predict that the woman in Village A is more likely to adopt a contraceptive method than her counterpart in Village B because of system effects: Mrs. A's friends and neighbors are more likely to encourage her to adopt since they themselves have adopted, and the village leaders in Village A are especially committed to family planning, while in Village B they are not.

This example shows how a system's structure can effect the diffusion and adoption of innovations, over and above the effect of such variables as the individual characteristics of the members of the system. Individual innovativeness is affected both by individuals' characteristics, and by the nature of the social system in which the individuals are members.

SYSTEM NORMS AND DIFFUSION. The Korean investigation by Rogers and Kincaid (1981) also illustrates the importance of village norms in affecting the rate of adoption of innovations. For example, this study of twenty-four villages found large differences from village to village, both in the level of adoption of family planning and in the adoption of particular types of family planning methods. One village had 51 percent adoption of the IUD (intrauterine device) and only one vasectomy adopter. Another village had 23 percent adoption of vasectomy. Yet another was a "pill village" in which all the adopters chose to use contraceptive pills. These differences were not due to the nature of the national family planning program in Korea, which promoted the same "cafeteria" of contraceptive methods in all villages for ten years prior to our data-gathering. The main explanation for the different contraceptive behavior from village to village was these systems' norms.

Norms are the established behavior patterns for the members of a social system. They define a range of tolerable behavior and serve as a guide or a standard for the members' behavior in a social system. The norms of a system tell an individual what behavior is expected.

A system's norms can be a barrier to change, as in the example of water-boiling in a Peruvian community. Such resistance to new ideas is often found in norms on food habits. In India, for example, sacred cows roam the countryside while millions of people are malnourished. Pork is not consumed by Moslems and Jews. Polished rice is eaten in most of Asia and the United States, even though whole rice is more nutritious. These are examples of cultural and religious norms. Norms can operate at the level of a nation, a religious community, an organization, or a local system like a village.

OPINION LEADERS AND CHANGE AGENTS. The most innovative member of a system is very often perceived as a deviant from the social system, and is accorded a somewhat dubious status of low credibility by the average members of the system. This individual's role in diffusion (especially in persuading others about the innovation) is therefore likely to be limited. Other members of the system function as opinion leaders. They provide information and advice about innovations to many in the system.

Opinion leadership is the degree to which an individual is able to influence other individuals' attitudes or overt behavior informally in a desired way with relative frequency. This informal leadership is not a function of the individual's formal position or status in the system. Opinion leadership is earned and maintained by the individual's technical competence, social accessibility, and conformity to the system's norms. When the social system is oriented to change, the opinion leaders are quite innovative; but when the system's norms are opposed to change, the behavior of the leaders also reflects this norm. By their close conformity to the system's norms, opinion leaders serve as an apt model for the innovation behavior of their followers. Opinion leaders thus exemplify and express the system's structure.

Any system may have both innovative opinion leaders and also leaders who oppose change. Influential persons can lead in the spread of new ideas, or they can head an active proposition. When opinion leaders are compared with their followers, they (1) are more exposed to all forms of external communication, and thus are more cosmopolite, (2) have somewhat higher social status, and (3) are more innovative (although the exact degree of innovativeness depends, in part, on the system's norms). The most striking characteristics of opinion leaders is their unique and influential position in their system's communication structure: They are at the center of interpersonal communication networks. A *communication network* consists of interconnected individuals who are linked by patterned flows of information. The opinion leader's interpersonal networks allow him or her to serve as a social model whose innovative behavior is imitated by many other members of the system. The respect with which the opinion leader is held can be lost, however, if an opinion leader deviates too far from the norms of the system. Opinion leaders can be "worn out" by change agents who overuse them. Opinion leaders may be perceived by their peers as too much like the professional change agents and may therefore lose their credibility with their former followers.

Opinion leaders are members of the social system in which they exert their influence. In some instances individuals with influence in the social system are professionals who represent change agencies external to the system. A *change agent* is an individual who influences clients' innovation-decisions in a direction deemed desirable by a change agency. The change agent usually seeks to obtain the adoption of new ideas, but may also attempt to slow down diffusion and prevent the adoption of undesirable innovations. Change agents use opinion leaders in a social system as their lieutenants in diffusion campaigns.

Change agents are often professionals with a university degree in a technical field. This professional training, and the social status that goes with it, usually means that change agents are heterophilous from their typical clients, thus posing problems for effective communication about the innovations that they are promoting. Many change agencies employ change agent aides. An *aide* is a less than fully professional change agent who intensively contacts clients to influence their innovation-decisions. Aides are usually homophilous with the average client, and thus provide one means of bridging the heterophily gap frequently found between professional change agents and their client audience.

TYPES OF INNOVATION-DECISIONS. The social system has yet another important kind of influence in the diffusion of new ideas. Innovations can be adopted or rejected (1) by an individual member of a system, or (2) by the entire social system, which can decide to adopt an innovation by a collective or an authority decision.

1. *Optional innovation-decisions* are choices to adopt or reject an innovation that are made by an individual independent of the decisions of the other members of the system. Even in this case, the individual's decision may be influenced by the norms of the system and by interpersonal networks. The decision of an individual housewife in Los Molinas to adopt or reject boiling water was an optional innovation-decision, although this choice was influenced by community-level factors, like the hot-cold complex. The distinctive aspect of optional innovation-decisions is that the individual is the unit of decision making, rather than the social system.

The classical diffusion model evolved out of early diffusion investigations of optional innovation-decisions: The diffusion of hybrid corn among Iowa farmers, the spread of a new antibiotic drug among medical doctors, and the like. In more recent decades, however, the scope of the diffusion paradigm included collective and authority innovation-decisions.

2. *Collective innovation-decisions* are choices to adopt or reject an innovation that are made by consensus among the members of a system. All of the units in the system usually must conform to the system's decision once it is made. For example, in Southern California, all organizations employing more than 100 workers are required by a state law to

gradually increase the average number of riders per vehicle over a five-year period, or else pay a stiff fine. The purpose is to reduce traffic congestion in Los Angeles, and thus to cut down on the smog caused by vehicle emissions. A work organization may choose to raise parking fees, encourage the use of mass transportation, or to provide car pools and van pools to employees. Freedom of choice is allowed the individual as long as the goal of reducing the number of commuter vehicles is served.

3. *Authority innovation-decisions* are choices to adopt or reject an innovation that are made by a relatively few individuals in a system who possess power, status, or technical expertise. The individual member of the system has little or no influence in the authority innovation-decision; he or she simply implements the decision. For instance, the president of a large U.S. computer corporation some years ago decided that all male employees should wear a white shirt, conservative necktie, and a dark suit; this authority decision had to be followed by every man who worked for the computer company.

These three types of innovation-decisions range on a continuum from optional decisions (where the adopting individual has almost complete responsibility for the decision), through collective decisions (where the individual has a say in the decision), to authority decisions (where the adopting individual has no influence in the innovation-decision). Collective and authority decisions are much more common than optional decisions in formal organizations, such as factories, schools, or government organizations, in comparison with other fields like agriculture and consumer behavior, where most innovation-decisions by farmers and consumers are optional.

Generally, the fastest rate of adoption of innovations results from authority decisions (depending, of course, on how innovative the authorities are). Optional decisions can usually be made more rapidly than collective decisions. Although made more rapidly, authority decisions may be circumvented during their implementation.

The type of innovation-decision for a given idea may change or be changed over time. Automobile seat belts, during the early years of their use, were installed in autos as optional decisions by the car's owner, who had to pay for the cost of installation. Then, in 1966, a federal law was passed requiring that seat belts be included in all new cars in the United States. An optional innovation-decision thus became a collective decision. But the decision by a driver or passengers to fasten the belts when in the car was still an optional decision—that is, except for 1974 model cars, which a federal law required to be equipped with a seat belt-ignition interlock system that prevented the driver from starting the engine until everyone in the auto's front seat had fastened their seat belts. So for one year, the decision to fasten seat belts became a collective authority-decision. The public reaction to this draconian approach was so negative that the U.S. Congress reversed the law, and the fastening of auto seat belts again became an individual-optional decision. Then, during the 1980s, many states passed laws requiring seat belt use; if the police apprehend someone not using a seat belt, they issue a traffic citation.

There is yet a fourth type of innovation-decision that is a sequential combination of two or more of the three types we just discussed. *Contingent innovation-decisions* are choices to adopt or reject that can be made only after a prior innovation-decision. For example, an individual member of a social system may be free to adopt or not adopt a new idea only after his/her system's innovation-decision. In the example just discussed, until the 1966 law (a collective innovation-decision by elected legislators representing the public), it was difficult for a vehicle owner to make an optional decision to install seat belts.

One can imagine other types of contingent innovation-decisions in which the first decision is of an authority sort followed by a collective decision. The distinctive aspect of contingent decision making is that two (or more) tandem decisions are required; either of the decisions may be optional, collective, or authority.

The social system is involved directly in collective, authority, and contingent innovation-decisions.

CONSEQUENCES OF INNOVATIONS. A social system is involved in an innovation's consequences because certain of these changes occur at the system level, in addition to those that affect the individual (Chapter 11).

Consequences are the changes that occur to an individual or to a social system as a result of the adoption or rejection of an innovation. There are at least three classifications of consequences:

1. *Desirable* versus *undesirable* consequences, depending on whether the effects of an innovation in a social system are functional or dysfunctional.
2. *Direct* versus *indirect* consequences, depending on whether the changes to an individual or to a social system occur in immediate re-

sponse to an innovation or as a second-order result of the direct consequences of an innovation.

3. *Anticipated* versus *unanticipated* consequences, depending on whether the changes are recognized and intended by the members of a social system or not.

Change agents usually introduce innovations into a client system that they expect will have consequences that will be desirable, direct, and anticipated. But often such innovations result in at least some unanticipated consequences that are indirect and undesirable for the system's members. For instance, the steel ax was introduced by missionaries to an Australian aborigine tribe (Sharp, 1952). The change agents intended that the new tool would raise levels of living and material comfort for the tribe. But the new technology also led to a breakdown in family structure, the rise of prostitution, and "misuse" of the innovation itself. Change agents can often anticipate and predict an innovation's *form*, the directly observable physical appearance of the innovation, and perhaps its *function*, the contribution of the idea to the way of life of the system's members. But seldom are change agents able to predict an innovation's *meaning*, the subjective perceptions of the innovation by the clients.

Diffusion of Hybrid Corn in Iowa

The Ryan and Gross (1943) study of the diffusion of hybrid seed corn in Iowa is the most influential diffusion study. The hybrid corn investigation includes each of the four main elements of diffusion that we have just discussed, and serves to illustrate these elements.

The innovation of hybrid corn was one of the most important new agricultural technologies when it was released to Iowa farmers in 1928. The new seed ushered in a whole set of agricultural innovations in the 1930s through the 1950s that amounted to an agricultural revolution in farm productivity. Hybrid seed was developed by agricultural scientists at Iowa State University and at other state land-grant universities. The diffusion of hybrid seed was heavily promoted by the Iowa Agricultural Extension Service and by salesman from seed corn companies. Hybrid corn yielded about 20 percent more per acre than the open-pollinated varieties that it replaced. It was also more drought-resistant and better suited to harvesting with mechanical corn-pickers. The seed lost its hybrid vigor after the first generation, so farmers had to purchase hybrid seed each year. Previously farmers had saved their own seed, selected from their best-looking corn plants. The adoption of hybrid corn meant that an Iowa farmer had to make important changes in his corn-growing behavior.

When Bryce Ryan, fresh from his Ph.D. studies at Harvard University, arrived at Iowa State University in 1939, he chose hybrid corn as the innovation of study in his investigation of social factors in economic decisions. This interest drew him to study how an Iowa farmer's social relationships with his neighbors influenced the individual's decision to adopt hybrid corn. Ryan had read anthropological work on diffusion while he was at Harvard, so he cast his Iowa study of hybrid corn in a diffusion framework. But unlike the qualitative methods used in anthropological studies of diffusion, the Iowa investigation mainly utilized quantitative data from survey interviews with Iowa farmers about their adoption of hybrid corn seed.

In the summer of 1941, Neal Gross, a new graduate student in rural sociology, was hired as a research assistant on the hybrid corn diffusion project. Ryan and Gross selected two small Iowa communities located west of Ames, and proceeded to interview personally all of the farmers living in these two systems. Using a structured questionnaire, Neal Gross, who did most of the data gathering, interviewed each respondent as to when he decided to adopt hybrid corn (the year of adoption was to become the main dependent variable in the data analysis), the communication channels used at each stage in the innovation-decision process, and how much of the farmer's corn acreage was planted in hybrid (rather than open-pollinated seed) each year. In addition to these recall data about the innovation, the two rural sociologists also asked each respondent about his formal education, age, farm size, income, travel to Des Moines and other cities, readership of farm magazines, and other variables that were later correlated with innovativeness (measured as the year in which each farmer decided to adopt hybrid corn).

Neal Gross was from an urban background, and initially felt somewhat uncomfortable interviewing Iowa farmers. Someone in Ames told Gross that farm people got up very early in the morning, so on his first day of survey data gathering, he arrived at a respondent's home at 6:00 AM, while it was still half-dark. By the end of the day, Gross had interviewed twenty-one respondents, and he averaged an incredible fourteen interviews per day for the entire study! Today, a survey interviewer who averages four interviews per day is considered hard-working. During one personal interview, an Iowa farmer asked Gross for advice about controlling horse nettles. Gross had never heard of horse nettles. He told the farmer that he should call a veterinarian to look at his sick horse (horse nettles are a kind of noxious weed).

Neal Gross personally interviewed 345 farmers in the two Iowa communities, but twelve farmers operating less than twenty acres were discarded from the data analysis, as were seventy-four respondents who started farming after hybrid corn began to diffuse. Thus, the data analysis was based on 259 respondents.

When all the data were gathered, Ryan and Gross coded the farmers' interview responses into numbers. The diffusion researchers analyzed the data by hand tabulation and with a desk calculator (computers were not available for data analysis until some years later). Within a year, Neal Gross (1942) completed his Master's thesis on the diffusion of hybrid corn, and shortly thereafter Ryan and Gross (1943) published their research findings in the journal, *Rural Sociology* (this article is the most widely cited publication from the study, although there are several others).

All but two of the 259 farmers had adopted hybrid corn between 1928 and 1941, a rather rapid rate of adoption. When plotted cumulatively on a year-by-year basis, the adoption rate formed an S-shaped curve over time. After the first five years, by 1933, only 10 percent of the Iowa farmers had adopted. Then, the adoption curve "took off," shooting up to 40 percent adoption in the next three years (by 1936). Then the rate of adoption leveled off as fewer and fewer farmers remained to adopt the new idea.

Farmers were assigned to adopter categories on the basis of when they adopted the new seed (Gross, 1942). Compared to later adopters, the innovators had larger-sized farms, higher incomes, and more years of formal education. The innovators were more cosmopolite, as measured by their number of trips to Des Moines (Iowa's largest city, located about seventy-five miles away).

Although hybrid corn was an innovation with a high degree of relative advantage over the open-pollinated seed that it replaced, the typical farmer moved slowly from awareness-knowledge of the innovation to adoption. The innovation-decision period from first knowledge to the adoption-decision averaged about nine years for all respondents, a finding that the innovation-decision process involved considerable deliberation, even in the case of an innovation with spectacular results. The average respondent took three or four years after planting his first hybrid seed, usually on a small trial plot, before deciding to plant 100 percent of his corn acreage in hybrid varieties.

Communication channels played different roles at various stages in the innovation-decision process. The typical farmer first heard of hybrid seed from a salesman, but neighbors were the most frequently cited channel leading to persuasion. Salesmen were more important channels for earlier adopters, and neighbors were more important for later adopters. The Ryan and Gross (1943) findings suggested the important role of interpersonal networks in the diffusion process in a system. The farmer-to-farmer exchange of their personal experiences with hybrid seed was at the heart of diffusion. When enough such positive experiences were accumulated by the innovators and early adopters, and exchanged with other farmers in the community, the rate of adoption took off. This threshold for hybrid corn occurred in 1935. After that point, it would have been impossible to halt the further diffusion of hybrid corn. The farm community as a social system, including the networks linking the individual farmers within it, was a crucial element in the diffusion process.

In order to understand the role of diffusion networks and opinion leadership, Ryan and Gross (1943) should have asked sociometric questions° of their respondents, such as, "From which other farmers have you obtained information about hybrid corn?" The sample design, which consisted of a complete enumeration in two communities, would have made the use of sociometric questions appropriate. But "information was simply collected from all community members as if they were unrelated respondents in a random sample" (Katz and others, 1963).

Even without sociometric data about diffusion networks, Ryan and Gross (1943) sensed that hybrid corn spread in the two Iowa communities as a kind of social snowball: "There is no doubt but that the behavior of one individual in an interacting population affects the behavior of his fellows. Thus, the demonstrated success of hybrid seed on a few farms offers new stimulus to the remaining ones." The two rural sociologists intuitively sensed what later diffusion scholars were to gather more detailed evidence to prove: That the heart of the diffusion process consists of interpersonal network exchanges and social modeling between those individuals who have already adopted an innovation and those who are then influenced to do so. Diffusion is fundamentally a social process.

° *Sociometry* is a means of obtaining and analyzing quantitative data about communication patterns among the individuals in a system by asking each individual to whom he or she is linked.

Study of the invisible college of rural sociologists investigating diffusion as of the mid-1960s identified the researchers who first utilized a new concept and/or methodological tool in studying diffusion (Crane, 1972). Ryan and Gross launched fifteen of the eighteen most widely used intellectual innovations in the rural sociology diffusion research tradition. So Bryce Ryan and Neal Gross played key roles in forming the classical diffusion paradigm. The hybrid corn study has left an indelible stamp on the history of diffusion research.

This case illustration is based on Ryan and Gross (1943), Gross (1942), Ryan and Gross (1950), and Valente and Rogers (1994).

Summary

Diffusion is the process by which an innovation is communicated through certain channels over time among the members of a social system. Diffusion is a special type of communication concerned with the spread of messages that are perceived as new ideas. *Communication* is a process in which participants create and share information with one another in order to reach a mutual understanding. Diffusion has a special character because of the newness of the idea in the message content. Thus some degree of uncertainty is involved in the diffusion process. An individual can reduce the degree of uncertainty by obtaining information. *Information* is a difference in matter-energy that affects uncertainty in a situation where a choice exists among a set of alternatives.

The main elements in the diffusion of new ideas are: (1) an *innovation*, (2) which is *communicated* through certain *channels*, (3) over *time*, (4) among the members of a *social system*. An *innovation* is an idea, practice, or object perceived as new by an individual or other unit of adoption. Almost all of the new ideas discussed in this book are technological innovations. A *technology* is a design for instrumental action that reduces the uncertainty in the cause-effect relationships involved in achieving a desired outcome. Most technologies have two components: (1) *hardware*, consisting of the tool that embodies the technology as a material or physical object, and (2) *software*, consisting of the knowledge base for the tool. The software information embodied in a technology serves to reduce one type of uncertainty, that concerned with the cause-effect relationships involved in achieving a desired outcome. But a technological innovation also creates another kind of uncertainty because of its newness to the individual, and motivates him or her to seek information by means of which the new idea can be evaluated. This *innovation-evaluation information* leads to a reduction in uncertainty about an innovation's expected consequences.

The characteristics of an innovation, as perceived by the members of a social system, determine its rate of adoption. Five attributes of innovations are: (1) relative advantage, (2) compatibility, (3) complexity, (4) trialability, and (5) observability.

Re-invention is the degree to which an innovation is changed or modified by a user in the process of its adoption and implementation.

A *communication channel* is the means by which messages get from one individual to another. Mass media channels are more effective in creating knowledge of innovations, whereas interpersonal channels are more effective in forming and changing attitudes toward a new idea, and thus in influencing the decision to adopt or reject a new idea. Most individuals evaluate an innovation, not on the basis of scientific research by experts, but through the subjective evaluations of near-peers who have adopted the innovation. These near-peers thus serve as role models, whose innovation behavior tends to be imitated by others in their system.

Another distinctive aspect of diffusion as a subfield of communication is that some degree of heterophily is present. *Heterophily* is the degree to which two or more individuals who interact are different in certain attributes, such as beliefs, education, social status, and the like. The opposite of heterophily is *homophily*, the degree to which two or more individuals who interact are similar in certain attributes. Most human communication takes place between individuals who are homophilous, a situation that leads to more effective communication. Therefore, the heterophily that is often present in the diffusion of innovations leads to special problems in securing effective communication.

Time is involved in diffusion in (1) the innovation-decision process, (2) innovativeness, and (3) an innovation's rate of adoption. The *innovation-decision process* is the mental process through which an individual (or other decision-making unit) passes from first knowledge of an innovation to forming an attitude toward the innovation, to a decision to adopt or reject, to implementation of the new idea, and to confirmation of this decision. We conceptualize five steps in this process: (1) knowledge, (2) persuasion, (3) decision, (4) implementation, and (5) confirmation. An individual seeks information at various stages in the innovation-decision process in order to decrease uncertainty about an innovation's expected consequences. The decision stage leads (1) to *adoption*, a decision to make full use of an innovation as the best course of action available, or (2) to *rejection*, a decision not to adopt an innovation.

Innovativeness is the degree to which an individual or other unit of adoption is relatively earlier in adopting new ideas than other members of a social system. We specify five *adopter categories*, classifications of the members of a social system on the basis of their innovativeness: (1) innovators, (2) early adopters, (3) early majority, (4) late majority, and (5) laggards. *Rate of adoption* is the relative speed with which an innovation is adopted by members of a social system.

A *social system* is a set of interrelated units that are engaged in joint problem-solving to accomplish a common goal. A system has *structure*, defined as the patterned arrangements of the units in a system, which gives stability and regularity to individual behavior in a system. The social and communication structure of a system facilitates or impedes the diffusion of innovations in the system.

Norms are the established behavior patterns for the members of a social system. *Opinion leadership* is the degree to which an individual is able to influence informally other individuals' attitudes or overt behavior in a desired way with relative frequency. A *change agent* is an individual who attempts to influence clients' innovation-decisions in a direction that is deemed desirable by a change agency. An *aide* is a less than fully professional change agent who intensively contacts clients to influence their innovation-decisions.

We distinguish three main types of innovation-decisions: (1) *optional innovation-decisions*, choices made by an individual independent of the decisions of other members of the system to adopt or reject an innovation, (2) *collective innovation-decisions*, choices made by consensus among the members of a system, and (3) *authority innovation-decisions*, choices made by relatively few individuals in a system who possess power, status, or technical expertise. A fourth category consists of a sequential combination of two or more of these types of innovation-decisions: *Contingent innovation-decisions* are choices to adopt or reject that are made only after a prior innovation-decision.

A final way in which a social system influences diffusion is *consequences*, the changes that occur to an individual or to a social system as a result of the adoption or rejection of an innovation.

2

A HISTORY OF
DIFFUSION RESEARCH

Diffusion research is thus emerging as a single, integrated body
of concepts and generalizations, even though the investigations
are conducted by researchers in several scientific disciplines.
—Everett M. Rogers with F. Floyd Shoemaker (1971),
Communications of Innovations: A Cross-Cultural Approach

Research on the diffusion of innovations started in a series of independent intellectual enclaves during its first several decades. Each of these
disciplinary cliques of diffusion researchers studied one kind of innovation; for example, rural sociologists investigated the diffusion of agricultural innovations to farmers while educational researchers studied the
spread of new teaching ideas among school personnel. Despite the distinctiveness of these approaches to diffusion research, each invisible
college uncovered remarkably similar findings; for example, that the diffusion of an innovation followed an S-shaped curve over time and that innovators had higher socioeconomic status than later adopters.

My main motivation for writing the first book on this topic, *Diffusion
of Innovations* (Rogers, 1962) was to point out the lack of diffusion of diffusion research, and to argue for greater awareness among the various
diffusion research traditions. A *research tradition* is a series of investigations on a similar topic in which successive studies are influenced by preceding inquiries. Essentially, each research tradition is an invisible college
of researchers, a network of scholars who are spatially dispersed but who
are closely interconnected by exchanging research findings and other scientific information.

By the mid-1960s the formerly impermeable boundaries between the

diffusion research traditions began to break down. Rogers with Shoemaker (1971) computed an index of cross-tradition citations for each diffusion publication available by 1968; this index was the number of
research traditions (other than the author's) represented in the footnotes
and bibliography of each empirical diffusion publication. The average index score (per diffusion publication) hovered at less than 1.0 during the
1940s, 1950s, and early 1960s. But from 1965 to 1968, the average score
suddenly doubled. The paper curtain separating the various diffusion research traditions had broken down.

This trend toward a more unified cross-disciplinary viewpoint in diffusion research continues today; every diffusion scholar is fully aware
of the parallel methodologies and results in the other traditions. All of
the diffusion research traditions have now converged, intellectually, toward a single large invisible college, although diffusion studies are conducted by scholars in many disciplines. This merger of diffusion
approaches has not been an unmixed blessing. Diffusion studies now
display a kind of bland sameness, as they pursue a small number of research issues with rather stereotyped approaches. The narrow perspectives of diffusion scholars in an earlier era have been replaced by
an unnecessary standardization in contemporary diffusion research approaches. Perhaps the old days of separate and varied research approaches were a richer intellectual activity than the present era of
well-informed sameness.

A major theme of this chapter is the story of the merging of the diffusion research traditions, and the consequences of this intellectual convergence. We address such questions as: Where did diffusion research
come from? How and why did it grow to its present position of popular
recognition by scholars, and its widespread use and application by policy-
makers? How has the acceptance of the classical diffusion model limited
the originality and appropriateness of the work of diffusion researchers?

The Beginnings of Diffusion Research in Europe

The roots of diffusion research extend back to the European beginnings
of social science.

Gabriel Tarde and Imitation

Gabriel Tarde, one of the forefathers of sociology and social psychology,
was a French lawyer and judge around the turn of the century who kept

an analytical eye on trends in his society as represented by the legal cases that came before his court. Tarde observed certain generalizations about the diffusion of innovations that he called the laws of imitation, and this became the title of his influential book. The purpose of his scholarly observations, Tarde (1903) said, was "to learn why, given one hundred different innovations conceived at the same time—innovations in the form of words, in mythological ideas, in industrial processes, etc.—ten will spread abroad while ninety will be forgotten."

Gabriel Tarde was far ahead of his time in his thinking about diffusion. Although he used slightly different concepts than those employed in the present book (for example, what Tarde called *imitation* is today called the adoption of an innovation), this sociological pioneer explored several of the main research issues that were pursued by diffusion scholars in later decades, using more quantitative approaches. For example, as the previous quotation indicates, Tarde identified the adoption or rejection of innovations as a crucial outcome variable in diffusion research. He observed that the rate of adoption of a new idea usually followed an S-shaped curve over time. Astutely, Tarde recognized that the take-off in the S-curve of adoption begins to occur when the opinion leaders in a system adopt a new idea. So diffusion network thinking was involved in Tarde's explanation of the S-curve, even though he did not use such present-day concepts as networks, homophily, and heterophily. Tarde's key word, imitation, implies that an individual learns about an innovation by copying someone else's adoption behavior. Tarde (1903,1969) proposed as one of his most fundamental laws of imitation that the more similar an innovation is to ideas that have already been accepted, the more likely the innovation will be adopted (today we say that the perceived compatibility of an innovation is related to its rapid rate of adoption).

To Tarde, the diffusion of innovations was a basic and fundamental explanation of human behavior change: "Invention and imitation are, as we know, the elementary social acts" (Tarde, 1969). Tarde was the main European forefather of the diffusion field. But his creative insights were not followed up immediately in empirical studies of diffusion. That was not to happen until after a lapse of forty years, with the Ryan and Gross hybrid corn study. Social scientists of Tarde's day lacked the methodological tools to conduct quantitative diffusion studies. His suggested approach to diffusion research lay fallow for several decades until an invisible college of American scholars was to coalesce around a latter-day paradigm based upon Tarde's laws of imitation.

The British and German-Austrian Diffusionists

Another root of diffusion research was a group of anthropologists that emerged in England and in Germany-Austria soon after the time of Gabriel Tarde in France (although they did not read his writings). These anthropologists are called the "British diffusionists" and the "German-Austrian diffusionists". The viewpoint of each school was similar. Diffusionism was the point of view in anthropology that explained social change in a given society as a result of the introduction of innovations from another society. The diffusionists claimed that all innovations spread from one original source, which, of course, argued against the existence of parallel invention (today we know that such parallel invention of new ideas frequently occurs).

The diffusionism viewpoint does not have much of a following today, owing to the extreme claim of the diffusionists that all social change could be explained by diffusion alone. The dominant viewpoint now is that social change is caused by both invention (the process by which a new idea is discovered or created) and diffusion, which usually occur sequentially. The main contribution of the European diffusionists was their calling the importance of diffusion to the attention of other social scientists (Kroeber, 1937).

The scholars who picked up on the work of the European diffusionists most directly, as one might expect, were anthropologists, especially those in the United States who, beginning in the 1920s, began to investigate the diffusion of innovations. Indirectly, this anthropological interest in the diffusion of innovations was to influence the Ryan and Gross (1943) investigation of hybrid seed corn in Iowa.

The Rise of Diffusion Research Traditions

The anthropological diffusion researchers constitute the oldest of the diffusion research traditions (Table 2–1). In this chapter we trace the intellectual ancestry of the ten main research traditions, as they help us to understand the history of diffusion research. Each research tradition consists of an academic discipline (for example, anthropology, marketing, geography) or a subdiscipline (for instance, early sociology, and rural sociology). Each tradition usually concentrated on investigating the diffusion of one main type of innovation: For example, rural sociologists specialized in farm innovations. Table 2–1 shows, for each tradition, the

Table 2–1. Comparison of the Major Diffusion Research Traditions.[a]

Diffusion Research Tradition	Number of Diffusion Publications (% of All Publications)	Typical Innovations Studied	Method of Data Gathering and Analysis	Main Unit of Analysis	Major Types of Findings
1. Anthropology	141 (4%)	Technological ideas (steel ax, the horse, water boiling)	Participant and nonparticipant observation and case studies	Tribes or peasant villages	Consequences of innovations; relative success of change agents
2. Early sociology	10 (—)	City manager government, postage stamps, ham radios	Data from secondary sources and statistical analysis	Communities or individuals	S-shaped adopter distribution; characteristics of adopter categories
3. Rural sociology[b]	845 (22%)	Agricultural ideas (weed sprays, hybrid seed, fertilizers)	Survey interviews and statistical analysis	Individual farmers in rural communities	S-shaped adopter distribution; characteristics of adopter categories; perceived attributes of innovations and their rate of adoption; communication channels by stages in the innovation-decision process; characteristics of opinion leaders
4. Education	359 (9%)	Teaching/learning innovations (kindergartens, modern math, programmed instruction, team teaching)	Mailed questionnaires, survey interviews, and statistical analysis	School systems, teachers, or administrators	S-shaped adopter distribution; characteristics of adopter categories
5. Public health and medical sociology	277 (7%)	Medical and health ideas (drugs, vaccinations, family planning methods, AIDS prevention	Survey interviews and statistical analysis	Individuals or organizations like hospitals or health departments	Opinion leadership in diffusion; characteristics of adopter categories; communication channels by stages in the innovation-decision process

6. Communication	484 (12%)	News events, technological innovations	Survey interviews and statistical analysis	Individuals or organizations	Communication channels by stages in the innovation-decision process: characteristics of adopter categories, and of opinion leaders; diffusion networks
7. Marketing and management	585 (15%)	New products (a coffee brand, the touch-tone telephone, clothing fashions)	Survey interviews and statistical analysis; field experiments	Individual consumers	Characteristics of adopter categories; opinion leadership in diffusion
8. Geography	160 (4%)	Technological innovations	Secondary records and statistical analysis	Individuals and organizations	Role of spatial distance in diffusion
9. General sociology	322 (8%)	A wide variety of ideas	Survey interviews and statistical analysis	Individuals	Characteristic of adopter categories; various others.
10. General economics	144 (5%)	Technological innovations	Economic analysis	Organizations, individuals	Economics of technological innovations
11. Other traditions[c]	563 (14%)	—	—	—	—
Total	3,890 (100%)				

[a] The exact number of major diffusion research traditions is arbitrary. We chose these because they represent the relatively greatest number of empirical diffusion publications (an exception is the early sociology tradition, which is included because of its influence on certain of the other traditions which developed later).

[b] The rural sociology tradition includes 150 publications by diffusion scholars in extension, whose work is closely related.

[c] Includes public administration and political science (129 publications), agricultural economics (101), psychology (73), industrial engineering (33), statistics (33), and others/unknown (194).

main types of innovations studied, methods of data-gathering and analysis, and the main findings. This overview and comparison of the diffusion research traditions is complemented by the following narrative description of each tradition.

Paradigms and Invisible Colleges

Any given field of scientific research is launched by a major breakthrough or reconceptualization, called a revolutionary paradigm by Kuhn (1970), that provides model problems and solutions to a community of scholars (Kuhn, 1970, p.viii). Recognition of the new paradigm sets off a furious amount of intellectual effort as promising young scientists are attracted to the field, either to advance the new conceptualization with their research or to disprove certain of its aspects. Gradually, a scientific consensus about the field is developed, and, perhaps after some years, the *invisible college* (the informal network of researchers who form around an intellectual paradigm to study a common topic) declines in scientific interest as fewer findings of an exciting nature turn up. These are the usual stages in the growth of science (Kuhn, 1970; Price, 1963; Crane, 1972). The research process is a very social activity in which crucial decisions are influenced by a network of scientists, organized around one important research idea.

An invisible college centered on an intellectual paradigm provides the typical scientist with the information that he or she needs to reduce the uncertainty of the research process. Of the many alternative directions that a research project might pursue, a paradigm structures a researcher toward one general approach. Thus, the paradigm and the invisible college of scientists that follow the paradigm provide a researcher with a source of security and stability in the uncertain world of research.

Research on the diffusion of innovations followed these rise-and-fall stages rather closely (Crane, 1972), although the final stage of demise does not seem to have begun (however, in some research traditions like rural sociology and education, the amount of diffusion research has slowed down). The hybrid corn diffusion study by Ryan and Gross (1943), described in Chapter 1, set forth the basic paradigm for studying diffusion. Its leads were soon followed by an increasing number of scholars (Figure 2–1). The amount of scientific activity devoted to investigating the diffusion of innovations then increased at a very sharp rate after the revolutionary paradigm appeared 50 years ago, as Kuhn's (1970) theory of the growth of science would predict.

Figure 2–1. Cumulative Number of Diffusion Research Publications by Year

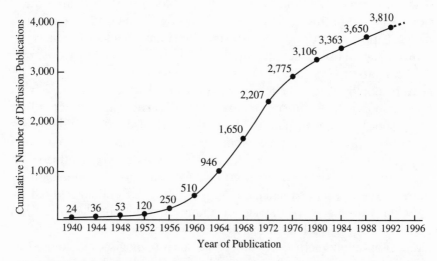

The field of research on the diffusion of innovations took off after formation of the diffusion paradigm by Ryan and Gross (1943). In each succeeding time period, the number of diffusion publications increased considerably, until very recent years, when the number of diffusion research publications completed per year slowed down somewhat.

Diffusion research is a particular type of communication research (as explained in Chapter 1), but it began outside of the academic field of communication. This was due to timing, as the Ryan and Gross (1943) hybrid corn study preceded the establishment of the first university institutes or departments of communication (Rogers, 1993b). The diffusion research approach was taken up in a variety of fields: education, anthropology, public health, marketing, geography, and rural sociology. Each of these disciplines pursued diffusion research in its own specialized way, without much interchange with the other diffusion research traditions, at least until the early 1960s when the boundaries between the traditions began to break down.

Now we turn to the beginnings of the anthropological research tradition in diffusion, in the 1920s.

The Anthropology Research Tradition

The anthropology tradition is not only the oldest of the research traditions analyzed in this book, it is also the most distinctive in its methodological approach to studying diffusion. Most anthropologists who study diffusion avoid using such quantitative tools as personal interviews, random sample surveys, and computer data analysis.

Anthropologists prefer to gather diffusion data more directly from their respondents, by means of *participant observation*, an attempt by a researcher to adopt the perspective of respondents by sharing their day-to-day experiences. An anthropologist often lives for several years in a peasant village or some other system of study, seeking to empathize with the everyday roles of respondents. Obviously, such a total immersion requires a great deal of patience on the part of the anthropologist field researcher, who may have to wait for a long time for what he or she has come to observe (such as diffusion and adoption behavior). The participant-observation method requires that anthropologists are limited to studying diffusion in small systems, like a single village. Most anthropological research is a one-person operation, and the investigator is therefore limited to what he or she can observe in a limited setting. The results of such inquiry provide valuable insights into the micro-level details of diffusion. There is less certainty that the results of anthropological diffusion studies are generalizable. For instance, to what extent can the administrators of the public health service in Peru apply the findings from Wellin's (1955) anthropological investigation of the failure of the water-boiling campaign in Los Molinas to other Peruvian villages? Does Los Molinas have special characteristics that affected the adoption and rejection of water boiling? Do similar diffusion circumstances occur in other Peruvian villages? We do not know.

There are also special advantages of anthropological research on diffusion. If the anthropologist is successful in attempting to empathize with the respondents of study, the ensuing account of diffusion will tell the story from the respondents' viewpoint, conveying their perceptions of the innovation and of the change agency with a high degree of understanding. This perspective helps the anthropologist overcome the pro-innovation bias that is displayed in much other diffusion research. Through total immersion in the respondents' system, the anthropologist gains a holistic perspective of the lifestyles, world views, and social relationships of the respondents. This capacity of anthropologists to understand the culture of their individuals of study, coupled with their long-term data-gathering over time, provides anthropological diffusion scholars with a unique means of understanding the consequences of innovation. Much of the research featured in Chapter 11 on consequences was carried out by anthropologists.

In addition to their useful contributions to our understanding of consequences, much anthropological research has also been conducted on the relationship of an innovation's rate of adoption.* Anthropologists often show that the planners and officials in charge of development programs failed to account fully for the cultural values of the expected adopters of an innovation. As a result, the diffusion program often failed, or at least it led to unanticipated consequences.

Compared to other research traditions, anthropology has been more concerned with the transfer of technological innovations from one society to another (as compared to the diffusion of a new idea within a society or system). This emphasis on intercultural diffusion is consistent with anthropologists' interest in the concept of culture, their favorite intellectual tool. An early illustration of this type of investigation was Wissler's (1923) study of the diffusion of horses from Spanish explorers to American Indian tribes in the West, and the spread of corn-growing from American Indians to European settlers. Contemporary studies of intercultural diffusion in the anthropological tradition evaluate development programs in which Western technologies are introduced in the developing countries of Latin America, Africa, and Asia.

In part owing to their early appearance on the diffusion research scene, anthropologists influenced the other diffusion research traditions, particularly early sociology and rural sociology. Other traditions have seldom used participant observation as their data-gathering methodology, but they have carried forward into quantitative research certain of the theoretical leads pioneered by anthropological diffusion scholars.

---

*Summaries of anthropological evidence on this point are provided by Spicer (1952), Barnett (1953), Arensberg and Niehoff (1964), and Niehoff (1966). Linton (1936) was one of the first scholars to recognize the relationship of the perceived characteristics of an innovation to its rate of adoption.

Miracle Rice in Bali: The Goddess and the Computer

One may have an image of an anthropologist as an Indiana Jones–like character, wearing native dress and a pith helmet, and speaking the local dialect with perfect fluency. USC anthropologist Steve Lansing indeed dresses in traditional Balinese dress and immerses himself completely in the exotic culture of Bali, the Indonesian island in the South Pacific. His research in Bali, continued over the past fifteen years, allows him to understand dimensions of the indigenous knowledge system affecting technological innovations that others, including Indonesian government officials, often cannot see. This in-depth comprehension by anthropologists comes from studying small systems over a lengthy time period. Like many other contemporary anthropologists, Professor Lansing used cutting-edge computer techniques in his research on the introduction and consequences of miracle rice varieties in Bali. In order to understand why the miracle rice failed in Bali, one must comprehend the religious aspects of the rice irrigation system.

Rice is central to life in Bali. The steep slopes of volcanic soil, stretching down from mist-covered mountain peaks to the sea, have been ingeniously terraced by Balinese farmers over the centuries so that irrigation water descends from a high crater lake, tumbling from one small rice plot to another, inching its way for miles down to the sea. These rice paddies for centuries have produced up to a ton of food per acre per year, with little or no added fertilizer. Because of ample rice yields, the small, densely populated island of Bali supports more than 2 million people. These high rice yields are made possible by a complex irrigation system coordinated by a hierarchical series of Hindu priests and water temples that regulate water flows. At the top of this indigenous system is the high priest, the Jero Gde (pronounced "Jeero G'day"), of the main water temple at Ulun Danu Batur, the crater lake near the peak of Batur volcano. Here offerings are made to Dewi Dano, the water goddess whom Balinese believe dwells in the crater lake.

The Jero Gde is overall manager of the irrigation system. Below him are a series of major dams, each with its Hindu priest and water temple, responsible for regulating water flows. The lower level of the irrigation system consists of smaller weirs, each with a minor water temple to regulate water flows. At the local level are 1,300 *subaks*, each a water-users' association of about 100 farmers. Each subak has a water shrine and a priest. Such an elaborate, hierarchically tiered social organization is necessary to operate the Balinese rice irrigation system. Water is a scarce resource, and some type of social organization is needed in order to distribute the water in an equitable manner. Presumably this is one reason why so many of the world's civilizations began in areas of irrigated agriculture.

But the water-temple system of Bali does far more than just deliver water to crops. Each rice terrace is a complex ecosystem, with the management of these carefully balanced ecological forces in the hands of the Jero Gde and his cadre of Hindu water priests. For instance, a single farmer cannot control the pests in his small rice plot unless he coordinates with his neighbors. Otherwise, the rats, brown leaf-hoppers, and other pests will simply migrate from field to field. The solution is for hundreds of farmers in several neighboring subaks to plant, irrigate, and harvest simultaneously, and then leave their rice fields to fallow for a period of several weeks. Evidence of such coordination is easily visible in Bali: All of the rice fields on an entire mountain slope will be the same growing green, harvest yellow, or fallow brown. But until anthropologist Lansing began to investigate, nobody understood how the actions of these hundreds of rice farmers were orchestrated. If rice experts knew of the indigenous irrigation system, they dismissed it as unimportant. Lansing says: "Modern irrigation experts thought the ancient temple system was mere religious nonsense."

Actually, the Balinese irrigation and ecology management system is extremely complex; the Jero Gde must seek an optimum balance of various competing forces. If all subaks were planted in symphony, pests would be reduced; however, water supplies would be inadequate due to peaks in demand. On the other hand, if all subaks staggered their rice planting schedules in a completely random manner, water demand would be spread out, and the water supply would be used efficiently. But the pests would flourish and wipe out the rice crop. So the Jero Gde must seek an ideal balance of pest control and water conservation between these competing policies, depending on the amount of rainfall flowing into the crater lake, levels of different pest populations in various subaks, and so forth. The high priest has considerable influence. On one occasion related by Professor Lansing, the Jero Gde concluded that a rodent plague was becoming widespread. "Instructions were sent down to all member subaks to build a special temporary shrine at all water inlets in every field, and perform a brief prayer and offering every third day for fifteen days. A widespread follow-up period was also suggested. . . . The small shrines duly appeared—on time—by the thousands" (Lansing, 1987). The Jero Gde was clearly managing the entire rice-growing ecosystem, not just irrigation.

Indonesian government officials eagerly introduced the Green Revolu-

tion rice varieties in Bali in the 1970s. They hoped to increase total food production, a national priority. Balinese rice farmers were told to grow three
rather than two crops per year, and to adopt chemical fertilizers and pesticides. These instructions broke down the centuries-old indigenous system
of fallow, managed by the Hindu priests. "As a consequence, the incidence
of bacterial and viral (rice) disease, together with insect and rat populations,
began to increase rapidly. Imported organochloride pesticides made some
dents in the rising pest populations, but also killed off eels, fish, and in some
cases, farmers in the rice fields" (Lansing, 1987). Rice yields dropped pre-
cipitously. Balinese rice farmers soon returned to the water-temple system
of water management, and discontinued the miracle rice varieties.

Anthropologist Steve Lansing has made his career studying Balinese culture, and was fully aware of how thoroughly Hindu religious thought per-
meated every aspect of daily life. He originally conducted anthropological
field research through participant observation of a rice-growing village. Naturally, he had observed the amazing uniformity among the tiny rice plots in
the subak that he studied; he explored the social organization of the subak,
including its water priest and his role in water allocation and the many religious attitudes involved in planting and growing rice. Most anthropologists
who studied irrigation systems stopped there. But Lansing became curious
about how water allocations, the simultaneous planting decisions, and the
periods of common fallow were decided upon for the entire mountain slope
of which his subak of study was one part. He accompanied his subak on their
annual pilgrimage to the Jero Gde at the High Temple on the Crater Lake.
Gradually, Lansing became fascinated with the entire system of rice irrigation in Bali, triggered by the failure of the miracle rice varieties.

At this point, in the late 1980s, Lansing, with the help of a USC ecological biologist, designed a computer simulation to calculate the effect on rice
yields in each subak of (1) rainfall, (2) planting schedules, and (3) pest proliferation. He called his simulation model "The Goddess and the Computer."
Lansing took his Macintosh computer and his simulation model from the
USC campus in Los Angeles to the Balinese High Priest at the temple on
the Crater Lake. After enthusiastically trying out various scenarios on the
computer, the Jero Gde concluded that the best rice harvests closely resembled those that the Balinese rice farmers had been following for more
than a millennium. When asked by Lansing what he thought of the computer analysis of this sacred system of water management, the Jero Gde
replied mysteriously, "Certainly you don't think that you came to work on
this by coincidence, do you?"

Today, two completely different systems for managing water resources exist side-by-side in Bali, each invisible to the other. "Downstream, foreign consultants dispatch airplanes to photograph Bali's rivers from above, and draw topographic maps of new irrigation systems. Upstream, a group of farmers drop frangipangi flowers in their [irrigation] canals before beginning a new ploughing. . . . two subaks arrive at the master water temple for advice on dealing with the brown planthoppers that have destroyed half their crop, and half a dozen men with picks and shovels shore up the sides of a field that has produced two crops of rice each year for the past eight centuries" (Lansing, 1987).

Are indigenous knowledge systems important in the introduction of technological innovations?

The present case illustration is based on Lansing (1987 and 1991) and Bardini (1994), and on numerous discussions with Professor J. Stephen Lansing, Department of Anthropology, University of Southern California.

Early Sociology

The intellectual tradition that we refer to as early sociology traces its ancestry to the French sociologist Gabriel Tarde, but most of the research publications in this tradition appeared from the late 1920s to the early 1940s (the same time period that the anthropology diffusion tradition was getting underway in America). The importance of the early sociology tradition is not because of its volume of investigations (there are only ten) nor to the sophistication of its research methods but rather to the considerable influence of early sociologists upon later diffusion researchers.

Early sociologists typically traced the diffusion of a single innovation over a geographical area like a state or a region. The early sociologists studied the diffusion of an innovation in order to understand social change. With the exception of Bowers (1937, 1938), who investigated the diffusion of ham radio sets, early sociologists did not emphasize the innovation-decision process nor did they concentrate on the process by which opinion leaders influenced others in their system to adopt or reject a new idea.

Bowers' investigation was probably the first study in the early sociology tradition that used primary data from respondents, in addition to data from secondary sources like government records. Bowers contacted a sample of 312 ham-radio operators in the United States by mailed questionnaire in order to determine the influences that led to their adoption of the radios. Bowers (1938) was the first researcher to find that interpersonal channels are more important than mass media channels for later adopters than for earlier adopters. The number of amateur radio operators in the United States had increased sharply from about 3,000 in 1914 to 46,000 in 1935. Bowers determined that this adopter distribution followed an S-shaped curve when the number of adopters was plotted by year. Bowers also related such ecological factors as city size and region in the United States to the rate of adoption of ham radios. Like others in the early sociology tradition, Bowers thus correlated ecological factors with innovativeness.

The ten studies in the early sociology diffusion tradition differed from their anthropological counterparts in that they used quantitative data analysis, a methodological approach that was to be followed by most other diffusion research traditions. The intellectual paradigm that was to set off widespread research on the diffusion of innovations had not yet happened. Creation of this paradigm had to wait for the rural sociology tradition.

Rural Sociology

The rural sociology research tradition formed the paradigm for diffusion research, and has produced the largest number of diffusion studies (see Table 2–1). Dominance of the diffusion field by rural sociology, indexed by the percentage of all diffusion studies completed by rural sociologists, has declined over past decades as other diffusion research traditions have grown more rapidly in size. Up to 1964, 423 of the 950 diffusion publications (45 percent) were in rural sociology. From 1965 to 1969, only 225 (26 percent) of the 849 diffusion publications were in rural sociology, and this percentage dropped further, to 14 percent (100 of 708 diffusion publications) from 1970 to 1974, to 8 percent (45 of 578 publications) from 1974 to 1981, and to 7 percent (54 of 805 publications from 1982 to 1994). Presently only a few rural sociology diffusion publications appear each year. But Table 2–1 shows that rural sociology is still the most important tradition in total number of diffusion studies.

Rural sociology is a subfield of sociology that focuses on the social problems of rural life. Most rural sociologists are employed in colleges of agriculture at land-grant universities. These agricultural schools have three main functions: (1) to teach students, (2) to conduct research on agricultural problems, so as to help farmers and agricultural businesses, and (3) to operate a state extension service to diffuse agricultural innovations (coming from research) to potential adopters, mainly farmers. The state colleges of agriculture and their research and extension subunits, the state agricultural experiment stations, and the state agricultural extension services are dominated by a high value on agricultural production through improved crop-growing, milk-production, beef-farming, and horticultural production. In an organization where the main value is on raising farm production, diffusion research by rural sociologists was considered very useful.

Diffusion research provided helpful leads to agricultural researchers about how to get their scientific results put into use by farmers. Diffusion research was greatly appreciated by extension service workers, who depend on the diffusion model as the main theory guiding their efforts to transfer new agricultural technologies to farmers (Rogers and others, 1982). So diffusion research fit well with the strong value on agricultural production that dominated colleges of agriculture. After about 1970, when surpluses of food production became a worldwide problem and when the farm crisis began in the United States, rural sociologists' interest in diffusion research began to fade. Today diffusion study is passé among rural sociologists.

THE HYBRID CORN STUDY AND THE DIFFUSION PARADIGM. Although a couple of pre-paradigmatic diffusion studies had been completed during the 1920s and 1930s, the Ryan and Gross (1943) investigation of the diffusion of hybrid-seed corn, more than any other study, influenced the methodology, theoretical framework, and interpretations of later students in the rural sociology tradition, and in other diffusion research traditions as well. Dr. Bryce Ryan was a professor of rural sociology at Iowa State University, the state land-grant school in Ames. In 1941, the Iowa Agricultural Experiment Station (the research branch of the college of agriculture) funded his proposed investigation of the spread of hybrid seed to Iowa farmers.

This innovation was a success story for Iowa State University. The development of hybrid seed corn had resulted from years of genetic research by agricultural scientists at Ames; finally, in 1928, hybrid seed was made available to Iowa farmers, promoted by the Iowa Agricultural Extension Service and by commercial seed companies that marketed the seed. The hybrid vigor of the new seed increased corn yields on Iowa farms, hybrid corn varieties withstood drought better than the open-pollinated seed they replaced, and hybrid corn was better suited to harvesting by mechanical corn pickers. Corn was the main farm crop in Iowa in the 1930s; in fact, Iowa's official state song boasts that it is "the tall corn state." The hybrid seed was adopted rapidly. By 1941, about thirteen years after its first release, the innovation was adopted by almost 100 percent of Iowa farmers.

Administrators of the Iowa Agricultural Experiment Station sponsored Professor Ryan's diffusion study in order to improve their understanding of lessons learned that might be applied to the diffusion of other farm innovations. These officials may also have been puzzled as to why such an obviously advantageous innovation as hybrid corn was not adopted more rapidly. For example, some farmers waited thirteen years to adopt, a period during which they were surrounded by neighbors who were using the innovation successfully.

Ryan and Gross (1950) investigated four main aspects of diffusion, which were to form the heart of the new paradigm: (1) the innovation-decision process for an individual farmer, including the sequential stages of awareness, trial, and adoption, (2) the roles of communication sources/channels in conveying the innovation, (3) the S-shaped rate of adoption, a curve that was tested as to whether it fit a normal distribution, and (4) the personal, economic, and social characteristics of various adopter categories, the classification of individuals on the basis of their relative earliness in adopting an innovation (Valente and Rogers, 1993).

The main findings from the hybrid corn study described in Chapter 1 will not be repeated here. This classic diffusion study headed later diffusion scholars toward pursuing certain research questions: Which variables are related to innovativeness? What is the rate of adoption of an innovation, and what factors (like the perceived attributes of the innovation) explain the speed of adoption? What role do different communication channels play at various stages in the innovation-decision process? These research directions have continued to dominate diffusion research since 1943. The intellectual influence of the hybrid corn study reached far beyond the study of agricultural innovations, and outside of the rural sociology tradition of diffusion research. The research paradigm created by the Ryan and Gross investigation became the academic template that was to be mimicked, first by other rural sociologists in their agricultural diffusion researches, and then by almost all other diffusion research traditions (whether they knew it or not).

The Iowa hybrid corn study left an indelible stamp on diffusion research up to the present. This lasting influence is not completely beneficial, intellectually speaking. An overly close copying of the classical diffusion paradigm by later researchers, who were often investigating diffusion of innovations of a quite different type, led to inappropriate methodologies and mistaken theoretical thrusts. Chapter 3 discusses criticisms of the dominance of the classical paradigm. We argue that the overwhelming relative advantage of hybrid corn (over the open-pollinated seed that it replaced) may have contributed to both the pro-innovation bias of later diffusion studies and to the lack of research attention paid to the consequences of technological innovations. Because the effects of hybrid corn were so obviously beneficial, it was assumed that the consequences of other innovations would also be positive.

In addition to structuring the diffusion paradigm theoretically, the Ryan and Gross hybrid corn study also established a prototypical methodology for conducting diffusion investigations: one-shot survey interviews with the adopters of an innovation, who are asked to recall their behavior and decisions regarding the innovation. Thus, the typical research design for studying diffusion was established in 1941. It has lived on, with only certain modifications, to the present day. The alternate methodological paths that were not taken by diffusion scholars represent a shortcoming in the field.

THE INVISIBLE COLLEGE OF RURAL SOCIOLOGY DIFFUSION RESEARCHERS. In the 1950s, a decade after Ryan and Gross set forth the diffusion paradigm in 1943, an explosion occurred in the number of diffusion studies by rural sociologists. Pioneering scholars in this tradition at the University of Wisconsin, the University of Missouri, and at Iowa State University carried forward the diffusion work launched by Ryan and Gross. New Ph.D's in rural sociology, produced at Madison, Columbia, and Ames in the 1950s, then became professors at other state land-grant universities where they, in turn, established diffusion research programs. I was one of these diffusion research missionaries, earning my Ph.D. degree at Iowa State and then teaching on the faculty at Ohio State University.

The invisible college of diffusion researchers in the rural sociology tradition was a highly interconnected network of scholars who shared a common theoretical-methodological framework (Crane, 1972). Dominating the network were two large cliques,* one composed of twenty-seven scholars and the other of thirty-two researchers; each centered in a lead-

---

*A *clique* is a subsystem whose elements interact with each other relatively more frequently than with other members of the communication system.

ing scholar of diffusion whose network links reached out to former Ph.D. students and to the students of those students. Smaller cliques of thirteen, twelve, seven, and so forth scholars were highly connected to the two major cliques (Figure 2–2). This network of rural sociology diffusion researchers provided consensus and coherence to the field; these scholars shared a common framework in studying diffusion, and they were abreast of each others' research findings. This invisible college helped the field to progress in an ordered direction toward its research goals. These research directions displayed a cumulative nature as each study built upon the accomplishments of previous work. Radical deviations from the diffusion paradigm were implicitly discouraged. Certain aspects of diffusion behavior were ignored, because they were not part of the accepted paradigm.

Another key factor in the 1950s' proliferation of the rural sociology diffusion research tradition, in addition to the interconnectedness of the invisible college of scholars, was the availability of research funds. During this period, state agricultural experiment stations, together with the U.S. Department of Agriculture, which partially funds the state agricultural research, were producing an outpouring of farm innovations: weed sprays, chemical fertilizers, new crop varieties, chemical feeds for livestock, and new farm machinery. The result was an "agricultural revolution" in which the number of persons fed and clothed by the average American farmer shot up from fourteen in 1950, to twenty-six in 1960, to forty-seven in 1970. This rapid increase in agricultural productivity resulted from the diffusion of farm innovations to American farmers.

The diffusion studies of rural sociologists helped show agricultural extension workers how to communicate new technological ideas to farmers, and thus how to speed up the diffusion process. Thanks to Ryan and Gross (1943), the rural sociologists had an appropriate paradigm to guide their diffusion studies. Thanks to the agricultural revolution of the 1950s, these diffusion scholars were in the right place (state university's colleges of agriculture) at the right time. The result was a proliferation of diffusion studies by the rural sociology tradition: 185 by 1960, 648 by 1970, and 791 by 1981. Then the volume of diffusion studies completed by rural sociologists per year slowed down further, and almost stopped (Figure 2–3).

RURAL SOCIOLOGY DIFFUSION RESEARCH IN THIRD WORLD NATIONS. In the early 1960s, American rural sociologists went international. This decade marked a large-scale attempt to export the land-grant university/agricul-

Figure 2–2. Communication Network Structure of Rural Sociologists Studying Diffusion as of 1967, on the Basis of Their Collaboration

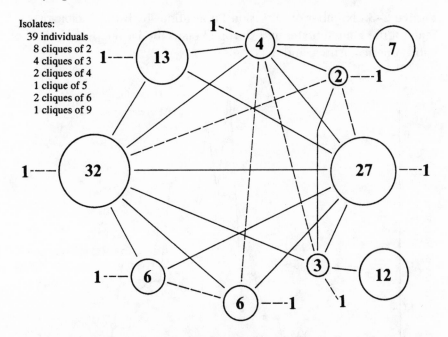

Isolates:
  39 individuals
  8 cliques of 2
  4 cliques of 3
  2 cliques of 4
  1 clique of 5
  2 cliques of 6
  1 cliques of 9

The invisible college of rural sociologists studying diffusion was highly interconnected in 1967 when Crane gathered these network data by mailed questionnaire from the 221 scholars in this diffusion research tradition. Each clique shown here includes individuals who interact more frequently with each other than with others. For the sake of simplicity, we have not shown the links within each clique, nor have we shown isolates. Direct collaboration between individuals in a pair of cliques is shown as a solid line, and a broken line indicates indirect collaboration (indicating that any member of a clique is linked to an individual in another clique through someone else). The two largest cliques, containing twenty-seven and thirty-two researchers, respectively, provide connectedness to the entire invisible college; if they were removed, the network would tend to decompose. The four largest cliques include all eight of the "high producers" (each of whom had ten or more diffusion publications); most of the clique members were their collaborators or students. All eight high producers were in communication with one another about current research. As in other invisible colleges that have been studied, the most productive scientists are leaders of cliques, and their contacts with each other link the cliques into a network. However, 101 of the 221 researchers are isolates or members of cliques not connected to the rest of the network. Few of these 101 individuals are productive scholars; many just completed their Master's or Ph.D. theses but had no further publications. Some do not live in the United States, having returned to their home country after finishing graduate study in America.

Source: Based on data reported by Crane (1972).

Figure 2–3. Number of Diffusion Publications by Rural Sociologists by Year, for the United States and Europe Versus the Developing Nations of Latin America, Africa, and Asia

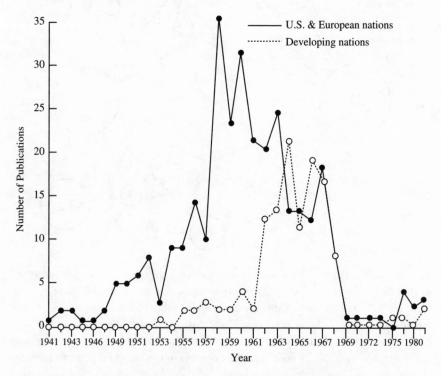

A total of 434 rural sociology publications on diffusion appeared from 1941 to 1981. Of the 331 U.S. and European diffusion publications, thirty-six (13 percent) were European, and one was Australian. A total of 103 publications reported diffusion research in Latin America, Africa, and Asia. The location of each diffusion study is determined on the basis of where the data were gathered, not where the research was published.

Source: Valente and Rogers (1994), based upon Rogers with Shoemaker (1971) and Rogers (1983).

tural extension service complex to the developing nations of Latin America, Africa, and Asia. With funding from the U.S. Agency for International Development (U.S. AID) and from private foundations, U.S. land-grant universities created overseas campuses in which American faculty members taught, conducted agricultural research, and advised extension services and other development programs (Rogers and others, 1982). Rural sociologists were part of this overseas operation, and they (in collaboration with graduate students from these developing nations that they had trained) launched diffusion studies in peasant villages. The main thrust of these international activities was agricultural development, so it was natural to pursue the topic of diffusion of farm innovations. In addition, rural sociologists investigated the diffusion of nutrition, health, and family planning innovations to villagers.

The early 1960s marked the beginning of a sharp take-off in the number of diffusion studies in developing countries (see Figure 2–3). Pioneering ventures by Syed A. Rahim (1961) in Bangladesh, and by Paul J. Deutschmann and Orlando Fals Borda (1962b) in Colombia, suggested that new ideas spread among peasants in villages in a generally similar pattern to their diffusion in more media-saturated settings like the United States and Europe. The diffusion process, and the concepts and models used to analyze it, seemed to be cross-culturally valid. Comparable results were found in the new settings. In later years, however, the applicability of the diffusion paradigm that was exported from the United States to Third World nations, began to be questioned.

The fast growth of diffusion studies in Third World countries in the 1960s occurred because technology was assumed to be the heart of development, at least as development was conceptualized at the time. So micro-level investigations of the diffusion of technological innovations among villagers were of direct relevance to development planners and to other government officials in developing nations. These research results, and the general framework of diffusion, provided both (1) a kind of theoretical approach to planning development programs, and (2) an evaluation procedure for measuring the success of development activities.

The proportion of all diffusion researches conducted in Third World nations is about 30 percent. Not all of these studies were conducted by rural sociologists, but this tradition played a pioneering role in launching diffusion research in developing nations. Since the 1970s, criticisms were made of the diffusion paradigm in Latin America, Africa, and Asia (which are discussed in Chapter 3).

DECLINE OF THE DIFFUSION PARADIGM IN RURAL SOCIOLOGY. The number of rural sociological diffusion publications in the United States declined dramatically after 1958, and after 1967 in developing nations. Thereafter, relatively few diffusion publications were authored by rural sociologists (see Figure 2–3). The major research problems had been solved, and anomalies and controversies arose. Intellectual criticisms of diffusion research increased during the late 1960s and early 1970s (Rogers, 1983). The diffusion paradigm that was developed by rural sociologists in the Midwest during the 1940s and 1950s, spread internationally among rural sociologists (although not to other scholars). So the subfield of rural sociological researchers fell, but not the diffusion paradigm.

The decline of interest in diffusion research by rural sociologists resulted from the success of the paradigm in answering the major theoretical questions. Crane (1972) concluded: "In the rural sociology area, a significant proportion of the innovative work in the area had already been done by the time [around 1960] the field began to acquire a significant number of new members." Few interesting intellectual questions remained to pursue, the number of new scholars attracted to the invisible college declined (Crane, 1972) and several of the leading diffusion scholars left the field.

Over the 25-year period from 1941 to 1966, the number of research innovations averaged about 40 for each of the five 5-year periods. During this 25-year period, the number of diffusion publications increased spectacularly from 6 to 187, with the take-off occurring over a decade after publication of the Ryan and Gross (1943) study. Hence the ratio of research innovations in rural sociological diffusion research (i.e., the introduction of a new variable of analysis) decreased drastically over the 25-year period, dropping almost to zero in the two final 5-year intervals. This decrease meant that the diffusion research front grew stale as the scholarly literature consisted increasingly of replications.

When a paradigm faces such a crisis, the rate of further research activity drops (Price, 1963; Kuhn 1962/1970). In this particular case, the paradigm was not found inadequate in its explanatory power, but rather it became stale as the main research questions were answered. Unlike the general case described by Kuhn and others, the Ryan and Gross paradigm was not replaced by an alternative paradigm to explain the diffusion of innovations.

Further, in this particular case, the mounting food surpluses produced by U.S. farmers led policy makers to question the previous value on raising agricultural production by diffusing farm innovations. Instead, rural sociologists turned their attention to finding solutions to the farm crisis caused by agricultural overproduction. So not only did the intellectual excitement of agricultural diffusion research burn out in the mid-1950s, but policy makers in agriculture (and rural sociologists themselves) began to see that the original conditions creating a need for diffusion research in agriculture had changed. Diffusion study by rural sociologists no longer promised to contribute toward solving the social problem of farm over-production. Instead, it could worsen the problem.

During the late 1960s and early 1970s, diffusion researchers in rural sociology began to assess their body of accumulated research more critically (Rogers, 1983). For instance, the anticipated and unanticipated consequences of diffusion were explored (Goss, 1979; Havens, 1975), and scholarly work by rural sociologists began to analyze the issue of whether the impacts of technological innovations were universally beneficial. Questions were raised about the environmental consequences of pesticides and other agricultural chemicals on the health of farmers and on the consumers of farm products. Several agricultural innovations like 2,4-D weed spray and diethyl stilbestrol for cattle feeding were banned by federal agencies because of their carcinogenic consequences. Such controversy and criticisms of a paradigm are typical (1) when the intellectual attraction of an invisible college is exhausted, and (2) when external conditions lead to questioning the application of the paradigm.

After 1975, some U.S. rural sociologists turned their scholarly attention to studying the diffusion of conservation and other ecology-related innovations, as the result of growing national concerns with environmental problems. This new type of diffusion study in the United States by rural sociologists accounts for the several diffusion publications per year completed since the late 1970s (see Figure 2–3). While the 1950s were decades of achieving greater farm productivity in the United States, and the 1960s were decades of attempts at increasing farm productivity in Latin America, Africa, and Asia via the Green Revolution, the 1980s and early 1990s were a period stressing the conservation of natural resources. The nature of rural sociological research on the diffusion of innovations, which continued at a low level of activity from 1969-1975, then changed to suit these contextual conditions after 1975.

Hard Tomatoes and Hard Times

During the 1970s some American rural sociologists began to question whether conducting research on the diffusion of agricultural innovations was indeed their most useful role, as social scientists of rural society. This critical attitude was boosted by a radical book written by James Hightower (1972), *Hard Tomatoes, Hard Times: The Failure of America's Land Grant Complex*. Mechanized tomato harvesting required that farmers plant tomato varieties that are very firm when they ripen. Both the harvesting machine and the hard tomato varieties were developed by agricultural researchers at state colleges of agriculture. These innovations benefited consumers through cheaper tomato prices, but unfortunately, many consumers did not like the hard tomatoes. They wanted ripe tomatoes that were soft. The hard tomatoes contained fewer vitamins than the older, soft varieties. Further, the mechanized tomato harvesters put thousands of farm laborers out of work, and drove thousands of small farmers, who could not afford to buy the expensive harvesting machines, out of tomato production (these consequences of the tomato harvester are detailed in Chapter 4).

Hightower claimed that the state colleges of agriculture were responsible for the agricultural revolution in the United States through their development and diffusion of farm innovations, but that they had almost totally ignored the consequences of these technical innovations. Hightower said this technological irresponsibility amounted to a failure on the part of U.S. colleges of agriculture. Almost all of the professional resources of the publicly supported land-grant colleges went into creating and diffusing agricultural production technology. Social science research on the consequences of innovation was severely shortchanged. Hightower's criticisms hit rural sociology especially hard; these scholars had been investigating diffusion for the past twenty years or so, in order to speed up the rate of adoption, instead of studying the technology's consequences, such as what could be done about the social problems stemming from the agricultural revolution in the United States.

This case illustration is based on Hightower (1972).

While a few diffusion studies continue to be conducted in the rural sociology tradition today, most of them deal with conservation innovations that farmers adopt in order to cope with environmental problems. Rural sociologists have become much more questioning of the emphasis placed upon agricultural production technology by colleges of agriculture. If the result is increased agricultural production in the United States at the cost of driving many farm families out of agriculture, some rural sociologists wonder if colleges of agriculture are really serving the U.S. farmer. Some rural sociologists have become a kind of social conscience for these colleges of agriculture. It is a quite different role from that played by the rural sociology tradition prior to recent decades.

Thus, the sharp decline of scholarly interest in diffusion research by rural sociologists resulted (1) from agricultural overproduction and the farm crisis of the 1930s, rural social problems that led to questioning the previous value on farm production, to which diffusion inquiry had previously contributed, and (2) from the usual pattern of the growth and decline of attention to a scientific paradigm. Eventually, all of the promising diffusion research questions had been pursued by rural sociologists, so they turned to the study of other scholarly topics. This falling-off of interest in a research issue is the final stage in the normal process of science (Valente and Rogers, 1993). While rural sociologists largely halted further diffusion research in the 1980s, their diffusion paradigm continued to catch the interest of scholars in other fields.

Education

Although it is an important diffusion research tradition in terms of the number of studies completed,* education is less important in terms of its contribution to the theoretical understanding of the diffusion of innovations. An exciting potential contribution could be made by the education research tradition, stemming from the fact that organizations are involved, in one way or another, in the adoption of educational innovations. U.S. farmers mainly make optional innovation-decisions, but most teachers and school administrators are involved in collective and/or authority innovation-decisions. Teachers, unlike farmers, work in organizations, and so organizational structures are inevitably involved in educational adoption decisions.

THE TEACHERS COLLEGE STUDIES.   Early educational diffusion studies were almost all completed at one institution, Columbia University's Teachers College, and under the direction of one scholar, Dr. Paul Mort. This tradition traces its roots to research in the 1920s and 1930s by Mort and others on whether local control over school financial decisions (as opposed to federal or state influence on these decisions) led to school innovative-

---

*Education diffusion publications numbered 23 in 1961 (5 percent of all diffusion work), 71 in 1968 (6 percent), 336 in 1981 (11 percent of all diffusion publications), and 359 in 1994 (9 percent). Education ranks fourth among the main diffusion traditions in terms of the number of publications (see Table 2–1).

ness. In short, the Columbia University education diffusion studies set out to show that local school control was related to innovativeness, which was thought to be a desirable characteristic of schools.

The data in these studies were most often gathered by questionnaires mailed to school superintendents or principals. The unit of analysis was the school system in most of these investigations. The Columbia University diffusion studies found that the best single predictor of school innovativeness was educational expenditure per pupil. The wealth factor appeared to be a necessary prerequisite for innovativeness among public schools. The stereotype of the rich suburban school in the United States as highly innovative was largely confirmed by the early Teachers College studies. Further, Mort and his fellow researchers found that a considerable time lag was required for the widespread adoption of new educational ideas: "The average American school lags twenty-five years behind the best practice" (Mort, 1953).

There is a wide range in the rate of adoption of educational innovations. For instance, it took kindergartens about fifty years (from 1900 to 1950) to reach complete adoption by U.S. schools (Mort, 1953). But driver training needed only eighteen years (from 1935 to 1953) to reach widespread adoption (Allen, 1956), and modern math took only five years, from 1958 to 1963 (Carlson, 1965). Driver training and modern math were heavily promoted by change agencies: Insurance companies and auto manufacturers in the case of driver training, and the National Science Foundation and the U.S. Department of Education in the case of modern math. The post-1958 aftermath of Sputnik caused public dissatisfaction with U.S. education and marked the beginning of an active federal government role in diffusing educational innovations. This involvement by federal and state-level governments in educational diffusion has somewhat eroded the degree of local school control which Mort had originally set out to show was so valuable.

LATER STUDIES IN EDUCATIONAL DIFFUSION. After Paul Mort's death in 1959, Teachers College at Columbia University lost its monopolistic control on educational diffusion. More recent studies focused (1) upon teachers as respondents, rather than on school administrators, (2) on within-school as well as school-to-school diffusion, and (3) on educational diffusion in Third World nations. Some studies in the education diffusion research tradition are sponsored by the U.S. Department of Education, as a means of evaluating the various diffusion programs that this government agency carries out. Many other diffusion studies are conducted by graduate students in education for their doctoral dissertations.

Two of the academic leaders in educational diffusion research in the 1960s and 1970s were Ronald G. Havelock and Matthew B. Miles. Each has written or edited a much-cited book (Miles, 1964; Havelock and others, 1969).

The Diffusion of Modern Math in Pittsburgh

The best piece of educational diffusion research is Richard O. Carlson's (1965) analysis of the spread of modern math among school administrators in Pennsylvania and West Virginia. He studied the role of opinion leaders in the diffusion networks for modern math among school superintendents, variables related to innovativeness, perceived characteristics of innovations and their rate of adoption, and the consequences of one educational innovation: Programmed instruction.

But Carlson's study is most impressive for the insight that it provides into the diffusion networks through which modern math spread from school to school in Allegheny County, Pennsylvania, the metropolitan area for Pittsburgh. Carlson conducted personal interviews with each of the thirty-eight superintendents who headed these school systems, asking each in what year they had adopted modern math, which other superintendents were their best friends, and for certain other data. Modern math entered the local educational scene of Allegheny County in 1958 when one school superintendent adopted. This innovator traveled widely outside of the Pittsburgh area, but he was a sociometric isolate in the local network; none of the thirty-seven other school administrators talked with him. The S-shaped diffusion curve did not take off until 1959–1960 after a clique of six superintendents adopted (see Figure 8–1 for a sociogram of the thirty-eight superintendents). These six included the three main opinion leaders among the Pittsburgh school administrators. The rate of adoption then climbed rapidly. There was only one adopter in 1958 (the innovator), five by the end of 1959, fifteen by 1960, twenty-seven by 1961, thirty-five by 1962, and all thirty-eight superintendents had adopted by the end of 1963. Thus, modern math spread to 100 percent adoption in about five years.

The initial adopter was too innovative to serve as an appropriate role model for the other superintendents. They waited to adopt until the opinion leaders in the six-member clique favored the innovation. Carlson's focus on interpersonal networks in diffusion represented a step forward from the Ryan and Gross (1943) hybrid corn study, which did not gather sociometric data. The school superintendent study reminds one of the investigation of the diffusion of a new drug among medical doctors, carried out in the public health tradition, and discussed in the following section.

This case illustration is based on Carlson (1965).

Public Health and Medical Sociology

This diffusion tradition began in the 1950s, and has continued growing since that time. The innovations studied are (1) new drugs or other new medical ideas, where the adopters are doctors or other health professionals, or (2) family-planning methods or health innovations, where the adopters are clients or patients.*

The Columbia University Drug Study

The classic study in this tradition was completed by three sociologists: Elihu Katz, Herbert Menzel, and James S. Coleman of Columbia University's Bureau of Applied Social Research, then America's most famous social science research institute. The drug diffusion investigation is perhaps second only to the Ryan and Gross analysis of hybrid corn in terms of its contribution to the diffusion paradigm. The most noted impact of the Columbia drug study was to orient future diffusion studies toward investigating the interpersonal networks through which subjective evaluations of an innovation are exchanged among individuals in a system. The drug study helped illuminate the nature of diffusion networks, suggesting the role that opinion leaders played in the "take-off" of the S-shaped diffusion curve. The Columbia study established that diffusion was a social process.

---

*The number of public health and medical sociology diffusion publications increased from thirty-six in 1967 (7 percent of all diffusion publications), to seventy-six in 1968 (7 percent), to 226 in 1981 (7 percent), and to 277 in 1994 (7 percent). So the number of publications in this research tradition has increased at a constant proportion of all diffusion publications (7 percent).

The market research department of Charles Pfizer and Company, a large pharmaceutical firm, provided a grant of $40,000 to the three Columbia sociologists for the drug diffusion research project, which began in 1954. Pfizer originally wanted to know if the advertisements they purchased in medical journals played an important role in diffusing the company's new drug products. Pfizer's prosaic research question was converted by the Columbia sociologists into one of the most important diffusion studies of all time (Rogers, 1994). A pilot study of the spread of a new drug was carried out among thirty-three doctors in a New England town (Menzel and Katz, 1955). The main investigation was conducted, after methodological techniques had been pretested in the pilot study, in four cities in Illinois in late 1954.

The drug study analyzed the diffusion of a new antibiotic that had appeared in late 1953, tetracycline. This innovation was referred to by the Columbia University researchers in most of their published reports by a pseudonym, "gammanym". The drug had been tried at least once by 87 percent of the Illinois doctors, who had been using two other closely related "miracle" drugs belonging to the same antibiotic family as gammanym. The new drug superseded an existing idea, just as hybrid corn had replaced open pollinated seed.

It is the patient rather than the doctor who pays for a new drug, although it is the doctor who makes the innovation-decision. The Columbia University sociologists interviewed 125 general practitioners, internists, and pediatricians in the four Illinois cities. These were 85 percent of the doctors practicing in specialties where "the new drug was of major potential significance" (Coleman and others, 1957). These 125 respondents sociometrically designated 103 additional doctors in other specialties, their network partners, who were also interviewed. Whereas many of the findings from the drug study are based upon the sample of 125 physicians, the sociometric analyses of diffusion networks comes from the responses of the total sample of 228 doctors, which constituted 64 percent of all doctors in active private practice in the four cities (Coleman and others, 1957).

The drug study used an *objective measure* of time of adoption, obtained from the record of drugstore prescriptions that were written by the doctors of study. The drug study is one of very few diffusion investigations in which the researchers were not forced to depend on recall-type data about innovativeness. Many doctors reported having adopted the drug earlier than their prescription records indicated (Menzel, 1957), although this might simply be because only a 10-percent sample of prescription records was consulted by the diffusion scholars.

This case illustration is based on Burt (1980 and 1987), Menzel and others (1959), Menzel and Katz (1955), Coleman and others (1957, 1959, and 1966), Katz (1956, 1957, and 1961), Katz and others (1963), Menzel (1957, 1959, and 1960), and Valente (1991, 1993, and 1994). The present discussion features data mainly from the four Illinois cities, rather than from the pilot study in New England.

The Columbia University investigators were not aware of other research traditions on diffusion at the time the gammanym data were gathered. The researchers make no secret of their surprise upon discovery of the hybrid seed study. Katz (1961) stated: "The drug study was completed . . . without any real awareness of its many similarities to the study that had been undertaken by Ryan and Gross almost fifteen years before."

There were striking parallels between the findings of the hybrid corn study and the drug study, which are impressive given the considerable differences between farmers and physicians. For instance, innovative doctors attended more out-of-town medical meetings than did later adopters, just as innovative Iowa farmers displayed their cosmopolite nature by more frequently visiting Des Moines. Later diffusion studies also reported that innovators have friendship networks that extend outside of their local system. And just as the innovative Iowa farmers had larger farms and higher incomes, the innovative doctors served richer patients and had a more wealthy medical practice. In both studies, socioeconomic status was positively related to innovativeness.

The most important findings from the Columbia University drug study dealt with interpersonal diffusion networks. Coleman and others (1966) found that almost all of the opinion leaders, defined as the doctors who received three or more sociometric choices as social friends, had adopted gammanym by the eighth month (of the seventeen-month diffusion period). At about this point, the S-shaped diffusion curve for the opinion leaders' followers really took off. In other words, one reason for the S-shaped curve is that once the opinion leaders in a system adopt, they then convey their subjective evaluations of the innovation to their many network partners, who are thereby influenced to adopt the new idea. This point in time at which a critical mass of doctors had adopted, and the S-shaped curve took off, is a key factor in the diffusion process (as will be discussed in Chapter 8).

Thus, a social system is a kind of collective-learning system in which the experiences of the earlier adopters of an innovation, transmitted through interpersonal networks, determine the rate of adoption of their followers. Such "learning by doing" in a social system can of course take a negative turn: If the new drug had not been very effective in curing the innovative doctors' patients, they would have passed their dissatisfactions with the new drug along to their peers. Then the S-shaped diffusion curve would have displayed a much slower rate of adoption. Or it might have reached a plateau and declined as a result of widespread discontinuance.

The doctors in the Columbia University diffusion study had more than adequate information about the new drug. Tetracycline had undergone clinical trials by pharmaceutical firms and by university medical professors prior to its release to doctors. The results of these scientific evaluations of the innovation were communicated in medical journal articles to the physicians in Coleman and others' (1966) sample, and by "detail men" (employees of the drug firms who contacted doctors with information about the new drug and who gave the doctors reprints of the journal articles and free samples of gammanym). These communication messages created awareness-knowledge of the innovation among the medical community, but such scientific evaluations of the new drug were not sufficient to persuade the average doctor to adopt. Subjective evaluations of the new drug, based on the personal experiences of a doctor's peers, were key to convincing the typical doctor to adopt gammanym for his own patients. When an office partner said to a colleague: "Look doctor, I prescribe gammanym for my patients, and it cures them more effectively than other antibiotics," that kind of message often had an effect.

This important research finding by Coleman and others (1966) led the Columbia University sociologists to investigate which doctors talked to whom. A doctor could talk to any one of the several hundred other doctors in his community. Why did he choose one, two, or three other doctors as his/her best friends? A dyadic network analysis disclosed that religion and age were the main determinants of friendship links, with home town and the medical school attended also of some importance. But the main reasons for who-to-whom links in the medical community were professional affiliations, such as belonging to the same hospital or clinic as another doctor or else participating with him or her in an office partnership. These findings suggested that the informal communication network of the medical doctors played an important role in the diffusion of the medical innovation, a topic to which we return in Chapter 8.

FAMILY PLANNING DIFFUSION IN THIRD WORLD NATIONS. Since the classic investigation of drug diffusion, a considerable number of other diffusion studies have been completed in the public health research tradition. Only a few of these studies have dealt with the spread of new medical ideas to doctors; most are investigations of the diffusion of health or family planning innovations to the public, especially in Third World countries.

An important boost to the internalization of the diffusion field was the rise of "KAP surveys" in the Third World countries during the 1960s. KAP studies are sample surveys of knowledge (K), attitudes (A), and adoption of the practice (P) of family planning innovations. K, A, and P are the logical dependent variables in evaluations of family planning communication campaigns. As national family planning programs arose in recent decades in Asia, Latin America, and in Africa to cope with a high rate of population growth, hundreds of KAP-type diffusion researches were carried out.

With the exception of the Taichung experiment in Taiwan (Freedman and Takeshita, 1969), described shortly, the intellectual contribution of these KAP surveys to scientific understanding of human behavior change has been dismal (Rogers, 1973). Although they may not have advanced the diffusion model, the KAP studies have served a practical function by showing (1) that most parents in Third World countries want fewer children than they actually have, and (2) that the majority of the public desires a government family planning program. The KAP surveys had an important impact on policy makers in developing nations, initially showing that national family planning programs were feasible, and later providing a means for evaluating the effectiveness of such programs.

Intellectually speaking, the family planning diffusion studies were generally disappointing, although several modifications in the classical diffusion model were formulated: the payment of incentives to promote the diffusion and adoption of contraceptives, the use of nonprofessional change agent aides, and various communication strategies to help overcome the taboo nature of family planning. Such modifications in the classical diffusion model emerged when family planning programs in Third World nations found the classical model wanting for purposes of promoting a preventive innovation (Rogers, 1973). In this case, programs outran the model on which they were based.

A *preventive innovation* is an idea that an individual adopts at one point in time in order to lower the probability that some future unwanted event will occur. The unwanted future event might not have happened anyway, even without adoption of the preventive innovation, and so the benefits of adoption are not clear-cut. Also, the prevented events, by definition, do not occur, and so they cannot be observed or counted. For instance, family planning officials estimate the consequences of contraception in "births averted," a behavior that is invisible to individual adopters, so the adopters have difficulty perceiving them. Preventive innovations like family planning generally have a low degree of observability, and have a relatively slow rate of adoption.

Further, most national family planning programs have found it much easier to diffuse knowledge about contraceptive methods (K) and to achieve favorable attitudes toward family planning (A), than to secure the widespread adoption and practice of contraception (P) by the target audience. Thus, KAP surveys often find a "KAP-gap," with a relatively high percentage of knowledge and favorable attitudes toward family planning methods (that is, K and A), but with a relatively low rate of adoption. In the developing nations of Latin America, Africa, and Asia, government policy makers realize the crucial need for lower rates of population growth. Otherwise, they cannot provide enough food, clothing, and schooling for the exploding number of children. So these governments carry out mass media campaigns for family planning, leading to widespread K and A. However, most parents do not share their government's desire for a lower rate of population growth. The public wants to continue their high fertility, as they prize children (especially boys) as low-cost farm labor, as an eventual source of support in old age, and as a means of carrying on the family name. The result is the KAP-gap. Knowledge gain and attitude change can be achieved more easily than can adoption of family planning methods.

The Taichung Field Experiment

The Taichung study in Taiwan by Berelson and Freedman (1964) was one of the earliest and most important of the KAP studies. Unlike the other KAP surveys, the Taichung study was a field experiment, that is, an experiment conducted in the real world rather than in a laboratory. In a field experiment, data are gathered from a sample of respondents at two points in time by means of a benchmark survey and a follow-up survey. After the benchmark survey, a treatment or treatments are applied to the sample. The effects of the treatment can be determined by measuring the change in some variable (for instance, adoption of an innovation) between the benchmark survey and the follow-up survey. One advantage of field experimental designs is that they allow the researcher to determine the *time-order* of an independent (treatment) variable on the dependent variable. As such, field experiments are an ideal research design for evaluating the effects of a diffusion program. The Berelson and Freedman study in Taiwan was one of the best, as well as one of the biggest: "This effort . . . is one of the most extensive and elaborate social science experiments ever carried out in a natural setting" (Berelson and Freedman, 1964).

The researchers implemented four different communication interventions (treatments) in approximately 2,400 *lins* (or neighborhoods, each composed of twenty to thirty families) in Taichung, a city in Taiwan: (1) neighborhood meetings about family planning, (2) neighborhood meetings, plus mailed information about family planning to local adopters, (3) neighborhood meetings, plus a personal visit to the home of likely adopters by a change agent who sought to persuade women to adopt family planning, and (4) neighborhood meetings, plus personal visits by the change agents to both husband and wife in families likely to adopt. In addition, all of the 2,400 neighborhoods in Taichung were blanketed with family planning posters.

The results of this diffusion experiment were truly spectacular: 40 percent of the eligible audience of about 10,000 women in Taichung adopted a family planning method. Pregnancy rates immediately decreased by about 20 percent. Seventy-eight percent of the contraceptives adopted were IUDs (intrauterine devices), the main family planning method promoted in the experiment and at the time a new contraceptive. The Taichung experiment showed that home visits by change agents were important for the success of a family planning program. Mass media communication (that is, the posters) created awareness-knowledge of family planning methods, but interpersonal communication throughout the group meetings and field worker visits led more directly to the adoption of contraceptives.

The Taichung researchers were surprised to find that considerable interpersonal diffusion (especially of the IUD) occurred *between* their treatment neighborhoods and the rest of the city (which was their control group). This unplanned diffusion spoiled their neat experimental design, but it may have been their most important finding (Freedman and Takeshita, 1969). Three types of evidence suggested that this unplanned, informal communication about family planning was effective in convincing potential adopters:

1. About 40 percent of the adopters of family planning in Taichung resided in the "Control" lins or in the "Mail" lins, while 60 percent of adopters lived in the neighborhoods contacted by field workers.

2. Even in the "Field Worker" lins, one-sixth of the adopters did so *before* they were visited by the family-planning field workers.
3. Twenty percent of the contraceptive adopters at Taichung's nine family planning clinics were women who lived *outside* of the city, and traveled some distance to secure contraceptive services.

Berelson and Freedman (1964) concluded: "The important thing is to develop a 'critical mass' that can generate enough personal motivation and social support to carry on without further home visits. . . . The task of a planned [population] program will thus be to develop enough knowledgeable and convinced users of contraceptives to start a movement that reaches out to the ill-informed or unconvinced." This fundamental lesson learned was emphasized by the finding that "nearly 75 percent of the new devices [IUDs] were accepted without the necessity of a home visit [by a family planning field worker]." So the partial contamination of the experimental design was of considerable benefit in informing us about the importance of interpersonal family planning communication.

The spectacular results of the Taiwan diffusion experiment provided optimism among development officials responsible for national family planning programs which were then being initiated in many developing countries. In the years since the Berelson-Freedman study, however, it has been impossible to secure results comparable to those achieved in Taiwan. So perhaps the Taiwan experiment led to an unrealistically rosy glow about family planning diffusion, an optimism that was to be dashed in the later 1960s and 1970s when many other nations launched family planning programs. In fact, the experience of these programs to date suggests that contraceptives are one of the most difficult types of innovations to diffuse (Rogers, 1973). One reason is because they are preventive innovations (see Chapter 6).

A methodological point made by the Taichung family planning study is that diffusion researches need not be limited to conducting one-shot surveys of the adopters of an innovation, with data gathering after a new idea has diffused. A field experimental design allows a diffusion researcher to draw on diffusion theory in order to plan one or more communication interventions that are then evaluated by analyzing differences in K, A, and P variables between benchmark and follow-up surveys. Diffusion field experiments can advance our understanding of diffusion behavior, and help policy makers design and implement more effective diffusion programs. Unfortunately, there have been very few field experiments in the three decades since the Taichung Project.

This case illustration is based on Berelson and Freedman (1964). A number of other publications report details on this research: Freedman (1964), Freedman and others (1964), Takeshita (1964, 1966), and Takeshita and others (1964). These publications are summarized in Freedman and Takeshita (1969).

Communication

The communication tradition of diffusion research today represents 484 (12 percent) of all diffusion publications. At the time of my 1962 edition of *Diffusion of Innovations*, there were few diffusion publications by communication scholars (1 percent of the total), and I did not even consider communication as a diffusion research tradition. Communication research on diffusion came on strong in ensuing decades.

Human communication as a scientific field of study was not fully appreciated until an influential book, *The Mathematical Theory of Communication*, was published by Claude E. Shannon and Warren Weaver (1949). Shannon defined the key concept of information and proposed a simple, linear model of communication. Then the field of communication research, initially centered on the effects of the media, began to grow. At first, in the 1930s and 1940s, established scientists from political science, sociology, and social psychology were attracted to communication research. They did not consider themselves communication scholars, nor did the new Ph.D.'s that they trained. In the period following World War II, departments of communication were established at many universities, with Wilbur Schramm playing the pioneer role at the University of Iowa, the University of Illinois, and at Stanford University (Rogers, 1994). Departments and schools of communication at various universities began producing Ph.D.'s in communication. These new scholars then were employed as professors in already-existing university departments of journalism and speech, where they injected the new scientific perspective of communication study into the existing curricula.

Today, more than 2,000 departments of communication, journalism, speech, advertising, and broadcasting are flourishing in U.S. universities. They award 50,000 bachelors' degrees in communication each year, about 5 percent of all bachelors' degrees granted by U.S. universities. In addition, about 2,000 masters' degrees and 250 Ph.D. degrees in communication are awarded per year (Rogers, 1994). The field of communication study is also quite strong in Mexico, Brazil, Korea, Egypt, and Northern European nations. So the new discipline of communication study has become well established.

One early concern of communication scholars was the diffusion of news events that were carried by the mass media. More than 50 such studies have been completed, dealing with such headline news items as President Kennedy's assassination, the *Challenger* disaster, the Gulf War, and various natural disasters. Unlike technological innovations, news events are ideas that do not have a material basis. Nevertheless, news events diffuse in a similar fashion: The distribution of knowers over time follows an S-shaped curve, interpersonal and mass media channels play comparable roles, and so on. One difference from the diffusion of other innovations is that news events spread much more rapidly; for example, 68 percent of the U.S. adult public were aware of the events in Dallas within thirty minutes of the shot that felled President Kennedy. Within another hour, 95 percent knew of this event.

Diffusion of News

Although it was not the first investigation of the diffusion of a major news event, the 1960 study by Paul J. Deutschmann and Wayne Danielson, more than any other, set the pattern for the many news diffusion researches that were to follow over future decades. Deutschmann and Danielson were two of the first individuals to earn Ph.D. degrees in communication study, both from Stanford University under Wilbur Schramm, who pioneered this new field of study. Deutschmann and Danielson looked at news diffusion as a communication process (both had been newspeople prior to graduate study), which led them to pursue certain research questions and thus to formulate the paradigm for news diffusion studies. Although Deutschmann was thoroughly familiar with rural sociological research on diffusion, and this knowledge certainly influenced their research on news diffusion, Deutschmann and Danielson (1960) did not cite diffusion research in their publication from this study.

News diffusion investigations mainly focus on tracing the spread of a spectacular news event like the assassination of a U.S. president, the Pope, or a prime minister; the *Challenger* disaster; or some other major world news event. At such times, each mass medium virtually crackles with the excitement of the news. Audience individuals often approach complete strangers on the street to tell them about the news event. As Deutschmann and Danielson (1960) stated: "Every so often a major news story 'breaks.' Reporters get the essential facts in a matter of minutes and send them on their way . . . Radio and television stations break into their programs to broadcast bulletins. Newspapers stop their presses for quick make-overs. In a flood of printed and spoken words, the message leaves the media."

What happens next as the news reaches the public and spreads from individual to individual is the concern of news diffusion scholars. They want to know the relative importance of radio, television, newspaper, and interpersonal channels in diffusing the news, and how quickly such diffusion occurs. It occurs very rapidly, Deutschmann and Danielson (1960) found: Within thirty hours of such major news events as President Eisenhower's heart attack, launching of the Explorer I Satellite, and Alaska statehood, from 75 to 95 percent of the public knew about the news event.

Because news diffusion is so rapid, the process is difficult to study by the usual methods of communication research. If a scholar applied for a research grant, designed and pretested a questionnaire, trained survey interviewers, and then contacted a sample of the public, several months or even years would elapse after the news event, and most respondents would have forgotten when and how they first heard about it. Thus a "firehouse research" design was followed by the two communication scholars. Deutschmann and Danielson planned a general questionnaire in advance of the three news events that they studied, and trained a cadre of graduate students to conduct telephone interviews with audience individuals. The costs of data gathering were extremely modest, as samples of several hundred individuals each were contacted in Lansing, Michigan; Madison, Wisconsin (Deutschmann was a professor at Michigan State University, and Danielson was at the University of Wisconsin); and in Palo Alto, California (where the two scholars had previously studied for their Ph.D. degrees). As a result of these quick-response data-gathering methods, Deutschmann and Danielson were able to begin telephone interviewing within twenty-four hours of the news events. A similar type of quick-response research design has been utilized by most other news diffusion scholars.

Deutschmann and Danielson found that radio, television, and newspapers were each cited by more respondents as their first sources/channels of communication about the news event than were interpersonal networks. The mass media, especially newspapers, were also important in providing more detailed information about a news event, but interpersonal channels were also important. "Two-thirds of our respondents reported being involved in conversations about the [news] events" (Deutschmann and Danielson, 1960).

In general, the two communication scholars documented the lightening speed of news diffusion, compared to the more usual rate of diffusion of technological innovations in agriculture, education, and medicine, where months and years, instead of hours, are required for the diffusion process. Relatively earlier knowers about a news event were characterized by more formal education and higher status occupations than were relatively later knowers. Deutschmann and Danielson (1960) concluded that on the basis of three major news events that they studied in the three university cities, "The diffusion process is far more regular than we suspected." Such common patterns of news event diffusion were later to be found by other scholars in the news-event diffusion research tradition.

The diffusion of news about a spectacular event can be very rapid. On January 28, 1986, the space shuttle *Challenger* exploded shortly after takeoff, killing all seven astronauts, including Christa McAuliffe, America's first teacher in space. Within thirty minutes of the explosion, half of a sample of 538 residents of Phoenix had heard about the *Challenger* disaster (Mayer, Gudykunst, Perrill, and Merrill, 1990). This amazing rapidity of news-event diffusion occurs because the individual only needs to gain awareness-knowledge of the news event, while the adoption of a technological innovation consists of the knowledge, persuasion, and implementation stages in the innovation-decision process (DeFleur, 1987a).

One of the important contributions of the news event diffusion studies has been to establish the conditions under which mass media versus interpersonal communication channels are relatively more important. News events of extremely high news value, like the assassination of President Kennedy or the shooting of Pope John Paul II in 1981 not surprisingly spread with great speed because while the media (especially radio and television) carry the news to a number of people, the news then fans out by word-of-mouth channels, even among strangers. Less spectacular, everyday news events of the kind that typically appear on the front page of a daily newspaper spread mainly via mass media channels. Events of relatively low news value, such as last night's decision by the city council to build a new sewer line, while reported in the local media, mainly spread by interpersonal channels among the few people who are interested (Greenberg, 1964).

A synthesis of the news diffusion studies by Melvin DeFleur (1987a) showed that "the tradition has all but run out." After flourishing in the 1960s and 1970s, scholarly interest in news diffusion declined as most of the intriguing research questions were answered, at least those suggested by the influential Deutschmann and Danielson (1960) study, which set the pattern for the other studies that followed. A few news-event diffusion studies are still being conducted by communication scholars in the 1990s. The main contribution of this work has been to help interest mass communication scholars in the diffusion paradigm.

This case illustration is based on Deutschmann and Danielson (1960) and DeFleur's (1987a) review of the news diffusion research tradition.

LATER COMMUNICATION RESEARCH ON DIFFUSION. In the early 1960s, communication scholars began to investigate the transmission of technological ideas, especially agricultural, health, educational, and family planning innovations in Third World nations. Paul J. Deutschmann's study of the diffusion of innovations in a Colombian village* stands as a landmark, and led other communication scholars to focus upon peasant audiences in the 1960s. During the 1970s communication scholars began to investigate the diffusion of technological innovations in the United States, sometimes when communities or organizations were the adopting units (see Chapter 10).

One of the special advantages of the communication research tradition is that it is open to analyzing any particular type of innovation. There are no limitations, such as the education research tradition's focus on educational innovations, the rural sociologist's main emphasis upon agricultural ideas, or the public health tradition's concern with family planning methods. This lack of a message-content orientation frees the communication researcher to concentrate on the process of diffusion. Further, the communication tradition has an especially appropriate intellectual toolkit of useful concepts and methods (for example, credibility, network analysis, and the semantic differential) for studying diffusion.

During the 1980s communication scholars began to carry out research on the diffusion of new communication technologies like VCRs, cable television, and E-mail systems. These technological innovations are unique in that they each represent a means for individuals to communicate with each other, and so a "critical mass" may occur in the rate of adoption (as we show in Chapter 8).

---

*The publications from this study are Deutschmann (1963), Deutschmann and Fals Borda (1962a, 1962b), and Deutschmann and Havens (1965).

Marketing

The marketing diffusion tradition has come on particularly strong since the 1960s, and especially since the 1970s when work on social marketing got underway. Marketing managers of private firms are concerned with how to launch new products successfully. Many new consumer products end in failure. In fact, it takes hundreds of attempts to introduce new consumer items each year to produce only one successful new product. Companies have a vital stake in the diffusion of new products, and a tremendous number of researches on this topic have undoubtedly been completed. However, a large portion of these diffusion research reports can be found only in the confidential files of the sponsoring company. The funding of marketing diffusion studies by private sources who use the results to gain a competitive advantage restricts scholarly access to the intellectual lessons learned from these diffusion studies in the marketing research tradition.

Even so, the number of available diffusion paradigms in the marketing tradition is impressive today. In 1961, there were only a handful of marketing diffusion studies, and I did not then consider that a marketing tradition existed (Rogers, 1962). By 1994, however, marketing diffusion research had exploded. The 585 publications constituted 15 percent of all diffusion publications, and thus marketing ranked second in its contribution to diffusion research (see Table 2–1). This marketing literature emphasizes prediction of the rate of adoption for new products, studies how the perceived attributes of an innovation affect its purchase, and includes publications about social marketing.

Marketing has a negative connotation in some academic circles because the term is narrowly construed as synonymous with manipulating human purchasing behavior for commercial advantage. On the contrary, marketing activities, if they are to be very successful over the long term, must match consumers' needs with commercial products and services. Marketing scholars and practitioners argue that they are providing a useful contribution to society by helping to identify consumer needs, and by fulfilling such needs by making appropriate commercial products available.

THE BASS FORECASTING MODEL. A tremendous expansion has occurred in the marketing literature on diffusion since the 1970s. The most important single impetus to this explosion is a model for forecasting the diffu-

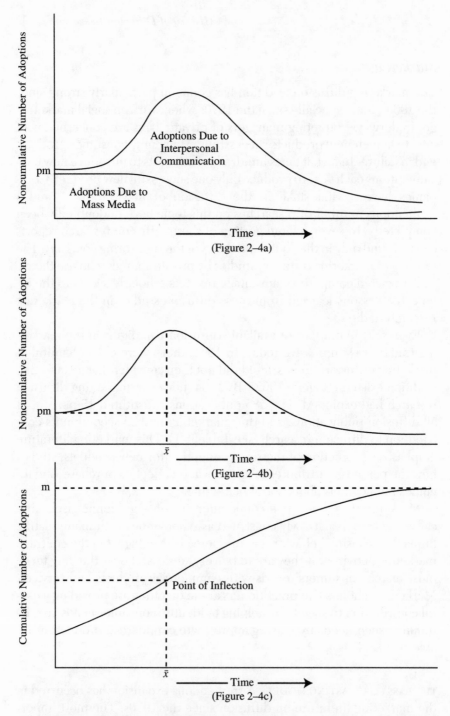

Figure 2–4. The Bass Model for Forecasting the Rate of Adoption of a New Product

sion of new consumer products proposed by Frank Bass in 1969, then a marketing professor at Purdue University and presently at the University of Texas at Dallas. The Bass forecasting model became so important in the marketing field because it offers some plausible answers to the uncertainty associated with the introduction of a new product in the marketplace. In fact, some of the largest U.S. corporations have used the Bass model: Eastman Kodak, IBM, RCA, Sears, and AT&T (Bass, 1986b). Most of the scholarly research inspired by the Bass forecasting model has been carried out by U.S. business school professors, but it has also been applied in other nations and in other academic fields. For example, Lawton and Lawton (1979) used the Bass model to predict the diffusion of educational ideas, and Akinola (1986) analyzed the diffusion of coco-spray chemicals among Nigerian farmers.

What is the Bass (1969) model? It assumes that potential adopters of an innovation are influenced by two types of communication channels: Mass media and interpersonal word-of-mouth channels. Individuals adopting a new product because of a mass media message occur continually throughout the diffusion process, but are concentrated in the relatively early time periods (Figure 2–4). Individuals adopting as a result of interpersonal messages about the new product expand in numbers during the first half of the diffusion process, and thereafter decline in numbers per time period, creating the S-shaped diffusion curve (Figure 2–4). Further the Bass forecasting model assumes that the rate of adoption during the first half of the diffusion process is symmetrical with that in the second half, as would necessarily occur for an S-shaped diffusion curve.

Figure 2–4.

Key elements in the Frank Bass (1969) forecasting model are (1) adopters due to mass media messages (p), (2) adopters due to interpersonal communication channels (q), and (3) an index of market potential (m) for the new product. Figure 2–4a shows that the number of adopters of a new product per time unit is due to mass media channels and to interpersonal channels, with the later much more important. Figure 2–4b shows that the crucial variable to predict is the number of adopters of the new product from the time of the prediction to the mean time of adoption, when a point of inflection occurs in the diffusion curve. The cumulative number of adopters can then be estimated (Figure 2–4c) because the S-shaped diffusion curve is symmetrical around the mean year of adoption.

Source: Based on Mahajan, Muller, and Bass (1990).

All of these elements of the Bass model are well known and are soundly based on the results of diffusion research. So what is the unique contribution of the Bass model? Most important, it is a *predictive* model that seeks to forecast how many adoptions of a new product will occur at future time periods, or on the basis of pilot launches of a new product, or even from managerial judgments made on the basis of the diffusion history of analogous products (Mahajan, Muller, and Bass, 1990). Note that the Bass model addresses the market in an aggregate way: The forecast is the total number of adopters who purchase the new product per time period, rather than the adoption or non-adoption by an individual customer. A second important contribution of the Bass model is to provide a mathematical formula for predicting the rate of adoption. The three parameters in the Bass model are: (1) a coefficient of mass media influence (p), (2) a coefficient of interpersonal influence (q), and (3) an index of market potential (m), which is estimated by data from the first few time periods of diffusion of a new product. For fifteen different uses of the Bass model, the average mass media influence coefficient, p, was .03, and the average interpersonal influence coefficient was .38 (Sultan, Farley, and Lehmann, 1990). This much greater weighing of word-of-mouth communication in the Bass model is consistent with the universal research finding in diffusion studies that diffusion is essentially a social process occurring through interpersonal networks. By expressing the essentials of the diffusion process in the form of a mathematical equation, Bass (1969) greatly simplified and codified our understanding of the diffusion of innovations, and also made such understanding very attractive to business school scholars, who tend to be mathematically inclined. Essentially, Bass repackaged diffusion knowledge into a form that was more usable by the business community and by marketing scholars. His original forecasts were for such consumer durable products as refrigerators, black-and-white television sets, dryers, and air conditioners (Bass, 1969). Soon an invisible college of marketing scholars were following up on the leads provided by Frank Bass, extending his forecasting model to other types of innovations, and adding various "bells and whistles" to his original model. A total of thirteen publications dealing with the Bass model appeared in the 1970s. Then the number jumped to eighty-two during the 1980s, and continues to grow in the 1990s.

Many of these follow-on researches extend the Bass model in order to test assumptions necessary for the basic simplicity of the original work (Mahajan, Muller, and Bass, 1990):

1. That the market potential, m, of a new product remains constant over time.
2. That the diffusion of the new product is independent of other innovations.
3. That the nature of an innovation does not change over time.
4. That the diffusion process is not influenced by marketing strategies, such as changing a product's price, advertising it more heavily, and so forth.
5. That supply restrictions do not limit the rate of diffusion of a new product.

SOCIAL MARKETING. We can *force* people to adopt innovations. For example, city and state governments enforce laws requiring motorcycle helmet use, utilization of automobile seatbelts, and driving under the 55-miles-per-hour speed limit. Cigarette-smoking is not permitted by domestic airline passengers in the U.S., or in nonsmoking sections of restaurants. In these cases, society imposes its will on individual behavior. Such a coercive approach to change is understandably not very popular with the public. A different approach to gaining the adoption of innovations that improve health, raise literacy levels, and extend life expectancy is *social marketing*, the application of commercial marketing strategies to the diffusion of nonprofit products and services.

Social marketing was launched about forty years ago with the rhetorical question "Why can't you sell brotherhood like you sell soap?" (Wiebe, 1952). In the past decade or so, the social marketing approach has been applied to energy conservation, smoking cessation, safer driving, decreasing infant mortality, AIDS prevention, family planning, preventing drug abuse, anti-littering, and improving nutrition. Often social marketing campaigns seek to convince people to do something that is unpleasant. For instance, many Americans wish to lose weight, stop smoking, get more exercise, and floss their teeth. But they do not do so. The main applications of social marketing are to change behavior in directions desired by individuals who are impeded by inertia or other resistances.

Social marketing has proven to be effective in attempts to cope with social problems and to bring about useful social changes in society. When done right, social marketing can make a difference. But it must be adequately funded and staffed by competent individuals, enough time must be provided for carrying out a social marketing campaign, and it should incorporate both formative and summative evaluation research in order to design effective messages. Social marketing is essentially a type of planned communication process.

An assessment of experiences with social marketing by Fox and Kotler (1980) concluded "that most social marketing problems will be more formidable than the typical marketing problems facing commercial marketers." One noted success for social marketing has been its use by government family planning programs to diffuse oral contraceptive pills and condoms in Third World countries. For example, a condom campaign in India in the 1970s involved renaming the product *Nirodh* (from a Sanskritic word meaning "protection"). Condoms had been known as "French letters" in India, and were considered taboo. After trying out their Nirodh campaign in a small test market in New Delhi, the social marketers expanded their coverage to one-fifth of India, and then by careful stages to the entire nation. A massive advertising campaign helped launch Nirodh, and the condoms were sold by thousands of tea shops and at cigarette stands on every street corner. The government of India subsidized the product so that each condom only cost about two cents. Market research was conducted at every step of the Nirodh campaign to provide feedback to the campaign planners: the selection of the name Nirodh over various alternatives, the selection of tea shops and cigarette stands as distribution outlets that would be accessible and acceptable to the intended audience, and what information was needed by Indian men about how to use condoms. The Nirodh campaign showed how marketing expertise could be used in a social marketing campaign for family planning.

There are certain important differences between commercial marketing and social marketing. By definition, commercial marketing is primarily motivated by a desire for profit. Social marketing is usually aimed at the poorest and least educated segments of society, who may be the most difficult to reach in a diffusion campaign. Commercial marketing is usually aimed at the relatively more elite segments of society, that potentially are most likely to buy a new product. Spectacular results are often expected of social marketing, such as by the ministry of health in a Third World county that wants a 50 percent reduction in infant mortality. A commercial marketer of beauty soap would be delighted with a 0.5 percent increase in market share. Sometimes, a social marketer and a commercial marketer are direct adversaries, such as when a tobacco company is marketing cigarettes and a government health campaign is urging smokers to quit. Or when milk companies promote their bottle-feeding products like powdered milk while a ministry of health in the same country is conducting a campaign to encourage breast-feeding. Social marketing is usually carried out by government and other nonprofit organizations, while commercial marketing is conducted by private companies.

What are the essentials of a social marketing campaign?

1. *Audience segmentation* is a communication strategy that consists of identifying certain subaudiences within a total audience, and then conveying a special message to each of these subaudiences. For example, the Stanford Heart Disease Prevention Project, with which the author was involved in the 1980s, identified individuals over forty-five years of age who smoked cigarettes and who were overweight as a priority subaudience for messages about preventing heart disease. Similarly, the Nirodh campaign in India identified young married couples as being particularly receptive to using condoms for spacing their children.

2. *Formative evaluation research* is conducted relatively early in a communication campaign in order to create more effective messages. Provisional versions of messages may be pretested with small samples of an intended audience in order to obtain feedback that allows the messages to be redesigned to make them more effective. Formative evaluation provides an audience orientation to social marketing campaigns.

3. The innovation is *positioned* relative to the intended audience's meanings so as to emphasize certain desired aspects. Sometimes this positioning can be facilitated by the name that is chosen for the innovation. An example is Nirodh in India ("protection"), *Panther* in Jamaica (a name for condoms that conveys an image of masculine vitality), and *Preethi* ("beautiful") in Sri Lanka. Often a logo is chosen to symbolize the innovation, particularly if the innovation is taboo (that is, too sensitive or embarrassing to talk about). For instance, in Sri Lanka, the logo for Preethi condoms was a circle made with the thumb and index finger (a nonverbal gesture meaning "okay" in the United States). An individual can enter a drugstore in Sri Lanka and silently indicate in a symbolic way that he or she wishes to purchase a Preethi. The logo is prominently displayed on the Preethi package, which is an eye-catching, pleasing color that has been chosen through pretesting. Sometimes, powerful symbolism is used to position an innovation; an example is the U.S. television ad of an egg frying in a skillet, accompanied by the caption, "This is your brain on drugs."

4. The *price* of the innovation is kept very low, as the purpose of social marketing is to change behavior, not to earn profits. Nirodhs only cost two cents. The conventional wisdom in social marketing campaigns is to charge a low price for a product or service, even though it could be given

away free. Further, distribution of the innovation should be convenient for its adopters. For example, condoms are distributed free on demand by policemen in Bangkok's redlight district, as part of a social marketing campaign jokingly referred to as "Cops and Rubbers" in Thailand.

5. Finally, a social marketing campaign should utilize communication channels (for instance, paid advertising) over which the campaign planners have control (rather than public service announcements, for example, which are often broadcast at times that miss the intended audience segment).

ADVANTAGES AND DISADVANTAGES OF THE MARKETING DIFFUSION TRADITION. The marketing tradition of diffusion research has certain advantages and some attendant disadvantages compared with other research traditions. Because marketing scholars usually conduct diffusion studies with the sponsorship, or at least the collaboration, of the manufacturers of a new product, the researchers are able to conduct field experiments (an especially powerful type of diffusion research design). Other than in marketing, diffusion scholars have seldom been in a position to control the intervention strategies through which an innovation is introduced, so it has not been possible to conduct field experiments (like the Taichung experiment in family planning described previously).

But such close siding with the sources of innovations in diffusion research can also lead to certain intellectual and ethical problems. For example, the needs of marketers are usually given priority over those of consumers. Sources wish to know how they can influence consumers' adoption behavior. In contrast, consumers may wish to know how to insulate themselves *from* such influence attempts or, more generally, how they can evaluate new products (Rogers and Leonard-Barton, 1978). The source bias in marketing diffusion studies may lead to highly applied research that, although methodologically sophisticated, deals with trivial diffusion problems in a theoretical sense.

As a result, we know more about consumer preferences for deodorant scents and the taste of beer than about how to best advance the theory of diffusion.

Geography

Although still one of the smallest of the ten main diffusion research traditions described in this book, the geography tradition has expanded considerably in recent decades, and it is unique in its emphasis upon space as a major factor affecting the diffusion of innovations. In 1961, there were only three diffusion publications in geography, all by Professor Torsten Hägerstrand at the University of Lund in Sweden (Rogers, 1962) By 1994, there were 160 diffusion studies by geographers, representing about 4 percent of the total number of diffusion publications.

Maps are one of the geographers' favorite tools. Space is the crucial variable for geographers, and they specialize in investigating how spatial distance affects other aspects of human existence. Professor Hägerstrand (1952; 1953) pioneered a simulation approach to investigating how spatial distance affected diffusion. First, Hägerstrand constructed a mathematical model of the diffusion process as it should theoretically occur over time and through space. For instance, Hägerstrand's model contained, as one of its elements, the "neighborhood effect," which expressed the greater likelihood for an innovation to spread from one adopter to another adopter (in the next unit of time) who was close by, rather than far away. This neighborhood effect was built into Hägerstrand's computer model of diffusion by means of mathematical probabilities of adoption that decreased with distance away from the adopter. Hägerstrand then entered a map of the Swedish countryside in his computer, and, beginning with the location of the first adopter of an agricultural innovation, he simulated the ensuing diffusion process. He then compared the resulting simulation of diffusion with data (1) on the innovation's actual rate of adoption, and (2) on the geographical spread of the farm innovation of study.

A diffusion simulation is an attempt to mimic the reality of diffusion. If the simulated process does not correspond to reality data, then the researcher adjusts the theoretical model of diffusion to more fully take reality into account. The eventual result is a series of abstracted rules about the diffusion process which represent a model. The geography research tradition shows clearly that space is important in determining the adoption of an innovation. Recent studies in the geography research tradition concentrate on the diffusion of geographically based computer systems among state and local governments.

General Sociology

The general sociology tradition of diffusion research is a residual category, consisting of all other diffusion studies by sociologists not included in early sociology, rural sociology, and public health/medical sociology. After the 1960s, diffusion studies by general sociologists proliferated; in 1994, this research tradition included 322 diffusion publications, 8 percent of the total (see Table 2–1). General sociology had climbed to fifth place among the diffusion research traditions. The rise of general sociology as a research tradition indicates that the diffusion approach is catching on among many sociologists today, in addition to those concerned with agricultural, medical, or public health innovations.

General Economics

The general economics research tradition has come on fast in the 1980s and early 1990s, to become one of the ten main diffusion research traditions. Some 155 publications, about 5 percent of the total, have appeared at the hand of general economists, and another 101 publications resulted from the research of agricultural economists, whom we regard as a separate, minor research tradition (see Table 2–1). General economists are mainly concerned with economic analyses of technological innovations.

A footnote to Table 2–1 mentions the five minor diffusion research traditions of public administration and political science, agricultural economics, psychology, statistics, and industrial engineering. These and other minor traditions make up 563 of the 3,890 diffusion publications in 1994, about 14 percent of the total. Today all of the behavioral science disciplines have at least some interest in the diffusion of innovations.

A Typology of Diffusion Research

Here we overview the various types of diffusion research, which we will detail in later chapters. Our present concern differs from the previous discussion of the history of diffusion research in that we now shall look at *types* of diffusion research, rather than at the various research traditions.

Table 2–2 shows eight different types of diffusion analysis and the relative amount of research attention paid to each. By far the most popular diffusion research topic has been variables related to individual innovativeness (Type 3 in Table 2–2). More than half (58 percent) of all the empirical generalizations reported in diffusion publications deal with innovativeness. We illustrate each of the eight types of diffusion research with one or two studies.

1. *Earliness of knowing about innovations.* Bradley S. Greenberg (1964) determined what, when, and how people first learned about the news of the assassination of President John F. Kennedy. Data were gath-

ered by telephone interviews with 419 adults in a California city. The respondents were classified as early knowers or late knowers. Most of the early knowers reported that they had heard of President Kennedy's death by radio or television, whereas most of the late knowers first learned of the assassination by means of interpersonal communication channels. Most individuals who first learned about this important news event from a mass medium then told other individuals about the message. Most individuals who first heard the news through an interpersonal network then turned to a mass media channel for further information and to obtain confirmation of the news event.

2. *Rate of adoption of different innovations in a social system.* Frederich Fliegel and Joseph Kivlin (1966b) conducted personal interviews with 229 Pennsylvania dairy farmers to measure their perceptions of fifteen attributes of each of thirty-three dairy innovations, in order to predict their rate of adoption. Innovations perceived as most economically rewarding and least risky were adopted more rapidly. The complexity, observability, and trialability of the innovations were less highly related to the innovations' rate of adoption, but innovations that were most compatible with farmers' values were adopted more rapidly.

3. *Innovativeness.* Paul J. Deutschmann and Orlando Fals Borda (1962b) conducted a diffusion survey in the Colombian village of Saucío to test the cross-cultural validity of correlates of innovativeness derived from prior U.S. diffusion Ïresearch (see Chapter 7). A striking similarity was found between the results obtained in the Colombia study and those from previous research in the United States.

Another correlates-of-innovativeness study is Lawrence Mohr's (1969) survey of the directors of county departments of public health in Michigan, Ohio, and Ontario (Canada). An innovativeness score was computed for each of the 120 health departments of study, indicating the degree to which each organization had adopted various new ideas in public health. The most innovative health departments were characterized by more financial resources, a director who was more highly committed to innovation, and by larger size. So research on factors related to innovativeness can be carried out with individuals or with organizations (or other systems) as the units of analysis.

4. *Opinion leadership.* The success or failure of diffusion programs rests in part on the role of opinion leaders and their relationship with change agents. Everett M. Rogers and Johannes van Es (1964) sought (1)

Table 2–2. Types of Diffusion Research

Type	Main Dependent Variable	Independent Variables	Units of Analysis	Approximate Percentage of Generalizations of This Type in Available Diffusion Publication[a]	Chapter in This Book Dealing with This Type of Research	Representative Diffusion Research Study
1	Earliness of knowing about an innovation by members of a social system	Characteristics of members (e.g., cosmopoliteness, communication channel behavior)	Members of a social system (usually individuals)	5%	Chapter 5—The Innovation-Decision Process	Greenberg (1964)
2	Rate of adoption of different innovations in a social system	Attributes of innovations (e.g., complexity, compatibility, etc.) as perceived by members of a system	Innovations	1%	Chapter 6—Perceived Attributes of Innovations and Their Rate of Adoption	Fliegel and Kivlin (1966b)
3	Innovativeness of members of a social system (the members may be individuals or organizations)	Characteristics of members (e.g., cosmopoliteness, communication channel behavior, resources, social status, contact with change agents); system-level variables	Members of a social system (individuals or organizations)	58%	Chapter7—Adopter Categories; and Chapter 10—Innovation in Organization	Deutschmann and Fals Borda (1962b), Mohr (1969)
4	Opinion leadership in diffusing innovations	Characteristics of members (e.g., cosmopoliteness); system norms and other system variables; communication channel behavior	Members of social system (usually individuals)	3%	Chapter 8—Diffusion Networks	Rogers and van Es (1964)

#						
5	Diffusion networks	Patterns in the network link between two or more members of a system	Dyadic network links connecting pairs of individuals (or organizations) in a system	Less than 1%	Chapter 8—Diffusion Networks	Rogers and Kincaid (1981), Coleman and others (1966)
6	Rate of adoption of innovations in different social systems	Systems norms; characteristics of the social system (e.g., concentration of opinion leadership); change agent variables (e.g., their strategies of change); types of innovations decisions	Social systems	2%	Some attention is given in Chapter 9—The Change Agent; and Chapter 10—Innovation in Organizations	Rogers and Kincaid (1981)
7	Communication channel use (e.g., whether mass media or interpersonal)	Innovativeness and other characteristics of members of a social system (e.g., cosmopoliteness; system norms; attributes of innovations	Members of systems (or the innovation-decision)	7%	Chapter 9—The Change Agent: and Chapter 5—The Innovation Decision Process	Ryan and Gross (1943)
8	Consequences of an innovation	Characteristics of members, the nature of the social system, and the nature and use of the innovation	Members or social systems or innovations	0.2%	Chapter 11—Consequences of Innovations	Sharp (1952)
	Others		Total	$\frac{24}{100}$		

[a] These percentages are based on a content analysis of the 6,811 generalizations identified in the diffusion literature available in 1968, which consisted of 1,084 publications reporting empirical research results.

to identify opinion leaders in five Colombian villages; (2) to determine their social characteristics, communication behavior, and cosmopoliteness; and (3) to determine the differences in these correlates of opinion leadership on the basis of villages with different norms. Data were gathered by personal interviews with 160 people in three modern villages and with ninety-five people in two traditional communities. Rogers and van Es found that opinion leaders, when compared to their followers in both modern and traditional systems, were characterized by more formal education, higher levels of literacy, greater innovativeness, higher socioeconomic status, and more mass media exposure. In the modern villages, however, the opinion leaders were young and innovative, reflecting the norms of these systems, whereas in the traditional systems the leaders were older and not particularly innovative (Rogers with Svenning, 1969). Thus, the behavior of the opinion leaders reflected the norms of their village.

5. *Diffusion networks*. Everett M. Rogers and D. Lawrence Kincaid (1981) conducted personal interviews with the sixty-nine married women in one Korean village in order to determine the role of interpersonal networks in the diffusion of family planning innovations. Each respondent was asked which other women in village she talked with about contraceptive methods. The spatial location of each respondent's home was a very important predictor of who talked with whom, even though the village was extremely small (with a diameter equivalent to only about two city blocks). But space was by no means a complete explanation of diffusion network links; in fact some women talked with a peer on the opposite side of the village. Physically lengthy links were especially characteristic of opinion leaders. One of the important roles of such leaders was to interconnect the cliques in the village, and thus to increase the network connectedness of the village's communication structure. Social similarity also helped to explain who was linked to whom; women of similar social status and age were more likely to interact with each other. Who-to-whom network studies generally find that space and social distance (that is, heterophily/homophily) are the main determinants of who talks to whom in diffusion networks.

In the drug diffusion study of James S. Coleman and others (1966), each respondent was asked to name the other doctors who were his best friends. Coleman and others then determined the main variables that explained who talked to whom via network links. Similarity in age, religion, hometown, and the medical school attended were important factors structuring who talked to whom. But the most important variables determining who-to-whom links in the medical community were such professional affiliations as practicing in the same clinic, hospital, or office partnership. Doctors were more likely to talk about the new drug if they worked together on a daily basis.

6. *Rate of adoption in different social systems.* Everett M. Rogers and D. Lawrence Kincaid (1981) sought to explain the rate of adoption of family planning innovations in twenty-four Korean villages. Unlike diffusion research Type 2, which seeks to explain why some innovations have a faster rate of adoption than others, in this type of research we study why the same innovation is adopted more rapidly in certain *systems* than it is in others. The Korean villages with the fastest rates of contraceptive adoption were composed of families with higher mass media exposure to family planning, had leaders with more highly connected networks in their village, and were villages with more change-agent contact. The economic resources of the village were less important in explaining the rate of adoption of family planning methods.

7. *Communication channel use.* The Bryce Ryan and Neal C. Gross (1943) investigation of the diffusion of hybrid seed corn in Iowa found that the typical Iowa farmer first heard of hybrid seed from a commercial salesman, but that neighbors were the most influential channel in persuading a farmer to adopt the innovation (later research generally showed that salesmen are not the most important communication channel at the knowledge stage). Ryan and Gross were the first researchers to suggest that an individual passes through different stages (knowledge and persuasion, for example) in the process of adopting a new idea. Different communication channels play different roles at these various stages in the innovation-decision process. Salesmen were more important channels about the innovation for earlier adopters, and neighbors were more important for later adopters. This finding suggests that communication channel behavior is different for the various adopter categories, a proposition supported by later diffusion researches.

8. *Consequences of innovation.* The consequences of the use of the steel ax by a tribe of aborigines were studied by the anthropologist Lauriston Sharp (1952). The Yir Yoront were relatively unaffected by modern civilization, owing to their isolation in the Australian bush, until some missionaries moved nearby. They distributed steel axes among the Yir Yoront as gifts and as pay for work performed. Before the introduction of

the steel ax, the stone ax had served as the Yir Yoront's principal tool and as a symbol of masculinity and respect. Only men could own stone axes, so women and children, who were the main users of these tools, borrowed them according to a system prescribed by custom. But the missionaries gave axes to anyone, which caused a major disruption of the Yir Yoront culture, and a revolutionary confusion of age and sex roles. Elders, once highly respected, now became dependent upon women and younger men for steel axes. The consequences of the steel ax were unanticipated, far-reaching, and disruptive (as we detail in Chapter 11).

We hope that the typology of diffusion research just described, although brief, will provide the reader with an overall research map of the entire field.

Summary

The present chapter shows that although diffusion research began as a series of scientific enclaves, it has emerged in recent years as a single, integrated body of concepts and generalizations, even though the investigations are conducted by researchers in different scientific disciplines. A *research tradition* is a series of investigations on a similar topic in which successive studies are influenced by preceding inquiries. The major diffusion traditions described are anthropology, early sociology, rural sociology, education, public health and medical sociology, communication, marketing and management, geography, general sociology, and general economics.

Eight main types of diffusion research were identified:

1. Earliness of knowing about innovations
2. Rate of adoption of different innovations in a social system
3. Innovativeness
4. Opinion leadership
5. Diffusion networks
6. Rate of adoption in different social systems
7. Communication channel use
8. Consequences of innovation.

When scholars accept an intellectual paradigm in a research field it enables them to pursue a coherent set of research directions. The paradigm also imposes and standardizes a set of assumptions and conceptual biases that, once begun, are difficult to recognize and overcome. That is the challenge for the next generation of diffusion scholars. In my first book on diffusion (Rogers, 1962) I stated: "This book suggests that students of diffusion have been working where the ground was soft. . . . The challenge for future research is to expand the area of digging and to search for different objectives than those of the past. Perhaps there is a need to dig deeper, in directions that theory suggests."

3

CONTRIBUTIONS AND CRITICISMS OF DIFFUSION RESEARCH

Innovation has emerged over the last decade as possibly the most
fashionable of social science areas.
— George W. Downs and Lawrence B. Mohr (1976),
"Conceptual Issues in the Study of Innovations"

This chapter reviews the main criticisms and shortcomings of diffusion research, and points out directions for future amelioration of current weaknesses of the diffusion approach. What are the assumptions and biases of diffusion research? How has acceptance of the classical diffusion model limited the originality and appropriateness of diffusion researches? Starting in the 1970s observers began to raise criticisms of diffusion. These criticisms should be taken seriously, for they offer directions for future improvement.

Despite these intellectual criticisms, we should not forget that the field of diffusion research has reached a point at which its contributions are highly regarded, both in providing theoretical understanding of human behavior change and in bringing about more effective programs of social change.

The Status of Diffusion Research Today

The contributions of diffusion research today are impressive. During recent decades the results of diffusion research have been incorporated in basic textbooks in social psychology, communication, public relations, advertising, marketing, consumer behavior, rural sociology, and other fields. Both practitioners (like change agents) and theoreticians regard the diffusion of innovations as a useful field of social science knowledge. Many U.S. government agencies have a division devoted to diffusing technological innovations to the public or to local governments; examples are the National Institutes of Health, the U.S. Department of Agriculture, and the U.S. Department of Education. These federal agencies also sponsor research on diffusion, as does the National Science Foundation and a number of private foundations. Federal research and development laboratories in the United States are required by law to transfer their technologies to private companies, who commercialize the technologies into new products that are then sold in the marketplace. We have already (in Chapter 2) discussed the applications of diffusion theory in development programs in Latin America, Africa, and Asia. Further, most commercial companies have a marketing department that is responsible for diffusing new products and a market research activity that conducts diffusion investigations in order to aid the company's marketing efforts. Because innovation is occurring throughout modern society, the applications of diffusion theory and research are found on all sides.

Diffusion research has achieved a prominent position today. Such has not always been the case. Some years ago, two members of the diffusion research fraternity, Frederick Fliegel and Joseph Kivlin (1966b), complained that: "Diffusion of innovation has the status of a bastard child with respect to the parent interests in social and cultural change: too big to ignore but unlikely to be given full recognition." The status of diffusion research has improved considerably in the eyes of academic scholars since the Fliegel and Kivlin assessment, as evidenced by the quote at the top of this chapter. Downs and Morh continued: "This popularity is not surprising. The investigations by innovation research of the salient behavior of individuals, organizations, and political parties can have significant social consequences. [These studies] imbue even the most obscure piece of research with generalizability that has become rare as social science becomes increasingly specialized."

What is the appeal of diffusion research to scholars, to sponsors of such research, and to students, practitioners, and policy makers who use the results of diffusion research? Why has so much diffusion literature been produced?

1. The diffusion model is a conceptual paradigm with relevance for many disciplines. The multidisciplinary nature of diffusion research cuts across various scientific fields; a diffusion approach provides a common conceptual ground that bridges these divergent disciplines and methodologies. There are few disciplinary limits as to who studies innovation. Most social scientists are interested in social change; diffusion research offers a particularly useful means to gain understandings of change because innovations are a type of communication message whose effects are relatively easy to isolate. Diffusion study is something like the use of radioactive tracers in studying the process of plant growth. One can understand social change processes more accurately if the spread of a new idea is followed over time as it courses through the structure of a social system. Because of their salience, innovations usually leave deep scratches on individual minds, thus aiding respondents' recall ability. The process of behavior change is illuminated in a distinctive way by the diffusion research approach, especially in terms of concepts like information and uncertainty. The focus of diffusion research on tracing the spread of an innovation through a system in time and/or in space has the unique quality of giving life to a behavioral change process. Conceptual and analytical strength is gained by incorporating time as an essential element in the analysis of human behavior change.

Diffusion research offers something of value to each of the social science disciplines. Economists are centrally interested in growth; technological innovation is an important variable for increasing the rate of economic growth in a society. Students of organization are concerned with processes of change within formal institutions, and in how an organizational structure is altered by the introduction of a new technology. Social psychologists try to understand the sources and causes of human behavior change, especially as such individual change is influenced by groups and networks to which the individual belongs. Sociologists and anthropologists share an academic interest in social change but use different methodological tools. The exchange of information in order to reduce uncertainty is central to communication study. So the diffusion of innovations is of note to each of the social sciences.

2. Diffusion research has a pragmatic appeal in helping get research results utilized. The diffusion approach promises a means to provide solutions (1) to individuals and/or organizations who have invested in research on some topic and are seeking to get it utilized, and/or (2) those

who desire to use the research results of others to solve a particular social problem or to fulfill a need. The diffusion approach helps connect research-based innovations and the potential users of such innovations in a knowledge-utilization process.

3. The diffusion paradigm allows scholars to repackage their empirical findings in the form of higher-level generalizations of a more theoretical nature. Such an orderly procedure in the growth of the diffusion research field allowed it to gradually accumulate empirical evidence. Were it not for the general directions for research activities provided by the diffusion paradigm, the impressive amount of research attention given to studying diffusion would not amount to much. Without the diffusion model, this huge body of completed research might just be "a mile wide and an inch deep." The diffusion paradigm provided a basis for creating a coherent body of generalizations.

4. The research methodology implied by the classical diffusion model is clear-cut and relatively facile. The data are not especially difficult to gather; the methods of data analysis are well laid out. Diffusion scholars have focused especially on characteristics related to individual innovativeness through cross-sectional analysis of survey data. Although the methodological straighforwardness of such diffusion studies encouraged many scholars to undertake such investigation, it also may have encouraged them to limit their theoretical advances.

Criticisms of Diffusion Research

Although diffusion research has made numerous important contributions to our understanding of human behavior change, its potential would be even greater were it not for the shortcomings and biases discussed in this section. If the 1940s marked the original formulation of the diffusion paradigm, the 1950s were a time of proliferation of diffusion studies in the United States, the 1960s involved the expansion of such research in developing nations, and the 1970s were the beginnings of introspective criticism for diffusion research. Until the 1970s, almost nothing of a critical nature was written about this field; such absence of critical viewpoints may have indeed been the greatest weakness of diffusion research.

Every scientific field makes certain simplifying assumptions about the complex reality that it studies. Such assumptions are built into the intellectual paradigm that guides the scientific field. Often these assumptions are not recognized, even as they affect such important matters as what is studied and what is ignored, and which research methods are favored and which are rejected. So when a scientist follows a theoretical paradigm, a set of intellectual blinders prevents the researcher from seeing much of reality. "The prejudice of [research] training is always a certain 'trained incapacity': The more we know about how to do something, the harder it is to learn how to do it differently" (Kaplan, 1964). Such trained incapacity is, to a certain extent, necessary; without it, a scientist could not cope with the vast uncertainties of the research process in a chosen field of study. Every research worker, and every field of science, has many blind spots.

The growth and development of a research field is a gradual puzzle-solving process by which important research questions are identified and eventually answered. The progress of a scientific field is helped by realization of its assumptions, biases, and weaknesses. Such self-realization is greatly assisted by intellectual criticism. That is why it is healthy for the diffusion field to face the criticisms raised about it.

The Pro-Innovation Bias of Diffusion Research

One of the most serious shortcomings of diffusion research is the pro-innovation bias. This problem was one of the first biases to be recognized (Rogers with Shoemaker, 1971) but little has been done to remedy this problem. What is the pro-innovation bias? Why does it exist in diffusion research? What could be done about it?

The *pro-innovation bias* is the implication in diffusion research that an innovation should be diffused and adopted by all members of a social system, that it should be diffused more rapidly, and that the innovation should be neither re-invented nor rejected. Seldom is the pro-innovation bias straightforwardly stated in diffusion publications. Rather, the bias is assumed and implied. This lack of recognition of the pro-innovation bias makes it especially troublesome and potentially dangerous in an intellectual sense. The bias leads diffusion researchers to ignore the study of ignorance about innovations, to underemphasize the rejection or discontinuance of innovations, to overlook re-invention, and to fail to study antidiffusion programs designed to prevent the diffusion of "bad" innovations (like crack cocaine or cigarettes, for example). The net result of the pro-innovation bias in diffusion research is a failure to learn certain very important aspects of diffusion; what we do know about diffusion is unnecessarily limited.

Pure Drinking Water in Egyptian Villages: Overcoming the Pro-Innovation Bias

When villagers in Third World countries are asked in surveys, "What is the most important problem in your life?" they consistently respond, "Water." Typically, village families walk several miles to obtain a reliable source of water, and three to four hours per day are spent by water-gatherers in carrying the water to their home. The water problem is particularly severe for Egyptian villagers living in the Nile River Delta. Here, water is available conveniently in the small canals that criss-cross this densely populated farming area. But the stagnant canal water represents a serious health threat because the canals are used by villagers for washing clothes and dishes and for urinating and defecating, as well as for drinking water. A green scum of algae often covers the stagnant canals, especially in the hot summer months. The aerial application of pesticides on the surrounding rice fields deposits dangerous hydrocarbon chemicals in the canal water.

The canals are also a breeding grounds for the snails that are hosts for the tiny parasites that cause schistosomiasis, a terrible disease endemic in the Nile Delta. Village children infested with schistosomiasis act like "walking zombies," sapped of their energy by the parasites in their liver, lungs, brain, and other vital organs. Many children die of schistosomiasis (also called snail fever or Bilharzia in Egypt). The canal water is also loaded with bacteria that cause infectious diarrhea among village babies, who can die within hours due to dehydration. Diarrheal disease in Egypt causes a high rate of infant mortality.

Given these unhealthy conditions associated with drinking canal water, it might seem surprising that the canals are the main source of drinking water for the villagers in the Egyptian Delta. A diffusion scholar, David Belasco (1989), sought to find out why. On one occasion, he observed a village woman gathering water for her family's consumption from a stagnant canal in which someone was urinating nearby. A dead donkey, its body bloated by the hot sun, floated in the canal. Why would anyone drink such obviously polluted water?

The main reason is that alternative water sources do not exist. In an effort to improve the public health conditions of villages, the government ministry of health, with funding from the U.S. Agency for International Development, constructed a system of pumps and pipes that delivers pure, chlorinated water to public spigots in many villages in the Nile Delta. Several villages studied by Belasco were served by this piped water system. Yet more than half of these villagers preferred the unhealthy canal water, and almost no one drank *only* the pure water. So the level of adoption of pure drinking water was extremely low, even though most villagers knew from a government health campaign on television and radio that canal water was contaminated with "microbes" that caused disease and death. Still they drank the canal water.

Belasco surveyed female water-gatherers in three villages in the Nile River Delta, and supplemented his survey interviews with his observations and ethnographic analysis of water-related behavior (this investigation is unique among diffusion studies in using both quantitative and qualitative data). Belasco found that the technological innovation of piped, chlorinated water was actually not so effective or advantageous as it might at first seem to be. The piped water system was not such an appropriate technology for Egyptian villagers as health experts and sanitation engineers claimed. Thus Belasco overcame the pro-innovation bias that characterizes past diffusion studies. The piped water system was inadequate because Egyptian politicians had promised pure water to all villagers in the populous Nile Delta. This popular goal severely overextended the water system that could be constructed with available resources. Further, much pure water was wasted. Each spigot was originally equipped with a spring-loaded shut-off valve, so that the flow of water would stop when the valve was not held open. However constant use of this valve led the spring to break. No one was responsible for its repair. In fact, many of the springs were intentionally broken by the villagers, who preferred constantly running water. So the pure water ran out of the spigot day and night, creating a filthy mudhole around the spigot, and also lowering the water pressure throughout the piped water system. Obviously, the technology for providing pure water supplies in villages of the Nile Delta was poorly planned, without an adequate consideration of human behavior and village culture. As in many technological systems, the context of user behavior was not fully taken into account by the hydraulic engineers who planned the pure-water system. The result was a technological innovation that did not match villagers' needs.

Belasco's respondents preferred canal water because the chlorinated water from the spigot tasted "chemical" or "medicinal" to them. Many believed that it weakened their sex drive. A popular rumor circulated that the government's unpopular family planning program had added chemicals to the piped water in order to decrease the rate of population growth in Egypt.

Most village water-gatherers stored the canal water in a *zir*, an earthen vase whose evaporation cools the water. The dirt and other solids in the canal water settle to the bottom of the *zir*, so that the resulting clear water appears to be pure. The bacteria and petrochemicals are still actually present, as are the microscopic schistosomiasis parasites. But villagers *perceive* that the zir purifies their drinking water. Alum, rose petals, and certain seeds are added to the canal water in the zir, helping create the perception that the water is purified. Most zirs do not have lids, so the dust and flies in the air further contaminate the water.

Social reasons also explain why canal water was preferred by most female water-gatherers. The women congregated on the canal banks in order to wash their clothes and dishes and to gather water, providing a social setting for the exchange of news and gossip. In comparison, standing in line at a water spigot was not a pleasant experience. The long lines of female water-gatherers congregated at each spigot in the very early morning, and these cueues lengthened as the day wore on. Only a tiny stream of water emerged from the spigot. Pushing frequently occurred and fighting often broke out, sometimes spreading to the male relatives of the water-gatherers. Worse, during the hot summer, when demand for the piped water was greatest, the government-installed water system was totally inadequate. The water supply was shut off completely for several hours each day, and often for days at a time. These highly unreliable conditions forced even those individuals who preferred piped water to drink canal water. Some women poured their inadequate supply of pure water into their zir of polluted canal water, contaminating the resulting mixture and negating the health effects of the piped water.

Belasco's respondents, all of whom were devout Moslems, washed their hands and feet prior to praying five times each day at the village mosque. Islamic belief calls for washing with pure water. Incredibly, Belasco found that villagers often cleaned their hands and feet with pure tap water from a spigot, but then drank the polluted canal water. Village religious leaders, who are highly respected opinion leaders, could have played an important role in promoting pure drinking water in Egypt, but this strategy was not pursued by government change agents.

A very few villagers *were* adopters of pure water. These adopters had high socio-economic status. Often they had relatives who worked in Saudi Arabia and sent their savings home. Such adopters often owned their own metered water tap, for which they paid a monthly fee on the basis of how much water they used. These village elites also could afford electricity and a pump to raise the water pressure in the government-provided piped water system. But even these well-educated, high-income villagers were forced to drink canal water when the piped water system was shut off for days or weeks at a time.

Clearly, the Egyptian villagers who reject the chlorinated, piped water and who drink polluted canal water do not appear to be so irrational as they might at first appear to be. One of the important contributions of diffusion researches like David Belasco's study in Egypt is to illuminate the complex nature of individuals' perceptions of an innovation. Understanding such perceptions can provide useful lessons to technological experts. After all, it is individuals' perceptions of an innovation that count.

The present case illustration is based on Belasco (1949).

REASONS FOR THE PRO-INNOVATION BIAS. How did the pro-innovation bias become part of diffusion research? The reason is historical. Hybrid corn *was* profitable for each of the Iowa farmers in the Ryan and Gross (1943) study, but most other innovations that have been studied since do not have this extremely high degree of relative advantage. Many individuals, for their own good, should not adopt them. Perhaps if the field of diffusion research had not begun with a highly profitable agricultural innovation in the 1940s, the pro-innovation bias would have been avoided, or at least recognized and dealt with properly.

During the 1970s, several critics of diffusion research recognized the pro-innovation bias. For example, Downs and Mohr (1976) stated: "The act of innovating is still heavily laden with positive value. Innovativeness, like efficiency, is a characteristic we want organisms to possess. Unlike the ideas of progress and growth, which have long since been casualties of a new consciousness, innovation, especially when seen as more than purely technological change, is still associated with improvement."

What causes the pro-innovation bias in diffusion research?

1. Much diffusion research is funded by change agencies: They have a pro-innovation bias (understandably so, since their purpose is to promote innovations) and this viewpoint has often been accepted by many of the diffusion researchers whose work they sponsor, whom they call upon for consultation about their diffusion problems, and whose students they hire as employees.

2. "Successful" diffusion leaves a rate of adoption that can be retrospectively investigated by diffusion researchers, while an unsuccessful

diffusion effort does not leave visible traces that can be very easily reconstructed. A rejected and/or a discontinued innovation is not so easily identified and investigated by a researcher through interrogating the rejectors and/or discontinuers. For somewhat similar reasons, the variety of forms taken by the re-invention of an innovation makes it difficult to study, posing methodological problems of classifying just what "adoption" means. The conventional methodologies used by diffusion researchers lead to a focus on investigating successful diffusion. Thus, a pro-innovation bias came into diffusion research.

One of the important ways in which the pro-innovation bias creeps into many diffusion researches is through the selection of the innovations that are studied. This aspect of the pro-innovation bias may be especially dangerous because it is implicit, latent, and largely unintentional. How are innovations of study usually selected in diffusion research?

First, the sponsor of an investigation may come to a diffusion researcher with a particular innovation (or class of innovations) already in mind. For example, the manufacturer of a laptop computer may request a diffusion researcher to study how this product is diffusing, and, on the basis of the ensuing research findings, make recommendations for speeding up the diffusion process. Or a federal government agency may provide funds to a university-based diffusion researcher for a research project on the diffusion of a technological innovation to the public, a new idea that government experts feel the public should adopt.

Second, in many other cases, the diffusion researcher selects an innovation to study (with little influence from a research sponsor) on the basis of which new ideas look intellectually interesting to the investigator. The researcher is likely to choose for study an innovation that is having a relatively rapid rate of adoption. Such innovations are often perceived as particularly noteworthy and dynamic. They are more likely to have policy implications. But the unintended result is that a pro-innovation bias is again injected into diffusion study.

Because of the pro-innovation bias, we know much more (1) about the diffusion of rapidly spreading innovations than about the diffusion of slowly diffusing innovations, (2) about adoption than about rejection, and (3) about continued use than about discontinuance. The pro-innovation bias in diffusion research is understandable from the viewpoint of financial, logistical, methodological, and policy considerations. The problem is that we know too much about innovation successes, and not enough about innovation failures.

In the future, we need a different kind of diffusion study from those of the past, so that we shed the pro-innovation bias. For balance, we need a number of diffusion researches with an "anti-innovation bias" in order to correct past tendencies.

OVERCOMING THE PRO-INNOVATION BIAS. How might the pro-innovation bias be overcome?

1. Alternative research approaches to after-the-fact data gathering about how an innovation has diffused should be explored. Diffusion research does not necessarily have to be conducted after an innovation has diffused completely to the members of a system (Figure 3–1). Such a rearward orientation to most diffusion studies helps lead them to concentration on successful innovations.

It is possible to investigate the diffusion of an innovation while the diffusion process is still underway (Figure 3–2). Data can be gathered at two or more points during the diffusion process, rather than just after the diffusion process is completed. This type of research design approaches that of a field experiment in which data are gathered before and after an in-

Figure 3–1. The Usual Diffusion Study Gathers Data from Adopters After the Innovation Has Diffused Widely by Asking Respondents to Look Backward Retrospectively in Time

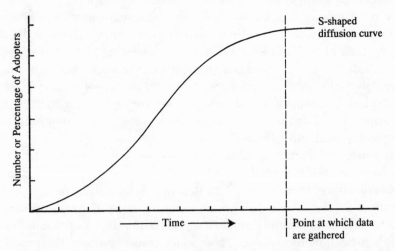

Because cases of successful diffusion are usually selected for study, a pro-innovation bias is introduced in much diffusion research

Figure 3–2. An Alternative Research Design for a Diffusion Study Is to Gather Data from Adopters at Several Points in Time During the Diffusion Process

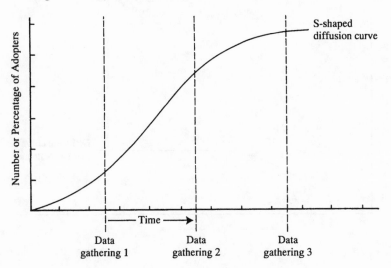

tervention, as in the Berelson and Freedman (1964) study of family planning diffusion in Taiwan (see Chapter 2). An in-process diffusion research design allows a scholar to investigate less successful, as well as more successful, cases of innovation diffusion, and therefore to avoid the pro-innovation bias.

2. Diffusion researchers should become much more questioning of, and careful about, how they select their innovations of study. Even if a successful innovation is selected for investigation, a diffusion scholar might also investigate an unsuccessful innovation that failed to diffuse widely among members of the same system (Figure 3–3). Such a comparative analysis would help illuminate the seriousness of the pro-innovation bias. In general a much wider range of innovations should be studied in diffusion research.

3. It should be acknowledged that rejection, discontinuance, and re-invention frequently occur during the diffusion of an innovation, and that such behavior may be rational and appropriate from the individual's point of view, if only the diffusion scholar could adequately understand the in-

Figure 3–3. Diffusion Research Can Also Help Shed the Pro-Innovation Bias by Investigating Unsuccessful Diffusion, Where the Rate of Adoption Has Plateaued

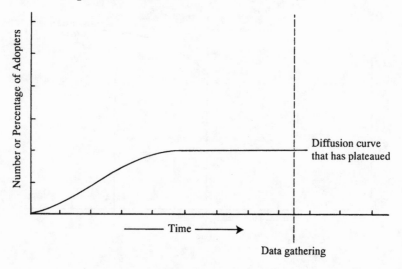

An example might be the use of seat belts in the United States, which has plateaued at 25 percent, or the public's use of ATMs (automatic teller machines), which has leveled off at 30 percent of all bank customers.

dividual's perceptions of the innovation and of his or her own situation, problems, and needs (Figure 3–4). For instance, adopters often feel that they know of relevant information about their local situation that the external change agent may not know or understand. Indigenous knowledge systems, like the hot-cold complex in the Peruvian village of Los Molinas (see Chapter 1), may affect the diffusion of a new idea. Re-invention is an important way in which the innovation is changed to fit the adopting unit's situation. For the first several decades of diffusion research, we did not recognize that re-invention existed. An innovation was regarded by diffusion scholars as an invariant during its diffusion process. Now it is realized, belatedly, that an innovation may be perceived somewhat differently by each adopter and modified to suit the individual's particular situation. Thus, diffusion scholars no longer assume that an innovation is perfect for all potential adopters in solving their problems and meeting their needs.

Figure 3–4. Diffusion Researchers Can Also Investigate How an Innovation Is Discontinued

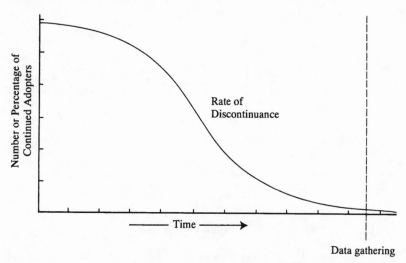

An example might be the discontinuance of cigarette smoking or the discontinuance of a technological innovation that has been found to have undesirable side effects (for example, certain chemical weedicides and pesticides).

4. Researchers should investigate the broader context in which an innovation diffuses, such as how the initial policy decision is made to diffuse the innovation to members of a system, how public policies affect the rate of diffusion, how the innovation is related to other innovations and to the existing practice(s) that it replaces, and how it was decided to conduct the R&D that led to the innovation in the first place (Figure 3–5). This wider scope to diffusion studies helps illuminate the broader system in which the diffusion process occurs.

5. We should increase our understanding of the motivations for adopting an innovation. Strangely, such "why" questions about adopting an innovation have only seldom been probed by diffusion researchers; undoubtedly, motivations for adoption are a difficult issue to investigate. Some adopters may not be able to tell a researcher why they decided to use a new idea. Other adopters may be unwilling to do so. Seldom are simple, direct questions in a survey adequate to uncover an adopter's rea-

Figure 3–5. Another Means of Avoiding the Pro-Innovation Bias Might Be to Investigate the Broader Context of Diffusion, Such as the Decision by the Change Agency to Diffuse the Innovation

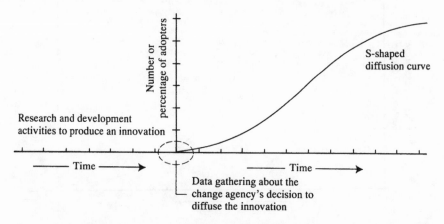

One might also study how the decision was made to begin R&D work to produce the innovation, and how the innovation was shaped into its final form.

sons for using an innovation. But we should not give up on trying to find out the "why" of adoption just because valid data about adoption motivations are difficult to obtain by the usual methods of survey research data gathering.

An economic motivation is often assumed to be the main thrust for an individual's adopting an innovation, especially if the new idea is expensive. Economic factors are undoubtedly very important for certain types of innovations and their adopters, such as the use of agricultural innovations by U.S. farmers. But the prestige secured from adopting an innovation prior to most of one's peers may also be important. For instance, Becker (1970a; 1970b) found that prestige motives were very important for county health departments in deciding to adopt new health programs. Mohr (1969) also found that a desire to gain social prestige was important in the adoption of technological innovations by health organizations. Mohr explained that "A great deal of innovation in [health] organizations, especially large or successful ones, is 'slack' innovation. After solution of immediate problems, the quest for prestige rather than the quest for organizational effectiveness or corporate profit motivates the adoption of most new programs and technologies." Perhaps prestige motivations are less important and profit considerations are paramount in private organizations, unlike the public organizations studied by Becker and Mohr. The desire for prestige is probably very important in decisions to adopt certain kinds of innovations like new clothing fashions, new-model cars, and laptop computers. We do not know because so few diffusion researchers have tried to assess motivations for adoption.

If diffusion scholars could more adequately see an innovation through the eyes of their respondents, including a better understanding of *why* the innovation was adopted or rejected, diffusion research would be in a better position to shed the pro-innovation bias of the past. A pro-innovation tilt is dangerous in that it may cloud the real variance in adopters' perceptions of an innovation. An astute observer of diffusion research, J.D. Eveland (1979), stated: "There is nothing inherently wrong with . . . a pro-innovation value system. Many innovations currently on the market are good ideas in terms of almost any value system, and encouraging their spread can be viewed as virtually a public duty." But even in the case of an overwhelmingly advantageous innovation, individuals in the potential audience for the innovation may perceive it in light of many possible values. If the researcher is to understand their behavior in adopting or rejecting the innovation, the researcher must be capable of taking their various points of view (Eveland, 1979). Simply to regard adoption of the innovation as *rational* (defined as use of the most effective means to reach a given end) and to classify rejection as wrong or stupid is to fail to understand that individual innovation-decisions are idiosyncratic and particularistic. They are based on the individual's perceptions of the innovation. Whether considered as right or wrong by a scientific expert who seeks to evaluate an innovation objectively, an adoption/rejection is always right in the eyes of the individual who made the innovation-decision (at least at the time the decision is made). Diffusion scholars would do well to remember the dictum by W.I. Thomas of the Chicago School of Sociology, stated in one of the first empirical studies of social behavior in America, "If men perceive a situation as real, that situation is real in all of its consequences" (Rogers, 1994). In other words, perceptions count.

In the past, we diffusion researchers placed an overreliance upon models of diffusion that are too rationalistic. The unfortunate consequence is that we often assumed that all adopters perceive an innovation in a positive light, as we ourselves may perceive it. We need to question this assumption of the innovation's advantage for adopters, and to gather data about how individuals perceive the innovation, much as David Belasco (1989) did in his study of the rejection of piped water in Egypt.

Certainly the first and most important step in shedding a pro-innovation bias in diffusion research is to recognize that it may exist.

Bottle-Feeding Babies in the Third World

Most diffusion programs in most countries have beneficial consequences for most people who adopt the innovations that are promoted (thus at least partially justifying the pro-innovation bias of past diffusion research). But in many cases, an innovation that is generally beneficial can be disastrous for certain adopters. And in some cases, a widely diffused innovation has disastrous consequences for *most* adopters.

One example is the diffusion of bottle-feeding among poor mothers in the Third World counties of Latin America, Africa, and Asia. Bottle-feeding with a prepared infant formula has been promoted as a replacement for breast-feeding of babies by several multinational corporations (headquartered mainly in the United States, Switzerland, and England). These multinationals use massive mass media campaigns to diffuse the innovation of bottle-feeding to poor parents in developing nations. The ads, carried mainly on radio and in newspapers, portray bottle-feeding as essential to raising healthy babies; the infants depicted in the print ads are fat and happy, and their mothers are shown as young and beautiful. One company's ads state: "Give your baby love and Lactogen." The advertising uses status and modernity appeals; bottle-feeding is depicted as a practice used by higher-income, well-educated families who live in attractive urban homes. By implication, if a poor peasant family adopts bottle-feeding, these people are encouraged to think that they will become more like the modern, high socioeconomic status parents in the ad. In many developing nations, bottle-feeding is one of the most widely advertised products in the mass media, surpassed only by alcoholic products and cigarettes. The result has been a major increase in the rate of adoption of bottle-feeding by mothers in Third World nations. In recent decades, bottle-feeding rose from 5 percent of all babies, to 10 percent, 25 percent, and to over 50 percent in many nations.

What's wrong with bottle-feeding? Nothing, under ideal conditions where a family has sufficient income to purchase the expensive powdered milk (which often costs up to one-third of a family's total income), and where sanitary conditions are available to prepare the baby formula. Most Third World families cannot afford to buy sufficient amounts of powdered milk products, so they water down their baby's formula. They lack pure water, or the resources to boil polluted water, for preparing the powdered milk formula. Often these poor families are unable to clean the bottles and other bottle-feeding equipment properly. Bacteria multiply in the emptied milk bottles, which are then refilled without being sterilized. Instead of contributing to infant health (as bottle-feeding could do under ideal conditions), the germ-ridden baby bottles become a lethal threat under the reality of village and urban slum conditions.

Consequently, bottle-feeding contributes directly to widespread infant diarrheal death in Third World countries. Diarrhea is the leading cause of infant deaths in many nations, often killing up to 50 percent of all babies. One sees many babies in developing nations with distended stomachs, stick-like arms and legs, and glazed eyes, the likely symptoms of "bottle-feeding disease." Even if such babies are hospitalized and fed intravenously in order to return them to good health, they are often bottle-fed again after their hospital discharge and thus succumb to diarrheal malnutrition.

During the late 1970s, a number of religious, student, and other protest groups began to raise public consciousness about the problem of bottle-feeding diffusion. Lawsuits were initiated against the multinational corporations, seeking to force them to halt their advertising campaigns aimed at poor parents in Third World nations. The World Health Organization (WHO) took a position against bottle-feeding, and began to assist national ministries of health in promoting breast-feeding as a healthier practice. Some Third World nations banned all public advertising of bottle-feeding products by the multinational corporations. Other nations forced these companies to halt their promotion of bottle-feeding products to new mothers in the delivery wards of hospitals by "milk nurses" (employees of the milk companies that wear nurses' uniforms).

The role of diffusion research in the infant diarrhea problem has changed over recent decades. In the 1950s and 1960s, multinational corporations based their advertising campaigns for bottle-feeding, in part, upon the results of diffusion research. Since the late 1970s, when public alarm about the bottle-feeding syndrome began to rise, diffusion researchers initiated investigations of how to persuade parents to discontinue bottle-feeding and to return to breast-feeding. Some diffusion scholars assisted government health campaigns to promote breast-feeding. Other scholars helped in the conduct of ORT (Oral Rehydration Therapy) campaigns intended to prevent the deaths of infants from diarrheal disease.

Bottle-feeding diffusion in Third World nations illustrates the pro-innovation bias of past diffusion research, and how we gradually overcame this bias. Blaming individual parents for the bottle-feeding cause of infant diarrhea does not go far toward solving the problem. It was necessary to recognize that the multinational milk companies played an important role in creating the problem. This recognition of system-blame for the problem may be a step toward its amelioration. But is has not proven easy to convince the multinational corporations to halt their dangerous sale of bottle-feeding products to poor parents in Third World nations.

This case illustration is based on various sources, including the author's personal experiences.

The Individual-Blame Bias in Diffusion Research

A source-bias is a tendency for diffusion research to side with the change agencies that promote innovations rather than with the individuals who are potential adopters. This source-bias is perhaps suggested by the words that we use to describe this field of research: "Diffusion" research might have been called something like "problem-solving," "innovation-seeking," or the "evaluation of innovations" had the audience originally been a stronger influence on this research. One cannot help but wonder how the diffusion research approach might have been different if the Ryan and Gross (1943) hybrid corn study had been sponsored by the Iowa Farm Bureau Federation (a farmers' organization) rather than by an agricultural research center like the Iowa Agricultural Experiment Station. And what if the Columbia University drug study had been sponsored by the American Medical Association, rather than by the Pfizer Drug Company? The source-sponsorship of early diffusion studies gave these investigations not only a pro-innovation bias but also structured the nature of diffusion research in other ways.

INDIVIDUAL-BLAME VERSUS SYSTEM-BLAME. As a result of who sponsors diffusion research, along with other pro-source factors, one can detect a certain degree of individual-blame, rather than system-blame, in diffusion research. *Individual-blame* is the tendency to hold an individual responsible for his or her problems, rather than the system of which the individual is a part (Caplan and Nelson, 1973). An individual-blame orientation implies that "If the shoe doesn't fit, there's something wrong with your foot." An opposite point of view would blame the system, not the individual; it might imply that the shoe manufacturer or the marketing system could be at fault for a shoe that does not fit.

Some factors underlying a particular social problem might indeed be individual in nature, and any effective solution to the problem may have to change these individual factors. But in many cases the causes of the social problem lie in the larger system of which the individual is a part. Ameliorative social policies that are limited to individual interventions will not be very effective in solving system-level problems. How a social problem is defined is an important determination of how we go about solving it, and ultimately of the effectiveness of the attempted solution. A frequent error is to overstress individual-blame in defining a social problem, and to underestimate system-blame. *System-blame* is the tendency to hold a system responsible for the problems of individual members of the system.

Consider the following cases in which a social problem was defined initially in terms of individual-blame.

1. Posters produced by a pharmaceutical manufacturer were captioned: "LEAD PAINT CAN KILL!" These posters place the blame on low-income parents for allowing their children to eat paint peeling off the walls of older housing. The posters blamed the parents, not the paint manufacturers or the landlords. This tendency toward stressing individual-blame rather than system-blame is common in many health and safety campaigns. One U.S. city with a high rate of lead-paint poisoning of children, pioneered in solving this problem by legally prohibiting landlords from using lead paint on the inside of residences. In the early 1990's, Federal Legislation was enacted to require homeowners to disclose that a residence is lead-free when a housing unit is rented or sold.

2. Motor vehicle accidents are the leading cause of death for individuals in the United States under thirty-five years of age. Until the mid-1960's, highway safety problems were defined in terms of speeding, reckless driving, and drunk drinking (see Chapter 4). Massive public communication campaigns were aimed at the individual driver, urging "Don't Drink and Drive," "Buckle Up for Safety," and "Slow Down and Live." Unfortunately, the highway accident rate continued to climb. Ralph Nader's (1965) book, *Unsafe at Any Speed*, helped to redefine the problem from mainly one of blaming "the nut behind the wheel" to a system-blame of unsafely designed automobiles and highways (Whiteside, 1972). Once the problem was redefined as one of system-blame as well as

individual-blame, federal legislative mandates for safer cars and highways followed, and the traffic fatality rate decreased (Walker, 1976, pp. 26–32; 1977). For instance, safety laws required more padding on auto dashboards and stronger car bumpers, as well as impact absorbers placed in front of the concrete columns supporting highway viaducts. But this redefinition of the traffic safety problem did not deny that individual drivers' behavior, if it could be effectively changed, could also contribute to safer driving. When the fifty-five-mile-per-hour speed limit was instituted in late 1973 (as an energy-saving policy), the number of highway deaths promptly dropped about 16 percent below the long-range downward trend. Further, MADD (Mothers Against Drunk Driving) secured tougher penalties for drunk driving in the 1980s and 1990s, leading to decreased highway deaths (Reinerman, 1988).

3. A large training program in Chicago sought to improve the employability of black inner-city men. The training course stressed the importance of punctuality in getting and holding a job. But such an individual-blame approach did not achieve good results. Nathan Caplan and Stephen D. Nelson (1973), social psychologists at the University of Michigan, were called upon to assess the punctuality problem. They found that only one-fourth of the trainees had alarm clocks or wrist watches, so most had to rely on someone else to wake them up in the morning. Further, the retrained workers had to depend upon unreliable means of public transportation and to cope with traffic congestion in traveling from their inner-city homes to suburban workplaces. Caplan recommended that the training program provide alarm clocks to the trainees. This suggestion was rejected by the government training program as inappropriate and unrealistic. The government reemployment program could spend thousands for training, but it would not spend a few dollars for alarm clocks.

4. In the 1960s and 1970s government leaders of many Third World nations launched national family planning programs in order to reduce the national rate of population growth. Government officials urged parents to have fewer children, usually only two or three. But most parents, especially the rural and urban poor, wanted four or five children, including at least two sons, to provide them with cheap family labor on their farms or in their businesses and with retirement care in their old age. Instead of seeking a system-blame solution, by creating public programs like agricultural mechanization and a social security system to substitute for large families, government officials criticized parents for not adopting contraceptives and for having too many children. Such an individual-

blame strategy for solving the overpopulation problem has not been very successful in most developing nations.

In each of these illustrations, a social problem was initially defined in terms of individual-blame. The resulting diffusion program to change human behavior was not very successful until, in some cases, system-blame factors were also recognized. These four cases suggest that we frequently make the mistake of defining social problems solely in terms of individual blame.

INDIVIDUAL-BLAME AND THE DIFFUSION OF INNOVATIONS. "The variables used in diffusion models [to predict innovativeness], then, are conceptualized so as to indicate the success or failure of the individual *within the system* rather than as indications of success or failure *of the system*" (Havens, 1975, emphasis in original). Examples of such individual-blame variables that have been correlated with individual innovativeness in past diffusion investigations include formal education, size of operation, income, cosmopoliteness, and mass media exposure. In addition, these past studies of individual innovativeness have included some predictor variables that might be considered system-blame factors, like change agent contact with clients and the degree to which a change agency provides financial assistance (such as in the form of credit to purchase an innovation). But seldom is it implied in diffusion research publications that the source or the channel of innovations might be at fault for not providing adequate information, for promoting inappropriate innovations, or for failing to contact less-educated members of the audience who may especially need a change agent's help.

Late adopters and laggards are often most likely to be individually blamed for not adopting an innovation and/or for being much later in adopting than the other members of their system. Change agents feel that such later adopters are not dutifully following the experts' recommendations to use an innovation. Such an improper response occurs because these individuals are "traditionally resistant to change," and/or "irrational." A more careful analysis may show that the innovation was not as appropriate for later adopters, perhaps because of their smaller-sized operations and more limited resources. Indeed they may have been extremely rational in not adopting. An approach with more emphasis on system-blame might question whether the R&D source of innovations was properly tuned to the actual needs of the later adopters in the system, and whether the change agency, in recommending the innovation, was fully informed about the actual life-situation of the later adopters.

One thinks of the piped water program in Egypt, described earlier in this chapter.

In fact, a stereotype of later adopters by change agents and others as traditional, uneducated, and/or resistant to change can become a self-fulfilling prophecy. Change agents do not contact the later adopters in their system because they feel, on the basis of their stereotypic image, that such contact will be unfruitful in leading to adoption. The eventual result is that without the information inputs and other assistance from the change agents, the later adopters are even less likely to adopt. Thus, the individual-blame image of the later adopters fulfills itself. Person-blame interpretations are often in everybody's interest, except those who are subjected to individual-blame.

Evidence of how an individual-blame bias can limit understanding of the diffusion process is provided by a study of recycling behavior in Edmonton and Calgary, Canada. In the early 1990s, when the data were gathered, the environment was very high on the public agenda. Yet Derksen and Gartrell (1993) found that individual attitudes toward the environment were related to the recycling of cans, bottles, and newspapers *only* for people who had access to a curbside recycling program. So in Edmonton, which had a city recycling program, a much more widespread adoption of recycling occurred, than in Calgary, which did not have a city program of curbside pickup. "Recycling has been conceptualized as an issue of individual behavior" (Derksen and Gartrell, 1993). Clearly, such an individual-blame perception is a mistake. Before individual attitudes toward the environment can be crystalized into recycling actions, a community-level decision must be made to adopt a recycling program.

REASONS FOR INDIVIDUAL-BLAME. It may be understandable (although regrettable) that change agents fall into the mental trap of individual-blame thinking about why their clients do not adopt an innovation. But why and how does diffusion research also reflect such an individual-blame orientation?

1. As implied previously, diffusion researchers sometimes accept a definition of the problem that they are to study from the sponsors of their research. So if the research sponsor is a change agency with an individual-blame bias, the diffusion scholar often picks up an individual-blame orientation. The ensuing research may then contribute, in turn, toward social policies of an individual-blame nature. "Such research frequently plays an integral role in a chain of events that results in *blaming people*

in difficult situations for their own predicament" (Caplan and Nelson, 1973, emphasis in original). The series of events is thus:

1. Experts and/or change agents perceive a social problem in individual-blame terms. $\longrightarrow$ 2. Diffusion researchers accept this individual-blame definition, and conduct research accordingly. $\longrightarrow$ 3. Social policies with an individual-blame orientation are formulated and implemented on the basis of this research, which do not effectively solve the social problem.

The essential error on the part of some diffusion researchers in the past is that they may have inadvertently equated the cause of an event or a condition, which is a matter to be scientifically and empirically ascertained, with the blame for an event or condition, which may be a matter of opinion, based upon certain values and beliefs (Capland and Nelson, 1973). Cause and blame are two different things. But the individual-blame bias in past diffusion research sometimes occurred, it seems, when the researchers uncritically accepted others' definitions of blame as a scientific cause. The investigators should have attributed cause among their variables of study only on the basis of empirical evidence, not on the basis of others' beliefs and judgments. Social scientists are not value-free in choosing or framing a research problem, although conduct of the research may be objective.

2. Another possible reason for the individual-blame bias in some diffusion research is that the researcher may feel that it is difficult or impossible to change system-blame factors, but that individual-blame variables may be amenable to change. System-level variables, especially if they involve changing the social structure of a system, may indeed be difficult to alter. But a first step toward system change might be for social scientists to define (or redefine) a social problem more accurately.

3. Individuals are often more accessible to diffusion researchers as objects for study than are systems, and the research tools of most diffusion investigators lead them to focus on individuals as units of analysis. The diffusion paradigm headed diffusion scholars in the direction of conducting surveys of individual adopters; for example. Ryan and Gross (1943) studied individual Iowa farmers. Data gathering from the change agencies diffusing the innovations and/or the R&D organizations that produced the innovations was not part of the prototypical diffusion study. Officials in

such systems may be at least equally to blame for certain diffusion problems as are the potential adopters (who are the usual objects of diffusion study). But it is not easy for diffusion scholars to study these officials.

Most social scientists who conduct diffusion research are specialists in conducting surveys of potential adopters. This particular research skill helps channel them into an individual-blame definition of diffusion problems, and away from a system-blame viewpoint. The anthropological diffusion research tradition on the other hand, because it conducts qualitative research instead of surveys, has been least accepting of an individual-blame point of view, and most likely to point to system-blame aspects of diffusion problems.

The overwhelming focus on the individual as the unit of analysis in diffusion research, while largely ignoring the importance of the individual's network relationships, is often due to the assumption that if the individual is the unit of *response*, he or she must consequently be the unit of *analysis* (Coleman, 1958). The use of survey methods in diffusion research tends to "destructure" human behavior: "Using random sampling of individuals, the survey is a sociological meat-grinder, tearing the individual from his social context and guaranteeing that nobody in the study interacts with anyone else in it. It is a little like a biologist putting his experimental animals through a hamburger machine and looking at every hundredth cell through a microscope; anatomy and physiology get lost; structure and function disappear, and one is left with cell biology" (Barton, 1968).

Even when the individual is the unit of response, network relationships can be the unit of analysis via some type of network analysis. *Communication network analysis* is defined as a method of research for identifying the communication structure in a system, in which relational data about communication flows are analyzed by using some type of interpersonal relationship as the unit of analysis (Rogers and Kincaid, 1981). Network analysis permits understanding communication structure as it channels the process of diffusion.

The influential Ryan and Gross (1943) study did not obtain data about diffusion networks. The refocusing of diffusion researches had to wait for later investigations, especially the drug study of medical doctors by Coleman and others (1966). It has become common for diffusion scholars to ask their respondents sociometric questions like: "From whom in this system did you obtain information that led you to adopt this innovation?" The sociometric dyad represented by each answer to this question can be the basic unit of analysis. Now the network link, rather than the individual, becomes the unit of analysis.

OVERCOMING THE INDIVIDUAL-BLAME BIAS. How can the person-blame bias be overcome?

1. Diffusion scholars should seek alternatives to using individuals as their units of analysis, and thus accepting mainly an individual-blame bias.
2. Researchers should keep an open mind about the causes of a social problem, at least until exploratory data are gathered, and guard against accepting change agencies' definitions of diffusion problems, which tend to be in terms of individual-blame.
3. All the participants should be involved, including potential adopters, in the definition of the diffusion problem, rather than just those persons who are seeking amelioration of a problem.
4. Social and communication structural variables should be considered, as well as intra-individual variables, in diffusion research. Past diffusion studies largely consisted of audience research, while seriously neglecting source research. The broader issues of who owns and controls (1) the R&D system that produces innovations, and (2) the communication system that diffuses them, and to whose benefit, also need attention in future diffusion investigations.

As in the case of the pro-innovation bias in diffusion research, perhaps one of the first and most important ways to guard against the individual-blame bias is to be aware that it exists. An individual-blame orientation is not always inappropriate. Perhaps individual-level variables *are* the most appropriate to investigate in a particular diffusion study. But in almost all cases such a psychological approach, centering on individual-level variables, is not a complete explanation of the diffusion behavior being investigated.

The Recall Problem in Diffusion Research

Time is one of the main methodological enemies in studying a process like diffusion. By definition, an innovation diffuses through time. It might seem a simple enough matter to obtain data from respondents about the time at which they decided to adopt an innovation, but it is not.

PROBLEMS IN MEASURING THE TIME OF ADOPTION. Diffusion inquiry differs from most other social science research by the fact that the time variable is not ignored. Time is one of the four essential elements of diffusion (see Chapter 1). Diffusion is a process that occurs over time, so there is no way to avoid including time when one studies diffusion. Although there are blessings that accrue from inclusion of the time variable in diffusion studies (for example, the tracerlike qualities of innovations), there are also some methodological curses.

One weakness of diffusion research is a dependence upon *recall data* from respondents as to their date of adoption of a new idea. Essentially, the respondent is asked to look back in time in order to reconstruct his or her past history of innovation experiences. This hindsight ability is not completely accurate (Menzel, 1957; Coughenour, 1965) for the typical respondent. It probably varies on the basis of the innovation's salience to the individual, the length of time over which recall is requested, and on the basis of individual differences in education, memory, and the like.

Diffusion research designs consist mainly of correlational analyses of cross-sectional data gathered in one-shot surveys of respondents (usually the adopters and/or potential adopters of an innovation), thus following the methods pioneered by Ryan and Gross (1943) in their hybrid corn study. Diffusion studies should rely on "moving pictures" of behavior, rather than "snapshots," because of their unique capacity to trace the sequential flow of an innovation as it spreads through a social system. Diffusion researchers have mainly relied, however, upon one-shot surveys of their respondents, a methodology that amounts to making the diffusion process almost timeless because of its effect of freezing the action of a continuous process over time. Survey research on the diffusion process is a convenient methodology for the researcher, but it is intellectually destructive of the "process" aspects of the diffusion of innovations. If data about a diffusion process are only gathered at one point in time, the investigator can only measure time through respondents' recall, and that is a rather weak reed on which to base the measurement of such an important variable.

More appropriate research designs for gathering data about the time dimension are: (1) field experiments, (2) longitudinal panel studies, (3) use of archival records, and (4) case studies of the innovation process with data from multiple respondents (each of whom provides a validity check on the others' data). These methodologies reflect the time dimension more accurately. Unfortunately, alternatives to the one-shot survey have not been widely used in past diffusion research. The research designs predominantly used in diffusion research do not tell us much about the process of diffusion over time, other than what can be reconstituted from respondents' recall data.

PROBLEMS IN DETERMINING CAUSALITY.   Cross-sectional survey data are unable to answer many of the "why" questions about diffusion. "Such factors [as wealth, size, cosmopoliteness, etc.] may be causes of innovations, or effects of innovativeness, or they may be involved with innovation in cycles of reciprocal causality through time, or both they and the adoption of new ideas may be caused by an outside factor not considered in a given study" (Mohr, 1966). One-shot surveys can't tell us much about time-order, or about the broader issue of causality.

The pro-innovation bias in diffusion research, and the overwhelming reliance on correlational analysis of survey data, often led in the past to avoiding or ignoring the issue of causality among the variables of study. We often speak of "independent" and "dependent" variables in diffusion research. A dependent variable usually means the main variable in which the investigator is interested; in about 60 percent of all diffusion researches, this dependent variable is innovativeness (see Table 2–2). Diffusion research usually implies that the independent variables "lead to" innovativeness, although it is often unstated or unclear whether this really means that an independent variable causes innovativeness. In order for variable X to be the *cause* of variable Y, (1) X must precede Y in time-order, (2) the two variables must be related, or co-vary, and (3) X must have a "forcing quality" on Y.

Here again we see the importance of research designs that allow us to more clearly understand the over-time aspects of diffusion. Field experiments are ideally suited to the purpose of assessing the effect of various independent variables (the interventions or treatments) on a dependent variable (like innovativeness). A *field experiment* is an experiment conducted under realistic conditions in which pre-intervention and post-intervention measurements are usually obtained by surveys. In the typical diffusion field experiment, the intervention is some communication strategy to speed up the diffusion of an innovation. For example, the diffusion intervention may be an incentive payment for adopting family planning that is offered in one village and not in another (Rogers, 1973). We recommend that *much greater use should be made of field experiments in diffusion research to help avoid the respondent recall problem and to evaluate diffusion policy alternatives.* To date, field experiments have especially been conducted by marketing scholars and by researchers investigating the effect of paraprofessional field workers and incentives in the diffusion of family planning innovations.

ALTERNATIVES TO DIFFUSION SURVEYS. Social science data-gathering techniques like the personal interview do not work very well when the researcher is asking the respondent to recall his or her previous mind-states over a long time period. For example, consider questioning a respondent as to his or her sources or channels of communication for an innovation that he or she adopted ten years previously. Obviously, we would not put much faith in such recall data, even if they were provided by a cooperative respondent who was sincerely trying to offer valid data.

In addition to field experiments, another kind of solution to the respondent recall problem in diffusion studies is to gather data at multiple points in the diffusion process. Instead of waiting until the innovation is widely diffused to gather the data via respondents' recall, the researcher gathers data at several points during the diffusion process (see Figure 3–2). At each data-point, respondents are asked whether or not they have adopted, and for the details about their innovation-decision. In essence, such a multiple data-points approach amounts to dividing the total length of the recall period up into smaller segments for the average respondent. Thus, more accurate recall is facilitated.

Another alternative solution to the respondent recall problem is a "point-of-adoption" study in which respondents are asked to provide details about their adoption of an innovation at the time that they adopt, such as when they come to a clinic (in the case of adopting a family planning innovation or AIDS prevention), a dealer or a warehouse (such as for an agricultural innovation), or to a store (to purchase a consumer innovation, for example). This data-gathering strategy solves the recall problem by gathering data at the time of adoption. Very few point-of-adoption studies have been conducted to date.

Various research strategies may be used to minimize the seriousness of the respondent recall problem in diffusion surveys:

1. Select innovations for study that have recently diffused rapidly and that are salient to the adopters (unfortunately, this strategy also increases the possibility of a pro-innovation bias).

2. Gather data about respondents' time of adoption from alternative sources, such as archival records. An example is the Coleman and others (1966) drug study in which doctors' recall data were checked against drugstore prescription records.
3. Carefully pretest the survey questions and do high-quality interviewing by well-trained interviewers, so as to maximize the likelihood of obtaining recall data that are as valid as possible.

The Issue of Equality in the Diffusion of Innovations

As we will show in Chapter 11, diffusion researchers have not paid much attention to the consequences of innovation. They have been especially inattentive to the issue of how the socioeconomic benefits of innovation are distributed within a social system. When the issue of equality has been investigated, we often find that the diffusion of innovations widens the socioeconomic gap between the higher and the lower status segments of a system. This tendency for the diffusion of innovations to increase socioeconomic inequality can occur in any system, but it has especially been noted in Third World nations. We therefore begin our discussion of equality issues with an examination of diffusion research in Latin America, Africa, and Asia.

THIRD WORLD DEVELOPMENT. As we showed in Chapter 2, research on the diffusion of innovations began in the United States. Then, during the 1960s, diffusion research caught on in the developing nations of Latin America, Africa, and Asia. The diffusion paradigm was followed closely. Many of the Third World diffusion studies were conducted by sojourners from the United States or Europe, or else by Latin American, African, or Asian scholars who had learned the diffusion approach during their graduate studies in the United States. A strong stamp of "made in America" characterized these diffusion researches in the Third World. At first, during the 1960s, it seemed that most diffusion research methods and theoretical generalizations were cross-culturally valid; that is, the diffusion process in Third World nations seemed to be generally similar to its counterpart in the richer, industrialized nations of Euro-America (Rogers with Shoemaker, 1971). Even though a peasant village in the Third World was characterized by much more limited financial resources, lower levels of formal education, and a paucity of mass media, innovations seemed to diffuse in approximately the same way as in the United States. For example, the rate of adoption followed the familiar S-shaped curve over time. As in the United States, innovators were characterized by higher social status, greater cosmopoliteness, and more tolerance for uncertainty than were other adopter categories in villages in Colombia (Deutschmann and Fals Borda, 1962a, 1962b) and in Bangladesh (Rahim, 1961).

But during the 1970s, questioning voices were raised about the cultural importation of a diffusion paradigm to Third World nations. Some of the critics were Americans or Europeans who had conducted diffusion studies in developing nations; other critics were Third World social scientists (especially in Latin America), who raised troubling questions about the conduct and the results of diffusion research as it was carried out in their nations. The key intellectual issue here is the cultural appropriateness of social science research as it originally grew to strength in the United States, and was then applied under very different sociocultural conditions in the Third World.

One reason that diffusion research is particularly subject to criticism in developing nations is because, compared to any other field of behavioral science, it received so much more attention in Latin America, Africa, and Asia. Today, approximately 16 percent of all diffusion studies have been conducted there. During the 1970s, an intellectual shift occurred in the basic conception of development. It was in this context of the passing of the dominant paradigm of development that diffusion research came to be evaluated by its critics in the 1970s, and found wanting. Four main elements in the dominant paradigm of development (Rogers, 1976) were:

1. *Economic growth* through industrialization and accompanying urbanization, approximately equivalent to passing through the Industrial Revolution.
2. Capital-intensive, labor-saving *technology*, mainly transferred from industrialized nations.
3. *Centralized planning*, mainly by government economists and bankers, in order to speed up the process of development.
4. *The causes of underdevelopment*, believed to lie mainly within the developing nation rather than in their trade or other external relationships with industrialized countries.

The classical diffusion model fit this dominant paradigm of development quite well. The paradigm of development implied that the transfer of technological innovations from development agencies to their clients lay at the heart of the development process. So diffusion studies began to proliferate in Latin America, Africa, and Asia, especially after about 1960.

Then a major shift in the conceptualization of development occurred. Today, *development* is defined as a widely participatory process of social change in a society intended to bring about both social and material advancement (including greater equality, freedom, and other valued qualities) for the majority of people through their gaining greater control over their environment.

The greater concern with equality of the benefits of development after the 1970s pointed toward the priority of villagers and urban poor (and, since the 1980s, of women) as the main target audience for development in developing nations. The empowerment of women gained attention, as it was realized that they were often subordinated to men, and that the technologies being introduced made them more so. Development policies became less elite-oriented, and more concerned with equalizing the socioeconomic benefits of technological innovations.

APPROPRIATENESS OF THE DIFFUSION PARADIGM TO THIRD WORLD NATIONS. An eminent Latin American communication scholar who conducted diffusion research on his continent, Juan Diaz Bordenave (1976), argues that the diffusion research questions asked by Latin American researchers do not get to the main issues affecting development. The typical research issues in past diffusion studies were:

1. How are technological innovations diffused in a social system?
2. What are the characteristics of innovators, early adopters, and other adopter categories?
3. What is the role of opinion leaders in the interpersonal networks through which a new idea diffuses in a system like a peasant village?

Bordenave (1976) suggests that the following research questions are more appropriate, if one is planning for a just social structure as the result of a development program:

1. What criteria guide the choice of innovations that are to be diffused: (1) the public welfare, (2) increased production of goods for export,

(3) maintaining low prices for urban consumers, or (4) increased profits for society's elites like large landowners and industrialists?
2. What influence does society's social structure have over individual innovation-decisions?
3. Are the technological innovations being diffused appropriate, well-proven, and adequate for the stage of socioeconomic development of the nation?
4. What are the likely consequences of technological innovation in terms of employment and unemployment, migration of rural people to already overcrowded cities, and to a more equitable distribution of individual incomes? Will the innovation widen or narrow socioeconomic gaps?

These important issues would carry diffusion research in directions to overcome its pro-innovation bias and individual-blame assumptions. The most important single way in which diffusion research in developing nations should be different from the past is in regard to the equity issue. In Latin America, Africa, and Asia, the social structure of a nation or of a local community is often in sharp contrast to that in Euro-America. Power, economic wealth, and information are usually more highly concentrated in a few hands, and this aspect of social structure affects not only the nature of an innovation's diffusion but also who reaps the main advantages and disadvantages of such technological change. The classical diffusion model was conceived in sociocultural conditions that were substantially different from those in Latin America (or Africa and Asia), and hence, Bordenave (1976) argued, when the diffusion model was used uncritically, it did not touch such basic issues as changing the social structure in these developing countries.

SOCIOECONOMIC GAPS AND DIFFUSION. The social structure in Third World nations is a powerful determinant of individuals' access to technological innovations. Development agencies tend to provide assistance especially to their innovative, wealthy, educated, and information-seeking clients. Following this progressive (or "easy to convince") diffusion strategy leads to a lower degree of equality. For example, more progressive farmers are eager for new ideas, and have the economic means to adopt; they can also more easily obtain credit if they need it. Because they have larger farms, the direct effect of their adoption on total agricultural production is also greater. Rural development workers follow this progressive client strategy because they cannot reach all of their clients, so they concentrate on their most responsive clients, with whom they are most homophilous. The result is a widening of the socioeconomic benefits gap among the change agent's client audience.

Does the diffusion of innovations necessarily have to widen socioeconomic gaps in a social system? Some reason for optimism on this issue has been provided by two field experiments in developing nations. Shingi and Mody (1976) in India and Röling and others (1976) in Kenya designed and evaluated diffusion approaches that narrowed, rather than widened, socioeconomic gaps. Essentially, these approaches sought, with some success, to overcome the inequity bias of the usual diffusion program. They introduced appropriate innovations to their lower socioeconomic clients through a special development program. These two studies (discussed in Chapter 11) suggest that if communication strategies are used effectively in narrowing the socioeconomic benefits gap, then the socioeconomic structure may no longer be a major barrier to the diffusion of innovations for the most disadvantaged segment of the population. Thus, it may be possible to bring about *greater* equality through appropriate diffusion strategies.

Summary

We discussed four major criticisms of diffusion research: (1) its *pro-innovative bias*, the implication of most diffusion research that an innovation should be diffused and adopted by all members of a social system, that it should be diffused more rapidly, and that the innovation should be neither re-invented nor rejected; (2) the *individual-blame bias*, the tendency to hold an individual responsible for his or her problems, rather than the system of which the individual is a part; (3) the *recall problem* in diffusion research caused by inaccuracies when respondents are asked to remember the time at which they adopted a new idea; and (4) the *issue of equality* in the diffusion of innovations, as socioeconomic gaps among the members of a social system are often widened as a result of the spread of new ideas. Alternatives to usual diffusion research approaches were proposed for overcoming each of these four criticisms of diffusion research.

We have reviewed four major shortcomings of diffusion research in this chapter. We conclude that the beginnings of diffusion research left an indelible stamp on the approaches, concepts, methods, and assumptions of the field. The biases that we inherited from our research ancestors have been inappropriate for the important diffusion research tasks of today. It is ironic that the study of innovation has itself become so traditional.

4

THE GENERATION
OF INNOVATIONS

The fundamental impulse that sets and keeps the capitalist
engine in motion comes from the consumer's goods, the new
methods of production or transportation, the new markets, the
new forms of industrial organization that capitalist enterprise
creates.
  —Joseph A. Schumpeter (1950), *Capitalism, Socialism, and
  Democracy*

Where do innovations come from? How do their origins cast a later
influence on their diffusion and consequences? As we pointed out in
Chapter 3, past diffusion studies typically began with the left-hand tail
of the S-shaped diffusion curve, that is, with the first adopters of an innovation. The decisions and events occurring previous to this point have
a strong influence on the diffusion process. In this wider-scope view of
the innovation-development process, diffusion is but one phase of the
larger sequence through which an innovation goes from the decision
to begin research on a recognized problem to the consequences of the
innovation.

Past diffusion investigations overlooked the fact that relevant activities and decisions usually occurred long before the diffusion process
began: A perceived problem, funding decisions about R&D activities
that led to research work, invention of the innovation and then its
development and commercialization, a decision that it should be diffused, transfer of the innovation to a diffusion agency, and its communication to an audience of potential adopters. *Then* the first
adoption occurs, and the diffusion process begins. This entire prediffusion series of activities and decisions is certainly an important part

131

of the innovation-development process, of which the diffusion phase is one component.

In this chapter we review researches completed on prediffusion aspects of the technology-development process. Unfortunately, there are relatively few such investigations of the early phases in the technology-development process. As a result, our grasp of the topics in this chapter is necessarily more tentative than in the rest of this book.

The Innovation-Development Process

In Chapter 1, we defined an *innovation* as an idea, practice, or object that is perceived as new to an individual or another unit of adoption. The *innovation-development process* consists of all the decisions and activities, and their impacts, that occur from recognition of a need or a problem, through research, development, and commercialization of an innovation, through diffusion and adoption of the innovation by users, to its consequences. Now we take up each of the main steps in the innovation-development process.

1. Recognizing a Problem or Need

The innovation-development process usually begins with recognition of a problem or need, which stimulates research and development activities designed to create an innovation to solve the problem/need (Figure 4–1). In certain cases, scientists may perceive a future problem and launch research to find a solution. An example is an agricultural scientist at the University of California at Davis who foresaw a severe labor shortage for California tomato farmers when the *bracero* program ended, and initiated a research and development program to breed hard tomato varieties that could be machine-picked (we described this case illustration in Chapter 2).

In other cases, a problem/need may rise to high priority on a system's agenda of social problems through a political process, as illustrated in Chapter 3 for the issue of automobile safety. Research and development to develop safer cars and highways had been conducted and accumulated for several years, but the results were not put into practice until the mid-1960s when a series of highly publicized legislative hearings and Ralph Nader's (1965) book, *Unsafe at Any Speed*, called national attention to the high rate of traffic fatalities. The social problem of auto safety rose to a high national priority owing to higher fatality rates in the early 1960s,

Figure 4–1. Six Main Phases in the Innovation-Development Process, Showing the Limited Scope of Past Tracer Studies and of Past Diffusion Studies

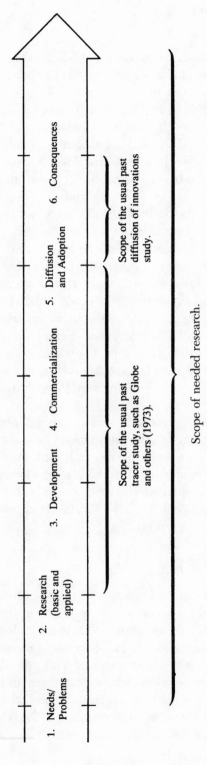

1. Needs/ Problems
2. Research (basic and applied)
3. Development
4. Commercialization
5. Diffusion and Adoption
6. Consequences

Scope of the usual past tracer study, such as Globe and others (1973).

Scope of the usual past diffusion of innovations study.

Scope of needed research.

These six phases are somewhat arbitrary in that they do not always occur in exactly the order shown here, and certain of the phases may be skipped in the case of certain innovations.

when the annual death rate reached 50,000. But the interpretation of this dangerous trend was in large part a political activity.

Havelock (1972) conducted a survey (1) of several hundred researchers specializing in auto safety, and (2) of several hundred decision makers who were members of the most prominent national highway safety organizations. The decision makers generally shared the public view of the traffic safety problem: That it was due to "the nut behind the wheel" (an individual-blame perspective). On the other hand, most of the research community rejected this "old guard" view of the safety problem and felt that solutions to vehicle fatality rates had to come from the redesign of autos and highways (a system-blame view). The invisible college of safety researchers who were employed mainly in universities was led by a cadre of research opinion leaders who were seen by their peer researchers as conducting the most important research in the field. These opinion leaders had a high degree of contact with decision makers, who were government officials or executives in private firms such as insurance companies. As a result, the old guard's perception of the traffic safety problem as due to the nut behind the wheel gradually gave way to a system-blame perspective of this social problem. Safety research was thus redirected, and new public policies were formed to effectuate safer cars and roads.

In this case, existing research results were put into use through a political process. And traffic safety researchers helped call attention to the social problem by means of their research, which led to the redefinition of the problem from one of individual-blame to system-blame. Here we see how the social construction of a problem is both a matter of scientific expertise and of political forces, as a prioritized agenda of innovation-needs is worked out over time.

2. Basic and Applied Research

Most innovations that have been investigated in diffusion researches have been technological innovations, and so the term "technology" is often used as a synonym for innovation. What is technology? As we stated in Chapter 1, *technology* is a design for instrumental action that reduces the uncertainty in the cause-effect relationships involved in achieving a desired outcome. This definition implies some need or problem that a tool can help to solve. The tool has a material aspect (the equipment, products, etc.) and a software aspect, consisting of knowledge, skills, procedures, and/or principles that are an information base for the tool. Almost every technology embodies software aspects, although they are generally less visible than the hardware aspects. Some technologies are almost purely software in nature; an illustration is Henry Ford's idea of assembly-line manufacturing, or the Japanese management concept of quality-control circles. These are mainly social technologies, centering around an idea.

As explained previously, most technological innovations are created by scientific research activities, although they often result from an interplay of scientific methods and practical problems. The knowledge base for a technology usually derives from *basic research*, defined as original investigations for the advancement of scientific knowledge that do not have a specific objective of applying this knowledge to practical problems. In contrast, *applied research* consists of scientific investigations that are intended to solve practical problems. Scientific knowledge is put into practice in order to design an innovation that will solve a perceived need or problem. Applied researchers are the main users of basic research. Thus, an invention* may result from a sequence of (1) basic research followed by (2) applied research leading to (3) development.

One measure of the success of research is whether or not it leads to a patent, through which the government protects the rights of the inventor for a period of seventeen years. The patent clause was introduced in the U.S. Constitution by our nation's founding fathers in order to provide a capitalistic motivation for invention. A patent guards the rights of the inventor during the period in which the new idea is being commercialized (that is, converted into a new product for sale). In order to be awarded a patent, an inventor must prove to the U.S. Patent Office that his or her new idea is genuinely original, that it does not overlap with existing knowledge.

Ordinarily, an inventor will sell a license to use the new idea for an initial fee plus a royalty (which is usually a percentage of sales from a product based on the patented idea). Many important research findings are not licensed, because no one has identified a profitable application for the new idea. Study is needed on how a patent facilitates or restricts the application of scientific findings to form useful innovations.

On certain occasions, R&D workers chance upon an invention while pursuing research to find a very different invention. The accidental dis-

---

Invention is the process by which a new idea is discovered or created. In contrast, innovation (as defined previously) occurs when a new idea is adopted or rejected. So invention and innovation are two different processes, although both deal with a new idea.

covery of a new idea is called serendipity. A case of serendipity occurred in the R&D laboratories of 3M, a company headquartered in Minneapolis that is best known for one of its products, Scotch tape. In the late 1970s, 3M researchers found a new bonding agent, but decided it was worthless because it did not stick paper very tightly to a surface. This failure was converted into a successful product when a 3M researcher used the new bonding agent to create Post-its™, the little stick-on squares of paper that can be used to attach a small note to a letter or other document. The 3M researcher gave some Post-it pads to the 3M president's executive secretary. She liked them. Then a box of Post-it pads were mailed to the executive secretary of the president of each Fortune 500 company in the U.S. The new product was on its way to becoming a big marketing success. Today Post-its are one of 3M's most profitable products, earning the company millions of dollars per year.

Another example of serendipity is Rogaine, a hair-restorer for balding men that is sold by the Upjohn Company. In the mid-1980s, Upjohn's R&D workers discovered Monoxidil, a drug that dilates the body's arteries and thus reduces blood pressure. To their great surprise the R&D workers on the Monoxidil project discovered that their own hair had begun to sprout luxuriantly. As an experiment, they applied a swatch of monoxidil on their forearms. Hair grew thickly. The monoxidil dilated the blood vessels, bringing more blood to the hair roots, and thus stimulated their hair's growth. Until this time, Upjohn had only sold drugs directly to medical doctors, and company officials did not think that selling a consumer product was appropriate. But the R&D workers were able to persuade the company's top manager to market Rogaine, the name given to Upjohn's hair growth stimulant after FDA (Food and Drug Administration) approval was granted. Rogaine sells for about $60 for a one month's supply, and once a man stops applying the product to a balding spot, the balding process proceeds rapidly, a feature which discourages discontinuance of the innovation. Once Rogaine was approved by the FDA and placed on the market, it earned large profits, and the value of Upjohn's stock shot up in the U.S. stock market.

An implicit assumption of the innovation-development process is that innovations are developed by the manufacturers who produce and sell these innovations. Research by Professor Eric Von Hipple (1988) at MIT, however, finds that this basic assumption is often wrong. In some fields, users develop most innovations, and then convince a manufacturing company to produce and sell the innovation, often after the user has created a prototype of the innovation. In other fields, companies that supply components and materials for a product develop innovations which a manufacturer then takes over to produce and sell. And in yet other fields, the conventional wisdom holds: Manufacturers indeed develop innovations.

Von Hipple (1988) found that "lead users" developed 77 percent of the innovations in the scientific instruments field, and 67 percent of the innovations in semiconductors and printed circuit boards. Yet in such other fields as tractor shovels, engineering plastics, and plastic additives, much of the innovation-development was by manufacturers.

Perhaps the general point here is that much innovation occurs when people talk, when information is exchanged about needs and wants versus possible technological solutions. Sometimes the initial impetus for an innovation comes from a lead user; under other conditions, a manufacturer may initiate the innovation's development. Thus the technology transfer process may essentially consist of technology exchange rather than a one-way flow of technology.

3. Development

The acronym "R&D" corresponds closely to the concept that it represents: "R" always appears together with "D" and, moreover, always precedes "D." Development is based closely on research. In fact, it is usually difficult or impossible to separate research and development, which is why the term "R&D" is so often used. But here we argue that research and development can be considered as distinct phases in the innovation-development process.

Development of an innovation is the process of putting a new idea in a form that is expected to meet the needs of an audience of potential adopters. This phase customarily occurs after research but prior to the innovation that stems from research. In the case illustration of the mechanized tomato harvester discussed later, the innovation was developed by agricultural researchers at the University of California at Davis. They designed a tomato-harvesting machine and built a prototype model, but then they contracted with a farm machinery company to manufacture the mechanized harvester. This later phase, called commercialization, will be discussed in a following section.

THE ROLE OF UNCERTAINTY IN R&D. If the adopter of an innovation is faced with a high degree of uncertainty, the inventor-developer of a new idea must understand not just his or her own problems but also anticipate the problems of various other individuals and organizations who will be the ultimate adopters of the innovation. In addition, the behavior of others in his or her own R&D organization, his or her competitors, government policy makers, and a host of others may all affect the success of an inventor's new idea. Information exchange about technological innovation is thus a crucial component affecting innovation. R&D workers devote much effort to obtaining and using information: Data about the performance of the innovation they are seeking to create and market, about the materials and components they are fabricating into the innovation, information about competitors' innovations, the nature of existing patents related to their proposed innovation, government policies affecting their proposed innovation, and the problems faced by the expected consumers and how the proposed innovation might help solve certain of these perceived problems.

So the innovation-development process is, most of all, driven by the exchange of technical information in the face of a high degree of uncertainty.

How the Refrigerator Got Its Hum

Every household refrigerator in the U.S. has a motor that drives a compressor that condenses a liquid, thus releasing heat into the room, which the liquid had previously absorbed in the refrigerator when the liquid vaporized. A superior alternative is the gas refrigerator, in which the ammonia refrigerant is vaporized by heating with a gas flame, and dissolves in water, thus cooling the refrigerator box. The gas refrigerator has no moving parts, and hence is unlikely to break down, or to make any noise. By about 1930, prototype refrigerators of both types were developed, and one might expect that the gas refrigerator, because of its overwhelming advantages, would capture the consumer market. It didn't.

The main reason was the extensive R&D investment in the electric refrigerator by General Electric, General Motors, Kelvinator, and Westinghouse. These large corporations decided that larger profits could be made from the electric refrigerator, and poured huge amounts of funding into R&D on the electric refrigerator, and in aggressive promotion of this product. Several companies who marketed the gas refrigerator could not compete with these larger opponents. So the technology available to the consumer was shaped by considerations of corporate profitability, determined mainly by General Electric during the R&D phase, rather than by consumer choice in the marketplace. As a result, the product that diffused was a refrigerator with a hum.

This case illustration is based on Cowan (1985).

THE SOCIAL CONSTRUCTION OF TECHNOLOGY. *Technological determinism* is the belief that technology causes changes in society. This viewpoint implies that technology is somehow autonomous (that is, outside of society). Obviously, it isn't. An opposite viewpoint is called the social construction of technology, which argues that technology is shaped by social factors. Technology is a product of society, and is influenced by the norms and values of the social system. For example, the previous case illustration on How the Refrigerator Got Its Hum shows that the technology selected was one that offered the greatest profits to the corporate manufacturers, not the technology that had the most advantages to consumers. So in this case economic factors such as profitability shaped the technological innovation that was diffused to consumers. Many important technologies are shaped by military demands. Examples are nuclear power, jet aircraft, and microelectronics.

SKUNKWORKS. Evidence that the usual bureaucratic structure of an organization is not very conducive to creating technological innovation is provided by the important role of "skunkworks," the small and often subversive units within a large organization that pioneer in creating innovation. So a skunkworks is an especially enriched environment that is designed to help a small group of individuals escape usual organizational procedures, so that innovation is encouraged. The R&D workers in a skunkworks are usually highly selective, given special resources, and work on a crash basis to create a needed innovation.

The distinctive name, skunkworks, originated during World War II, in 1943, when the P-80 Shooting Star was designed in Lockheed's Advanced Development Projects Division in Burbank, California. A closely guarded incubator was set up in a circus tent next to a plastics factory in Burbank. The strong smells that wafted into the tent made the Lockheed R&D workers think of the foul-smelling "Skunk Works" factory in Al Capp's Li'l

Abner comic strip. The name stuck, and came to be generalized to similar crash R&D units that have been created by various companies down through the years.

One particularly famous skunkworks was established by Steve Jobs of Apple Computer, Inc. in the early 1980s to design the Macintosh computer. This skunkworks was secretly located behind the Good Earth Restaurant in Cuppertino (in Northern California's Silicon Valley). About fifty highly dedicated young computer designers labored day and night, under the aggressive and abusive leadership of Jobs. After the Macintosh was announced, and then disappointingly postponed several different times, the revolutionary new computer was finally displayed at Apple's annual stockholders' meeting in January, 1984. The Macintosh received rave notices—several million American consumers visited computer stores the next day in order to look at the new machine. The fifty young computerists who had toiled so long in the Apple Skunkworks suddenly found themselves celebrities. Several were millionaires.

Why are skunkworks needed in order to develop technological innovations like the P-80 Shooting Star and the Apple Macintosh? Most R&D organizations are bureaucracies, structured to provide stability and continuity, but not very flexible in nurturing innovation. Here we see an illustration of the inherent conflict between organizational structure and technological innovation. A skunkworks provides a means to get the best of both.

TECHNOLOGY TRANSFER. *Technology transfer* is the exchange of technical information between the R&D workers who create a technological innovation and the users of the new idea. The conventional conception of technology transfer is that it is a process through which the results of basic and applied research are put into use. This view implies that technology transfer is a one-way process, usually from university-based basic researchers to individuals in private companies who develop and commercialize the technological innovation. Further, in this traditional and limited view of technology transfer, the technology is seen mainly as hardware technology, a physical product.

Clearly, if one understands that a technology usually consists of software as well as hardware, and thus that a technology is essentially composed of information (matter-energy that affects an individual's choice of alternatives in a decision-making situation), technology transfer is a communication process (Eveland, 1986). Further, especially if recent years, most scholars have realized that technology transfer is a two-way exchange. Even when a technology moves in one direction, such as from a university or a federal R&D lab to a private company, the two or more parties must participate in a series of communication exchanges as they seek to establish a mutual understanding about the meaning of the technology.

In the past decade or so, technology transfer has become a very important policy issue for the United States government. In industry after industry, from cars to VCRs to semiconductor memory chips, Japanese high-technology companies have taken market share away from their American counterparts. The result has been a monumental trade deficit with Japan that the U.S. cannot continue to afford in the long term. Something must be done, and federal policy makers have been desperately exploring alternatives, many dealing with technology transfer. Even though U.S. R&D leads Japan far and away in creating technological innovations, Japanese firms have been much more effective in transferring this technology into commercial products, which are manufactured with higher quality and at a lower price. If American firms are to compete successfully with Toyota, NEC, and Sony, they must learn to do a better job of technology transfer.

The VCR is an illustration of the inadequacies of American-style technology transfer, as compared to this process in Japan. The VCR was invented in the late 1950s by Ampex Corporation, a company known for its high-quality audiotape, headquartered in Redwood City, California, just south of San Francisco. Ampex sold their product to television stations, who used the VCRs to replace film with videotape. The VCRs used one-inch tape, were about the size of a refrigerator, and cost $50,000. Sales boomed and the Ampex company flourished. R&D workers at Ampex suggested to management that they should design and sell a miniaturized version of their VCR for consumers to use in their homes. But the company management insisted they were not in that market, and instead sold the rights to the technology to Sony Corporation of Japan, who then commercialized the idea into a home VCR.

Sony and other Japanese manufacturers have racked up billions of dollars in sales each year from VCRs. Today, no American company produces the product. This illustration is one of many examples in which American inventiveness is converted into commercial advantage by a Japanese company through more adroit commercialization, manufacturing, and marketing.

Following the end of the Cold War, federal R&D labs, especially weapons labs like Los Alamos, Sandia, and Oak Ridge, had to convert to transferring their military technologies to private companies in order to produce peacetime products. Such technology transfer is extremely difficult. For more than fifty years, the federal weapons labs were secret, closed systems, enclosed in wire fences and tightly guarded. Their organizational culture emphasized the prevention of technology leakage. Suddenly, the mission of these R&D labs was redirected by the Federal government to technology transfer. But the organizational culture of these Federal R&D labs has not changed as quickly as have world events, so relatively few technological innovations are actually transferred to private firms.

In general, the international competitiveness of the United States is threatened by its difficulties with technology transfer, compared to the apparent ease with which the Japanese manage this process. What is so difficult about technology transfer? One problem in answering this question is to understand correctly what technology transfer is, and then to measure when it has occurred.

There are three possible levels (or degrees) of technology transfer (Gibson and Rogers, 1994):

1. *Knowledge*. Here the receptor knows about the technological innovation, perhaps as the result of mass communication messages about the new idea.

2. *Use*. Here the receptor has put the technology into use in his or her organization. This type of technology transfer is much more complex than just knowing about the technology (above). The difference is equivalent to the knowledge stage in the innovation-decision process versus the implementation stage (Chapter 5).

3. *Commercialization*. Here the receptor has commercialized the technology into a product that is sold in the marketplace. For such commercialization to occur, a great deal of time and resources must be invested by the technology receptor. So commercialization requires interpersonal communication exchanges about the technology over an extended period of time, an even more intensive exchange of information than does the use level of technology transfer.

These three degrees of technology transfer have often not been recognized in the past, with the result that thinking and writing about technology transfer have been confusing. Scholars who study technology transfer agree, however, that this process often fails. Technology transfer is very difficult, in part because we have underestimated just how much effort is required for it to occur.

4. Commercialization

Innovations often result from research activities; they thus are scientific results packaged in a form ready to be adopted by users. Because such packaging of research results is usually done by private firms, this stage in the technology-development process is called commercialization. *Commercialization* is the production, manufacturing, packaging, marketing, and distribution of a product that embodies an innovation. It is the conversion of an idea from research into a product or service for sale in the marketplace.

Not all innovations come from research and development, of course. They may instead arise from practice as certain practitioners seek new solutions to their needs/problems. For example, most medical innovations are the product of research and development by specialized experts, but occasionally an innovation comes from practice. An illustration is radial keratotomy, a surgical procedure for correcting certain eyesight problems.* This innovation was adopted by several thousand practitioners before its scientific evaluation was begun by the National Institutes of Health (NIH) in the early 1980s. There are similar examples of innovations coming out of practice in education, public transportation, agriculture, and other fields.

Two or more innovations are often packaged together in order to facilitate their diffusion because the several innovations have a functional interrelatedness, or at least they are so perceived by potential adopters. A *technology cluster* (also called an innovation package in Chapter 5) consists of one or more distinguishable elements of technology that are perceived as being interrelated closely.

The Trail of the Mouse: From SRI to Xerox to Apple

The bottom line for technology transfer is the commercialization of technology into the form of useful products that are sold to consumers in the marketplace. A well-known failure of technology transfer is the case of the microcomputer, which was developed at Xerox PARC (Palo Alto Research

---

*By making a series of tiny incisions in the eye. One concern is whether the long-term effect of radial keratotomy might be loss of vision.

Center) located in a research park on the Stanford University campus. Founded in 1970, by 1977 PARC had developed an incredible set of important microcomputer technologies, including:

1. The world's first computer designed for an individual, called the Alto (a personal computer)
2. The mouse, a means for an individual to interact with a computer
3. Icons and pull-down menus
4. Laser printing
5. Ethernet technology, a cable linking computers into a local area network

These technologies were developed by about two dozen key individuals in Xerox PARC. The Xerox Corporation, then the world's leading paper copier company, invested 150 million dollars in Xerox PARC during its first 14 years (Uttal, 1983). Unfortunately for Xerox, none of these personal computing technologies, except for laser printing, were commercialized by the Xerox Corporation into useful products. Instead, most of the personal computing technologies invented and developed at Xerox PARC from 1970 to 1975 were marketed by Apple Computer, Inc. after 1984.

Steven Jobs of Apple visited Xerox PARC in November, 1979, and was impressed by the personal computing technologies that he saw there. Within six months, Jobs had hired Larry Tesler, the PARC researcher who conducted the tour, and later several other key PARC employees, to play a leading role in developing the widely sold Macintosh, announced in 1984. So Apple commercialized many of the personal computing technologies developed at Xerox PARC. The book about the failure of technology transfer from Xerox PARC to the Xerox Corporation is entitled *Fumbling the Future: How Xerox Invented, and Then Ignored, the First Personal Computer* (Smith and Alexander, 1988). This case history examines that failure.

Xerox PARC was founded in 1970 in order to create "the office of the future" soon after its parent company, the Xerox Corporation, purchased a mainframe computer company and decided that office copying and computers would eventually merge. PARC was "one of the most unusual corporate research organizations of our time" (Perry and Wallich, 1985). This expensive R&D lab was not tied to any of the Xerox Corporation's existing product lines. Instead, the president of the Xerox Corporation gave PARC the vague mission of developing "the architecture of information." No one knew quite what that meant.

Nevertheless, Xerox PARC was located on the Stanford Industrial Park, and a director was hired. PARC attracted a set of very talented computer R&D workers. "In the mid-1970s, close to half of the top 100 computer scientists in the world were working at PARC . . ." (Perry and Wallich, 1985). PARC was a spectacular success in developing technological innovations, particularly during its first five years, from 1970 to 1975. What led to the amazing performance of Xerox PARC in developing many of the important microcomputing innovations?

1. Outstanding R&D personnel, most of whom were identified by Dr. Robert Taylor, a PARC administrator who had been the research grants manager for computing at the U.S. Department of Defense's Advanced Research Projects Agency (ARPA). This agency funded many of the computer science departments then emerging in U.S. universities, such as at MIT, Carnegie-Mellon, and at Stanford University. So Taylor was widely acquainted in the computer science field. He was able to recruit talented individuals to Xerox PARC's Computer Science Laboratory because he had plenty of funding, and Palo Alto had an attractive climate and was then rapidly becoming a high-technology center (called Silicon Valley). "It happened that 1970–71 was a good time to recruit able people in the information sciences. The computer business had not yet really taken off, and there was a moderately serious economic recession" (Pake, 1985). Further, a nearby company, the Berkeley Computer Corporation, had just failed, and Taylor hired several of its key people at Xerox PARC. Once a critical mass of outstanding computer scientists were employed at PARC, it became easier to recruit additional R&D employees to PARC.

Several key R&D employees moved to PARC from nearby SRI International, where they had been working for a visionary computer scientist, Douglas C. Engelbart, who had invented the mouse as an alternative to the keyboard for people to interface with a computer. During the 1960s, Englebart experimented with the mouse as a means of controlling terminals connected to a mainframe computer. However, Englebart was not oriented to microcomputers, and so he refused to devise a mouse for these much smaller computers. As a result, several of his staff (who felt that microcomputers represented the future) moved to Xerox PARC, which was then getting underway. PARC was only five miles from SRI. The SRI defectors took the mouse with them. This movement of individuals from SRI to PARC was one means of technology transfer.

2. Taylor's management style was conducive to creating technological innovation. He encouraged the free exchange of technical information among

his research workers at PARC. Their regular meeting room at PARC was equipped with bean-bag chairs and the walls were lined with China boards. Long hair, sandals, tee-shirts, and jeans symbolized the personal freedom that was allowed the researchers. PARC's organizational culture facilitated information exchange and encouraged creativity. Research goals were set by consensus. There was little hierarchy within PARC, and resources were plentiful.

3. R&D employees at Xerox PARC used the innovations that they created in their daily work: The Alto computer, Ethernet, computer languages, the mouse, and icons. The R&D workers who created the microcomputing innovations were also the users.

4. The time was ripe for technological innovation in microcomputing in the early 1970s. A crucial prior innovation, the microprocessor, had been invented by Ted Hoff and others at nearby Intel Corporation (Noyce and Hoff, 1981). The microprocessor is a computer's central processing unit on a single computer chip. Invention of the microprocessor made possible the microcomputer, a stand-alone personal computer. Rapid advances in miniaturizing semiconductor functions, with a corresponding decrease in price per unit of computer memory, occurred in the early 1970s. The decreasing price of semiconductor memory meant that microcomputers could be priced for a mass consumer market.

So Xerox PARC R&D workers were located in the right place, and at the right time, to make important advances in microcomputer technologies. But they were unable to commercialize them into consumer products for the marketplace.

Why did Xerox PARC fail to transfer the mouse and other important microcomputing technologies to the marketplace?

1. The Xerox Corporation was the leading company in the paper copier business in the 1970s, and it saw its specialty as chemicals-on-paper. The Xerox Corporation envisioned electronic computing technologies as its future. But the microcomputer technologies developed at Xerox PARC occurred so rapidly that the parent corporation was largely unprepared for them. It perceived of itself as still in the office copier business, not in the microcomputer business. The one PARC technology that was commercialized effectively by the Xerox Corporation, laser printing, was incorporated into a Xerox copier. So the Xerox Corporation's image of itself was an impediment to the transfer of microcomputer technologies from its expensive R&D center in Palo Alto.

On the other hand, Apple Computer, Inc., was in the microcomputer business from its beginning, so the people at Apple Computer understood the marketing of personal computers. Computer scientists and engineers at Apple had full support from Steve Jobs, the founder and top executive in the company, for developing the technologies they obtained from PARC into a commercial product.

2. No effective mechanisms were created for technology transfer from Xerox PARC to the manufacturing and marketing/sales divisions of the Xerox Corporation. When such a development unit was later created at Xerox PARC, the Systems Development Division (SDD), it was generally unable to form an effective bridge for technology transfer to the Xerox Corporation's operating units. PARC was located in Palo Alto, CA, an ideal location for conducting R&D in personal computing, but unfortunately at a great physical distance from the Corporation's headquarters in Stanford, Connecticut; its manufacturing center in Rochester, NY; or its Office Systems Division in Dallas. Geographical distance diminishes the opportunities for frequent personal contact, and thus makes technology transfer more difficult (Gibson and Rogers, 1994). "PARC had weak ties to the rest of Xerox, and the rest of Xerox had no channel for marketing products based on the researchers' efforts" (Uttal, 1983).

However, transfer of the mouse technology occurred when several key individuals went from SRI to Xerox PARC. Another important technology transfer of the mouse and other microcomputing technologies occurred from PARC to Apple Computer in 1979 when Steve Jobs, cofounder of Apple Computer, visited PARC with several of his engineers. These visitors immediately understood the microcomputing technologies they observed, such as the mouse, pull-down menus, and icons. Jobs and his followers then converted these technologies into a commercial product, the Macintosh, which became one of the most widely selling computers of all time.

Technology transfer of the mouse and related microcomputer technologies from SRI to PARC, and from PARC to Apple Computer, did not require a long time period to occur. But the conversion of these technologies into a commercialized product (the Macintosh) required a relatively longer time. For example, Jobs visited PARC in 1979, but the Macintosh was not announced until 1984. Commercialization of the SRI/PARC microcomputer technologies by Apple had to await the emergence of appropriate supporting technologies such as low-price semiconductor memories and powerful microprocessors.

This case illustration draws directly on Rogers and Bardini (1994).

5. Diffusion and Adoption

Gatekeeping is controlling the flow of messages through a communication channel. One of the most crucial decisions in the entire innovation-development process is the decision to begin diffusing an innovation to potential adopters. On the one hand, there is usually pressure to approve an innovation for diffusion as soon as possible, as the social problem/need that it seeks to solve may have a high priority. Public funds may have been used to conduct the research and such financial support is an unrealized public investment until the innovation is adopted by users. On the other hand, the change agency's reputation and credibility in the eyes of its clients rests on only recommending innovations that will have beneficial consequences for adopters. Scientists are usually very cautious when it comes time to translate their scientific findings into practice.

Innovation gatekeeping, controlling whether or not an innovation should be diffused to an audience, occurs in a variety of ways in different fields. Agricultural experiment stations in each of the fifty states develop farm innovations and then turn them over to their state agricultural extension services to diffuse; each innovation that is judged ready for diffusion is recommended to farmers for their adoption by agricultural experts. The innovation may be given blanket approval, or it may just be recommended for certain farmers, or for certain climatic or soil conditions. An organizational interface is often involved at the point of deciding to begin diffusing an innovation, as the new idea passes from R&D workers in an agricultural experiment station to a diffusion agency (the agricultural extension service). A similar organizational interface between an R&D unit and a diffusion agency is involved in many other fields, and the decision point is managed in a variety of ways.

There is a strong concern in medical diffusion with exerting "quality control" over the technologies that spread to practitioners. This concern is understandable, given the possible threat to human life that might be involved in diffusing an unsafe medical innovation to practitioners. A novel approach to gatekeeping medical innovations was pioneered by the National Institutes of Health through the conduct of consensus development conferences. *Consensus development* is a process that brings together scientists, practitioners, consumers, and others in an effort to reach general agreement on whether or not a given innovation is both safe and effective (Lowe, 1980). The medical innovation may be a device, a drug, or a medical or surgical procedure. A consensus conference differs from the usual state-of-the-art scientific meeting in that a broadly based panel is constituted to address a set of predetermined questions regarding the particular medical innovation under review. A consensus conference at the NIH typically ends with preparation of a brief consensus statement which is published by the U.S. government and widely disseminated to physicians by means of medical journals and by other means.

Consensus development conferences were begun in 1978 in recognition of the fact that the medical fields lacked a formal gatekeeping process to assure that medical research discoveries were identified and scientifically evaluated to determine if they were ready to be used by doctors and other health-care workers. It was feared that some new technologies might have diffused without an adequate scientific evaluation, while other well-validated medical technologies might be diffusing too slowly.

The NIH consensus development conferences approve or disapprove of medical innovations for diffusion to users on the basis of the evaluation of these innovations in clinical trials, which may have been conducted at the commercialization phase of the innovation-development process. *Clinical trials* are scientific experiments designed to determine prospectively the effects of an innovation in terms of its efficacy, safety, and other factors. The purpose of clinical trials is to evaluate the effects of an innovation under real-life (rather than laboratory) conditions, as a basis for making a go/no-go decision as to the diffusion of the innovation. Once several clinical trials of a medical innovation have been conducted, perhaps with funding provided by the NIH, the results are pulled together in a consensus development conference. So the consensus development process serves an important function in gatekeeping the flow of medical innovations from research into practice.

Several evaluations of the NIH consensus development conferences have been carried out to determine whether or not the consensus development statements, each recommending or not recommending a medical innovation, have a direct impact on practitioners' decisions to adopt or reject the innovation. These evaluation results are rather discouraging (Lomas, 1991; Ferguson, 1993). Only some of the practitioners in a medical specialty know about the NIH recommendation concerning an innovation, and only some of those medical doctors act accordingly.

The consensus development approach has also been used by the National Institute of Mental Health, the U.S. Department of Education, and other federal agencies. A similar function to the consensus development conferences is performed by means of other mechanisms in other change agencies. Often, however, the crucial decision as to which innovations to diffuse is made less formally and hence responsibility for this choice may be rather loose.

6. Consequences

The final phase in the innovation-development process is the *consequences* of an innovation, defined as the changes that occur to an individual or to a social system as a result of the adoption or rejection of an innovation. Here the original problem/need that set off the innovation-decision process is either solved or not. Further detail on the consequences of an innovation is presented in Chapter 11.

We have implied in the present section that the six stages in the innovation-development process occur in the linear sequence in which they were discussed. On the contrary, in many cases certain of these phases do not occur, or the time-order of the phases may be changed.

Serendipity in the Discovery of Warfarin

The story of warfarin, the most widely used rat poison in the world today, helps illustrate how scientific research aimed at solving one problem can lead to a technological innovation that is tremendously effective at solving a different problem. Previously, we explained that serendipity is the chance, unplanned discovery of a new idea.

Research by Professor K.P. Link and his associates at the University of Wisconsin in 1934 was designed to find the chemical in spoiled sweet clover hay that led to cattle hemorrhage. Many farmers fed their cattle sweet clover in those days, in part because planting sweet clover was recommended by agronomists as a crop with the ability to "sweeten" an acidic soil, and to minimize soil erosion. But when the sweet clover hay was fed to cattle, they sometimes became ill and, unless treated, died from internal bleeding. Farmers called this mysterious illness sweet clover disease.

Professor Link set out to isolate the hemorrhaging agent in spoiled sweet clover. He found an anticoagulant called coumarin. Biomedical researchers soon began to test the usefulness of this agent in certain types of surgery and on some heart conditions. But the most important application of Dr. Link's findings from research on sweet clover disease occurred a dozen years later,

when Link began to experiment in 1945 with using coumarin and its deriv-
atives as a rodenticide. He found to his surprise that the anticoagulant was
a very effective rat-killer.

Dr. Link applied to the Wisconsin Alumni Research Foundation
(WARF), a University of Wisconsin "kitty," for funds to pursue his research
on coumarin as a rat-killer. In 1948, a chemical derivative of coumarin was
found to be a particularly effective rat poison. Called "warfarin" (after
WARF), this poison was released to commercial manufacturers with the licensing royalties going back to WARF. These returns from warfarin fund
many of the Madison professors' pet research projects, provide research as-
sistantships for doctoral students, and pay for other research expenses.

Warfarin poison is highly lethal to rats. Because warfarin kills rats by causing internal bleeding, the stricken rodents seek water and thus do not usually die in their burrows. So farmers and homeowners can readily observe
the effectiveness of warfarin in eradicating rats; the observability of the innovation is thus enhanced (see Chapter 6). Warfarin is not dangerous to
dogs, cats, or humans who happen to consume it.

Today, over 3.5 million tons of warfarin are sold each year, with about
half of this rat poison being used by farmers. Total retail sales of warfarin-
based rodenticides are $50 to 100 million per year. Overall savings from war-
farin in the form of avoiding grain loss and property damage are undoubtedly
many times this figure.

Professor Link began his research that eventually led to the rat-killer by
investigating "sweet clover disease." The innovation-development process
for warfarin was uncertain and unpredictable, with serendipity and accident
playing major roles. So our present model of the six-phased process of innovation-development should be considered only a general guide from
which many innovations deviate.

This case illustration is based on Lowe (1981).

Socioeconomic Status, Equality, and Innovation-Development

One of the important policy shifts in international development work during the 1970s was to pay much greater attention to issues of socioeconomic equality. This policy emphasis on equality is directly related with
every phase of the innovation-development process.

For example, a consistent finding from past researches on the diffusion phase is that individuals' socioeconomic status is highly related to their degree of change agent contact, and that status (and change agent contact) are in turn highly related to their degree of innovativeness (see Chapter 9). Thus, change agencies cause increased socioeconomic inequality among their audience through their usual introduction of innovations.

Further, the socioeconomic status of individual adopters is interfaced with the nature of the innovation-development process. For example, whether a new agricultural machine like the tomato-harvestor in California is produced as a four-row, a six-row, or as an eight-row model has an important influence on whether larger or smaller farmers will purchase it. The larger, more expensive machines will be less affordable by smaller farmers. In fact, whether a research topic likely to benefit larger or smaller farmers is investigated by public R&D workers has much to say about who will eventually adopt the results of such research (Hightower, 1972).

Can technologies be developed and diffused in a way that would lead to greater equality (rather than inequality)in their socioeconomic consequences? The answer lies in an analysis of how socioeconomic status factors affect each step in the innovation-development process. One example of this type of investigation is provided by the following study of tomato-harvesting.

Hard Tomatoes in California

The nature of an innovation's diffusion and its consequences are often determined in part during the R&D work to create the innovation. How the diffusion process is predetermined by decisions and events that occurred much prior to the first adoption is illustrated by the case of the mechanized tomato harvester in California.

California is the number one agricultural state in America, and tomatoes are one of California's most important farm products. Prior to the introduction of the mechanized harvester in 1962 about 4,000 farmers produced tomatoes in California; nine years later, only 600 of these growers were still in business. Before the new machine, 50,000 farmworkers, mostly immigrant Mexican men, were employed as tomato pickers in California. They were replaced by 1,152 machines (each costing about $65,000), plus about 18,000 workers who rode the harvesters to sort out the damaged and immature tomatoes. About 80 percent of these sorters were women; only a few were Mexican-Americans.

Other consequences of the mechanized harvesters included moving tomato-growing out of California's San Joaquin County into Yolo and Fresno Counties, where the soil and weather conditions were more ideally suited to growing tomatoes for mechanized picking. To enable machine-picking, agricultural scientists bred hard tomatoes that would not bruise easily. Unfortunately, American consumers prefer soft tomatoes. Even though the hard tomatoes tasted the same, they contained somewhat fewer vitamins.

So the development of the mechanized tomato picker had many far-reaching consequences. Were the effects anticipated by the R&D workers who developed the mechanized pickers at the University of California at Davis? Not at all, say the analysts of this case, Friedland and Barton (1975) who conclude that these agricultural scientists were "social sleepwalkers." The creators of the mechanical harvesters were motivated to save the tomato industry for California when it was threatened by termination of the Mexican *bracero* program in 1964 (which meant the end of cheap labor). The scientists showed little concern for how the social consequences of this new technology would adversely affect human lives, leading James Hightower (1972) to entitle his book, *Hard Tomatoes, Hard Times*. Almost all of the research to develop this technology was conducted by agricultural professors at the University of California at Davis, using more than 1 million dollars of public funds (Schmitz and Seckler, 1970). The chief researcher was G.C. "Jack" Hanna, a professor of vegetable crops. He took the lead in breeding a hard-tomato variety that could be machine-harvested, despite the vigorous opposition of his colleagues and administrators who believed that his idea of mechanical picking was ridiculous. In fact, they feared that his bizarre project would damage the reputation of their department and of the University of California.

In 1971, Hanna developed a tomato variety, VF-145, that was ideal for machine picking. It was firm enough for machine harvesting, the fruits were easily detachable from the vine, and most of the tomatoes ripened at about the same time. Hanna teamed with an agricultural engineer at UC Davis named Coby Lorenzen to design a tomato-harvesting machine that would cut off the tomato plant at soil level, pluck the fruits from the vine, and elevate them past a crew of tomato-sorters into a gondola truck for transportation to market. The harvester, designed by Lorenzen, was then produced by

Hanna's friend, Ernest Blackwelder, a farm machinery manufacturer who contracted with the University of California.° In 1964, 224 tomato-picking machines brought in 25 percent of all tomatoes grown. This sudden increase in adoption occurred because the U.S. Congress ended the *bracero* program through which Mexican farmer workers were brought to California. Professors Hanna and Lorenzen had rushed to develop the mechanized harvester because they had foreseen this legislative change. The tomato industry honored Hanna as the individual who "saved the tomato for California." Six years later, in 1970, 1,152 of the machines harvested 99.9 percent of the tomato crop and 32,000 former hand pickers were out of work.

In retrospect, one might wonder how differently the diffusion and adoption of this innovation might have been had the R&D workers designed a smaller machine, one that more of the 4,000 tomato farmers (as of 1962) could have adopted. What if the impending threat of a severe labor shortage in 1964 had not forced Hanna, Lorenzen, and Blackwelder to rush their prototype machine into production? What if the University of California at Davis had conducted social and economic research on the impacts of farm mechanization prior to 1962, so that the destructive consequences of the new technology on employment, and the unhappiness of tomato consumers with hard tomatoes, might have been anticipated, and perhaps mitigated?

The decisions and activities occurring in the R&D phase of the technology development process directly affect the later diffusion phase. Diffusion scholars have ignored this fact too long.

This case illustration is based on Rasmussen (1968), Schmitz and Seckler (1970), Hightower (1972), Friedland and others (1981), Fiske (1980), and especially, Friedland and Barton (1975).

° By 1969, Blackwelder paid $225,000 in technology royalties to the University of California for the right to produce the tomato harvester (Schmitz and Seckler, 1970).

Tracing the Innovation-Development Process

Considerable research has been devoted to tracing the research, development, and commercialization phases of the innovation-development process (as we showed in Figure 4–1). Such retrospective tracer studies reconstruct the sequence of main events and decisions in the innovation-development process. The sources of data are usually personal interviews with key investigators and other participants, research publications, and archival records of research grants, patents, and change agency records.

One of the first, and best-known, retrospective tracer studies of the research and development phases of the innovation-development process is Project Hindsight (Isenson, 1969). This massive tracer study investigated the role of various R&D variables in the research and development activities leading to twenty different military weapons systems, such as the Minuteman missile, the Polaris submarine, the C-141 transport aircraft, and the M-61 nuclear warhead. The key events and decisions in the process of creating each of the twenty technological innovations were identified, an average of about thirty-five events per innovation. Project Hindsight concluded that most of the research that contributed to creation of the twenty innovations was highly applied, and was funded in order to produce the particular weapons system that eventually resulted. The findings of Project Hindsight are usually interpreted to mean that applied research contributes more directly to creation of a technological innovation than does basic research—hardly a surprising conclusion.

Project Hindsight led to further innovation tracer studies, first by the Illinois Institute of Technology Research (in 1968) in Project TRACES (Technology in Retrospect and Critical Events in Science), and later by the Batelle-Columbus Laboratories in what was termed TRACES II (Globe and others, 1973) and TRACES III (Batelle-Columbus Laboratories, 1976). These investigations, along with Project Sappho in England (Achilladelis and others, 1971), represent further improvements in the methodology of retrospective tracer studies, and a broadening of the technological innovations studied from military weapons to a variety of biomedical, agricultural, consumer, and other innovations.

These tracer studies generally show that a major technological advance in such fields as military weapons, medicine, or agriculture requires not just one innovation, but a cluster of innovations, often as many as a dozen. For example, the heart pacemaker was an innovation cluster that depended upon the prior invention of electronic transistors, compact batteries, and several other developments (Globe and others, 1973). We should not forget this functional interdependence of innovations, which diffusion scholars generally overlook by investigating single innovations as if they were completely independent (see Chapter 6).

Further, the innovation tracer studies show that a lengthy period, often about twenty years, occurs between an invention in basic research and its application in a weaponry or medical innovation. It seems that the basic research results have to "age" before they can be packaged into a useful innovation. For example, the length of time from first conception of a technological innovation to its first realization was nine years (from

1951 to 1960) for oral contraceptives (Globe and others, 1973). The comparable period for two agricultural innovations was much longer; twenty-five years for hybrid corn (1908 to 1933), and thirteen years for insecticides (1934 to 1947). The ten innovations studied in the TRACES II study required an average of nineteen years from first conception to first realization (Globe and others, 1973).

Finally, the tracer studies show that research is often conducted without a practical application to a social problem in mind. This point is made by Comroe (1977), who traced the innovation-development process for the ten most important technologies in cardiopulmonary medicine. Of the 500 or so key research articles leading to these innovations, 41 percent reported research that, at the time it was conducted, had no relationship whatever to the disease that it helped treat. This widely quoted finding implies that the innovation-development process does not always begin with a perceived problem or need, and that a considerable degree of serendipity may occur.

Several of the case illustrations included in this chapter, such as "The Trail of the Mouse," "Serendipity in the Discovery of Warfarin," and "Hard Tomatoes in California," resulted from tracer studies.

Shortcomings of the Tracer Studies

There are several weaknesses in the innovation tracer studies that need to be improved upon in future research. These tracer studies are *retrospective*; much could also be learned from conducting *prospective* studies of the innovation-development process. Further, past tracer studies focused upon very important technological innovations like the heart pacemaker, oral contraceptives, and the Minuteman missile. We do not know if similar results would obtain for less socially significant innovations.

Further, the data-sources for tracer studies are rather limited:

1. These tracer studies depended almost entirely upon the availability of research publications about the technology, in order to reconstruct a partial view of the R&D phases of the innovation-development process.
2. In light of dependence upon these limited data sources, the tracer studies generally describe the research and development phases of the process but do not tell much about the diffusion/adoption phase, and almost nothing about the consequences of the innovation. Investigations of the *entire* innovation-development process are needed.

3. Also because of the nature of the data sources, the tracer studies give the impression that the research and development phases are relatively rational and planned. Serendipitous and accidental aspects of the innovation-development process are unlikely to be fully reported in research publications written by the inventors and researchers.

Future Research on the Innovation-Development Process

At the beginning of this chapter we pointed out that our discussion of the innovation-development process is based on a rather thin research base. What research questions should be studied in the future to improve our understanding of the innovation-development process?

1. How is the agenda of research priorities in a scientific field set? How are users' needs and problems communicated to R&D workers? What role does a change agency play in translating users' needs into R&D projects?
2. What is the impact on users' credibility in a change agency when it reverses its policy concerning an innovation, for example, by recommending an innovation's discontinuance that it previously recommended?
3. To what extent are technological innovations actually developed by "lead" users, rather than by R&D experts? Research by Von Hippel (1988) indicates that many innovations are created by end-users, who then encourage a manufacturer to commercialize the innovation. Is this a general pattern?
4. What are the consequences of a technological innovation on socio-economic equality, and how is this impact of an innovation affected by its size and cost, which were determined at the development and commercialization phases?
5. What are the key linkages and interrelationships among the various organizations involved in the innovation-development process? Particularly, how do researchers interface with change agents in making the decision to launch the diffusion of an innovation?

The Agricultural Extension Model

The government agency that has been by far the most successful in securing users' adoption of its research results is the agricultural extension services. Although this system is commonly called the agricultural extension model, it actually consists of three main components: (1) a research subsystem, consisting of professors of agriculture supported by the fifty state agricultural experiment stations and the U.S. Department of Agriculture, (2) county extension agents, who work as change agents with farmers and other rural people at the local level, and (3) state extension specialists who link agricultural researchers to the county agents (Rogers and others, 1982). Both the researchers and the extension specialists are located in state agricultural universities, and have similar levels of expertise (both are usually Ph.D.'s in agriculture). So the agricultural extension model is an integrated system for the innovation-development process, although this fact is not widely understood (Rogers, 1988a).

The agricultural university teaching component of the agricultural extension model was established first, by the Morrill Act of 1862, which established land-grant universities, one in each state. Originally, these universities were called state colleges and often had the clumsy phrase "of agriculture and mechanical arts" in their title, for instance, the Iowa State College of Agriculture and Mechanical Arts or the Michigan Agricultural College. Eventually these institutions were called universities, and their names were shortened to Ohio State University, New Mexico State University, and so forth. Because they retained a college of agriculture as one unit (along with a college of education, a college of medicine, etc.), many students today refer to the land-grant universities as "cow colleges." It is not intended to be a compliment, but from the viewpoint of transferring agricultural research into practice, the cow colleges are exemplars.

For twenty-five years, the land-grant universities mainly engaged in teaching agriculture and engineering, but in 1887 a federal law, the Hatch Act, provided funding for agricultural research. Now the professors of agriculture began to lay out experimental plots for testing whether one variety of crop outyielded another. The professors also conducted experiments with different feeding rations for cattle, pigs, and other livestock. Next, the agriculture professors began to convey their research findings to farmers. The agricultural experiments were applied research and the professors wanted their findings to be utilized.

Finally, in 1914, the state agricultural extension services were established by the Smith-Lever Act, which stated their purpose as: "To aid in diffusing among the people of the United States useful and practical information on subjects relating to agriculture and home economics, and to encourage application of the same." So the agricultural extension service has a long history; in fact, it is probably the oldest diffusion system in the United States. Certainly, by reputation it is the most successful.

The budget for the extension services comes from federal, state, and county governments, and for this reason the term "Cooperative Extension Service" is often used for the entire system to indicate the collaboration of these three levels of government. The total annual budget for the agricultural extension services is approximately equal to the annual public investment in agricultural research. This fifty-fifty level of funding for diffusion activities in agriculture is one reason for the success of the agricultural extension services; no other Federal mission agency spends more than a few percent of its research expenditures on diffusion activities (see Chapter 9).

Several other government agencies have tried to copy the agricultural extension model, but with little success. These attempts to extend the agricultural extension model often ignored one or more of the main elements in the model (Rogers and others, 1982). Some federal agencies installed a diffusion system with the equivalent of extension specialists, but they failed to establish local-level change agents to contact clients directly (the counterpart of county extension agents). Other federal agencies forgot that the agricultural extension services were established in 1914, and that it took more than forty years before this change agency set off the "agricultural revolution" in the 1950s and 1960s, in which the extension services diffused farming innovations so effectively that a tremendous increase in U.S. agricultural productivity resulted. Still other extensions of the agricultural extension model overlooked the important fact that much agricultural research is highly applied, conducted in order to be put into use to solve farmer's problems. The attempts to copy the agricultural extension model in such fields as education, public transportation, vocational rehabilitation, energy conservation, and family planning have therefore not been very successful to date.

Summary

Past diffusion researches usually began with the first adopters of an innovation, that is, with the left-hand tail of the S-shaped diffusion curve. Events and decisions occurring previous to this point have a considerable influence upon the diffusion process. We urge that the scope of future diffusion research should be broadened to include study of the entire process of how an innovation is generated.

The *innovation-development process* consists of all the decisions and activities, and their impacts, that occur from recognition of a need or problem, through research, development, and commercialization of an innovation, through diffusion and adoption of the innovation by users, to its consequences. Recognition of a problem or need may happen by means of a political process through which a social problem rises to a high priority on the agenda of problems that deserve research. In other cases, a scientist may perceive a future problem or sense a present difficulty and begin a research program to seek solutions.

Many, but not all, technical innovations come out of research. *Basic research* is defined as original investigations for the advancement of scientific knowledge that do not have the specific objective of applying this knowledge to practical problems. The results of basic research are used in *applied research*, which consists of scientific investigations that are intended to solve practical problems.

The usual next phase in the innovation-development process is *development*, defined as the process of putting a new idea into a form that is expected to meet the needs of an audience of potential adopters. The next phase, *commercialization*, is defined as the production, manufacturing, packaging, marketing, and distribution of a product that embodies an innovation. Commercialization is usually done by private firms, as the name of this phase implies.

A particularly crucial point in the innovation-development process is the decision to begin diffusing an innovation to potential adopters. This choice represents an arena in which researchers come together with change agents. How are innovations evaluated? One way is through *clinical trials*, scientific experiments that are designed to determine prospectively the effects of an innovation in terms of its efficacy, safety, and the like.

Finally, the innovation diffuses, is adopted, and eventually causes consequences, the final step in the innovation-development process. The six phases described here may not always occur in a linear sequence, the time-order of the phases may be different, or certain phases may not occur at all.

5

THE INNOVATION-DECISION PROCESS

One must learn by doing the thing, for though you think you know
it, you have no certainty until you try.
                                    —Sophocles, 400 B.C.

The *innovation-decision process* is the process through which an individual (or other decision-making unit) passes (1) from first knowledge of an innovation, (2) to forming an attitude toward the innovation, (3) to a decision to adopt or reject, (4) to implementation of the new idea, and (5) to confirmation of this decision. This process consists of a series of actions and choices over time through which an individual (or an organization) evaluates a new idea and decides whether or not to incorporate the innovation into ongoing practice. This behavior consists essentially of dealing with the uncertainty that is inherently involved in deciding about a new alternative to those previously in existence. The perceived newness of an innovation, and the uncertainty associated with this newness, is a distinctive aspect of innovation decision making, compared to other types of decision making.

This chapter describes a model of the innovation-decision process and five stages in this process, and summarizes the research evidence that these stages exist. Our main concern here is with optional innovation-decisions that are made by individuals, although much of what is said contributes a basis for our later discussion of the innovation-decision process in organizations (Chapter 10).

A Model of the Innovation-Decision Process

Diffusion scholars have long recognized that an individual's decision about an innovation is not an instantaneous act. Rather, it is a *process* that occurs over time, consisting of a series of actions and decisions. What is the nature of these sequential stages in the process of innovation decision making?

Our present model of the innovation-decision process is depicted in Figure 5–1. This conceptualization consists of five stages:

1. *Knowledge* occurs when an individual (or other decision-making unit) is exposed to an innovation's existence and gains some understanding of how it functions.
2. *Persuasion* occurs when an individual (or some other decision-making unit) forms a favorable or unfavorable attitude toward the innovation.
3. *Decision* occurs when an individual (or some other decision-making unit) engages in activities that lead to a choice to adopt or reject the innovation.
4. *Implementation* occurs when an individual (or other decision-making unit) puts an innovation into use.
5. *Confirmation* occurs when an individual (or some other decision-making unit) seeks reinforcement of an innovation-decision already made, or reverses a previous decision to adopt or reject the innovation if exposed to conflicting messages about the innovation.

Now we describe the behaviors that occur at each of the five stages in the innovation-decision process.

Knowledge Stage

The innovation-decision process begins with the *knowledge* stage which occurs when an individual (or other decision-making unit) is exposed to an innovation's existence and gains some understanding of how it functions.

Which Comes First, Needs or Awareness of an Innovation?

Some observers claim that an individual plays a passive role in being exposed to awareness-knowledge about an innovation. It is argued that an individual becomes aware of an innovation by accident, since the individual cannot actively seek an innovation until he/she knows that it exists. For example, Coleman and others (1966) concluded that initial knowledge about a new medical drug mainly occurred through communication channels and messages (such as salespersons and advertising) that physi-

Figure 5–1. A Model of Stages in the Innovation-Decision Process

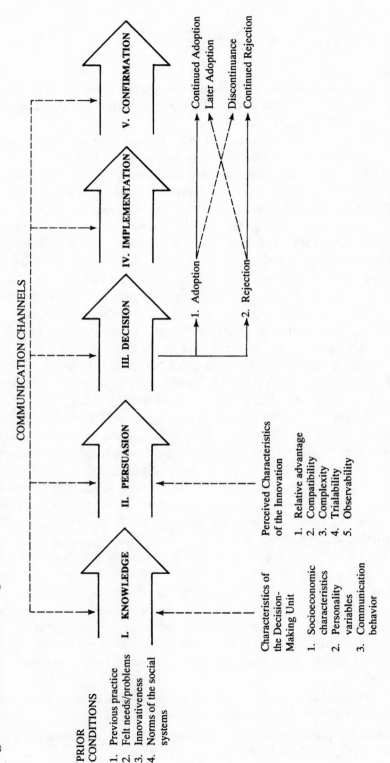

The *innovation-decision process* is the process through which an individual (or other decision-making unit) passes from first knowledge of an innovation, to forming an attitude toward the innovation, to a decision to adopt or reject, to implementation of the new idea, and to confirmation of this decision.

cians did not seek; at later stages in the innovation-decision process, however, doctors became active information-seekers, usually from their peers in communication networks.

Other scholars of diffusion feel that an individual gains awareness-knowledge through behavior that must be initiated, and that awareness-knowledge is not just a passive activity. The predispositions of individuals influence their behavior toward communication messages and the effects that such messages are likely to have. Individuals tend to expose themselves to ideas that are in accordance with their interests, needs, and existing attitudes. Individuals consciously or unconsciously avoid messages that are in conflict with their predispositions. This tendency is called selective exposure.* Hassinger (1959) argued that individuals will seldom expose themselves to messages about an innovation unless they first feel a need for the innovation, and that even if such individuals are exposed to these innovation messages, such exposure will have little effect unless the innovation is perceived as relevant to the individual's needs and as consistent with the individual's attitudes and beliefs.† For example, a farmer can drive past a hundred miles of hybrid corn in Iowa and never "see" the innovation. A Californian can walk past a house with solar panels on the roof and not perceive this innovation. Selective exposure and selective perception act as particularly tight shutters on the windows of our minds in the case of innovation messages, because such ideas are new. We cannot have consistent and favorable attitudes about ideas that we have not previously encountered. There is, then, much in the ideas of selective exposure and selective perception to support Hassinger's viewpoint that the need for an innovation must usually precede awareness-knowledge of the innovation.

How are needs created? A *need* is a state of dissatisfaction or frustration that occurs when one's desires outweighs one's actualities, when "wants" outrun "gets." An individual may develop a need when he or she learns that an innovation exists. Therefore, innovations *can* lead to needs, as well as vice versa. Some change agents create needs among their clients through pointing out the existence of desirable new ideas. Thus knowledge of the existence of an innovation can create motivation for its adoption.

Selective exposure is the tendency to attend to communication messages that are consistent with one's existing attitudes and beliefs.

†This is *selective perception*, the tendency to interpret communication messages in terms of one's existing attitudes and beliefs.

By no means are perceived needs or problems a very complete explanation of why individuals begin the innovation-decision process. In part, this is because individuals do not always recognize when they have a problem, nor do individuals' needs always agree with what experts might think the individuals need. Professor Edgar Dale was fond of saying: "We may want food and not need it. And we may need vitamins and minerals and fail to want them."

Does a need precede knowledge of a new idea, or does knowledge of an innovation create a need for a new idea? Perhaps this is a chicken-or-egg problem. Research does not provide a clear answer to this question of whether awareness of a need or awareness of an innovation (that creates a need) comes first. The need for certain innovations, such as a pesticide to treat a new bug that is destroying a farmer's crops, probably comes first. But for many other new ideas, the innovation may create the need. This sequence may be especially likely for consumer innovations like clothing fashions and electronic products like compact discs.

Types of Knowledge About an Innovation

The innovation-decision process is essentially an information-seeking and information-processing activity in which the individual is motivated to reduce uncertainty about the advantages and disadvantages of an innovation. The individual wishes to understand the innovation, and to give meaning to it. This is a social process, involving talking with others.

An innovation typically contains *software information*, which is embodied in the innovation and which serves to reduce uncertainty about the cause-effect relationships that are involved in achieving a desired outcome (such as meeting a need of the individual). Questions such as "What is the innovation?" "How does it work?" and "Why does it work?" are the main concerns of an individual about an innovation. The first of these three types of knowledge, *awareness-knowledge*, is information that an innovation exists. Awareness-knowledge then motivates an individual to seek "how-to" knowledge and principles knowledge. This type of information-seeking is concentrated at the knowledge stage of the innovation-decision process, but it may also occur at the persuasion and decision stages.

How-to knowledge consists of information necessary to use an innovation properly. The adopter must understand what quantity of an innovation to secure, how to use it correctly, and so on. In the case of innovations that are relatively more complex, the amount of how-to knowledge needed for proper adoption is much greater than in the case of less complex ideas. And when an adequate level of how-to knowledge is not obtained prior to the trial and adoption of an innovation, rejection and discontinuance are likely to result. To date, few diffusion investigations are available that deal with how-to knowledge.

Principles-knowledge consists of information dealing with the functioning principles underlying how the innovation works. Examples of principles-knowledge are: The notion of germ theory, which underlies the functioning of water boiling, vaccinations, and latrines in village sanitation and health campaigns; the fundamentals of human reproduction, which form a basis for family planning innovations; and the biology of plant growth, which underlies the adoption of fertilizer by farmers and gardeners. It is usually possible to adopt an innovation without principles-knowledge, but the danger of misusing the new ideas is greater, and discontinuance may result. Certainly, the competence of individuals to decide whether or not to adopt an innovation is facilitated by principles know-how. If a problem occurs in an individual's use of an innovation, principles-knowledge may be essential in solving it.

What is the role of change agents in bringing about the three types of knowledge? Most change agents concentrate their efforts on creating awareness-knowledge, although this goal often can be achieved more efficiently in many client systems by mass media channels. Change agents could perhaps play their most distinctive and important role in the innovation-decision process if they concentrated on how-to knowledge, which is probably most essential to clients in their trial of an innovation (at the decision stage in the innovation-decision process). Most change agents perceive that creation of principles-knowledge is outside the purview of their responsibilities and is a more appropriate task for formal schooling. It is often too complex a task for change agents to teach basic understanding of principles. But when such understanding is lacking, the change agent's long-run task is often more difficult.

Early Versus Late Knowers of Innovations

The following generalizations summarize the results of findings regarding early knowing about an innovation:

5–1. *Earlier knowers of an innovation have more formal education than later knowers.*

5–2. *Earlier knowers of an innovation have higher socioeconomic status than late knowers.*

5–3. Earlier knowers of an innovation have more exposure to mass media channels of communication than later knowers.

5–4. Earlier knowers of an innovation have more exposure to interpersonal channels than later knowers.

5–5. Earlier knowers of an innovation have more change agent contact than later knowers.

5–6. Earlier knowers of an innovation have more social participation than later knowers.

5–7. Earlier knowers of an innovation are more cosmopolite than later knowers.

The characteristics of earlier knowers of an innovation are similar to the characteristics of innovators: More formal education, higher socioeconomic status, and the like. But earlier knowers are not necessarily innovators.

Knowing about an innovation is often quite different from using a new idea. Most individuals know about many innovations that they have not adopted. Why? One reason is because an individual may know about a new idea but not regard it as relevant to the individual's situation, and as potentially useful. Attitudes toward an innovation, therefore, frequently intervene between the knowledge and decision functions. In other words, the individual's attitudes or beliefs about the innovation have much to say about his or her passage through the innovation-knowledge process. Consideration of a new idea does not go beyond the knowledge function if an individual does not define the information as relevant to his or her situation or if sufficient knowledge is not obtained to become adequately informed so that persuasion can take place.

Persuasion Stage

At the *persuasion** stage in the innovation-decision process, the individual (or some other decision-making unit) forms a favorable or unfavor-

---

*We do not define persuasion with exactly the same connotation as many other communication scholars, who use the term to imply a source's communication with an intent to induce attitude change in a desired direction on the part of a receiver. Our meaning for persuasion is equivalent to attitude formation and change on the part of an individual, but not necessarily in the direction intended by some particular source, such as a change agent.

able attitude* toward the innovation. Whereas the mental activity at the knowledge stage was mainly cognitive (or knowing), the main type of thinking at the persuasion function is affective (or feeling). Until the individual knows about a new idea, of course, he or she cannot begin to form an attitude toward it.

At the persuasion stage the individual becomes more psychologically involved with the innovation; he or she actively seeks information about the new idea, *what* messages he or she receives, and *how* he or she interprets the information that is received. Thus, selective perception is important in determining the individual's behavior at the persuasion stage, for it is at the persuasion stage that a general perception of the innovation is developed. Such perceived attributes of an innovation as its relative advantage, compatibility, and complexity are especially important at this stage (see Figure 5–1).

In developing a favorable or unfavorable attitude toward the innovation, an individual may mentally apply the new idea to his or her present or anticipated future situation before deciding whether or not to try it. This is a kind of vicarious trial. The ability to think hypothetically and counter-factually and to project into the future is an important mental capacity at the persuasion stage where forward planning regarding the innovation is involved.

All innovations carry some degree of uncertainty for the individual, who is typically unsure of the new idea's results and thus feels a need for social reinforcement of his or her attitude toward the new idea. The individual wants to know that his or her thinking is on the right track, in comparison with the opinion of peers. Mass media messages are too general to provide the specific kind of reinforcement that the individual needs to confirm the individual's beliefs about the innovation.

At the persuasion stage, and especially at the decision stage, an individual is motivated to seek *innovation-evaluation information*, the reduction in uncertainty about an innovation's expected consequences. Here an individual usually wants to know the answers to such questions as "What are the innovation's consequences?" and "What will its advantages and disadvantages be in my situation?" This type of information, while often easily available from scientific evaluations of an innovation, is usually sought by most individuals from their near-peers whose sub-

---

Attitude is a relatively enduring organization of an individual's beliefs about an object that predisposes his or her actions.

jective opinion of the innovation (based on their personal experience with adoption of the new idea) is most convincing. When someone who is like us tells us of their positive evaluation of a new idea, we are often motivated to adopt it.

The main outcome of the persuasion stage in the innovation-decision process is either a favorable or unfavorable attitude toward the innovation. It is assumed that such persuasion will lead to a subsequent change in overt behavior (that is, adoption or rejection) consistent with the attitude held. But in many cases attitudes and actions are quite disparate. For example, such a discrepancy between favorable attitudes and actual adoption is frequently found for contraceptive ideas in Third World nations. For instance, surveys of parents of childbearing age in many of these nations show that almost all of these individuals say they are informed about family planning methods and have a favorable attitude toward using them. But only 15 or 20 percent of the parents have actually adopted contraceptives (Rogers, 1973). This attitude-use discrepancy is called the "KAP-gap" (KAP refers to knowledge-attitude-practice) in the family planning field. One reason this gap occurs is because the available family planning methods are not acceptable to parents, owing to certain undesirable side-effects that are associated with them in the minds of potential adopters.

In many other circumstances, formation of a favorable or unfavorable attitude toward an innovation does not lead to an adoption or rejection decision. Nevertheless, there is a tendency in this direction, that is, for attitudes and behavior to become consistent. Why aren't attitudes and actions more closely related? In some cases overt behavior change is beyond an individual's control. Let's say that an individual intends to get a blood test for HIV/AIDS tomorrow but the health clinic is closed. Adoption of a new idea often entails obtaining the innovation in the form of a product or service, which may not always be available to an individual, or which may be too expensive for the individual to adopt. Such intervening factors can cause a KAP-gap.

Another reason why attitudes are not converted into action may be the communication channels utilized by an individual who is a potential adopter. We know from past research that interpersonal communication from a near-peer who is a satisfied adopter often pushes a potential adopter over the edge of decision into adoption of an innovation. Some potential adopters are so located in the diffusion network of their system that they do not have interpersonal communication about the innovation with a near-peer. Perhaps the individual is a social isolate in the network, or else just happens not to have any satisfied adopters as near-peers. Even though this individual has favorable attitudes toward the innovation, adoption may not occur until the individual has interpersonal communication with a satisfied adopter.

Certain individuals are more likely to have an attitudes/adoption gap than are others. For example, later in this chapter we show that earlier adopters of an innovation are characterized by a relatively shorter innovation-decision period (the length of time from awareness-knowledge of an innovation to its adoption). In comparison, later adopters require a longer time period, once aware of a new idea, to move to adoption. So at any given point in time, these later adopters are likely to have a discrepancy between knowledge/attitudes versus adoption. They may have low *efficacy*, defined as the degree to which an individual feels they can control their future. Someone with relatively low self-efficacy would not possess the self-confidence to think that they could adopt the innovation.

An attitude-adoption gap is particularly characteristic of certain innovations, such as new ideas that are preventive in nature. A *preventive innovation* is a new idea that an individual adopts in order to avoid the possible occurrence of some unwanted event in the future (see Chapter 6). The undesired event may, or may not, occur if the innovation is not adopted. So the desired consequences of a preventive innovation are relatively uncertain. Further, adoption and use of a preventive innovation may be unpleasant (such as getting a blood test for HIV/AIDS). Under such circumstances, the individual's motivation to adopt the innovation is weak. Examples of preventive innovations are contraceptives, getting a mammogram test for breast cancer, stopping smoking, the use of automobile seat belts, buying insurance, and preparing a preventive for a possible disaster such as an earthquake or hurricane. Even when an individual perceives a need for innovation, and when the innovation is accessible, adoption often does not occur. So the rate of adoption of preventive innovations is relatively slower than for nonpreventive innovations.

The persuasion-adoption discrepancy for preventive innovations can sometimes be closed by a *cue-to-action*, an event occurring at a certain time that crystallizes a favorable attitude into overt behavior change. Some cues-to-action occur naturally; for instance, many women adopt a contraceptive after they experience a pregnancy scare or an abortion (Rogers, 1973). In other cases, a cues-to-action can be created by a change agency; for instance, some national family planning programs pay incentives in order to provide a cue-to-action to potential adopters. Holding a campaign may provide a cue-to-action for certain individuals. An example is the one-day national "Smoke Out," held each November in the United States, in which thousands of people stop smoking.

Decision Stage

The *decision* stage in the innovation-decision process occurs when an individual (or other decision-making unit) engages in activities that lead to a choice to adopt or reject an innovation. *Adoption* is a decision to make full use of an innovation as the best course of action available. *Rejection* is a decision not to adopt an innovation.

One way to cope with the inherent uncertainty about an innovation's consequences is to try out the new idea on a partial basis. Most individuals will not adopt an innovation without trying it first on a probationary basis in order to determine its usefulness in their own situation. This small-scale trial is often part of the decision to adopt. In some cases, an innovation cannot be divided for trial and so it must be adopted or rejected in toto. Innovations that can be divided for trial are generally adopted more rapidly (see Chapter 6). Most individuals who try an innovation then move to an adoption decision, if the innovation has at least a certain degree of relative advantage. Methods to facilitate the trial of innovations such as the distribution to clients of free samples of a new idea, will speed up the rate of adoption. A field experiment among Iowa farmers found that the free trial of a new weed spray speeded the innovation-decision period by about a year (Klonglan, 1962, 1963; Klonglan and others, 1960a).

For some individuals and for some innovations, the trial of a new idea by a peer like themselves can substitute, at least in part, for their own trial of an innovation. This "trial-by-others" provides a kind of vicarious trial for an individual. Change agents often seek to speed up the innovation-process for individuals by sponsoring demonstrations of a new idea in a social system (see Chapter 9). This demonstration can be quite effective in influencing adoption by individuals, especially if the demonstrator is an opinion leader (Magill and Rogers, 1981).

The innovation-decision process can just as logically lead to a rejection decision as to adoption. In fact, each stage in the innovation-decision process is a potential rejection point. For instance, it is possible to reject an innovation at the knowledge stage by simply forgetting about it after gaining initial awareness-knowledge. And, of course, rejection can occur even after a prior decision to adopt. This is discontinuance, which usually occurs in the confirmation stage of the innovation-decision process. Two different types of rejection are (Eveland, 1979):

1. *Active rejection*, which consists of considering adoption of the innovation (including even its trial) but then deciding not to adopt it.
2. *Passive rejection* (also called nonadoption), which consists of never really considering the use of the innovation.

Obviously, these two types of rejection represent quite different types of behavior. Unfortunately, they have not been distinguished in past diffusion researches. Perhaps owing to the pro-innovation bias that pervades much diffusion inquiry (Chapter 3), investigation of rejection behavior of all kinds has not received much scientific attention.

Further, there is usually an implicit assumption in diffusion studies of a linear sequence of the first three stages in the innovation-decision process: Knowledge-persuasion-decision. In some cases, the actual sequence of stages may be knowledge-decision-persuasion. For example, in a Korean village that I once studied, a meeting of married women was called, and, after a lecture by a government family planning official about the IUD (intrauterine device), there was a show of hands to indicate the women who wanted to adopt (Rogers and Kincaid). Eighteen women (of the forty present) volunteered, and promptly marched off to a nearby health clinic to have IUDs inserted. In this case, a presumably optional innovation-decision almost became a collective innovation-decision as a result of strong group pressure. A similar group-oriented strategy for family planning is followed in the "group planning of births" in the People's Republic of China (Rogers and Chen, 1980). The community decides who should have babies in a group meeting held annually, and then parents are influenced to follow these group birth plans. Such strong group pressure for adoption of an innovation would be abhorrent to values on individual freedom in many cultures, but they are not in Korea and China. So the knowledge-persuasion-decision sequence proposed in our model of the innovation-decision process may be somewhat culture-bound. In some sociocultural settings, the knowledge-decision-persuasion sequence may frequently occur, at least for certain innovations.

Implementation Stage

Implementation occurs when an individual (or other decision-making unit) puts an innovation into use. Until the implementation stage, the innovation-decision process has been a strictly mental exercise. But implementation involves overt behavior change, as the new idea is actually put into practice. It is often one thing for an individual to decide to adopt a new idea, but quite a different thing to put the innovation into use. Problems in exactly how to use the innovation crop up at the implementation stage. Implementation usually follows the decision stage rather directly unless it is held up by some logistical problem, like the temporary unavailability of the innovation.

A certain degree of uncertainty about the expected consequences of the innovation still exists for the individual at the implementation stage, even though the decision to adopt has been made previously. When it comes to implementation, an individual particularly wants to know the answers to such questions as "Where do I obtain the innovation?" "How do I use it?" "How does it work? " and "What operational problems am I likely to encounter, and how can I solve them?" So much active information-seeking usually takes place at the implementation stage. Here the role of the change agent is mainly to provide technical assistance to the client as he or she begins to use the innovation.

Problems of implementation are much more serious when the adopter is an organization rather than an individual. In an organizational setting, a number of individuals are usually involved in the innovation-decision process, and the implementers are often a different set of people from the decision makers. Also, the organizational structure that gives stability and continuity to an organization may be a resistant force to implementation of an innovation. As we show in Chapter 10, it was not until diffusion scholars began to study the innovation-decision process in organizations that the importance of the implementation stage for individual/optional innovation-decisions became apparent. The implementation of innovations in organization has been heavily studied in the 1980s and early 1990s.

When does the implementation stage end? It may continue for a lengthy period of time, depending on the nature of the innovation. But eventually a point is reached at which the new idea becomes an institutionalized and regularized part of the adopter's ongoing operations. The innovation finally loses its distinctive quality as the separate identity of the new idea disappears. This point is usually considered the end of the implementation stage, and is often referred to as routinization or institutionalization, especially when it occurs in organizations (see Chapter 10).

Implementation may also represent the termination of the innovation-decision process, at least for most individuals. But for others, a fifth stage of confirmation may occur, as we explain in a following section. First, we shall discuss the concept of re-invention, which often occurs at the implementation stage.

Re-Invention

In the early years of diffusion study, we assumed that adoption of an innovation meant the exact copying or imitation of how the innovation had been used previously in a different setting. Sometimes the adoption of an innovation does indeed represent identical behavior; for example, the California Fair Trade Law of 1931, the first law of its kind, was adopted by ten other states complete with three serious typographical errors that had appeared in the California bill (Walker, 1971). In many other cases, however, an innovation is not invariant as it diffuses. The new idea changes and evolves during the diffusion process.

Diffusion scholars now recognize the concept of *re-invention*, defined as the degree to which an innovation is changed or modified by a user in the process of its adoption and implementation. Until the 1970s, re-invention was ignored completely, or was considered at most a very infrequent behavior. When a respondent in a diffusion survey told about his or her re-invention of a new idea, it was considered as a very unusual kind of behavior, and was treated as a "noise" in diffusion research. Adopters were considered to be passive acceptors of an innovation, rather than active modifiers and adapters of a new idea. Once diffusion scholars made the mental breakthrough of recognizing that re-invention could happen, they began to find that quite a lot of it occurred.

Re-invention could not really be investigated until diffusion researchers began to gather data about implementation, for most re-invention occurs at the implementation stage of the innovation-decision process. We now know that a great deal of re-invention occurs for certain innovations which suggests that previous diffusion research may have erred, by measuring adoption as a stated intention to adopt (at the decision stage). The fact that re-invention often happens is a strong argument for measuring adoption at the implementation stage, and as action by the adopter, rather than just as an intention to act.

Most scholars in the past have made a distinction between invention and innovation. *Invention* is the process by which a new idea is discovered or created, while adoption is a decision to make full use of an innovation. Thus adoption of an innovation is the process of *using* an existing idea, which may have been previously invented by someone. This heuristic difference between invention and innovation, however, is not so clear-cut once we acknowledge that an innovation is not necessarily a fixed entity as it diffuses within a social system. "Re-invention" seems like an appropriate word to describe the degree to which an innovation is changed or modified by the user in the process of its adoption and implementation.

How Much Re-Invention Occurs?

The recent research focus on re-invention was launched by Charters and Pellegrin (1972), who were the first scholars to recognize the occurrence of re-invention (although they did not use the term per se). These researchers traced the adoption and implementation of the educational innovation of "differentiated staffing" in four schools over a one-year period. They concluded that "differentiated staffing was little more than a word for most [teachers and administrators], lacking concrete parameters with respect to the role performance of participants. . . . The word could (and did) mean widely differing things to the staff, and nothing to some. . . . The innovation was to be invented on the inside, not implemented from the outside." These scholars noted the degree to which the innovation was shaped differently in each of the four organizations they studied.*

When an invention is designed with the concept of re-invention in mind, a certain degree of re-invention often occurs as the innovation diffuses. For instance, previous research on innovation in organizations had assumed that a new technological idea enters a system from external sources and is then adopted (with relatively little adaptation of the innovation) and implemented as part of the organization's ongoing operations. Thus it is assumed that adoption of an innovation by individual A or organization A will look much like adoption of this same innovation by individual B or organization B. Recent investigations call this assumption into serious question. For instance:

1. A national survey of schools adopting educational innovations promoted by the National Diffusion Network, a decentralized diffusion system, found that 56 percent of the adopters implemented only selected aspects of an innovation. Much such re-invention was relatively minor, but in 20 percent of the adoptions, important changes were made in the innovations (Emrick and others, 1977).

---

*Charters and Pellegrin became aware of re-invention (1) because they used a process research approach, and (2) due to their focus on the implementation stage in the innovation-decision process for the innovation of differentiated staffing.

2. An investigation of 111 innovations in scientific instruments field by Von Hippel (1976) found that in about 80 percent of the cases, the innovation process was dominated by the user (that is, a customer). The user typically built a prototype model of the new product and then turned it over to a manufacturer for volume production. So the "adopters" played a very important role in designing and redesigning these industrial innovations.

3. Of the 104 adoptions of innovations by mental health agencies that were studied in California, re-invention occurred somewhat more often (in fifty-five cases) than did unchanged adoption (in forty-nine cases) (Larsen and Agarwala-Rogers, 1977, p. 37; 1977b).

4. A study of the adoption by fifty-three local government agencies of a computer-based planning tool (called GBF/DIME) that was promoted to them by a Federal agency, found that about half of the "adoptions" represented at least some degree of re-invention (Eveland and others, 1977; Rogers and others, 1977a).

5. Research on the rapid diffusion of a school-based drug abuse prevention program called D.A.R.E. (Drug Abuse Resistance Education) disclosed a high degree of re-invention. D.A.R.E. began in 1983 in Los Angeles, and ten years later, over 5 million fifth and sixth graders were taught the seventeen-lesson D.A.R.E. curriculum in their classroom by a uniformed policeman. This speedy rate of adoption occurred because the drug problem was high on the public agenda in the late 1980s. A good deal of re-invention took place (Rogers, 1993a, pp. 139–162). For instance, one of the seventeen D.A.R.E. lessons encouraged school children not to join gangs. However, schools in which there was not a gang problem did not teach the D.A.R.E. material on that topic. The basic idea of D.A.R.E., that of having a uniformed policeman teach the drug prevention lessons, however, was used by all adopters.

Generalization 8 states that: *At least some degree of re-invention occurs at the implementation stage for many innovations and for many adopters.*

Re-Invention Is Not Necessarily Bad

Whether re-invention is considered good or bad depends on one's point of view. Re-invention generally does not receive much favorable attention from research and development agencies, who may consider re-invention a distortion of their original technology. In fact, some designers of innovation shape a new idea so that it is particularly difficult to re-invent. They feel that "re-invention proofing" is a means of maintaining quality control over their innovation. Diffusion agencies may also be unfavorable toward re-invention, feeling that they know best as to the form of the innovation that the users should adopt. Change agents find it difficult to measure their performance if an innovation they are promoting changes over time and across different adopters. Their usual measure, the rate of adoption of an innovation, can become an ambiguous index when a high degree of re-invention occurs. In extreme cases of re-invention, the original innovation may even lose its identity.

Adopters, on the other hand, generally think that re-invention is a desirable quality. They emphasize or even overemphasize the amount of re-invention that they have accomplished (Rice and Rogers, 1980). The choices available to a potential adopter are not just adoption or rejection; modification of the innovation or selective rejection of some components of the innovation may also be options (as in the case of D.A.R.E.). Some implementation problems by an individual or an organization are unpredictable by nature, so changes in the originally planned innovation often should occur.

Re-invention often is beneficial to the adopters of an innovation. Flexibility in the process of adopting an innovation may reduce mistakes and encourage customization of the innovation to fit it more appropriately to local situations or changing conditions. As a result of re-invention, an innovation may be more appropriate in matching an adopter's preexisting problems and more responsive to new problems that arise during the innovation-decision process. A national survey of innovation in public schools found that when an educational innovation was re-invented by a school, its adoption was more likely to be continued and less likely to be discontinued (Berman and Pauley, 1975). Discontinuance happened less often because the re-invented innovations better fit a school's circumstances. This investigation disclosed that a rather high degree of re-invention occurred: The innovations and the schools engaged in a kind of mutually influencing interaction, as the new idea and the school moved closer to each other (Berman and McLaughlin, 1974, 1975, 1978; Berman and others, 1975, 1977). Usually, the school changed very little, and the innovation substantially.*

---

*Eveland and others (1977) used one procedure for measuring the degree of re-invention: They identified the number of elements in each implementation of an innovation that were similar to, or different from, the "mainline" version of the innovation (that was promoted by a change agency). Most innovations can be decomposed analytically into constituent elements, thus offering one means of indexing the degree of re-invention.

Why Does Re-Invention Occur?

Some of the reasons for re-invention lie in the innovation itself, while others involve the individual or organization that is adopting the new idea.

1. Innovations that are relatively more complex and difficult to understand are more likely to be re-invented (Larsen and Agarwala-Rogers, 1977). Re-invention thus may be a simplification of the innovation.

2. Re-invention can occur because of an adopter's lack of full knowledge about the innovation, such as when there is a relatively little direct contact between the adopter and the change agents or previous adopters (Rogers and others, 1977; Eveland and others, 1977; Larsen and Agarwala-Rogers, 1977, p.38). For example, re-invention of a geographically based computer software system (GBF/DIME) occurred more frequently when change agents only created awareness-knowledge of the innovation, than when consultation was provided to the adopting organization at the implementation stage. So re-invention sometimes happens due to ignorance and inadequate learning.

3. An innovation that is an abstract concept or that is a tool (like a computer software program) with many possible applications is more likely to be re-invented (Rogers, 1978). The elements comprising an innovation may be tightly or loosely bundled or packaged (Koontz, 1976). A tightly bundled innovation is a collection of highly interdependent components; it is difficult to adopt one element without adopting the other elements. A loosely bundled innovation consists of elements that are not highly interrelated; such an innovation can be flexibly suited by adopters to their conditions. So the designer or manufacturer of an innovation can affect the degree of re-invention by making the innovation easy or difficult to re-invent (Von Hippel and Finkelstein, 1979).

4. When an innovation is implemented in order to solve a wide range of users' problems, re-invention is more likely to occur. A basic reason for re-invention is that one individual or organization applies the innovation to a different problem than does another. The perceived problem that originally motivated an individual to search for an innovation determines in part how the innovation will be used. The degree of re-invention of an innovation is greater when a wide degree of heterogeneity exists in the individual and organizational problems with which the innovation is matched.

5. Local pride of ownership of an innovation may also be a cause of re-invention. Here the innovation is often modified in certain rather cosmetic or minor ways so that it appears to be a local product. In some cases

of such pseudo-re-invention, the innovation may just be given a new name, without any fundamental changes in the innovation itself. Such localization may be motivated by a desire for status on the part of the adopter, or by a desire to make the innovation more acceptable to individuals in the local system. Often, "Locals say that the innovation is local," as Havelock (1974) found in a survey or 353 U.S. school superintendents. Perhaps as one observer suggested, an innovation may be somewhat like a toothbrush in that people do not like to borrow it from someone else. They want their own. Or at least they want to put their own "bells and whistles" on the basic innovation, so that it looks different from others' adoption of the innovation. A strong psychological need to re-invent seems to exist for many individuals.

An illustration is provided by the diffusion of computers to local government in the United States, who used them for such data-handling tasks as accounting, issuing payrolls, and recordkeeping. A high rate of re-invention occurred when twelve cities and counties adopted the innovation of computer data processing (Danziger 1977). Computer programmers working for a local government viewed such modifications of software packages as a challenging and creative task. It was more fun to re-invent a computer software program than simply to transfer it from another local government or to purchase it from a commercial supplier, which was viewed as unstimulating drudgery. Further, Danziger (1977) found that local government officials emphasized their degree of re-invention, stressing the uniqueness of their adoption. The relatively petty "bells and whistles" that the adapters had re-invented appeared to them to be major improvements.

6. Finally, re-invention may occur because a change agency encourages its clients to modify an innovation. While most change agencies generally oppose re-invention, decentralized diffusion systems may encourage their clients to re-invent new ideas. For example, the diffusion of D.A.R.E. was not managed or directed by a federal agency, so each school was left to do its own thing with the seventeen-lesson D.A.R.E. curriculum (Rogers, 1993a).

Recognition of the existence of re-invention brings into focus a different view of adoption behavior: Instead of simply accepting or rejecting an innovation as a fixed idea, potential adopters on many occasions are active participants in the adoption and diffusion process, struggling to give their own unique meaning to the innovation as it is applied in their local context. Adoption of an innovation is thus a process of social construction. This conception of adoption behavior, involving re-invention, is more in line with what certain respondents in diffusion research have been trying to tell researchers for many years.

Re-Invention of Horse Culture by the Plains Indians

When the European colonists encountered the Plains Indians in the vast grasslands west of the Mississippi River, the horse was the central element of Indian culture. The Indians killed buffalo from horseback, fought other tribes while mounted on their ponies, and utilized their horses to move their wigwams from place to place. But the horse was not indigenous to the Plains Indians. Instead, the horse had only been introduced to the Indian tribes by Spanish explorers around 1650. Within a decade or two, French fur traders found that men, women, and children in the Plains Indian tribes were riding horses. The Indians had copied saddles, stirrups, the crupper, and the lariat from the Spanish explorers, who, in turn had borrowed these innovations from the Moors (Arabic people from North Africa, who had previously occupied Spain for 500 years). In short, the Plains Indians "copied the whole [horse] culture from a to z" (Wissler, 1923). Extensive contact occurred with the Spanish, and the horse had originally appeared with Spanish riders, so the Plains Indians easily learned how to ride the new animal. Horse culture then spread quickly throughout the American grasslands.

But one important aspect of horse culture was re-invented: The travois. Previous to the coming of the horse, the Plains Indians used dogs as beasts of burden. Tents and baggage were transported on the travois, a kind of drag frame. So when the Indians first saw the horse, they called it a dog. Many Indian tribes in the United States still speak of the horse by a name meaning dog. They enlarged the travois, and harnessed the horse to it. Only somewhat later did the Plains Indians begin to ride on horseback.

This case illustration is based on Wissler (1914 and 1923).

Confirmation Stage

As explained previously,* a decision to adopt or reject is often not the terminal stage in the innovation-decision process. For example, Mason (1962) found that Oregon farmers sought information *after* they had de-

---

*And as indicated by such researchers as Mason (1962) and Francis and Rogers (1960).

cided to adopt, as well as before. At the *confirmation* stage the individual (or some other decision-making unit) seeks reinforcement of the innovation-decision already made or reverses a previous decision to adopt or reject the innovation if exposed to conflicting messages about the innovation. At the confirmation stage, the individual seeks to avoid a state of dissonance or to reduce it if it occurs.

Dissonance

Human behavior change is motivated in part by a state of internal disequilibrium or dissonance, an uncomfortable state of mind that the individual seeks to reduce or eliminate (Festinger, 1957). An individual who feels dissonant will ordinarily be motivated to reduce this condition by changing his or her knowledge, attitudes, or actions. In the case of innovative behavior, this dissonance reduction may occur:

1. When the individual becomes aware of a felt need and seeks information about an innovation to meet this need. Here, a receiver's need for the innovation can motivate the individual's information-seeking activity about the innovation. This behavior occurs at the knowledge stage in the innovation-decision process.

2. When the individual knows about a new idea and has a favorable attitude toward it, but has not yet adopted. Then the individual is motivated to adopt the innovation by dissonance between what he or she believes versus what he or she is doing. This behavior occurs at the decision and implementation stages in the innovation-decision process.

3. After the innovation-decision to implement the innovation, when the individual secures further information that persuades him or her that he or she should *not* have adopted. This dissonance may be reduced by discontinuing the innovation. Or if he or she originally decided to reject the innovation, the individual may become exposed to pro-innovation messages, causing a state of dissonance that can be reduced by adoption. These types of behavior (discontinuance or later adoption) occur during the confirmation stage in the innovation-decision process (Figure 5–1).

These three types of dissonance reduction consist of changing behavior so that attitudes and actions are more closely in line. But it is often difficult to change one's prior decision to adopt or reject; activities have been set in motion that tend to stabilize the original decision. Perhaps a considerable expense was involved in adoption of the innovation. Therefore, individuals frequently try to avoid becoming dissonant by seeking only that information that they expect will support or confirm the decision they already made. This behavior is an example of selective exposure.* During the confirmation stage the individual wants supportive messages that will prevent dissonance from occurring. Nevertheless, some information reaches the individual that leads to questioning the adoption-rejection decision made previously in the innovation-decision process.

At the confirmation stage in the innovation-decision process, the change agent can play a special role. In the past, change agents have primarily been interested in achieving adoption decisions. At the confirmation stage they have the additional responsibility of providing supporting messages to individuals who have previously adopted. Change agents often assume that once adoption is secured, it will continue. But there is no assurance against discontinuance, because negative messages about an innovation circulate via interpersonal networks in most client systems.

Discontinuance

Discontinuance is a decision to reject an innovation after having previously adopted it. A rather surprisingly high rate of discontinuance has been found for certain innovations. Leuthold (1967) concluded from his study of a statewide sample of Wisconsin farmers that the rate of discontinuance was just as important as the rate of adoption in determining the level of adoption of an innovation at any particular time during the diffusion process. In any given year there were about as many discontinuers of an innovation as there were first-time adopters.

Two types of discontinuance are: (1) replacement and (2) disenchantment. A *replacement discontinuance* is a decision to reject an idea in order to adopt a better idea that supersedes it. In many fields, there are constant waves of innovations. Each new idea replaces an existing practice that was an innovation in its day. For example, the adoption of "gammanym" (tetracycline) led to the discontinuance of two other antibiotic drugs in the Columbia drug study (Coleman and others, 1966). Hand calculators replaced slide rules. Microcomputers replaced the use of mainframe computers. CDs (compact discs) replaced vinyl plastic for music. Many other examples of replacement discontinuances occur in everyday life.

A *disenchantment discontinuance* is a decision to reject an idea as a result of dissatisfaction with its performance. Such dissatisfaction may come

---

*Similarly, dissonance can be reduced by selective perception (message distortion) and by the selective forgetting of dissonant information.

about because the innovation is inappropriate for the individual and does not result in an adequate level of perceived relative advantage over alternative practice. Perhaps a government agency has ordered that the innovation is no longer safe and/or that it has side-effects that are dangerous to health. Or discontinuance may result from the misuse of an innovation that could have functioned advantageously for the individual if it had been used correctly. This later type of disenchantment seems to be more common among later adopters than among earlier adopters, who have more formal education and greater understanding of the scientific method, so they know how to generalize more carefully the results of an innovation's trial to its full-scale use. Later adopters also have fewer resources, which may either prevent adoption or cause discontinuance because the innovations do not fit their limited financial position. On the basis of past research we suggest Generalization 5–9: *Later adopters are more likely to discontinue innovations than are earlier adopters.*

Diffusion scholars previously assumed that later adopters are relatively less innovative because they did not adopt or were slower to adopt. But the evidence on discontinuance behavior suggests that many laggards adopt but then discontinue, usually owing to disenchantment. For instance, Bishop and Coughenour (1964) reported that the percentage of discontinuance for Ohio farmers ranged from 14 percent for innovators and early adopters, to 27 percent for early majority, to 34 percent for late majority, to 40 percent for laggards. Leuthold (1965) reported comparable figures of 18 percent, 24 percent, 26 percent, and 37 percent, respectively, for a sample of Canadian farmers.

High discontinuers are characterized by less formal education, lower socioeconomic status, less change agent contact, and the like, which are the opposite of the characteristics of innovators (Chapter 7). Discontinuers share the same characteristics as laggards, who indeed are characterized by a higher rate of discontinuance.

The discontinuance of an innovation is one indication that the new idea may not have been fully institutionalized and routinized into the ongoing practice and way of life of the adopter at the implementation stage of the innovation-decision process. Such routinization is less likely (and discontinuance more frequent) when the innovation is less compatible with the individual's beliefs and past experiences. Perhaps (1) there are innovation-to-innovation differences in rates of discontinuance, just as there are such differences in rates of adoption, and (2) the perceived attributes of innovations (for example, relative advantage and compatibility) are negatively related to the rate of discontinuance. For instance, we would expect an innovation with a low relative advantage to have a slow rate of adoption and a fast rate of discontinuance.

In some special cases, adopting an innovation consists mainly of discontinuing a previously adopted idea. An illustration is smoking-cessation. A lifestyle revolution has occurred in the United States in the past several decades as half of all individuals who ever smoked regularly (and who are still alive today) have stopped smoking. As a result of smoking cessation, these millions of Americans will extend their life expectancy for an average of twelve years. Smoking cigarettes is an addictive behavior, one that is extremely difficult to change in that the decision not to smoke is not fully controlled by the individual. How did this U.S. smoking revolution take place? First, such widespread discontinuance did not happen as the result of economic factors. Unlike some other nations, the U.S. government has not slapped on a high cigarette tax, which research evidence indicates can discourage young people from starting to smoke and cause some adults to stop. Canada in the early 1990s raised cigarette taxes so high that a pack cost six dollars. Some states in the U.S. have instituted higher cigarette taxes; for example, California in 1989 voted a special twenty-five cents per pack tax that is used to provide cigarette-cessation advertising and educational programs.

The main thrust for cigarette-cessation in America began with the 1964 Surgeon General's report that smoking was dangerous to health. This report was based on scientific studies of the health effects of smoking cigarettes. Warnings were placed on cigarette packs and in all cigarette advertising. In 1971, tobacco companies were stopped from running their radio and television advertising. Scientific studies of "second-hand smoke" found that nonsmokers inhaled the smoke of others, and their health suffered. City governments and private companies began to restrict places in which it was acceptable to smoke. For example, until the mid-1960s, airline flight attendants distributed free packets of cigarettes with after-meal coffee. In the late 1980s, U.S. airlines banned smoking from all domestic flights. Many restaurants provided non-smoking eating areas, and most workplaces banned smoking. Within a decade or so, the social norm on cigarette-smoking changed from one of perceiving it as a "cool" act (remember Humphrey Bogart with his ever-present cigarette dangling?) to a very negative behavior ("Only losers smoke").

Thus the lifestyle revolution of smoking-cessation in the United States was caused by advances in research-based knowledge about health risks, which provided a basis for regulations on the marketing of cigarettes and for restrictions on where an individual can smoke (Rabin and Sugarman, 1993). Decades were necessary to change the social norms on smoking. So the widespread discontinuance of cigarette smoking in America did not happen overnight.

Forced Discontinuance and the Rise of Organic Farming

A unique and theoretically interesting type of discontinuance occurred in recent decades when federal regulatory agencies, especially the Food and Drug Administration, banned the use of certain chemical innovations. Such forced discontinuance often results from research-based evidence that a chemical innovation may cause cancer or involve some other threat to consumer health.

My Ph.D. dissertation study in 1954 was based on data gathered from 155 farmers in an Iowa farm community about their adoption of such agricultural innovations as 2, 4-D weed spray, antibiotic swine feeding supplements, and chemical fertilizers. These chemical innovations represented the wave of post–World War II agricultural technologies that were recommended to farmers by agricultural scientists at Iowa State University and by the Iowa Extension Service. Like most other diffusion investigators, I accepted the recommendations of the agricultural scientists about the chemical innovations as valid. So did most of the Iowa farmers that I interviewed in my diffusion study. I remember, however, one farmer who rejected all of these agricultural chemicals because, he claimed, they killed the earthworms and songbirds in his fields. At the time, I personally regarded his organic attitude as irrational. Certainly his farming behavior was measured as laggardly by my innovativeness scale (composed of a dozen or so agricultural innovations recommended by agricultural experts).

But the rise of the environmental movement in the United States in the 1960s and research on the long-term effects of agricultural chemicals made me begin to wonder. In 1972, the U.S. Environmental Protection Agency banned the use of DDT as an insecticide because of its threats to human health. Then DES (diethyl stilbestrol) was banned for cattle feeding, as were antibiotic swine-feeding supplements and 2, 4, 5-D weed spray. It had been found that the concentration of such chemicals increased to dangerous levels owing to biomagnification in the food chain, until levels dangerous to human health sometimes occurred.

Since the early 1980s an increasing proportion of U.S. consumers have patronized health food stores where they paid a premium price for organically grown foods. Correspondingly, the number of organic farmers and gardeners increased, as a result of growing concern about the effects of chemical pesticides and fertilizers. Organic farmers harvest somewhat lower crop yields than do chemical farmers (due to crop destruction by insects and other pests), but their costs of production are also lower and they secure a higher price for their organic food production from natural food stores.

In 1980, the U.S. Department of Agriculture reversed its policy of opposing organic farming and gardening, and began to advise U.S. farmers and gardeners to consider using fewer chemicals. The USDA also began a research program to develop appropriate seed varieties for organic farming and gardening. Surveys of organic farmers indicated that most were not "hippies," nor were they lower-educated traditional farmers. In fact, most organic farmers are commercial operators with the general characteristic of progressive farmers such as above-average education, larger farms, and so on. These characteristics are what one would expect from the innovators in adopting organic farming.

The USDA in the 1980s realized that chemical pesticides were being overused by many farmers, and launched a program called "integrated pest management" (IPM). A key factor in initiating the IPM program was the fact that hundreds of insect varieties developed resistance to existing pesticides, along with a concern for the consumer health problems resulting from biomagnification through the food chain. Integrated pest management consists of careful scouting of a farmer's fields, usually by trained scouts, who advise the farmer when a pest problem has increased above an economic threshold, and when spraying with a chemical pesticide would thus be justified. Farmers who adopt IPM typically report important savings from decreased use of pesticides. Some farmers save thousands of dollars.

Today, looking back to my 1954 Iowa diffusion investigation, the organic farmer that I interviewed certainly has had the last laugh over agricultural experts. My research procedures classified him as a laggard in 1954; by present day standards he was a superinnovator of organic farming. So for two different (and opposing) innovations, this farmer was in two extremely different adopter categories.

This case illustration is based on the author's experience.

Are There Stages in the Process?

What empirical evidence is available that the stages posited in our model of the innovation-decision process (see Figure 5–1) exist in reality? A definitive answer is difficult to provide. It is not easy for a researcher to probe the intrapersonal mental process of an individual respondent. Nevertheless, there is tentative evidence from various studies supporting the concept of stages in the innovation-decision process.

Evidence of Stages

Empirical evidence of the validity of stages in the innovation-decision process comes from an Iowa study (Beal and Rogers, 1960) that shows that most farmer-respondents recognized that they went through a series of stages as they moved from awareness-knowledge to a decision to adopt.* Specifically, they realized that they had received information about an innovation from different channels and sources at different stages in the process. Of course, it is possible for an individual to use the same sources or channels at each stage, but if he or she does not, this indicates some differentiation of the stages. Beal and Rogers (1960) also found that none of their 148 respondents reported adopting immediately after becoming aware of a new weed spray and 63 percent of the adopters of a new livestock feed reported different years for knowledge and for the decision to adopt. Most Iowa farmers seemed to require a period of time that could be measured in years to pass through the innovation-decision process. This finding provided evidence that adoption behavior is a process that contains various stages and that these stages occur over time.

Yet another type of evidence provided by Beal and Rogers (1960) deals with skipped stages. If most respondents report not having passed through a stage in the innovation-decision process for a given innovation, a question would thus be raised as to whether that stage should be included in the model. Beal and Rogers found, however, that most farmers described their behavior at each of the first three stages in the process: knowledge, persuasion, and decision. None reported skipping the knowledge or decision stages, but a few farmers did not report a trial prior to adoption.

---

*The conception of stages in the innovation-decision process does not necessarily require that individuals passing through the process would be conscious of what stage they are at.

How do we know that our innovation-decision process model also describes the behavior of other types of individuals than farmers as they adopt nonagriculture innovations? Coleman and others (1966) found that most physicians reported different communication channels about a new drug at the knowledge stage from those reported at the persuasion stage. LaMar (1966) studied the innovation-decision processes of 262 teachers in twenty California schools. The teachers went through the stages in the process, much as had been found in the studies of farmers. Kohl (1966) found that all fifty-eight Oregon school superintendents in his sample reported that they passed through each of the stages for such innovations as team teaching, language laboratories, and flexible scheduling.

In summary, we suggest Generalization 5–10: *Stages exist in the innovation-decision process*. The evidence is most clear-cut for the knowledge and decision stages and somewhat less so for the persuasion stage. Only rather poor data are available on the distinctiveness of the implementation and confirmation stages. Given the importance of the stages concept in diffusion research, why has more research not been directed toward understanding the innovation-decision process? Perhaps it is because the "process" nature of this research topic does not fit the "variance" type of research methods (utilizing variables measured quantitatively) used by most diffusion researchers.

Variance and Process Research

Research designed to answer the question whether stages exist in the innovation-decision process obviously needs to be quite different from the study of independent variables associated with the dependent variable of innovativeness. The first is *process research*, defined as a type of data gathering and analysis that seeks to determine the time-ordered sequence of a set of events. In contrast, *variance research* is a type of data gathering and analysis that consists of determining the co-variances among a set of variables, but not their time-order.

Most diffusion research (and most social science research) is variance-type investigation. It uses highly structured data gathering and quantitative data analysis of cross-sectional data, such as from one-shot surveys. Because only one point in time is represented in cross-sectional data, variance in a dependent variable is related to the variance in a set of independent variables. For example, variance research is appropriate for investigating variables related to innovativeness. But it cannot probe backward in time to understand what happened first, next, and so on, and how each of these events influenced the next.

In order to explore the nature of the innovation-decision process, one needs a dynamic perspective to explain the causes and sequences of a series of events over time. Data-gathering methods for process research are less structured and the data are typically more qualitative in nature. Seldom are statistical methods used to analyze the data in process research. Diffusion scholars have frequently failed to recognize the important distinction between variance and process research in the past (Mohr, 1978 and 1982).

The general point here is that research on a topic like the innovation-decision process must be quite different from the variance research that has predominated in the diffusion field in the past.

The Hierarchy of Effects

The notion of a hierarchy of communication effects is that an individual usually must pass from knowledge change to overt behavior change in a cumulative sequence of stages that are generally parallel to the stages in the innovation-decision process (Table 5–1). Communication effects thus occur in an ordered sequence for most individuals who pass through the process. Interpersonal communication channels are generally more effective in causing the persuasion effects, and mass media channels are more effective in bringing about the knowledge effects.

A different but closely related model of stages in the innovation-decision process has been proposed by Professor James O. Prochaska, a cancer prevention researcher at the University of Rhode Island. Prochaska's five-stage model of how individuals change an addictive behavior is widely utilized in the public health field to explain the adoption of preventive health innovations like safe sex, contraception, getting a mammogram for early detection of breast cancer, and so forth. Prochaska, DiClemente, and Norcross (1992) define the five stages in changing addictive behavior as:

1. *Precontemplation*, where an individual is aware that a problem exists and begins to think about overcoming it.
2. *Contemplation*, when an individual is aware that a problem exists and is seriously thinking about overcoming it, but has not yet made a commitment to take action.

Table 5–1. The Hierarchy of Effects Corresponds to Stages in the Innovation-Decision Process and to Stages of Change

Stages in the Innovation-Decision Process	*Hierarchy of Effects*	*Porchaska's Stages of Change*
I. *Knowledge Stage*		I. Precontemplation
1. Recall of information.		
2. Comprehension of messages.		
3. Knowledge or skill for effective adoption of the innovation.		
II. *Persuasion Stage*		II. Contemplation
4. Liking the innovation.		
5. Discussion of the new behavior with others.		
6. Acceptance of the message about the innovation.		
7. Formation of a positive image of the message and the innovation.		
8. Support for the innovative behavior from the system.		
III. *Decision Stage*		III. Preparation
9. Intention to seek additional information about the innovation.		
10. Intention to try the innovation.		
IV. *Implementation Stage*		IV. Action
11. Acquisition of additional information about the innovation.		
12. Use of the innovation on a regular basis.		
13. Continued use of the innovation.		
V. *Confirmation Stage*		V. Maintenance
14. Recognition of the benefits of using the innovation.		
15. Integration of the innovation into one's ongoing routine.		
16. Promotion of the innovation to others.		

Source: Based on McGuire's (1989, p. 45) hierarchy of effects, as modified by Population Communication Services at Johns Hopkins University, and with the addition of Prochaska's stages of change (Prochaska, DiClemente, and Norcross, 1992).

3. *Preparation*, the stage at which an individual intends to take action in the immediate future, but has not yet done so.
4. *Action*, when an individual changes behavior or the environment in order to overcome the problem.
5. *Maintenance*, the stage at which an individual consolidates and continues the behavior change that was made previously.

Prochaska finds that the vast majority of addicted individuals are not at the action stage. For example he estimates that 10 to 15 percent of smokers are prepared for action, 30 to 40 percent are in the contemplation stage, and 50 to 60 percent are in the precontemplation stage. A professional change agent will be disappointed if he/she assumes all three categories are equally ready to break their smoking addiction. This misperception may be one reason why so many individuals drop out of training classes in smoking cessation, drug abuse treatment, and weight control, or else relapse to their addiction after completing the training. The more general point is that the stages in the innovation-decision process matter. An individual must pass through them in sequence.

We turn now to the role of different communication channels in the innovation-decision process.

Communication Channels by Stages in the Innovation-Decision Process

The five stages in the innovation-decision process help us understand the role of different communication channels, as is illustrated by the diffusion of gammanym among medical doctors.

Communication Channels in the Innovation-Decision Process for Tetracycline

The role of different communication channels at different stages of the innovation-decision process is provided by the classic study of the diffusion of gammanym, a new antibiotic "wonder drug" among the doctors in a medical community (Coleman and others, 1966). This innovation had spectacular results, and it was adopted very rapidly. Within two months of its release, 15 percent of the physicians had tried it; this figure reached 50 percent four months later, and at the end of seventeen months, gammanym dominated doctors' antibiotic prescriptions. Gammanym had such a striking relative advantage over previous antibiotic drugs that most of a doctor's peer networks conveyed very positive messages about the innovation. One of the most important contributions of the drug study was to establish the importance of interpersonal networks as a communication channel in the innovation-decision process.

Information that creates awareness-knowledge of an innovation seldom comes to individuals from a source or channel of communication that they actively seek. Information about a new idea can only be actively sought by individuals (1) after they are aware that the new idea exists, and (2) when they know which sources or channels can provide information about the innovation. Further, the relative importance of different sources or channels of communication about an innovation depends in part on what is available to the audience of potential adopters. For example, if a new idea is initially promoted only by the commercial firm that sells it, it is unlikely that other sources or channels will be very important, at least at the knowledge stage of the innovation-decision process. Coleman and others (1966) found that 80 percent of the medical doctors in their drug study reported first learning about gammanym from drug companies (57 percent from the pharmaceutical detail men, 18 percent from drug-house mailings, 4 percent from drug-house magazines, and 1 percent from drug ads in medical journals).

Later in the innovation-decision process, at the persuasion and decision stages, near-peer networks were the major sources or channels of communication about the new drug, and the commercial role was unimportant.[*] Awareness-knowledge that a new drug existed could be credibly communicated by commercial sources or channels, but doctors relied on the experiences of their peers for evaluative information about the innovation. The pharmaceutical firms that sold tetracycline were not regarded as credible by medical doctors.

---

[*]The Coleman and others (1966) finding that medical doctors did not perceive drug company detailmen as credible sources/channels of communication about a new drug was not supported by a replication study in Australia. Peay and Peay (1988) investigated the diffusion of temazepam, a new drug that was an important improvement in medical practice but not a "wonder drug" like tetracycline. The Australian doctors who had contact with detailmen (61 percent of the total sample) adopted the innovation earlier than did other doctors.

Scientific evaluations of tetracycline were communicated to the doctors, but such information did not convince them to adopt the innovation. Coleman and others (1966) concluded that, "The extensive trials and tests by manufacturer, medical schools, and teaching hospitals—tests that a new drug must pass before it is released—are not enough for the average doctor." They found that "teaching at the expert level cannot substitute for the doctor's own testing of the new drug; but testing through the everyday experiences of colleagues on the doctor's own level can substitute, at least in part." Individuals depend on their near-peers for innovation-evaluation information, which decreases their uncertainty about the innovation's expected consequences.

One type of evidence that the interpersonally communicated experience of near-peers can substitute, in part, for one's personal experience with an innovation is provided by analyses of the degree to which earlier versus later adopters of an innovation adopt a new idea completely at the time of their first trial. The first medical doctors to adopt gammanym did so on a very partial basis; the nineteen physicians who adopted the new drug in the first and second months of its use only wrote prescriptions for an average of 1.5 patients. The twenty-two doctors who adopted the innovation in the third or fourth months wrote 2.0 prescriptions, while the twenty-three doctors adopting in the fifth through eighth months wrote an average of 2.7 prescriptions (Coleman and others, 1966).*

Why are the first individuals in a system to adopt an innovation usually most tentative in their degree of trial of use of the new idea? The reason concerns the role of uncertainty in the diffusion process. Even though most innovative adopters of gammanym and hybrid corn were fully informed of the scientific evaluations that had been made of the new idea, this information did not reduce their uncertainty about how the innovation would work out for them. The innovators had to conduct their own personal experimentation with the new idea in order to assure themselves that it was indeed advantageous. They could not depend on the experience of peers with the innovation, because no one else had adopted the innovation at the time that

---

*Similarly, Ryan (1948) found that Iowa farmers adopting hybrid corn prior to 1939 initially planted only 15 percent of their corn acreage with hybrids, but those who adopted in 1939 and 1940 planted 60 percent of their acreage in hybrid seed in their first year of adoption. This figure was 90 percent for those starting in 1941–42 (the laggards).

the innovators adopted (at least in their system). Later adopters profit from their peers' accumulated personal experiences with the innovation; thus, much of the uncertainty of the innovation is removed by the time the later adopters first use a new idea, making a personal trial of the new idea less necessary for them.

This case illustration is based on Coleman and others (1966).

Categorizing Communication Channels

It is often difficult for individuals to distinguish between the source of a message and the channel that carries the message. A *source* is an individual or an institution that originates a message. A *channel* is the means by which a message gets from the source to the receiver. In the present section, we mainly speak of "channels" but often "source/channel" would be more accurate.

Researchers categorize communication channels as either (1) interpersonal or mass media in nature, or (2) originating from either local or cosmopolite sources. These channels play different roles in creating knowledge versus persuading individuals to change their attitude toward an innovation. The channels also are different for earlier adopters than for later adopters.

Mass media channels are means of transmitting messages involving a mass medium, such as radio, television, newspapers, and so on, that enable a source of one or a few individuals to reach an audience of many. Mass media can: (1) reach a large audience rapidly, (2) create knowledge and spread information, and (3) lead to changes in weakly held attitudes.

The formation and change of strongly held attitudes, however, is usually accomplished by interpersonal channels. *Interpersonal channels* involve a face-to-face exchange between two or more individuals. These channels have greater effectiveness in dealing with resistance or apathy on the part of the communicatee. What can interpersonal channels do best?

1. Provide a two-way exchange of information. One individual can secure clarification or additional information about the innovation from another individual. This characteristic of interpersonal networks often allows them to overcome the social-psychological barriers of selective exposure, perception, and retention.

2. Persuade an individual to form or to change a strongly held attitude. This role of interpersonal channels is especially important in persuading an individual to adopt an innovation.

Mass Media Versus Interpersonal Channels

Generalization 5–11 states: *Mass media channels are relatively more important at the knowledge stage and interpersonal channels are relatively more important at the persuasion stage in the innovation-decision process.* The importance of interpersonal and mass media channels in the innovation-decision process was first investigated in a series of researches with farmers, and then largely confirmed in studies of other types of respondents. For example, Sill (1958) found that if the probability of adoption were to be maximized, communication channels must be used in an ideal time sequence, progressing from mass media to interpersonal channels. Copp and others (1958, p. 70) found that "A temporal sequence is involved in agricultural communication in that messages are sent out through mass media directed to awareness, then to groups, and finally to individuals. A farmer upsetting this sequence in any way prejudices progress at some point in the adoption process." The greatest thrust out from the knowledge stage was provided by the use of the mass media, while interpersonal channels were salient in moving individuals out of the persuasion stage. Using a communication channel that was inappropriate to a given stage in the innovation-decision process (such as an interpersonal channel at the knowledge stage) was associated with later adoption of the new idea by an individual because such a channel use delayed progress through the process.

Data on the relative importance of interpersonal and mass media channels at each stage in the adoption of 2, 4-D weed spray were obtained by Beal and Rogers (1960) from 148 Iowa farmers. Mass media channels, such as farm magazines, bulletins, and container labels, were more important than interpersonal channels at the knowledge stage for this innovation. The percentage of respondents mentioning an interpersonal channel increased from 37 percent at the knowledge stage to 63 percent at the persuasion stage.

The evidence just presented in support of Generalization 5–11 came from research done in the United States, where the mass media are widely available. The mass media, however, may not be so widely available in Third World countries. For example, Deutschmann and Fals Borda (1962b) found that interpersonal channels were heavily used even at the knowledge stage by Colombian villagers. In Bangladesh villages, Rahim (1961, 1965) found that mass media channels were seldom mentioned as channels about agricultural innovations, whereas cosmopolite-interpersonal channels were very important, and in some ways seemed to perform a similar role to that played by mass media channels in more developed countries. An example of a cosmopolite-interpersonal channel is an Iowa farmer attending a farm machinery show in Des Moines, or a doctor traveling to an out-of-town medical specialty meeting.

Rogers with Shoemaker (1971) made a comparative analysis of the role played by mass media and cosmopolite-interpersonal channels by stages in the innovation-decision process for twenty-three different innovations (mostly agricultural) in the United States, Canada, India, Bangladesh, and Colombia. Mass media channels are of relatively greater importance at the knowledge stage in both developing and developed countries, although there was a higher *level* of mass media channel usage in the developed nations, as we would expect. Mass media channels were used by 52 percent of the respondents in developed nations at the persuasion stage, and 18 percent at the decision stage. The comparable figures for respondents in Third World nations were 29 percent and 6 percent. This meta-research showed that cosmopolite-interpersonal channels were especially important at the knowledge stage in developing nations.

Cosmopolite Versus Localite Channels

Generalization 5–12 states: *Cosmopolite channels are relatively more important at the knowledge stage, and localite channels are relatively more important at the persuasion stage in the innovation-decision process.* Cosmopolite communication channels are those from outside the social system of study; interpersonal channels may be either local or cosmopolite, while mass media channels are almost entirely cosmopolite. The meta-research for twenty-three different innovations in ten nations (mentioned previously) showed that if cosmopolite-interpersonal and mass media channels are combined to form the category of cosmopolite channels, in the Third World nations the percentage of such channels was 81 percent at the knowledge stage and 58 percent at the persuasion stage. In developing nations, the percentages were 74 percent at the knowledge stage and 34 percent at the persuasion stage. These meta-research data hint that the role played by mass media channels in developed countries (creating awareness-knowledge) is perhaps partly replaced by cosmopolite-interpersonal channels in developing countries. These channels include change agents, visits outside the local community, and visitors to the local system from the city.

Communication Channels by Adopter Categories

The preceding discussion of communication channels by stages in the innovation-decision process ignored the effects of the respondent's adopter category. Now we explore channel usage by different adopter categories.

Generalization 5–13 states: *Mass media channels are relatively more important than interpersonal channels for earlier adopters than for later adopters.* At the time that innovators adopt a new idea there is almost no one else in the system who has experience with the innovation. Later adopters do not need to rely so much on mass media channels because a store of interpersonal, local experience has accumulated in their system by the time they decide to adopt. Perhaps interpersonal influence is not so necessary to motivate earlier adopters to decide favorably on an innovation. They possess a more venturesome orientation, and the mass media message stimulus is enough to move them over the mental threshold to adoption. But the less change-oriented later adopters require a stronger and more immediate influence, like that from interpersonal networks.

There is strong support for Generalization 5–13 from researches in both developed and developing nations. Data illustrating this proposition are shown in Figure 5–2 for the adoption of a chemical weed spray by Iowa farmers.

Reasoning similar to that just presented leads to Generalization 5–14: *Cosmopolite channels are relatively more important than localite channels for earlier adopters than for later adopters.** Innovations enter a system from external sources; those who adopt first are more likely to depend upon cosmopolite channels. These earlier adopters, in turn, act as interpersonal and localite channels for their later-adopting peers.

The Innovation-Decision Period

The *innovation-decision period* is the length of time required for an individual or organization to pass through the innovation-decision

---

*This proposition bears close resemblance to Generalization 7–25, which states that earlier adopters are more cosmopolite than later adopters. Generalization 5–14, however, refers to cosmopolite *channel* usage, rather than to cosmopolite behavior in general.

Figure 5–2. Interpersonal Channels Are Relatively Less Important for Earlier Adopters Than for Later Adopters of 2, 4-D Weed Spray in Iowa

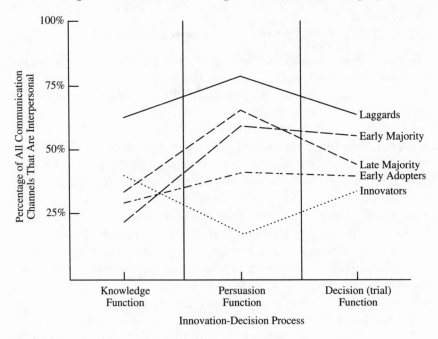

Source: Beal and Rogers (1960).

process.* The time elapsing from awareness-knowledge of an innovation decision for an individual is measured in days, months, or years. The period is thus a gestation period during which a new idea ferments in an individual's mind.

Rate of Awareness-Knowledge and Rate of Adoption

Most change agents wish to speed up the process by which innovations are adopted. One method of doing so is to communicate information about new ideas more rapidly or more adequately so that knowledge is created at an earlier date. Another method is to shorten the amount of

---

*The length of the innovation-decision period is usually measured from first knowledge until the decision to adopt (or reject), although in a strict sense it should perhaps be measured to the time of confirmation. This later procedure is often impractical or impossible because the confirmation function may continue over an indefinite period.

time required for the innovation-decision after an individual is aware of a new idea. Many potential adopters are aware of an innovation but are not motivated to try it. For example, almost all of the Iowa farmers in the hybrid corn study heard about the innovation before more than a handful were planting it. "It is evident that . . . isolation from knowledge was not a determining factor in late adoption for many operators" (Ryan and Gross, 1950). Shortening the innovation-decision period is thus one of the main methods of speeding the diffusion of an innovation.

Figure 5–3 illustrates the interrelationships between the rate of awareness-knowledge, rate of adoption, and the innovation-decision period for a new weed spray. The slope of the curve for the rate of awareness is steeper than that for the rate of adoption. These data, along with evidence from other studies, suggest Generalization 5–15: *The rate of awareness-knowledge for an innovation is more rapid than its rate of adoption.* Later adopters have longer innovation-decision periods than earlier adopters, a point to which we shall soon return.

There is a great deal of variation in the average length of the innovation-decision period from innovation to innovation. For instance, 9.0 years was the average period for hybrid corn in Iowa (Gross, 1942), while 2.1 years was the average for weed spray depicted in Figure 5–3 (Beal and Rogers, 1960). How can we explain these differences? Innovations with certain characteristics are generally adopted more quickly; they have a shorter innovation-decision period. For example, innovations that are relatively simple in nature, divisible for trial, and compatible with previous experience usually have a shorter innovation-decision period.

Length of the Period by Adopter Category

One of the important individual differences in length of the innovation-decision period is on the basis of adopter category. We pointed out previously that the data in Figure 5–3 show a longer period for later adopters. We show this relationship in greater detail in Figure 5–4,where the average length of the period is shown for the five adopter categories. These data and those from other studies support Generalization 5–16: *Earlier adopters have a shorter innovation-decision period than later adopters.* Thus the first individuals to adopt a new idea (the innovators) do so not only because they become aware of the innovation somewhat sooner than their peers, but also because they require fewer months or years to move from knowledge to decision. Innovators perhaps gain part of their innovative position (relative to late adopters) by learning about innovations at

Figure 5–3. Rate of Awareness-Knowledge, Rate of Adoption, and Length of the Innovation-Decision Period for Iowa Farmers Adopting a Weed Spray by Year

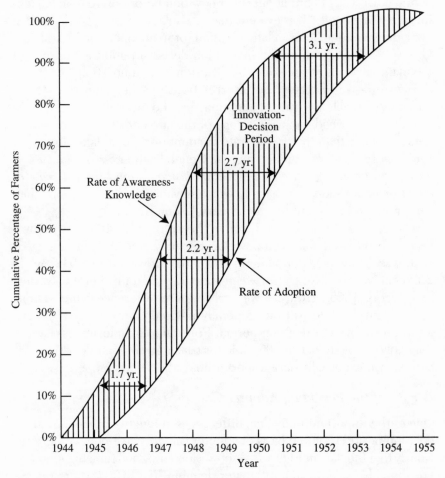

The shaded area in this figure illustrates the aggregate innovation-decision period between awareness-knowledge and adoption of weed spray. Knowledge proceeds at a more rapid rate than does adoption, a finding that suggests that relatively later adopters have a longer average innovation-decision period than earlier adopters. For example, there are 1.7 years between 10 percent awareness and 10 percent adoption, but 3.1 years between 92-percent awareness and 92 percent adoption.

Source: A reanalysis of data originally gathered by Beal and Rogers (1960).

Figure 5–4. Innovators Have Shorter Innovation-Decision Periods Than Laggards in Adopting 2, 4-D Weed Spray

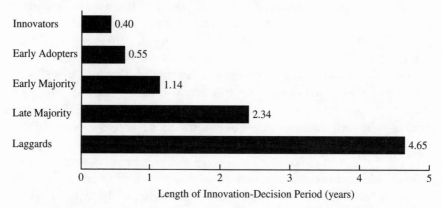

Source: This figure is based on data from 148 Iowa farmers, gathered by Beal and Rogers (1960).

an earlier time, but the present data suggest that innovators are the first to adopt because they require a shorter innovation-decision period.

Why do innovators require a shorter period? Research studies show that innovators have more favorable attitudes toward new ideas and so less resistance to change must be overcome by communication messages about innovations. Innovators may also have shorter innovation-decision periods because (1) they use more technically accurate sources and channels about innovations, such as direct contact with scientists, and (2) they place higher credibility in these sources than the average individual. Innovators may also possess a type of mental ability that better enables them to cope with uncertainty and to deal with abstractions. An innovator must be able to conceptualize relatively abstract information about innovations and apply this new information to his or her own situation. Later adopters can observe the results of innovations by earlier adopters and may not require this type of mental ability.

Summary

The *innovation-decision process* is the process through which an individual (or other decision-making unit) passes from first knowledge of an innovation, to forming an attitude toward the innovation, to a decision to adopt or reject, to implementation of the new idea, and to confirmation of this decision. This process consists of five stages: (1) *knowledge*—the individual (or decision-making unit) is exposed to the innovation's existence and gains some understanding of how it functions; (2) *persuasion*—the individual (or other decision-making unit) forms a favorable or unfavorable attitude toward the innovation; (3) *decision*—the individual (or other decision-making unit) engages in activities that lead to a choice to adopt or reject the innovation; (4) *implementation*—the individual (or other decision-making unit) puts an innovation into use; and (5) *confirmation*—the individual (or other decision-making unit) seeks reinforcement for an innovation-decision already made, but may reverse this decision if exposed to conflicting messages about the innovation.

Earlier knowers of an innovation, when compared to later knowers, are characterized by more formal education, higher social status, greater exposure to mass media channels of communication, greater exposure to interpersonal channels of communication, greater change agent contact, greater social participation, and more cosmopoliteness (Generalizations 5–1 to 5–7).

Re-invention is the degree to which an innovation is changed or modified by a user in the process of its adoption and implementation. Re-invention occurs at the implementation stage for certain innovations and for certain adopters (Generalization 5–8).

Discontinuance is a decision to reject an innovation after having previously adopted it. Two types of discontinuance are: (1) *replacement discontinuance*, in which an idea is rejected in order to adopt a better idea that superseded it, and (2) *disenchantment discontinuance*, in which an idea is rejected as a result of dissatisfaction with its performance. Later adopters are more likely to discontinue innovations than are earlier adopters (Generalization 5–9).

We conclude, on the basis of research evidence, that stages exist in the innovation-decision process (Generalization 5–10). Needed in the future is *process research*, a type of data gathering and analysis that seeks to determine the time-ordered sequence of a set of events. Most past diffusion study has been *variance research*, a type of data gathering and analysis that consists of determining the covariances among a set of variables but not their time-order.

A *communication channel* is the means by which a message gets from a source to a receiver. We categorize communication channels (1) as either interpersonal or mass media in nature, and (2) as originating from either local or cosmopolite sources. *Mass media channels* are means of transmitting messages involving a mass medium such as radio, television, newspapers, and so on, that enable a source of one or a few individuals to reach an audience of many. *Interpersonal channels* involve a face-to-face exchange between two or more individuals.

Mass media channels are relatively more important at the knowledge stage, and interpersonal channels are relatively more important at the persuasion stage in the innovation-decision process (Generalization 5–11). Cosmopolite channels are relatively more important at the knowledge stage, and local channels are relatively more important at the persuasion stage in the innovation-decision process (Generalization 5–12). Mass media channels are relatively more important than interpersonal channels for later adopters (Generalization 5–13). Cosmopolite channels are relatively more important than local channels for earlier adopters than for later adopters (Generalization 5–14).

The *innovation-decision period* is the length of time required for an individual or organization to pass through the innovation-decision process. The rate of awareness-knowledge for an innovation is more rapid than its rate of adoption (Generalization 5–15). Earlier adopters have a shorter innovation-decision period than do later adopters (Generalization 5–16).

6

ATTRIBUTES OF
INNOVATIONS AND THEIR
RATE OF ADOPTION

Make a better mousetrap, and the world will beat a path to your
door.

—Ralph Waldo Emerson

Some innovations diffuse from first introduction to widespread use in a
few years. For example, Nintendo video games achieved very rapid adoption since the 1980s when they were introduced in the United States. By
1994, Nintendo was found in 30 million U.S. homes! Yet another consumer innovation like home computers leveled out at about 30 percent
use in recent years. What characteristics of innovations affect the rate at
which they diffuse and are adopted? This chapter identifies five characteristics by which an innovation may be described, and shows how individuals' perceptions of these characteristics predict the rate of adoption
of the innovation.

The diffusion research literature indicates that much effort has been
spent in studying "people" differences in innovativeness (that is, in determining the characteristics of the different adopter categories) but
that relatively little effort has been devoted to analyzing "innovation"
differences (that is, in investigating how the properties of innovations
affect their rate of adoption). This latter type of research can be of great
value in predicting people's reactions to an innovation. These reactions
can be modified by the way in which an innovation is named and positioned, and how it is related to existing beliefs. Diffusion researchers in
the past tended to regard all innovations as equivalent units from the

204

viewpoint of their analysis. This is an oversimplification, and a dangerous one.

Black Music in White America: Rap

If one were to write a scenario for an innovation that would *not* diffuse in
America, it might be a new musical form originating with low-income
black men from distressed urban areas who used this lyrical content to
draw attention to their feelings of anger, frustration, and violence. The
African rhythmic quality of the new music is in stark contrast to the European notions of melody that dominate American music. Most radio stations refused to play the new music, mainly because its fans were not an
important audience for advertisers. Most popular music climbs the popularity charts in the U.S. because of air play, so the radio embargo on the
new music pushed it onto the fringes of society, and practically guaran-
teed its failure.

But rap music, despite the above attributes and limitations, has become
enormously popular in white America, and in the world. It is *the* contemporary musical form, ranking with such earlier types of black-originated music as jazz, blues, ragtime, and the cakewalk. Rap has been called "musical
graffiti" (vandalism to some, art to others). How does one explain its popularity? Steve Greenberg, an authority on the diffusion of music in America,
reasons that rap, because of its underclass origins, is appealing to middle and
upper-class youth who wish to rebel against the status quo establishment of
their parents and the society in which they live. Suburban white teenagers,
who one might expect would object to rap's radical tone, instead are its
biggest fans.

Their parents regard rap as just an ugly noise. The parental generation of
suburban whites is attracted to European classical music that "expresses feelings of class and worth that speak to a certain segment of society—one which
possesses the power and wealth to maintain the institutions necessary to the
perpetuation of the classical music world" (Greenberg, 1992). These upper-
class aspects of classical music include concert halls, expensive opera cos-
tumes and stage sets, and the high-priced tickets of these events.

Rap music flourished without access to the music establishment. Most
rap is performed by artists in their own homes, using inexpensive, widely accessible equipment, in contrast to the sound studios and sophisticated

recording equipment of other musical genres. Rap music is mainly disseminated on homemade cassettes and by locally owned independent record
companies. For a decade, the major recording companies resisted rap, and
even in the mid-1990s only a small portion of the music on the *Billboard* rap
singles chart was produced by the major labels. As mentioned previously,
the radio industry (which usually makes or breaks the success of any piece
of music) ignored rap because its audience is not a priority for radio advertisers to reach. For example, New York does not have a single rap station,
although it has two full-time classical radio stations.

Nevertheless, rap music is more popular with U.S. teenagers each year,
especially those who are upper-middle class suburban whites. Rap has attributes perceived by these youth as compatible with values that they wish
to express.

This case illustration is based on Greenberg (1992), and on numerous discussions of the diffusion of popular music with Steve Greenberg, who is president of Big Beat Records, a subsidiary
of Atlantic Records, in New York.

Explaining Rate of Adoption

Rate of adoption is the relative speed with which an innovation is adopted
by members of a social system. It is generally measured as the number
of individuals who adopt a new idea in a specified period, such as each
year. So the rate of adoption is a numerical indicator of the steepness of
the adoption curve for an innovation.

The perceived attributes of an innovation are one important explanation of the rate of adoption of an innovation. From 49 to 87 percent of the
variance in rate of adoption is explained by five attributes: Relative advantage, compatibility, complexity, trialability, and observability (Rogers,
1983). In addition to these five perceived attributes of an innovation, such
other variables as (1) the type of innovation-decision, (2) the nature of
communication channels diffusing the innovation at various stages in the
innovation-decision process, (3) the nature of the social system in which
the innovation is diffusing, and (4) the extent of change agents' promotion efforts in diffusing the innovation, affect an innovation's rate of adoption (Figure 6–1).

The type of innovation-decision is related to an innovation's rate of
adoption. Innovations requiring an individual-optional innovation-
decision are generally adopted more rapidly than when an innovation is
adopted by an organization (see Chapter 10). The more persons involved

Figure 6–1. Variables Determining the Rate of Adoption of Innovations

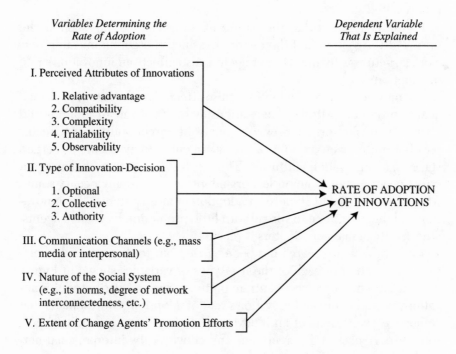

| *Variables Determining the Rate of Adoption* | *Dependent Variable That Is Explained* |

I. Perceived Attributes of Innovations

   1. Relative advantage
   2. Compatibility
   3. Complexity
   4. Trialability
   5. Observability

II. Type of Innovation-Decision

   1. Optional
   2. Collective
   3. Authority

III. Communication Channels (e.g., mass media or interpersonal)

IV. Nature of the Social System (e.g., its norms, degree of network interconnectedness, etc.)

V. Extent of Change Agents' Promotion Efforts

RATE OF ADOPTION OF INNOVATIONS

in making an innovation-decision, the slower the rate of adoption. One means of speeding the rate of adoption of an innovation is to attempt to alter the unit of decision so that fewer individuals are involved.

The communication channels used to diffuse an innovation also may influence the innovation's rate of adoption (see Figure 6-1). For example, if interpersonal channels (rather than mass media channels) create awareness-knowledge, as frequently happens for later adopters, their rate of adoption is slowed. The relationship between communication channels and the attributes of the innovation often interact to slow down or speed up the rate of adoption. For example, Petrini and others (1968) found differences in communication channel use on the basis of the perceived complexity of innovations among Swedish farmers. Mass media channels, such as agricultural magazines, were satisfactory for less complex innovations, but interpersonal contact with extension change agents was more important for innovations that were perceived by farmers as more complex. If an inappropriate communication channel were used, such as mass media channels for complex new ideas, a slower rate of adoption resulted.

Figure 6–1 shows that the nature of the social system, such as the norms of the system and the degree to which the communication network structure is highly interconnected, also affects an innovation's rate of adoption.

An innovation's rate of adoption is also affected by the extent of change agents' promotion efforts. The relationship between rate of adoption and change agents' efforts, however, may not be direct and linear. Greater payoff from a given amount of change agent activity occurs at certain stages in an innovation's diffusion. The greatest response to change agent effort occurs when opinion leaders adopt, which usually occurs somewhere between 3 and 16 percent adoption in most systems. The innovation will then continue to spread with little promotion by change agents, after a critical mass of adopters is reached.

Little diffusion research has been carried out to determine the relative contribution of each of the five types of variables shown in Figure 6–1. In this chapter we concentrate on the perceived attributes of innovations in explaining an innovation's rate of adoption. Our theme is that subjective evaluations of an innovation, derived from individuals' personal experiences and perceptions and conveyed by interpersonal networks, drives the diffusion process.

Research on the Attributes of Innovations

We need a standard classification scheme for describing the perceived attributes of innovations in universal terms. We would then not have to study each innovation as a special case to predict its rate of adoption. We could say, for example, that innovation A is more like innovation B (in the eyes of the adopters) than it is like innovation C. Such a general classification system is an eventual objective of diffusion research on innovation attributes. While this goal has not been reached, the present section discusses one approach that has been widely used for the past thirty years or so. Five different attributes of innovations are described. Each is somewhat empirically interrelated with the other four, but they are conceptually distinct. Selection of these five characteristics is based on past writing and research, as well as on a desire for maximum generality and succinctness. The five attributes of innovations are (1) relative advantage, (2) compatibility, (3) complexity, (4) trialability, and (5) observability.

The crucial importance of perceptions in explaining human behavior was emphasized by an early dictum of the Chicago School of Sociology: "If men perceive situations as real, they are real in their consequences" (Thomas and Znaniecki, 1927). In other words, perceptions count. The receivers' perceptions of the attributes of an innovation, not the attributes as classified by experts or change agents, affect its rate of adoption.

The first research on attributes of innovations and their rate of adoption was conducted with farmers, but studies of teachers and school administrators suggest that similar attributes predict the rate of adoption for educational innovations. Holloway (1977) designed his research with 100 high school principals around the five attributes described in this chapter. Holloway (1977) factor-analyzed Likert-type scale items measuring his respondents' perceptions of new educational ideas to derive the attributes. General support for the present framework was found, although the distinction between relative advantage and compatibility was not very clear-cut, and the status-conferring aspects of educational innovations emerged as a sixth dimension predicting rate of adoption.

Moore and Benbasat (1990) developed a set of general scale items to measure each of the five main attributes of innovations (plus several others) that can be applied to any particular innovation. This is a valuable methodological contribution to future research.

Most research on the attributes of innovations and their rate of adoption utilized individuals as the units of analysis, but this need not necessarily be so. For instance, why not use organizations or communities or some other kind of system as the unit of analysis? Goldman (1992) investigated the perceived attributes of a Campaign for Healthier Babies that was promoted by a national organization, the March of Dimes, to its local chapters for their implementation. Some 116 directors of local chapters reported their perceptions of the campaign five months after it was launched. Four attributes (each measured with a multiple item scale)— perceived compatibility with the local chapter's needs, simplicity (the opposite of complexity), relative advantage, and observability—were related to the degree of implementation of the Campaign for Healthier Babies.

One possible problem with measuring the five attributes of innovations is that they may not in all cases be the five most important perceived characteristics for a particular set of respondents. The solution, of course, is to elicit the main attributes of innovations from the respondents as a prior step to measuring these attributes as predictors of the rate of adoption. This procedure was followed by Kearns (1989 and 1992) in a study of the adoption of eight computer innovations among the 127 suburban municipalities of Pittsburgh, Pennsylvania. The eight innovations were identified by contacting computer consultants and city officials. The name of each of the eight innovations was written on a 3×5 inch card, with a one-sentence description of each innovation. Each of the 127 respondents was handed three of the innovation-cards, and asked, "Can you think of any way in which two of these innovations are alike and different from the third?" A respondent might say, for example, that two of the innovations are technologically complex, while the third was costly. Then the same respondent was handed another triplet of innovation-cards, and asked the same question. Kearns (1992) utilized this procedure to elicit twenty-five attributes of the eight innovations.

These twenty-five attributes included the five main attributes discussed in this chapter (relative advantage, compatibility, etc.), along with several additional attributes, such as flexibility in the way an innovation is implemented, the need for approval of the innovation by the city council, and so forth. Note that the additional attributes were specific to the eight computer innovations and to the city officials who were the respondents. The respondents were asked to rank the eight innovations on each of the twenty-five attributes. For example, each respondent ranked the eight innovations from most costly to least costly. Then these perceived attribute ratings were correlated with the rate of adoption of the eight innovations. The twenty-five perceived attributes explained 27 percent of the variance in the rate of adoption of the eight innovations. The five attributes (relative advantages, compatibility, etc.) explained 26 percent of the variance, only slightly less. Presumably the difference occurred because the twenty-five attributes were grounded more fully in the respondents' own frames of reference.

Tornatzky and Klein (1982) carried out a meta-research of seventy-five publications about perceived attributes and rate of adoption. Relative advantage and compatibility were usually, but not always consistently, related to rate of adoption in a positive direction, and complexity was negatively related to rate of adoption (as expected).

We conclude that the main attributes of innovations for most respondents can be described by the five attributes in our general framework.

Postdiction Versus Prediction

The usefulness of research on the attributes of innovations is mainly to predict their *future* rate of adoption and use. Most past research, however, has been *postdiction*, not *prediction*. That is, the attributes of innovations are considered as independent variables in explaining variance in the dependent variable of rate of adoption of innovations. This dependent variable is measured in the recent past, and the independent variables are measured in the present; so attributes can hardly be *predictors* of the rate of adoption. Generalizations, however, about such attributes as relative advantage or compatibility to explain rate of adoption have been derived from past research, and these generalizations could be used to predict the rate of adoption of innovations in the future. Such forward-looking investigations are sometimes called acceptability research because their purpose is to identify a basis for positioning an innovation so that it will be more acceptable (that is, have a more rapid rate of adoption).

An ideal research design would measure the attributes of innovations at t_1 in order to predict the rate of adoption for these innovations at t_2 (Tornatzky and Klein, 1981). Several approaches are useful for helping predict into the future:

1. Extrapolation from the rate of adoption of past innovations into the future for other similar innovations.
2. Describing a hypothetical innovation to its potential adopters, and determining its perceived attributes, to predict its rate of adoption.
3. Investigating the acceptability of an innovation in its prediffusion stages, such as when it is just being test-marketed and evaluated in trials.

None of these methods of studying the attributes of innovations is an ideal means for predicting the future rate of adoption of innovations. Research on predicting an innovation's rate of adoption would be more valuable if data on the attributes of the innovation were gathered prior to, or concurrently with, individuals' decisions to adopt the innovation (Tornatzky and Klein, 1981).

Predicting the Rate of Adoption of Norplant

Norplant is a promising new contraceptive that resulted from biomedical research by the Population Council (a Rockefeller Foundation–supported international family planning organization headquartered in New York) in the mid-1980s. This contraceptive innovation was then tested in clinical trials with about 5,000 women in several African nations, and approved by the

FDA (Food and Drug Administration) for use in the United States in 1991. The contraceptive was found to be safe (from unwanted side-effects) and efficacious (in preventing pregnancy). Norplant is the first important advance in contraceptive technology since the oral pill and the IUD (intrauterine device) became available in the early 1960s. A woman adopts Norplant by having six small plastic tubelets of the contraceptive hormone inserted with a needle under the skin on the underside of her forearm. The plastic tubelets, each about one inch long, slowly leak the contraceptive into the woman's bloodstream. Pregnancy is prevented over a five-year period. The Norplant insertion is considered an operation and can only be done by a medical doctor. It is almost painless and takes only about five minutes. The Norplant tubelets can be removed at any time by a doctor. So discontinuance is relatively easy.

The cost of Norplant in the United States is $500, which puts this innovation beyond the reach of poor women. However, the cost of Norplant adoption is covered by health insurance in several states, and one state provides free Norplant for all welfare recipients. The first adopters of Norplant in the U.S. were well-educated, higher-income women; only about 10 percent were below the poverty line. Adoption of Norplant is almost impossible to detect, even when short-sleeved clothes are worn, when a woman's skin is white. But under a dark skin, the Norplant tubelets, made of white plastic, are often visible. So the personal privacy of adopting Norplant may vary for white-skinned versus dark-skinned women. By 1993, only a few thousand of the 40 million fertile-aged, sexually active American women had adopted Norplant. Almost none of the adopters were women of color.

Knowing only these bare facts, would you predict the rate of adoption of Norplant in the U.S. for the next decade? What kinds of data would you need? What perceptions of Norplant would you want to measure?

This case illustration is based on various sources.

Relative Advantage

Relative advantage is the degree to which an innovation is perceived as being better than the idea it supersedes. The degree of relative advantage is often expressed as economic profitability, social prestige, or other benefits. The nature of the innovation determines what specific type of relative advantage (such as economic, social, and the like) is important to adopters, although the characteristics of the potential adopters also affect which subdimensions of relative advantage are most important.

Economic Factors and Rate of Adoption

A new product may be based on a technological advance or advances that result in a reduced cost of production for the product, leading to a lower selling price to consumers. Economists call this learning by doing (Arrow, 1962). An example is the VCR (video cassette recorder), which sold for more than $1,200 in 1980. Within a few years, thanks to technological improvements and to increasing competition, a similar VCR sold for only about $200.

When the price of a new product decreases so dramatically during its diffusion process, a rapid rate of adoption is encouraged. In fact, one might even question whether an innovation like the VCR is really the same in 1993, when it cost $200, as in 1980 when it cost six times as much. Certainly, its absolute relative advantage increased tremendously. Here we see that a characteristic of the innovation changed as its rate of adoption progressed. Thus, measuring the perceived characteristics of an innovation cross-sectionally at one point in time provides only a partial picture of the relationship of such characteristics to an innovation's rate of adoption.

A controversy regarding the relative importance of profitability versus noneconomic attributes of innovations for U.S. farmers occurred in past diffusion literature. Griliches (1957), an economist, explained about 30 percent of the variation in rate of adoption of hybrid corn on the basis of the innovation's profitability. He concluded: "It is my belief that in the long run, and cross-sectionally, [sociological] variables tend to cancel themselves out, leaving the economic variables as the major determinants of the pattern of technological change." Market forces undoubtedly are of importance in explaining the rate of adoption of farm innovations. For some innovations (such as high-cost and highly profitable new ideas) and for some farmers, economic aspects of relative advantage may be the most important single predictor of rate of adoption. But to expect that economic factors are the sole predictors of rate of adoption is unlikely. Other studies found that a combination of an innovation's profitability plus its observability were most important in determining its rate of adoption.

Status Aspects of Innovations and Overadoption

One motivation for many individuals to adopt an innovation is the desire to gain social status. Gabriel Tarde (1903) observed that status seeking was a main reason for imitating the innovation behavior of others. For certain innovations, new clothing fashions for example, the social prestige that the innovation conveys for its adopter is almost the sole benefit that the adopter receives. In fact, when many other members of a system have also adopted the same fashion, an innovation like shorter skirts or designer jeans may lose much of its prestige value to the adopters. This gradual loss of status-giving on the part of a particular clothing innovation provides pressure for yet newer fashions. Many clothing fashions are fads. A *fad* is an innovation that represents a relatively unimportant aspect of culture, which diffuses very rapidly, mainly for status reasons, and then is rapidly discontinued. Other examples of fads are hula hoops, mood rings, flip-up sunglasses, and umbrella-hats.

Clothing fashions are by no means the only class of innovations for which status-conferring considerations are a main reason for adoption, and upper-class women are by no means the only members of a population who are attracted to status-giving innovations. The adoption of other highly visible innovations like new cars and hair styles is especially likely to be status motivated. A spectacular example of the status-providing capacity of certain farm innovations is provided by the diffusion of "Harvestore" silos in the rural United States. These silos are constructed of steel and glass, painted navy blue, and prominently display the maker's name. Their height dominates a farm's skyline, so they are easily visible from public roads. Because Harvestores are extremely expensive (from $50,000 to $90,000, depending on the size), most agricultural experts recommend that U.S. farmers buy a much cheaper type of silo for storing their corn and hay silage. But the status-conferring quality of the Harvestores appeals to many farmers. In fact, some American farmers own, and prominently display, two Harvestores, perhaps the rural equivalent of the two-car garage in a suburban home.

Certain individuals who adopt an innovation at a particular time are more highly motivated by status seeking than are other individuals. For example, many lower-income individuals do not care about clothing fashions. Status motivations for adoption seem to be more important for innovators, early adopters, and early majority, and less important for the late majority and laggards.

The status motivations for adopting innovations have been understudied in past diffusion research. Respondents may be reluctance to admit that they adopted a new idea in order to secure the status aspects associated with the innovation. Direct questioning of adopters about this motivation is likely to underestimate its real importance in adoption decisions. Improved measurement approaches are needed to investigate different motivations for adopting an innovation, particularly such non-economic factors as status conferral.

Overadoption

Even though every innovation is judged on economic grounds to a certain degree by its potential adopters, every innovation also has at least some degree of status conferral. Overadoption is one result of the prestige-conferring aspect of adopting an innovation.

Overadoption is the adoption of an innovation by an individual when experts feel that he or she should reject. Overadoption occurs because of insufficient knowledge about the new idea on the part of the adopter, an inability to predict the innovation's consequences, and/or the status-conferring aspect of a new idea. Certain individuals have such a penchant for anything new that they occasionally appear to be suckers for change. They adopt when they shouldn't.

Whether an individual should or should not adopt an innovation is often difficult to determine. *Rationality*, defined as the use of the most effective means to reach a given goal (Merton, 1949/1968), is not easily measured in many cases. The classification as to whether or not an adoption is rational or not can sometimes be made by an expert on the innovation under study. Through lack of knowledge or through inaccurate perceptions, the individual's evaluation of an innovation may not agree with an expert's. Most individuals perceive their actions to be rational. Our main concern in the present case is with objective rationality rather than with subjective rationality as perceived by the individual.

The notion of overadoption implies that one role of the change agent is to prevent too much adoption of an innovation, as well as to try to speed up the diffusion process. Overadoption is a major problem in many fields. We mentioned previously the adoption of Harvestore silos by American farmers; this innovation is not recommended by agricultural experts. In the field of medicine, expensive hospital equipment is sometimes purchased when its use cannot be justified. For example, Scannel and others (1971) indicated that there were at least twice as many hospital establishments for open-heart surgery in the United States as were needed. As a result, many surgical teams were not operating frequently enough to keep their skills at a safe level of performance.

Overadoption sometimes happens when some attribute, or subattribute, of an innovation is perceived as so attractive to an individual that it overrules all other considerations. For example, the status-conferring aspect of a consumer innovation may be so important to an individual that adoption occurs, even though other perceptions of the new idea would lead one to expect that the innovation might be rejected. Further study of the phenomenon of overadoption is needed.

Relative Advantage and Rate of Adoption

Throughout this book we have emphasized that the diffusion of an innovation is an uncertainty-reduction process. When individuals (or an organization) pass through the innovation-decision process, they are motivated to seek information to decrease uncertainty about the relative advantage of an innovation. Potential adopters want to know the degree to which a new idea is better than an existing practice. So relative advantage is often an important part of message content about an innovation. The exchange of such innovation-evaluation information lies at the heart of the diffusion process.

Diffusion scholars have found relative advantage to be one of the best predictors of an innovation's rate of adoption. Relative advantage indicates the benefits and the costs resulting from adoption of an innovation. The subdimensions of relative advantage include the degree of economic profitability, low initial cost, a decrease in discomfort, social prestige, a savings in time and effort, and the immediacy of the reward. This last factor explains in part why preventive innovations generally have an especially low rate of adoption, as discussed in the following section. The relative advantage of preventive innovations is difficult for change agents to demonstrate to their clients, because it occurs at some future, unknown time.

Past investigations of the perceived attributes of innovations almost universally report a positive relationship between relative advantage and rate of adoption. We summarize these research findings on relative advantage with Generalization 6–1: *The relative advantage of an innovation, as perceived by members of a social system, is positively related to its rate of adoption.* Unfortunately, for purposes of generalizability, the respondents in most of these studies were U.S. commercial farmers, and their motivation for adoption of these innovations is centered on the economic aspects of relative advantage. As Frederick Fliegel and Joseph Kivlin (1966a), who are the deans of such research, point out: "Since we are dealing here with innovations having direct economic significance for the acceptor, it is not surprising that innovations perceived as most rewarding and involving least risk and uncertainty should be accepted most rapidly." In fact, a study by Fliegel and Kivlin (1966a) that included U.S. small-scale farmers (who are oriented less to profit considerations) found that a decrease in discomfort, one subdimension of relative advantage, but not economic profitability, was positively related to rate of adoption.

Economic aspects of relative advantage may be even less important for peasant farmers in Third World nations. Fliegel and others (1968) found that Punjabi farmers in India behaved more like small-scale Pennsylvania farmers (actually, even more so) than like large-scale U.S. farmers, regarding their perceptions of innovations: "Much more than financial incentives will be necessary to obtain widespread and rapid adoption of improved practices. . . . Unlike the Pennsylvania dairy farmers, the Punjabi respondents apparently attach greater importance to social approval and less to financial return" (Fliegel and others, 1968).

Preventive Innovations

A preventive innovation has a particularly slow rate of adoption because individuals have difficulties in perceiving its relative advantage. The sought-after consequence is distant in time, and so the relative advantage of a preventive innovation is a delayed reward. In contrast, an incremental (that is, non-preventive) innovation provides a desired outcome in the near future. An example is an Iowa farmer who planted hybrid seed corn to obtain a 20 percent increase in crop yield. Compare this behavior with a preventive innovation like "safe sex" to avoid contracting HIV/AIDS. Adoption by an individual now may prevent getting AIDS at some future time. But the individual might not have contracted AIDS even without adopting the idea of safe sex. So the rewards of adoption are not only delayed in time, but uncertain as to whether they actually will be needed (Figure 6–2).

Further, the unwanted event that is avoided by adopting a preventive innovation is difficult to perceive because it is a non-event, the absence of something that otherwise might have happened. For example, an individual's not contracting HIV/AIDS is invisible, unobservable, and hence difficult or impossible to comprehend. Family planning experts, in calculating the effects of contraceptive campaigns, estimate the number of births averted by calculating the pregnancies that would have occurred if contraceptives had not been adopted; the concept of births averted is not very meaningful to a peasant family in a Third World country that is being urged to adopt a preventive innovation like family planning.

Given these complex difficulties in perceiving the relative advantage

Figure 6–2. Preventive Innovations Are More Difficult to Diffuse Than Are Incremental Innovations

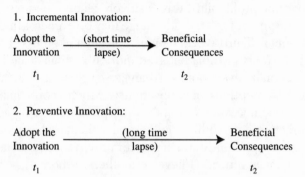

1. Incremental Innovation:

Adopt the   (short time   Beneficial
Innovation   lapse)   Consequences

t_1 t_2

2. Preventive Innovation:

Adopt the   (long time   Beneficial
Innovation   lapse)   Consequences

t_1 t_2

of preventive innovations, it is understandable why individuals often do not adopt. But in recent decades several preventive health campaigns have been carried out with successful results. One noted example is the Stanford Heart Disease Prevention Program conducted in the 1970s and 1980 in several California communities (Rogers, 1992). Large numbers of individuals at risk for heart disease changed their personal lifestyles regarding cigarette and alcohol use; jogging, aerobics, and other forms of regular exercise; nutritional habits like eating less red meat and using less salt; and reducing stress. How was this revolution in healthy lifestyles brought about?

The Stanford Program consisted of a series of communication campaigns, each aimed at a preventive innovation like smoking-cessation or weight reduction. A *communication campaign* (1) intends to generate specific effects, (2) on the part of a relatively large number of individuals, (3) within a specified period of time, (4) through an organized set of communication activities (Rogers and Storey, 1988). The word campaign derives from the Latin word for "field," as when Julius Caesar went to the field with a military campaign. The leaders of the Stanford Heart Disease Prevention Program carefully planned their use of mass media communication to recruit at-risk individuals into small group-training classes, such as for aerobic exercise and smoking-cessation. The health promotion messages were aimed at especially high-risk individuals in the California communities, such as older men who were overweight and who had high-cholesterol diets. The Stanford campaigns used *formative evaluation*, a type of research that is conducted while an activity is ongoing, in order to improve its effectiveness. Health-promotion messages were pretested with their intended audience, to be sure that they were understood and had the intended effects.

The Stanford program also based its communication activities on strategies drawn from diffusion theory, social marketing, and from social learning theory (Bandura, 1977). Campaign messages showed positive role models for healthy living, such as highly credible individuals who had lost weight through jogging and by eating more nutritious foods.

The results of the Stanford Heart Disease Prevention Program showed an important reduction in the risk of heart disease in the California communities (Flora with others, 1993). Further, the success of the Stanford Program encouraged the conduct of numerous other healthy lifestyle communication campaigns, aimed at drug abuse prevention and smoking prevention among school children, family planning, heart disease prevention among adults, and HIV/AIDS prevention. The Stanford Heart Disease Prevention Program, and its many intellectual "sons" and "daughters," show that the adoption of preventive health innovations can be facilitated effectively, but that special efforts are needed, particularly to emphasize the relative advantage of the preventive innovations.

Effects of Incentives

Many change agencies award incentives or subsidies to clients to speed up the rate of adoption of innovations. The main function of an incentive for adopters is to increase the degree of relative advantage of the new idea. *Incentives* are direct or indirect payments of either cash or in kind that are given to an individual or a system to encourage some overt behavioral change. Often, the change entails the adoption of an innovation.

Incentives have been paid to speed up the diffusion of innovations in a variety of fields: Agriculture, health, medicine, and family planning. In recent decades more research has been conducted on family planning incentives than on any other type. Incentives can take a variety of different forms (Rogers 1973).

1. *Adopter versus diffuser incentives.* Incentives may be paid either directly to an adopter, or to another individual to persuade an adopter. An illustration of a diffuser incentive is that paid to vasectomy canvassers in India (described in Chapter 9). These canvassers had each had the vasectomy operation themselves, and then earned a small incentive by convincing other men like themselves to adopt. Often the canvassers showed

their small vasectomy scar to a potential adopter in order to persuade him that only a minor operation was involved. A diffuser incentive mainly increases the observability of an innovation, rather than its relative advantage.

2. *Individual versus system incentives*. Payments may be made to individual adopters or to change agents, or to social systems to which they belong. For example, the government family planning agency in Indonesia paid a community incentive to villages that achieved a high rate of adoption of contraceptives; such an incentive policy increases the relative advantage of family planning and encourages word-of-mouth communication about adoption.

3. *Positive versus negative incentives*. Most incentives are positive in that they reward a desired behavior change (like adoption of a new idea), but it is also possible to penalize an individual by imposing an unwanted penalty or by withdrawing some desiderata for not adopting an innovation. For example, the government of Singapore decreed that the mother in any family that has a third (or further) child is not eligible to receive maternity leave and that the parents must pay all hospital and delivery costs (which are otherwise free to all citizens). Also, government-owned apartments in Singapore are quite small (something like married-student apartments in U.S. universities), so that a three-child family is very crowded.

4. *Monetary versus nonmonetary incentives*. While incentives are often financial payments, they may also take the form of some commodity or object that is desired by the recipient. For instance, in one state in India a sari with red triangles (the symbol for family planning in India) was awarded to each woman who was sterilized.

5. *Immediate versus delayed incentives*. Most incentives are paid at the time of adoption, but others can only be awarded at a later time. For example, some Third World nations provide a cost-free education to children of a couple who have a small family.

Any combination of these five types of incentive policies can be awarded in a given situation, depending on which particular combination of incentives has the desired influence on the diffusion of innovations. Offering incentives is one diffusion strategy that affects the perceived attributes of innovations, especially relative advantage, and thus an innovation's rate of adoption. Some incentive policies are designed only to encourage trial of a new idea; an illustration is the free samples of a new product that many commercial companies offer to their customers. The strategy here is that by facilitating trial use, full-scale adoption will follow (if the innovation possesses a potential relative advantage that can be perceived by the receiver). Other incentive policies are designed only to secure adoption of a new idea by the earlier adopters; once a level of 20- or 30-percent adoption is reached in a social system, the economic incentive is discontinued by the change agency. For example, the federal government and several state governments offered tax-rebate incentives for the adoption of residential solar heating in the early 1980s. The cost of such incentives became too large to be affordable by these governments, and they were halted once a level of 5- or 10-percent adoption was reached. These pump-priming incentives were utilized to launch the diffusion process, in the expectation that further diffusion would then become a self-generating process.

On the basis of research and experience with family planning innovations, Rogers (1973) drew the following conclusions:

1. *Incentives increase the rate of adoption of an innovation.* Adopter incentives increase relative advantage, and diffuser incentives increase the observability with which an innovation is perceived. Further, an adopter incentive can act as a *cue-to-action* (an event occurring at a point in time that crystallizes an individual's favorable attitude into overt behavior change) in triggering the adoption of an innovation.

2. *Adopter incentives lead to adoption of an innovation by individuals different from those who would otherwise adopt.* Innovators and early adopters usually have higher socioeconomic status and other characteristics that set them off from later adopters (see Chapter 7). But when a large adopter incentive is paid to family planning acceptors, for example, individuals of *lowest* socioeconomic status adopt. Thus it seems that paying an adopter incentive can change the audience segment that pioneers in adopting an innovation. Such a change has important implications for socioeconomic equality in the diffusion process.

3. *Although incentives increase the quantity of adopters of an innovation, the quality of such adoption decisions may be relatively low, limiting the intended consequences of adoption.* If individuals adopt an innovation partly in order to obtain an incentive, there is relatively less motivation to continue using the innovation (if it can be discontinued).

Serious ethical issues are involved in paying incentives, which deserve to be explored in future studies. Also, the effectiveness of incentive policies can be improved by conducting empirical studies to evaluate the effects of incentives on the rate of adoption, continuation, and consequences of innovations.

Mandates for Adoption

Providing incentives is one means through which a higher level of social organization like a government, community, or a commercial company can exert its influence on the behavior of individual members of the system. Certain types of behavior change may be desired or demanded by a government, for example, but not by individual members of the public. One example is the rate of population growth in a Third World nation: The national government often wishes to slow the population growth rate, so that it can better provide schools and jobs for the next generation. But parents may wish to have large families to carry on the family name, to obtain cheap labor, or for purposes of security in old age. Under these conditions, a national government often provides strong incentives to parents to persuade them to have fewer children. Where there is strong public resistance to voluntary incentives which the individual is free to accept or reject, a government may mandate adoption of family planning innovations or the desired consequences of such adoption (a small family).

Since the early 1980s, the government of the People's Republic of China has mandated the one-child family, in a policy of desperation. China is the world's most populous nation, with more than 1.1 billion people, a population which was growing rapidly. During the 1970s, the Chinese government turned away from Chairman Mao's belief that a rapidly growing population was an engine of national economic growth, and began to encourage Chinese parents to adopt contraceptives and have only two children. Such policies were inadequate to stem the rate of population increase. Chinese parents simply loved their babies, especially boys. So the one-child ideal began to be encouraged by the government, increasingly with a vengeance. Factory work groups, urban neighborhoods, and rural villages began the "group planning of births." Group discussions were held regularly to decide which parents could next have their one child. After the birth of the first child, a couple was strongly encouraged to adopt sterilization. If a couple did not follow the group plan or if pregnancy with a second baby occurred, the mother faced group pressure to have an involuntary abortion. Such draconian mandates for adoption of the one-child family norm led to a sharp decrease in the population growth rate of China.

Environmental behavior also frequently involves a conflict between what is best for the system, say a city or a nation, and what the individual would prefer to do. For example, smog and traffic congestion became worse each year in large cities like Los Angeles. The cost of building additional freeways was prohibitive, and the existing thoroughfares became so clogged with vehicles that they increasingly become mile-long "parking lots," with stop-and-go traffic moving at a snail's pace. Each year the number of vehicles in Southern California increased by 3 percent. Something had to be done. In 1990 a new regulation called Article XV went into effect, requiring that every organization employing 100 or more people had to increase the average number of employees coming to work per vehicle over a five-year period until an average of 1.5 was reached. A variety of innovative means could be utilized by the employing organization to reach this goal: Higher charges for employee parking, free bus passes, the organization of ride pools, and providing free commuter van service. If an employer organization did not make year-by-year progress toward the goal of 1.5 employees per vehicle, the organization faced stiff fines under Article XV. The main purpose of this regulation was to mandate a major reduction in commuter traffic, and a corresponding improvement in air quality through less smog.

A different, but equally draconian, approach to mandating a reduction in smog was taken by California's Clean Air Act: By 1998 2 percent of each auto manufacturer's new cars that are sold in California, about 40,000 autos, must be emission-free. This figure rises to 5 percent by 2001, and to 10 percent by 2003. Only electric vehicles meet the smog-free standards, so in essence the Clean Air Act mandated a rapid adoption of electric vehicles. Otherwise, auto manufacturers face severe fines and other penalties if they sell vehicles in California. A car-maker cannot afford to withdraw from the California market because the state represents 15 percent of all U.S. auto sales.

The main shortcoming of electric cars is that existing lead-and-acid batteries are relatively heavy and must be recharged after only about a ninety-minute drive. Up to eight hours are required for recharging. Further, electric vehicles are relatively more expensive than gasoline-powered cars. The Clean Air Act motivated U.S. automakers to launch major R&D efforts to develop improved batteries and to design more efficient electric vehicles.

Each of these mandates for adoption represents a mechanism through which the system exerts pressure on the individual to recognize the relative advantage of an innovation.

Compatibility

Compatibility is the degree to which an innovation is perceived as consistent with the existing values, past experiences, and needs of potential adopters. An idea that is more compatible is less uncertain to the potential adopter, and fits more closely with the individual's life situation. Such compatibility helps the individual give meaning to the new idea so that it is regarded as familiar. An innovation can be compatible or incompatible (1) with sociocultural values and beliefs, (2) with previously introduced ideas, or (3) with client needs for the innovation.

Compatibility with Values and Beliefs

An innovation's incompatibility with cultural values can block its adoption. Chapter 1 showed how the residents of the Peruvian village of Los Molinos perceived water-boiling as incompatible with their culturally defined hot-cold classification. American farmers place a strong value on increasing farm production; soil-conservation innovations are perceived as conflicting with this production value, and have generally been adopted very slowly.

In modern urban India there is a strong norm against eating food with the left hand, which is believed to be unclean. This habit began centuries ago when Indian villagers used their left hand for certain functions associated with defecation. At that time there were inadequate washing and sanitary facilities and the left-hand-as-unclean complex was functional. But today it is easy for urban, middle-class Indians to wash their hands before meals. Nevertheless, the unclean-hand belief persists strongly as a cultural element in urban India. How would you like to be the change agent responsible for persuading 900 million Indians to eat with their left hand? Many change agents face equally difficult assignments in promoting innovations that run counter to strongly held values.

One of the most important agricultural innovations of all time was the so-called miracle varieties of rice bred at the International Rice Research Institute (IRRI) in the Philippines in the mid-1960s. These improved rice varieties, when grown with heavy applications of chemical fertilizers, the use of pesticides, thicker planting, and other management practices, often *tripled* a farmer's rice yields. The IRRI miracle rice varieties spread very rapidly throughout Asia, causing a "green revolution." But the agronomists and plant breeders at IRRI only bred the miracle rice varieties for high yields and resistance to pests. No attention was given to the taste of the new rice. The present author was involved in the mid-1960s in the first diffusion studies of miracle rice in South India. He found that the new varieties did not taste "right" to the farm people who were planting the innovative seed. They sold the harvest from the IRRI varieties in the marketplace, while continuing to plant the traditional rice seed for their own family consumption. The author informed the rice-breeders of IRRI about the taste incompatibility problem, but in the 1960s they scoffed at this recommendation: "We triple rice yields. Farm people will soon learn to like the taste of IRRI rice!"

Thirty years later, South Indian farmers, like their counterparts in many other Asian nations, are still planting small amounts of traditional rice varieties for their own consumption, while growing the IRRI rice for sale. And the miracle rice sells for a price that is about 20 percent less than the tastier, local varieties. In the 1980s, the International Rice Research Institute finally began breeding its new rice varieties for consumer taste, as well as high yield. Compatibility is important in determining rate of adoption.

Other examples of the cultural incompatibility of an innovation sometimes occur when an idea is designed for use in one culture but then spreads to a different culture, with different cultural values. An illustration is a bar-code reader that IBM designed in the 1970s for check-out stands in U.S. supermarkets. This equipment could sum a series of product prices to a six-digit total, for example, $9,999.99. This total was more than adequate at the time, when the bill for most customers was less than $100. Unfortunately, the IBM designers of the bar-code readers did not think globally. In Italy, which was experiencing an exorbitant rate of inflation, 10,000 *lira* would hardly buy a loaf of bread. Similarly, Lotus 1-2-3, the popular computer spreadsheet program, encountered incompatibility problems in India, where *lakhs* (10,000) and *crores* (10,000,000) are used instead of terms like thousands, millions, and billions, and where the meaning of a comma and a period (a decimal point) are often reversed, so that $9,999.99 would be written $9.999,99.

Compatibility with Previously Introduced Ideas

An innovation may be compatible not only with deeply imbedded cultural values but also with previously adopted ideas. Compatibility of an innovation with a preceding idea can either speed up or retard its rate of adoption. Old ideas are the main mental tools that individuals utilize to assess new ideas. One cannot deal with an innovation except on the basis of the familiar, with what is known. Previous practice provides a familiar standard against which an innovation can be interpreted, thus decreasing uncertainty.

Examples of the use of past experience to judge new ideas come from an early diffusion study in a Colombian peasant community (Fals Borda, 1960). At first, farmers applied chemical fertilizers on top of their potato seed (as they had done with cattle manure), thereby damaging the seed and causing a lower yield. Other peasants excessively sprayed their potatoes with insecticides, transferring to the new idea their old methods of watering their plants. Given their lack of understanding of the principles-knowledge of how chemical fertilizer and insecticides affected potato yields, the Colombian farmers gave meaning to these innovations in terms with which they were familiar.

In these cases, the perceived compatibility of the new idea with previous experience led the adopters to incorrectly utilize the innovations. Here, compatibility led to adoption of a new idea, but then to incorrect use to the innovation. So presumed compatibility with a previously introduced idea can cause overadoption or missadoption. An illustration comes from the introduction of tractors in the Punjab, a prosperous farming area in Northern India (Carter, 1994). Tractors were perceived as giving social prestige to the owner, much as had the bullocks that the tractor replaced as a means of farm power and as transportation to market towns. Punjabi farmers, however, did not carry out basic maintenance of their tractors, such as cleaning the air filters and replacing the oil filter. As a result, a new tractor typically broke down after a year or two, with the farmer often failing to repair it. A foreign consultant was invited to investigate the problem. He made an engine maintenance chart, and had it translated into Punjabi. The chart was printed in five colors, and distributed to all farmers (who had tractors) by agricultural extension agents, who explained to farmers why regular maintenance was important. But still the tractors broke down.

Then a salesman came to the Punjab who had sold blankets to farmers the previous year for covering their bullocks in cold weather. Within a few days several tractors were observed with a blanket covering the hood. The foreign expert warned farmers that the blanket could cause the tractor engine to overheat. Nevertheless, within ten days, virtually every tractor had a blanket covering the hood. To Punjabi farmers, it made sense to keep their source of farm power warm during winter weather. But cleaning the air filter and changing the oil filter on their tractor was not compatible with their previous experience with caring for their bullocks.

Hawley (1946) sought to determine why the Roman Catholic religion, promoted by proselytizing Spanish priests, was readily accepted by Eastern Pueblo Indians in Arizona and New Mexico, whereas the Western Pueblos, "after a brief taste of Catholicism, rejected it forcefully, killed the priests, burned the missions, and even annihilated the village of Awatobi when its inhabitants showed a tendency to accept the acculturation so ardently proffered." Hawley concluded that the Eastern Pueblos, whose family structure was heavily patrilineal and father-oriented, were attracted by the new religion in which the deity was a male figure. Catholicism, however, was incompatible with the mother-centered beliefs of the Western Pueblos. Perhaps if the change agents had been able to emphasize the female-image aspects of Catholicism (such as the Virgin Mary), they would have achieved greater success among the Western Pueblo tribes.

The rate of adoption of a new idea is affected by the old idea that it supersedes. Obviously, however, if a new idea were completely congruent with existing practice, there would be no innovation, at least in the minds of the potential adopters. In other words, the more compatible an innovation is, the less of a change in behavior it represents. How useful, then, is the introduction of a very highly compatible innovation? Quite useful, perhaps, if the compatible innovation is seen as the first step in a series of innovations that are to be introduced sequentially. The compatible innovation can pave the way for later, less compatible innovations.

An interesting example of how *low* compatibility of an innovation can be related to a rapid rate of adoption comes from an investigation of the diffusion of art. One of the relatively few studies of the diffusion of a nontechnological innovation is Lievrouw and Pope's (1994) investigations of new art and new artists. Such aesthetic innovations seem to display some unique qualities regarding their diffusion. For example, while most innovations that are higher in perceived compatibility have a more rapid rate of adoption, the reverse may be true for artworks. If aesthetic innovations are too closely derivative of older works, they are unlikely to meet much critical or economic success. Artworks must be somewhat radical if they are to diffuse rapidly.

A negative experience with one innovation can damn the adoption of future innovations. Such innovation negativism (Arensberg and Niehoff, 1964) can be an undesirable aspect of compatibility. *Innovation negativism* is the degree to which one innovation's failure conditions a potential adopter to reject future innovations. When one idea fails, potential adopters are conditioned to view all future innovations with apprehension. For this reason, change agents should begin their efforts with a particular audience with an innovation that has a high degree of relative advantage, so that they can then build successively on this initial success. The national family planning program in India began by promoting the IUD, a method that was widely discontinued in the 1960s. Family planning in India has never been able to recover from this disastrous failure, because of innovation negativism.

Compatibility with Needs

One dimension of the compatibility of an innovation is the degree to which it meets a felt need. Change agents seek to determine the needs of their clients, and then to recommend innovations that fulfill these needs. Discovering felt needs is not a simple matter; change agents must have a high degree of empathy and rapport with their clients in order to assess their needs accurately. Informal probing in interpersonal contacts with individual clients, client advisory committees to change agencies, and surveys of clients are sometimes used to determine needs for innovations.

Potential adopters may not recognize that they have a need for an innovation until they are aware of the new idea or of its consequences. In these cases, change agents may seek to generate needs among their clients but this must be done carefully or else the felt needs upon which a diffusion campaign is based may be only a reflection of the change agent's needs, rather than those of clients. Thus one dimension of compatibility is the degree to which an innovation is perceived as meeting the needs of the client system. When felt needs are met, a faster rate of adoption usually occurs, as we see in the following case illustration.

The War on Drugs and the Diffusion of D.A.R.E.

D.A.R.E. (Drug Abuse Resistance Education) experienced a phenomenal rate of diffusion in the first decade following its creation in Los Angeles in 1983. Five million school children in the U.S., along with their counterparts in Australia, New Zealand, Canada, and Europe were taught a 17-hour curriculum of saying "no" to drugs. Their classroom teachers were uniformed policemen, each of whom had several years of experience in fighting drugs on the street.

During the 1980s the War on Drugs (as it was termed by the White House) was an issue very high on the national agenda. In September, 1989, 54 percent of the public rated drugs as "the most important problem facing the U.S. today." Four years previously, in 1985, this percentage was zero. And one year later, in 1990, only 9 percent of the U.S. public considered drugs as the number one problem facing the nation. By 1992, this figure dropped to only 4 percent (Figure 6–3). The timing of this rise-and-fall of the drug issue on the national agenda is a fundamental reason for the rapid diffusion of D.A.R.E. President Ronald Reagan and the nation's First Lady, Nancy Reagan, told children "Just Say No to Drugs." The mass media devoted many news stories and television documentaries to the drug issue in the late 1980s. Basketball star Len Bias died from a drug overdose in 1986, humanizing the drug problem. The White House appointed a "drug czar" to command the War on Drugs. Federal funding for drug prevention programs became available, and drug addiction became a $2 billion a year industry. Concerned parents demanded that their local school mount a drug prevention program.

But the U.S. drug problem of the 1980s was mainly a social construction by national leaders, by the U.S. media, and the public. In fact, a long-term downward trend in the number of deaths caused by drugs in the United States continued during the late 1980s rise-and-fall of the drug issue. The U.S. public was not well-informed about this fact. What was new in the 1980s was the particular drug that became an important killer: Crack cocaine.

In any event, the high priority of the drug issue on the national agenda, even though it was mainly a matter of perception rather than of reality, drove the rapid diffusion of D.A.R.E.

Birth of the D.A.R.E. Program

D.A.R.E. was conceived in 1983 by former Los Angeles Policy Chief Darryl F. Gates, a "champion" for the D.A.R.E. program. At that time, the drug problem had not yet started to climb the national agenda. Chief Gates launched D.A.R.E. three years prior to the first peaking of the drug issue on the U.S. media and public agendas that occurred in 1986, and six years prior to the major peak in 1989. This timing was exquisite.

Darryl Gates in 1983 had been chief of the LAPD (Los Angeles Police Department) for five years and a member of the police force for twenty-four

Figure 6–3. The Drug Issue on the U.S. Media Agenda and the Public Agenda

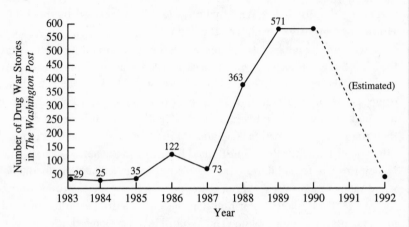

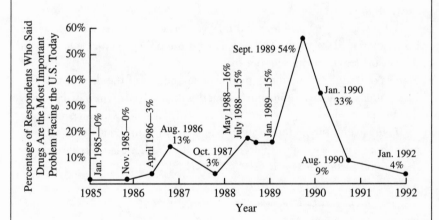

Source: Dearing and Rogers (in press).

years. He was a highly respected city police chief and had pioneered law enforcement's first SWAT team, which became an international model. Prior to the D.A.R.E. program, the LAPD had conducted twice-yearly school drug busts, using police officers disguised as students. These school drug busts were highly criticized and in 1983 Chief Gates was searching for an alternative approach to the school drug problem in Los Angeles. Prevention looked like an attractive approach.

Chief Gates assigned uniformed police officers to make classroom presentations about drug-abuse prevention to school children. Gates knew that he needed the cooperation of the Los Angeles Unified School District, and so he initiated collaboration with the Los Angeles Board of Education in mid-1983. After preliminary approval of the basic idea of D.A.R.E., police officials began to collaborate with educators in planning the core curriculum for the D.A.R.E. program.

The essence of the D.A.R.E. program is:

1. To aim at a target audience of 5th and 6th-graders, school children who are nine, ten, or eleven, an age (1) at which most have not yet become drug users, and (2) when they still regard police officers as highly credible.

2. To incorporate assertiveness training, resisting peer pressure, and building self-esteem in the D.A.R.E. program, as well as material about drug abuse and the consequences of drug use. As a 1990 brochure from D.A.R.E. America states: "It [D.A.R.E.] doesn't tell them to say 'no'; it teaches them how to say 'no'." As part of their D.A.R.E. training, students rehearse various ways of refusing offers to try alcohol or drugs.

3. To use police officers as external trainers to teach the curricular materials, rather than depending on the regular classroom teacher or on special school personnel such as health educators. Uniformed police officers are trained in a two-week course on child development, teaching methods, classroom management, and communication skills, and then make the classroom presentations. Police have high perceived credibility about drugs in the eyes of most school children. As a D.A.R.E. brochure states: "The police officers assigned to D.A.R.E. have come straight from the streets. Their years of direct experience with the ruined lives and street crimes caused by substance abuse gives them a credibility unmatched by teachers, movie or television celebrities, or professional athletes" (D.A.R.E. America, 1990). Black officers are assigned to predominantly black schools, Hispanic officers to predominantly Hispanic schools, and so on.

4. To schedule teaching the seventeen D.A.R.E. presentations, each of forty-five to sixty minutes, to 5th- and 6th-graders on a once-a-week basis during the school semester.

5. To provide high school student leaders as positive role models for the 5th-and 6th-graders.

6. To contact (1) kindergarten students through 4th-graders, in order to acquaint these school children with their school's D.A.R.E. police officer

and to lay the groundwork for the 5th and 6th grade intensive program; (2) junior high school students, who receive a ten-lesson follow-up to the earlier seventeen-lesson D.A.R.E. curriculum; and (3) high school students, who receive an eleven-lesson program enhancing the drug resistance skills previously introduced in elementary and junior high school.

7. To create and maintain personal relationships of the police officers with the 5th- and 6th-graders in the elementary school to which they are assigned. As an official description of the D.A.R.E. program (Bureau of Justice Assistance, 1988) stated: "In addition to their formal classroom teaching, D.A.R.E. officers spend time on the playground, in the cafeteria, and at student assemblies to interact with students informally. They may organize a soccer match, play basketball, or chat with students over lunch. In this way students have an opportunity to become acquainted with the officer as a trusted friend who is interested in their happiness and welfare."

Diffusion of D.A.R.E.

Why did the D.A.R.E. program diffuse so rapidly?

1. The late 1980s were a period during which the drug issue rose rapidly on the national media agenda and the public agenda to a peak in 1989 (see Figure 6–3). The perceived importance of the drug issue meant that federal, state, and local government funding was available for the rapid expansion of the D.A.R.E. program in the United States. It also meant that parents, school board members, and other citizens often demanded that a local drug-abuse prevention campaign be launched in their community. The perceived importance of the drug problem in the United States during the 1980s encouraged the spontaneous diffusion of D.A.R.E. through horizontal channels from one community to another. Although the D.A.R.E. program began in one city, rather than as a federal innovation originating in Washington, D.C., White House enthusiasm for the drug problem gave a tremendous push to D.A.R.E., and federal funding was provided to local police departments through the U.S. Department of Justice for dissemination of the D.A.R.E. program.

2. In addition to public funding, many private resources were contributed to D.A.R.E. Such contributions are facilitated by the national organization for D.A.R.E. programs called "D.A.R.E. America." For example, KFC (Kentucky Fried Chicken) was the first national corporate cosponsor of the D.A.R.E. programs. In 1989, a California bank contributed $500,000 to D.A.R.E. and promised $1 million over the next five years.

3. Numerous evaluations of the D.A.R.E. program were conducted, and generally showed that students who received the D.A.R.E. program had a slightly lower rate of use of cocaine than non-D.A.R.E. students. Differences in the use of other drugs are also in the expected direction. But D.A.R.E.'s effects on school children are very modest, and generally are less than for other drug abuse prevention programs (Ennett and others, 1994). Nevertheless, the fact that several early evaluations showed generally positive effects encouraged decision makers to conclude that D.A.R.E. works. Local communities point to their D.A.R.E. program with pride, to show that they are doing something about the drug problem.

4. The spread of D.A.R.E. occurred through a decentralized type of diffusion system, in which re-invention frequently occurred, with each adopting community customizing the main elements in the core D.A.R.E. program to suit its local conditions. Such flexibility in the nature of local D.A.R.E. programs undoubtedly sped the rate of adoption of this innovation, although it may also have resulted in somewhat less successful D.A.R.E. programs (Wulf, 1987). Whether or not the customization of the D.A.R.E. concept in a local community leads to a less effective program of drug-abuse prevention, or whether it just represents an appropriate adaptation to local conditions, is not clear. D.A.R.E. America opposed re-invention.

5. The D.A.R.E. program was launched by an influential individual, Los Angeles Police Chief Darryl Gates, who continued to champion the innovation for a decade. Chief Gates addressed the national conference of police chiefs about the D.A.R.E. program, and articles about it appeared in police trade journals. Los Angeles may have been an ideal location in which to launch D.A.R.E. in that most Americans think of the city as a national center for drug problems and other gang-related difficulties. Thus, if D.A.R.E. were effective in Los Angeles, other communities might expect that it would work for them, where drug and gang problems are less serious.

Re-Invention of D.A.R.E Programs

Headquarters personnel of D.A.R.E. America felt that the D.A.R.E. innovation package should be adopted *in toto* by implementing communities, in essence without re-invention. The original, Los Angeles version of the D.A.R.E. program is taken as the template, and deviations from this model are considered to be "errors." This viewpoint assumes that all of the adopting communities have similar conditions to Los Angeles and that modification of the D.A.R.E. program is unnecessary.

Many adopting communities do not accept this assumption. A considerable degree of re-invention of the D.A.R.E. program occurs. Professor Kathleen Wulf (1987) at the University of Southern California conducted a mailed questionnaire survey of eighty-four law enforcement agencies nationwide that had sent police officers to the Los Angeles training center for two weeks of instruction in the D.A.R.E. program from 1984 to 1987. Although 95 percent of the local programs were called "D.A.R.E." a certain degree of re-invention of the innovation occurred. For example, 34 percent of the adopting communities did not include all seventeen D.A.R.E. lessons in their local program. Most likely not to be included was Resisting Gang Pressure: 24 percent of all local D.A.R.E. programs did not include this lesson (these communities may have thought that they did not have a serious gang problem). Forty-two percent said they had made some modifications in the D.A.R.E. program.

The D.A.R.E. program diffused among U.S. schools at a phenomenal rate, compared to any other educational innovation. During the 7 years from 1983 to 1990, the number of students taught the D.A.R.E. program increased from zero to 5 million. Undoubtedly, D.A.R.E.'s successful diffusion moved U.S. schools into directly combating the drug problem. But at what cost of alternative paths not taken? Some critics of D.A.R.E. point out that the adoption of this innovative program represents 17 fewer hours devoted to the teaching of math, reading, and other basic subjects in the 5th- and 6th-grade curriculum.

Overall, the rapid diffusion of D.A.R.E. occurred because it met the felt needs of the U.S. public to do something to prevent the perceived drug problem in America.

This case illustration is based on Rogers (1993a).

Compatibility and Rate of Adoption

The example just reviewed, and other evidence, support Generalization 6–2: *The compatibility of an innovation, as perceived by members of a social system, is positively related to its rate of adoption.* Past diffusion research suggests that compatibility may be of relatively less importance in predicting rate of adoption than relative advantage. This finding may be in part an artifact of difficulties in measuring perceived compatibility.

Technology Clusters

Innovations often are not viewed singularly by individuals. They may be perceived as an interrelated bundle of new ideas. The adoption of one new idea may trigger the adoption of several others. A *technology cluster* consists of one or more distinguishable elements of technology that are perceived as being interrelated. The boundaries around any given innovation are often not clear-cut or distinct. In the minds of potential adopters, one innovation may be perceived as closely related to another new idea. If this is the case, a change agency may find it useful to promote a cluster or package of innovations to clients, rather than to treat each new idea separately.

For instance, in India and in other Asian nations, a package of agricultural innovations, including the IRRI rice varieties, chemical fertilizers, and other agricultural chemicals, was recommended *in toto* to farmers. Villagers adopted the package more rapidly than they would adopt if each of the innovations had been diffused individually. More important, by adopting all at once, farmers achieved the total yield effects of all the innovations, plus the interaction effects of each new idea on the others.

Unfortunately, the effects of using a package approach has seldom been investigated in diffusion research, although it makes sense intuitively. Naturally, the packaging should be based on the user's *perceptions* of the interrelated innovations, but this has not been done.

One of the few investigations of a complex of new ideas is Silverman and Bailey's (1961) analysis of the adoption of three corn-growing innovations by 107 Mississippi farmers. The three ideas (fertilization, hybrid seed, and thicker planting) were functionally interrelated in such a way that adoption of the latter innovation without concurrent use of the other two ideas actually resulted in *lower* corn yields than if none of the three new ideas were used. Most farmers either adopted all three of the ideas or none of them, but 8 percent used unsuccessful combinations. Silverman and Bailey suggested the need for agricultural change agents to show farmers the interrelationships among the three ideas in their corn-growing complex.

Some merchandisers offer tie-in sales, a technique that recognizes the compatibility among several new products. A new clothes washer may be offered to housewives as a package deal along with a dryer, for example. Some marketing schemes hook an unwanted product onto a compatible innovation that possesses a high degree of relative advantage.

Future research needs to analyze complexes of innovations, to study new ideas in an evolutionary sequence, and to determine the degree of compatibility perceived by individuals among interrelated ideas. Such study would provide a sounder basis for assembling innovations in easier-to-adopt packages.

Naming an Innovation

The name given to an innovation often affects its perceived compatibility, and therefore its rate of adoption. Inadequate attention has been paid to what innovations are called by potential adopters, and as a result many serious mistakes have been made. For instance, a major U.S. soap company introduced its trademarked product "Cue" into French-speaking nations, where the word has an obscene connotation. Another well-known example is a certain model of U.S. automobile, the Nova, which means "no-go" (*No va*) in Spanish. Such egregious errors have shown commercial companies the importance of market research to pretest the name for a new product prior to its release. On the other hand, public change agencies generally have not realized the importance of what an innovation is called, at least until the social marketing approach began to gain attention in recent years (see Chapter 2).

The perception of an innovation is colored by the word symbols used for it. The selection of an innovation's name is a delicate and important matter. Words are the thought-units that structure perceptions. And of course it is the potential adopter's perceptions of an innovation that affect its rate of adoption. Sometimes a medical or a chemical name is used for an innovation that comes from medical or chemical research and development; unfortunately, such names are not very meaningful to potential adopters (unless they are physicians or chemists). Examples are "2, 4-D weed spray," "IR-20 rice variety," and "intrauterine device," terms that were confusing and misunderstood by potential adopters. A new intrauterine device, the "Copper-T," was introduced in South Korea some years ago without careful consideration of an appropriate Korean name. The letter "T" does not exist in the Korean alphabet, and copper is considered a very base metal with a very unfavorable perception. A worse name could hardly have been chosen (Harding and others, 1973).

In contrast, the word "Nirodh" was carefully selected in India in 1970 as the most appropriate term for condoms. Prior to this time, condoms had a very negative perception as a contraceptive method; they were thought of mainly as a means of preventing venereal disease. When the government of India decided to promote condoms as a contraceptive method, a variety of terms were pretested. *Nirodh*, a Sanskrit word meaning "protection," was selected, and then promoted in an advertising campaign to the intended audience (Rogers, 1973). The result was a sharp increase in the rate of adoption of Nirodhs.* In 1992, 700 million Nirodhs were given away free by the Indian government, and 300 million were sold at a cheap price.

We recommend such a receiver-oriented, empirical approach to naming an innovation, so that the word symbol for a new idea has the desired meaning for the intended audience.

Positioning an Innovation

A basic assumption of the positioning strategy, based on market research, formative evaluation, and on social marketing, is that an individual will behave toward a new idea in a similar manner to the way the individual behaves toward other ideas that are perceived as similar to the new idea. For instance, consider a category of existing ideas consisting of products A, B, and C. If a new product, X, is introduced to the audience for these products, and if they perceive X as similar to B, but unlike A and C, then consumers who purchased B will be as likely to buy X as B. If other factors (like price) are equal, X should attain about one-half of the former B consumers, but the introduction of X should not affect the sales of products A and C. Further, if we can learn why consumers perceive B and X as similar, but different from A and C, X can be positioned (through its name, color, packaging, taste, and the like) so as to maximize its distance from A, B, and C in the minds of the consumers, and thus to gain a unique niche for the new idea. Obviously, the positioning of an innovation rests on accurately measuring its compatibility with previous ideas.

Research to position new products is often conducted by market researchers, and the methods for positioning an innovation have been developed by commercial researchers. But these positioning techniques can be used to facilitate the introduction of a social marketing innovation. For instance, Harding and others (1973) used positioning methods to introduce the Copper-T, then a new intrauterine contraceptive device in Korea. First, they asked a small sample of potential adopters to help identify twenty-nine perceived attributes of eighteen contraceptive methods in a

---

*In part, because use of the word "Nirodh" helped overcome the tabooness of condoms. *Taboo communication* is a type of message transfer in which the messages are perceived as extremely private and personal in nature because they deal with proscribed behavior.

relatively open-ended, unstructured approach. Then a different sample of Korean respondents were asked to rate each of the eighteen family planning methods (including the Copper-T, the only new method) on these twenty-nine attributes (which included numerous subdimensions of the five main attributes of innovations discussed in this chapter). The results led to recommendations about which attributes of the Copper-T to stress in its diffusion campaign, in order to maximize its rate of adoption. For instance, Harding and others (1973) recommended stressing the Copper-T's long lifetime, its reliability (in preventing unwanted pregnancies), its lack of interference with sexual behavior, and its newness. The researchers also recommended a change in the physical nature of the innovation. "Certain features of the Copper-T, such as the string [a plastic thread used to remove the intrauterine device], perhaps should be altered since the string is associated with causing bacteria to enter the womb and with causing an inflammation of the womb" (Harding and others, 1973).

Positioning research can help identify the ideal niche for an innovation relative to perceptions of existing ideas in the same category. This ideal niche is determined by the new idea's perceived position relative (1) to previous ideas, and (2) to the characteristics of the new idea that make it similar to, and different from, existing ideas. The positioning approach views an innovation's perceived characteristics (at least some of them) as dynamic and changeable. Positioning research puts the diffusion researcher in the role of designer (or at least a co-designer) of the innovation.

One special kind of positioning research is conducted to provide guidance to R&D activities on what kind of innovations to produce. If innovations of type X will not be accepted by potential adopters but innovations of type Y will be accepted, R&D workers should direct their efforts toward developing type-Y innovations. An example of this approach is provided by the World Health Organization's (WHO) Human Reproduction Unit in Geneva, which directs a research program on contraceptives for use in Third World nations. Most past contraceptive methods faced difficult problems of acceptability (Rogers, 1973). So WHO conducts special diffusion studies to determine what types of contraceptives would be most acceptable. These recommendations give direction to WHO biomedical researchers who seek to create a new contraceptive with an "ideal" set of attributes for its future acceptability.

For example, acceptability studies of contraceptive behavior show that men and women in Third World nations are very adverse to using a family planning method that requires manipulation of the human genitals. Unfortunately, the main contraceptives promoted by government family planning programs in Third World nations in the past required genital manipulation: The IUD (intrauterine device), condoms, and the diaphragm, for instance. Perhaps the incompatibility of these contraceptive methods with the aversion to genital handling is one reason why their rate of adoption has been discouraging in most nations. So WHO biomedical research was directed, in part, toward developing contraceptives that did not require genital handling (Rogers and Pareek, 1982). Examples are an injectable contraceptive like Depo Provera or an implant like Norplant. Yet a basic difficulty remains for national family planning programs in the nations of Latin America, Africa, and Asia: A highly compatible contraceptive method does not yet exist. No amount of acceptability research can completely make up for this lack of an appropriate contraceptive technology that is effective, safe from undesirable side effects, and highly acceptable to potential adopters. Nevertheless, several Third World countries have been able to achieve a relatively high rate of adoption of family planning methods and a corresponding decline in the rate of population growth. For example, Korea, Indonesia, and China each have a rate of adoption of about 66 percent of all fertile-age married couples. This high level of contraceptive use has been attained by an effective delivery system of family planning clinics and field workers, social marketing strategies, and, in the case of China, considerable group pressure for the one-child family.

A major health problem facing the world today is the AIDS epidemic. Since the first AIDS cases were detected in the United States in 1981 among gay men, the human immune-deficiency virus (HIV) has spread to millions of people in the U.S., Mexico, Brazil, Thailand, Haiti, India, and African nations like Tanzania, Kenya, Uganda, and Zaire. Within a few years after contracting HIV, the typical individual is diagnosed with the symptoms of AIDS, and, a few years later, dies. While the main means of HIV transmission in the United States involve gay men and IV (intravenous) drug users who share needles, the virus is mainly transmitted by heterosexual contact in other nations, with prostitutes playing a key role in the early stages of the epidemic.

How can the HIV/AIDS epidemic be contained? Prevention campaigns warn high-risk individuals, such as commercial sex workers (the term used by WHO and the U.S. government for prostitutes), IV drug users, or individuals with a high number of sexual contacts. HIV/AIDS prevention agencies also urge individuals to have "safe sex," which means using a condom. But condoms are widely perceived as incompatible with sexual pleasure, as messy, and as requiring genital handling. So even in nations in which the AIDS epidemic is widespread, like the United States, health officials have only been able to convince 5 to 10 percent of sexually active individuals to adopt safe sex. Until more effective technologies of AIDS prevention or cure are found through biomedical research, the only way to combat the AIDS epidemic is through more effective educational campaigns to diffuse condom use. Is it possible to position condoms so they are perceived as relatively more compatible?

Indigenous Knowledge Systems

The innovation positioning strategy consists of depicting an innovation, X, relative to existing ideas A, B, and C that are already familiar to potential adopters. The basic notion of the compatibility attribute is that a new idea is perceived in relationship to existing practices that are already familiar to the individual.

Change agents and others who introduce an innovation often commit the *empty vessels fallacy* by assuming that potential adopters are blank slates who lack a relevant experience with which to associate the new idea. In the past decade the empty vessels fallacy has been overcome in agriculture, health, and family planning by attention to indigenous knowledge systems. Scholars, often anthropologists, probe the traditional experiences of individuals in Third World nations to understand how these indigenous knowledge systems can serve as a bridge for innovations. For example, Juan Flavier, a family planning official in the rural Philippines, found that villagers understood that when chicken hens ate the brown-colored seeds of the iping-iping tree, they stopped laying eggs. So Flavier explained to villagers that oral contraceptive pills for humans acted in a similar way to the iping-iping seeds.

Steve Lansing, an anthropologist at the University of Southern California, studied the irrigation system of the island of Bali in Indonesia (Lansing, 1991). As explained in Chapter 2, he found that the seasonal flow of water among the rice fields was controlled by a series of Hindu water temples and their priests. This indigenous system of irrigation control would fallow a large area of several square miles, so that the rice pests would die; then the water would be released for planting the next crop of rice. When the IRRI miracle rice varieties were introduced by Indonesian extension workers, they ignored the indigenous irrigation system. The miracle rice had a shorter growing session than the existing varieties on Bali, and was incompatible with the irrigation schedule of the Hindu priests. The eventual result was lower, instead of higher, yields from the new rice, and then its discontinuance by Balinese farmers. This problem could have been avoided, Lansing (1991) points out, if the extension workers had not ignored the indigenous knowledge system for rice irrigation.

Why are indigenous knowledge systems often ignored by those individuals introducing an innovation? A strong belief in the relative advantage of the new idea often leads technocrats to assume that existing practices are so inferior that they need not be considered at all. The practitioner specialists of indigenous knowledge systems, like the Hindu priests in Bali, the traditional birth attendants (midwives) in many nations, and the *curenderos* of Latin America may be considered quacks by their modern-technology counterparts. Such a superior attitude often leads to the empty vessels fallacy, and to the introduction of an innovation that is perceived as incompatible with the ideas that it seeks to replace.

Change agents frequently overlook the fact that almost every innovation is evaluated by clients in terms of their prior experience with something similar. The innovation may be "new wine," but it is poured into old bottles (that is, the clients' existing perceptions). The solution to the empty vessels fallacy is for a change agent to understand her or his clients' prior experiences with the practice that the innovation replaces. So an effective change agent must comprehend his clients' indigenous knowledge systems.

A great deal of useful knowledge is usually represented in indigenous knowledge systems. For example, Squanto and the other Native Americans of his tribe taught the Pilgrims in colonial Massachusetts to fertilize their corn by dropping in a small fish along with each seed kernel when planting corn. Similarly, a large number of "modern" drugs come from traditional herbal medications: Morphine, quinine, and codeine, for example. Oral contraceptive pills were originally obtained from a tropical yam in Mexico. In the People's Republic of China today, more than 5,000 plant species are used for medical purposes. When I studied "barefoot doctors" in China some years ago, I noticed that each such change agent aide cultivated a small garden of herbal medicines, thus greatly reducing the cost of health care (Rogens and Chen, 1980).

Many types of indigenous knowledge systems are represented by a cadre of practitioners of the traditional knowledge system. A majority of babies in Third World countries today are delivered by traditional midwives, who are usually older, uneducated, and low-income women who were taught to deliver babies by their mother or another older relative. These traditional midwives in Latin America, Africa, and Asia are perceived as highly credible by the rural and urban poor women who have the highest fertility rates. Thus, national family planning programs in many countries targeted the traditional midwives for special training courses on antiseptic methods of infant delivery, in which each trainee is rewarded with a birth-delivery kit containing disinfectant, bandages, and so forth. Traditional birth attendants typically regard these kits as desirable status symbols. In some countries these trained traditional midwives are paid a small incentive for each family planning adopter they recruit and are urged to refer their difficult birth cases to a government health clinic.

However, most professional change agents regard traditional practitioners as quacks, and either ignore them or attack them. This antagonism is an example of the empty vessels fallacy. In many nations, in addition to traditional birth attendants, every peasant village contains a traditional veterinarian, a masseuse, and a traditional medical doctor. In Latin America, *curanderos* (traditional practitioners of mental health) are widely found. For a change agent to ignore these traditional practitioners, and the indigenous knowledge systems that they represent, is to court disaster. For example, when traditional midwives were ignored or attacked by medical doctors employed by government family planning programs, the traditional birth attendants planted rumors about the contraceptive methods that were being introduced by the national family planning program, and a high rate of discontinuance resulted (Rogers, 1973). This problem occurred for the IUD in India and in Pakistan in the 1960s, for example.

Complexity

Complexity is the degree to which an innovation is perceived as relatively difficult to understand and use. Any new idea may be classified on the complexity-simplicity continuum. Some innovations are clear in their meaning to potential adopters whereas others are not. Although the research evidence is not conclusive, we suggest Generalization 6–3: *The complexity of an innovation, as perceived by members of a social system, is negatively related to its rate of adoption.*

The very first adopters of home computers in the U.S. were hobbyists, individuals who simply loved technological gadgets. Many were engineers or other individuals who had had extensive experience with mainframe and/or minicomputers before home computers became available in the late 1970s. These hobbyist adopters of home computers did not perceive the innovation as complex. It wasn't, to them. But the individuals who adopted home computers later (in the early 1980s) did not have such a high level of technical expertise, and they typically went through a period of intense frustration during the several weeks after they came home with a new Apple, Tandy, Radio Shack, or IBM personal computer. They were baffled by how to connect the various components, how to get word-processing and other software programs to run, and so forth. The frustrated adopter was puzzled when trying to read the computer manual, and could get little help from the salespeople, who talked a confusing technical jargon. Rogers, Daley, and Wu (1980) found that a period of six to eight weeks of extreme frustration characterized the new adopter of a home computer. Eventually, however, most individuals joined a computer users' club, obtained help from friends, or found other means to cope with the complexity of their home computer. But the perceived complexity of home computers was an important negative force in their rate of adoption in the early 1980s. Eventually, home computers became more user friendly, and their rate of adoption rose gradually to about 30 percent of all U.S. households by 1994.

Trialability

Trialability is the degree to which an innovation may be experimented with on a limited basis. New ideas that can be tried on the installment plan are generally adopted more rapidly than innovations that are not divisible. Some innovations are more difficult to divide for trial than are others. The personal trying-out of an innovation is a way to give meaning to an innovation, to find out how it works under one's own conditions. This trial is a means to dispel uncertainty about the new idea. We suggest Generalization 6–4: *The trialability of an innovation, as perceived by members of a social system, is positively related to its rate of adoption.*

Relatively earlier adopters of an innovation perceive trialability as more important than do later adopters (Gross, 1942; Ryan, 1948). More innovative individuals have no precedent to follow when they adopt, whereas later adopters are surrounded by peers who have already adopted the innovation. These peers act as a kind of vicarious trial for later adopters, and hence their own personal trial of the new idea is less crucial for them. So laggards move from initial trial to full-scale use more rapidly than do innovators and early adopters (see Chapter 5).

Observability

Observability is the degree to which the results of an innovation are visible to others. The results of some ideas are easily observed and communicated to others, whereas some innovations are difficult to observe or to describe to others. We suggest Generalization 6–5: *The observability of an innovation, as perceived by members of a social system, is positively related to its rate of adoption.*

Most of the innovations studied in past diffusion research are technological ideas. A technology has two components: (1) a *hardware* aspect that consists of the tool that embodies the technology as material or physical objects, and (2) a *software* aspect that consists of the information base for the tool. An example, cited in Chapter 1, is computer hardware (the electronic equipment) and software (the computer programs). The software component of a technological innovation is not so apparent to observation, so innovations in which the software aspect is dominant possess less observability, and usually have a relatively slower rate of adoption. An example is safe sex, the preventive approach recommended to individuals by health experts to avoid contracting HIV/AIDS. Safe sex is a rather ambiguous idea, perhaps including abstinence and sexual monogamy, as well as the very specific material referent of using condoms. As a result, the preventive innovation of safe sex has spread slowly, to only a few percent of the individuals at high risk for HIV/AIDS in the United States.

Cellular Telephones in the United States

The innovation of cellular telephones was first offered to American consumers in 1983, and an amazing 13 million were sold in the following 10 years. This telephone operates with a built-in rechargeable battery, so that it is portable. It is called cellular because each metropolitan area is divided into cells, each from 1 to 25 miles in radius. As one drives from one cell to another, the telephone system automatically switches a call from one cell to another without interrupting service. The usual charges for a cellular telephone are a one-time activation fee of $35, a flat rate per month of $30, and an air charge of from 25 to 50 cents per minute (depending on whether it is a peak calling time or not) for both incoming and outgoing calls.

The first adopters of cellular phones in 1983 were male executives whose companies provided a cellar phone as an office perk. At that time, a cellular phone cost about $3,000. Soon the quality of cellular service improved, the price of a cellular phone dropped to only $250, and the product became so miniaturized that it could fold into a shirt pocket. Rather quickly cellular telephones became a general consumer product. In 1993, one in three cellular phones was sold for nonbusiness use.

Cellular phones have an almost ideal set of perceived attributes, and this is undoubtedly one reason for the innovation's very rapid rate of adoption in the U.S.

1. *Relative advantage*: One of the main benefits of the cellular telephone is that it saves an estimated two hours per week in avoiding missed appointments and delayed schedules, and improves time management. These time savings are especially important for individuals living in cities like Los Angeles, New York, and Chicago, who are frequently trapped in traffic congestion. The portable nature of cellular phones frees users from being in any fixed place. One special advantage of a cellular phone in one's car is that it can be used for disabled vehicle calls or for medical emergency calls.

From the beginning, cellular phones have been an important status symbol. This is one reason why they are so often used by individuals in public places like restaurants and bars. Evidence of the prestigious nature of the innovation is provided by the widespread sale of replicas of cellular phones; more than 40,000 "Cellular Phoneys," a $16 nonworking model manufactured by a California company, Fax Systems, were sold (Teisberg, 1992). The falling cost of a cellular phone and its decreasing size (already mentioned), also spurred the rate of adoption. Gradually, cellular telephones came out of the automobile trunk and into people's pockets and purses.

2. *Compatibility*: A cellular phone connects into the existing telephone system, and allows the user to talk with anyone who has a regular telephone. Thus formation of a critical mass of cellar phone users was not necessary in the early stages of this innovation's diffusion.

3. *Complexity*: From the user's perspective, a cellular telephone operates exactly the same as a regular phone, and so it was unnecessary to learn any new skills.

4. *Observability*: Uses of cellular phones in automobiles, restaurants, and other public places helped emphasize their status-conferral to potential buyers. The innovation was highly observable.

5. *Trialability*: It is possible to borrow a friend's cellular phone for trial use. Rental cars often came equipped with a cellular telephone, which provided a trial of the innovation for many individuals.

This case illustration is based on Teisberg (1992) and various other sources.

Nintendomania: Rapid Adoption of an Entertainment Innovation

Nintendo home video game-players may be the fastest-diffusing consumer electronics product of all time. In the seven years following the introduction of this innovation in the United States in 1986, an unbelievable 50 million Nintendos were sold; they were found in about one-third of all U.S. households, representing practically every American family with boys. In comparison, only about half as many U.S. households adopted a personal computer (actually, the Nintendo game-player *is* a computer, carefully disguised), after twice as many years of diffusion. During this same fourteen years in which Nintendo game-players diffused, twice as many U.S. homes adopted VCRs (a consumer electronics product costing approximately the same price as one of Nintendo's little gray boxes), but there are some major differences. One Japanese company, Nintendo, sold *all* of the video game-players. Further, Nintendo sold *all* of the games played; this is the equivalent of one company selling all of the videos that are played on VCRs! The home video industry in the United States is big, about $6.5 billion in sales in 1993 (thus bigger than the movie box-office take), but it is fragmented among numerous companies.

Nintendo is a 100-year-old company headquartered in Kyoto, Japan, that makes playing cards, and, in recent decades, electronic entertainment equipment. Nintendo has only 850 employees in Japan, where the game-players and the video game cartridges are created and manufactured; the company earns an incredible $1.5 million per employee (there are additional employees in sales and distribution in the United States and Europe and some of the manufacturing in Japan is done by subcontractors). In 1992, Nintendo's U.S. sales were responsible for 10 percent of the immense U.S./Japanese trade deficit! So the Nintendo company is tremendously profitable.

Much of Nintendo's success with these video game-players traces to some very astute product planning by Hiroshi Yamauchi, the company president, in which he intuitively utilized the five perceived attributes of innovations to achieve a very rapid rate of adoption in Japan, where the game-player was introduced several years before it was sold in America. The Nintendo Famicom (for "family computer") was not the first video game-player, not by a long ways. That distinction belongs to Nolan Bushnell and his Atari Corporation, which pioneered the video game industry in 1972 with the game of "Pong." Bushnell built this simple game around a new type of semiconductor chip called a microprocessor, in his home workshop in Northern California's Silicon Valley. Bushnell placed his "Pong" console in Andy Capp's tavern in Sunnyvale, California. The next day, Capp telephoned Bushnell to complain that the video machine was broken. Bushnell soon found the problem: The coin box was so filled with quarters that it had plugged the machine. He quickly installed a larger coin box, knowing that he was on the way to becoming a multi-millionaire. Bushnell called his new company Atari, a Japanese word equivalent in meaning to "check" in the Oriental game of Go. Unfortunately, Bushnell was a poor manager, his Atari Corporation grew too fast, Warner Communication purchased it, and then managed it even more poorly. The quality of many of the Atari games was poor, and in 1984, after selling 20 million home-game-players, the Atari company faced bankruptcy, leaving a very bad taste with consumers. The home video industry seemed to be dead.

Nintendo's Yamauchi didn't think so. He asked his R&D engineers to come up with a video game-player that took advantage of advances in microelectronics, and with games that would be fun to play. Yamauchi decided to leave off the computer keyboard and disk drives (as disks can be copied). Instead, one inserts a video game in the Nintendo Famicom game-player as a cartridge. Yamauchi shrewdly planned a razor-and-razor-blade strategy: The Famicom game-player sold relatively cheaply (about $100), while the games were relatively expensive ($60 per game). Nintendo introduced each new game as an arcade game, in order to generate excitement among young boys. Then the game would be made available for the Famicom home game-player. Each new game had a relatively short period of popularity of only several months; then it was replaced by a yet-newer game. Many games were violent, dealing with street fighting, racing, and sports like football. But some games centered on wit and humor and surprise, such as Nintendo's popular character, Mario the plumber. Nintendo maintained complete control over all games. Special circuitry was built into the Famicom game-player so that it would reject any game cartridge not made by Nintendo; this circuitry was changed from time to time, so that a competing company could not sell its games to run on Nintendo game-players. In short, Nintendo had a complete lock on the home video game industry in Japan. Soon, the Nintendo Famicoms were in 40 percent of all Japanese households.

Now it was time to invade the U.S. market. President Yamauchi selected his son-in-law, Minoru Arakawa, who held a masters degree in engineering from MIT and had worked in North America, to head Nintendo's U.S. operations. These two Japanese executives knew that introducing a new video game-player would be extremely difficult in the United States, following on the heels of Atari's 1984 disaster. Their prior success in Japan helped; for one thing, the parent Nintendo company could provide $50 million for launching the innovation in the United States. Arakawa, with help from his father-in-law, carefully positioned the new product's attributes to suit U.S. consumers, while retaining the basic hardware of the Famicom game-player.

1. *Relative advantage*: The fun, high-quality games that had been created in Japan were immediately available for use in the Nintendo game-players in America. The Nintendo game-player had higher resolution graphics and thus more lifelike features that the old Atari machines. The Nintendo Company created shortages of their most popular games so as to fan the heat of "Nintendomania" by creating the impression that the games were even more widely popular than they actually were, and thus raising their perceived relative advantage.

2. *Compatibility*: Nintendo's "razor blade" strategy, mentioned previously, meant that the hardware was priced relatively low, so that the game-player was very affordable. Nintendo expected to make its main profits on the software games. Parents bought the game-players, usually as a Christmas or birthday present for a son, and often after considerable urging from their child. Nintendo aimed its advertising mainly at children, expecting them to persuade their parents.

3. *Complexity*: The video game-players were called "Nintendo Entertainment Systems" (rather than "Famicoms") in the United States. Every effort was made to avoid identifying the product as a computer: It was sold in toy stores (like Toys 'Я' Us), not in computer stores. As in Japan, the little gray box did not come with a keyboard or a disk drive (although a panel in the bottom can be removed to reveal a port for a cable connector to a keyboard, modem, or other computer equipment). The game-player was easy to attach to a television set, and use of the two hand-controllers was simple to understand. Even the instruction booklet that came with each game car-

tridge was extremely simple, so simple that many players did not even bother to read it. Further, Nintendo in America provided an 800-number to call if a player encountered problems; soon this number received half a million calls per week (it eventually was discontinued for reasons of cost).

4. *Observability*: Nintendo launched a huge advertising campaign for its Nintendo Entertainment System, and for the most popular games ("Mario," "Super Mario," and "Tetris"). As in Japan, new games were introduced first in video arcades. Nintendo mounted tie-in sales and advertising campaigns with Pepsi Cola, McDonalds, and a Hollywood film. Kids exchanged information about new Nintendo games on the playground, at school, and on other occasions when they were together. High visibility for the game-players and the games was provided in toy stores, where special "World of Nintendo" areas were created (the toy stores were willing to do so because Nintendo products made up 20 percent or more of their total sales).

5. *Trialability*: Any kid passing a Nintendo display in a toy store could stop and play a Nintendo game. The cheap-hardware-expensive-software strategy of Nintendo, already mentioned, also helped achieve a rapid rate of adoption of the Nintendo Entertainment Systems. The company wanted individuals to experiment with their new product, to convince themselves of its superiority over the old Atari machines.

Despite this careful product positioning by Nintendo, it was very difficult to introduce their game-players in 1986 in America. When Minoru Arakawa and his staff contacted toy distributors in the pilot launch in New York, the distributors typically said: "I got this job a year or two ago when my predecessor was fired for overstocking on Atari video games. So don't talk to me about a new video game-player." At first, Nintendo had to guarantee that it would buy back any unsold product. Bit by bit, some toy stores were convinced to carry the Nintendo Entertainment Systems. After several months, 25,000 game-players were sold in New York. Then it was on to Los Angeles to start the diffusion of Nintendo Entertainment Systems there. Gradually, the entire U.S. was covered. Sales began to pick up. The persistence that is characteristic of Japanese management began to pay off. Young boys became addicted to the Nintendo games, particularly those featuring Mario the plumber. Soon each new Nintendo game created a sensation, as toy stores quickly sold out of their supply. By 1993, the Nintendo Company of America, headquartered in the Seattle area, was selling an unbelievable 600,000 games and game-players *per day*!

A worthy competitor finally challenged Nintendo in 1990, when Sega Enterprises (another Japanese company) released the Genesis game-player, a machine with better graphics than the Nintendo Entertainment System. Nintendo countered with its Super Nintendo Entertainment System in 1991. The following year, 1992, Sega announced a CD-ROM attachment for its Genesis game-player; the games had such high resolution that they resembled movies. Unlike a CD disc which can just store music, a compact-disc-record-only-memory (or CD-ROM) can carry music, still and moving pictures, voices, and computer programs. In Japan, the Nintendo Company then made the next technological advance. The computer port in the bottom panel of each Nintendo game-player was utilized to connect the little machines into electronic networks for telebanking and stock trading. By 1993, half a million Japanese homes had joined the Nintendo electronic network. Something similar would probably be introduced in the U.S.

This case illustration is based on Sheff (1993) and Tetzeli (1993).

Summary

This chapter suggested five attributes of innovations by which an innovation can be described, and showed that individual receiver's perceptions of these attributes predict an innovation's rate of adoption.

Rate of adoption is the relative speed with which an innovation is adopted by members of a social system. In addition to the perceived attributes of an innovation, such other variables affect its rate of adoption as (1) the type of innovation-decision, (2) the nature of communication channels diffusing the innovation at various stages in the innovation-decision process, (3) the nature of the social system, and (4) the extent of change agents' efforts in diffusing the innovation.

Relative advantage is the degree to which an innovation is perceived as better than the idea it supersedes. The relative advantage of an innovation, as perceived by members of a social system, is positively related to its rate of adoption (Generalization 6–1). *Overadoption* is the adoption of an innovation when experts feel that it should be rejected.

Compatibility is the degree to which an innovation is perceived as consistent with the existing values, past experiences, and needs of potential adopters. The perceived compatibility of an innovation is positively related to its rate of adoption (Generalization 6–2).

Complexity is the degree to which an innovation is perceived as relatively difficult to understand and to use. The perceived complexity of an innovation is negatively related to its rate of adoption (Generalization 6–3).

Trialability is the degree to which an innovation may be experimented with on a limited basis. The perceived trialability of an innovation is positively related to its rate of adoption (Generalization 6–4).

Observability is the degree to which the results of an innovation are visible to others. The perceived observability of an innovation is positively related to its rate of adoption (Generalization 6–5).

7

INNOVATIVENESS AND ADOPTER CATEGORIES

Be not the first by whom the new is tried, Nor the last to lay the old aside.
　　　　—Alexander Pope, *An Essay on Criticism*, Part II.

A slow advance in the beginning, followed by rapid and uniformly accelerated progress, followed again by progress that continues to slacken until it finally stops: These are the three ages of . . . invention. . . . If taken as a guide by the statistician and by the sociologists, [they] would save many illusions.
　　　　—Gabriel Tarde, *The Laws of Imitation*, p.127.

The individuals in a social system do not adopt an innovation at the same time. Rather, they adopt in an over-time sequence, so that individuals can be classified into adopter categories on the basis of when they first begin using a new idea. We could describe each individual adopter in a system in terms of time of adoption, but this would be extremely tedious. It is much more efficient to use adopter categories consisting of individuals with a similar degree of innovativeness.

We know more about *innovativeness*, the degree to which an individual or other unit of adoption is relatively earlier in adopting new ideas than other members of a system, than about any other concept in diffusion research. Because increased innovativeness is the main objective of change agencies, it became the main dependent variable in diffusion research. Innovativeness indicates overt behavioral change, the ultimate goal of most diffusion programs, rather than just cognitive or attitudinal change. So innovativeness is a bottom-line type of behavior in the diffusion process.

This chapter suggests a method of categorizing adopters and demonstrates the usefulness of this technique with research findings about the characteristics of adopter categories.

The Diffusion of Farm Innovations in Saucío, A Colombian Village in the Andes

The Saucío study in the early 1960s was a turning point for diffusion research in several important respects. This investigation in Colombia was the first diffusion study in a peasant village in Latin America, Africa, or Asia (a diffusion study by Syed Rahim was underway in Bangladesh at about the same time). All of the 500 or so diffusion researches completed by 1960 were conducted in North America and Europe, despite the fact that 80 percent of the world's population lived in the Third World. At the time that the Saucío study was carried out in 1962, it was not known whether or not the diffusion of innovations would be similar in peasant villages. These systems were characterized by high levels of illiteracy, poverty, and by very limited mass media exposure.

The Saucío study was conducted by Paul J. Deutschmann, a professor of communication from Michigan State University, and Orlando Fals Borda, an American-trained Ph.D. who founded the field of sociology in Colombia. Fals Borda had been carrying out research in Saucío for a decade, and had introduced various new ideas in the village as experiments in social change: A new school building, a sewing cooperative, a cooperative store, and two important agricultural innovations (the vaccination of chickens against cholera, and a new potato variety, *Papas Monserrate*). The seventy-one farmers of Saucío depended on potatoes as their main crop, and also raised some poultry, livestock, and wheat.

Paul Deutschmann had studied the diffusion of news events in the United States (Deutschmann and Danielson, 1960), and was well acquainted with research on the diffusion of agricultural innovations. Fals Borda also had become familiar with agricultural diffusion research when he was earning his doctorate at the University of Minnesota. In 1961, Deutschmann moved from East Lansing to San José, Costa Rica, where he directed a program on communication research in Latin America. He provided funds for the collaborative restudy of Saucío, with Fals Borda and his students at the National University of Colombia (in Bogotá), using a diffusion approach.

Saucío was a small village located more than two miles high in the steep volcanic soils of the Andes Mountains. The residents of Saucío had originally been Indians, conquered by Spanish explorers 450 years ago. By 1962 most aspects of Indian culture had disappeared. The Saucíans were poor, with half of the farms under four acres in size. Forty-two percent of the farmers were illiterate, and only two of the seventy-one farmers had more than four years of formal education. Illiteracy and poverty limited their mass media exposure. Only 14 percent of the households owned a radio, and but 44 percent listened to radio even occasionally. Compared to a media-saturated nation like the United States, Saucío appeared to be an unlikely setting for the diffusion of innovations.

However two of the six innovations of study, chemical fertilizers and spray guns for insecticides and fungicides, had diffused over the past 30 years in Saucío, reaching almost 100-percent adoption. The rate of adoption for these two innovations was similar to that for hybrid seed corn in Iowa (Ryan and Gross, 1943). Two other innovations, a concentrated poultry and livestock feed and a potato fungicide, diffused in the ten years prior to the 1962 diffusion study, with both reaching 75-percent adoption. All six innovations of study (including the two introduced by Fals Borda) followed an S-shaped curve over time. During the first years of the introduction of an innovation in the village, only a few farmers adopted each year. Then a critical mass of adopters was reached, and the cumulative rate of adoption speeded up as many farmers adopted each year. Finally, the rate of adoption gradually leveled off as fewer and fewer farmers remained to adopt the innovation.

Deutschmann and Fals Borda combined all six innovations into a composite measure of innovativeness, the general tendency for individuals to adopt new ideas. Four farmers in Saucío had adopted all six innovations. In contrast, one farmer had not adopted any of the innovations. Each villager who had adopted an innovation was asked when such adoption had taken place, and greater weight was given in the innovativeness scores for relatively earlier adoption. The cumulative distribution of the innovativeness scores for the seventy-one farmers was S-shaped and approached normality. Thus the respondents were classified into five adopter categories:

1. *Innovators:* The two farmers with the highest innovativeness scores
2. *Early adopters:* The ten farmers with the next highest innovativeness scores
3. *Early majority:* The twenty-three farmers with the next highest innovativeness scores
4. *Late majority:* The twenty-three farmers with the next highest innovativeness scores
5. *Laggards:* The thirteen farmers with the lowest innovativeness scores

Deutschmann and Fals Borda (1962b) then proceeded to determine the characteristics of the five adopter categories, and to compare these results with the present author's study of Ohio farmers (Rogers, 1961). In both Saucío and in Ohio, farm size, formal education, mass media exposure, and opinion leadership (measured as the degree to which a farmer was sought by others for information and advice about agricultural innovations) were the variables most highly related to innovativeness. That is, innovators and laggards differed most sharply on these socioeconomic and communication variables in both Saucío and Ohio. The diffusion of agricultural innovations seemed to display rather striking similarities in the two quite different settings. The diffusion process seemed to represent a general pattern of human behavior.

However, there were also certain sharp differences between the two systems of study regarding the diffusion of innovations. For example, the range in average farm size from innovators to laggards in Ohio was 339 to 128 acres (Rogers, 1961). In Saucío, the most innovative farmer had 100 times the amount of farm land as the least innovative farmer! Such extremes in socioeconomic status are generally characteristic of peasant villages in Third World nations. As in other diffusion researches, the innovators in Saucío were much more cosmopolite than the laggards, traveling outside of the village to market towns and cities, and also learning about new ideas from the mass media.

The diffusion process in Saucío was mainly via interpersonal communication channels within the village. In previous farm diffusion research in the United States, the mass media were most important at the knowledge stage in the innovation-decision process. However, in Saucío 43 percent of the sources/channels reported by farmers at the knowledge stage involved face-to-face communication with other farmers in the village. Only five farmers reported using mass media sources/channels at the knowledge stage in adopting an innovation. This heavy dependence on interpersonal communication in Saucío seemed to slow the diffusion process, especially for the first two innovations to diffuse, in the 1930s. Their S-curves of adoption had a long "tail" to the left, in which five to ten years were required for the rate of adoption to take off. So word-of-mouth was particularly important in the diffusion process in Saucío.

The Ryan and Gross (1943) hybrid seed corn study found that most farmers did not adopt an innovation until they had tried it on an experimental basis on their own farm. In fact, the typical Iowa farmers adopted the new seed only after seven years of trial planting. In contrast, most of the Saucío villagers went directly to full-scale use of the six innovations without first trying them out. Perhaps such impulsive behavior occurred because the Colombian villagers did not have a "scientific" learning-from-experience attitude, due to their low level of formal education. Deutschmann and Fals Borda (1962b) suggest that such plunge-adoption decisions may have been due to the conditioning of Colombian peasants to respond immediately to authoritarian sources. The more recently introduced innovations in Saucío were more likely to be adopted on a trial basis, suggesting that the peasant farmers were learning to evaluate the agricultural innovations on the basis of their own experimental experience.

Although mass media exposure in Saucío was quite limited, innovators had much higher exposure than did laggards, averaging a mass media exposure score (composed of radio, newspapers, and books) of twenty-six, while laggards averaged only four. Innovators were more likely than laggards to utilize mass media sources/channels at the knowledge stage, 11 percent to 2 percent. Innovators were also more cosmopolite at the knowledge stage, using sources/channels from outside the village, 33 percent to 17 percent. So the innovators played an important role for the village system in getting the diffusion process underway for an innovation. Once an innovation was introduced from cosmopolite, mass media sources, the diffusion process then became self-sustaining by means of interpersonal communication channels within the village.

The Saucío study became a diffusion classic, opening the way for hundreds of diffusion investigations to be conducted in Third World countries in the years that followed. The Deutschmann and Fals Borda study demonstrated the usefulness of the conceptual tools of innovativeness and adopter categories.

This case illustration is based on Deutschmann and Fals Borda (1962b), and on discussions with them about their study.

Classifying Adopter Categories on the Basis of Innovativeness

Titles of adopter categories were once about as numerous as diffusion researchers themselves. The inability of researchers in the early days of diffusion research to agree on common semantic ground in assigning terminology led to this plethora of adopter descriptions. The most innovative individuals were termed "progressists," "high-triers," "experimentals," "lighthouses," "advance scouts," and "ultraadopters." The least innovative individuals were called "drones," "parochials," and "diehards." This fertile disarray of adopter categories and methods of categorization emphasized the need for standardization. How could a reader compare research findings about adopter categories from one study to another until there was standardization of both the nomenclature and the classification system? Fortunately, one method of adopter categorization gained a dominant position. It is based upon the S-shaped curve of adoption.

The S-Shaped Curve of Adoption and Normality

The time element of the diffusion process allows us to classify adopter categories and to draw diffusion curves. The adoption of an innovation usually follows a normal, bell-shaped curve when plotted over time on a frequency basis. If the cumulative number of adopters is plotted, the result is an S-shaped curve. Figure 7–1 shows that the same adoption data can be represented by either a bell-shaped (frequency) curve, or an S-shaped (cumulative) curve.

The S-shaped adopter distribution rises slowly at first when there are few adopters in each time period. It then accelerates to a maximum until half of the individuals in the system have adopted. Then the S-curve increases at a gradually slower rate as fewer and fewer remaining individuals adopt the innovation. This S-shaped curve is normal. Why? The reasoning rests on the role of information and uncertainty reduction in the diffusion process.

Individuals learn a new skill, or item of knowledge, or set of facts, through a learning process that, when plotted over time, typically follows a normal curve. When an individual is confronted with a new situation in a psychologist's laboratory, the subject initially makes many errors. After several trials, the errors decrease until a certain learning capacity has been reached. When plotted, these data yield a curve of increasing gains at first and later become a curve of decreasing gains. The gain in learning per

Figure 7–1. The Number of New Adopters Each Year, and the Cumulative Number of Adopters, of Hybrid Seed Corn in Two Iowa Communities

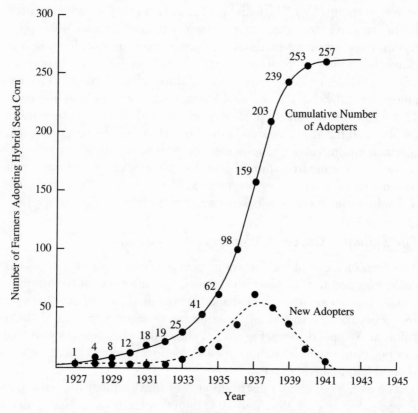

The cumulative number of adopters of hybrid seed corn approaches an S-shaped curve over time, while the frequency distribution of the number of mean adopters per year approaches a normal, bell-shaped curve.

Source: Based on Ryan and Gross (1943).

trial is proportionate to (1) the product of the amount already learned, and (2) the amount remaining to be learned before the limit of learning is reached. This nature of the learning curve provides a reason to expect an adopter distribution to be normal.

Many human traits are normally distributed, whether the trait is a physical characteristic, such as weight or height, or a behavioral trait, such as intelligence or the learning of information. Hence, a variable such as the degree of innovativeness is expected also to be normally distributed. If a social system is substituted for the individual in the learning curve, it seems reasonable to expect that experience with the innovation is gained as each successive member in the social system adopts it. Each adoption in the social system is in a sense equivalent to a learning trial by an individual.

We expect a normal adopter distribution for an innovation because of the cumulatively increasing influences upon an individual to adopt or reject an innovation, resulting from the activation of peer networks about the innovation in a system. This influence results from the increasing rate of knowledge and adoption (or rejection) of the innovation in the system. We know that the adoption of a new idea results from information exchange through interpersonal networks. If the first adopter of an innovation discusses it with two other members of the system, and each of these two adopters passes the new idea along to two peers, and so forth, the resulting distribution follows a binomial expansion, a mathematical function that follows a normal shape when plotted over a series of successive generations. The process is similar to that of an unchecked infectious epidemic (Bailey, 1957, pp. 29-37, 155-159).

Of course, several assumptions underlying this hypothetical example are seldom found in reality. For instance, members of a system do not have completely free access to interact with one another. Status differences, geographical barriers, and other variables affect who talks to whom about an innovation. The S-shaped diffusion curve begins to level off after half of the individuals in a social system have adopted, because each new adopter finds it increasingly difficult to tell the new idea to a peer who has not yet adopted, for such nonknowers become increasingly scarce.

The S-shaped curve of diffusion "takes off" once interpersonal networks become activated in spreading subjective evaluations of an innovation from peer to peer in a system (see Figure 7–1). The part of the diffusion curve from about 10 percent adoption to 20 percent adoption is the heart of the diffusion process. After that point, it is often impossible to stop the further diffusion of a new idea, even if one wished to do so.

Ryan and Gross (1943) tested the S-shaped diffusion curve for hybrid seed corn in Iowa, using the chi square goodness-of-fit test to determine whether or not the rate of adoption deviated significantly from a cumulative normal curve. It did. In the years from 1932 to 1935, prior to the average year of adoption in 1937, fewer Iowa farmers adopted the innovation than were expected to do so on the basis of the normal curve (see Figure 7-1). Then, in the following period from 1937 to 1939, many more farmers adopted the new seed than predicted by a normal curve. There seemed to be rather strong resistance to the new idea in the early part of the diffusion process, which was then overcome, perhaps after a critical mass of satisfied adopters was achieved. Nevertheless, the actual rate of adoption over time generally approached a normal S-curve, with year-to-year deviations from normality (noted above) tending to cancel each other out over the total diffusion process.

In 1994, Joey Donahue at Los Alamos National Laboratories, used a powerful supercomputer program called MINUIT to reanalyze the Ryan and Gross (1943) hybrid corn data. The results of this analysis supported Ryan and Gross's original conclusions that the rate of adoption deviated from normality, even though the rate of adoption of hybrid seed was generally S-shaped. The main deviation from normality occurred near the mean year of adoption, around 1937, when a peak in annual adoption took place.

Generalization 7–1 states: *Adopter distributions follow a bell-shaped curve over time and approach normality*. Evidence supporting this statement comes from investigations of agricultural, consumer, and other innovations in a variety of systems, in the United States and in other nations (for example, Rogers, 1958; Bose, 1964; Ryan, 1948; Beal and Rogers, 1960; Dimit, 1954; and Hamblin and others, 1973). A variety of different mathematical formulas have been proposed to fit the shape of adopter distributions. This work is generally in agreement that the S-shaped diffusion curves are essentially normal. This point has very useful implications for classifying adopter categories.

The S-shaped curve only describes cases of successful innovation, in which an innovation spreads to almost all of the potential adopters in a social system. Many, many innovations are not successful. After only a few adopters in a system, the innovation may meet with rejection, so that its rate of adoption levels off and, through discontinuance, nosedives. The S-curve, it must be remembered, is innovation-specific and system-specific, describing the diffusion of a particular new idea among the member-units of a particular system.

The S-curve of diffusion is so ubiquitous that students of diffusion may expect every innovation to be adopted over time in an S-shaped pattern. However, some innovations do not display an S-shaped rate of adoption, perhaps for some idiosyncratic reason or another. The innovation may be taboo in nature, so that individuals cannot discuss it freely. Perhaps the new idea is applicable only to certain unique population groups within the total population. For example, adopting safe sex may only be appropriate for individuals who are at high risk for contracting HIV/AIDS. In this case, the diffusion curve for the idea of safe sex will not be S-shaped for the entire population.

The main point here is not to assume that an S-shaped rate of adoption is an inevitability. Rather, the shape of the adopter distribution for an innovation ought to be regarded as an open question, to be determined empirically. In most cases when this has been done, an adopter distribution follows a bell-shaped, normal curve, or is S-shaped on a cumulative basis.

The Method of Adopter Categorization

Anyone seeking to standardize adopter categories must decide: (1) on the number of adopter categories, (2) on the portion of the members of a system to include in each category, and (3) on the method, statistical or otherwise, of defining the adopter categories.

The criterion for adopter categorization is *innovativeness*, the degree to which an individual or other unit of adoption is relatively earlier in adopting new ideas than other members of a social system. Innovativeness is a relative dimension, in that an individual has more or less of it than others in a system. Innovativeness is a continuous variable, and partitioning it into discrete categories is a conceptual device, much like dividing the continuum of social status into upper, middle, and lower classes. Such classification is a simplification that aids the understanding of human behavior, although it loses some information as a result of grouping individuals.

Ideally, a set of categories should be (1) *exhaustive*, or include all the units of study, (2) *mutually exclusive*, or exclude a unit of study that appears in one category from also appearing in any other category, and (3) derived from a single *classificatory principle*.

We have previously demonstrated that S-shaped adopter distributions closely approach normality. This is important because the normal frequency distribution has several characteristics that are useful in classifying adopters. One characteristic or parameter is the mean ($\bar{x}$), or average, of the individuals in the system. Another parameter of a distribution is its standard deviation (*sd*), a measure of dispersion or variation about the mean. The standard deviation indicates the average amount of variance from the mean for a sample of individuals.

These two statistics, the mean (*x*) and the standard deviation (*sd*), are used to divide a normal adopter distribution into categories. Vertical lines are drawn to mark off the standard deviations on either side of the mean so that the normal curve is divided into categories with a standardized percentage of respondents in each category. Figure 7–2 shows the normal frequency distribution divided into the five adopter categories. These five adopter categories and the approximate percentage of individuals included in each are located on the normal adopter distribution in Figure 7–2.

The area lying to the left of the mean time of adoption (of innovation) minus two standard deviations includes the first 2.5 percent of the individuals in a system to adopt an innovation—the *innovators*. The next 13.5 percent to adopt the new idea are included in the area between the mean minus one standard deviation and the mean minus two standard deviations; they are labeled *early adopters*. The next 34 percent of the adopters, called *early majority*, are included in the area between the mean date of adoption and the mean minus one standard deviation. Between the mean and one standard deviation to the right of the mean are the next 34 percent to adopt the new idea, the *late majority*. The last 16 percent to adopt are called *laggards*.

Figure 7–2. Adopter Categorization on the Basis of Innovativeness

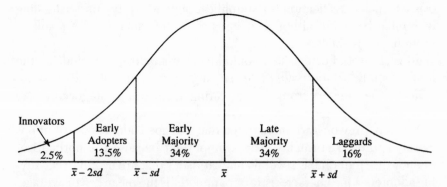

The innovativeness dimension, as measured by the time at which an individual adopts an innovation or innovations, is continuous. The innovativeness variable is partitioned into five adopter categories by laying off standard deviations from the average time of adoption (*x*).

This adopter classification is not symmetrical in that there are three adopter categories to the left of the mean and only two to the right. One solution would be to break laggards into two categories, such as early and late laggards, but laggards seem to form a fairly homogeneous category. Similarly, innovators and early adopters could be combined into a single category in order to achieve symmetry, but their quite different characteristics suggest they are two distinct adopter categories.

One difficulty with our method of adopter classification is incomplete adoption, which occurs for innovations that have not reached 100 percent use. This incomplete adoption means that our fivefold classification scheme is not exhaustive. The problem of incomplete adoption or non-adoption is eliminated when a series of innovations are combined into a composite innovativeness scale.

Three principles of categorization were suggested previously. Innovativeness as a criterion for adopter categorization fulfills each of these requirements. The five adopter categories are exhaustive (except for nonadopters), mutually exclusive, and derived from one classification principle. The method of adopter categorization just described is the most widely used in diffusion research today. It is practically the only method of adopter categorization.

Adopter Categories as Ideal Types

The five adopter categories set forth in this chapter are ideal types. *Ideal types* are conceptualizations based on observations of reality that are designed to make comparisons possible. Ideal types are not simply an average of all observations about an adopter category. Exceptions to the ideal types can be found. If no exceptions or deviations existed, ideal types would not be necessary. Ideal types are based on abstractions from empirical investigations. Pronounced breaks in the innovativeness continuum do not occur between each of the five categories.

We now present an overview of the dominant characteristics and values of each adopter category, which will be followed by more detailed generalizations.

Innovators: Venturesome

Venturesomeness is almost an obsession with innovators. This interest in new ideas leads them out of a local circle of peer networks and into more cosmopolite social relationships. Communication patterns and friendships among a clique of innovators are common, even though the geographical distance between the innovators may be considerable. Being an innovator has several prerequisites. Control of substantial financial resources is helpful to absorb the possible loss from an unprofitable innovation. The ability to understand and apply complex technical knowledge is also needed. The innovator must be able to cope with a high degree of uncertainty about an innovation at the time of adoption.

The salient value of the innovator is venturesomeness, due to a desire for the rash, the daring, and the risky. The innovator must also be willing to accept an occasional setback when a new idea proves unsuccessful, as inevitably happens. While an innovator may not be respected by the other members of a local system, the innovator plays an important role in the diffusion process: That of launching the new idea in the system by importing the innovation from outside of the system's boundaries. Thus, the innovator plays a gatekeeping role in the flow of new ideas into a system.

Early Adopters: Respect

Early adopters are a more integrated part of the local social system than are innovators. Whereas innovators are cosmopolites, early adopters are localites. This adopter category, more than any other, has the greatest degree of opinion leadership in most systems. Potential adopters look to early adopters for advice and information about the innovation. The early adopter is considered by many as "the individual to check with" before using a new idea. This adopter category is generally sought by change agents as a local missionary for speeding the diffusion process. Because early adopters are not too far ahead of the average individual in innovativeness, they serve as a role model for many other members of a social system.

The early adopter is respected by his or her peers, and is the embodiment of successful, discrete use of new ideas. The early adopter knows that to continue to earn this esteem of colleagues and to maintain a central position in the communication networks of the system, he or she must make judicious innovation-decisions. The early adopter decreases uncertainty about a new idea by adopting it, and then conveying a subjective evaluation of the innovation to near-peers through interpersonal networks.

Early Majority: Deliberate

The early majority adopt new ideas just before the average member of a system. The early majority interact frequently with their peers, but seldom hold positions of opinion leadership in a system. The early majority's unique position between the very early and the relatively late to adopt makes them an important link in the diffusion process. They provide interconnectedness in the system's interpersonal networks. The early majority are the most numerous adopter categories, making up one-third of the members of a system.

The early majority may deliberate for some time before completely adopting a new idea. Their innovation-decision period is relatively longer than that of the innovator and the early adopter. "Be not the first by which the new is tried, Nor the last to lay the old aside," quoted at the top of the present chapter, particularly fits the thinking of the early majority. They follow with deliberate willingness in adopting innovations, but seldom lead.

Late Majority: Skeptical

The late majority adopt new ideas just after the average member of a system. Like the early majority, the late majority make up one-third of the members of a system. Adoption may be both an economic necessity for the late majority, and the result of increasing network pressures from peers. Innovations are approached with a skeptical and cautious air, and the late majority do not adopt until most others in their system have done so. The weight of system norms must definitely favor an innovation before the late majority are convinced. The pressure of peers is necessary to motivate adoption. Their relatively scarce resources mean that most of the uncertainty about a new idea must be removed before the late majority feel that it is safe to adopt.

Laggards: Traditional

Laggards are the last in a social system to adopt an innovation. They possess almost no opinion leadership. Laggards are the most localite in their outlook of all adopter categories; many are near isolates in the social networks of their system. The point of reference for the laggard is the past. Decisions are often made in terms of what has been done previously, and these individuals interact primarily with others who also have relatively traditional values. Laggards tend to be suspicious of innovations and change agents. Their innovation-decision process is relatively lengthy, with adoption and use lagging far behind awareness-knowledge of a new idea. Resistance to innovations on the part of laggards may be entirely rational from the laggards' viewpoint, as their resources are limited and they must be certain that a new idea will not fail before they can adopt. The laggard's precarious economic position forces the individual to be extremely cautious in adopting innovations.

"Laggard" might sound like a bad name. This title of the adopter category carries an invidious distinction (in much the same way that "lower class" is a negative nomenclature). Laggard is a bad name because most nonlaggards have a strong pro-innovation bias (see Chapter 3). Diffusion scholars who use adopter categories in their research do not mean any particular disrespect by the term "laggard." Indeed, if they used any other term instead of laggards, such as "late adopters," it would soon have a similar negative connotation. But it is a mistake to imply that laggards are somehow at fault for being relatively late to adopt. System-blame may more accurately describe the reality of the laggards' situation.

A People Who Said No to Innovation: The Old Order Amish

If you were an Old Order Amish person living in the United States today, you would not believe in using buttons (instead you would fasten your clothing with hooks and eyes), tractors, automobiles (which are considered "worldly"), family planning, wallpaper, cigarettes, wristwatches, or neckties; you would not engage in dating, military service, or voting; and you would not be educated beyond the eighth grade. You would believe that large families are good (the average Amish family has seven to nine children), that the only proper occupation is farming, and in marrying an Amish mate.

The Amish are a religious sect that began in Switzerland during the 1690s when the followers of Jakob Ammann (hence the name "Amish") split off from existing Christian religions. The Amish were persecuted in Europe, and began migrating to Pennsylvania prior to the Revolutionary War of 1775. About 500 Amish came during this initial wave; a later wave of 3,000 more Amish came after the War of 1812.

Today about 100,000 Old Order Amish live in rural communities in the U.S. In the past 80 years, the number of Amish in America has increased by 700 percent. Ohio has the largest Amish population, followed by Pennsylvania and Indiana, with Amish communities also located in Michigan, Iowa, Kansas, Kentucky, and Florida.

It is impossible to remain Amish without marriage to an Amish mate, so inbreeding is a problem. Only eight family names account for nearly 80 percent of all Amish people in Ohio, Pennsylvania, and Indiana. Virtually all of the several thousand Amish people in Lancaster County, Pennsylvania, are descendants of Christian Fisher, who was born in 1757. The selection of marriage partners among the Amish is limited by their horse-and-buggy transportation, as they seldom marry an individual living outside of their local community.

When an Amish person deviates from church teachings, he or she is punished by a form of excommunication known as shunning (or *Meidung*). When a person is shunned, no other Amish individual may speak to the individual. As a member of the Old Order Amish only knows others of the same faith, shunning means that the individual hasn't a friend in the world. Even the member's children, brothers, sisters, and spouse must refuse to speak to the individual, or even to eat at the same table. Marital relations are forbidden. Only upon public repentance by the sinner is the excommunication lifted. For example, a young Amishman in Ohio was shunned for being seen driving a car. After a week of such punishment, he came before the local congregation and repented symbolically by tearing up his driver's license.

Despite the social pressure exerted by Amish parents on their youth, not all remain in the religion. An estimated 20 percent defect. The high birth rates of the Amish, however, more than make up for this attrition. Many who leave the Amish faith join the Mennonite church, which is closely related in its lifestyle, but is less strict.

Amish children have almost no contact with the non-Amish world around them. TV, radio, magazines, and non-Amish schooling are forbidden. Friendships with non-Amish children are also banned. Amish teenagers are forbidden to attend public high schools where their parents fear they will be lost to popular music, fast cars, and the practice of going steady. A distinctive language also is important in maintaining socialization of the young into the Old Order Amish culture. The Amish speak a special German dialect, which also sets them apart from the non-Amish.

The religious persecution of the Amish during their European beginnings several centuries ago led to a strong value on separation from the society within which they live. The Amish stress this history of persecution in socializing their children; each schoolchild reads about the Amish martyrs who were tortured, raped, and killed by their Christian countrymen in Europe.

One key ingredient in Amish survival is rich soil, which the Amish farm in a labor-intensive manner, growing tobacco, vegetables, fruit, and specialty crops. They also carry on such intensive livestock enterprises as dairying and raising chickens. The Amish family seeks to set up each of their offspring in farming. Tractors are rejected to maintain labor opportunities for Amish children. Hard work and high fertility go hand-in-hand for the Amish, as they seek to balance their rapidly increasing population with their local environment. In recent years, escalating land prices threaten the Amish way of life. Today about half of the adult Amish people in Lancaster County work in such nonfarm employment as carpentry, blacksmithing, crafts, cheese-making, or in restaurants. One Amish business converts tractor-drawn farm implements to horse-drawn equipment, replacing pneumatic tires with metal rims.

While the Amish must say "no" to most consumer innovations and to many agricultural innovations, they are generally very innovative in adopting new ideas that fit with their religious and family values. For example, Sommers and Napier (1993) gathered personal interview data from a sample of 366 Amish and non-Amish farmers living in three Ohio counties. The Amish farmers were greatly concerned with the problem of ground water pollution by agricultural chemicals. Such protection of soil and water resources is believed by the Amish to have a religious significance. Living in harmony with nature is highly valued, understandably so because the Amish way of life is dependent on high agricultural productivity. Community norms among the Amish reflect this value on conservation, so the same interpersonal pressures that oppose adoption of farm machinery, automobiles, and tractors encourage farmers to apply less fertilizer and pesticides.

Amish families are culturally forbidden to use modern technologies like household water filtering systems or to purchase bottled water (Sommers and Napier, 1993). Accordingly, the adoption of such farm conservation innovations as lower chemical applications is the most appropriate means for Amish farm families to avoid ground water pollution.

So while the Amish are relatively uninnovative in a general sense, they are very innovative in adopting innovations that are consistent with Amish cultural values.

This case illustration is based upon Hostetler (1980, 1987) and numerous other sources.

Characteristics of Adopter Categories

A voluminous research literature has accumulated about variables related to innovativeness. Here we summarize this diffusion research in a series of generalizations under three headings: (1) socioeconomic status, (2) personality values, and (3) communication behavior.

Socioeconomic Characteristics

7–2. Earlier adopters are not different from later adopters in age. There is inconsistent evidence about the relationship of age and innovativeness; about half of the some 228 studies on this subject show no relationship, a few show that earlier adopters are younger, and some indicate they are older.*

7–3. Earlier adopters have more years of formal education than later adopters.

7–4. Earlier adopters are more likely to be literate than are later adopters.

7–5. Earlier adopters have higher social status than later adopters. Status is indicated by such variables as income, level of living, possession of wealth, occupational prestige, self-perceived identification with a social class, and the like. However measured, social status is usually positively related with innovativeness.

7–6. Earlier adopters have a greater degree of upward social mobility than later adopters. Evidence suggests that earlier adopters are not only of higher status but are on the move in the direction of still higher levels of social status. In fact, they may be using the adoption of innovations as one means of getting there.

7–7. Earlier adopters have larger units (farms, schools, companies, and so on) than later adopters. The social characteristics of earlier adopters mark them as more educated, of higher social status, and the like. They are wealthier and have large units. Socioeconomic status and innovativeness appear to go hand in hand.

Do innovators innovate because they are richer, or are they richer because they innovate? The answer to this cause-and-effect question cannot be answered solely on the basis of available cross-sectional data. But there are understandable reasons why social status and innovativeness vary together. Some new ideas are costly to adopt and require large initial outlays of capital. Only the wealthy units in a system may be able to adopt these innovations. Greatest profits usually go to the first to adopt; therefore, the innovator gains a financial advantage through relatively early adoption of the innovation. The innovators become richer and the laggards become relatively poorer through this process.

---

*Rogers (1962) re-analyzed Gross' (1942) original data to demonstrate that there are wider differences in age between adopter categories when age at the time of *adoption* of hybrid seed was used, rather than age at the time of the data-gathering *interview*.

Because the innovator is the first to adopt, risks must be taken that can be avoided by later adopters who do not wish to cope with the high degree of uncertainty concerning the innovation when it is first introduced into a system. Certain of the innovator's new ideas are likely to fail. He or she must be wealthy enough to absorb the loss from these occasional failures. Although wealth and innovativeness are highly related, economic factors do not offer a complete explanation of innovative behavior (or even approach doing so). For example, although agricultural innovators tend to be wealthy, there are many rich farmers who are *not* innovators.

THE "CANCIAN DIP." All of the generalizations just presented concerning socioeconomic status and innovativeness assume a positive and linear relationship between these two variables. It is assumed that individuals adopt innovations in direct proportion to their socioeconomic status; with each added unit of income, education, and other socioeconomic status variables, an individual is expected to become more innovative by an equivalent amount.

This linearity of the socioeconomic-innovativeness relationship, however, was questioned by Professor Frank Cancian, an anthropologist at the University of California at Irvine. Cancian's theory says that innovativeness and socioeconomic status go together at the extremes; that is, individuals of highest socioeconomic status are highly innovative, and those of lowest socioeconomic status are least innovative. Cancian argues that between these two extremes, individuals of low-middle socioeconomic status are more innovative than individuals of high-middle status, especially in the early stages of the diffusion of an innovation (say until about 25-percent adoption has occurred in the social system) when the degree of uncertainty concerning the innovation is highest. Later, when perhaps 50 percent adoption has been reached, Cancian proposes that the high-middle individuals catch up and pass the low-middle individuals, thus resulting in a more linear relationship between socioeconomic variables and innovativeness.

This "Cancian dip" is depicted in Figure 7–3. Cancian's theory argues that the degree of uncertainty regarding an innovation's performance gradually decreases as the rate of adoption of an innovation increases in a system. When uncertainty is high (early in an innovation's diffusion), low-middle socioeconomic status (SES) individuals will be more innovative than the high-middle SES individuals in a system because they have less to lose. Later, when the innovation has diffused more widely and is perceived as less uncertain, the greater socioeconomic resources of the

Figure 7–3. The Cancian Dip Between Innovativeness and Measures of Socioeconomic Status Argues that Low-Middle Socioeconomic Status (SES) Individuals Are More Innovative than High-Middle SES Individuals, at Least in the Early Phase of the Diffusion Process

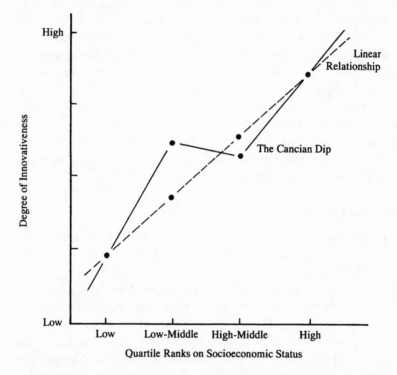

Professor Frank Cancian proposed a nonlinear theory of innovativeness and socioeconomic status, in which low-middle SES individuals are more innovative than high-middle individuals because they stand to gain more and to lose less by such innovativeness.

high-middle individuals enable them to adopt at a faster rate than the low-middle individuals, and to catch up and surpass them in innovativeness.

The Cancian dip hypothesis is complicated and difficult to test with empirical data. Cancian pioneered such research, proposing the main measures and methodologies (Cancian, 1967, 1976b, 1977, 1979a, 1979b, 1980, 1981). His work set off a wide variety of retests, refutations, and discussions of this theory.* Much of this research consists of re-analysis of existing data-sets that were originally collected without the intention of testing the Cancian dip hypothesis.† The most enthusiastic of these re-analyses consists of data from over 6,000 farmers who were interviewed in twenty-three different research studies; each of these original investigators provided their data to Cancian (1976b). What conclusions were reached from this massive analysis? In twenty-three of the forty-nine data-sets (each representing a farming system in which an agricultural innovation was at approximately 25-percent adoption), the Cancian dip was supported in that the low-middle individuals were more innovative than the upper-middle. In twenty-six of the forty-nine situations, the Cancian dip was not found (Cancian, 1979b).

Even though overwhelming evidence in support of the Cancian dip hypothesis was not found, it is no longer safe to assume that socioeconomic status and innovativeness are related in a linear fashion, especially at an early stage in the diffusion process.

Personality Variables

Personality variables associated with innovativeness have not yet received full research attention, in part because of difficulties in measuring personality dimensions in field interviews.

7–8. *Earlier adopters have greater empathy than later adopters. Empathy* is the ability of an individual to project himself or herself into the role of another person. This ability is an important quality for an innovator, who must be able to think counterfactually, to be particularly imaginative, and to take the roles of heterophilous others in order to exchange information effectively with them. To a certain extent, the innovator must be able to project into the role of individuals who are outside of the local system, such as innovators in other systems, change agents, and even scientists and R&D workers.

7–9. *Earlier adopters may be less dogmatic than later adopters. Dogmatism* is the degree to which an individual has a relatively closed belief

---

*These publications include Boyd (1980), Gartrell (1977), Gartrell and others (1973), Frey and Freeman (1981), Frey and others (1979), Morrison and others (1976), Rogers and others (1970), Wagener and others (1981), and Wilkening and others (1969).

†Thus these researches represent a special type of *meta-research*, defined as the synthesis of empirical research results into more general conclusions at a theoretical level.

system, that is, a set of beliefs that are strongly held. A highly dogmatic person would not welcome new ideas; such an individual would instead prefer to hew to the past. Evidence in support of this generalization is not very strong, consisting of only several research studies.

7–10. *Earlier adopters have a greater ability to deal with abstractions than do later adopters.* Innovators must be able to adopt a new idea largely on the basis of rather abstract stimuli, such as are received from the mass media. Later adopters can observe the innovation in the here-and-now of a peer's operation. They need less ability to deal with abstractions.

7–11. *Earlier adopters have greater rationality than later adopters. Rationality* is use of the most effective means to reach a given end.

7–12. *Earlier adopters have greater intelligence than later adopters.*

7–13. *Earlier adopters have a more favorable attitude toward change than later adopters.*

7–14. *Earlier adopters are better able to cope with uncertainty and risk than later adopters.*

7–15. *Earlier adopters have a more favorable attitude toward science than later adopters.* Because most innovations are the products of scientific research, it is logical that innovators are more favorably inclined toward science.

7–16. *Earlier adopters are less fatalistic than later adopters. Fatalism* is the degree to which an individual perceives a lack of ability to control his or her future. An individual is more likely to adopt an innovation if he or she is efficacious and believes that he or she is in control, rather than thinking that the future is determined by fate.

7–17. *Earlier adopters have higher aspirations (for formal education, occupations, and so on) than later adopters.*

Communication Behavior

We can state the following generalizations:

7–18. *Earlier adopters have more social participation than later adopters.*

7–19. *Earlier adopters are more highly interconnected through interpersonal networks in their social system than later adopters. Connectedness* is the degree to which an individual is linked to others.

7–20. *Earlier adopters are more cosmopolite than later adopters.* Innovators' interpersonal networks are more likely to be outside, rather than within, their system. They travel widely and are involved in matters beyond the boundaries of their local system. For instance, Iowa hybrid corn innovators traveled to urban centers like Des Moines more often than the average farmer (Ryan and Gross, 1943). Medical doctors who innovated in adopting a new drug attended more out-of-town professional meetings than noninnovators (Coleman and others, 1966). *Cosmopoliteness* is the degree to which an individual is oriented outside a social system.

Innovators act like the German sociologist Georg Simmel's (1908/1964) "stranger," whose special perspective stems from a lack of integration into the local system: "He is not radically committed to the unique ingredients and peculiar tendencies of the group, and . . . is bound by no commitments which could prejudice his perception, understanding, and evaluation of the given." The stranger's orientation outside of the group allows the importing of information from the wider society.

7–21. *Earlier adopters have more change agent contact than later adopters.*

7–22. *Earlier adopters have greater exposure to mass media communication channels than later adopters.*

7–23. *Earlier adopters have greater exposure to interpersonal communication channels than later adopters.*

7–24. *Earlier adopters seek information about innovations more actively than later adopters.*

7–25. *Earlier adopters have greater knowledge of innovations than later adopters.*

7–26. *Earlier adopters have a higher degree of opinion leadership than later adopters.* Although innovativeness and opinion leadership are positively related, the degree to which these two variables are related depends in part on the norms of the social system. In a system with norms favorable to change, opinion leaders are more likely to be innovators (see Chapter 8).

Audience Segmentation and Adopter Categories

In summary, we see that in most of the previous generalizations, an independent variable is positively related to innovativeness. This relationship means that innovators score higher on these independent variables than laggards. For instance, Rogers with Svenning (1969) found that in traditional Colombian villages the innovators averaged thirty trips a year to cities whereas the laggards averaged only 0.3 trips. A few variables, such as dogmatism and fatalism, are negatively related to innovativeness, and opinion leadership is greatest for early adopters, at least in most systems.

Thus, a set of general characteristics of each adopter category has emerged from diffusion research. The important differences among these adopter categories suggest that change agents should use somewhat different approaches with each adopter category, thus following a strategy of audience segmentation. *Audience segmentation* is a strategy in which different communication channels or messages are used with each sub-audience. This strategy breaks down a heterophilous audience into a series of relatively more homophilous sub-audiences. Thus, one might appeal to innovators who adopted an innovation because it was soundly tested and developed by credible scientists, but this approach would not be effective with the late majority and laggards, who do not have a favorable attitude toward science. They will not adopt a new idea until they feel that most uncertainty about the innovation's performance has been removed; these later adopters place greatest credibility in the subjective experiences of their peers with the innovation, conveyed to them through interpersonal networks.

The Innovativeness-Needs Paradox

The individuals or other units in a system who most need the benefits of a new idea (the less educated, less wealthy, and the like) are generally the last to adopt an innovation. The units in a system who adopt first generally least need the benefits of the innovation. This paradoxical relationship between innovativeness and the need for benefits of an innovation tends to result in a wider socioeconomic gap between the higher and lower socioeconomic individuals in a social system. Thus, one consequence of many technological innovations is to widen socioeconomic gaps in a social system (see Chapter 11).

One illustration of the innovativeness-needs paradox is the adoption of contraceptive innovations in Third World nations. Elite families in these societies are already relatively small in size, even though these families could well afford to raise many children. When a national family planning program is launched by the government, these elite families are the first to adopt contraceptives (Rogers, 1973). While elite families average only two or three children, lower-status families average five or six children (which they often cannot afford to feed, clothe, or educate). The poorer families generally do not adopt contraceptive innovations, even though one might think these families would feel a stronger need for family planning. Thus, the paradox occurs in which those who might need an innovation most are the last to adopt it.

What creates this paradox? In the case of family planning, poor families believe that having many children (especially sons) is an economic asset, in that the sons can assist with farm and other work. Poor parents do not believe the government officials who tell them that the small family is a happy family. A second reason for the paradoxical tendency of those individuals who most need an innovation to adopt it last, is that change agents often follow a segmentation strategy of *least resistance*, in that they especially contact the socioeconomic elites, who are most receptive to innovations. Most contraceptive methods require resources, skills, and/or training to adopt, which the nonelite members of a system are less likely to possess. For example, family planning innovations are used more easily and more effectively by elite parents, as these contraceptive technologies require the planning of behavior, understanding the human reproduction function, and other skills. So even when family planning methods are provided to individuals at no cost by a government program, the socioeconomic elites tend to adopt first.

The innovativeness-needs paradox need not occur. Change agents could pursue a segmentation strategy of *greatest resistance*, in which communication efforts are concentrated on the sub-audiences who are lowest in socioeconomic status, who feel the least need for the innovation, and who would otherwise be the last to adopt. An unfortunate consequence of the tendency of change agents to concentrate their efforts on their elite clients, while largely ignoring the hard-to-get sub-audience of late majority and laggards, is widening gaps between the information-rich and the information-poor in a social system (see Chapter 11).

Innovativeness Among Fishermen

A study of eighty-three U.S. commercial fishermen in the Pacific Ocean found that different independent variables explained the adoption of six innovations in commercial fishing (Dewees and Hawkes, 1988). For example, the innovation of midwater trawling was adopted by fishermen who were more cosmopolite (measured as the number of ports in which the fishermen landed fish), had more relatives in fishing, and were more optimistic about future fishing conditions. In comparison, adopters of the innovation of survival suits were relatively younger and sought information about innovations from more expert sources. Adopters of chromoscopes (which locate fish underwater with a sound beam) had a larger fishing business, and perceived the innovation as less complex.

These different characteristics of the adopters of each innovation could be understood on the basis of the perceived attributes of the innovations. For example, a chromoscope cost from $3,000 to $5,000 and so the fishermen with larger firms were better able to afford them. Adopters of midwater trawling often combined family resources to purchase a larger fishing vessel, which traveled over a wider area. Hence having more relatives in fishing was understandably related to adoption, as was optimism about the fishing industry . Survival suits were a safety innovation of a relatively low-cost nature that greatly increased chances of survival in the cold water of the Pacific. Younger fishermen were more likely to adopt.

Dewees and Hawkes (1988) suggest the methodological advantages of combining two types of diffusion research: Independent variables related to innovativeness, and perceived attributes of innovations related to their rate of adoption. Findings from each type of research aided the understanding of the other. The conclusion that different independent variables explained adoption versus nonadoption of each innovation undoubtedly resulted because Dewees and Hawkes (1988) studied six innovations that were quite diverse in their perceived attributes (such as low-cost safety innovations, very expensive electronic innovations, etc.). It is hardly surprising that such diverse innovations were perceived differently, and that the fishermen adopting them had quite different characteristics.

Dewees and Hawkes (1988) followed a methodological lead suggested by Downs and Mohr (1976) in a critique of innovativeness research calling for a disaggregation of the units of analysis in diffusion study. For example, instead of utilizing an innovativeness scale composed of the six fishing innovations, Dewees and Hawkes (1988) regarded the adoption (or nonadoption) of each of the six innovations as a separate independent variable. So instead of having eighty-three units of analysis (that is, their sample of eighty-three commercial fishermen), Dewees and Hawkes had $83 \times 6 = 258$ units of analysis. Their study's disaggregation strategy allowed them to better understand innovation-to-innovation differences in variables related to innovativeness.

But such a disaggregation of the measurement of the innovativeness concept necessarily leads to a kind of inconsistency or unreliability in their innovation-to-innovation findings. Such inconsistent results always will accompany disaggregation, and in fact illustrate one good reason to utilize composite innovativeness scales to measure the dependent variable. Dewees and Hawkes (1988) make much of their finding that different independent variables (age, size of fishing enterprise, importance of family ties, etc.) are related to the adoption of one innovation but not another. This finding is an artifact of their disaggregation methodology.

A similar type of dissaggregated research strategy characterizes another investigation of the diffusion of eighteen innovations among 190 commercial fishermen in Maine and New Hampshire by Acheson and Reidman (1982). The innovations ranged very widely, from buying a larger fishing boat (at a cost of from \$80,000 to \$350,000), to adopting a CB radio costing about \$100, to purchasing scanning sonar costing a minimum of \$3,500 and requiring a great deal of experience to operate effectively. These scholars concluded: "The innovations studied are very different and are adopted to solve distinct problems. In fact, no two innovations in our study could be explained by identical sets of factors. . . . Innovations are adopted when they match the needs of potential adopters. . . . The desirability of adopting an innovation depends on the problem the innovation promises to solve for the adopter in question" (Acheson and Reidman, 1982).

What can one conclude from these two studies of fishermen's innovativeness?

1. There are useful advantages of disaggregating the units of analysis in innovativeness research from individuals adopting a set of innovations, to an individual adopting a single innovation. Such disaggregation greatly increases the total units of analysis, and allows greater insight into the micro-level of adoption behavior.

2. A scholar should hardly be surprised that such disaggregation of an innovativeness measure leads to different independent variables being related to the adoption of different innovations, especially when the innovations of study are quite different from each other.

Useful alternatives to the usual variables-related-to-innovativeness approach of most past diffusion studies are illustrated by the investigations of Dewees and Hawkes (1988) and Acheson and Reidman (1982). Their research approach need not be limited to the study of innovativeness among fishermen.

This case illustration is based mainly on Downs and Mohr (1976), Dewees and Hawkes (1988), and Acheson and Reidman (1982).

Summary

Adopter categories are the classifications of members of a social system on the basis of *innovativeness*, the degree to which an individual or other unit of adoption is relatively earlier in adopting new ideas than other members of a system. A variety of categorization systems and titles for adopters have been used in past studies. This chapter suggested the standard set of five adopter categories that is widely followed today.

Adopter distributions tend to follow an S-shaped curve over time and to approach normality (Generalization 7–1). The continuum of innovativeness can be partitioned into five adopter categories (innovators, early adopters, early majority, late majority, and laggards) on the basis of two characteristics of a normal distribution, the mean and the standard deviation. Dominant attributes of each category are: Innovators—venturesome; early adopters—respect; early majority—deliberate; late majority—skeptical; and laggards—traditional. The relatively earlier adopters in a social system are no different from later adopters in age (Generalization 7–2), but they have more years of formal education (Generalization 7–3), are more likely to be literate (Generalization 7–4), have higher social status (Generalization 7–5), a greater degree of upward social mobility (Generalization 7–6), and larger-sized units, like farms, companies, schools, and so on (Generalization 7–7). These characteristics of adopter categories indicate generally that earlier adopters have higher socioeconomic status than later adopters. The "Cancian dip" questions whether the relationship between innovativeness and socioeconomic status is linear. This theory proposes that individuals of low-middle socioeconomic status are more innovative than individuals of high-middle status, especially in the early stages of the diffusion of an innovation when the degree of uncertainty about the innovation is greatest. Reanalysis of various data-sets provides some support for the Cancian dip, but there is also a good deal of contradictory evidence.

Earlier adopters in a system also differ from later adopters in personality variables. Earlier adopters have greater empathy (Generalization 7–8), less dogmatism (Generalization 7–9), a greater ability to deal with abstractions (Generalization 7–10), greater rationality (Generalization 7–11), greater intelligence (Generalization 7–12), a more favorable attitude toward change (Generalization 7–13), a better ability to cope with uncertainty and risk (Generalization 7–14), a more favorable attitude toward science (Generalization 7–15), less fatalism (Generalization 7–16), and higher aspirations for formal education, occupations, and so on (Generalization 7–17).

Finally, the adopter categories have different communication behavior. Earlier adopters have more social participation (Generalization 7–18), are more highly interconnected in the interpersonal networks of their system (Generalization 7–19), are more cosmopolite (Generalization 7–20), have more change agent contact (Generalization 7–21), greater exposure to mass media channels (Generalization 7–22), greater exposure to interpersonal communication channels (Generalization 7–23), engage in more active information seeking (Generalization 7–24), have greater knowledge of innovations (Generalization 7–25), and a higher degree of opinion leadership (Generalization 7–26).

Past research thus shows many important differences between earlier and later adopters of innovations in (1) socioeconomic status, (2) personality variables, and (3) communication behavior. The distinctive characteristics of the five adopter categories mean that these adopter categories can be used for audience segmentation.

8

DIFFUSION NETWORKS

Every herd of wild cattle has its leaders, its influential heads.
—Gabriel Tarde, *The Laws of Imitation*

In the previous chapters of this book we emphasized the importance of interpersonal network influences on individuals both in their coping with the uncertainty of new ideas and in convincing them to adopt innovations. Here we explore what is known about such diffusion networks and how they function to convey innovation-evaluation information to decrease uncertainty about a new idea. We begin with a discussion of *opinion leadership*, the degree to which an individual is able informally to influence other individuals' attitudes or overt behavior in a desired way with relative frequency. Opinion leaders are individuals who lead in influencing others' opinions about innovations. The behavior of opinion leaders is important in determining the rate of adoption of an innovation in a system. In fact, the S-shape of the diffusion curve occurs because once opinion leaders adopt and tell others about the innovation, the number of adopters per unit of time takes off. We explore in this chapter the role of social modeling in diffusion networks, and how interpersonal communication drives the diffusion process through creating a "critical mass" of adopters.

Opinion Leadership in the Diffusion of Modern Math

Insight into the nature of opinion leadership is provided by a study of the spread of an important educational innovation, modern math, among the thirty-eight school superintendents in Allegheny County, Pennsylvania, which is essentially the city of Pittsburgh.

The innovation of modern math began in the early 1950s when top mathematicians in the United States completely overhauled the nature of mathematics training being offered in public schools. Out of their efforts came modern math, a radically new approach to mathematics packaged to include textbooks, audiovisual aides designed for teaching the new concepts, and summer institutes to retrain school teachers in the new subject matter. The innovation spread relatively quickly because of powerful federal sponsorship by the National Science Foundation and the U.S. Department of Education. Modern math was widely hailed by educators as a major improvement. It was quite different from the "old" math in that it used set theory, Venn diagrams, and an emphasis upon probability. Math teachers had to learn an entirely new approach to their subject.

Modern math entered the schools of Allegheny County through one school superintendent, shown in Figure 8–1 as "I," who adopted in 1958. This innovator was a sociometric isolate in that he had no interpersonal network links with any of the other school superintendents in the Pittsburgh area. Innovators like "I" are frequently disdained by their fellow members in a local system. They interact primarily with cosmopolite friends who are outside of the local system.

Figure 8–1 is a sociogram, a communication map tracing the network links in the diffusion of an innovation. The arrows show the patterns of friendship among the superintendents. The shaded area encircles six friends who constitute a clique or informal friendship group. The superintendents in this clique interact more with each other than they do with outsiders.

This clique played a central role in the diffusion of modern math in Pittsburgh's schools. Once the clique members (especially the three main opinion leaders who decided to use the innovation in 1959 and 1960) adopted, the rate of adoption for modern math began to climb rapidly in the system. Figure 8–1 shows there was only one adopter in 1958 (the innovator), five by the end of 1959, fifteen by 1960, twenty-seven by 1961, thirty-five by 1962, and thirty-eight by the end of 1963. The rapid spurt in 1959, 1960, and 1961 appeared to occur as a direct result of the opinion leaders' behavior.

Later in the present chapter we show that opinion leaders are highly conforming to the norms of their system. We see support for this generalization in the present case. The cosmopolite innovator was *too* innovative to serve as an appropriate role model for the other thirty-seven superintendents; they

Figure 8–1. Opinion Leadership Patterns in the Diffusion of Modern Math among School Superintendents in Allegheny County, Pennsylvania (the three opinion leaders are identified as "OL," and the innovator is labeled "I").

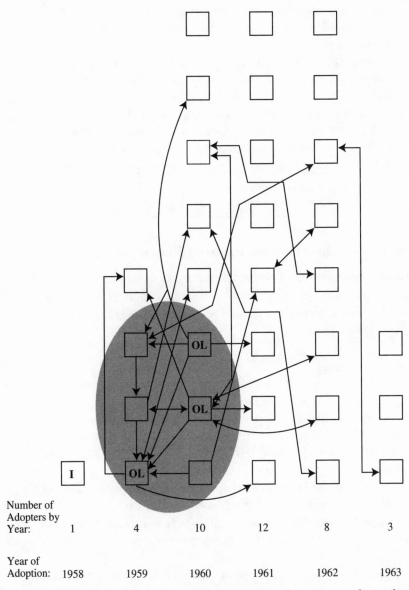

Number of Adopters by Year:	1	4	10	12	8	3
Year of Adoption:	1958	1959	1960	1961	1962	1963

For the sake of simplicity, only thirty-two of the thirty-eight superintendents who adopted modern math are shown. Two adopters in 1960 and four adopters in 1961 are not shown here.

Source: Constructed from data provided by Carlson (1965).

waited to adopt until the three opinion leaders in the six-member clique favored the innovation. A change agent responsible for diffusing another innovation in Allegheny County should concentrate promotional efforts on these opinion leaders.

Further, Figure 8–1 shows a rather high degree of homophily in the time of adoption of modern math by the superintendents. Many of the friendship arrows are between superintendents who adopted in the same year or within one year of each other. When two superintendents in a dyadic relationship adopted in different years, the difference is slight, suggesting that in this case the source is different enough from the receiver to be perceived as competent but not so much different as to be an inappropriate role-model.

This case illustration is based on Richard O. Carlson (1965), and details the brief description of the modern math study provided in our Chapter 2.

Models of Mass Communication Flows

In order to understand better the nature of opinion leadership and diffusion networks, we now examine several models of mass communication flows, roughly in the temporal sequence of their entrance on the stage of communication study.

Hypodermic Needle Model

The *hypodermic needle model* postulated that the mass media had direct, immediate, and powerful effects on a mass audience. The mass media in the 1940s and 1950s were perceived as a powerful influence on behavior change. The omnipotent media were pictured as conveying messages to atomized masses of individuals (Katz and Lazarsfeld,1955). Evidence of the power of the mass media was drawn from such historical events as: (1) the role of the Hearst newspapers in arousing public support for the Spanish-American War, (2) the power of Nazi leader Joseph Goebbels' propaganda apparatus during World War II in Europe, and (3) the influence of Madison Avenue advertising on consumer and voting behavior in the U.S.

Eventually, when more sophisticated methods were used in communication research, considerable doubt was cast on the hypodermic needle model. This survey research was directed by Paul F. Lazarsfeld of Columbia University, a pioneering mass communication scholar (Rogers, 1994). The hypodermic needle model was based primarily on intuitive theorizing from unique historical events and was too simple, too mechanistic, and too gross to give an accurate account of mass media effects.

Two-Step Flow Model

The decisive end of the hypodermic needle model resulted serendipitously from a classic study of the 1940 presidential election in Erie County, Ohio (Lazarsfeld and others, 1944). This inquiry was designed with the hypodermic needle model in mind and was aimed at analyzing the role of the mass media in changing political decisions. A panel study conducted with a sample of 600 voters over the six months prior to the November election found, to the researchers' surprise, that very few voting choices were directly influenced by the mass media. "This study went to great lengths to determine how the mass media brought about such changes. To our surprise we found the effect to be rather small. . . . People appeared to be much more influenced in their political decisions by face-to-face contact with other people . . . than by the mass media directly" (Lazarsfeld and Menzel, 1963). Instead the data suggested "that ideas often *flow* from radio and print *to* opinion leaders and *from* these to the less active sections of the population" (Lazarsfeld and others, 1944). The first step, from media sources to opinion leaders, is mainly a transfer of *information*, whereas the second step, from opinion leaders to their followers, also involves the spread of interpersonal *influence*. This *two-step flow hypothesis* suggested that communication messages flow from a source, via mass media channels, to opinion leaders, who in turn pass them on to followers. This model has since been tested for a variety of communication behaviors, including the diffusion of innovations, and found generally to provide some useful understandings of the flow of mass communication.

The two-step flow model helped focus attention upon the interface between mass media channels and interpersonal communication channels. The model implied that the mass media were not so powerful nor so direct as was previously thought. Of course an individual can be exposed to a new idea either through mass media or interpersonal channels, and then engage in communication exchanges about the innovation with peers. The mass communication process does not necessarily consist of just two steps. In some instances there may be only one step, as when the mass media have a direct impact on an individual. In other instances a multistage communication process may occur.

Different communication sources/channels function at different stages in an individual's innovation-decision process. The original two-step flow model did not recognize the role of different communication sources/channels at various stages in the innovation-decision process. We know that individuals pass from (1) *knowledge* of an innovation, (2) to *persuasion*, (3) to a *decision* to adopt or reject, (4) to *implementation*, and then (5) to *confirmation* of this decision. Mass media channels are primarily knowledge-creators, whereas interpersonal networks are more important in persuading individuals to adopt or reject. This notion was masked in the original statement of the two-step model because the time sequence involved in an individual's decision-making process was ignored. Such source/channel differences between the knowledge and persuasion stages usually exist for *both* opinion leaders and followers. Thus, the opinion leaders are not the only individuals to use mass media channels, as the original statement of the two-step flow model suggested.

The two-step flow model as it was originally postulated did not tell us enough. The flow of communication in a mass audience is far more complicated than just two steps. What is known about the mass communication process is too detailed to be expressed in one sentence or in two steps. Nevertheless, one important intellectual benefit from the two-step flow hypothesis occurred in communication study: a focus upon opinion leadership.

Homophily-Heterophily in Communication Networks

Understanding of the nature of communication flows through interpersonal networks is enhanced by the concepts of homophily and heterophily. The structure of *who* relays messages to *whom* is brought out in such network analysis.

Homophily and Heterophily

A fundamental principle of human communication is that the exchange of ideas occurs most frequently between individuals who are alike, or homophilous. *Homophily* is the degree to which a pair of individuals who communicate are similar. The similarity may be in certain attributes, such as beliefs, education, social status, and the like. The conceptual label of homophily was given to this phenomenon several decades ago by Paul F. Lazarsfeld and Robert K. Merton (1964), but the general idea of homophilous behavior was noted almost a century ago by Gabriel Tarde

(1903): "Social relations, I repeat, are much closer between individuals who resemble each other in occupation and education." *Heterophily* is the degree to which pairs of individuals who interact are different in certain attributes. Heterophily is the opposite of homophily.

Homophily occurs frequently because communication is more effective when source and receiver are homophilous. When two individuals share common meanings, beliefs, and mutual understandings, communication between them is more likely to be effective. Individuals enjoy the comfort of interacting with others who are similar. Talking with those who are markedly different from ourselves requires more effort to make communication effective. Heterophilous communication between dissimilar individuals may cause cognitive dissonance because an individual is exposed to messages that are inconsistent with existing beliefs, an uncomfortable psychological state. Homophily and effective communication breed each other. The more communication there is between members of a dyad, the more likely they are to become homophilous;* the more homophilous two individuals are, the more likely that their communication will be effective. Individuals who depart from the homophily principle and attempt to communicate with others who are different from themselves often face the frustration of ineffective communication. Differences in technical competence, social status, beliefs, and language, lead to mistaken meanings, thereby causing messages to be distorted or to go unheeded.

A study of the diffusion of computers among the top administrators in 127 Pittsburgh suburban communities found that these innovations mainly spread by means of interpersonal networks. The networks mainly connected city officials whose municipalities were neighboring, and who were most similar in formal education and length of governmental experience (Kearns, 1992). Again, we see that most diffusion networks are homophilous.

But heterophilous communication has a special informational potential, even though it may occur only rarely. Heterophilous network links often connect two cliques, thus spanning two sets of socially dissimilar individuals in a system. These heterophilous interpersonal links are especially important in carrying information about innovations, as is implied

---

*Although similarities in static variables like age and other demographic characteristics obviously cannot be explained as the result of communication leading to increased homophily.

in Granovetter's (1973) theory of the strength of weak ties. So homophilous communication may be frequent and easy but may not be so
crucial as the less frequent heterophilous communication in diffusing innovations. Homophily accelerates the diffusion process, but limits the
spread of an innovation to individuals connected in the same network.

Homophily as a Barrier to Diffusion

Homophily can act as an invisible barrier to the flow of innovations within
a system. New ideas usually enter a system through higher status and
more innovative members. A high degree of homophily means that these
elite individuals interact mainly with each other, and thus the innovation
does not "trickle down" to non-elites. Homophilous diffusion patterns
cause new ideas to spread horizontally, rather than vertically, within a system. Homophily therefore can act to slow down the rate of diffusion in a
system. If homophily is a barrier to diffusion, change agents should work
with different sets of opinion leaders in a system. If the interpersonal networks in a system were characterized by a high degree of heterophily, a
change agent could concentrate attention on only a few opinion leaders
near the top in social status and innovativeness. This is seldom the case.

Available evidence suggests Generalization 8–1: *Interpersonal diffusion networks are mostly homophilous*. For instance, individuals of highest status in a system seldom interact directly with those of lowest status.
Likewise, innovators seldom converse with laggards. Although this homophily pattern in interpersonal networks acts to slow the diffusion of
innovations within a system, it also has benefits. For example, a high-
status opinion leader might be an inappropriate role model for someone
of lower status, so interaction between them might not be beneficial to
the latter. An illustration of this point comes from an investigation by Van
den Ban (1963) in a Netherlands agricultural community. He found that
only 3 percent of the opinion leaders had farms smaller than fifty acres
in size, but 38 percent of all farms in the community were smaller than
fifty acres. The wisest farm management decision for the large farmers
was to purchase mechanized farm equipment, such as tractors and milk-
ing machines, as a substitute for hired labor, which was expensive. The
best economic choice for the smaller farmers, however, was to ignore the
expensive equipment and concentrate on intensive horticultural farming
that required a great deal of labor per acre. As might be expected, however, the small farmers were following the example of the opinion leaders with large farms, even though the example was inappropriate for their

situation. In this case a greater degree of homophily, so that small farmers would interact mainly with opinion leaders who were themselves small farmers, would have been beneficial.

An illustration of homophilous and heterophilous diffusion networks is provided by Rao, Rogers, and Singh (1980), who studied two Indian villages. One village was very innovative, while the other village had more traditional norms. Diffusion networks for a new rice variety were more homophilous in the traditional village. The opinion leaders here were elderly and had little formal education. In comparison, the opinion leaders in the innovative village were younger, highly educated, and of a high social caste. In the more traditional village, diffusion network links were highly homophilous; Brahmins talked to Brahmins, Harijans talked to Harijans, and so forth. But in the progressive village, the new rice variety started at the top of the social structure, and then spread rapidly downward across the caste lines through heterophilous network links. So the heterophilous network links aided rapid diffusion.

Following are generalizations about characteristics of opinion leaders and followers under various degrees of heterophily in a system:

Generalization 8–2: *When interpersonal diffusion networks are heterophilous, followers seek opinion leaders of higher socioeconomic status.*

Generalization 8–3: *When interpersonal diffusion networks are heterophilous, followers seek opinion leaders with more formal education.*

Generalization 8–4: *When interpersonal diffusion networks are heterophilous, followers seek opinion leaders with a greater degree of mass media exposure.*

Generalization 8–5: *When interpersonal diffusion networks are heterophilous, followers seek opinion leaders who are more cosmopolite.*

Generalization 8–6: *When interpersonal diffusion networks are heterophilous, followers seek opinion leaders with greater change agent contact.*

Generalization 8–7: *When interpersonal diffusion networks are heterophilous, followers seek opinion leaders who are more innovative.*

The six generalizations indicate a general tendency for followers to seek information and advice from opinion leaders who are perceived as more technically competent than themselves. When heterophily occurs, it is usually in the direction of a greater degree of competency, but not *too* much greater. We should not forget that the general pattern of interpersonal networks is one of homophily in diffusion networks. This homophily means that the dyadic followers of opinion leaders usually learn appropriate lessons about an innovation through their ties with their near-peer opinion leaders. But these homophilous diffusion networks also slow the percolation of an innovation through the structure of a social system.

Measuring Opinion Leadership and Network Links

Four main methods of measuring opinion leadership and diffusion network links have been used in the past: (1) sociometric, (2) informants' ratings, (3) self-designating techniques, and (4) observation (Table 8–1).

The *sociometric* method consists of asking respondents whom they sought (or hypothetically might seek) for information or advice about a given topic, such as a particular innovation. Opinion leaders are those members of a system who receive the greatest number of sociometric choices (and thus who are involved in the largest number of network links). Undoubtedly, the sociometric technique is a highly valid measure of opinion leadership, as it is measured through the perceptions of followers. It necessitates, however, interrogating a large number of respondents to locate a small number of opinion leaders. And the sociometric method is most applicable when all members of a social system provide network data, rather than when a small sample within the total population is contacted.[*]

It is common to specify the number of sociometric network partners who can be named by a respondent; for example, "Who are the *three* (or four, or five) other women in this village with whom you have discussed family planning methods?" Such limited-choice questioning leads a respondent to name only the strongest network partners. It is possible that others with whom a respondent converses less often may exchange information with the respondent that is most crucial in the diffusion process. Perhaps sociometric questions should allow an unlimited number of choices, letting the respondent name any number of network partners with whom a topic is discussed. Another approach is to conduct a roster study, in which each respondent is presented with a list of all the other members of the system, and asked whether he or she talks with each of them, and how often. The roster technique has the advantage of measuring weak as well as strong links.

---

[*]Although it is possible to locate sociometric opinion leaders in surveys by means of snowball sampling in which an original sample of respondents in a system is interrogated. Then the individuals sociometrically designated by this sample are interviewed as a second sample, and so on (Rogers and Kincaid, 1981).

Table 8–1. Advantages and Limitations of Four Methods of Measuring Opinion Leadership in Diffusion Networks

Measurement Method	Description	Questions Asked	Advantages	Limitations
1. Sociometric method	Ask system members to whom they go for advice and infomation about an idea	Who is your leader?	Sociometric questions are easy to administer and are adaptable to different types of settings and issues Highest validity	Analysis of sociometric data can be complex. Requires a large number of respondents to locate a small number of opinion leaders. Not applicable to sample designs where only a portion of the social system is interviewed.
2. Informants' ratings	Subjectively selected key informants in a system are asked to designate opinion leaders	Who are leaders in this system?	A cost-saving and time-saving method as compared to sociometric method	Each informant must be thoroughly familiar with the system.
3. Self-designating method	Ask each respondent a series of questions to determine the degree to which he/she perceives himself/herself to be an opinion leader	Are you a leader in this system?	Measures the individual's perceptions of her/his opinion leadership, which influence her/his behavior	Dependent upon the accuracy with which respondents can identify and report their self-images.
4. Observation	Identify and record communication network links as they occur	None	High validity	Obtrusive, works best in a very small system, and may require much patience by the observer.

An alternative to using sociometry to identify opinion leaders is to ask key *informants* who are especially knowledgeable about the networks in a system. Often a handful of informants can identify the opinion leaders in a system, with a precision that is almost as accurate as sociometric techniques, particularly when the system is small and the informants are well-informed.

The *self-designating* technique asks respondents to indicate the tendency for others to regard them as influential. A typical self-designating question is: "Do you think people come to you for information or advice more often than to others?" The self-designating method depends upon the accuracy with which respondents can identify and report their self-images. This measure of opinion leadership is especially appropriate when interrogating a random sample of respondents in a system, a sampling design that often precludes effective use of sociometric methods.

A fourth means of measuring opinion leadership is *observation,* in which an investigator identifies and records the communication behavior in a system. One advantage of observation is that the data usually have a high degree of validity. If network links are appropriately observed, there is no doubt about whether they occur or not. Observation works best in a very small system, where the observer can actually see and record interpersonal interactions as they occur. Unfortunately, in such small systems observation may be a very obtrusive data-gathering technique. Because the members of a system know they are being observed, they may act differently.° Further, an observer may need to be very patient if the diffusion network behavior that he or she wants to observe occurs only rarely.

In practice, observation is seldom used to measure diffusion networks and opinion leadership. By far the most popular means of measurement is survey sociometry.

When two or three types of opinion leadership measurement have been utilized with the same respondents, positive correlations among the measures have been obtained, although these relationships are far from perfect. This finding suggests that the choice of any one of the four methods can be based on convenience, as all four are about equally valid.

°Very unobtrusive methods of measuring network links may sometimes be used, where the data were recorded for other purposes (Rogers and Kincaid, 1981). For example, an electronic mail system leaves a computer record of who talks to whom, and what they said; these data can sometimes be accessed as an unobtrusive measure of network links, with the permission of the respondents.

In a typical distribution of opinion leadership in a social system, a few individuals receive a great deal of opinion leadership, while most individuals have none or very little. The most influential opinion leaders are key targets for the efforts of change agents.

Monomorphic and Polymorphic Opinion Leadership

Is there one set of all-purpose opinion leaders in a system, or are there different opinion leaders for different issues? *Polymorphism* is the degree to which an individual acts as an opinion leader for a variety of topics. Its opposite, *monomorphism*, is the degree to which an individual acts as an opinion leader for only a single topic. The degree of polymorphic opinion leadership in a given social system seems to vary with such factors as the diversity of the topics on which opinion leadership is measured, whether system norms are innovative or not, and so on. An analysis of opinion leadership among housewives in Decatur, Illinois, for four different topics (fashions, movies, public affairs, and consumer products) by Katz and Lazarsfeld (1955) found that one-third of the opinion leaders exerted their influence in more than one of the four areas. Other studies report more, or less, polymorphism. For instance, village leaders in Third World countries are frequently opinion leaders for health, agricultural, and educational ideas, as well as political and moral issues in the community.

Characteristics of Opinion Leaders

How do opinion leaders differ from their followers? The following seven generalizations summarize a considerable volume of empirical studies designed to answer this question. In each we refer to "opinion leaders" and "followers" as if opinion leadership were a dichotomy and as if all nonleaders were followers. These oversimplifications are necessary for the sake of clarity.

External Communication

Generalization 8–8: *Opinion leaders have greater exposure to mass media than their followers*. The original conception of the two-step flow hypothesis stated that opinion leaders attend more to mass media channels (Lazarsfeld and others, 1944). Opinion leaders gain their perceived competency by serving as an avenue for the entrance of new ideas into their system. The external linkage may be provided via mass media channels, by the leader's cosmopoliteness, or by the leader's greater change agent contact.

Generalization 8–9: *Opinion leaders are more cosmopolite than their followers*.

Generalization 8–10: *Opinion leaders have greater change agent contact than their followers*.

Accessibility

For opinion leaders to spread messages about an innovation, they must have extensive interpersonal network links with their followers. Opinion leaders must be socially accessible. One indicator of such accessibility is social participation; face-to-face communication about new ideas occurs at meetings of formal organizations and through informal discussions.

Generalization 8–11: *Opinion leaders have greater social participation than their followers*.

Socioeconomic Status

We expect that a follower typically seeks an opinion leader of somewhat higher status, as suggested in Generalization 8–2. So opinion leaders, on the average, should be of higher status than their followers. This point was stated by Gabriel Tarde (1903): "Invention can start from the lowest ranks of the people, but its extension depends upon the existence of some lofty social elevation."

Generalization 8–12: *Opinion leaders have higher socioeconomic status than their followers*.

Innovativeness

If opinion leaders are to be recognized by their peers as competent and trustworthy experts about innovations, the opinion leaders should adopt new ideas before their followers. There is strong empirical support for Generalization 8–13: *Opinion leaders are more innovative than their followers*. But opinion leaders are not necessarily innovators. Sometimes they are, but often they are not. At first glance, there appears to be contradictory evidence as to whether or not opinion leaders are innovators. What explains this apparent paradox? We must consider the effect of system norms on the innovativeness of opinion leaders, because the degree to which opinion leaders are innovative depends in large part on their followers.

Innovativeness, Opinion Leadership, and System Norms

How can opinion leaders be most conforming to system norms and at the same time lead in the adoption of new ideas? The answer is expressed as Generalization 8–14: *When a social system's norms favor change, opinion leaders are more innovative, but when the norms do not favor change, opinion leaders are not especially innovative.* In systems with more traditional norms, the opinion leaders are usually a separate set of individuals from the innovators. The innovators are perceived with suspicion and often with disrespect by the members of such systems, who do not trust their sense of judgment about innovations. For instance, in a study of Colombian farmers in traditional villages, Rogers with Svenning (1969) found that opinion leaders were only slightly more innovative than their followers and were older and less cosmopolite. But in progressive villages, opinion leaders were young and innovative. So the system's norms determine whether or not opinion leaders are innovators.

Data from inquiries in various nations support the notion of opinion leaders as highly conforming to system norms. For instance, Herzog and others (1968) concluded from their study of Brazilian villages that: "In the most traditional communities, neither the leaders nor their followers are innovative, and as a result, the community remains traditional. In the most modern communities, community norms favor innovativeness and both the leaders and followers are innovative. In the middle range communities, where modernization is just getting underway, divisions occur and the community opinion leaders lead the way toward modernization, by trying new ideas before the other farmers in the community."

A common error made by change agents is that they select opinion leaders who are too innovative. Change agents work through opinion leaders in order to close the heterophily gap with their clients (see Chapter 9). But if opinion leaders are too much more innovative than the average client, the heterophily that formerly existed between the change agent and his or her clients now exists between the opinion leaders and their followers. Innovators are poor opinion leaders in systems with traditional norms: They are too elite and too change-oriented. The innovator serves as an unrealistic model for the average client, and he or she knows this. The norms of the system determine which adopter category the opinion leaders in a system belong to.

A parallel case to that among farmer opinion leaders is found in the case of the former "laboratory schools" in the United States. These schools were usually affiliated with a college of education, located on a university campus, and served to introduce new teaching methods. The first lab school was founded by John Dewey at the University of Chicago around 1900, and served as the site for implementing his radical ideas in elementary education, such as "learning by doing" and "teach the whole child" (Rogers, 1994). Like the Dewey School, the typical lab school was wealthy, and its student body was composed of bright faculty children. Supposedly, the lab school was an attempt to demonstrate educational innovations that would then spread to other schools. But the lab schools, with their enriched environments and talented students, were perceived as too different by the average school. Teachers and administrators would visit the lab schools, impelled by curiosity, but went away unconvinced of the innovations they had observed. As a result, laboratory schools throughout the United States have fallen into disrepute as a means of educational diffusion. Almost all of them have been terminated. They were failures in demonstrating the usefulness of educational innovations.

Sometimes change agents identify potentially effective opinion leaders among their clients, but they concentrate their contacts too much on these leaders, who become innovators and lose their former followers. The relationship of respect between opinion leaders and their followers is a delicate balance. If an opinion leader becomes too innovative, or adopts a new idea too quickly, followers may begin to doubt the opinion leaders' judgment. One role of the opinion leader in a social system is to help reduce the uncertainty about an innovation for his or her followers. To fulfill this role, the opinion leader should demonstrate prudent judgment in decisions about adopting new ideas. So the opinion leader must continually look over his or her shoulder, and consider where the rest of the system is at regarding new ideas.

The opinion leaders' influence in a social system may vary not only on the basis of his or her innovativeness relative to the norms of the system, but also on the basis of the nature of the innovation that is diffusing. An interesting illustration of the role of opinion leaders in the diffusion of a high-uncertainty innovation and a low-uncertainty innovation is provided by Marshall Becker's (1970b) survey of ninety-five directors of local health departments.* The low-uncertainty innovation was a measles immunization program, a new idea that fit easily with the purpose of health

---

*Becker (1970b) actually referred to these two innovations as "high adoption potential" and "low adoption potential," with the former having a larger audience of potential adopters that the latter innovation.

departments and that was compatible with the professional norms of the directors of the health departments (who were medical doctors). The measles immunization program spread quickly among the health departments of study. The innovators in adopting this new program were the opinion leaders among the ninety-five health department directors. The adoption behavior of the opinion leaders served to speed up the diffusion process.

The high-uncertainty innovation was diabetes screening, a program that was a radical departure from the usual activities of public health departments. This innovation was socially risky because it infringed upon an activity usually performed by medical doctors in private practice (screening for chronic diseases). So this innovation did not fit with the norms of the public health system. The innovators in adopting this innovation were not opinion leaders; instead they were the directors of health departments whom their peers rated as socially marginal. The opinion leaders knew about this innovation, but they waited to adopt. Once the innovators had implemented the innovation of diabetes screening and found that its social risks were not excessive, the opinion leaders adopted. The innovation of diabetes screening then diffused rapidly, but only after an slow start.

Becker (1970b) interpreted these findings to mean that the time at which an individual adopted an innovation depended on whether or not the individual was an opinion leader, and whether the innovation was considered highly risky or not. Typically, innovative individuals hold back in adopting a high-uncertainty innovation to maintain their opinion leadership.

Becker's (1970b) investigation of health department directors is distinctive in that the respondents were heads of organizations. Can organizations have opinion leadership, as individuals do? A study by Jack Walker (1966) suggested that innovations can diffuse from organization to organization through interorganizational networks, in a parallel process to that among individuals in a social system.* The organizations studied by Professor Walker were the fifty state governments in America. Each state was scored as to its innovativeness in adopting (such as by enacting a new state law) each of eighty-eight new state programs in welfare, health, education, conservation, highways, civil rights, police, and the

---

*The publications bearing on the Walker study of innovativeness among the U.S. states are Walker (1966, 1971, 1973, 1976, 1977) and Gray (1973a, 1973b).

like. Each adoption by a state amounted to offering a new service, establishing a new regulation, or creating a new state agency. Examples are having a gasoline tax, enacting a civil rights bill, providing for slaughterhouse inspection, and having a state health board. The five most innovative states, Walker (1971) found, were New York, Massachusetts, California, New Jersey, and Michigan. The pioneering states, which Professor Walker called the national league, have large populations and are urbanized and industrialized. Perhaps they face social problems some years before the more rural and smaller states, and therefore enact new types of laws to cope with these problems. They are also richer states, so they have the resources to adopt innovations.

In each region of the United States, certain states emerged as opinion leaders; once they adopted a new program, other states in their region followed their lead. If an innovation was first adopted by a state other than one of these leader states, it then spread to the other states slowly or not at all. Thus, a network communication structure existed for innovation diffusion among the American states.

In a further analysis, Walker (1971) gathered sociometric data from personal interviews with state officials in ten of the states in order to determine the diffusion networks linking the American states. State officials looked to their immediate neighbors when searching for information about innovations: "State administrators communicate most readily with their counterparts in states that they believe have similar resources, social problems, and administrative styles" (Walker, 1971). For instance, Iowa officials followed Michigan's and California's lead in certain innovations, although they were much more influenced by Wisconsin, a bordering state to Iowa that was considered a more appropriate model. Walker (1971) found that the follower states in his study often copied the exact wording of a law previously adopted by an opinion leader state, including in several cases, a typographical error! Wisconsin ranked tenth on Walker's index of innovativeness; Iowa ranked twenty-ninth among the fifty states.

In summary, one can think of the diffusion process among the fifty American states as beginning with a new law that is adopted by one or more of the five "national league" states. After a few years, the new law may be adopted by one of the regional opinion leader states. Then the innovative law spreads rapidly among the surrounding states in that region. Note that the opinion leader states generally mediated between the five innovators and the other forty-five states. They provided connectedness to the nationwide diffusion network. Here we are beginning to look at more than just the characteristics of individual opinion leaders versus followers. We have taken a step toward gaining an improved understanding of diffusion networks by looking at the network structure of the system.

Networks in the Diffusion of a Medical Drug

Early diffusion scholars simply counted the number of network links reported for each individual in a system, in order to measure the degree of opinion leadership, and then determined the characteristics of opinion leaders and followers. In this type of investigation individuals were the units of analysis, even though the variable of opinion leadership was measured for individuals as the number of interpersonal choices they received. They next began using diffusion network *links* as units of analysis. This intellectual shift was a profound change in the nature of diffusion research. Such network analysis allowed deeper understanding of the previously hidden interpersonal mechanisms of the diffusion process.

The first diffusion investigation to explore the nature of diffusion networks was the classic study by James S. Coleman and others (1966) of a new drug's spread among medical doctors. This splendid investigation is distinctive in the insightful way in which Coleman and his colleagues investigated the interpersonal networks that impel the diffusion process. Like previous diffusion scholars, Coleman and others first studied various independent variables related to individual innovativeness (the month of adoption of the new drug tetracycline—code-named Gammanym—by medical doctors). Unlike most previous scholars, however, Coleman and his coresearchers included various indicators of network communication behavior among their independent variables of study; they found these network variables to be the most important predictors of innovativeness (more important than such individual characteristics as age, cosmopoliteness, and socioeconomic status).

But Coleman and others (1966) did not stop there, as previous diffusion researchers had done. Instead, they studied the way in which interpersonal networks explained the nature of the diffusion process. In this way, they departed from the previous reliance of diffusion scholars on the individual as the unit of analysis; they pioneered in using diffusion network links as their units of data analysis. This methodological advance provided important understandings of the interpersonal mechanisms creating the S-shaped diffusion curve.

Tetracycline was a powerful antibiotic drug, widely used in the treatment of acute conditions. The innovation had a potential for almost daily use by a physician in general practice. Tetracycline's efficacy in any particular case could be quickly and easily determined. The new drug seemed to be the approximate equivalent for doctors of what hybrid corn meant to Iowa farmers: A major change in previous behavior, whose results (in terms of relative advantage) were strikingly evident. Unlike the Iowa farmers, who adopted hybrid corn for themselves, the medical doctors were making adoption decisions for their patients. So the doctors may have faced less risk in adopting tetracycline; they could hardly have lost their medical practice because of the new drug. But the farmers had to pay for the hybrid corn they planted, and faced the prospect of crop failure.

Only two months after the new drug became available, 15 percent of the doctors tried it, and four months later this figure reached 50 percent (Coleman and others, 1966). Undoubtedly, the perceived attributes of tetracycline affected its rapid rate of adoption (it reached almost complete adoption by the doctors in the Illinois cities of study in only seventeen months), and emphasized the importance of peer networks in its diffusion. Although there was the usual uncertainty in a doctor's first use of the new drug, its results were strikingly positive and almost all of the interpersonal network messages about the innovation encouraged other doctors to adopt. Practically no discontinuance of tetracycline occurred during the seventeen-month period of its diffusion. Tetracycline was an ideal innovation to trace as it spread through diffusion networks in the four medical communities of study.

Coleman and others (1966) found that innovativeness in adopting the new drug was associated with several measures of network *interconnectedness* (defined as the degree to which the units in a social system are linked by interpersonal networks) for their sample of medical doctors:

1. Affiliation with a hospital as a regular staff member.
2. More frequent attendance at hospital staff meetings.
3. Sharing an office with one or more other doctors.
4. Being named sociometrically as a source of information and advice by other doctors.
5. Being named sociometrically by other doctors as someone with whom they discussed their patients' cases.
6. Being named sociometrically as a best friend by other doctors.

7.   Reciprocating the sociometric network links reported by other doctors
     who chose a respondent as a discussion partner.

For each of these seven network variables, doctors with more network
links were the most innovative in adopting tetracycline, while doctors who
were isolates (that is, who received no sociometric choices from their peers)
were latest in adopting the new drug (Figure 8–2). In fact, the degree of net-

Figure 8–2. The Rate of Adoption for Interconnected Doctors "Took-Off" in a Snowballing Contagion Process, While the Rate of Adoption for
Relatively Isolated Doctors Approached a Straight
Line

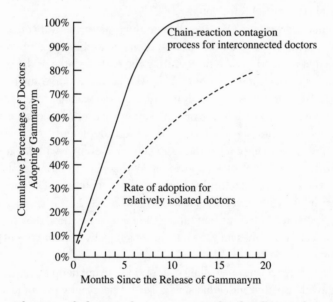

The rates of adoption above are a generalized and somewhat
stylized version of the actual rates of adoption of tetracycline
reported by Coleman and others (1966, p. 89) for interconnected versus isolated doctors, for each of the seven network
measures. The chain-reaction contagion process occurs for
interconnected doctors because they are closely linked by interpersonal networks.

Source: Based upon Coleman and others (1966).

work interconnectedness of a physician was a better predictor of innovativeness than any of the other independent variables investigated by Coleman and others (1966), such as a doctor's personal characteristics, exposure
to communication channels, patients' average incomes, and the like. "Be-
tween-people" variables were more important than the "within-people" variables. Among the various network connectedness measures, the best
predictor of innovativeness was the friendship variable (the sixth variable in
the list above); in fact, more than half of the forty-six isolate doctors (who
received only one or no friendship sociometric choices, and who practiced
medicine alone rather than in an office partnership) had still not adopted
the new drug ten months after it began to diffuse in the medical community
(Coleman and others, 1966). In comparison, at this same ten-month point,
almost all of the interconnected doctors (who received two or more network
choices) had adopted tetracycline.

Coleman and others (1966) explained the greater innovativeness of the
interconnected doctors on the basis of a chain-reaction kind of contagion
process that seemed to take place during the early months of the diffusion
process for tetracycline. Figure 8–2 shows that the S-curve for the interconnected doctors takes off rapidly in a kind of snowballing process: An early
adopter conveys his or her personal experience with the innovation to two
or more of his or her peers, who each may then adopt, and, in the next time
period, interpersonally convey their subjective experience with the new idea
to two or more other doctors, and so on. Within several months, almost all
of the interconnected doctors have adopted, and their rate of adoption then
necessarily begins to level off. This contagion process occurred because of
the interpersonal networks that linked the medical doctors, thus providing
communication avenues for the exchange of subjective evaluations of the innovation.

The chain-reaction snowballing of adoption did not happen, however, for
the relatively isolated individuals, who lacked peer-network contacts from
which to learn about others' subjective evaluations of the innovation. So the
isolated individuals' rate of adoption is almost a straight line, curving slightly
because the number of new adopters in each period remains a constant percentage of those who have not already adopted the innovation (see Figure
8–2). There is no sudden take-off in the rate of adoption for the isolated individuals. But eventually most or all of these isolated individuals adopted.
Interconnected doctors were more innovative in adopting the new drug because of their interpersonal networks: "The impact [of networks] upon the

integrated doctors was quick and strong; the impact upon isolated doctors was slower and weaker, but not absent" (Coleman and others, 1966).

When the doctors were confronted with making a decision about the new drug in an ambiguous situation that did not speak for itself, they turned to each other for information that would help them make sense out of the new idea. Thus, the meaning of the new drug was socially constructed. Doctors closely linked in networks tended to interpret the innovation similarly. In the case of tetracycline, the medical community studied by Coleman and others (1966) gradually arrived at a positive perception of the innovation. This shared opinion led the interconnected doctors to adopt the new drug more rapidly, but eventually the medical community's favorable view of the innovation trickled out to the relatively isolated doctors on the social margins of the network. We see that diffusion is a very social process.

We conclude this discussion with Generalization 8–15, which states that: *The network interconnectedness of an individual in a social system is positively related to the individual's innovativeness.* If individuals are convinced to adopt new ideas by the experience of near-peers with an innovation, then the more interpersonal communication an individual has with such near-peers, the more innovative the individual will be in adopting the new idea.

In recent years, several scholars reanalyzed the Coleman and others' drug diffusion data in order to question and extend several of the original conclusions about the role of social networks in the diffusion process. Ronald S. Burt (1980 and 1987) concluded that the similarity in the time of adoption of tetracycline by two doctors was not due mainly to a network link, but rather to "structural equivalence" (which occurs when two individuals occupy the same social space in the structure of a network). Peter V. Marsden and Joel Podolny (1990) also reanalyzed the data using the technique of event history analysis. They concluded that network variables had little influence on doctors' innovativeness in adopting tetracycline. Finally, Thomas W. Valente (1991,1993, and 1994) reanalyzed the data using a threshold model, in which each doctor has an individual threshold of resistance to the medical innovation which has to be overcome by network influences about the innovation from near-peers. Valente (1993) found that a combination of external influence from cosmopolite sources (particularly medical journals) plus the network interconnectedness of doctors best explained their innovativeness in adopting tetracycline. These recent reanalyses of the drug diffusion data illustrate how several scholars, each with a unique theoretical model and with distinctive methodological tools, come to different conclusions about the way in which network influences explain the adoption of an innovation.

This case illustration is based upon Coleman and others (1966).

Diffusion Networks

As we have just shown, the heart of the diffusion process is the modeling and imitation by potential adopters of their near-peers' experiences who have previously adopted a new idea. In deciding whether or not to adopt an innovation, individuals depend mainly on the communicated experience of others much like themselves who have already adopted. These subjective evaluations of an innovation mainly flow through interpersonal networks. We must understand the nature of networks if we are to understand fully the diffusion of innovations.

One evidence for the importance of network influences on individuals in the diffusion of innovations comes from investigations in Third World villages. For example, Rogers and Kincaid (1981) studied the diffusion of several different family planning innovations in twenty-five Korean villages. They found that certain of these villages were "pill villages," others were "IUD villages," and one of the villages was a "vasectomy village." In a "pill village" all of the adopters of family planning methods were using oral contraceptive pills, and, similarly in the other villages of study, all contraceptive adopters were using the same family planning method. Certainly such amazing homogeneity in choice of contraceptive innovation could not have occurred by chance. Each of the Korean villages had been the target of the same national family planning program, in which a standard cafeteria of contraceptive methods were promoted throughout the country.

Closer study by Rogers and Kincaid (1981) disclosed that in an "IUD village," for example, certain opinion leaders had first adopted a particular family planning innovation, the IUD, and their experiences were then shared with fellow villagers via interpersonal networks. The result, after several years of diffusion, was the tendency for every adopter in that village to be using the same method of family planning. These findings suggest that in Korea, the diffusion of family planning mainly occurs within villages, even though the government program was aimed at the national population.

Further evidence of this point came from the wide range in the percent of married, fertile-aged couples adopting family planning (Rogers and Kincaid, 1981). In some villages, more than 50 percent of the target audience had adopted. In other villages, the rate of adoption was only 10 or 15 percent. Such differences trace to the nature of intravillage communication networks. So an individual's network links are one important predictor of the individual's adoption of an innovation.

Similar clustering of adopters of an innovation has been observed in other settings. For example, William H. Whyte (1954) noted that window air conditioners were adopted by clusters of neighboring houses in a Philadelphia suburb. In the mid-1950s, the diffusion of air conditioners was well underway in America. Adoption of this relatively expensive item of household equipment was easily identifiable in the aerial photographs that Whyte took, as the air conditioners protruded out the windows of the Philadelphia row houses in the suburb that he studied. When Whyte followed up with personal interviews with the adopters of window air conditioners, he found that neighboring adopters seldom had purchased an identical brand of the cooling equipment. Satisfied adopters told their network partners about the pleasures of air conditioning, but they did not push the particular brand of equipment that they had adopted. Instead, they said that all brands of air conditioners were pretty much alike.

Patient Zero and Sexual Networks in the Early Spread of AIDS

The first Americans with AIDS were diagnosed by medical doctors in New York, San Francisco, and Los Angeles, and reported to the Centers for Disease Control and Prevention (CDC) in May, 1981. All of the patients were gay young men, otherwise in a state of good health. Many had a rare kind of skin cancer, Karposi's Sarcoma, previously only found in old men of Mediterranean descent. Others died of an unusual form of pneumonia. The new epidemic baffled the CDC investigators. When they interviewed the first forty patients to be diagnosed with AIDS symptoms, they found that nineteen of these men who lived in Los Angeles were linked by sexual contact with the twenty-one other patients who resided in San Francisco, New York, and elsewhere in the U.S. Clearly, something was being transmitted from man to man through sexual contact. What could it be? CDC investigators checked out various lubricants used in gay sex. They also looked into poppers and other types of drugs.

The forty patients with the mystery disease had one quality in common. They said they had sexual contacts with an average of 227 different individuals per year, with one patient reporting 1,560 sexual contacts. The CDC researchers identified one of the forty AIDS patients, whom they called "Patient Zero," as playing a particularly key role in the diffusion network. He named 72 different male partners during 1979 to 1981. Eight were among the other 39 AIDS patients. Further, Patient Zero connected the Los Angeles cluster with the New York cluster of AIDS patients.

Patient Zero was named Gaetan Dugas. He was a flight attendant for Air Canada, and traveled widely. He was strikingly handsome, and had a hyperactive sexual drive. These special characteristics represented a lethal factor in the sexual network for early AIDS transmission. Similarly in England, two of the first British patients with AIDS were homosexual airline stewards. And in India and East Africa, truck drivers and commercial sex workers at truck stops played a major role in spreading AIDS during the first phase of its diffusion.

The CDC investigators invited Professor Alden S. Klovdahl, a noted network scholar at Australian National University, to analyze the data on the network links among the 40 men with AIDS. Klovdahl used a special computer program, ORTEP, similar to that used by chemists to visualize molecular structures. On one of the three dimensions of the network of the forty men, Klovdahl plotted the date at which each individual reported the onset of AIDS symptoms (Figure 8–3) Now the crucial role of Patient Zero was even more apparent. While not the first individual with AIDS (he was the sixth), once Patient Zero got AIDS, many others soon followed. His eight direct sexual contacts in turn linked him to eight other men with AIDS, who in turn linked him to ten more of the men. So in three steps, Patient Zero infected 26 (63 percent) of the 39 other individuals with AIDS. Figure 8–3 indicates that some individuals seem to have infected others who reported AIDS symptoms earlier than their infectors. This is possible, because of the different lengths of individuals' infection periods (the time from being infected with the virus until the individual has AIDS symptoms).

The computer graphics of Klovdahl's computer program allowed the CDC researchers to better understand the nature of the AIDS network among the forty men. The CDC assumed that a virus was being transmitted through sexual contact, and that it caused an immune deficiency in the hu-

Figure 8–3. A Three-Dimensional Sociogram of the Sexual Links Among the First Forty Gay Men with AIDS, Showing the Key Role of Patient Zero (near the center of the network)

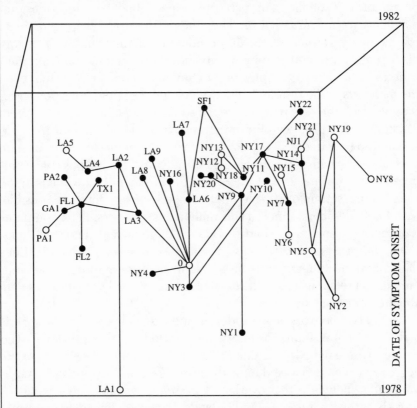

The vertical axis represents the date at which AIDS symptoms were first diagnosed for each respondent. A designation of "LA1" indicates the respondent was the first individual in Los Angeles to experience the onset of AIDS symptoms.

Source: Klovdahl (1985).

man body which allowed various infections to run unchecked. Later, this explanation was supported by other evidence, and AIDS was given its name, Acquired Immune Deficiency Syndrome.

Based on Klovdahl (1985) and on personal discussions with Alden S. Klovdahl.

Communication Network Analysis

A *communication network* consists of interconnected individuals who are linked by patterned flows of information. Networks have a certain degree of structure, of stability. This patterned aspect of networks provides predictability to human behavior. The study of networks helps illuminate *communication structure*, the differentiated elements that can be recognized in the patterned communication flows in a system. This communication structure is so complex that in any but a very small system even the members of the system do not understand the communication structure of which they are part. There are so many possible network links in a system, that a problem of information overload is caused for the individual who tries to detect the communication structure. For instance, in a social system with 100 members, 4,950 network links are possible (computed by the formula $(\frac{N[N-1]}{2})$ where N is the number of individuals in the system). In a system of 200 members, 19,900 network links are possible; with 1,000 members, almost a half-million links are possible. A computer is necessary to analyze the patterns among these myriad of network links. *Communication network analysis* is a method of research that identifies the communication structure in a system by using interpersonal communication relationships as the units of analysis in analyzing network data about communication flows.

Methods of network analysis identify individuals in cliques on the basis of their communication proximity in network links, so that individuals who are closer are assigned to the same clique. *Communication proximity* is the degree to which two linked individuals in a network have personal communication networks that overlap. A *personal communication network* consists of those interconnected individuals who are linked by patterned communication flows to a given individual. One can think of each individual possessing such a personal network, consisting of the set of other individuals to whom the focal individual is linked in network relationships. The focal individual's behavior is determined, in part, by information and influence that is communicated through the individual's personal network.

Some personal networks consist of a set of individuals, all of whom interact with each other; these are *interlocking personal networks*. In contrast, *radial personal networks* consist of a set of individuals linked to a focal individual but not interacting with each other. Such radial personal networks are less dense and more open,* and thus allow the focal indi-

---

Openness is the degree to which a unit exchanges information with its environment.

vidual to exchange information with a wider environment. Obviously, such radial networks are particularly important in the diffusion of innovations because the links reach out into the entire system, while an interlocking network is more ingrown in nature.

The Strength of Weak Ties Theory

The general notion of classifying network links on the basis of the degree to which they convey information began with Mark S. Granovetter's (1973) theory of "the strength of weak ties." This network scholar sought to determine how people living in the Boston suburb of Newton got jobs. Granovetter gathered data from a sample of 282 respondents who had taken a new job within the past year. To his surprise, most of these individuals said that they heard about their positions from heterophilous individuals who were not very close friends. These "weak ties" occurred with individuals "only marginally included in the current network of contacts, such as an old college friend or a former workmate or employer, with whom sporadic contact had been maintained" (Granovetter, 1973). Chance meetings with such acquaintances sometimes reactivated these weak ties, leading to the exchange of job information with the individual. Sometimes the lead to a new job came from a complete stranger.

An example of successful job searching through weak network links was an accountant who flew to Boston to attend a convention. The accountant shared a taxi at Logan Airport with a Bostonian businessman. They began a conversation, and the businessman disclosed that his company was seeking to hire an accountant. You can imagine what happened next. The accountant, who later resided in Newton, was one of Granovetter's respondents.

Only 17 percent of Granovetter's Newton respondents said they found their new job through close friends or relatives.* Why were weak ties so much more important than strong network links? Because an individual's close friends seldom know much that the individual does not also know. One's intimate friends are usually friends of each other's, forming a close-knit clique (an interlocking personal network). Such an ingrown system

---

*Similar evidence of the importance of weak ties in the diffusion of information about new jobs is provided by Langlois (1977), Lin and others (1981), and Friedkin (1980), but not by Murray and others (1981). An overall summary of research findings is provided by Granovetter (1982).

is an extremely poor net in which to catch new information from one's environment. Much more useful as a channel for gaining such information are an individual's more distant (weaker) acquaintances; they are more likely to possess information that the individual does not already possess, such as about a new job or about an innovation. Weak ties connect an individual's small clique of intimate friends with another, distant clique; as such, weak ties are often bridging links,* connecting two or more cliques. If these weak ties were somehow removed from a system, the result would be an unconnected set of separate cliques. So even though weak ties are not a frequent path for the flow of communication messages, the information flowing through them plays a crucial role for individuals and for the system. This great importance of weak ties in conveying new information is why Granovetter (1973) called his theory "the [informational] strength of weak [network] ties."

This weak-versus-strong-ties dimension is more precisely defined as *communication proximity*, the degree to which two individuals in a network have overlapping personal communication networks. Weak ties are low in communication proximity because they connect two individuals who do not share network links with a common set of other individuals. At least some degree of heterophily must be present in network links for the diffusion of innovations to occur. Low-proximity weak ties are often heterophilous, and this is the reason for their central importance in the diffusion process. For example, Liu and Duff (1972) and Duff and Liu (1975) found that a family planning innovation spread rather quickly among the members of small cliques of Filipino housewives. But this new idea did not diffuse throughout the total community until information about the contraceptive was conveyed by weak ties from one tight-knit clique to another. The weak ties were usually heterophilous on socioeconomic status, thus linking, for example, a higher-status clique with a lower-status clique.

We summarize this discussion with Generalization 8–16: *The information-exchange potential of communication network links is negatively related to their degree of (1) communication proximity, and (2) homophily*. Heterophilous links of low proximity (Granovetter's weak ties), while rare, play a crucial role in the flow of *information* about an innovation. This information may also be *influential* if it consists of a personal

---

*A *bridge* is an individual who links two or more cliques in a system from his or her position as a member of one of the cliques.

evaluation of an innovation by an individual who has already adopted it. Perhaps there is a strength of weak ties component in networks that convey information about an innovation, and a "strength of *strong* ties" in networks that convey interpersonal influence. Certainly the influence potential of network ties with an individual's intimate friends is stronger than the opportunity for influence from an individual's weak ties with seldom-contacted acquaintances. Closely linked peers in an interlocking network seldom exert their potential influence because this type of homophilous, high-proximity personal network is seldom activated by information about an innovation. An individual's intimates rarely possess much information that the individual does not already know. Information must flow into such an interlocking network to provide energy for further information exchange.

Who Is Linked to Whom in Networks?

Generalization 8–17 states: *Individuals tend to be linked to others who are close to them in physical distance and who are relatively homophilous in social characteristics.* Individuals form network links that require the least effort and that are most rewarding. Both spatial and social proximity can be indicators of least effort. Communication network links with neighboring and homophilous partners are relatively easy and require little effort. But we have just shown that such low-effort network links are usually of limited value for obtaining information about innovations. In contrast, heterophilous links with socially and spatially distant others are usually stronger in carrying information about new ideas to an individual. Easy network links are thus of less informational value.

The implication for individuals in managing their personal networks, if they wish to improve their reception of information, is to break out of the comfort of close links and to form more heterophilous and spatially distant network links.

Networks in Recruitment to Freedom Summer

Joining a protest, demonstration, social movement, or some other form of activism amounts to adopting an innovation, although in this case the new idea is an ideology rather than a hardware technology. An illustration of this point is provided by Doug McAdam's (1986) study of university students who joined the 1964 Mississippi Freedom Summer project. Hundreds of young people volunteered to travel to Mississippi to register black voters and to dramatize their denial of civil rights. They gave up their opportunity for summer jobs to support themselves while in the South. They lived with black families, enduring their poverty and fear. Three of the Freedom Summer activists were killed by segregationists that included Mississippi law enforcement officers. The volunteers endured arrests, beatings, and bombings. Certainly the adoption of volunteering for the 1964 Freedom Summer was a major decision. Recruitment of the volunteers typically resulted from a speech by a civil rights activist at a meeting on a university campus; then the recruit filled out a five-page application form and was personally interviewed by a recruiter for Freedom Summer.

Twenty years later, Professor Doug McAdam, a sociologist at the University of Arizona, obtained access to the applications of 720 volunteers and 239 other students who were selected but who then withdrew prior to departing for Mississippi in 1964. McAdam also conducted indepth personal interviews with eighty of the participants and withdrawals from the Freedom Summer project. The application form asked each student to list the names of ten people that they wished to be kept informed of their summer activities. These data allowed McAdam to measure each student's network links (1) with others who went on the Mississippi Freedom Summer, and (2) with students who withdrew. Further, indirect network links could be measured, such as with a student who was not named directly, but who was named by someone else that a respondent named. These indirect network ties were weak ties (Granovetter, 1973).

Weak ties did not have much impact in explaining whether a student volunteer went to Mississippi or withdrew. Neither did such other variables as prior activism, race, distance from Mississippi, college major, or other personal characteristics. Being male, of older age, and active in campus organizations were somewhat related to participation in Freedom Summer versus withdrawal. But by far the best predictor of going to Mississippi was having strong network relationships with other participants or to a Freedom Summer activist. Having a close friend who withdrew from the project influenced a respondent to also withdraw. Some of the withdrawals resulted from the opposition of parents or other adults. One example is a freshman woman who said: "I heard an SNCC [Student Nonviolent Coordinating Committee] person speak. . . . at [the university] and was absolutely mesmerized. It was like I now had a mission in life. I remember filling out the application and racing back to my dorm to call my parents, thinking, of course, that they would be as thrilled with my 'mission' as I was." But the student's mother started crying, and her father threatened to stop paying for tuition. Faced with these negative influences, the student withdrew from Freedom Summer.

As in the adoption of technological innovations reviewed previously in this book, the diffusion of an ideological innovation is a social process. Interpersonal network links, more than any other single factor, explain whether or not university students risked their lives by participating in the 1964 Mississippi Freedom Summer. Perhaps because an ideological innovation does not have a material referent (that is, hardware) to the extent that a technological innovation does, its social construction through interpersonal communication with others is especially important.

A crucial concept in understanding the social nature of the diffusion process is the *critical mass*, a point in the process when diffusion becomes self-sustaining. The notion of the critical mass comes from scholars of social movements, and in recent years the concept has become useful in studies of the diffusion of interactive innovations.

The present case illustration is based upon McAdam (1986) and McAdam and Paulson (1993).

The Critical Mass in the Adoption of Interactive Innovations

The rate of adoption of interactive media such as electronic messaging systems, fax, and teleconferencing often displays a certain distinctive quality called the critical mass. The *critical mass* occurs at the point at which enough individuals have adopted an innovation so that the innovation's further rate of adoption becomes self-sustaining. The interactive quality of the new media creates a certain degree of interdependence among the adoption decisions of the members of a system. An interactive innovation is of little use to an adopting individual unless other individuals with whom the adopter wishes to communicate also adopt. Thus, a critical mass of individuals must adopt an interactive communication technology before it has utility for the average individual in the system. With each additional adopter, the utility of an interactive communication technology increases for all adopters. An illustration is provided by the very first individual to adopt a telephone in the 1870s. This interactive technology had no utility until a second individual also adopted. Until a critical mass occurs at a relatively early stage in the diffusion process, the rate of adoption is slow. After a critical mass is achieved, the rate of adoption accelerates (Figure 8–4).

Interactivity is the degree to which participants in a communication process can exchange roles in, and have control over, their mutual discourse (Williams, Rice, and Rogers, 1988). "Mutual discourse" is the degree to which a given communication act is based on a prior series of communication acts. Thus, each message in a sequence of exchanges affects the next message in a kind of cumulative process. *Exchange of roles* means the empathic ability of individual A to take the position of individual B (and thus to perform B's communication acts), and vice-versa. Having *control* means the extent to which an individual can choose the timing, content, and sequence of a communication act, search out alternative choices, enter the content into storage for other users, and perhaps create new communication capabilities (Williams, Rice, and Rogers,

Figure 8–4. The Rate of Adoption (1) for a Usual Innovation, and (2) for an Interactive Innovation, Showing the Critical Mass

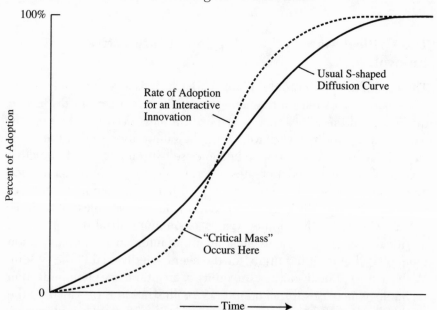

The *critical mass* occurs at the point at which enough individuals have adopted an innovation so that the innovation's further rate of adoption becomes self-sustaining.

1988). Such control of the communication process is broadly shared in the case of interactive communication.

Interactive communication technologies facilitate multidirectional information exchanges. In the case of noninteractive innovations, the earlier adopters have a *sequential* interdependence effect on later adopters. As more and more individuals in a system adopt, the noninteractive innovation is perceived as increasingly beneficial to future adopters. But in the case of interactive innovations, not only do earlier adopters influence later adopters, but later adopters also influence earlier adopters, in a process of *reciprocal* interdependence (Markus, 1990). The benefits from each additional adoption of an interactive innovation increase not only for all future adopters, but also for each previous adopter. The distinctive aspect of interactive communication technologies, in a diffusion sense, is "reciprocal interdependence, in which later adopters influence earlier adopters as well as the other way around" (Markus, 1990). So the benefits of an interactive innovation flow backward in time to previous adopters, as well as forward in time to future adopters.

Diffusion of an Interactive Innovation: BITNET and INTERNET

BITNET and INTERNET are typical of new communication technologies that are interactive in nature; a kind of interpersonal communication occurs via an electronic communication channel, rather than face-to-face. Examples of interactive communication technologies are e-mail (like BITNET and INTERNET), telephones, and, to a certain extent, fax.

BITNET stands for "Because It's Time NETwork." This interconnection of university computers was begun in 1981 by Ira Fuchs, the Vice Chancellor for University Systems at CUNY (the City University of New York), and Greydon Freemen, director of the computer center at Yale University. Both university campuses had made considerable use of local computer networking on their own campus, which seemed to fit with the collaborative nature of much academic work. BITNET began when the two university computer centers were connected via a leased telephone line, thus allowing anyone at either of the two university local networks to exchange messages that were typed into a computer. By the end of the first year, 1981, four additional universities joined BITNET. Each subscribing university joined by leasing a telephone line to the nearest university that already belonged to BITNET.

Here we see an illustration of sequential interdependence; each additional adopting university increased the benefits of BITNET for every institution that was a potential adopter through a decreased initial cost of adoption. The first adopters of BITNET were elite East Coast institutions, who were highly competitive in applying for government and foundation research grants. They had the usual characteristics of innovators (see Chapter 7).

Then, in 1982, the University of California at Berkeley leased a long, expensive telephone line to join BITNET. This adoption was key to opening up BITNET to other West Coast universities, and a number joined shortly, each paying a part of the transcontinental phone line. This is an illustration of reciprocal interdependence, in which each additional adopter increases the utility of the innovation for both future adopters and previous adopters. Suddenly, the rate of adoption of BITNET took off; by 1983, nineteen universities joined. Then, between 1984 and 1985, BITNET doubled in size every six months. Telephone leased lines to Canadian, European, and Japanese universities were established. Federal R&D laboratories also joined BITNET, and connections to ARPANET (a prior electronic network of defense-related R&D organizations) were established. Eventually, in the early 1990s, BITNET joined with numerous other networks to form INTERNET, an electronic network of networks. At this point, an academic person at a U.S. research university could safely assume that any other such individual with whom they wished to communicate could be reached via BITNET.

The growth of computer networks has increased at an exponential rate in recent years. The main impetus for this expansion was the formation of INTERNET, a network linking over 20,000 existing computer networks, including BITNET. The origins of INTERNET go back to ARPANET, which was created in 1969 to allow U.S. Department of Defense contractors to share computer services. E-mail was added as an afterthought, but soon came to be the dominant function for the network's users. ARPANET was designed in the Cold War era to survive a nuclear attack, so there was no single control point. When INTERNET was formed out of ARPANET in 1983, it continued this many-to-many, decentralized network structure. Thousands and thousands of computers are linked by telephone lines through thousands and thousands of different network paths. A particular message courses its way toward its intended destination, passed along from computer to computer. So nobody really runs INTERNET. Such is the true nature of a network.

By mid-1993, INTERNET connected 15,000,000 computers, a number that was doubling annually. These INTERNET users included people in 200 nations, and 800 million messages were transmitted during 1994. What do people use INTERNET for? Authors collaborate in writing books on INTERNET. Some users fall in love, and plan their wedding on the network. Other individuals utilize the humor bulletin boards, some of which feature soft porn. Many users seek, and exchange, information about a particular topic. A computer company offers free use of its new computer to those who wish to try it out with their own software programs, linked to the new computer via INTERNET. Many INTERNET users are university professors and R&D workers who exchange technical information with other members of their invisible college.

What if someone "misbehaves" on INTERNET? They quickly receive negative feedback until they change their behavior. For instance, one company sent copies of its catalogue of products to a large number of INTERNET users. This inappropriate act led to an immediate and critical response from thousands of network participants. The catalogue company evidently had not realized that a network is a two-way street. Such "mailbox bombing" occurs when individuals send thousands of messages to someone's e-mail account in order to overload it, as punishment for misconduct on INTERNET. So the decentralized network has a self-policing function. Even though no single authority is in charge of INTERNET, social norms are upheld.

Gurbaxani (1990) fit various curves to the data on rate of adoption for BITNET, and concluded that the distribution closely approximated an S-shaped curve. The critical mass occurred just after 1982 when UC Berkeley joined BITNET. "Once the critical mass was reached, however, the growth rate increased dramatically to where the number of nodes doubled every six months" (Gurbaxani, 1990). A crucial strategy for managers of an interactive innovation is to identify those units in a system whose adoption will most rapidly influence potential users to subscribe: In the present case, UC Berkeley, a highly respected California university, triggered the critical mass with its adoption of BITNET. Once it adopted, many other universities followed. With each additional adopter, the innovation of BITNET became more valuable to each future adopter, and also to every previous adopter. Then, when BITNET joined with other computer networks in INTERNET, the total number of users skyrocketed because of reciprocal interdependence.

This case illustration is based on Gurbaxani (1990), and on various other sources.

*Background of the Concept of the Critical Mass** *

The notion of the critical mass originated in physics, where it was defined as the amount of radioactive material necessary to produce a nuclear reaction. "An atomic pile 'goes critical' when a chain reaction of nuclear fission becomes self-sustaining" (Schelling, 1978). Various illustrations of critical mass situations, in which a process becomes self-sustaining after some threshold point has been reached, abound in everyday life. A single log in a fireplace will not continue to burn by itself; a second log must be present so that each log reflects its heat onto the other. When the ignition point is reached, the fire takes off, and the two logs will burn to ashes.

The critical mass bears on the relationship between the behavior of individuals and the larger system of which they are part. It thus centers on a crucial cross-level analysis that is "characteristic of a large part of the social sciences, especially the more theoretical part" (Schelling, 1978). "The principle of 'critical mass' is so simple that it is no wonder that it shows up in epidemiology, fashion, survival and extinction of species, language systems, racial integration, jaywalking, panic behavior, and political movements" (Schelling, 1978).

The concept of the critical mass is so fundamental to an understanding of such a wide range of human behavior because individual's actions often depend on how many other individuals around them are behaving in a particular way (Schelling, 1978). Much of the theory and research concerning the critical mass in recent decades was inspired by Mancur Olson's (1965) *The Logic of Collective Action*: "Even if all the individuals in a large group are rational and self-interested, and would gain if, as a group, they acted to achieve their common interest or objective, they would still not voluntarily act to achieve that common or group interest." This seeming irrationality has attracted a great deal of scholarly attention to the study of collective action by communication scholars, sociologists, social psychologists, economists, and scholars of public opinion. Why is individual behavior in a system so seemingly illogical? The basic reason is that each individual acts in ways that are rational in pursuing *individual* goals without fully considering that he or she might be disadvantaging the system at the *collective* level.

Olson's "logic of collective action" is similar to Garrett Hardin's (1968) "tragedy of the commons," in which each individual pursues a rational

---

*The present discussion of the critical mass draws directly on Rogers (1990b and 1991b).

course of behavior that ironically drives the system (that is, the "commons") to disaster. Hardin's concept derives its name from the commons pasture in Medieval European villages, which was filled to its grazing capacity. Each herdsman calculated that the addition of one more animal would not exceed the capacity of the commons. But each of several hundred herdsmen calculated similarly, with a result of excessive grazing, erosion, and destruction of the commons pasture. A contemporary analogue occurs in the use of air conditioners by urban dwellers during a heat wave. "Each individual is most comfortable using his/her air conditioner at full power; yet if everyone does so, the result is a power overload that leaves everyone with no cooling at all" (Brewer, 1985).

Watching While Being Watched

Now consider a new electronic messaging system being introduced in an organization. This electronic messaging system has greater and greater utility for all users as additional individuals adopt. If the first adopters were to think only of their own *immediate* benefits, rather than about how they might *eventually* benefit, or how their organization might benefit, no one would adopt and the S-shaped diffusion process for the innovation would never begin. Until there is a critical mass of adopters, an interactive innovation has little advantage (and considerable disadvantage) for individual adopters. So we see another illustration of individual/system relationships, as in the previously discussed case of the logic of collective action and the tragedy of the commons. When a critical number of individuals have adopted an interactive innovation, a further rate of diffusion becomes self-sustaining. The critical mass is thus a kind of tipping point or social threshold in the diffusion process. After the critical mass is reached, the social system encourages further adoption by individual members of the system.

The notion that individuals adopt an innovation in part on the basis of their expectations regarding others' future adoption is suggested by Allen (1983): "It seems likely that individuals base their choice on what they expect the others to decide. Thus, the individual's effort to decide hinges upon 'watching the group'—the other members in the community of actual/potential subscribers—to discern what the group choice may be. . . . The outcome for the group then turns literally upon everybody watching while being watched."

The critical mass can also affect *discontinuance* of an interactive innovation, as well as adoption. As noted previously, diffusion theory allows for a certain degree of one-directional interdependence in individuals' decisions to adopt: Later adopters are influenced by earlier adopters (but not vice versa). For noninteractive innovations, this one-way influence relationship is called sequential interdependence. The notion of a critical mass implies that reciprocal interdependence also occurs, in which early adopters are influenced by later adopters (and discontinuers and rejecters), as well as vice versa. "As users defect, the benefits to the remaining users will decrease and the costs increase, thus stimulating further defection" (Markus, 1987). Thus, just as the critical mass affects the rate of adoption of an interactive innovation, it may also affect the rate of discontinuance by speeding up this process.

For example, consider an individual in an organization who stops responding to e-mail messages. This discontinuance of the e-mail system soon becomes evident to other individuals who are sending electronic messages to the discontinuer. They conclude that e-mail is no longer an effective way to reach the discontinuer. Thus everyone else becomes slightly more likely to discontinue using e-mail. So discontinuance of the interactive innovation by one individual may lead eventually to a critical mass of discontinuers, and then to complete rejection of e-mail by the entire organization.

Until this point in our discussion of the critical mass, we have treated all adopters as equivalent in their influence potential. Obviously they are not. A small number of highly influential individuals who adopt a new idea may represent a stronger critical mass than a very large number of individual adopters who have little influence. The critical mass typically includes the opinion leaders in a system, which implies that the communication network structure of the system is vitally involved in contributing to the power of the critical mass in the diffusion process of interactive innovations.

Individual Thresholds for Adoption

A *threshold* is the number of other individuals who must be engaged in an activity before a given individual will join that activity (Granovetter, 1978; Markus, 1987). In the case of the diffusion of an innovation, a threshold is reached when an individual is convinced to adopt as the result of knowing that some minimum number of other individuals in the system (or, more likely, in the individual's personal communication network) have adopted, and are satisfied with their use of the innovation. Notice that a threshold is at the *individual* level of analysis, whereas the critical mass operates at the *system* level. Individuals have adoption thresholds; systems such as communities and organizations have a critical mass. Individual thresholds explain the microlevel process through which aggregated individual decisions make up the critical mass in a system.

Granovetter (1978) provided an illustration of how the two-level phenomenon of individual thresholds and system-level critical mass are interrelated: "Imagine 100 people milling around in a square—a potential riot situation. Suppose their riot thresholds are distributed as follows: There is one individual with threshold 0, one with threshold 1, one with threshold 2, and so on up to the last individual with threshold 99. This is a distribution of thresholds. The outcome is clear and could be described as a 'bandwagon' or 'domino' effect: The person with threshold 0, the 'instigator,' engages in riot behavior—breaks a window, say. This activates the person with threshold 1. The activity of these two people then activates the person with threshold 2, and so on, until all 100 people have joined."

If we removed the individual with threshold 1 and replaced the individual by someone with threshold 2, the riot would end with just one rioter. No critical mass would be reached.

Threshold models assume that an individual decision to adopt an innovation depends on the number of other individuals in the system who have already made the behavior change (Krassa, 1988). Although the conceptual notion of a distribution of individual thresholds facilitates our understanding of the diffusion process (especially for an interactive innovation), few empirical studies of this topic have been conducted. Thomas W. Valente (1991, 1993, and 1994) has pioneered in advancing our understanding of thresholds (and critical mass) in the diffusion of innovations.

Why Do Individuals Adopt Prior to the Critical Mass?

A key question in understanding the role of the critical mass in the diffusion process is why an individual adopts an interactive technology before the point at which a critical mass is reached. At any earlier point, the perceived cost of adopting the innovation outweighs its perceived benefits. An early adopting individual may decide to adopt in anticipation that the innovation's rate of adoption will take off in the near future when others adopt, although past diffusion research suggests that most individuals do not adopt an innovation until after learning of their peers' successful experiences (Rogers, 1986b).

Typical adoption behavior is illustrated by a Korean woman, a respondent in a diffusion survey conducted by Rogers and Kincaid (1981) in 1973, who adopted a family planning innovation (Figure 8–5). As an increasing percentage of her personal network (the dozen other women in her village with whom she talked most often about family planning) adopted family planning methods, she gradually was influenced to adopt. The percentage of network partners who had adopted rose from 33 percent in 1969 to 50 percent in 1970 and 1971 and to 62 percent in 1972, when a "tipping point" (the respondent's individual threshold) was reached. Then the respondent adopted. The Korean villages in the study were systems in which, in Allen's (1983) words, everybody was watching while being watched in the process of family planning diffusion.

The threshold for adoption varies for different individuals in a system, which explains the S-shaped diffusion curve. The innovators who adopt an innovation first have a very low threshold for adoption, attributable to their venturesomeness. Later adopters have higher thresholds (that is, stronger resistance to the innovation) that are reached only when many other individuals in their personal network have adopted. Whereas later adopters are much more heavily socialized into the local system, innovators, due to their cosmopolite orientation, are almost social isolates in the system. Individual thresholds for adoption are normally distributed, thus creating the S-curve of diffusion.

Valente (1994) showed that network thresholds can be used to classify individuals according to (1) their innovativeness with respect to their system, and (2) their innovativeness with respect to their personal network partners. This type of analysis locates individuals who have adopted early in the diffusion process, but late relative to their personal network partners. Similarly, Valente's analysis showed that some individuals were late adopters who were exposed to the innovation through their network partners, but who still did not adopt. Other individuals were late adopters because of a lack of network exposure to the innovation. Here we see the analytical advantages of exploring the individual's innovativeness as a function of his/her network partners' innovativeness in adopting an innovation.

The general point here is expressed in Generalization 8–18, that *An individual is more likely to adopt an innovation if more of the other individuals in his or her personal network have adopted previously* (Rogers and Kincaid, 1981). Diffusion is highly social in nature: An individual's threshold for adoption is reached when a certain number of the individ-

Figure 8–5. Illustration of an Individual's Threshold for Adoption (indexed as the percentage of adopters in the individual's personal communication network) of Family Planning Innovations for a Woman in a Korean Village

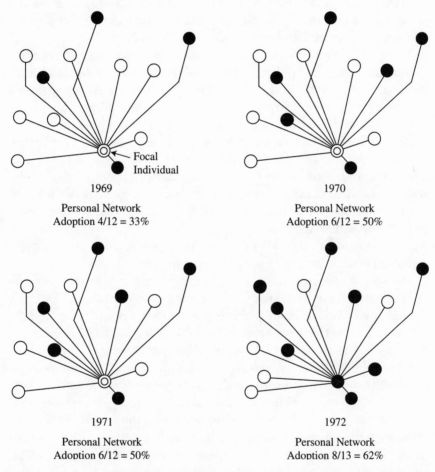

1969

Personal Network
Adoption 4/12 = 33%

1970

Personal Network
Adoption 6/12 = 50%

1971

Personal Network
Adoption 6/12 = 50%

1972

Personal Network
Adoption 8/13 = 62%

The Korean woman who is the focal individual in this personal communication network of a dozen village women adopted a family planning innovation only after half of her network partners adopted, in 1972. Thus this individual had a relatively high threshold of resistance to family planning methods, which had to be overcome by extensive network influences from near-peers who had adopted previously.

Source: Rogers and Kincaid (1981).

ual's peers have adopted. Innovators, having a very low threshold, adopt an innovation relatively early and thus launch the diffusion process for an innovation in a system. By adopting early, the innovators help other, later-adopting individuals to reach their adoption threshold. When the critical mass in the rate of adoption of an interactive innovation is reached, the percentage of all individuals' network partners takes a sudden jump, triggering a much more rapid rate of adoption thereafter.

To explain the effect of the critical mass on the adoption behavior of a system's members, we utilized thinking about microlevel personal communication networks. Many key questions about the critical mass can only be answered by investigating the networks through which the critical mass occurs and by which it exerts its effects. For example, in our discussion of the Korean woman's adoption of family planning (see Figure 8–5), we measured her adoption threshold as the percentage of her personal communication network partners who adopted prior to her. We did not measure her adoption threshold as the percentage of all of the other thirty-eight women in her *village*, as she did not communicate about family planning with two-thirds of these fellow villagers. Measures of individuals' adoption thresholds are more precise when measured at the personal network level than at the level of the entire system.

The notion of a critical mass calls for important modifications of diffusion theory in the particular case of interactive innovations. The critical mass may also occur for noninteractive innovations. For example, a new article of clothing becomes fashionable when a critical mass of social elites begins wearing it. The fashionable dressers are watching while being watched. Other individuals then rapidly adopt the new fashion, which will eventually be supplanted by a yet-newer clothing fashion. Yesterday's fashions are sold in second-hand stores and at garage sales.

A good deal of interdependence occurs among the adopters of any innovation in the sense that adopters influence their peers to adopt by providing them with a positive (or negative) evaluation of the innovation. Such peer influence usually makes the diffusion curve take off somewhere between the 5-percent and 20-percent level of adoption. Once this take-off is achieved, little additional promotion of the innovation is needed, as further diffusion is self-generated by the innovation's own social momentum. This explanation for the S-shaped curve of adoption for a noninteractive innovation sounds much like the critical mass. What is different in the special case of interactive innovations is that there is a built-in "forcing quality" in the adopter-to-decider relationship, which stems from the reciprocal interdependence of interactive innovations. "It takes two to tango," as Katz (1962) pointed out. At least two.

The Critical Mass in the Diffusion of Fax

Since 1983, when the diffusion of facsimile ("fax") machines began, the rate of adoption has been more rapid than that for personal computers or VCRs, and it rivals that of cellular telephones in the U.S. This rapid diffusion of fax occurred, however, after a wait of 150 years while the technology was shaped into its present form, the appropriate telephone infrastructure to support fax was put in place, and until a critical mass of users slowly accumulated.

Fax was invented in 1843 by Alexander Bain, a Scottish clockmaker who called it a recording telegraph because the message was transmitted over telegraph lines. There were no adopters. A century later, in 1948, RCA announced a fax machine that transmitted messages via radio waves; it was called ultra-fax. During the 1960s, Xerox manufactured a fax machine called a "telecopier" that was sold to the Associated Press, UPI, and Reuters news agencies to send photographs and documents over telephone lines to mass media newsrooms. But at this point, accessing phone lines still required operator assistance, telecopiers were slow (it took eight minutes to transmit a single page), and the machines emitted an unpleasant smell.

Next, automatic telephone dialing and direct connection of a fax machine to regular phone lines was allowed. Faster transmission was demanded by users. A fax machine scans a page and converts the material on it into electric signals, which are sent over phone lines. The time required for telephone transmission limited the speed of sending a fax. A universal standard was adopted by the manufacturers of fax machines in 1965. But the equipment was still relatively expensive, about $8,000. The price began to fall, and transmission speed increased, when Japanese companies entered the market around 1980. Sharp introduced the first low-priced machine ($2,000) in 1984, and large companies in the U.S. began to buy fax machines. About 80,000 machines were sold that year. The price of a fax machine began to drop further in ensuing years, to $500 in 1980, and to $250 in 1993. It was estimated that a single page could be faxed from Los Angeles to Washington, D.C. for as little as a dime, compared to a first-class stamp of 29 cents. The main advantage of sending a fax is speed; so it mainly competes with overnight mail, which is much more expensive, depends on a third party for delivery, and does not provide a written confirmation that the message has been received, as does fax. A fax-message conveys a sense of urgency to the individual receiving it, that the message must be important.

Although the fax boom began in the United States around 1983, the rate of adoption remained quite slow until 1987, the year in which a critical mass of users occurred. About one million machines were sold in 1987, and in 1989, two million fax units were adopted. Starting in 1987, Americans began to assume that "everybody else" had a fax machine (Holmlöv and Warneryd, 1990). "What is your fax number?" became a common query among American businesspeople. Fax numbers began to appear on individual's business cards. Dating services used fax messages, and many takeout restaurants, such as pizza shops, began to encourage customers to fax in their orders. One U.S. company markets special fax stationery via ads transmitted by fax, and promises a Sony Walkman to anyone who supplies the company with 100 fax numbers. Fax advertising makes up about 1 percent of all fax transactions. In recent years, some states passed legislation banning all junk mail by fax.

So it took 150 years for fax to become an overnight success!

This case illustration is based upon Holmlöv and Warneryd (1990), and various other sources.

Strategies for Getting to Critical Mass

What are some possible strategies that may be used to reach critical mass for an innovation in a system?

1. Target top officials in an organization's hierarchy for initial adoption of the interactive innovation. For example, when the president of an organization champions an interactive technology and is the first to adopt and utilize the new medium to send messages to other individuals in the organization, an obvious metacommunication message is implied: Other individuals should adopt the new technology to respond to the president's electronic messages. In 1982, a photograph of Stanford University president Donald Kennedy using a new electronic mail system appeared in the university's faculty newsletter. It was a clear signal that professors should adopt the e-mail system.

   Clearly, the organizational context for the critical mass can be important in providing organizational pressures to adopt an interactive innovation. An organization's hierarchy, reward system, and regulations can encourage, or discourage, the adoption of a new idea. The organization can provide resources for the adoption of an interactive technology and thus lower individuals' perceived cost of adopting.

2. Shaping individuals' perceptions of the innovation; for example, by implying that adoption of the innovation is inevitable, that the innovation is very desirable, or that the critical mass has already occurred or will occur soon.

3. Introducing the innovation to intact groups in the system whose members are likely to adopt at once. The city of Santa Monica, California, an upper-middle class community adjoining Los Angeles, launched Public Electronic Network (PEN) in 1989. PEN was one of the first municipal electronic communication systems in the United States that was free to citizens. The PEN project provided computer bulletin boards to individuals, including the members of a Neighborhood Watch group, a PTA, or a church group. Many members of these intact groups adopted at the same time, thus helping achieve a critical mass.

4. Provide incentives for early adoption of the interactive innovation, at least until the critical mass is reached.

"The most direct approach [to reaching critical mass] is to give the service free to a selected group of people for a limited time" (Rohlfs, 1974). An illustration of this strategy is provided by the French government, which in the 1980s gave free Minitel units to hundreds of thousands of heavy telephone users. Although very expensive, this strategy for achieving critical mass was successful. Within a dozen years, more than 6.0 million French households (about 25 percent of all telephone subscribers) had adopted the Minitel videotext system. Videotext is a system of delivering colored frames of information to a home or office television or computer screen by means of a cable or telephone line. The Minitel experience is all the more noteworthy because other attempts to introduce videotext services, in the United States and elsewhere, have been unsuccessful. Despite very heavy initial investments, these efforts failed to achieve a critical mass of users.

Minitel in France: Getting to Critical Mass

The French Minitel system consists of a microcomputer function, a small screen, and a connection to a home or office telephone in order to provide electronic telephone directory services. In addition to linking a telephone subscriber to France's 35 million phone numbers, Minitel provides weather, home banking, ticket reservation, teleshopping, games, and other information services. But the function that helped most in getting Minitel to critical mass was completely unplanned by the French engineers who designed the system: Conversational chatting on the *messagerie* bulletin boards. Minitel was designed as a kind of newspaper, but functions most importantly as a kind of interactive telephonic service.

By 1993, 6 million French telephone subscribers had adopted Minitel, about 25 percent of the total, and the number of Minitel users was continuing to increase at 24 percent per year. More than a billion connections were made by Minitel users each year. The amazing success of Minitel is all the more impressive in comparison to other videotext systems in the world, none of which have been adopted by even 10 percent as many users. Minitel's success was achieved in the first three or four years of its diffusion, by the mid-1980s, when it reached a critical mass of users. How did Minitel get to critical mass?

The story begins with a vision of France as an information society and as a major world producer of computer-related technology. This vision statement was expressed by Simon Nora and Alain Minc in their 1978 report, *The Computerization of Society*, which became a best-selling book in France. The French felt threatened by the British Prestel system, which the French feared would become the world standard for videotext. The French telephone system at this time was simply awful, and was very underused. The French telecommunications agency launched a trial of a new videotext system in Vélizy, a Paris suburb, in 1981. At this point, the system was called Antiope, a name that caused public confusion with the animal by a similar name. French newspapers felt that Antiope was unfair government competition in delivering the news, and threatened legal action against the government telecommunications agency.

The new videotext system was renamed "Minitel," and the pilot project at Vélizy was expanded to several other relatively wealthy areas in France. Soon Minitel service was available in an entire province. Then the Minitel project was expanded to another province, and within five years, Minitel was available nationwide. French Telécom provided an annual subsidy of $800 million to launch Minitel, hoping that this huge investment would be returned once a critical mass of adopters was achieved. By 1990, Minitel broke even, and since then has earned a return on investment of 8 to 12 percent per year.

The monthly charges for using Minitel were not separated from regular telephone usage on subscribers' bills, so most individuals did not actually know how much they were paying for Minitel. Actually, the monthly bills of Minitel subscribers are about 150 percent those of non-Minitel phone subscribers, so there is a considerable extra cost.

French Telécom also provided incentives to various companies that used Minitel to connect with their customers. An example of such kiosk services is a newsstand from which a Minitel subscriber can order *Le Monde* or some other newspaper delivered to his or her home address. Business use of Minitel is considerable; 95 percent of French companies with more than 500 employees have adopted Minitel.

Despite these incentives, the rate of adoption for Minitel during the early 1980s was discouragingly slow for French Telécom, who wanted to achieve a high level of use and thus regain their huge investment of about $1.8 billion as quickly as possible. In October 1981, a key event of a completely unplanned nature occurred. Some computer hackers in the city of Strasbourg began to exchange chatty messages via Minitel. These live conversations took place via a *messagerie* service that the computer pirates called Gretel, identified by a logo of a heart with fluttering eyelashes. Participants in this electronic mail system were anonymous (even the monthly billing from French Telécom does not indicate which services were used), and much of the message content was sex-related. The Telécom design engineers were scandalized, and threatened to close Gretel down. But Minitel Rosé ("Pink Minitel") rapidly became too popular to kill. Within a year, chatting bulletin boards on Minitel were receiving 1,200 calls per day, with an average length of one hour per call, at a cost of $12 (U.S.) per hour. Pink Minitel was addictive; one French woman ran up a monthly bill of $14,000. Soon the sex-related messaging services on Minitel represented 8 percent of all calls, 19 percent of the time spent using Minitel, 22 percent of total sales, and half of Minitel's profits. Minitel was now well on its way to reaching critical mass. French people use the *messageries* as the electronic equivalent of singles bars. In a nation known for its love of talk and its talk of love, perhaps Pink Minitel should not have come as a surprise to the engineers who designed the Minitel system. The names of the Minitel Rosé messaging services imply their soft pornographic content: Sextel, Désiropolis, Aphrodite, Aíme-Moi. Minitel subscribers must pay for such titillation: French Telécom imposed a special extra tax of 33 percent on users of Minitel Rosé.

French Telécom made Minitel so easy to adopt that discontinuance was also very easy. About 20 percent of the 6 million adopters of this videotext system do not use it at all, and another 30 percent of adopters use it very little. Some 20 percent of subscribers only use Minitel for telephone directory services. Heaviest users are white-collar employees. Minitel has only negligible use in rural areas of France. Public Minitel terminals are available in post offices throughout France, to provide electronic directory services.

The key to the success of Minitel was in getting to a critical mass of users rapidly, and the unplanned role of Minitel Rosé drove this early rate of adoption.

This case illustration draws on Kramer (1993) and numerous other published accounts of the diffusion of Minitel.

Social Learning Theory

A social psychological theory with direct applicability to diffusion networks is social learning theory. Most psychological approaches to human learning look within the individual to understand how learning occurs. But the social learning approach looks outside of the individual at a specific type of information exchanges with others to explain how behavior changes. The intellectual leader of social learning theory is Professor Albert Bandura (1977) of Stanford University.

The central ideal of social learning theory is that an individual learns from another by means of observational modeling; that is, one observes another person's behavior, and then does something similar. The observer's behavior is not exactly the same as the model's, which would be simple imitation or blind mimicry. Rather, in social modeling the observer extracts the essential elements from an observed behavior pattern in order to perform a similar behavior. Modeling allows the learner to adapt the observed behavior (much like the re-invention of an innovation).

The basic perspective of social learning theory is that the individual can learn from observation of other people's activities, so the individual does not necessarily have to experience a verbal exchange of information for the individual's behavior to be influenced by the model. Thus, nonverbal communication is important in behavior change (as well as verbal communication). Because social learning theory recognizes external factors to the individual as important in behavior change, it is essentially social, by viewing communication as a cause of behavior change. The individual can learn a new behavior by observing another individual in person or via the mass media (especially visual media like television or film). Social modeling often occurs through interpersonal networks, but it can also occur through a public display by someone with whom one is unacquainted. Ideally, an individual learns more from a social model if the model is positively rewarded for the behavior that is displayed, rather than punished.

Social learning and diffusion have much in common: Both theories seek to explain how individuals change their overt behavior as a result of communication with other individuals. Both theories stress information exchange as essential to behavior change, and view network links as the main explanation of how individuals alter their behavior.

Sociologists at the University of Arizona (Hamblin and others, 1973, 1979; Pitcher and others, 1978; Kunkel, 1977) have applied social learning theory to the diffusion of innovations, such as the rate of airplane hijackings. Their viewpoint is that "Diffusion models portray society as a huge learning system where individuals are continually behaving and making decisions through time but not independently of one another. . . . Everyone makes his own decisions, not just on the basis of his own individual experiences, but to a large extent on the basis of the observed or talked about experiences of others" (Hamblin and others, 1979).

While there is a basic similarity between social learning theory and the diffusion of innovations, there are also important differences.

1. In comparison to social learning, diffusion research has been more aggregate in the way that the effects of modeling are measured (as either adoption or rejection of an innovation). Social learning perspectives would encourage diffusion researchers to measure more exactly *what* the individual learns through a network link with an adopter of an innovation. This detailed learning might include what resources of time, money, effort, skills, and mastery of technical jargon are necessary for the individual to adopt an innovation. Will the innovation solve the focal individual's perceived problem/need? What is the innovation's relative advantage over previous practice? How satisfied is the adopter-peer with the innovation? Such issues as these would focus diffusion research on the informational content that is exchanged in diffusion networks.

2. A diffusion perspective, if more fully brought into social learning research, might provide greater attention to time as a variable in behavior change, thus helping social learning focus more centrally on behavior change as a *process*.

3. Both social learning and recent diffusion research recognize that the individual does not always exactly mimic the model (as is implied by re-invention). Instead, the individual learner-adopter usually abstracts or generalizes the information learned from the model.

4. Both social learning and diffusion researchers have recently emphasized the exchange/convergence aspects of behavior change, emphasizing interpersonal information exchange as the basis for behavior change.

Summary

Opinion leadership is the degree to which an individual is able to influence informally other individuals' attitudes or overt behavior in a desired way with relative frequency. Opinion leaders play an important role in diffusion networks. The concept of opinion leadership originated as part of the *two-step flow model*, which hypothesized that communication messages flow from a source, via mass media channels, to opinion leaders, who in turn pass them on to followers. The two-step flow model challenged the previous *hypodermic needle model*, which postulated that the mass media had direct, immediate, and powerful effects on individual members of a mass audience.

Homophily is the degree to which a pair of individuals who communicate are similar. *Heterophily* is the degree to which pairs of individuals who interact are different in certain attributes. Interpersonal diffusion networks are mostly homophilous (Generalization 8–1). Such homophily can act as an invisible barrier to the rapid flow of innovations within a social system, as similar people interact in socially horizontal patterns.

When interpersonal diffusion networks are heterophilous, followers seek opinion leaders of higher socioeconomic status, with more formal education, greater mass media exposure, more cosmopoliteness, greater change agent contact, and more innovativeness (Generalizations 8–2 through 8–7).

Compared to followers, opinion leaders have greater mass media exposure, more cosmopoliteness, greater change agent contact, greater social participation, higher social status, and more innovativeness (Generalizations 8–8 through 8–13). Opinion leaders conform more closely to a system's norms than do their followers. When a social system's norms favor change, opinion leaders are especially innovative (Generalization 8–14).

A *communication network* consists of interconnected individuals who are linked by patterned flows of information. An individual's network links are important determinants of his or her adoption of innovations. The network interconnectedness of an individual in a social system is positively related to the individual's innovativeness (Generalization 8–15). *In-*

terconnectedness is the degree to which the units in a social system are linked by interpersonal networks.

Networks provide a certain degree of structure and stability in the predictability of human behavior. *Communication structure* is the differentiated elements that can be recognized in the patterned communication flows in a system. This structure consists of the cliques within a system and the network interconnections among them through bridges and liaisons. Individuals are identified as belonging to cliques on the basis of *communication proximity*, the degree to which two linked individuals in a network have personal communication networks that overlap. A *personal network* consists of those interconnected individuals who are linked by patterned communication flows to a given individual.

Personal networks that are radial (rather than interlocking) are more open to an individual's environment, and hence play a more important role in the diffusion of innovations. The information-exchange potential of communication network links is negatively related to their degree of (1) communication proximity, and (2) homophily. This generalization (8–16) is an expression of Granovetter's theory of the strength of weak ties." Individuals tend to be linked to others who are close to them in physical distance and who are relatively homophilous in social characteristics (Generalization 8–17).

The *critical mass* occurs at the point at which enough individuals have adopted an innovation that the innovation's further rate of adoption becomes self-sustaining. The critical mass is particularly important in the diffusion of interactive innovations like e-mail, cellular telephones, and teleconferencing, where each additional adopter increases the utility of adoption for all adopters. *Interactivity* is the degree to which participants in a communication process can exchange roles in, and have control over, their mutual discourse. As more individuals in a system adopt a noninteractive innovation, it is perceived as increasingly beneficial to future adopters (this is a *sequential* interdependence effect on later adopters). However, in the case of an interactive innovation, the benefits from each additional adoption increase not only for all future adopters, but also for each previous adopter (this is *reciprocal* interdependence).

A *threshold* is the number of other individuals who must be engaged in an activity before a given individual will join that activity. An innovator has a low threshold of resistance to adopting a new idea, and so few (or no) interpersonal network influences are needed for adoption. In contrast, a late majority individual has a much higher threshold that must be overcome by near-peer network influences in order to overcome resistance to the innovation. Thresholds act for individuals in a somewhat parallel way to the critical mass at the system level. An individual is more likely to adopt an innovation if more of the other individuals in his or her personal network have adopted previously (Generalization 8–18).

Social learning theory states that individuals learn from others whom they observe, and then imitate by following a similar (but not necessarily identical) behavior. Such social modeling frequently occurs through diffusion networks.

9

THE CHANGE AGENT

One of the greatest pains to human nature is the pain of a new idea. It . . . makes you think that after all, your favorite notions may be wrong, your firmest beliefs ill-founded. . . . Naturally, therefore, common men hate a new idea, and are disposed more or less to ill-treat the original man who brings it.

—Walter Bagehot *Physics and Politics*

This chapter is about the role of the change agent, relationships with clients, and various diffusion strategies that may be employed to change clients' behavior. A *change agent* is an individual who influences clients' innovation-decisions in a direction deemed desirable by a change agency. A change agent usually seeks to secure the adoption of new ideas, but he or she may also attempt to slow the diffusion process and prevent the adoption of certain innovations with undesirable effects.

Much of this chapter deals with directed change programs in which one-way communication is intended to change the innovation behavior of clients. But even in these influence attempts by change agents, the communication relationship between the agent and the client is important and a good deal of two-way information-exchange takes place. In decentralized diffusion systems, certain of the adopters serve as change agents for other adopters. Even in relatively centralized diffusion systems, the long-range goal of many change agents is to create conditions in which clients can help themselves, and thus work the change agent out of a job. *Communication*, defined as a process in which participants create and share information with one another in order to reach a mutual understanding, describes the contact between a change agent and clients.

335

Change Agents as Linkers

Many different occupations fit our definition of change agent: Teachers, consultants, public health workers, agricultural extension agents, development workers, and salespeople. All of these change agents provide a communication link between a resource system of some kind and a client system. One of the main roles of a change agent is to facilitate the flow of innovations from a change agency to an audience of clients. For this type of communication to be effective, the innovations must be selected to match client's needs. For the linkage to be effective, feedback from the client system must flow through the change agent to the change agency so that it appropriately adjusts its programs to fit the changing needs to clients.

Change agents would not be needed in the diffusion of innovations if there were no social and technical chasms between the change agency and the client system. The change agency system is usually composed of individuals who possess a high degree of expertise regarding the innovations that are being diffused; change agency personnel may be Ph.D.s in agriculture, science, or other technical fields. Their superior know-how makes it difficult for them to communicate directly with clients. Accompanying their heterophily in technical competence usually is heterophily in subcultural language differences, socioeconomic status, and beliefs and attitudes. Change agents, even though they link the two systems, may be quite heterophilous in relation to both their clients and to the technical experts in the change agency. This heterophily gap on both sides of the change agent creates role conflicts and certain problems in communication. As a bridge between two differing systems, the change agent is a marginal figure with one foot in each of two worlds.

In addition to facing this problem of social marginality, change agents also must deal with the problems of *information overload*, the state of an individual or a system in which excessive communication inputs cannot be processed and utilized, leading to breakdown. The large volume of information about innovations flowing from the change agency may overcome the change agent's capacity to select the most relevant messages for the client system. By understanding the needs of the clients, a change agent can selectively transmit to them relevant information only.

The Sequence of Change Agent Roles

Seven roles can be identified for the change agent in the process of introducing an innovation in a client system.

1. *To develop a need for change.* A change agent often initially helps clients become aware of the need to alter their behavior. In order to initiate the change process, the change agent points out new alternatives to existing problems, dramatizes the importance of these problems, and may convince clients that they are capable of confronting these problems. The change agent assesses client's needs at this stage, and also may help to create needs.

2. *To establish an information-exchange relationship.* Once a need for change is created, a change agent must develop rapport with his or her clients. The change agent can enhance relationships with clients by being perceived as credible, competent, and trustworthy, and by empathizing with the clients' needs and problems. Clients must accept the change agent before they will accept the innovations that he or she promotes. The innovations are judged on the basis of how the change agent is perceived.

3. *To diagnose problems.* The change agent is responsible for analyzing clients' problems to determine why existing alternatives do not meet their needs. In arriving at such diagnostic conclusions, the change agent must view the situation emphathically from the clients' perspective.

4. *To create an intent in the client to change.* After a change agent explores various avenues of action that clients might take to achieve their goals, the change agent seeks to motivate their interests in the innovation.

5. *To translate an intent to action.* A change agent seeks to influence clients' behavior in accordance with recommendations based on the clients' needs. Interpersonal network influences from near-peers are most important at the persuasion and decision stages in the innovation-decision process. The change agent can operate only indirectly here, by working with opinion leaders to activate near-peer networks.

6. *To stabilize adoption and prevent discontinuance.* Change agents may effectively stabilize new behavior through reinforcing messages to clients who have adopted, thus "freezing" the new behavior. This assistance is given when a client is at the implementation or confirmation stage in the innovation-decision process.

7. *To achieve a terminal relationship.* The end goal for a change agent is to develop self-renewing behavior on the part of clients. The change agent should seek to put him or herself out of business by developing the clients' ability to be their own change agents. In other words, the change agent seeks to shift the clients from a position of reliance on the change agent to one of self-reliance.

Failing Through Success: Building Village Wells in India

The Indian government is led by an elite cadre of highly selected officers, the Indian Administrative Service (IAS), who are chosen in their early twenties from some 200,000 applicants each year through a system of competitive examinations. The annual cohort of 100 or so IAS candidates are then given a trial by fire: Assignment as a change agent in charge of a huge development project.

In 1988, "Hari Singh" was selected by the IAS, and assigned to direct the SWACH (Sanitation, Water, and Community Health) Project in a district in a highly traditional state in Western India. A survey showed that villagers in this desertlike area rated a need for safe drinking water as their priority problem. The SWACH Project was designed to eradicate guineaworms, which were endemic to the area, and which were transmitted by drinking contaminated water. The Project was supported by UNICEF, the United Nations' Childrens' Fund, which supplied trucks and drilling rigs. When Singh took up his duties, he found that UNICEF had a cumbersome procedure for procuring this equipment (it did not arrive for three more years). However, the young IAS officer was able to contract with local well-drillers, so that the SWACH Project could get underway immediately.

Then he encountered another, more serious problem. The state government refused to release the $400,000 that it had committed to the SWACH Project. After a great deal of effort with his superiors, Singh was able to secure somewhat less than half of these funds. But he made do by redesigning the well-drilling procedures, so that each village well cost only about $165 to contract, one-third the original estimate. The target for the first year of the SWACH Project was to build 800 wells. Using his cost-cutting design, Singh was able to complete an incredible 2,037 village wells during the first seven months. Further, his staff carried out an extensive educational program with villagers, so that they understood the importance of drinking the well water in order to avoid guineaworm. His junior engineers, who supervised the project at the village level, surveyed the families in each village to determine where the well should be located. So far, so good.

Soon, however, problems began to arise with the local power structure. Two junior engineers on the project were caught selling cement and other building materials to local *pramukhs*, influential politicians. Hari Singh replaced the two with honest technicians. Then he received a deputation of *pramukhs* who complained about the locations of the village wells. A *pra-*

mukh typically demanded that the village well be sited in the courtyard of his home. Instead, Singh insisted that the well be centrally located in the village, so that it could be used by everyone.

The *pramukhs* sought to have Hari Singh removed from the SWACH Project. They went over his head to his boss and to his boss's boss, recommending that he be "promoted" to a bigger job elsewhere. Despite his refusal to leave the project, the IAS transferred Singh to an obscure administrative position in a remote corner of India.

What do you think the young IAS officer did that was wrong in introducing change?

The following case illustration was related to the present author by an Indian government officer, identified here by a pseudonym.

Factors in Change Agent Success

Change Agent Effort

One factor in change agent success is the amount of effort spent in communication activities with clients. Generalization 9–1 states: *Change agent success in securing the adoption of innovations by clients is positively related to the extent of change agent effort in contacting clients*. The degree of success of change agents is usually measured in terms of the rate of adoption of innovations by members of the client system (see Chapter 6). This success measure is frequently used because the main objective of most change agencies is to secure the adoption of new ideas by their clients. An improved measure of change agent success might be the degree to which desired consequences of innovation adoption occur among the clients (see Chapter 11).

The sheer amount of client contact is by no means the sole explanation of change agent success, however. For instance, the timing of the client contact, relative to the stage of diffusion of an innovation, is also a factor in success. Stone (1952) analyzed the amount of effort expended by agricultural extension agents in promoting a new idea to Michigan farmers. In the first years of a diffusion campaign the rate of adoption of the innovation roughly paralleled the amount of change agents' efforts, as measured by the number of agent days per year devoted to the innovation. After about 30-percent adoption was reached, however, the extension agents' efforts decreased, whereas the farmers continued to adopt the new idea at an almost constant rate. Once the opinion leaders adopt and a critical mass is reached, the adoption curve shoots upward in a self-generating fashion, and a change agent can begin to retire from the scene (at least for that innovation). The S-curve of adoption will then continue to climb, independent of change agents' efforts, under further impetus from opinion leaders.

Client Orientation

A change agent's social position is midway between the change agency and the client system. The change agent is necessarily subject to role conflict. A change agent is often expected to engage in certain behaviors by the change agency, and at the same time is expected by clients to carry out quite different actions. How is this role conflict best resolved, from a viewpoint of achieving change agent success? Perhaps the case of Hari Singh and the introduction of village wells in India bears on this issue.

Generalization 9–2 states: *Change agent success in securing the adoption of innovations by clients is positively related to a client orientation, rather than to a change agency orientation.* Client-oriented change agents are more likely to be feedback-minded, to have closer rapport with their clients and higher credibility in the eyes of their clients, and to base their diffusion activities on clients' need.

Compatibility with Clients' Needs

An important and difficult role for the change agent is to diagnose clients' needs. We suggest Generalization 9–3: *Change agent success in securing the adoption of innovations by clients is positively related to the degree to which a diffusion program is compatible with clients' needs.**

Change projects that ignore clients' felt needs often go awry or produce unexpected consequences. For example, one Indian village was provided with development funds to construct irrigation wells that could double crop yields. But the villagers wanted wells for drinking because they had to carry their water several miles from a river. The peasants built the wells in the village center, rather than in their fields, and drank the water, instead of irrigating their crops. If the change agent had based his program upon the felt needs of the villagers, one well might have been provided for drinking purposes. Perhaps a stronger need for irrigation

---

* This generalization is similar to Generalization 6–2: *The compatibility of a new idea, as perceived by members of a social system, is positively related to its rate of adoption.*

could have been developed by pointing out the financial pay offs from adopting this innovation.

A change agent can allow clients to pursue the solution to their needs so completely that they commit errors or misdirect priorities. An example is provided by an unsupervised self-help program in Southeast Asia that led to unexpected results (Niehoff, 1964). Leaders in each village were allowed to decide on their own development projects; then a change agency provided construction materials, such as cement, hardware, and roofing materials. Hundreds of village projects were carried out, including building schools, roads, markets, irrigation canals, and dams. But it soon became apparent that more than half of the construction projects were Buddhist temples, a result that was not expected or desired by the government change agency.

Change agents should be aware of their clients' felt needs and adapt their change programs to them. They should not, however, relinquish their role in shaping these needs, so as to optimize the clients' welfare in the long run.

Sustainability: "Chicken" Davis in Nigeria

In recent years, the sustainability of change agents' programs has received much more attention than previously, both in the United States and in the Third World nations of Latin America, Africa, and Asia. Unless an innovation is highly compatible with clients' needs and resources, and unless clients feel so involved with the innovation that they regard it as "theirs," it will not continue over the long term. The importance of sustainability is emphasized by the case of the introduction of American chickens in Eastern Nigeria in the late 1960s by Dr. "Chicken" Davis, a U.S. poultry science expert.

When Davis arrived in Nigeria, he immediately saw the need for improved poultry raising. Chicken was considered a national delicacy, consumers liked eggs, and the protein in poultry products improved nutrition of the people, but there was a severe shortage of these foods. Village chickens ran wild, eating whatever feed they might find, and did not provide much meat. Many of the eggs they laid could not be found. "Chicken" Davis introduced Western methods of poultry farming: Caged chickens, who were fed imported grain. High-producing, rapidly growing baby chickens were flown in from U.S. hatcheries (for several years, I waited for my luggage at local airports in Nigeria while thousands of baby chicks in cardboard boxes were unloaded). Western chicken raising was very popular, and the poultry-farming enterprises promoted by "Chicken" Davis spread rapidly through-out Eastern Nigeria. During the three years of Davis' program, millions of baby chicks were imported to Nigeria. Protein consumption in the national diet increased, and the small-scale poultry farmers reaped handsome prof-its. When Dr. Davis retired from the international development agency for whom he worked, at the end of his three-year assignment in Nigeria, he was awarded a hero's medal by the President of Nigeria.

Two weeks later, a poultry epidemic swept through Eastern Nigeria, killing all the imported birds. The wild village chickens were immune to the disease. Within a year of "Chicken" Davis' departure, only an unpleasant memory remained of his work. Not a Western chicken survived.

What mistakes did "Chicken" Davis make from a viewpoint of the sus-tainability of the innovation that he introduced?

This case illustration is based on the present author's field notes from research in Nigeria.

Change Agent Empathy

Empathy is the degree to which an individual can put himself or herself into the role of another person. Change agent empathy with clients is es-pecially difficult when the clients are extremely different from the change agents. We expect change agents to be more successful if they can em-pathize with their clients. We suggest Generalization 9–4: *Change agent success in securing the adoption of innovations by clients is positively re-lated to empathy with clients.*

Change agents are generally oriented to achieving client adoption of innovations. In many cases they might be more effective in the long run if they achieved higher-quality adoptions, that is, adoption by clients who were more satisfied and who passed this positive attitude along to other individuals who are potential adopters. Family planning programs have recognized that if the quality of client services is improved, more adop-tion of contraceptives will occur, discontinuance rates will drop, and the rate of adoption will increase. One means of improving the quality of clinic services has been to train nurses and other clinic staff to greet clients when they enter the clinic, to listen to them as they describe their need for family planning, to establish eye contact with the client, to smile, and to establish rapport with the client. These interpersonal skills were taught to clinic staff in Nigeria in a three-day training course, which was then evaluated by means of data from clinic records. The results? The "quality" of adoption of family planning methods increased, and this satisfaction on the part of adopters was passed on to others (Kim and others, 1992). In a similar field experiment in Ghana, "mystery clients" were used to evaluate the effects of training the clinic staff in how to treat their clients in a courteous manner. Mystery clients are specifically trained to act like ordinary clients when they enter a clinic to seek family planning services; they serve as unobtrusive observers of how they are treated. The results from the mystery clients study in Ghana showed that increased empathy with the clients, and a more positive relationship of change agents with clients in general, contributed to greater change agent success in securing the adoption of innovations by clients (Huntington and others, 1990).

Communication Campaigns

Conventional wisdom a decade or two ago was that communication campaigns were futile. Even when well-planned and carried out with considerable resources, campaigns often failed. A well-known early example was the Cincinnati campaign for the United Nations, which was intended to build public support for the UN. At this time, soon after the founding of the United Nations, the UN was perceived as a new idea. This Cincinnati campaign was massive in scope, with 60,000 pieces of literature distributed, speeches presented at 2,800 organizations, and with radio stations broadcasting sixty radio spots each week (Star and Hughes, 1950). The campaign was targeted at segments of the city's population known to be poorly informed about the United Nations, which, according to pre-campaign formative evaluation surveys, were females, the elderly, the poor, and the less educated.

The six months' campaign unfortunately reached the wrong audience (the younger and better educated) and had only minor effects. For instance, individuals who were found to know anything about the United Nations changed from 70 to 72 percent, an evaluation survey indicated. The campaign messages did not get through to the targeted audience because of *selective exposure*, the tendency of individuals to attend to messages that are consistent with an individual's prior attitudes and experiences (Hyman and Sheatsley, 1974).

Another reason why the Cincinnati campaign failed was due to its abstract nature. The campaign slogan, "Peace Begins with the United Nations—and the United Nations Begins with You," was not connected to any specific behavior on the part of audience members. A local resident remarked: "Why, yes. I heard it over and over again. . . . But I never did find out what it means."

After some years of thinking that communication campaigns only have minimal effects, scholars began to realize that campaigns *could* succeed if they were carried out in a different and more effective manner (Mendelsohn, 1973). Successful campaign strategies consisted of (1) utilizing *formative evaluation*, conducting research on the campaign's intended audience and on the messages in order to plan the campaign more effectively, (2) setting specific but reasonable campaign goals, (3) using *audience segmentation*, the strategy of dividing a heterogeneous mass audience into relatively homogeneous audience segments, and (4) designing the campaign's mass media messages to trigger interpersonal network communication among members of the intended audience. So a campaign can succeed if it is carried out in a way that is based on communication strategies like the above.

What is a campaign? The term derives from military origins and from Latin, meaning "to go to the field." Military terminology, like "target," for example, still is utilized in describing campaigns, as in "reaching the target audience." So a campaign is purposeful, intended to bring about certain specific effects (the Cincinnati campaign for the United Nations failed because it was so ambiguous). Further, a campaign is usually aimed at a large audience, and carried out in a more or less specifically defined time period, say a few weeks or months. Finally, a campaign usually entails an organized set of activities and messages, such as posters, television spots, and so forth. Thus a *campaign* intends to generate specific outcomes or effects in a relatively large number of individuals, usually within a specified period of time and through an organized set of communication activities (Rogers and Storey, 1988).

One illustration of a successful campaign is a television-centered project for family planning in the city of Enugu, Nigeria, carried out by local health officials with the help of scholars from Johns Hopkins University (Piotrow and others, 1990). In Nigeria at this time, the idea of family planning was an unfamiliar and sensitive topic. So the campaign planners decided to introduce the idea through entertaining and dramatic episodes inserted in a popular television variety program, *In a Lighter Mood*. The family planning episodes showed positive and negative role models, that is, television characters who adopted a family planning innovation and also those who resisted the idea. Thus, Bandura's (1986) social learning theory, the notion that individuals can learn by observing others' behavior (see Chapter 8), was used as a basis for the television character portrayals of family planning. The negative resisters to family planning were socially punished in the television shows, and the positive role models were rewarded. For example, a traditional couple who had a large number of children later could not afford to provide them with adequate education, to their chagrin.

This approach is an example of *entertainment-education*, putting an educational idea in an entertainment message to achieve behavior changes (Nariman, 1993). Further, focus group interviews with members of the intended audience for the entertainment-education messages (fertile-aged men and women in Enugu) were carried out by the campaign planners, so as to be sure that the educational messages were understood but were not offensive. In all, forty-three entertainment-education episodes about family planning were produced, pretested in formative research with the audience, and broadcast in the weekly *In a Lighter Mood* show. Audience members were encouraged to ask questions about family planning, and certain of these questions were answered on the air. The location of the government's family planning clinic in Enugu was mentioned in every television episode, so that potential adopters, once motivated, could easily find available contraceptive services. The clinic staff gathered source-of-referral data from individual client-adopters, so that the effects of the television episodes could be determined from clients when they came to the family planning clinic to adopt.

During the six months prior to broadcast of the television episodes, the clinic averaged about fifty adopters of family planning per month. Once the entertainment-education episodes were broadcast on *In a Lighter Mood*, the average number of adopters increased to 150 per month, a rate of adoption that continued for the next year or so (Piotrow and others, 1990). The clinic's clients were asked their source of referral: About 50 percent mentioned *In a Lighter Mood*.

Why was this campaign so effective? It was planned on the basis of formative evaluation research with the intended audience, the messages were pretested with the audience, the entertainment-education messages were lively and relevant, and an appropriate access point (the family planning clinic) was provided for potential adopters.

So communication campaigns can be quite effective when change agents conduct them according to appropriate strategies.

Homophily and Change Agent Contact

As previously defined (see Chapter 8), *homophily* is the degree to which pairs of individuals who interact are similar, and *heterophily* is the degree to which they differ. Change agents usually differ from their clients in most respects, and have most contact with clients who are most like themselves. This general statement leads to a series of generalizations about change agent contact with clients for which there is strong empirical support.*

Generalization 9–5: *Change agent contact is positively related to higher social status among clients.*

Generalization 9–6: *Change agent contact is positively related to greater social participation among clients.*

Generalization 9–7: *Change agent contact is positively related to higher formal education among clients.*

Generalization 9–8: *Change agent contact is positively related to cosmopoliteness among clients.*

All of the generalizations above suggest that more effective communication between change agents and their clients occurs when they are homophilous with each other. Such effective communication is rewarding, and encourages change agents to contact clients who are much like themselves.

NIDA (the National Institute on Drug Abuse) estimates that about 15,000 individuals work in drug treatment programs in the United States, mostly as drug abuse counselors. These counselors are relatively low-paid (averaging about $16,000 per year in 1990), have a low level of formal education, and are mostly former drug addicts. Thus they are relatively homophilous with their clients. The counselors' role is mainly disciplinary: Urging clients to take their methadone, requiring them to have regular urine tests to guarantee that they are drug-free, and so forth. Such near-peer change agents seem to be relatively successful as drug abuse counselors, where homophily with clients on such variables as socioeconomic status, cultural and minority status, and prior personal experience in drug use are important.

---

* In addition, three generalizations about change agent contact were encountered in previous chapters: Generalization 5–5: *Earlier knowers of an innovation have greater change agent contact than later knowers*; Generalization 7–25: *Earlier adopters of innovations have more change agent contact than later adopters*; and Generalization 8–12: *Opinion leaders have greater change agent contact than their followers.*

The number of agricultural change agent contacts per year for a sample of 1,307 Brazilian farmers (Rogers and others, 1970) was:

Average Number of
Change Agent Contacts per Year

Innovators	20
Early adopters	15
Early majority	12
Late majority	5
Laggards	3

These data are typical of a number of studies of client contact with change agents. Change agent contact is one of the variables most highly related to innovativeness. Rogers and others (1970) concluded, on the basis of investigating fifteen variables related to innovativeness among some 4,000 farmers in three Third World nations: "The single variable that emerges as most highly related to change agent contact, even when the effect of other variables is controlled, is agricultural innovativeness." In turn, socioeconomic status was highly related to innovativeness for these peasant farmers in Brazil, Nigeria, and India. These three variables may be diagrammed as:

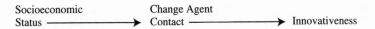

Socioeconomic Status ———————> Change Agent Contact ———————> Innovativeness

This circle of relationships means that change agents are helping those clients least who most need their help.

When Yes Means No

When a professional change agent and his/her clients do not share a common culture, their communication relationship is extremely heterophilous, which can lead to misunderstandings. An illustration comes from the interaction between medical professionals and the Southeast Asian refugees who were transported to American reception centers in the late 1970s and 1980s, given a health examination, and placed in training and work positions. These thousands of Asians, mainly from Vietnam, Cambodia, and Laos, do not share a common language or culture with the U.S. medical professionals who treat them. Interpreters were used in the health clinics to help bridge this communication gap.

Nevertheless, severe misunderstandings occurred, as Katalanos (1994) found. For instance, here is a typical exchange between a female medical professional and a recently arrived Southeast Asian refugee woman:

MEDICAL DOCTOR: "Are you married?"

INTERPRETER [to the Southeast Asian patient]: "This doctor asks if you are married. She does not mean to insult you. In America, a woman can have a baby without being married. It is not a shameful matter. Please do not be offended."

PATIENT [to Interpreter]: "I do not understand. In my country this would bring great shame to my parents. My husband would be very angry if he heard this question. It shows him no respect."

INTERPRETER [to medical doctor]: "She says she is married."

A particular cause of confusion and frustration for the American clinic doctors are the words "yes" and "no." When a Vietnamese patient does not understand a question, the Vietnamese answers "yes" when the individual really means "no." A negative response is impolite, and it might hurt the doctor's feelings. So when the doctor asks:

MEDICAL DOCTOR: "Are you happy here in America?"

PATIENT: "Oh yes" [meaning: I am not happy at all, but I do not want to hurt your feelings. After all, your country took me in].

Further, "yes" may simply mean "I hear you, and I will answer your question," as the following exchange illustrates:

MEDICAL DOCTOR: "Did you take your medicine?"

PATIENT: "Yes [I hear you]. No [I did not take it]."

MEDICAL DOCTOR, [TRYING AGAIN]: "You did not take your medicine?"

PATIENT: "Yes [I hear you]. Yes [I did not take it. The medicine was too strong]."

MEDICAL DOCTOR: "Ah, so you did not take it!"

PATIENT: "Yes. No."

Here, "Yes" actually means "Yes, I hear you, and "Yes, I will answer your question." Such responses leave the American health care provider feeling completely frustrated, as the following exchange indicators:

MEDICAL DOCTOR: "Did you have any more chest pain?"

VIETNAMESE PATIENT: "Yes. Chest pain."

MEDICAL DOCTOR: "Did you take those pills that I gave you? The ones that you put under your tongue?"

PATIENT: "Yes. I take pills."

MEDICAL DOCTOR: "Did they help?"

PATIENT: "Yes. Help."

MEDICAL DOCTOR: "How many did you need to take?"

PATIENT: "One. Two. Ten. Help pain."

MEDICAL DOCTOR: "I told you not to take more than three. After three tablets, you need to go to the hospital if there is still pain."

PATIENT: "Yes, I take. No pain. No hurt chest. No hurt leg."

MEDICAL DOCTOR: "You took the pills for leg pain!?"

PATIENT: "Yes. No leg pain."

MEDICAL DOCTOR: "The pills are for chest pain. For your heart! Not your leg!"

PATIENT:"Yes. I take pills. Leg not hurt."

These exchanges make the American doctor feel helpless to find words that will convey appropriate questions. The Vietnamese patient does not understand why the doctor seems displeased. After all, the patient carefully avoided any responses that might have offended the doctor.

This case illustration is based on Nikki Katalanos (1994).

Change Agent Contact with Lower-Status Clients

Less-educated, lower-income clients need the assistance of change agents more than do more elite clients. Then why don't change agents concentrate their efforts on their most disadvantaged clients? The answer reflects the innovativeness-needs paradox discussed in Chapter 7.

More elite clients are homophilous with change agents, and so communication between the two is easier and more effective. Lower-status clients are socioeconomically different from the change agent, and this heterophily gap impedes effective communication. If the change agent is an employee of a government agency or some other establishment institution, the lower-status client may distrust the change agent. Further, less-privileged clients often lack the necessary resources to adopt innovations that the change agent is promoting.

Finally, many change agents do not try to contact their more needy, lower-status clients because of a self-fulfilling prophecy that the change agents have developed from their past experience (Röling, 1981; Röling and others, 1976). Change agents think that their lower-status clients are not responsive to the change agents' efforts at diffusing innovations: This stereotype in the change agent's mind discourages the change agent from initiating contact with less-advantaged clients.

What could be done to encourage the lower-status and least-innovative clients to have more change agent contact? One answer is to select change agents who are as much like their clients as possible. If most clients possess only a few years of formal education, a university-trained change agent will likely face greater communication difficulties than if he or she has fewer years of education. This is one reason why many diffusion programs employ change agent aides. Generalization 9–9 states: *Change agent success in securing the adoption of innovations by clients is positively related to homophily with clients.*

The problems of change agent–client heterophily are illustrated by an analysis of the ineffective diffusion of family planning ideas from welfare workers to their clients in a city in Tennessee (Placek, 1975). Federal regulations required that welfare mothers be informed about contraceptives by their welfare workers. The social workers tried to act as change agents in diffusing family planning methods to welfare mothers, but almost no adoption resulted. Why? It was not because the welfare mothers wanted to have more children; Placek found that 51 percent of the 1,141 pregnancies occurring to his 300 respondents were unwanted at the time of conception. The lack of adoption of family planning was mainly because of the extreme heterophily between the professional change agents and their clients. The welfare workers were mainly white, middle-class, university graduates. Eighty percent of the welfare mothers were black and most had not completed high school. Both the social workers and the welfare mothers were females, but the professionals were married without children, while the mothers were unmarried and averaged three or more children. The clients did not trust the welfare workers because of their disciplinary role; the social workers sometimes conducted midnight raids to determine if illicit sexual relationships existed that would allow a welfare mother to be dropped from the welfare rolls, under man-in-the-house laws.

What could be done to close the heterophily gap between the social workers and the welfare mothers? Placek (1975) recommended employing certain of the welfare mothers as change agent aides to disseminate family planning information to their near-peers.

Paraprofessional Aides

An *aide* is a less than fully professional change agent who intensively contacts clients to influence their innovation-decisions. One of the important advantages of aides is their much lower cost per client contacted. In family planning programs in Asian nations, thirty aides can be employed for the same cost as one medical doctor. But the main advantage of paraprofessional aides over professional change agents is that the aides are socially closer to the lower-status members of the user system that they serve.

Technical expertise may not be the most important quality of a change agent in the eyes of clients. Personal acceptability of the change agent is as important, or more important, than technical expertise. Paraprofessional aides are much less technically expert than are professionals, but they often more than make up for their lower degree of technical expertise through their greater social expertness. For example, family planning aides in most Third World nations are female paraprofessionals, who are better able to discuss the culturally sensitive topic of contraception with female clients than are predominately male doctors (Rogers, 1973).

Thus, selection of change agent aides according to sex, formal education, and personal acquaintance with the client system can minimize the social distance between the change agent system and the client system. Aides often halve the social distance between professionals and low-status clients.

Change Agent Credibility

Even though change agent aides have less *competence credibility*, defined as the degree to which a communication source or channel is perceived as knowledgeable and expert, they have the special advantage of *safety credibility*, the degree to which a communication source or channel is perceived as trustworthy. Because an aide is perceived as a near-peer by clients, they are not likely to suspect the aide of having selfish motives or manipulative intentions.

Heterophilous sources/channels (like professional change agents) are perceived as having competence credibility, while homophilous sources/channels (like aides) are perceived as having safety credibility. An ideal change agent would have a balance of competence and safety credibility. A change agent might be homophilous with his or her clients in social characteristics (such as socioeconomic status, ethnicity, and the like) but heterophilous in regard to technical competence about the innovations being diffused.

A change agent aide who has previously adopted an innovation that he or she is promoting approaches an ideal combination of homophily/heterophily and of competence credibility/source credibility. An illustration is vasectomy canvassers in India, who were paid a small fee for each adopter of male sterilization that they brought to a health clinic for the operation (Repetto, 1969). The canvassers were as poor, uneducated, and low in socioeconomic status as members of the client system, but the aides also possessed a kind of competence credibility in that they had all previously had vasectomies. So the Indian canvassers had both safety credibility on the basis of their social homophily, and competence credibility owing to their having already adopted the innovation.

The canvassers were supersalesmen for vasectomy, ranging over a one-hundred-mile radius in search of adopters, and working a seven-day week. A crucial point in the adopter's innovation-decision process occurred when the canvasser showed him his operation scar, as evidence that he knew what he was talking about. This private act helped establish the aide's competence credibility with potential adopters.

Generalization 9–10 states: *Change agent success in securing the adoption of innovations by clients is positively related to credibility in the clients' eyes.*

One type of change agent that suffers from generally low credibility is the commercial salesperson. The adoption of a new idea almost always entails the purchase of a new product. Clients often regard commercial change agents with low credibility. For example, the author found that 97 percent of a sample of Ohio farmers said they would more likely be convinced of an agricultural innovation if they talked about it with a neighbor rather than with a salesman (Rogers, 1961).

The commercial agent's motives, as perceived by his or her clients, may be one reason for the low credibility placed in his or her recommendations for adoption. Clients feel that salespeople promote the overadoption of new ideas to secure higher commissions from sales. Commercial change agents are relatively more important as a source/channel at the implementation stage than they are at other stages in the innovation-decision process for agricultural innovations (Ryan and Gross, 1943; Beal and Rogers, 1957; and Copp and others, 1958): The client may purchase a small amount of the new product for trial. At this point the individual relies heavily upon commercial change agents for information on how to use the innovation. Their credibility is limited to how-to information, and does not usually extend to an ability to persuade the individual to form a favorable attitude toward the innovation. Such persuasive credibility is accorded to near-peers, noncommercial change agents, and other sources who have nothing to gain, at least not to the extent that a commercial salesman has.

Commercial channels/sources in some cases can create awareness-knowledge of an innovation. For instance, the Coleman and others (1966) drug study found that drug detailmen and the commercial publications of pharmaceutical companies were reported by about 80 percent of the medical doctors as their source of knowledge about tetracycline. Detailmen are employees of pharmaceutical firms who call on doctors to provide them with details about medical innovations, and to give them free samples of new drugs. The drug detailmen are not credible at the persuasion and decision stages in the innovation-decision process, when a doctor is deciding whether or not to adopt (Coleman and others, 1966).

Inauthentic Professionalization of Aides

Inauthentic professionalization is the process through which an aide takes on the dress, speech, or other identifying marks of a professional change agent. For instance, the vasectomy canvassers in India demanded uniforms, identification badges, and other symbols of professional change agents (Repetto, 1969). Aides usually identify with the professional change agents who supervise them, and so, quite naturally, they want to become more like them. They cannot gain the university degree that the professional possesses, and so they try to act like them or at least look like them. But such inauthentic professionalization destroys the very heterophily-bridging function for which the aides were employed (Rogers, 1973). If aides are made aware of the problem of inauthentic professionalization, however, they usually will act in ways to correct this threat to their effectiveness with clients.

Opinion Leaders

Opinion leadership is the degree to which an individual can informally influence other individuals' attitudes or overt behavior in a desired way with relative frequency (see Chapter 8). Diffusion campaigns are more likely to be successful if change agents identify and mobilize opinion leaders. Generalization 9–11 is: *Change agent success in securing the adoption of innovations by clients is positively related to the extent that he or she works through opinion leaders.*

The time and energy of the change agent are scarce resources. By focusing communication activities on opinion leaders in a social system, the change agent can leverage these scarce resources and hasten the rate of diffusion of an innovation among clients. Economy of effort is achieved because contacting opinion leaders takes far less of the change agent's resources than if each member of the client system were to be consulted. The opinion leader approach magnifies the change agent's efforts. Furthermore, by enlisting the aid of opinion leaders, the change agent provides the aegis of local sponsorship and sanction for the new ideas that are introduced. Network messages from near-peers like opinion leaders are regarded as credible in convincing an individual to adopt an innovation. After the opinion leaders in a system adopt an innovation, it may be impossible to stop its further spread.

Change agents sometimes mistake innovators for opinion leaders. Opinion leaders have followers, whereas innovators are the first to adopt new ideas. When the change agent concentrates communication efforts on innovators, rather than on opinion leaders, the results may be to increase awareness-knowledge of the innovations, but few clients will be persuaded to adopt. The innovators' behavior does not necessarily convince the average members of a system to follow suit. A change agent may correctly identify the opinion leaders in a system but then proceed to concentrate his or her attention so much on these few leaders that they may become *too* innovative in the eyes of their followers, or become perceived as overly identified with the change agent. Thus, a change agent can wear out the credibility of opinion leaders by making them too innovative.

The Role of Demonstrations

Potential adopters of a new idea are aided in evaluating an innovation if they are able to observe it in use under conditions similar to their own. Such observation often occurs naturally, when one individual views another's experience in using the innovation. Change agents may try to increase the observability of an innovation, and thus speed its rate of adoption, by organizing a demonstration of the innovation.

Since the early days of the agricultural extension service, extension agents have conducted demonstrations of agricultural innovations in farmers' fields. For example, a chemical fertilizer might be demonstrated by laying out plots of corn (or some other crop) with, and without, fertilizer. At the end of the crop season, the extension agent would help the farmer harvest the plots, measure the yields on both plots, and invite neighboring farmers to observe the demonstration's results. The change agent might lead a discussion of how fertilizer affects plant growth, or of the cost-benefits of applying fertilizer. Evaluation of such on-farm demonstrations by diffusion researchers show that they can be an effective strategy, especially for innovations that are easily observable and that are in the early stages of the diffusion process (prior to reaching critical mass, when the S-curve takes off under its own self-generated impetus). The demonstration method was so important in the early days of the agricultural extension service that county home economics agents were commonly referred to as home demonstration agents. They conducted demonstrations of home canning, new recipes, and sewing techniques for farm housewives.

The demonstration strategy is widely utilized today, not only in agriculture, but also in energy conservation, mass transportation, education, environmental protection, substance abuse prevention, and many other fields. Demonstrations may account for 10 percent of the federal government's R&D budget (Baer and others, 1977). A current example of the demonstration approach is provided by the U.S. Department of Energy's (DOE) integrated demonstrations of nuclear waste cleanup technologies in Albuquerque, New Mexico, and at Savannah River, South Carolina. The technologies, developed by federal weapons laboratories like Sandia National Lab, are demonstrated under actual field conditions to private companies who contract with DOE to clean up contaminated nuclear waste storage sites, of which there are hundreds in the United States. These demonstrations are "integrated" in the sense that a package of technologies is used, representing the current best practice in nuclear waste cleanup. Such integration means that it is not possible to evaluate the effects of each separate technology so demonstrated.

We should distinguish two types of demonstrations, which are quite different in the functions that they perform: (1) *experimental demonstrations,* which are conducted to evaluate the effectiveness of an innovation under field conditions, and (2) *exemplary demonstrations,* which are conducted to facilitate diffusion of the innovation to other units (Myers, 1978). Often these two types of demonstrations are confused, or a single demonstration is expected to fulfill both functions. An experimental demonstration is successful if the innovation demonstrated is evaluated adequately, whether this evaluation is positive or negative. In either case, knowledge is advanced about the effectiveness of the innovation. An example of an experimental demonstration is the field trials of a new cure for AIDS. The main audiences for experimental demonstrations are the sponsors of the innovation being evaluated, and the demonstration usually has low public visibility. The attitude of the demonstration's managers should be one of healthy skepticism toward the innovation (Magill and Rogers, 1981).

In contrast, an exemplary demonstration, whose purpose is to facilitate the diffusion of an innovation, is intended to persuade potential adopters: It should be conducted with high public visibility, and the demonstration's managers should have an attitude of optimistic assurance about the innovation's effectiveness. The DOE integrated demonstrations of nuclear waste cleanup technologies, mentioned previously, are mainly exemplary demonstrations, in that there is little doubt about the effectiveness of the technologies, which were evaluated previously. The main purpose of the DOE integrated demonstrations is to speed up the diffusion process.

We see that the demonstration of an innovation under field conditions can be a useful strategy for change agents to diffuse an innovation. The demonstration is often effective because it combines the perceived competence credibility of the change agent with the perceived safety credibility of the demonstrator. A demonstration can be particularly effective if the demonstrator is a respected opinion leader.

Clients' Evaluative Ability

One of the change agent's unique inputs to the diffusion process is technical competence. But if the change agent takes a long-range approach to change, he or she should seek to raise the clients' technical competence and their ability to evaluate potential innovations themselves. Then the clients could become their own change agents. This suggests Generalization 9–12: *Change agent success in securing the adoption of innovations by clients is positively related to increasing client ability to evaluate innovations.*

Unfortunately, change agents often are more concerned with such short-range goals as escalating the rate of adoption of innovations. Instead, in many cases, self-reliance should be the goal of change agencies, leading to termination of client dependence on the change agent. This goal, however, is seldom reached by most change agencies; they usually promote the adoption of innovations, rather than seeking to teach clients the basic skill of how to evaluate innovations themselves.

The Agricultural Extension Service

The agricultural extension service of the United States is reported to be the world's most successful change agency. Certainly it is the most admired and most widely copied (see Chapter 4). The main evidence for the success of the agricultural extension model is the agricultural revolution, a dramatic increase in U.S. farm productivity in the decades following World War II. "It is impossible for anyone to speak ten words about diffusion without two of them being 'agricultural extension.' . . . In many ways, it constitutes the defining metaphor for all technology transfer efforts" (Eveland, 1986).

The *agricultural extension model* is a set of assumptions, principles, and organizational structures for diffusing the results of agricultural research to farmers in the United States.

Historical Development of the Extension Services

Both the U.S. Department of Agriculture (USDA) and land-grant universities were begun by Congressional legislation passed in 1862. Several previous attempts to pass a land-grant college bill had been defeated by states' rights legislators who viewed a federal grant of land to each state as a threat to the states' power. In 1862, during the Civil War, when the Southern states' rights enthusiasts were absent from the U.S. Congress, the Morrill Act (named for Senator Justin Morrill of Vermont) was passed. the law provided that in each state an acreage of federal land was to be set aside, and the income from this property was to support a college or university for teaching "agriculture and the mechanic arts."* the Morrill Act was a general, vaguely worded document and its meanings were not entirely clear at the time of its passage. This ambiguity may have been a deliberate strategy to gain the political support needed for passage of the Act. The ambiguity has served to allow the land-grant universities, and their extension services, to adjust to suit the changing times over the decades.

Not only did the 1862 Morrill Act set in motion state-level educational institutions that were to become the basic component of the agricultural extension model, but the land-grant colleges also provided a big boost to engineering. Their focus on agriculture and engineering marked the early land-grant colleges as a radical innovation of the day, sharply contrasting with the classical, liberal arts, and scientific education provided by the European universities (such as Cambridge University, Oxford University, and the University of Paris) that were the models for most private universities in the United States.

The early professors of scientific agriculture in the land-grant colleges soon realized that they lacked sufficient research-based knowledge about agriculture. This realization caused a demand for agricultural research on farm problems in agronomy, animal breeding and nutrition, horticulture, and other fields. Twenty-five years after the land-grant college act, the Hatch Act of 1887 provided federal funds to state agricultural experiment stations. These research centers became a second component of the land-grant college of agriculture. About one dollar out of four spent at the state experiment stations is of federal origin, channeled through the USDA.

In the early 1900s, state extension activities became another component of the land-grant colleges. Early professors of agriculture in the land-grant

---

* Twenty-eight years later, the U.S. Congress passed a second Morrill Act to provide support to sixteen black land-grant institutions in Southern and border states, so these states each have two land-grant institutions. The black institutions are euphemistically called 1890 land-grant colleges of agriculture. Examples are Prairie View A&M University in Texas, Tuskegee Institute in Alabama, and Alcor State University in Mississippi.

colleges wanted their research-based knowledge to be used by farmers. Until about 1914, there was no effective means for transmitting such information from the colleges at Ames, Davis, Ithaca, and elsewhere to farm audiences. The agricultural professors wrote bulletins intended for farmers, but many farmers could not read or understand the technical content of the bulletins, and there was no effective system for distributing the bulletins. Special campaigns were organized around a trainload of college professors who would tour their state to stump local communities in favor of some agricultural innovation, like seed corn selection in Iowa. Their knowledge was often received eagerly, but follow-up was lacking, and eventually the "corn seed gospel train" approach fell into disrepute. Agricultural improvement societies were formed in local communities to promote agricultural innovations among the gentleman-farmer class. Their main activities were county and state fairs, which provided rural entertainment but were much less effective as tools of agricultural diffusion. These piecemeal approaches to effective diffusion were tried, and found wanting. The agricultural extension model was not yet created.

The first extension approach whose format is still largely followed today was pioneered in Broome County, New York, in 1911. The Binghamton Chamber of Commerce in Broome County was particularly concerned about the welfare of farmers, as agriculture was the local industry. Accordingly, the chamber's "Farm Bureau" (so named in accordance with such other divisions of the Chamber of Commerce as the Roads and Alleys Bureau, the Better Business Bureau, etc.) decided to employ a recent agricultural graduate from Cornell University to diffuse innovations to farmers in Broome County. Part of his first year's salary was donated by the Delaware and Lackawanna Railroad, and so he was called a county agent (all railroad employees were termed agents in those days, as for example, ticket agents, station agents, etc.). The Binghamton Chamber of Commerce's Farm Bureau included several leading farmers, who solicited their neighbors for donations to help pay the county agent's salary. Soon these donations were institutionalized into annual memberships in the Broome County Farm Bureau.

The idea of a county extension agent, and of a local Farm Bureau, spread rapidly across the United States after 1911. This movement was spurred (1) by provision of federal financing through the Smith-Lever Act of 1914, and (2) by the need for higher agricultural production during World War I.

As the county agent movement spread, so did the county agents' sponsoring body, the Farm Bureaus. Soon the county Farm Bureaus federated into state organizations, and then in 1919 into the American Farm Bureau Federation (AFBF). This organization began to operate as a legislative pressure group, a function incompatible with its original purpose of being the local sponsor of county extension agents. The Farm Bureau and the extension services split in 1919, but the two organizations remain friendly until the present day. The legislative assistance of the AFBF, and of state Farm Bureaus, is one reason for the financial strength and stability of the extension services. The annual amount of money and personnel invested in the agricultural extension effort since 1920 has increased sharply. By 1920 there were 3,000 extension employees. Today, the total is 17,000.

Funds for extension services in the United States come from federal (40 percent), state (40 percent), and county government (20 percent) sources, which is why the total extension system is often referred to as the *cooperative* extension service. The extension service has maintained a high level of growth at a time when federal spending on agriculture generally has not kept pace with increases in the federal budget.

State Extension Specialists

Of the 17,000 professional staff members of the extension services, about 68 percent are county-level extension agents, specializing in agriculture, home economics, and youth (4-H Club) work. In addition, there are 4,000 extension subject-matter "specialists" at the state level (17 percent of all extension employees). These specialists interpret current research findings in their specialized fields to county extension employees, and thus indirectly to clients. American farmers increasingly are cotton-growers, milk-producers, mink-growers, and so forth, rather than general farmers, so specialized knowledge is increasingly important. Consider an extension agronomy specialist, whose office is in the department of agronomy at the state agricultural college. The specialist travels over the state to address farmer meetings and to keep county extension agents abreast of new developments in agronomy. Likewise, there are extension specialists in farm management, marketing, animal husbandry, dairying, entomology, home economics, and other fields.

Essentially the state extension specialist links the sources of research-based knowledge to the county extension agents. He or she is "the county agent's extension agent." To effectively fulfill this linkage function, the extension specialist must bridge the scientific/intellectual world of the land-grant university with the pragmatic world of the farmer and his or her county extension agent. Usually, a specialist has had previous experience as a county extension agent, and then moved, through graduate study, into a specialized agricultural field.

The success of a state extension specialist rests directly on how well the needs of clients are served. If a specialist cannot effectively relate his or her technical knowledge to farmers' problems, the specialist's career will be short-lived.

Similarly, the reward system for research workers in the USDA and the state agricultural experiment stations strongly encourages publishing research results in a form that is useful to farmers. All participants in the research/transfer process pull together to produce utilizable knowledge, and to get it diffused and adopted by farm people. The linking function of the state extension specialists and of the county extension agents is facilitated by the orientation of agricultural researchers toward potential utilization of their innovations. The specialization of U.S. agriculture helped create a need for state extension specialists, and the agricultural extension model was capable of adjusting to cope with changes in the nature of agriculture.

Broadening the Extension Service Mission

In 1911, extension activities were solely concerned with biological agriculture: Agronomy, animal husbandry, poultry, and so forth. County extension agents placed their main emphasis upon production-increasing innovations like new seeds, fertilizers, improved livestock, and farm equipment. Soon the farmer's wife began to demand that her information needs for better nutrition, child care, and home management also receive attention by the extension service. Accordingly, the county agricultural agent, usually with a college degree in technical agriculture, was paired with a colleague: a county home economics agent (originally called a "home demonstration agent") usually with a bachelor's degree in home economics from a land-grant university.

The county extension staff then expanded to include a county agent responsible for 4-H Club activities. This 4-H Club agent usually possessed a bachelor's degree in technical agriculture, and was considered a future county agricultural agent in training. After some years' experience as a 4-H agent, he or she might be promoted to be a country agricultural agent.

By the 1930s and 1940s state extension services began to turn some of their attention to problems of agricultural marketing and to consumer information programs. These changes shifted the extension services away from strictly an agricultural production focus. This change away from sole dependence upon production agriculture meant that the extension service appealed to new, nonfarm audiences. The Smith-Lever Act of 1914 that provided federal aid to the state extension services did not specify that the extension services should work only with farm people. The number of farmers dropped from 35 percent of the total U.S. population in 1910, to less than 3 percent in recent years. These demographic shifts in the U.S. population led the extension service to concentrate more efforts upon rural-nonfarm and urban audiences.

Conclusions About the Agricultural Extension Model

Eight main elements characterize the agricultural extension model:

1. *A critical mass of new technology*, so that the technology transfer system has a body of innovations with potential usefulness for its clients.
2. *A research subsystem oriented to utilization*, due to the rewards for researchers, research funding policies, and the personal ideologies of agricultural researchers.
3. *A high degree of user control over the technology transfer process*, as evidenced through client participation in program determination (such as in county extension advisory councils), attention to user needs in guiding research and extension decisions, and the importance accorded feedback from clients on the system's effectiveness.
4. *Linkages among the extension system's components*, as provided by a shared conception of the total system, use of a common language by members of the system, and by a common sense of mission.
5. *A high degree of client contact by the extension subsystem.*
6. *A spanable social distance across each interface between components in the technology transfer system*, in which the social distance (heterophily) reflects levels of professionalism, formal education, technical expertise, and specialization. For example, when the heterophily gap between agricultural scientists and county extension agents became too great, state extension specialists were created as spanners or linkage agents.
7. *Evolution as a complete system*, rather than having the extension system grafted onto an existing research system.
8. *A high degree of control by the technology transfer system over its environment*, so that the system is able to shape its environment rather

than passively react to changes. Such an efficacious system is less likely to face unexpected crises, and can obtain adequate resources.

What lessons have been learned to date about the agricultural extension model?

1. The agricultural extension model has changed in response to shifts in its environment in major ways since its origin in 1911 and this flexibility is a key reason for its relative success.
2. The agricultural extension model is based on client participation in identifying local needs, program planning, and evaluation and feedback.
3. Agricultural research activities are oriented toward the utilization of research results, such as through reward systems for researchers, and this pro-utilization orientation facilitates the effectiveness of the extension service.
4. State extension specialists are in close social and spatial contact with agricultural researchers and professors in their academic specialty, and this closeness facilitates their linking research-based knowledge to farmer problems.
5. The agricultural extension model has been more effective in diffusing agricultural production technology to farmers than in diffusing other subject-matter content to farm and nonfarm audiences.
6. The agricultural extension model includes not only a systematic procedure for the diffusion of innovations from researchers to farmers, but also institutionalized means of orienting research activities toward users' needs (thus the land-grant college/agricultural experiment station/extension service complex is a total technology transfer system).
7. The U.S. extension services have been highly successful, if success is measured mainly by continued growth in funds and personnel, due (1) to their ability to adjust to environment changes, and (2) to the strong support of the American Farm Bureau Federation, and of elite farm leaders.
8. The extension services are criticized for an overemphasis on production agriculture and for a lack of concern with rural social problems, some of which resulted from the extension services' previous success in diffusing technological innovations in agriculture.

If the first county agent in 1911 could meet his contemporary extension counterparts in Broome County, New York today, we wonder if he would recognize their activities as representing extension work: Long-distance phone calls to state extension specialists in Ithaca. Golden hamsters instead of baby beeves for 4-H Club projects. Holding a public meeting on recycling. Assisting suburban gardeners in pruning their roses.

We doubt it.

This case illustration is based mainly on Rogers, Eveland, and Bean (1982), Rogers (1986a), and Rogers (1988a).

Centralized and Decentralized Diffusion Systems

For decades, the classical diffusion model dominated the thinking of scholars, policy makers, and change agencies. In this model, an innovation originates from some expert source (often an R&D organization). This source then diffuses the innovation as a uniform package to potential adopters who accept or reject the innovation. The individual adopter of the innovation is a passive accepter. This classical model owes much of its popularity to the success of the agricultural extension services and to the fact that the basic paradigm for diffusion research grew out of the Ryan and Gross (1943) hybrid corn study. Much agricultural diffusion in the United States is relatively centralized, in that key decisions about which innovations to diffuse, how to diffuse them, and to whom, are made by a small number of technically expert officials near the top of a diffusion system. Most diffusion systems in nonagricultural fields are also quite centralized.

The classical diffusion model was challenged by Schön (1967), who noted that diffusion theories lagged behind the reality of emerging diffusion systems. He particularly criticized classical diffusion theory (which he called a "center-periphery model") because of its assumption that innovations should originate from a centralized source and then diffuse to users. While recognizing that this classical model may fit much of reality, Schön noted that it fails to capture the complexity of relatively decentralized diffusion systems in which innovations originate from numerous sources and then evolve as they diffuse via horizontal networks.

In recent decades, I gradually became aware of diffusion systems that did not operate at all like centralized diffusion systems. Instead of coming out of formal R&D systems, innovations often bubbled up from the operational levels of a system, with the inventing done by certain lead-users. Then the new ideas spread horizontally via peer networks, with a high degree of re-invention occurring as the innovations are modified by users to fit their particular conditions. Such decentralized diffusion systems usually are not run by technical experts. Instead, decision making in the diffusion system is widely shared, with adopters making many decisions. In many cases, adopters served as their own change agents.

Comparing Centralized Versus Decentralized Systems

How does a decentralized diffusion system differ from its centralized counterpart? Table 9–1 and Figure 9–1 show the differences between centralized and decentralized diffusion systems. Our distinction is somewhat oversimplified because it suggests a dichotomy (rather than a continuum) of centralized/decentralized diffusion systems. In reality, an actual diffusion system is usually some hybrid of the elements of a centralized and of a decentralized system (Figure 9–2).

In general, centralized diffusion systems are based on a more linear, one-way model of communication. Decentralized diffusion systems more closely follow a convergence model of communication, in which participants create and share information with one another to reach a mutual understanding. A fundamental assumption of decentralized diffusion systems is that members of the user system have the ability to make sound decisions about how the diffusion process should be managed. This capacity of the users to run their own diffusion system is greatest (1) when the users are highly educated and technically competent practitioners (for example, cardiovascular surgeons), so that all the users are experts, or (2) when the innovations being diffused do not involve a sophisticated level of technology (for example, home energy conservation or organic gardening versus building a nuclear power plant), so that intelligent laymen have sufficient technical expertise.

Decentralized diffusion systems exist in a wide variety of fields and locations which suggests that we have severely underestimated the degree to which a user system is capable of managing its own diffusion processes. Our understanding of decentralized diffusion systems is still limited, owing to the general lack of investigations of such user-dominated diffusion.

Advantages and Disadvantages of Decentralized Diffusion

Compared to centralized systems, innovations diffused by decentralized systems are likely to fit more closely with users' needs and problems. Users feel a sense of control over a decentralized diffusion system, as they participate in making key decisions, such as which of their perceived

Table 9–1. Characteristics of Centralized and Decentralized Diffusion Systems

Characteristics of Diffusion Systems	Centralized Diffusion System	Decentralized Diffusion Systems
1. The degree of centralization in decision-making and power.	Overall control of decisions by national government administrators and technical subject-matter experts.	Wide sharing of power and control among the members of the diffusion system; client control by local systems; much diffusion is spontaneous and unplanned.
2. Direction of diffusion.	Top-down diffusion from experts to local users of innovations.	Peer diffusion of innovations through horizontal networks.
3. Sources of innovations.	Innovations come from formal R&D conducted by technical subject-matter experts.	Innovations come from experimentation by nonexperts, who often are users.
4. Who decides which innovations to diffuse?	Decisions about which innovations should be diffused are made by top administrators and technical subject-matter experts.	Local units decide which innovations should diffuse on the basis of their informal evaluations of the innovations.
5. How important are clients' needs in driving the diffusion process?	An innovation-centered approach; technology-push, emphasizing needs created by the availability of the innovation.	A problem-centered approach; technology-pull, created by locally perceived needs and problems.
6. Amount of re-invention?	A low degree of local adaptation and re-invention of the innovations as they diffuse among adopters.	A high degree of local adaptation as they diffuse among adopters.

Figure 9–1. Centralized and Decentralized Diffusion Systems

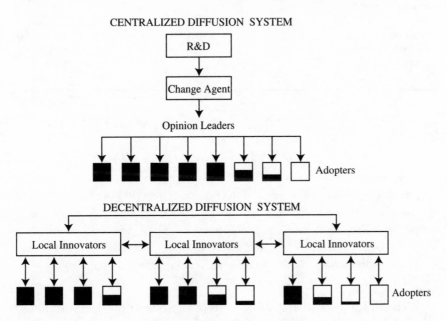

In decentralized diffusion systems, innovations spread by horizontal networks among near-peers in a relatively spontaneous fashion. Innovations are created by certain local users, and may be re-invented by other adopters.

problems most need attention, which innovations best meet these needs, how to seek information about each innovation and from what source, and how much to modify an innovation as they implement it in their particular setting. The high degree of user control over these key decisions means that a decentralized diffusion system is geared closely to local needs. Problems of change agent–client heterophily do not exist, or are greatly minimized. User motivations to seek innovations mainly drive a decentralized diffusion process, and this may be more cost-efficient than situations in which professional change agents manage the diffusion process. User self-reliance is encouraged in a decentralized system. Finally, decentralized diffusion is publicly popular; users generally like such systems.

Several disadvantages, however, usually characterized decentralized diffusion systems (in comparison with centralized diffusion systems):

Figure 9–2. The Continuum of Decentralized and Centralized Diffusion Systems

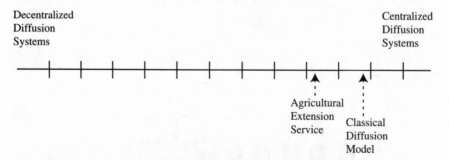

The classical diffusion model, based on the Ryan and Gross (1943) hybrid corn study, is relatively centralized. Only in recent years did diffusion scholars began to realize that actual diffusion systems ranged on a continuum. The agricultural extension service in the United States is relatively centralized, as are many diffusion systems modeled loosely after it, but other diffusion systems are relatively decentralized.

1. Technical expertise is difficult to bring to bear on decisions about which innovations to diffuse and to adopt, and it is possible for ineffective innovations to diffuse through a decentralized system because of the lack of quality control. So when a diffusion system is disseminating innovations that involve a high level of technical expertise, a decentralized diffusion system may be less appropriate than a more centralized diffusion system.

2. Furthermore, nonexperts in decentralized diffusion systems lack an understanding of diffusion strategies that might be utilized. As a result, site-visits to observe an innovation in use by an adopter are the main channels of diffusion. Such site-visiting can be an effective means of diffusion, but it may create an overload problem for the site that is visited, as has occurred for individuals, organizations, or cities that have thousands of site-visitors per year. Completely decentralized diffusion systems may suffer from the fact that local users, who control the system, lack adequate knowledge of users' problems and about available innovations that could solve them.

3. Sometimes a national government wants an innovation diffused for which the people do not feel a need. In a highly decentralized system, such an innovation simply will not diffuse. An example is family planning in Third World nations, which a government may regard as a high prior-

ity but which local people may not want. Decentralized diffusion systems for contraceptive innovations do not exist in Latin America, Africa, and Asia. Similarly, environmental innovations like recycling and car pooling may be a national priority but not be popular with people. A decentralized diffusion approach would not work here.

Our present discussion suggests that:

1. Decentralized diffusion systems are most appropriate for certain conditions, such as for diffusing innovations that do not involve a high level of technical expertise, among a set of users with relatively heterogeneous conditions. When these conditions are homogeneous, a relatively more centralized diffusion system may be more appropriate.

2. Certain elements of centralized and decentralized diffusion systems can be combined to form a hybrid diffusion system that uniquely fits a particular situation. For example, a diffusion system may combine a central-type coordinating role, with decentralized decisions being made about which innovations should be diffused and which users should site-visit. Technical evaluations of promising innovations can be made in an otherwise decentralized diffusion system.

Summary

A *change agent* is an individual who influences clients' innovation-decisions in a direction deemed desirable by a change agency. Change agents face two main problems: (1) their social marginality, due to their position midway between a change agency and their client system, and (2) *information overload*, the state of an individual or a system in which excessive communication inputs cannot be processed and used, leading to breakdown. Seven roles of the change agent are: (1) to develop a need for change on the part of clients, (2) to establish an information-exchange relationship, (3) to diagnose problems, (4) to create an intent to change in the client, (5) to translate an intent into action, (6) to stabilize adoption and prevent discontinuance, and (7) to achieve a terminal relationship with clients.

Generalizations 9–1 through 9–4, and 9–9 through 9–12, suggest that a change agent's relative success in securing the adoption of innovations by clients is positively related to: (1) the extent of change agent effort in contacting clients, (2) a client orientation, rather than a change agency orientation, (3) the degree to which the diffusion program is compatible with clients' needs, (4) the change agent's empathy with clients, (5) his or her homophily with clients, (6) credibility in the client's eyes, (7) the extent to which he or she works through opinion leaders, and (8) increasing clients' ability to evaluate innovations.

Further, we propose that change agent contact is positively related to: (1) higher social status among clients, (2) greater social participation, (3) higher formal education, and (4) cosmopoliteness (Generalizations 9–5 through 9–8)

An *aide* is less than a fully professional change agent who intensively contacts clients to influence their innovation-decisions. Not only do aides provide lower-cost contacts with clients than is possible with professional change agents, but they are also able to help bridge the heterophily gap between professionals and clients, especially lower-socioeconomic clients. Aides have less *competence credibility*, the degree to which a communication source or channel is perceived as knowledgeable and expert, but they have greater *safety credibility*, the degree to which a communication source or channel is perceived as trustworthy. An aide's safety credibility is a result of his or her homophily with the client system. *Inauthentic professionalization* is the process through which an aide takes on the dress, speech, or other identifying marks of a professional change agent.

In recent decades diffusion scholars have become aware that an alternative to the classical diffusion model exists in the form of decentralized diffusion systems. These diffusion programs have outrun the classical model (which is now recognized to be a relatively centralized approach). In *centralized* diffusion systems such as the agricultural extension service in the United States, overall control of diffusion decisions such as which innovations to diffuse, which diffusion channels to use, and to whom to diffuse innovations, is held by government officials and technical subject-matter experts. Diffusion in centralized systems flows top-down, from experts to users.

In contrast, *decentralized* diffusion systems are client controlled, with a wide sharing of power and control among the members of the diffusion system. Instead of coming out of R&D systems, innovations in decentralized systems come from local experimentation by nonexpert users. Local units decide which innovations should diffuse through horizontal networks, allowing a high degree of re-invention. Decentralized diffusion systems are based upon a convergence-type of communication, in which participants create and share information with one another in order to reach a mutual understanding. Decentralized diffusion systems are: (1) most appropriate for certain conditions, and (2) combinable with elements of centralized systems to form a hybrid diffusion system.

10

INNOVATION IN ORGANIZATIONS

Ideas confine a man to certain social groups and social groups confine a man to certain ideas. Many ideas are more easily changed by aiming at a group than by aiming at an individual.
—Josephine Klein, Working with Groups: The Social Psychology of Discussion and Decision

The present book thus far has been concerned with the diffusion of innovations to *individuals*. Many innovations, however, are adopted by *organizations*. And in many cases, an individual cannot adopt a new idea until an organization has previously adopted.

The present chapter particularly deals with collective and authority innovation-decisions: These two types usually entail an organization as the system in which the innovation-decision occurs. Here we trace the important change from the early studies of organizational innovativeness, in which data were gathered typically from a large sample of organizations to determine the characteristics of more- and less-innovative organizations, to investigations of the innovation process in organizations. These latter studies provide important insights into the nature of the innovation process and the behavior of organizations as they change.

The innovation-process studies stress the implementation stages involved in putting an innovation into use in an organization. These innovation-process studies improve upon previous diffusion research which generally stopped short of investigating implementation. Once a decision to adopt has been made in an organization, implementation does not always follow directly. Compared to the innovation-decision process by individuals, the innovation process in organizations is much more com-

371

plex. Implementation typically involves a number of individuals, each of whom plays a different role in the innovation-decision process. Further, implementation amounts to mutual adaptation in which both the innovation and the organization change in important ways.

Types of Innovation-Decisions

Three types of innovation-decisions are:

1. *Optional innovation-decisions*, choices to adopt or reject an innovation that are made by an individual independent of the decisions by other members of a system
2. *Collective innovation-decisions*, choices to adopt or reject an innovation that are made by consensus among the members of a system
3. *Authority innovation-decisions*, choices to adopt or reject an innovation that are made by a relatively few individuals in a system who possess power, status, or technical expertise

In addition, *contingent innovation-decisions* are choices to adopt or reject that can be made only after a prior innovation-decision. Thus, a doctor's decision to adopt a new medical procedure can be made only after the doctor's hospital has decided to purchase the necessary item of medical equipment. This example illustrates an optional decision that follows a collective decision. Other sequential combinations of two or more of the three types of innovation-decisions can also constitute a contingent decision.

One illustration of a contingent innovation-decision, consisting of an authority innovation-decision followed by optional innovation-decisions, is provided by Regulation XV in Los Angeles, a government edict that forces employing organizations to strongly discourage their workers from commuting to work as single passengers. Los Angeles has the worst air quality in the United States, in part because the Southern California basin is surrounded by mountains that trap air masses to create an inversion layer. Further, Los Angeles is a sprawling region with an inadequate mass transportation system; most people (79 percent) drive to work alone in private automobiles, with average commuter drives of an hour twice a day. As Los Angeles continues to grow in population and in the number of cars on its freeways, something drastic has to be done.

The state of California acted by establishing an agency, the South Coast Air Quality Management District (AQMD) to clean up the smog. Its Regulation XV required that all employers with at least 100 employees implement a system of incentives and disincentives to discourage driving to work alone. The goal is to persuade the 7 million commuters in the Los Angeles region to change a very deep-seated behavior. AQMD's Regulation XV seeks to increase the average number of riders per vehicle from 1.13 to 1.5 by the late 1990s. This 33 percent increase in vehicle occupancy is to be achieved by employing organizations who are expected to encourage their employees to travel to work in carpools, vanpools, and buses; to telecommute (work at home); to work a flexible schedule; to make parking more costly and difficult; and to provide bicycle parking racks and showers for bicyclists. Note that the individual employee makes an optional innovation-decision, but chooses among options that the employing organization is mandated by Regulation XV (an authority innovation-decision) to provide to its employees. Thus organizations often constrain or determine the innovation behavior of their individual members.

How Thermos Designed a New Electric Grill

The Thermos Corporation of Schaumburg, Illinois, is a well-established firm noted for its Thermos bottles and lunch boxes. It also is a major manufacturer of gas and electric cookout grills, where it competes head-to-head with several other big companies in the $1-billion-a-year barbecue grill market. Until 1992, these grills all looked pretty much alike. When Monte Peterson took over as the chief executive officer of Thermos in 1990, he decided to replace its traditional bureaucratic organizational structure (divisions for engineering, manufacturing, marketing, and so forth) with flexible, interdisciplinary work teams. Peterson began this changeover by forming a group to design a revolutionary new product: The Thermos Thermal Electric Grill, which uses an entirely new technology to give food a barbecued taste, while burning cleaner than gas or charcoal-burning competitive products. Thermos' electric grill is easy to clean, does not require heavy propane tanks, and has a space-age look. Introduced in 1992, first-year sales of the Thermal Electric Grill sizzled, and Thermos boosted its market share for electric grills from 2 percent to 20 percent.

How did Thermos create this successful new product? The innovation-generation process began in 1990 when CEO Peterson appointed six of his middle managers from engineering, marketing, manufacturing, and finance to a product development team. At first there was resistance to leaving their parent departments to work on the interdisciplinary team, but Peterson convinced his people to collaborate. The team was told to go into the field and learn all about people's cookout needs, and then to design a new grill to meet these needs. They called themselves the Lifestyle Team, rather than the New Grill Team, thus avoiding a dominant emphasis on grill technology, at the expense of focusing on the customer. Outside consultants from an industrial design company, Fitch Inc. of Worthington, Ohio, were added to the Thermos team in order to provide expertise in conducting marketing research and in designing the product.

The Lifestyle Team set a series of rugged deadlines, aiming to launch their new grill at the National Hardware Show in Chicago in August, 1992, two years off. Team members were freed of all other duties. Their time schedule allocated many months for planning the product, and a relatively short time for execution, an emphasis on planning followed by Japanese companies (Thermos is owned by Nippon Sanso). The Lifestyle Team first spent about one month on the road, conducting focus group interviews with customers, visiting people's homes, and videotaping home barbecues. They learned some surprising facts: More women were barbecuing, and they complained of messy charcoal. Many grills were rusted and unattractive. Southern California had banned the use of charcoal starter (due to its creating smog); New Jersey prohibited the use of gas grills on apartment and condo balconies. The new grill would have to be electric.

The problem was that customers hated electric grills, mainly because they used a heat rod located six inches below the grill which bakes the food rather than grilling it. Here is where Thermos' core competency came in handy (a core competency is what an organization does best). For Thermos, its core competency is the vacuum technology that keeps liquids hot or cold in Thermos bottles. The engineering experts on the Lifestyle Team drew on this core competency by designing a domed vacuum top for the grill that kept the heat inside the grill. They moved the heat rod up into the surface of the grill so that it seared the meat, giving it those brown barbecue lines. The legs of the grill formed a tripod, so that it fit into a corner of an apartment terrace. The Team gave the first 100 Thermos electric grills to Thermos employees for a pilot test in mid-1992. Employees were told to "use them hard," such as in the rain and loaded with heavy platters of food. The Lifestyle team thus discovered that the grill's shelves broke easily. They were subsequently redesigned with stronger plastic.

Finally, Team members loaded the new electric grill into a U-Haul truck, and drove to the headquarters of such important retail chains as Target, Service Merchandise, and so forth. They barbecued shrimp and vegetables for the presidents of these companies. The $299 retail price seems substantial, but reception of the Thermos Thermal Electric Grill at the 1992 National Hardware Show was enthusiastic. The Thermos Company's revenues increased by 13 percent in 1993, with most of the increase coming from new products like the electric grill. Shortly thereafter, Thermos began forming other interdisciplinary teams to design other new products.

Notice that in this case, *both* the innovation and the organization changed: The Thermos Corporation adopted the innovation of flexible work groups as a basis of organizing to create new products. The perceived success of the Lifestyle Team in designing the new electric grill encouraged Thermos to adopt this change in its organizational structure. Thermos adopted its own particular kind of interdisciplinary work group, bringing in special expertise from a consulting agency. Thus, Generalization 10–1 states that *Both the innovation and the organization usually change in the innovation process in organizations*. Further, when Target and the other retail chains began selling the Thermos Thermal Electric Grills in their stores, this innovative product necessitated changes in store organization, such as establishing a new department of electric grills and hiring special salespeople to handle the new product.

This case illustration is based on Dumaine (1993).

Organizations

An *organization* is a stable system of individuals who work together to achieve common goals through a hierarchy of ranks and a division of labor (Rogers and Agarwala-Rogers, 1976). Organizations are created to handle large-scale routine tasks through a pattern of regularized human relationships. Their efficiency as a means of orchestrating human endeavors is in part a result of this stability, which stems from the relatively high degree of structure that is imposed on communication patterns. A predictable organizational structure is obtained through:

1. *Predetermined goals*. Organizations are formally established for the explicit purpose of achieving certain goals. The objectives of the organization determine to a large extent the structure and function of the organization. For example, the Federal Express Company exists to provide

overnight delivery of letters and packages; its organizational structure is highly centralized, almost like a paramilitary unit.

2. *Prescribed roles*. Organizational tasks are distributed among the various positions as roles or duties. A role is a set of activities to be performed by an individual occupying a given position. Positions are the "boxes" on an organizational chart. Individuals may come and go in an organization, but the positions continue, as do the roles expected of individuals filling these positions.

3. *Authority structure*. In a formal organization all positions do not have equal authority. Instead, positions are organized in a hierarchical authority structure that specifies who is responsible to whom, and who can give orders to whom.

4. *Rules and regulations*. A formal, established system of written procedures governs decisions and actions of organizational members. There are prescribed procedures for hiring new members, for promotion, for discharging unsatisfactory employees, and for coordinating the control of various activities to ensure uniform operations.

5. *Informal patterns*. Every formal organization is characterized by various kinds of informal practices, norms, and social relationships among its members. These informal practices emerge over time and represent an important part of any organization. Nevertheless, the intent of bureaucratic organizations is to depersonalize human relationships as much as possible by standardizing and formalizing them.

Given the relative stability of organizations, one might expect that innovation would be very rare. On the contrary, innovation goes on all the time in most organizations. Many barriers and resistances to change exist in an organization. But we should not forget that innovation is one of the fundamental processes underway in all organizations.

Organizational Innovativeness

Diffusion research began with investigations of individual decision makers such as farmers. When this paradigm was extended to medical doctors and teachers, the early diffusion studies ignored the fact that teachers are school employees and that most doctors work in hospitals or in a group practice. Several decades later, researches began conducting diffusion studies in which the unit of adoption was an organization, rather than an individual. These early studies of organizational innovativeness were oversimplifications in that the data were obtained from a single individual (usually the chief executive). In essence, each organization in these studies was reduced to the equivalent of an individual. The entire organization was treated as a single unit of analysis.

Nevertheless, much useful knowledge was gained from the organizational innovativeness studies and some are still carried out today. Important innovations spread among the firms in an industry in a diffusion process that is similar to the way that an innovation diffuses among the individuals in a community or some other system. Evidence for this point comes from Czepiel's (1975) investigation of the diffusion of the innovation of the continuous casting process among eighteen companies in the U.S. steel industry: "A functioning informal community [links] the firms together." Again, we see that diffusion is a social process.

Until the 1970s scholars simply transferred to the study of organizations the models and methods of investigating innovativeness earlier developed for individuals, often without carefully thinking through the ways in which the two levels of systems were alike or differed (Eveland, 1979). Several hundred studies of organizational innovativeness were completed by the 1970s. Then a different kind of diffusion research in organizations began, looking at the innovation process *within* the organization. Instead of determining the variables related to more-innovative and less-innovative organizations, the process of innovation was traced in a single organization over time.

The early studies of organizational innovativeness helped illuminate the characteristics of innovative organizations; many of these characteristics were equivalent to the characteristics of innovative individuals. For example, larger organizations are more innovative, just as are individuals with larger incomes and higher socioeconomic status. But certain of the organizational characteristics do not have an individual counterpart; for instance, organizational structural characteristics like system openness* and formalization† were found to be related positively and negatively, respectively, to organizational innovativeness. A fair degree of conceptual

---

* *System openness* is the degree to which the members of a system are linked to other individuals who are external to the system. An open system exchanges information across its boundaries. Perhaps system openness for an organization is somewhat equivalent to cosmopoliteness for an individual.

† *Formalization* is the degree to which an organization emphasizes following rules and procedures in the role performance of its members. So formalization is the degree to which an organization is bureaucratic.

originality took place in the organizational innovativeness studies, even though their research methodologies were directly copied from the individual-level innovativeness studies.

Why have studies of organizational innovativeness generally become passé?

1. The organizational innovativeness studies found rather low relationships between the independent variables (measured qualities of the organization) investigated and the dependent variable of innovativeness. Often a hundred or more organizations were the units of study, and the typical investigation followed a highly quantitative approach to data analysis. Independent variables like organizational structural dimensions of centralization, formalization, and the like were measured for each organization. The dependent variable of innovativeness was typically measured as a composite score, composed of the adoption of from ten to twenty innovations. The innovation process for each innovation in each organization of study was thus submerged through aggregation into an overall innovativeness score for each organization. This cross-sectional approach to data analysis also meant that time as a variable was lost; thus, the process (that is, the over-time) aspects of the innovation process could not be measured. The relatively modest correlations of organizational structural variables with innovativeness helped demonstrate the futility of understanding innovation in organizations through innovativeness surveys.

2. One vexing problem of the organizational innovativeness studies was how adequately the data provided by the chief executive represented the innovation behavior of the entire organization. Because the organizational innovativeness investigations typically gathered data only from the top executive of each organization in a sample of organizations, there was no way to determine how adequately these data truly represented the entire organization's behavior with regard to a technological innovation. For example, questionnaire data were gathered from eight city officials (the chief administrator, finance officer, police chief, etc.) in each of 276 U.S. cities about the adoption of three planning/budgeting innovations (Bingham and Frendreis, 1978). One would expect that the chief executive and the finance officer would agree about such a basic matter as to whether or not their city had adopted a budgeting innovation, but such agreement between these two top officials occurred only about two-thirds of the time. This was a troubling finding for diffusion scholars studying organizational innovativeness. Gathering data only from a few

individuals at the top of a large sample of organizations did not seem to provide very valid measures of the concepts of study.

Size and Organizational Innovativeness

The size of an organization has consistently been found to be positively related to its innovativeness. Generalization 10–2 states: *Larger organizations are more innovative.*

Mytinger (1968) asked: "Is [innovativeness a result of] the man, the agency, or the place?" The innovativeness of forty local health departments in California was related to (1) their size, measured in the number of staff and the amount of their budget, which in turn rested on (2) the size of the city they served, and (3) the cosmopoliteness, accreditation, and prestige of the health director among his or her peer health officials. Overall, "This study suggests that *size*—size of community and size of [the health] department—is perhaps the most compelling concomitant to innovativeness" (Mytinger, 1968).

Why do researchers consistently find that size is one of the best predictors of organizational innovativeness? First, size is a variable that is easily measured, presumably with a relatively high degree of precision. So size is included for study in almost every organizational innovativeness investigation.

Second, size is probably a surrogate measure of several dimensions that lead to innovation: Total resources, slack resources, technical expertise of employees, organizational structure, and so on. These unidentified variables have not been clearly understood, or adequately measured in most researches. These lurking variables may be a fundamental reason for the finding that size and innovativeness are related. Few scholars have much theoretical interest in size as a variable, but it is a convenient stand-in for other variables of interest.

Structural Characteristics and Organizational Innovativeness

Innovativeness is related to such independent variables as (1) individual (leader) characteristics, (2) internal organizational structural characteristics, and (3) external characteristics of the organization (Figure 10–1). Here we look at the organizational structure variables related to the innovativeness of organizations.

Centralization is the degree to which power and control in a system are concentrated in the hands of relatively few individuals. Centralization

Figure 10–1. Independent Variables Related to Organizational Innovativeness

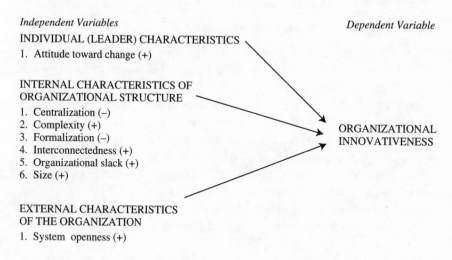

Independent Variables

INDIVIDUAL (LEADER) CHARACTERISTICS
1. Attitude toward change (+)

INTERNAL CHARACTERISTICS OF
ORGANIZATIONAL STRUCTURE
1. Centralization (−)
2. Complexity (+)
3. Formalization (−)
4. Interconnectedness (+)
5. Organizational slack (+)
6. Size (+)

EXTERNAL CHARACTERISTICS
OF THE ORGANIZATION
1. System openness (+)

Dependent Variable

ORGANIZATIONAL
INNOVATIVENESS

has usually been found to be negatively associated with innovativeness; that is, the more that power is concentrated in an organization, the less innovative the organization tends to be. The range of new ideas in an organization is restricted when a few strong leaders dominate the system. In a centralized organization, top leaders are poorly positioned to identify operational-level problems, or to suggest relevant innovations to meet these needs. Although the initiation of innovations in a centralized organization is less frequent than in a decentralized organization, the centralization may encourage the implementation of innovations, once the innovation-decision is made.

Complexity is the degree to which an organization's members possess a relatively high level of knowledge and expertise, usually measured by the members' range of occupational specialties and their degree of professionalism expressed by formal training. Complexity encourages organizational members to conceive and propose innovations, but it may make it difficult to achieve consensus about implementing them.

Formalization is the degree to which an organization emphasizes following rules and procedures in the role performance of its members. Such formalization acts to inhibit the consideration of innovations by organization members, but encourages the implementation of innovations.

Interconnectedness is the degree to which the units in a social system are linked by interpersonal networks. New ideas can flow more easily among an organization's members if the organization has higher network interconnectedness. This variable is positively related to organizational innovativeness.

Organizational slack is the degree to which uncommitted resources are available to an organization. This variable is positively related to organizational innovativeness, especially for innovations that are higher in cost.

The results of the several hundred studies of organizational innovativeness show rather low correlations of each of the independent variables (in Figure 10–1) with the innovativeness of organizations. One reason for these results is that each of the organizational structural variables may be related to innovation in one direction during the initiation phases of the innovation process, and in the opposite direction during the implementation phases. Low centralization, high complexity, and low formalization facilitate initiation in the innovation process, but these structural characteristics make it difficult for an organization to implement an innovation (Zaltman and others, 1973). Thus, we see how bringing the initiation and implementation subprocesses of the innovation process into our analysis better explains the results of past research on variables related to organizational innovativeness.

While scholarly interest in organizational innovativeness studies has decreased in recent years, such investigations continue, often with interesting results. For example, Fennell (1984) studied the diffusion and adoption of two related innovations (alcoholism counseling programs for employees, and the provision of insurance coverage for alcoholism treatment of employees) by 173 private companies employing at least 250 workers in Illinois. The two innovations were linked synergistically; if a company adopted the alcoholism insurance coverage program, the adoption of alcoholism counseling was also facilitated. Larger size and greater complexity were related to adoption of the alcoholism insurance program, which in turn often led to the adoption of alcoholism counseling, despite the opposition of labor unions and medical departments.

A particularly interesting investigation representing a new type of organizational innovativeness study was reported by Alan D. Meyer and James B. Goes (1988). These scholars studied twelve medical innovations (CAT scanners, ultrasonic imaging, laser surgery, electronic fetal monitoring, fiberoptic endoscopy, and so forth) as they were adopted in the twenty-five hospitals in a Midwestern city. These 300 innovation-decisions, each representing an innovation in an organization, were the units of analysis. Note this important departure from the usual organizational innovativeness study in which each of the twenty-five hospitals would have been scored on their relative innovativeness in adopting the twelve innovations. Instead, Meyer and Goes (1988) used a nine-point scale for each innovation-decision process, ranging from a hospital's staff being aware of the innovation (1 point), through adoption and regular use of the innovation (8 points), to expanding and upgrading the new technology (9 points). Essentially, this dependent variable is the degree to which a hospital has progressed through the stages in the innovation process for each of the twelve innovations of study.

One of the medical doctor respondents in this study described the complicated innovation process in a hospital as follows:

> A lot of us [doctors] want the very latest medical equipment—both for our patients' sake and for our own sake. Medicine's extremely competitive . . . there's competition for referrals and competition to be known as the guy who can handle a really tough, challenging case.
>
> [The board members] ask, "How are we ever going to pay for all this?" As a rule, doctors and boards never meet, so the decisions are made separately, at different levels, according to different criteria.
>
> But sandwiched in the middle, between the doctors and the board, you have the administrators.

From remarks like these, one senses the complexity of the innovation process for a new medical technology in a hospital. Meyer and Goes (1988) found that the degree of progress of an innovation through the innovation process in a hospital (their dependent variable of study) was explained (1) by the perceived attributes of the innovations, with observability, low risk, and low complexity explaining 40 percent of the variance in the dependent variable), and (2) by hospital environmental, organizational, and leadership variables, which explained 11 percent of the variance in the dependent variable. Large hospitals with complex structures, which used aggressive marketing strategies and were located in an urban environment, were particularly innovative. Especially important in the progress of a medical technology through the innovation process was a hospital chief executive officer (CEO) who exerted substantial influence as the innovation's champion. Thus, innovation champions were crucial in moving a medical innovation through the innovation process in a hospital.

Other investigations of the innovation process in an organization have also found that an innovation champion can play an important role in boosting a new idea. Of course, anti-innovation champions can detract from the success of a new technology in reaching the routinization stage of the innovation process.

Tightening the Iron Cage Through Self-Managing Work Teams

The great German sociologist Max Weber (1958) described bureaucratic organizations like factories, armies, and government agencies as characterized by a form of authoritarian control that he called the iron cage. Rules are made and orders are issued by individuals of authority, and carried out by organizational members who accept the system of authority. At first, this control system operates in a rational and efficient manner, but the organizational effectiveness of the bureaucracy usually gets lost over time. Rules are enforced overzealously, and applied in an inappropriate way to all cases. Bureaucratic leaders become impersonal and the former rationality of the control system disappears. Nevertheless, organization members continue to support the bureaucratic authority system, trapped in an iron cage of control.

Recently, some organizations have implemented an alternative to the bureaucratic system of control in an effort to escape the iron cage. These post-bureaucratic organizations have replaced hierarchical authority with a system of self-managing work teams, each composed of a small number of individuals who take on the responsibilities of their former supervisors (as we saw in the case of the Lifestyle Team at the Thermos Corporation, cited previously in this chapter). Top management of the organization provides a vision for the individuals in work teams, who then manage their own day-to-day activities including coordination with other units of the organization. The self-managing work teams set their own work schedule, order the materials that they need, and convey their completed work to consumers. One advantage of organizing in work groups is to save the cost of lower-level managers, who are no longer needed. Work teams also usually have increased employee motivation, satisfaction, and productivity. Finally, self-managed work teams should free organization members from the shackles of bureaucracy, from Weber's iron cage.

But do they? Professor James R. Barker (1993) studied a high-tech electronics company, ISE Communications, before, during, and after it adopted the innovation of self-managed work teams. ISE manufactures circuit boards for sale to telephone companies. Workers assemble semiconductors, resistors, potentiometers, and other parts onto a printed circuit board, and then solder these components to the board. After testing and trouble-shooting, the circuit board is packaged and shipped. This work is monotonous in nature, and the industry is highly competitive.

Barker met a company executive from ISE Communications at a social function, where the official learned of Barker's interest in studying the implementation and consequences of work groups. Barker was invited to visit the company and he spent several days a week there for the next two and one-half years. His ethnographic research consisted of observation and repeated, in-depth personal interviews with workers and company officials at ESL.

The company's adoption of self-managed work teams began in 1986, when Jack Tackett, vice-president for manufacturing and a co-founder of ISE, decided that the company's survival depended on converting to self-management: "We could not meet customer demands anymore. Hierarchy insulates people from the customer. . . . The demands of the market are too dynamic for a company to be controlled by a handful of managers" (quoted in Barker, 1993). Tackett managed to persuade others in the company to give the innovation a try, and in 1988 one work team was established. The new team performed better than anyone had imagined. Then, over a weekend, Tackett had the company's manufacturing area completely remodeled into an arrangement for three more work teams. Machines, worktables, and other equipment were moved to create the three work areas. On Monday morning, Tackett assigned employees to the teams. Three former supervisors were organized into a support group which helped each team solve its technical problems.

A worker told Professor Barker (1993) what happened next: "Well, it was mass confusion. Nobody knew where they were sitting, what team they were on. . . . As far as details, no idea! So basically, everybody was just kind of like WOW, this is kinda fun." Workers were assigned to the three teams by drawing numbers out of a hat. One former manager was assigned to each work team as a coach; Tackett instructed each coach to teach the team members how to manage themselves. Tackett also worked with the company president in crafting a vision, which stated, in part: "We will be an organization where each of us is a self-manager. . . ." Each team met formally for about 15 minutes at the start of each workday to plan their work activities.

In mid-1990, ISE almost went bankrupt, and employee lay-offs were necessary. Soon, however, the financial crisis eased and the company began to prosper, in part because of the work teams. Costs were lowered, by saving the salaries formerly paid to supervisors and managers. New employees were hired, creating four new work teams. Commitment to the organization was high, and team members took pride in their success. The self-managed work groups took responsibility for many decisions, including whether or not to work overtime. For example, the "Blue Team" had promised to get out a customer order on a particular day, but were held up by a lack of potentiometers, which only arrived in midday. The Blue Team's coordinator, Lee Ann, told her colleagues that they would have to work two hours past the regular quitting time. Larry, a member of the Blue Team, groaned: "Damn, I've got plans for five-thirty." Suna said: "My daughter's school play is tonight!" But the team members decided that they would have to work overtime, as they had promised delivery to their customer. They informed Jack Tackett of their decision to work overtime (they could decide to do so without his approval). One team member volunteered to arrange for the building to stay open after 5 o'clock. The Blue Team agreed that Suna could leave, and she promised to work late the next time that overtime was necessary.

As this example suggests, the work teams at ISE had a great deal of responsibility, and displayed considerable initiative. For instance, new employees were hired on a provisional basis for several months, with the final employment decision made by the other members of their work team. Gradually, the work groups began to exert more influence over the behavior of their members, such as the time at which they came to work. The work groups made rules about tardiness and absenteeism. If an individual was more than five minutes late, the worker was charged with an "occurrence," and counted as absent for the entire day. If a worker accumulated four or more occurrences per month, the work team coordinator placed a written warning in the individual's personnel file. A large wall chart was erected in the Red Team's work area, listing each members' name and with color-coded dots to indicate whenever they were "on time," "tardy," or had an "occurrence" that day. One employee, Ronald, told Professor Barker: "Now the

whole team is around me, and the whole team is observing what I am doing" (Barker, 1993).

Changes also began to take place in each work team's leadership. At first,
a "coordinator" was elected by each team on a monthly basis. Later, this time
period was expanded to six months. Soon the coordinator's role began to take
on the aura of supervisor (Barker, 1993). Team members looked to their coordinator for direction. Next, in 1992, the team leader's role was made per-
manent, and the title was changed from "coordinator" to "facilitator." A
10-percent pay boost was given to the facilitators, in recognition of their
added responsibilities. But the team members still kept primary control over
their own self-management.

The gradual formalization of their work life seemed natural to the work
team members. Jim Barker observed that the employees of ISE Communication were recreating a control system. They made rules concerning ab-
sences, and they enforced them. The work team members held authority
over each other, but it was unlike the bureaucratic control of hierarchical
authority that had originally prevailed. The post-bureaucratic control system
was an iron cage too, but it was a self-imposed iron cage, mainly controlled
by the work teams themselves.

This case illustration is based on Barker (1993), Barker, Melville, and Pacanowsky (1993), and
discussions with James R. Barker about the present study.

Evolution of Airline Computer Reservations Systems

The U.S. airline industry changes its fare prices 12 million times a day, and
airline reservation systems process 1,500 transactions a second! In recent
decades, the main basis of competition between U.S. airlines has been their
computerized reservations systems, which have become a tool for competitive advantage, in several cases deciding which airlines went bankrupt and
which survived. This evolutionary process is driven by advances in communication technologies that extend the boundaries of an airline company to
include travel agencies and, ultimately, customers. Information thus becomes an asset for gaining competitive advantage in the airline industry.

In the years just after World War II, U.S. airlines manually maintained a
list of seats on each flight in a looseleaf folder at the city of departure. Customers made a reservation by telephone. During the 1950s, these availabil-

ity listings were put on a computer system. The president of American Airlines was acutely aware of the deficiencies of this reservations system: Double bookings, unfilled seats on many flights, etc. Thus American Airlines initiated development of the SABER (Semi-Automatic Business Environment Research) reservation system through a joint agreement with IBM: The computerized system should match passengers to seats, print passenger itineraries, issue boarding passes, and, importantly, move reservations terminals to the offices of travel agents. Another twenty years was needed before American Airlines was able to establish this vision, a period during which the name of the system was changed from "SABER" to "SABRE" (to suggest speed, accuracy, and competitive advantage), and during which American Airlines employees accumulated considerable technical experience with the computer reservation system.

Finally, in 1967, the SABRE system was implemented. American Airlines placed 200 of its terminals with large-volume, geographically well-situated travel agents. At this point, travel agents sold 30 percent all airline tickets. It quickly became apparent to American Airlines that their computer reservations strategy generated substantial extra income. The first 200 installations had been expected to contribute $3.1 million in increased passenger sales per year; the actual contribution was $20 million, a return on investment of 500 percent! This income came from two sources (1) a fee of somewhat less than $2.00 was charged all other airlines by American Airlines for every flight segment booked on the SABRE system, and (2) a display bias, in which all American flights between two cities were displayed in the top lines of the computer screen, followed by the flights of American Airlines' "co-hosts" (who did not compete in the same market and who paid American a fee). The flights of American's most direct competitors, like United, were listed last, often on a second screen. Approximately 70 percent of all flights are sold from the first computer screen that is displayed. This display bias allows the airline owning the computer reservation system to gain an extra 25 percent of flight bookings. This is a very considerable advantage in a highly competitive industry.

Meanwhile, United Airlines also sought to exploit the competitive advantage that could be gained through developing a computer reservation system. But United initially saw its APOLLO system primarily as a means to reduce clerical costs, and only slowly did the airline realize the marketing potential of its reservation system. Development of APOLLO was relegated to a low-level unit in the United Airlines organization; in contrast, American

Airlines' President Robert Crandell established a separate organizational unit, Travel Agency Automation, and championed it. In 1976, United furloughed thirty computer programmers working on APOLLO as part of a 3-percent across-the-board layoff, with the cuts based solely on seniority. Thus United lost some of its most relevant expertise; these computer programmers were immediately hired by American Airlines for its computer reservation unit.

The Airline Deregulation Act of 1978 augured the end of government approval of airline rates and fares. No longer could airline bosses "graze sleepily on a peaceful playing field." Fare changes, previously made on a semi-annual basis, were made daily. Passenger inquiries changed from questions about seat availability to price shopping. Travel agents became more important as airlines closed many of their city ticket offices; by 1985, 86 percent of all flight reservations were made by travel agents. American Airlines aggressively promoted its SABRE system to travel agencies, spending $20 million per year on the promotion. By the late 1980s, 95 percent of the 29,000 travel agents in the United States had airline computer terminals, with American's SABRE system installed at 38 percent of travel agents and with United's APOLLO at 30 percent. American's nine co-hosts paid $7 million annually in fees, and another $80 million was generated for American by increased passenger ticket sales (mainly from the display basis).

In 1980, American Airlines launched the first frequent flyer program, in which loyal customers were rewarded with free flights after accumulating a certain number of miles flown. Other airlines perceived frequent flyer programs as just a strategy to foster customer loyalty, and quickly followed American's lead. Astutely, American assigned each frequent flyer an identification number, which was entered into the SABRE computer system. United had each passenger fill out a 3×5 inch card for each flight segment, which was stapled to the flight coupon. Soon, United had accumulated a warehouse full of these frequent flyer cards, and had to hire an army of clerks to enter them into the computer system. But the United frequent flyer system was not tied into United's APOLLO reservation system, so the airline could not utilize the data generated by its frequent flyer program in management decisions about airline routes and prices. Meanwhile, American Airlines, which had conceived of its frequent flyer program as a means to obtain valuable information about the several hundred thousand businessmen who do so much flying that they are the key market niche for U.S. airlines. American used its frequent flyer data to arrange flight connections and special promotions to attract and hold these special customers.

For instance, say that you are one of American's most frequent flyers. As your morning flight takes off from Dallas–Fort Worth International Airport, the SABRE system transmits to an on-board computer in the cockpit a message that you are sitting in Seat 2B (you were previously upgraded to this first-class seat by SABRE). The American Airlines stewardess brings you a Bloody Mary, compliments of the captain (SABRE knows that you prefer this drink before 11:00 A.M., and a gin martini on the rocks, very dry, after lunchtime). SABRE has scheduled your connection in Atlanta, so that you have a convenient thirty minutes before your continuing flight to New York. Yes, SABRE is looking after you.

One can see from this example how information, and the new communication technology that controls this information, can be an important weapon for competitive advantage. American Airlines managed the technological innovation of its computer reservation system judiciously, and thus gained a competitive advantage over United Airlines and its other rivals in the airlines industry.

This case illustration is based upon Copeland and McKenney (1988), and other sources.

The Innovation Process in Organizations

An important turning point in the history of research on innovation in organizations occurred with publication of the book *Innovations and Organizations* by Gerald Zaltman and others (1973). These authors specified the distinctive aspects of innovation when it took place in an organization. For one thing, the main dependent variable of study often became implementation, putting an innovation into use, rather than adoption (the decision to use an innovation). Until this point, most studies of innovations and organizations concerned organizational innovativeness, measured as the adoption or nonadoption of a battery of innovations by a sample of organizations. After the early 1970s, research on innovations and organizations centered on investigations of a single innovation in an organization or organizations. Often the innovation of study was a new communication technology like electronic messaging, a management information system, or some other computer-based technological innovation. "The field of innovation in organizations has been invigorated in the 1980s by the study of new communication technologies" (Van de Ven and Rogers, 1988).

The innovation process in organizations has been traced by diffusion scholars to identify the main sequence of decisions, actions, and events in this process. Data about the innovation process are obtained by synthesizing the recallable perceptions of key actors in the innovation process, written records of the organization adopting, and other data sources.

An explosion occurred in the number of studies about innovation in organizations published in 1980s and 1990s. Why? One reason is that business school scholars, particularly in departments of management and organization, became fascinated with the innovation process. Further, a large and well-funded research program on this topic, the Minnesota Innovation Research Program, was launched in the business school of the University of Minnesota in 1983. This program, lead by Professor Andrew H. Van de Ven, consisted of thirty scholars who conducted fourteen in-depth case studies of technological innovations in a variety of fields: industry, education, agriculture, health, defence, and so forth. Van de Ven and his colleagues pursued a common theoretical framework in gathering and analyzing their data on innovation. The results are an integrated set of studies of the innovation process in organizations (Van de Ven and others, 1989).

Another important reason for the increasing research attention accorded to innovation in organizations is the widespread introduction of computer-related technologies in all kinds of organizations. The implementation of many of these innovations failed, causing a great deal of practical interest in better understanding how to effectively introduce computer-related technologies.

Such interactive innovations as e-mail have little functional advantage (and often have a considerable disadvantage) for the first user of these technologies in an organization. Obviously, the very first adopter of electronic mail has no one with whom to communicate. Thus the rate of adoption for the new interactive technologies proceeds very slowly at first in an organization, at least until a critical mass is reached (see Chapter 8). A distinctive intellectual advantage of studying new communication technologies is that such investigations provide a new type of data, and allow scholars to study new variables with new theories (Van de Ven and Rogers, 1988).

Van de Ven and Rogers (1988) stated: "Today, there is probably as much scholarly research conducted on innovation in organizations as there are innovation studies with individuals in the general society as the units of analysis. So the intellectual intersection of innovations and organizations has indeed become a popular dwelling spot for contemporary research activity."

The general assumption of research on innovation in organizations is that organizational variables act on innovation behavior in a manner over and above that of the aggregate of individual members of the organization. Thus the organizational context of these innovation process studies adds a kind of intellectual supercharger to the analysis. "Organizations are often seen in this research as constraints or resistances to innovations, at least to the extent that many problems are usually encountered in attempts to implement an innovation in an organization. Alternatively, these difficulties can be seen as evidence that a particular innovation may not fit well with an organization's perceived problem, or that the innovation's expected consequences are perceived by the organization's members as more negative than positive" (Van de Ven and Rogers, 1988).

The innovation process consists of a usual sequence of five stages (Figure 10–2), two in the initiation subprocess and three in the implementation subprocess. Later stages in the innovation process cannot be undertaken until earlier stages have been settled, either explicitly or implicitly.

1. Agenda-Setting

Agenda-setting occurs in the innovation process when a general organizational problem that may create a perceived need for an innovation is defined. The agenda-setting process goes on all the time in every system. It has to, so that the system knows what to work on first, next, and so forth. Agenda-setting is the way in which needs, problems, and issues bubble up through a system and are prioritized in a hierarchy for attention (Dearing and Rogers, in press). The agenda-setting stage in the innovation process in organizations amounts both to identifying and prioritizing needs and problems on one hand, and to searching the organization's environment to locate innovations of potential usefulness to meet the organization's problems.

The agenda-setting stage requires an extended period of time, often several years. The case studies of the innovation process conducted as part of the Minnesota Innovation Research Program led to the conclusion that "Innovations are not initiated on the spur of the moment, nor

Figure 10-2. Five Stages in the Innovation Process in an Organization

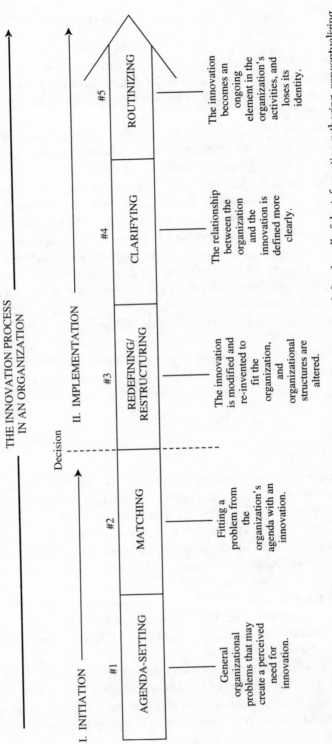

THE INNOVATION PROCESS
IN AN ORGANIZATION

I. INITIATION

II. IMPLEMENTATION

Decision

| #1 | #2 | #3 | #4 | #5 |

AGENDA-SETTING

MATCHING

REDEFINING/RESTRUCTURING

CLARIFYING

ROUTINIZING

General organizational problems that may create a perceived need for innovation.

Fitting a problem from the organization's agenda with an innovation.

The innovation is modified and re-invented to fit the organization, and organizational structures are altered.

The relationship between the organization and the innovation is defined more clearly.

The innovation becomes an ongoing element in the organization's activities, and loses its identity.

The innovation process in an organization consists of two broad activities: (1) *initiation*, defined as all of the information gathering, conceptualizing, and planning for the adoption of an innovation, leading up to the decision to adopt, and (2) *implementation*, all of the events, actions, and decisions involved in putting an innovation into use. The decision to adopt (shown as a vertical dotted line in the figure above) divides initiation, composed of the agenda-setting and matching stages, from implementation, composed of the three stages of redefining/restructuring, clarifying, and routinizing.

392

by a single dramatic incident, nor by a single entrepreneur" (Schroeder, Van de Ven, Scudder, and Polley, 1986).

Agenda-setting is continuously underway in every organization. We consider agenda-setting as part of the sequence of the innovation process, for it is here that the initial motivation is generated to impel the later steps in the innovation process. At the agenda-setting stage, one or more individuals in an organization identify an important problem and then seek an innovation as one means of coping with the problem.

A *performance gap* is the discrepancy between an organization's expectations and its actual performance. This difference between how an organization's members perceive its performance, in comparison to what they feel it should be, can be a strong impetus to search for an innovation. Generalization 10–3 states: *A performance gap can trigger the innovation process*. The Minnesota Innovation Research Program provides evidence for this statement. These case studies of innovation show that in most cases a shock to the organization reached a threshold of attention by the organization's participants, leading to action. This shock, often caused by direct personal confrontations with needs or problems, leads the organization to initiate the innovation process (Schroeder, Van de Ven, Scudder, and Polley, 1986).

Most organizations engage in an opportunistic surveillance by scanning the environment for new ideas that might be beneficial to the organization. As March (1981) noted, innovation in organizations "often seems to be driven less by problems than by solutions. Answers often precede questions." Most organizations face many problems, but possess knowledge of only a few innovations that offer solutions. So the chance of identifying an innovation to cope with a particular problem is relatively small. But if one begins with a solution, there is a good chance that the innovation will match some problem faced by the organization. Consequently, most organizations continuously scan for innovations, and match a promising innovation with one of their relevant problems.

Sometimes, knowledge of the existence of an innovation launches the innovation process, without an initial recognition of a problem or need by an organization which leads to the search for a solution. For example, an investigation by Wildemuth (1992) of the forty-three adoptions of computer-related innovations in three large corporations found that a rational identification of organizational problems at the agenda-setting stage and a search for innovations to meet these needs (at the matching stage) did not occur. "Instead, participants took an opportunistic approach to the acquisition of computing resources. Prior to the purchase of hardware and software, there were no specific plans for its use" (Wildemuth, 1992). There was little intentionality in the early stages of the innovation process for computer-related ideas.

On the basis of his analysis of how new safety laws were passed by the U.S. Senate, Jack Walker (1977) concluded: "Those who manage to shape the legislative agenda, in other words, are able to magnify their influence many times over by determining the focus of attention and energy in the entire political process." The agenda-setting role for innovation in an organization is a tremendously powerful one for the individuals who are involved in it.

2. Matching

Matching is defined as the stage in the innovation process at which a problem from the organization's agenda is fit with an innovation, and this match is planned and designed. At this second stage in the innovation process, the problem is conceptually matched with the innovation to establish how well they fit. This is a kind of reality testing in which the organization's members attempt to determine the feasibility of the innovation in solving the organization's problem. Such symbolic planning entails thinking about the anticipated problems that the innovation might encounter if it were implemented. Of course, the organization's decision makers may conclude that a mismatch of the innovation with the problem would occur. This decision will lead to rejection, terminating the innovation process prior to implementation.

The agenda-setting and the matching steps in the innovation process together constitute *initiation*, defined as all of the information gathering, conceptualizing, and planning for the adoption of an innovation, leading up to the decision to adopt. So this decision marks a watershed in the innovation process between initiation and *implementation*, all of the events, actions, and decisions involved in putting an innovation into use.

The implementation subprocess consists of three stages: Redefining/restructuring, clarifying, and routinizing.

3. Redefining/Restructuring

At this stage, the innovation imported from outside the organization gradually begins to lose its foreign character. *Redefining/restructuring* occurs when the innovation is re-invented to accommodate the organization's needs and structure more closely, and when the organization's structure is modified to fit with the innovation.

Both the innovation and the organization are expected to change, at least to a certain degree, during the redefining/restructuring stage of the innovation process. However, a study of several innovations in three organizations by Tyre and Orlikowski (1994) found that only a brief window of opportunity existed in an organization during which an innovation can be modified. Thereafter, the innovation is rapidly routinized and embedded in the organization's structure, and is then unlikely to change.

INNOVATION AND ORGANIZATION STRUCTURE. Not only is the innovation modified to fit the organization, the structure of the organization may be changed to accommodate the innovation. Sometimes a new organizational unit is created with responsibility for the innovation, such as when an organization installs a new computer, and establishes a computer center to operate it. In other cases, the innovation may affect the structure of the entire organization, such as when an electronic messaging system is introduced in a company. Suddenly, every employee has direct communication access to the chief executive.

The implementation of a technological innovation in an organization amounts to a mutual adaptation of the innovation and the organization. Typically, each one changes during the subprocess of implementation. "Innovations not only adapt to existing organizational and industrial arrangements, but they also transform the structure and practice of these environments" (Van de Ven, 1986). This mutual adaptation must occur because the innovation almost never fits perfectly in the organization in which it is to become embedded. Thus a fair degree of creative activity is required to avoid, or to overcome, the misalignments that occur between the innovation and the organization.

An illustration of this point is provided by a case study of implementation conducted by Harvard Business School Professor Dorothy Leonard-Barton, an investigation of an innovation called Solagen by the Eastman Kodak Company. The previous practice for obtaining gelatin, used by Kodak to make film, consisted of a 150-year-old process of decomposing animal bones and hide in lime oil for six weeks. Kodak Research Laboratories developed Solagen, a chemical process that reduced the decomposition process to forty-eight hours. The Solagen process was tested in a pilot plant, with good results, and Kodak made plans for building a plant costing millions of dollars. Very precise calibration of the Solagen process was required because it occurred so rapidly. The plant operators were accustomed to thrusting a six-foot pole into the lime pit in order to determine if undecomposed bones remained at the bottom.

In the new plant, operators had to determine the degree of decomposition by readings on a dial; decisions had to be made in a matter of minutes, rather than days. The plant operators could not cope with this new need for rapid decisions. Because of this complexity of the new technology, implementation of the Solagen process failed at Kodak (Leonard-Barton, 1988a).

Note that in this case, the innovation came from within the Eastman Kodak Company, rather than being imported from across the corporation's boundaries. Generally, such internally generated innovations are more likely to be successfully implemented, as the innovation more closely fits the organization's situation, and the organization's participants identify the innovation as theirs. The case studies conducted by the Minnesota Innovation Research Program led to the conclusion that: "Innovation receptiveness, learning, and adoption speed are facilitated when the innovation is initially developed within the user organization, and inhibited when end-users [adopters] are provided with no opportunities to re-invent innovations that were initially developed elsewhere. Organizational units not involved in the development or re-invention of an innovation tend to view it as an external mandate" (Schroeder, Van de Ven, Scudder, and Polley, 1986).

Technology has often been assumed to be an objective and external force that affects organizational structure. A more recent and realistic view of technology in an organization is to see it as the product of human interaction, as its meaning is gradually worked out through discussion (Orlikowski, 1992). The viewpoint is that of the social construction of technology.

The redefining/restructuring stage in the innovation process in an organization amounts to social constructionism, in which perceptions of the organization's problem and the innovation come together, and each are modified. If the innovation derives from inside the organization, individuals regard it as familiar and compatible and hence find it easier to give meaning to the new idea. Similarly, when the innovation enters the organization from external sources, but the exact form that it takes can be extremely flexible and a good deal of re-invention takes place, the organization's participants can define the new idea so that it becomes theirs. An example is often provided by computer software innovations, which by their nature are inherently very flexible. Software programs are essentially intellectual tools, which can be applied to a specific problem in an organization.

Research on the adoption of computer innovations in organizations shows that a lack of technical knowledge often is a barrier to implementation, and that companies delay adoption of these complex technologies until they obtain sufficient know-how to implement the computer innovations successfully. "In response to knowledge barriers, new institutions come into existence which progressively lower those barriers, and make it easier for firms to adopt and use the technology without extensive in-house expertise. Service bureaus, consultants, and simplification of the technology are examples" (Attewell, 1992).

INNOVATION AND UNCERTAINTY. Computer-related innovations create uncertainty in an organization, an uncomfortable state in a system that often leads to resistance to the technology. This uncertainty is one reason for the special difficulties that computer technologies frequently encounter in the implementation subprocess. The more "radical" an innovation, indexed by the amount of knowledge that organization members must acquire in order to adopt, the more uncertainty it creates and the more difficult its implementation. Dewar and Dutton (1986) found in their study of six innovations by forty companies in the U.S. footwear industry that large firms were more likely to have technical specialists, and thus to adopt radical innovations. Incremental innovations that did not create so much uncertainty, and that did not require so much technical expertise to implement, were more equally adopted by both larger and smaller shoe manufacturers.

Gerwin (1988) found it useful to identify three different types of uncertainty in investigating computer-aided manufacturing technologies:

1. *Technical uncertainty*, the degree to which it is difficult for an organization to determine the reliability, capacity, and precision of the new technology, or whether newer technology will soon appear to make the innovation obsolete.

2. *Financial uncertainty*, the degree to which the implementation of the innovation will yield an attractive return on investment, and whether future returns can be forecast accurately.

3. *Social uncertainty*, the degree to which conflict is likely to occur during implementation of the innovation. For instance, will a labor union oppose the innovation, because of its labor-saving consequences?

Some innovations are so radical, and create such a high degree of uncertainty, that they must be adopted through an innovation process that is relatively unstructured/and almost completely unroutine. An *unstruc-*

tured decision process is one that has not been encountered previously in quite the same form and for which no predetermined set of ordered responses and routines exists in the organization (Mintzberg, Raising-hani, and Théôrét, 1976). Most past research on organizations deals with routine decisions, for which customary and widely understood proce-dures exist. However, the nature of innovations in organizations, espe-cially radical innovations, means that they represent a type of unstructured decision. For example, Gibson and Rogers (1994) investi-gated the process of implementing the first R&D consortium, the Mi-croelectronics and Computer Technology Corporation (MCC), in the United States in the 1980s. An R&D consortium is a cooperative activity of member corporations which conducts research for the benefit of each participating company. Twenty large U.S. electronics companies launched the MCC in 1982; it was the first of its kind, and the member firms had to learn over a period of several years how to collaborate in the R&D consortium at the same time that they competed with each other in the marketplace. Gradually, with further experience, U.S. corporations became accustomed to the idea of R&D consortia, which became per-ceived as less radical, and could be adopted through more structured de-cisions. By 1994, more than 300 R&D consortia had been founded in the United States.

INNOVATION CHAMPIONS. An individual role that is often important in the innovation process in organizations is that of the innovation champion, as mentioned previously. Generalization 10–4 states that *The involvement of an innovation champion contributes to the success of an innovation in an organization*. In fact, Schön (1963) stated: "The new idea either finds a champion or dies." The champion is a charismatic individual who throws his/her weight behind the innovation, thus overcoming the indifference or resistance that a new idea often provokes in an organization (Howell and Higgins, 1990). When a sample of twenty-five innovation champions were matched with twenty-five non-champions, Howell and Higgins (1990) found the champions were higher risk-takers and more innova-tive, and initiated more attempts to influence others.

One usually thinks of an innovation champion as a powerful individ-ual with a high office in the organization, say a company president or a division chief. Day (1994) found this picture of innovation champions to be true for innovations that are costly, visible, or radical (in the sense that the new idea represents a new direction for the organization). Champions of innovations that are highly uncertain but not technology-driven often serve both as an innovation champion and as the organizational sponsor for the new idea.

4. Clarifying

Clarifying occurs as the innovation is put into more widespread use in an organization, so that the meaning of the new idea gradually becomes clearer to the organization's members. Too-rapid implementation of an innovation at the clarifying stage often leads to disastrous results. An illustration of undue haste in implementing an innovation is provided by the account of the Santa Monica Freeway Diamond Lane experiment in Los Angeles, which appears later in this chapter.

Misunderstandings or unwanted side-effects of the innovation may occur. If identified, corrective action can be taken. Stable arrangements are made for the innovation in the organization at the clarifying stage in the innovation process. The innovation is becoming imbedded in the organizational structure.

The clarifying stage in the innovation process in an organization consists of social construction. When a new idea is first implemented in an organization, it has little meaning to the organization's members. The innovation is surrounded by uncertainty. How does it work? What does it do? Who in the organization will be affected by it? Will it affect me? These are typical of the questions that individuals seek to answer at the clarifying stage. Through a process of the people in an organization talking about the innovation, they gradually gain a common understanding of it. Thus their meaning of the innovation is constructed over time through a social process of human interaction.

5. Routinizing

Routinization occurs when the innovation has become incorporated into the regular activities of the organization, and the innovation loses its separate identity. At that point, the innovation process in an organization is complete. Organizational members no longer think of the innovation as a new idea. It has been completely absorbed into the organization's ongoing activities.

Studying innovation in an organization offers the advantage of easier access to respondents (compared to surveys of respondents in a community or in the public, for example), so that it is more facile to gather data at more than one point in time. For example, Bach (1989) gathered data from the sixty-seven physicians and physician assistants in a medical clinic (1) two weeks prior to the introduction of an innovation, (2) the day after the innovation was launched, and (3) fourteen weeks later. This three-point data-gathering meant that data on the rate of adoption were determined by actual behavior, rather than depending on recall. The innovation was a pocket-sized booklet containing daily log sheets on which a physician's clinic work was recorded, in order to facilitate more accurate charges and payments. Rather amazingly, one-third of the respondents adopted the innovation within two weeks of its introduction (at a series of group meetings at which its advantages were explained). This rapid rate of adoption of the innovation may have occurred because the innovation met a specific need of the organization, and it originated from within the organization. The clarifying stage of the innovation process was almost unnecessary, with routinization occurring almost immediately for many adopters.

Discontinuance of an innovation can occur during the routinization stage, and sometimes does, as the Santa Monica Freeway Diamond Lane experiment demonstrates. In fact, the implementation subprocess often ends in failure.

The Santa Monica Freeway Diamond Lane Experiment: How Not to Implement an Innovation

Back in the mid-1970s, one lane in each direction of the four-lane, twelve-mile length of Interstate 10, which runs from the Pacific Ocean beaches of Santa Monica through downtown Los Angeles, was removed from regular commuter traffic, painted with large diamonds, and restricted to buses and carpools with at least three passengers. The objectives of this Santa Monica Freeway Diamond Lane project were to improve traffic flow, to lower gasoline consumption, and to lessen air pollution caused by auto exhausts.

Viewed in light of these objectives, the Diamond Lane experiment was a complete success. The Diamond Lane carried 90 percent as many people as it had before the lane was restricted, and it did so in only 30 percent as many vehicles. Travel time from Santa Monica to downtown Los Angeles on the Santa Monica Freeway's Diamond Lane was cut from 20 minutes to 15 minutes, and even on the non-preferential lanes, travel time decreased by a minute. The vehicle occupancy rate increased from a pre-project 1.20 persons per vehicle to 1.35 persons per vehicle. Bus ridership increased by 250 percent and the number of carpools tripled. These were remarkable changes in commuting behavior.

Despite these objective indicators of success, the public reaction toward the Santa Monica Diamond Lane experiment was very negative. After five months of troubled existence, the Diamond Lane experiment was discontinued. How could such an objectively successful implementation of an innovation end as a failure?

The answer lies in the subjective perceptions of the public, and how they were formed. For example, although the Diamond Lane moved people at a much faster rate, this special lane appeared, especially to motorists stalled in the bumper-to-bumper traffic on the other lanes of the Santa Monica Freeway, to only have a vehicle on it every quarter mile or so (of course this apparent spacing was because the vehicles moved at a much faster rate on the Diamond Lane). Motorists in the slow-moving vehicles reacted against the Diamond Lane in a variety of ways. One driver threw a can of nails on the Diamond Lane; another tried to paint out the diamonds. Some people rented themselves out as riders for one dollar a day to bring a car pool up to the required minimum of three passengers. Some drivers made cardboard cutout passengers or used stuffed dummies. An organization, Citizens Against Diamond Lanes, was formed to lobby against the project. CALTRANS (the California Department of Transportation), the state agency implementing the project, received several thousand letters; 90 percent opposed the Diamond Lane experiment. Nevertheless, CALTRANS, an organization dominated by engineers, felt that the public's negative reaction was just a temporary problem of transition. But then the Los Angeles City Council voted against the project. Several lawsuits were filed, calling for an end to the Diamond Lane project. Eventually, after five months, one of these lawsuits was supported by the courts, and the Diamond Lane experiment ended.

The Santa Monica Freeway Diamond Lane experiment had been developed in haste as a result of several crises. The 1974 OPEC oil shortage heightened concern about reducing gas consumption. Further, the mid-1970s marked the end of building freeways in Los Angeles, as a result of a lack of federal highway funding and the rise of environmental issues. Yet the number of vehicles on the city's streets increased by 3 percent a year. And as traffic congestion worsened in Los Angeles, auto pollutants contributed to the pall of smog over the city. One possible solution to these problems seemed to be the designation of diamond lanes on the Santa Monica Freeway, the world's busiest highway. A year or two previously, a Diamond Lane experiment had been highly successful on the Shirley Highway, south of Washington, D.C. The Urban Mass Transportation Administration provided CALTRANS with $800,000 in federal funds for the Santa Monica Freeway project.

Mistakes in implementation were made from the beginning. A fundamental error was to overlook the fact that the Shirley Highway *added* a Diamond Lane to existing lanes, while in Los Angeles, one lane in each direction was *taken away* from the eight existing lanes of traffic. The result was to throw traffic on the non-designated lanes into a bumper-to-bumper crawl. The Diamond Lane project began on Monday, March 15, 1976, which was characterized by heavy traffic flow, causing the *Los Angeles Times* to call the day "Mad Monday" and to refer to the experiment as "Chaos on the Freeway." Mass media in the Los Angeles area mounted a strong attack on the Diamond Lane project, which the CALTRANS professional employees ignored. They were more concerned with technical aspects of the project. A major increase in the number of traffic accidents occurred on the Santa Monica Freeway; from eleven per week prior to the experiment, to fifty-nine during the first week of the project (this figure later dropped to twenty-five accidents per week). The media made much of these accident rates. Collaboration of CALTRANS with other agencies was poor. For example, the California Highway Patrol (CHIPs) issued citations to drivers with less than three passengers per vehicle. As public support for the project dwindled, CHIPs became less willing to police these offenders, and finally, when the court ordered the experiment to end a week later, CHIPs simply stopped giving tickets, and all vehicles immediately began using the Diamond Lane.

What lessons were learned from the failure of the Santa Monica Freeway Diamond Lane project? Perceptions of an innovation shape public acceptance, not objective indicators like the number of car pools or the number of vehicle passengers moving per hour on a Diamond Lane. The mass media coverage given to an innovative project can be important in shaping its public acceptance. Finally, constructing an extra lane for a Diamond Lane, rather than taking one away from existing traffic, is important. In fact, this lesson has been utilized in the hundreds of Diamond Lane projects in U.S. cities that have been implemented successfully since the Santa Monica Freeway experience. More generally, the Santa Monica Diamond Lane demonstrated the crucial importance of the implementation subprocess in the in-novation process. Implementation cannot be rushed.

This case illustration draws on Aberg and others (1976) and Schwalbe (1976).

Summary

An *organization* is a stable system of individuals who work together to achieve common goals through a hierarchy of ranks and a division of labor. Individual behavior in an organization is relatively stable and predictable because organizational structure is characterized by prede-termined goals, prescribed roles, an authority structure, rules and regu-lations, and informal patterns. Although behavior in organizations is relatively stable, innovation is going on all the time. Both the innovation and the organization usually change in the innovation process within or-ganizations (Generalization 10–1).

Until about twenty years ago, innovation in organizations was mainly studied by correlating independent variables with organizational innov-ativeness in cross-sectional data analysis. A consistent finding in organi-zational innovativeness research is that larger organizations are more innovative (Generalization 10–2). The chief executive in an organization was typically asked to provide data in these large-scale surveys. Rather low correlations of characteristics variables with organizational innova-tiveness were found, and today this type of research is largely passé.

It was replaced by research on the innovation process in organizations. We divide the innovation process into two subprocesses (1) *initiation*, all of the information gathering, conceptualizing, and planning for the adop-tion of an innovation, leading up to the decision to adopt, and (2) *imple-mentation*, all of the events, actions, and decisions involved in putting an innovation into use. The two initiation stages are (1) agenda-setting, and (2) matching, and the three implementation stages are (1) redefining/re-structuring, (2) clarifying, and (3) routinizing.

Agenda-setting occurs in the innovation process when a general orga-nizational problem that may create a perceived need for an innovation is defined. A *performance gap*, the discrepancy between an organization's expectations and its actual performance, can trigger the innovation process (Generalization 10–3). *Matching* is the stage in the innovation process at which a problem from the organization's agenda is fit with an innovation, and this match is planned and designed.

Redefining/restructuring occurs when the innovation is re-invented to accommodate the organization's needs and structure more closely, and when the organization's structure is modified to fit with the innovation. The involvement of an innovation champion contributes to the success of an innovation in an organization (Generalization 10–4). *Clarifying* occurs as the innovation is put into more widespread use in an organization, so that the meaning of the new idea gradually becomes clearer to the organization's members. *Routinization* occurs when the innovation has become incorporated into the regular activities of the organization and the innovation loses its separate identity. This fifth stage marks the end of the innovation process in an organization.

11

CONSEQUENCES OF INNOVATIONS

Changing people's customs is an even more delicate responsibility than surgery.

—Edward H. Spicer, *Human Problems in Technological Change*

Consequences are the changes that occur to an individual or to a social system as a result of the adoption or rejection of an innovation. Invention and diffusion are but means to an ultimate end: the consequences of adoption of an innovation.

In spite of the importance of consequences, they have received little study by diffusion researchers. Further, the data that we have about consequences are rather "soft" in nature, based mainly on case studies. It is difficult to generalize about consequences. We can describe consequences and establish categories for classifying consequences, but we cannot predict when and how these consequences will happen.

Change agents also give little attention to consequences. They often assume that adoption of a given innovation will produce only beneficial results for adopters. This assumption is the pro-innovation bias. Change agents should recognize their responsibility for the consequences of innovations that they introduce. They should be able to predict the advantages and disadvantages of an innovation before introducing it to their clients, but this is seldom done.

The introduction of snowmobiles to Lapp reindeer herders in Northern Finland illustrates how difficult it is to predict the effects of technology, which in this case were far-reaching and negative.

405

The Snowmobile Revolution in the Arctic

In the United States the snowmobile is a means of winter recreation. Since the invention of the "Ski-Doo," a one-person snow vehicle, in 1958, the adoption of snowmobiles spread dramatically, and within a dozen years over a million were in use in North America. Some outcry against the ski-doo (which quickly became a generic name for snowmobiles) was voiced, owing to the noise pollution they caused in previously peaceful outdoor areas of the United States and Canada.

But among the Skolt Lapps, a reindeer-herding people of Northern Finland who live above the Arctic Circle, the rapid introduction of snowmobiles caused far-reaching consequences that were termed "disastrous" (Pelto, 1973). One method of investigating the consequences of technological innovation is for a social scientist (an anthropologist in the present case) to intensively study a small community. Dr. Pertti Pelto of the University of Connecticut had lived among the Skolt Lapps in the Sevettijärvi region of Northern Finland for several years, beginning in 1958, prior to the introduction of snowmobiles in 1962–1963. Pelto returned to this community repeatedly over the next decade to assess the impact of the snowmobile revolution through participant observation, personal interviews with the Lapps, and via collaboration with a research assistant/key informant (who was the first Skolt Lapp to buy a snowmobile). Pelto chose to concentrate on a single technological innovation because its consequences were so striking and hence relatively easier to identify. Many of the impacts of the ski-doo were unfavorable. Pelto argues that the snowmobile represents a class of technological innovations that shifts energy sources from local and autonomous origins (reindeer sleds in this case) to a dependence on external sources (snowmobiles and gasoline).

Prior to the introduction of snowmobiles, the Skolt Lapps herded semi-domesticated reindeer for their livelihood. Reindeer meat was the main food. Reindeer sleds were the principal means of transportation, and reindeer hides were used for making clothing and shoes. Surplus meat was sold at trading stores for cash to buy flour, sugar, tea, and other staples. The Lapps saw themselves mainly as reindeer-herders, and prestige was accorded to men who had a good string of draught reindeer. Lapp society was an egalitarian system in which each family had approximately equal numbers of animals. Skolt children received a "first tooth reindeer," a "name-day reindeer," and gifts on various other occasions, including wedding gifts of reindeer, so that a new household began with a small herd of the beloved animals. The Lapps felt a special relationship with their reindeer, and treated them with much care. The reindeer was the central object in Lapp culture.

In 1961 a Bombardier Ski-Doo from Canada was displayed in Rovaniemi, the capital city of Finnish Lapland. A schoolteacher purchased this snowmobile for recreational travel, but soon found that it was useful for hauling wood and storebought supplies. The Lapps began using snowmobiles for reindeer herding. Within the following year, two ski-doos were purchased for herding reindeer in an area where the land was forested and rocky. The herders had to drive their machines by standing on the footboards or kneeling on the seat, instead of riding in the usual seated straddle position (like on a motorcycle), in order to spot reindeer at a greater distance and to steer around rocks, trees, and other obstacles. But the erect riding style was dangerous as the driver was thrown forward when the snowmobile hit an obstruction. Additionally, the snowmobiles broke down often in the rough terrain of Lapland.

Despite these problems, the rate of adoption of snowmobiles was very rapid among the Lapps. Three snowmobiles were adopted in the second year of diffusion, five more the next year, then eight more, and sixteen in 1966 and 1967. By 1971, almost every one of the seventy-two households in Sevettigärvi (the village studied by Professor Pelto) had at least one snowmobile. An improved model, the Motoski, was introduced from Sweden. It had a more powerful motor and was better suited to driving in rough terrain.

The main advantage of the snowmobile was much faster travel. The round trip from Sevettigärvi to buy staple supplies in Norwegian stores was reduced from three days by reindeer sled, to five hours by snowmobile. Within a few years of their initial introduction, snowmobiles completely replaced skis and reindeer sleds as a means of herding reindeer. Unfortunately, the noise and the smell of the machines drove the reindeer into a near-wild state. The friendly relationships between the Lapps and their animals was disrupted by the high-speed machines. Frightened running by the reindeer decreased the number of reindeer calves born each year. The average number of reindeer per household in Sevettigärvi dropped from fifty-two in presnowmobile days, to only twelve in 1971, a decade later. This average is misleading because about two-thirds of the Lapp households completely dropped out of reindeer-raising as a result of the snowmobile. Most could not find other work and were unemployed. On the other hand, one family in Sevettigärvi, who were relatively early in purchasing a snowmobile, built up a large herd, and by 1971 owned one-third of all the reindeer in the community.

Not only did the frightened reindeer have fewer calves, but the precipitous drop in the number of reindeer also occurred because many of the animals had to be slaughtered for their meat, so the Lapps could purchase the snowmobiles, gasoline for their operation, and spare parts and repairs. A new machine cost about $1,000, and gas and repairs typically cost about $425 per year. Despite this relatively high cost (for the Skolt Lapps, who lived on a subsistence income), snowmobiles were considered a household necessity, and the motorized herding of reindeer was considered much more prestigious than herding by skis or with reindeer sleds. The snowmobile revolution pushed the Skolt Lapps into a tailspin of cash dependency, debt, and unemployment.

Why didn't the Lapps, given their love for the reindeer and the disastrous effects of snowmobiles, resist this technological innovation? Pelto (1973) suggests the reason is that at no point in the introduction and diffusion of snowmobiles could the Skolt Lapps have predicted the possible future outcomes of the technology, and decided on whether the innovation should proceed unchecked. An assessment of the technology's impacts could have been made in the 1960s, but it was not, because the Lapps were not technically able to anticipate the far-reaching consequences of the snowmobile. Further, Lapp society is very individualistic, and given the technology's advantages for the first adopters (who were wealthier and younger than the average), initial adoption was impossible to prevent. Thereafter, the diffusion process quickly ran its course.

As a result, the reindeer-centered culture of the Skolt Lapps was severely disrupted. Most families today are unemployed and depend upon the Finnish government for subsistence payments. The snowmobile revolution in the Arctic led to disastrous consequences for the reindeer, and for the Lapps who depended on the animals for their livelihood.

Since the anthropological study of the snowmobile revolution by Pertti Pelto, further technological developments have occurred in Lapland. During the summer months, the Lapps began using motorcycles to herd their reindeer. Certain affluent Lapps even began using helicopters. An increasing number of reindeer slaughtered for meat were found to have stomach ulcers.

Certainly technological innovation has not been kind to the Skolt Lapps.

This case illustration of the consequences of the snowmobile among the Skolt Lapps is based upon Pelto (1973), Pelto and Müller-Wille (1972), and Pelto and others (1969).

Studying Consequences

The consequences of innovation have been understudied in past diffusion research. Instead of asking, as much past research has done: "What variables are related to innovativeness?" future investigations need to ask: "What are the *effects* of adopting innovations?" Figure 11–1 contrasts these two research objectives.

Innovativeness, the main dependent variable in much past research, now becomes a predictor of a more ultimate dependent variable, the consequences of innovation. This called-for research seeks to explain consequences, a research goal that is actually closer to the objectives of most change agencies. Change agents usually want to bring about desirable consequences among their clients, not just the adoption of innovations. But most diffusion research has stopped with an analysis of the *decision* to adopt a new idea, ignoring how this choice is implemented, and with what consequences.

Why are there so few studies of consequences?

1. *Change agencies, who often sponsor diffusion research, overemphasize adoption per se, tacitly assuming that the consequences of innovation-decisions will be positive.* Change agencies assume that an innovation is needed by their clients, that its introduction will be desirable, and that adoption of the innovation represents success. These pro-innovation assumptions are not always valid.

2. *The usual survey research methods are less appropriate for the investigation of innovation consequences than for studying innovativeness.* Extended observation over time, or an in-depth case study, are usually utilized to study consequences. Diffusion researchers rely almost entirely upon survey methods of data gathering. But studying the consequences of innovation with the usual one-shot survey methods is not very effective. Case study approaches are more appropriate, but they often yield idiosyncratic, descriptive data from which generalization to other innovations and to other systems is difficult.

The study of consequences is complicated by the fact that they usually occur over extended periods of time. An innovation's consequences cannot be understood simply by adding an additional question or two to a survey instrument, another 100 respondents to a sample population, or another few days of data-gathering in the field. Instead, scholars must take a long-range research approach in which consequences are analyzed as they unfold over a period of time, which may be years.

Figure 11–1. A Model for Studying the Consequences of Innovation

CORRELATES (OR ANTECEDENTS) OF INNOVATIVENESS		INDICATORS OF INNOVATIVENESS	CONSEQUENCES OF INNOVATION	
(INDEPENDENT VARIABLES)	→	(PRIOR DEPENDENT VARIABLE)	(NEW DEPENDENT VARIABLE)	

CORRELATES (OR ANTECEDENTS) OF INNOVATIVENESS

(INDEPENDENT VARIABLES)

1. Socioeconomic characteristics
2. Personality variables
3. Communication behavior

INDICATORS OF INNOVATIVENESS

(PRIOR DEPENDENT VARIABLE)

Relative earliness in adopting new ideas

CONSEQUENCES OF INNOVATION

(NEW DEPENDENT VARIABLE)

Functional, Direct, or Manifest Consequences:

1. Increased production or effectiveness
2. Higher income
3. More leisure
4. Others

Dysfunctional, Indirect, or Latent Consequences:

1. Greater expense
2. Need for more capital
3. Less equitable distribution of income, land, or other resources
4. Others

NOTE: The area outlined in dotted lines represents the additional element of consequences that should be emphasized in diffusion research.

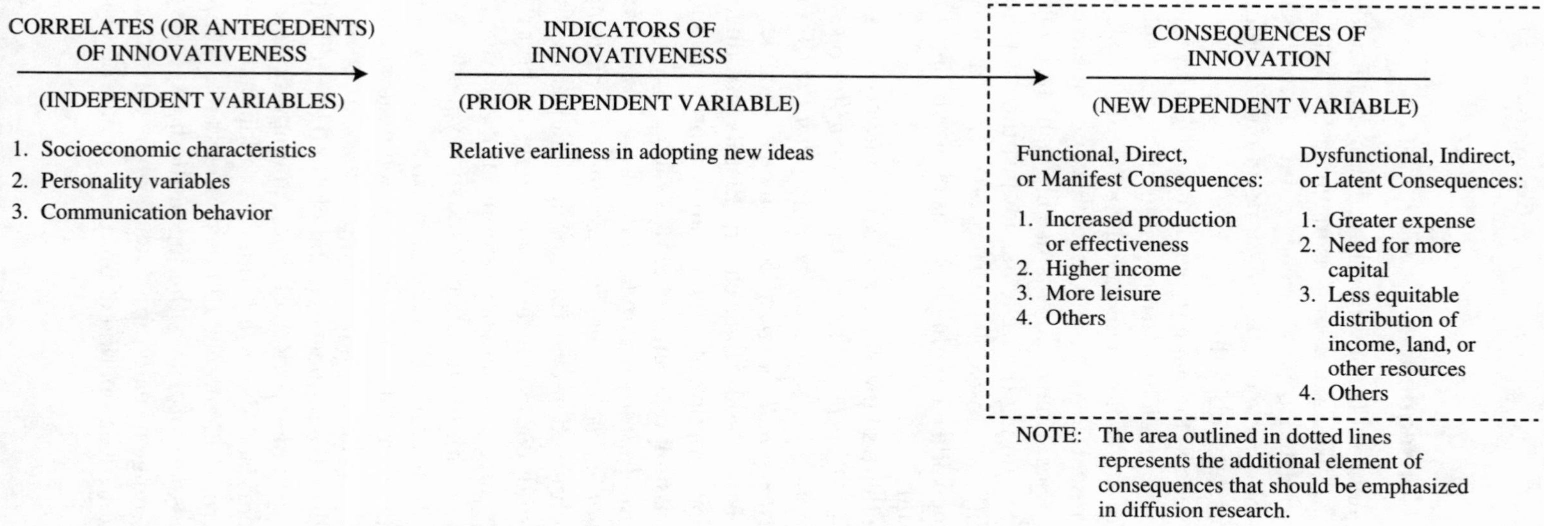

A panel study in which respondents are interviewed both before and after an innovation is introduced can yield desired information about consequences. Data about consequences can also be obtained from field experiments in which an innovation is introduced on a pilot basis, and its results evaluated under realistic conditions, prior to its widespread diffusion. The panel study and the pilot field experiment can provide quantitative data about an innovation's consequences which can lead to generalizations, rather than mere description. Such generalizations can be predictive rather than being just a post-mortem of consequences that have already occurred. We draw upon several panel studies and field experiments in our following discussion of the equality consequences of innovations.

3. *Consequences are difficult to measure.* Individuals using an innovation are often not fully aware of all of the consequences of their adoption. Therefore, attempts to study consequences that rest on respondents' reports often lead to incomplete and misleading conclusions.

Judgments concerning consequences are almost unavoidably subjective and value-laden, regardless of who makes them. A researcher from one culture may find it particularly difficult to make completely objective judgments about the desirability of an innovation in another country. *Cultural relativism* is the viewpoint that each culture should be judged in light of its own specific circumstances and needs. No culture is actually best in an absolute sense. Each culture works out its own set of norms, values, beliefs, and attitudes that function most effectively for itself. For instance, a newcomer to India may be puzzled by the millions of sacred cows that roam the countryside freely, while many people live under famine conditions. The foreigner is unlikely to understand that Indian cattle provide manure that is essential for fuel, fertilizer, and housing construction. The holiness of cows in the Hindu religion is quite functional, rather than being just a cultural oddity.

Cultural relativism poses problems for the measurement of consequences. Data about the results of an externally introduced innovation that are gathered from clients, change agents, or scientific observers are subjectively flavored by their own cultural beliefs. Consequences should be judged as to their functionality in terms of the user's culture, without imposing outsiders' normative beliefs about the needs of the client system.

A further problem in measuring the consequences of an innovation is that these consequences are often confounded with other effects. For example, in assessing the results of a new fertilizer or pesticide on crop yields, one cannot ignore the consequences caused by natural events like droughts, floods, or volcanic eruptions. One problem in measuring the consequences of innovations is untangling cause-and-effect relationships. Ideally, we should only measure the consequences that are exclusively the outcome of an innovation, the changes that would not have occurred if the innovation had not been introduced. But many important consequences are unanticipated and indirect; these effects of an innovation are difficult to determine in a precise manner. For instance, the classification of unanticipated consequences rests on an investigator's ability to determine the original objectives for introducing an innovation in a system; such purposes may be partly concealed by subsequent rationalizations on the part of the members of the system (Goss, 1979).

Classifications of Consequences

One step toward an improved understanding of the consequences of innovations is to classify them in a taxonomy. Consequences are not unidimensional; they can take many forms and are expressed in various ways. We find it useful to analyze three dimensions of consequences: (1) desirable versus undesirable (2) direct versus indirect, and (3) anticipated versus unanticipated.

Desirable Versus Undesirable Consequences

Desirable consequences are the functional effects of an innovation for an individual or for a social system. *Undesirable consequences* are the dysfunctional effects of an innovation to an individual or to a social system. The determination of whether consequences are functional or dysfunctional depends on how the innovation affects the adopters. An innovation can cause consequences for individuals other than its adopters. For instance, rejectors of a new idea may be affected because an innovation benefits the other members of the system that adopt it, widening a socioeconomic gap over the rejectors. Often everyone in a system is touched by the consequences of a technological innovation.

Certain innovations have undesirable impacts for almost everyone in a social system. The snowmobile in Lapland had ill consequences for almost everyone, although a few Lapps became very rich reindeer owners as a result of the innovation. Every social system has certain qualities that should not be destroyed if the welfare of the system is to be maintained.

These might include family bonds, respect for human life and property, maintenance of individual respect and dignity, and appreciation for others, including appreciation for contributions made by ancestors. Other sociocultural elements are more trivial and can be modified, discontinued, or supplanted with little impact.

An innovation may be functional for a system but not functional for certain individuals in the system. The adoption of miracle varieties of rice and wheat in India and other nations led to what is called the Green Revolution. The resulting higher crop yields and heightened farm income were important benefits for farmers and for society. Yet the Green Revolution also led to fewer farmers, immigration to urban slums, higher unemployment rates, and political instability. Although many individuals profited from the adoption of the new seeds, the Green Revolution led to unequal conditions for the system as a whole. So whether the consequences are desirable or undesirable depends on whether one takes certain individuals, or the entire system, as a point of reference.

WINDFALL PROFITS. Positive consequences of an innovation may occur for certain members of a system at the expense of others. By the time that laggards adopt a new idea, they are often forced to do so by economic pressures. By being the first in the field, innovators frequently secure a kind of economic gain called windfall profits.

Windfall profits are a special advantage earned by the first adopters of a new idea in a system. Their unit costs are usually lowered and their additions to total production have little effect on the price of the product. But when all members of a system adopt a new idea, total production increases, and the price of the product or service eventually often goes down. This change offsets the advantage of lowered unit costs.

The innovator must take risks to earn windfall profits. All new ideas do not turn out successfully, and occasionally the innovator gets his/her fingers burned. Adoption of a noneconomic or unsuccessful innovation can result in *windfall losses* for the first individuals to adopt. An example of windfall losses occurred in the diffusion of pocket calculators. The first model sold (in 1971) measured three-by-five inches, cost $249, and could only add, subtract, multiply, and divide. Within a year the price of a four-function calculator dropped to $100; in another year the price was only $50, and within a decade the calculator cost less than $10. Its size shrank to the thickness of a credit card. *Later* adopters gained a windfall benefit in this case, by waiting to adopt.

Usually new ideas make the rich richer and the poor poorer, widening the socioeconomic gap between the earlier and later adopters of a new idea. Data from the Iowa hybrid seed corn study by Gross (1942) were reanalyzed by Rogers (1962). The innovators of this new idea, who adopted in the late 1920s, earned almost $2,500 more than the laggards, who adopted hybrid seed in 1941. The innovators earned these windfall profits because of (1) a higher market price for corn which lasted only until most farmers adopted hybrid seed, thus increasing corn production; (2) their larger corn acreage (for example, the innovators who adopted in 1927, averaged 124 acres of corn while the typical laggard, who adopted in 1941, raised only 70 acres of corn); and (3) the greater number of years they received the higher yields from hybrid seed.

Separatability of Desirable and Undesirable Consequences

Most innovations cause both desirable and undesirable consequences. Understandably, individuals generally want to obtain the functional effects of an innovation and to avoid the dysfunctional effects. To do so assumes that certain of the desired consequences from a technological innovation can be separated from the consequences that are not wanted. Such an assumption of separability usually involves desired advantages from a new technology such as increased effectiveness, efficiency, or convenience, versus such unwanted consequences as changes in social values and institutions. Previously we discussed the desired advantage of the snowmobile among the Finnish Lapps such as faster transportation, which unfortunately brought with it the decline in reindeer raising and its accompanying consequences of widespread unemployment and other social problems.

We conclude with Generalization 11–1: *The effects of an innovation usually cannot be managed to separate the desirable from the undesirable consequences.*

As we discussed in Chapter 7, the Old Order Amish in the United States have maintained a distinctive culture for hundreds of years. The Amish do not adopt technological innovations like cars and tractors, electricity, and household conveniences, because the social consequences of these innovations would lead to the breakdown of Amish society. The Amish understand the principle of inseparability in managing technological innovations; they willingly forego the desired advantages of tractors and modern farm equipment (such as larger farms, higher crop yields, and increased incomes) to avoid the undesirable consequences of increased dependence on non-Amish businesses (such as farm machinery dealers), lessened farm labor requirements, and the pressure for larger farms (Ericksen and others, 1980).

The largest Amish community is in Lancaster County, Pennsylvania, where this religious sect has survived for more than 200 years by following a general rule of not adopting technological innovations. The fertile soil allows the Amish to succeed financially on small farms of about fifty acres, which they operate on a labor-intensive basis. Their high fertility provides the workforce, so that mechanized equipment is not needed. Recently skyrocketing land prices, however, make it difficult for Amish parents to set up their grown children in farming. When the young people enter urban occupations like carpentry and construction work, they often drop out of Amish society. So the Old Order Amish in Lancaster now face an uncertain future (Ericksen and others, 1980).

But the Amish adherence to the principle of inseparability has served them well. They forego most modern technological innovations in farming and household living because they fear the social consequences that would inevitably accompany them.

Direct Versus Indirect Consequences

The intricate, often invisible web of interrelationships among the elements in a culture means that a change in one part of a system often initiates a chain reaction of indirect consequences stemming from the direct consequences of an innovation. *Direct consequences* are the changes to an individual or a social system that occur in immediate response to an innovation. *Indirect consequences* are the changes to an individual or a social system that occur as a result of the direct consequences of an innovation. There are consequences of consequences.

An illustration of this framework for understanding the direct and indirect consequences of an innovation is diagrammed in Figure 11–2, based on an anthropological study of the adoption of wet rice farming by a tribe in Madagascar (Linton & Kardiner, 1952). The nomadic tribe had cultivated rice by dry-land methods. After each harvest they would move to a different location. Then they changed to wet-land rice farming. A pattern of land ownership developed, social status differences appeared, the nuclear family replaced the extended clan, and tribal government changed. The consequences of the technological innovation were both direct and far-reaching, in that several generations of indirect consequences from wet-rice growing spread from the more direct results.

Figure 11–2. The Direct and Indirect Consequences of the Adoption of Wet Rice Growing in Madagascar

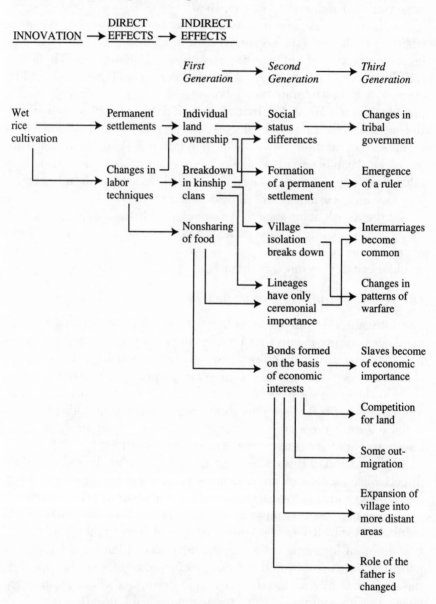

Source: Based on Linton and Kardiner (1952, pp. 221–231).

ORT: Consequences of Consequences

Until the 1980s, an estimated 5 million young children died each year from diarrhea-related causes, representing about 30 percent of all infant deaths in the world. Diarrhea is often transmitted by contaminated water resulting from inadequate sanitation and poor personal hygiene. In babies, diarrhea can cause a 10-percent loss of body weight, and can kill in a matter of hours through dehydration.

Powdered milk products such as Nestlé's Lactogen contribute to infant deaths caused by diarrhea, as explained in Chapter 3. During the 1980s, widespread public alarm and the actions of the World Health Organization (WHO) helped to convince Nestlé and other powdered milk companies to change their marketing practices. But babies in Third World nations continued to die from diarrhea. Social marketing campaigns were launched in Latin America, Africa, and Asia to promote breast feeding, and to discourage the use of powdered milk for baby feeding.

The most promising breakthrough in the struggle to prevent infant diarrheal deaths occurred in the mid-1970s when a young medical doctor in Bangladesh invented ORT (oral rehydration therapy). Despite its elegant scientific name, ORT is remarkably simple: One part salt and eight parts sugar, in three soft drink bottles of clean water. The salt and sugar ingredients are available in every peasant household in the Third World. In a pilot project in The Gambia in West Africa, parents were instructed to measure the salt and sugar with a bottle cap from an empty Coke bottle, and then to mix the ingredients in the bottle. ORT is essentially Gatorade without the green color. It is also similar to the chicken soup given by Jewish mothers to their sick children. ORT is an electrolyte mixture that functions to rehydrate the body (that is, to return water to the body so that a baby does not die from dehydration), and to provide lost salt to the body. The sugar provides quick energy to help the body recover.

ORT is a lifesaver, but it can also be dangerous. If the ratio of salt and sugar is reversed, the baby may die. If clean water is not used, the baby gets diarrhea again. ORT does not cure the bacterial infection that causes diarrhea. ORT only prevents the progression from diarrhea to dehydration and to death. The ORT innovation is almost purely information. Can the correct mixing of the ORT formula be taught through the mass media? In the first ORT campaigns, conducted in Honduras in 1980 and in The Gambia in

1981, a poster illustrating the correct mixing of the ORT formula was designed without words (because of widespread illiteracy on the part of the public). But salt and sugar look alike, and formative evaluation of the poster showed that some misinformation occurred. Some national ORT programs decided that it is more effective to distribute small foil packets of the salt and sugar ingredients, which are then mixed with water, and given to a sick baby. These ORT salts are sold for a few cents in groceries, or given free in government health clinics.

The early ORT campaigns in Honduras and The Gambia indicated that certain traditional beliefs about infant diarrhea would have to be considered if ORT were to diffuse widely and be used effectively. In Honduras, for example, the traditional cure for diarrhea was to administer a purge (similar to Exlax). Further, in Honduras, it was widely believed that a sack of worms exists in everyone's abdominal cavity, and that when the worms become agitated and leave the sack, diarrhea results. So the prevention of infant diarrhea depended on not disturbing the sack of worms. In The Gambia, infant diarrhea was believed to be caused by supernatural forces, such as by the will of Allah (God). The concept of dehydration ran counter to these traditional beliefs. Pilot studies on the social marketing of ORT in The Gambia and in Honduras indicated that a communication campaign could raise the levels of public knowledge and adoption of ORT, but it was much more difficult to convey effectively the concept of dehydration. Most people who used ORT did not have a scientifically correct understanding of how it worked. Such principles knowledge rests on understanding the chemical process of electrolytes. Health officials asked the rhetorical question, "Does one need to know how a motor works in order to drive a car?"

The social marketing efforts to diffuse ORT could not be sustained over time in some Third World nations. For example, in The Gambia, funding of the ORT social marketing campaign ended soon after the pilot campaign was completed in 1981, and so little sustainability of the innovation occurred.

In 1987, the original two-country ORT program was expanded to seventeen other Third World nations. By the mid-1990's, almost every Third World nation had launched an ORT campaign. Integrated child survival campaigns typically emphasize ORT, along with breast-feeding, the immunization of children, improving the quality of drinking water, and promoting personal sanitation (like using latrines and washing one's hands regularly).

As ORT diffused widely in Third World countries during the late 1980s and early 1990s, the rate of infant mortality dropped accordingly. But as a result, the rates of population growth in these nations climbed. How were schooling, housing, and jobs to be provided for millions of infants whose lives were saved by ORT? Clearly, the answer is a faster rate of adoption of family planning methods. But in many of the poorest countries, where ORT campaigns were highly successful, national family planning programs were relatively ineffective. Here we see how beneficial consequences of the rapid adoption of one innovation led to the worsening of another social problem.

The diffusion of ORT suggests that the indirect consequences of an innovation are often especially difficult to plan for, and manage, as they are often unanticipated.

This case illustration is based upon the present author's personal experience.

Anticipated Versus Unanticipated Consequences

Anticipated consequences are changes brought about by an innovation that are recognized and intended by the members of a social system. An example of such a manifest consequence is the snowmobiles' advantage to the Lapps of providing rapid transportation. The Lapps could not, however, anticipate such latent consequences of this innovation as its disastrous effects on their reindeer. Although they are less discernible to observers, the subsurface consequences of an innovation may be just as important as the anticipated consequences. *Unanticipated consequences* are changes from an innovation that are neither intended nor recognized by the members of a social system. The disintegration of respect for their elders among the Yir Yoront, in the case study that follows, is an example of an unanticipated consequence of the adoption of steel axes. This change in family relations was of tremendous importance to the tribe, even though such a consequence was not readily apparent when steel axes were first introduced by well-meaning missionaries.

No innovation comes without strings attached. The more technologically advanced an innovation is, the more likely its introduction is to produce many consequences—some of them anticipated, but others unintended and hidden. A system is like a bowl of marbles: Move any one of its elements and the positions of all the others are inevitably changed also.

This interdependency is often not fully understood by the adopters of an innovation, and may not be comprehended by the change agents who introduce a new idea in a system. Unanticipated consequences represent a lack of understanding of how an innovation functions and of the internal and external forces at work in a social system (Goss, 1979). Awareness of a new idea creates uncertainly about how the innovation will actually function for an individual or other adopting unit in a system. This uncertainty motivates active information-seeking about the innovation, especially through interpersonal peer networks. Individuals particularly seek to reduce the uncertainty about an innovation's expected consequences. Such uncertainty can be decreased to the point where an individual feels well enough informed to adopt the new idea. But uncertainty about an innovation's consequences can never be completely removed.

Some 2 million women adopted breast implants, many with injections of liquid silicone, before the Food and Drug Administration (FDA) in 1965 classified the injections as a drug that was under their jurisdiction. In 1988, silicone breast injections were named a "highest risk device" by the FDA. Later, in 1992, silicone injections were banned completely. Typically, plastic surgeons had injected the silicone gel inside a woman's breast, using a kind of plastic envelope to prevent the liquid silicone from migrating to other parts of the body. However, these plastic envelopes often proved to be ineffective over time. The human body might attack the plastic envelope by forming a cellular shell around it and squeezing the implant until it became hard, and thus painful to the woman. If the plastic envelope broke, as it sometimes did, or if it leaked, the liquid silicone spread throughout the body, enlarging lymph nodes and causing serious health problems. As a result, many adopters of silicone breast implants had to have an operation to remove them.

Starting in 1988, women began to file lawsuits against the manufacturers of silicone implants. One jury awarded a $7 million settlement. In 1994, a $4.22 billion global settlement agreement was offered to women with breast implants by the major manufacturers. Individuals with breast implants have up to thirty years to file a claim; allowance is also provided to second-generation claims to be filed by the children of women with implants to whom the silicone gel was transmitted with breast milk.

How might this expensive and painful experience with silicone breast implants have been avoided? In retrospect, the manufacturers of breast implants can be criticized for not conducting adequate research on the consequences of this innovation prior to its introduction. Unfortunately, the unanticipated consequences did not become evident for several years after initial adoption. Further, the several million women who adopted silicone implants to enlarge the appearance of their breasts might be criticized for using this cosmetic and ultimately dysfunctional innovation. Perhaps questions should be raised about the impacts of mass media advertising and other influences that persuaded women that their figure needed enhancement.

The adopter is often able to obtain adequate information from peers about the desirable, direct, and anticipated consequences of an innovation. But the unanticipated consequences are by definition unknown by individuals at their time of adoption. Such unforeseen impacts of a new idea represent a type of innovation-evaluation information that cannot be obtained by an individual from other members of his or her system. Professional change agents often cannot know the unanticipated consequences of an innovation until after its widespread adoption has occurred (if then), as we see in the following case of the steel ax, introduced by missionaries to an Australian tribe.

We conclude this discussion of the three classifications of consequences with Generalization 11–2: *The undesirable, indirect, and unanticipated consequences of an innovation usually go together, as do the desirable, direct, and anticipated consequences.*

Steel Axes for Stone-Age Aborigines

The consequences of the adoption of steel axes by a tribe of Australian aborigines vividly illustrates the need for consideration of the undesirable, indirect, and unanticipated consequences of an innovation. The Yir Yoront traveled in small nomadic groups over a vast territory in search of game and other food. The central tool in their culture was the stone ax, which the Yir Yoront found indispensable in producing food, constructing shelter, and heating their homes. A complete revolution was precipitated by the replacement of the stone ax by the steel ax.

Anthropologist Lauriston Sharp (1952) conducted his investigation of the Yir Yoront by the method of participant observation. He studied Yir Yoront culture by taking part in its everyday activities. Because of their isolation, the tribe was relatively unaffected by Western civilization until the establishment of a nearby missionary post. The missionaries distributed many steel axes among the Yir Yoront as gifts and as payment for work performed.

Previously, the stone ax had been a symbol of masculinity and of respect for elders. Only men owned stone axes, although women and children were the principal users of these tools. Axes were borrowed from fathers, husbands, or uncles according to a system of social relationships prescribed by custom. The Yir Yoront obtained their stone ax heads in exchange for spears through bartering with other tribes, a process that took place as part of elaborate rituals at seasonal fiestas.

When the missionaries distributed the steel axes to the Yir Yoront, they hoped that a rapid improvement in living conditions would result. There was no important resistant to using the steel axes, because the tribe was accustomed to securing their tools through trade. Steel axes were more efficient for most tasks, and the stone axes rapidly disappeared among the Yir Yoront.

But the steel ax contributed little to social progress; to the disappointment of the missionaries, the Yir Yoront used their new-found leisure time for sleep, "an act they had thoroughly mastered." The missionaries distributed the steel axes equally to men, women, and children. Young men were more likely to adopt the new tools than were the elders, who did not trust the missionaries. The result was a disruption of status relations among the Yir Yoront and a revolutionary confusion of age and sex roles. Elders, once highly respected, now became dependent upon women and younger men, and were often forced to borrow steel axes from these social inferiors.

The trading rituals of the tribe also became disorganized. Friendship ties among traders broke down, and interest declined in the annual fiestas, where the barter of stone axes for spears had formerly taken place. The religious system and social organization of the Yir Yoront became disorganized as a result of the tribe's inability to adjust to the innovation. The men began prostituting their daughters and wives in exchange for the use of someone else's steel ax.

Many of the consequences of the innovation among the Yir Yoront were undesirable, indirect, and unanticipated; these three types of consequence often go together, just as desirable, direct, and anticipated consequences are often associated.

This case illustration is adapted from Sharp (1952, pp. 69–92).

Form, Function, and Meaning of an Innovation

The case of the steel ax among the Yir Yoront also illustrates a common error made by change agents in regard to an innovation's consequences. They are able to anticipate the form and function of an innovation's consequences, but not its meaning for potential adopters. What do we mean by the form, function, and meaning of an innovation?

1. *Form* is the directly observable physical appearance and substance of an innovation. Both the missionaries and the Yir Yoront recognized the form of the new tool because of its similarity in appearance to the stone ax.

2. *Function* is the contribution made by an innovation to the way of life of members of a social system. The tribe immediately perceived the steel ax as a cutting tool, to be used in much the same way as the stone ax had been.

3. *Meaning* is the subjective and frequently unconscious perception of an innovation by members of a social system. "Because of its subjective nature, meaning is much less susceptible to diffusion than either form or [function]. . . . A receiving culture attaches new meanings to the borrowed elements of complexes, and these may have little relation to the meanings which the same elements carried in their original setting" (Linton, 1936).

What mistakes did the missionaries make in the introduction of the steel ax? These change agents understood the form and function of the steel ax. They believed the Yir Yoront would use the new tool in much the same way as they had the stone ax, such as for cutting brush. But the missionaries made an egregious error in not predicting the meaning of the new idea to the Yir Yoront. They did not anticipate that the steel ax would lead to more sleep, prostitution, and a breakdown of social relationships and customs. Change agents frequently do not sense or understand the social meaning of the innovations that they introduce, especially the negative consequences that accrue when an apparently desirable innovation is used under different conditions. Change agents are especially likely to make this mistake if they do not empathize with the innovation's users, which is particularly likely when the change agents are heterophilous with their clients.

We conclude with Generalization 11–3: *Change agents more easily anticipate the form and function of an innovation for their clients than its meaning.*

The Irish Potato Famine

One of the worst famines in history was the Irish potato famine of 1850, which left 2 million people dead of starvation, forced another 2 million to migrate to the United States, and left 4 million to live in abject poverty. What caused this famine?

The story begins a century earlier when a new wonder food, the potato, was introduced from North America. Ireland's climate was perfect for the potato, and Ireland was relatively free from disease and insects. Potato yields were abundant. A Green Revolution occurred. The number of people began to increase, from the 2 million Irish in the 1700s to 4.5 million by 1800, and to a burgeoning 8 million in 1845. Catholic priests blessed this increased human fertility, which gave them more souls to save. Thanks to the potato, the human population continued to expand. Absentee landlords who visited their estates were amazed at the hordes of dirty, wretched people who lived in poverty. Even with the prospering potato, most of the Irish lived on the edge of hunger.

Then in 1845, a fungus, *Phytophothora infestans*, arrived from America, and wiped out the entire potato crop. Previously, during the long Atlantic crossing, often requiring a month or more, infected potatoes from America rotted, destroying the fungus. But the new clipper class of ships made the transatlantic crossing so quickly, in 12 to 14 days, that infected potatoes did not have time to rot. The fungus survived the trip. The weather in 1845 and 1846 was cool and rainy, perfect for the fungus. The potato crop in Ireland was wiped out completely.

Who was responsible for the devastating potato famine in Ireland? Was it the unwitting do-gooder who first brought the potato to Ireland? Was it the fungus, *Phytophothora infestans*? Was it the improved sailing technology of the clipper ships, which shortened the crossing, allowing the fungus to arrive on Irish shores? Or was it the Catholic culture of the Irish, which favored large families?

This case illustration is based on Paddock (1992).

Achieving a Dynamic Equilibrium

Perhaps the missionaries introduced too many steel axes to the Yir Yoront too rapidly. What rate of change will allow a system to achieve the benefits of an innovation, and yet not produce disequilibrium in the social system?

There are three types of equilibrium in a system.

1. *Stable equilibrium* occurs when there is almost no change in the structure or functioning of a social system. Perhaps a completely isolated and traditional system in which the rate of change is almost zero, provides an example of stable equilibrium.

2. *Dynamic equilibrium* occurs when the rate of change in a social system is commensurate with the system's ability to cope with it. Change oc-

curs in a system in dynamic equilibrium, but it occurs at a rate that allows the system to adapt to it.

3. *Disequilibrium* occurs when the rate of change is too rapid to permit a social system to adjust. An analogy is a traffic circle with one too many cars in it; all movement stops. The social disorganization that accompanies disequilibrium marks it as a painful and inefficient way for change to occur in a system.

The long-range goal of most change agents is to produce a condition of dynamic equilibrium in a client system. Innovations should be introduced into the system at a deliberate rate that allows for careful balancing of the system's ability to adjust to the changes. This delicate gauging of the optimum rate of change in a system is very difficult. The missionaries among the Yir Yoront misjudged the rate at which the aborigines' system could absorb the consequences of the steel ax.

Organic Farming and the Discontinuance of Pesticides

Back in 1954, one of the Iowa farmers that I personally interviewed for my Ph.D. dissertation research rejected all of the chemical innovations that I was then studying: Weed sprays, cattle and hog feeds, chemical fertilizers, and a rodenticide. He insisted that his neighbors, who had adopted these chemicals, were killing their songbirds and the earthworms in the soil. I had selected the new farm ideas in my innovativeness scale on the advice of agricultural experts at Iowa State University; I was measuring the best recommended farming practice of that day. The organic farmer in my sample earned the lowest score on my innovativeness scale, and was categorized as a laggard.

In the forty years or so since this interview, several of the farm chemicals that I studied have been banned because of their unhealthy effects on humans. I have come to understand that the organic farmer respondent in Iowa may actually have been the most innovative individual in my study, leading the new wave of organic farmers and gardeners that were soon to emerge (as was mentioned in Chapter 7). By 1990, about half of one percent of all U.S. food sales were organic, and were sold at about 10- to 20-percent higher prices than nonorganic products. Organic sales are increasing 40 percent per year in the United States.

Since DDT was invented in 1946, most of the world's farmers have been stuck on a dizzying treadmill of ever-increasing dependence on pesticides.

Although intended to wipe out pests, the undesirable, indirect, and unanticipated consequences of the Pesticide Revolution includes health risks to humans and to the environment, as well as creation of hordes of chemically resistant, seemingly indestructible bugs. In 1946, there were only fourteen species of pesticide-resistant pests. By 1994, there were more than 500.

Integrated Pest Management (IPM) is the use of alternative methods of pest control such as careful monitoring of pest numbers and damage, using natural pest predators, and other means (Corbet, 1981; Grieshop and others, 1988). The purposes of IPM are to control pests at a lower cost, and to decrease dependence on chemical pesticides. In essence, integrated pest management amounts to trading off heavy, regular applications of pesticides which are relatively expensive for more economic decisions based on field counts of pest damage that indicate pesticide spraying is justified. The use of chemicals is considered a last resort, when more organic methods of pest control are inadequate. Integrated Pest Management reduces farmer dependence on pesticides. IPM includes (1) use of natural enemies such as spiders to destroy pests, (2) need-based chemical spraying that is only applied when the insect infestation justifies it, (3) pest-resistant plant varieties, and (4) biotic methods to control pest reproduction such as breeding with sterile insects.

Despite its seeming advantages, IPM is very difficult to diffuse. Agricultural change agents attempting to promote IPM are faced with a paradox: Their counterparts three decades ago extolled the virtues of chemical sprays. Farmers today therefore wonder if they should believe change agents who tell them to stop using pesticides. Further, IPM calls for complex behavioral changes that demand more labor than does routine chemical spraying.

The roots of the overadoption of pesticides trace to the Green Revolution in many countries in the 1960s. Along with high-yielding seeds, fertilizers, and improved farm management, pesticides were distributed by government extension agents, usually at subsidized rates. The result was often a tripling of rice and wheat yields. Multinational corporations established a network of pesticide sales outlets throughout most nations. These salespeople are formidable opponents of Integrated Pest Management.

IPM is targeted at meeting the human and economic cost of pesticide overuse. Approximately 10,000 people die each year and 4 million suffer acutely from pesticide poisoning (Repetto, 1985). Most rice growers in Asia spray with pesticides every week, while only about one spraying per year is justified economically. Why do Asian rice-farmers use approximately fifty times as much pesticides as would be justified economically? When they adopted pesticides as part of the Green Revolution, the chemicals were spectacularly effective in killing rice pests. However the pests soon developed resistance to the pesticides, forcing farmers to apply heavier and heavier doses of pesticides, and to use pesticides that were more threatening to human health.

Farmers originally had the following notion of causation in mind when they adopted pesticides:

But spraying pesticides led to an accelerated natural selection that produced resistant strains of the insects and other pests, a natural selection process that worked as a self-corrective device.

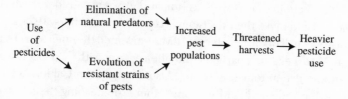

An IPM program was launched in California's Sacramento Valley in 1984 to control tomato worms. This area, consisting mainly of Yolo County, produces 30 to 40 percent of the state's tomatoes for processing (for catsup, pizza, and tomato juice). California tomato-growers in this area operate huge enterprises, with farms averaging 2,235 acres (3.5 square miles), including 600 acres of tomatoes. These farmers are highly experienced, having raised tomatoes for twenty-one years on average (Grieshop and others, 1988). The IPM program was introduced by entomologists in the California Agricultural Extension Service, headquartered at Davis. Farmers were invited to educational meetings at which they were taught to identify the tomato fruitworm, the beet armyworm, and the Western yellowstriped armyworm. Instruction was also provided on how to sample tomato worm infestation by walking through fields in specific routes, by counting worm eggs, and by randomly selecting fruits to estimate worm infestation. Bulletins and other printed materials about IPM were disseminated, and on-farm demonstrations of the innovation were held. The Extension Service also trained local youth as pest control advisors, who, for a small fee, regularly sampled a farmer's tomato fields for worm infestation.

"Integrated Pest Management" is a rather vacuous terminology to most California tomato farmers, so the IPM program was called the "worm sampling methods for processing tomatoes" by extension agents. They also knew that farmers conceived of this innovation mainly in economic terms, so an evaluation of IPM's consequences was made in the first year of the program; an economic benefit (mostly a result of reduced pesticide purchases) of $7.10 per acre ($4,260 for the average farmer with 600 acres of tomatoes) was achieved. One might expect that all of the tomato farmers in the Sacramento Valley would immediately adopt IPM. They did not. Even though a survey of eighty-four tomato farmers showed that most had awareness-knowledge of the innovation, the rate of adoption followed an S-shaped curve, reaching 60-percent adoption only after five years. Clearly economic relative advantage was not enough. "Although economic factors are important, much more than economics is at work as [tomato] growers consider these [IPM] innovations and make their decisions" (Grieshop and others, 1988).

More than half of the adopters of IPM re-invented the innovation by modifying IPM to meet their particular situation or to fit with their extensive previous experience in tomato-growing. Also, many of the California farmers previously had adopted IPM for some other crop, leading them to change one or more of the components of the tomato IPM innovation that was recommended to them by extension service experts. The farmers were particularly likely to alter the methods of sampling tomato worm infestation. Indigenous knowledge systems led to modification of the innovation, as did local pride of ownership: "It was often stated by farmers that they had been using IPM for years (as many as twenty-one) and that they had developed some of their own techniques that resulted in the modification of the university-recommended model" (Grieshop and others, 1988).

California tomato-growers perceived of IPM as highly complex. The idea of random sampling the worm infestation of their fields left them somewhat baffled. It seemed much simpler just to regularly apply a heavy dose of pesticides. IPM consisted of techniques that were essentially information (for example, counting eggs and worms, keeping records of such infestation, etc.), a software component of the innovation that was not very observable. IPM became more concrete only with a farmer's direct hands-on experience with the innovation. Thus IPM is a difficult innovation in terms of its complexity. Certainly, if IPM is to achieve a faster rate of adoption, "It is essential that IPM methods be simplified as much as possible, particularly the use of monitoring and action thresholds [that is, when to spray]" (Wearing, 1988).

This case illustration draws from a variety of sources.

Equality in the Consequences of Innovations

One specific mistake made by the missionaries among the Yir Yoront was to whom they introduced the innovation. Unaware of the cultural emphasis on respect for elder males among the Yir Yoront, the change agents gave steel axes to women, children, and young men indiscriminately. In general, one of the ways in which change agents shape the consequences of an innovation is who they work with most closely. If a change agent were to contact the poorer and less educated individuals in a social system, rather than the socioeconomic elites (as is usually the case), the benefits from the innovations that are so introduced would be more equal. Usually, however, change agents have most contact with the more-educated, higher-status individuals in a system, and thus tend to widen socioeconomic gaps through the innovations that they introduce.

In addition to the desirable-undesirable, direct-indirect, and anticipated-unanticipated aspects of the consequences of innovation, one might classify consequences as to whether they increase or decrease equality among the members of a social system. Here we are mainly talking about the consequences of an innovation at the system level (that is, whether some resource such as income or socioeconomic status is distributed more or less equally), rather than at the individual level.

The diffusion of innovations generally causes wider socioeconomic gaps within an audience. This increased inequality occurs because:

1. Innovators and early adopters have favorable attitudes toward new ideas and are more likely to search actively for innovations. They also possess the available resources to adopt higher-cost innovations, while later adopters do not.

2. Professional change agents concentrate their client contacts on innovators and early adopters in hopes that the opinion leaders among these earlier adopting categories will then pass along the new ideas they have learned to their followers. But most interpersonal network links connect individuals who are similar in adopter category and socioeconomic sta-

tus. So innovations generally "trickle across" rather than "trickle down" in the interpersonal communication networks of a system.

3. By adopting innovations relatively sooner than others in their system, innovators and early adopters achieve windfall profits, thereby widening the socioeconomic gap between these earlier adopting categories and the laggards. Thus the earlier adopters get richer, and the later adopters' economic gain is comparatively smaller.

So the diffusion of innovations usually decreases the degree of equality in a social system. But this tendency toward gap-widening need not occur, if special strategies are followed to narrow gaps.

Our previous example of the impact of the snowmobile among the Skolt Lapps illustrated two dimensions of consequences: (1) the first dimension of helping everyone travel more rapidly (thus achieving a higher average *level* of "Good," some widely desired objective or desideratum), and (2) the second dimension of the *unequal distribution* of the "Good" (the tendency for reindeer ownership to become concentrated in the hands of just a few Lapps). Figure 11–3 depicts these two dimensions of consequences; in the first situation, the average level of Good in a system increases as a result of the innovation, but the distribution remains equal. In the second situation shown, however, the average level of Good again increases, but the Good also becomes more concentrated in the hands of the socioeconomic elite as a consequence of the innovation; so the degree of equality in the system has decreased because of the innovation.

When diffusion scholars and change agents began to distinguish between (1) the level of Good, and (2) the equality of distribution of Good as consequences of diffusion activities, the next logical step was to begin investigating the gap-widening and gap-narrowing impacts of diffusion.

The Communication Effects Gap

Most past diffusion studies attempted to determine what effects a particular source, channel, message, or combination of such elements has on an audience's behavior. This research on the first dimension of communication effects pursues the question: "What are the effects of a communication activity?" Effects are indexed mainly as the average change in the knowledge, attitudes, or overt behavior of a set of individuals.

The nature of research on the second dimension of communication effects is quite different. Here one asks: "Has the communication activity had a greater, or different, effect on certain individuals than on others?" The communication scholar seeks to ascertain the *equality* of effects of

Figure 11–3. The Two Dimensions of Consequences of an Innovation in a System: Level of Good and Degree of Equality

1. Before the Innovation

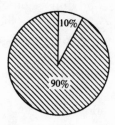

2. After the Innovation

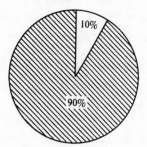

The total amount of income or other Good in the system is held by a wealthy minority (of, say, 10 percent)

The total amount of Good is now larger, but the proportion held by the wealthy minority remains the same.

I. **The level of Good in a system increases, but its distribution remains at the same degree of equality-inequality.**

1. Before the Innovation

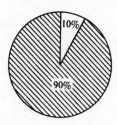

2. After the Innovation

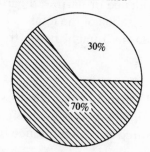

The prior conditions are the same as above.

Both the total amount of Good in the system and the proportion of Good held by the wealthy increase as a consequence of the innovation. Hence there is less equality.

II. **The level of Good in a system increases, and its distribution also becomes more concentrated and hence less equal.**

communication, not just how much effect occurred *on the average* (or in the aggregate).

About the time that diffusion researchers began to turn to this second dimension, dealing with the equality issue, Tichenor and others (1970) proposed a useful research paradigm for studying gaps, suggesting that data should be gathered at two or more points in time, both before and after a communication activity. The measure of effects should be not just the average amount of behavior change in the audience (the first dimension), but whether gaps in socioeconomic status and/or in knowledge of information increased or decreased (this is the second dimension of effects). In essence, Tichenor and others (1970) suggested that we should look at who in an audience was affected most, and who least. Figures 11–4a and 11–4b depict this research paradigm that was very influential on diffusion scholars studying the equality of consequences of innovation.

One of the main implications of the communication effects gap paradigm, inspired by Tichenor and others (1970) and carried forward in numerous other studies, was to look *within* an audience to determine whether certain segments were more affected by an innovation than other segments. This analytic approach to looking also for differential effects, rather than just for average effects or aggregate effects on the entire audience, took diffusion scholars in the direction of focusing upon equality issues.

Scholars began to investigate the degree to which a diffusion program widened or narrowed gaps among the members of a system. The categorization of the total audience into two or more segments ("ups" versus "downs") might be on the basis of socioeconomic status (for example,

Figure 11–4a. The First Dimension of Communication Effects (for All Members of the System) Is an Average Increase of Four Units, Measured as the Difference from t_1 to t_2.

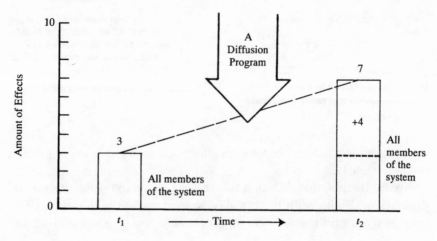

Figure 11–4b. The Second Dimension of Communication Effects (Which Analyzes Effects Separately for Downs and Ups) Indicates That the Effects Gap Is Widened by the Diffusion Program.

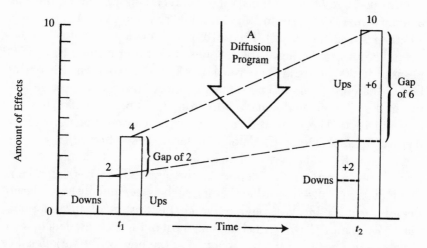

Note that the Downs are *absolutely* better off as a result of the diffusion program (+2), but *relatively* worse off (as the Ups gained +6). So the rich get richer (informationally), and the poor get less poor.

larger versus smaller farmers in a village), adopter category (for instance earlier adopters versus later adopters), or the level of information that individuals possessed (the information-rich versus the information-poor). Almost no matter how the ups and downs were classified, certain regularities about equality in the consequences of diffusion were found.

Gap-Widening Consequences of the Diffusion of Innovations

Generalization 11–4 states: *The consequences of the diffusion of innovations usually widen the socioeconomic gap between the earlier and later adopting categories in a system.* A second, related conclusion, Generalization 11–5 is: *The consequences of the diffusion of innovation usually widen the socioeconomic gap between the audience segments previously high and low in socioeconomic status.*

Now we take up several researches that illustrate the generalizations stated above. Havens and Flinn (1974) examined the consequences of new coffee varieties among Colombian farmers over the period from 1963 to 1970. Of their original sample of fifty-six coffee growers, seventeen adopted the new varieties, which considerably increased their yields; it was important to adopt chemical fertilizers and weedicides along with the new coffee varieties to achieve these high yields. As a result of adopting this package of innovations, the seventeen adopters raised their net income from 6,700 pesos in 1963 to 21,000 pesos in 1970, an increase of 14,300 pesos (213 percent). The thirty-nine nonadopting coffee farmers (who did not use the new varieties) raised their net income from 4,500 pesos to 12,000 pesos, an increase of only 7,500 (166 percent). So one effect of the coffee variety innovations was to widen the income gap between the adopters and nonadopters from 2,200 pesos in 1963 to 9,000 pesos in 1970. The improved coffee varieties caused much greater income inequality among the Colombian farmers (see Figure 11–4b).

How much of this increased inequality among the Colombian coffee growers was a result of the adoption of the new coffee varieties, and how much of it was caused by other factors, such as the initially larger farms, higher formal education, and other characteristics of the adopters? Havens and Flinn (1974) conclude that most of the increased income inequality was a result of the introduction of the new coffee varieties. For example, they computed the net income per acre of coffee grown, thus removing the effect of the larger farms of the adopters. The adopters and nonadopters both began at about the same level of income per acre in 1963; 290 pesos per acre and 222 pesos per acre, respectively. But by 1970, when the adopters were securing the higher yields that resulted from growing the new varieties, their income per acre shot up to 1,642 pesos per acre (an increase of 1,352 pesos), while the nonadopters' income per acre rose to 632 pesos (an increase of 415 pesos). Much of the increased income inequality between the adopters and nonadopters was, thus, caused by the introduction of the coffee variety innovations.

What did the adopters do with their higher income? Some bought larger farms, with some of the land coming from the nonadopters. In 1963, the adopters averaged farms of nineteen acres and the nonadopters eight acres; by 1970, the adopters had increased their farms to thirty-three acres, while the nonadopters' farms shrank to an average size of six acres. In addition, eleven of the nonadopters dropped out of farming, and either became day laborers or else migrated to the city; presumably, their farms were purchased by the adopters.

If adoption of the new coffee varieties were to have such important consequences, why didn't the thirty-nine nonadopters also start growing the new varieties? Adopting a new coffee variety is a major decision in Colombia because three years are required before the new trees come to production; many farmers need credit to tide them over this period until their investment in the new variety begins to pay off. Smaller *campesinos* who did not have much land to put up as collateral, were generally unable to borrow funds to enable them to adopt the new coffee varieties, and they therefore lost the potential advantage of the higher yields and farm incomes that they could have achieved by adopting the new coffee varieties.

This vicious circle explains how adoption of the coffee variety innovations widened the socioeconomic gaps (1) between the adopters and non-adopters, and (2) between those individuals originally high and low in socioeconomic status. The innovation was a lever, prying wider the gap between the rich and the poor.

Social Structure and the Equality of Consequences

How an innovation is introduced determines, in part, the degree to which it causes unequal consequences. Evidence for this point comes from an investigation of the impacts of adopting irrigation wells by villagers in Bangladesh and in Pakistan (Gotsch, 1972). In each country, an irrigation well cost about the same amount and provided water for fifty to eighty acres of farmland. The introduction of Green Revolution wheat and rice varieties created a need for irrigation in both nations. But the equality of the consequences of an identical innovation was quite different in Pakistan from those in Bangladesh, mainly because of the different social organization that accompanied the new technology.

In Pakistan, 70 percent of the irrigation wells were purchased by farmers with twenty-five acres or more (considered to be very large farms); only 4 percent of the villagers with farms of less than thirteen acres adopted. When the irrigation water was accompanied by the use of fertilizers and other agricultural chemicals, a farmer typically could increase his net farm income by about 45 percent. So the irrigation wells in Pakistan made the rich richer; the poor farmers became *relatively* poorer.

But in Bangladesh, average farm size was only one or two acres, not large enough to justify the private ownership of an irrigation well. So in Bangladesh, village cooperatives typically purchased a well, and provided irrigation water to everyone who belonged to the co-op. Farm incomes were doubled because farmers could raise a winter crop of rice during the season when rainfall was scarce. In Bangladesh, the rate of adoption of the wells was slower than in Pakistan because the innovation-decision was collective rather than individual-optional in nature. But the consequences of the innovation were distributed much more equally than they were in Pakistan, where an initially high degree of social stratification led to a concentration of the irrigation wells' impact among the rich farmers.

The social structure in which the innovation was introduced in Bangladesh and Pakistan, rather than the innovation itself, determined the distribution of its socioeconomic impacts. This investigation along with others, suggests Generalization 11–6: *A system's social structure partly determines the equality versus inequality of an innovation's consequences.* When a system's structure is already very unequal, it is likely that when an innovation is introduced (especially if it is a relatively high-cost innovation), the consequences will lead to even greater inequality in the form of wider socioeconomic gaps.

The irrigation consequences research in Bangladesh and Pakistan illustrates, as does the Colombian coffee study, that an innovation's adoption and its impacts are related to characteristics of the social system, as well as to variables at the individual level of analysis. The fact that village co-ops already existed in Bangladesh when irrigation wells were introduced, and that small coffee-growers in Colombia could not obtain credit to adopt the new coffee varieties, largely determined who adopted and who could not. The determining factors were mainly at the system level, although their impacts occurred through individuals' actions. Why didn't the smaller farmers in Pakistan and Colombia adopt the innovations? The answer is system-blame, not individual-blame (see Chapter 3).

Social structural factors are not necessarily static barriers or facilitators of the adoption of innovations and their consequences. A rural development agency in Bangladesh had organized the village cooperatives just prior to the introduction of irrigation wells, for exactly the purpose that they served: to enable small farmers, through banding together, to adopt relatively high-cost innovations such as tractors and irrigation wells.

Strategies for Narrowing Gaps

As the Bangladesh-Pakistan study of irrigation wells suggests, innovations do not inevitably widen socioeconomic gaps within a system. But such gap-widening inequality will usually occur unless a change agency devotes special efforts to prevent it. In the Bangladesh illustration, the change agency had organized cooperatives so that this social organization in which the technology of irrigation wells was imbedded helped prevent widening of the socioeconomic gap.

What strategies for gap-narrowing can be used by change agencies? We list possible strategies here, organized under the major reasons why socioeconomic gaps ordinarily widen as a consequence of innovations.

I. THE UPS HAVE GREATER ACCESS TO INFORMATION, CREATING AWARENESS ABOUT INNOVATIONS, THAN DO THE DOWNS.

1. Provide messages that are redundant or that are of less interest and/or benefit to the higher socioeconomic subaudience. This strategy enables the lower socioeconomic subaudience to catch up. This "ceiling effect" strategy was used successfully for narrowing the socioeconomic gap among Indian villagers by special television programming (Shingi and Mody, 1976).

2. Tailor communication messages especially for the lower socioeconomic subaudience in terms of their particular characteristics, such as formal education, beliefs, communication habits, and the like. Communication materials are seldom especially designed for this audience segment, and hence most messages are ineffective in gap-closing. Although the basic content of these messages may be the same as for the Ups, to be effective in reaching the lower socioeconomic audience, the message design, treatment, and presentation may need to be different; for example, more line drawings, photographs, and other visual aids may be needed because of the lower levels of formal education among the Downs. Formative evaluation* may be especially helpful in producing effective messages for the Downs, such as by pretesting prototype messages before they are produced in large quantities.

3. Use communication channels that are particularly able to get through to the Downs so that access is not a barrier to gaining awareness-knowledge of innovations. In the United States, for example, lower socioeconomic audiences are especially heavy television viewers but depend less on print media than do the Ups. In Third World nations, many Downs do not possess literacy skills, so print media are out; the Downs are much more likely to have radio exposure than to view television.

4. Organize the Downs in small groups in which they can learn about innovations and discuss these new ideas. The group context for listening,

---

* *Formative evaluation* is a type of research that is conducted while an activity, process, or system is ongoing, to improve its effectiveness. In contrast, *summative evaluation* is a type of research that is conducted to reach a decision about the effectiveness of an activity, process, or system after it has run its course.

discussion, and action provides a basis for the Downs to gain efficacy, a feeling that they have control over their environment.

5. Shift the concentration of change agent contact from the innovators and early adopters to the late majority and laggards. These later adopting categories tend to place less credibility in professional change agents, and they seldom actively search for information from them, as they place greater trust in interpersonal networks with their peers. But when change agents directly contact late majority and laggards, and where the innovations are appropriate to their needs, the response has often been encouraging (Röling and others, 1976).

There is a cost to gap-narrowing activities by change agents; they cannot increase the total Good in a system while they are attempting to secure a more equitable distribution of Good. There is a trade-off between the first and the second dimensions of diffusion consequences. Consider the case of a change agent working in a single village. One farmer owns 100 acres, while each of the remaining 100 farmers operates an average of one acre. If the change agent contacts the one hundred smaller farmers, he/she may be able to get them to adopt new crop varieties, chemical fertilizers, and other agricultural innovations, so that their yields increase an average of ten bushels per acre within a few years. But with much less effort, the change agent could contact the one large farmer, who is already innovative and receptive to new ideas; an increase of ten bushels per acre on the elite individual's farm equals the consequences of the much greater efforts by the change agent with all one hundred smaller farmers.

II. THE UPS HAVE GREATER ACCESS TO INNOVATION-EVALUATION INFORMATION FROM PEERS THAN DO THE DOWNS. If the trickle-down theory were operating perfectly, the Downs would rapidly learn of the Ups' personal experience with an innovation, and quickly follow suit. But in the communication networks in many systems, Ups talk to Ups, and Downs talk to Downs (Röling and others, 1976). So the Downs are often not connected in interpersonal networks about innovations. How can this problem be overcome?

1. Identify opinion leaders among the disadvantaged segment of a system and concentrate change agents contacts on them, to activate peer networks about an innovation.

2. Select change agent aides from among the Downs who contact their homophilous peers about innovations.

3. Form groups among the Downs to provide them with leadership and social reinforcement in their innovation-decision making. Such small

groups give the Downs greater economic, political, and social strength (as we saw in the example of the Bangladesh village cooperatives).

III. THE UPS POSSESS GREATER SLACK RESOURCES FOR ADOPTING INNOVATIONS THAN DO THE DOWNS. The Ups are usually much more able to adopt innovations, particularly if these new ideas are expensive, technologically complex, and provide economies of scale. What strategies can overcome these gap-widening tendencies?

1. Recommend appropriate innovations for the Downs. For such appropriate technologies to be available, R&D activities should be directed at the problems of the lower socioeconomic members of the system.

2. Create a social organization so that the Downs can command the slack resources needed to adopt certain high-cost innovations. An illustration of this social organization strategy is the village co-ops in Bangladesh that facilitated the adoption of irrigation by small farmers.

3. Provide a means through which the Downs can participate in the planning and execution of diffusion programs, including the setting of program priorities.

4. Establish special diffusion agencies to work only with the Downs, thus enabling change agents to meet the particular needs of the lower socioeconomic audience. If such an agency had existed among the Colombian coffee growers studied by Havens and Flinn (1974), it might have provided agricultural credit to the small farmers so that they could have afforded to adopt the new coffee varieties.

5. Shift emphasis from diffusing innovations coming out of formal R&D to spreading information about experience-based ideas through a more decentralized diffusion system. Depend more on indigenous knowledge systems (see Chapter 6).

Wider Gaps Are Not Inevitable

Field experiments by Shingi and Mody (1976) and Röling and others (1976) suggest Generalization 11–7: *When special efforts are made by a diffusion agency, it is possible to narrow, or at least to maintain the size of, socioeconomic gaps in a social system.*

The Shingi and Mody (1976) field experiment in India evaluated the ceiling effect strategy, identified previously in this chapter as Strategy I–1: Provide messages that are redundant or that are of less interest and/or benefit to the Ups, but that are appropriate to the lower socioeconomic subaudience. Two Indian communication scholars, Prakash M. Shingi and Bella Mody, content-analyzed agricultural television programs (before they were broadcast) to determine the twenty-one main items of information about wheat-growing and potato-raising innovations that they contained. The television programs were designed to provide useful information to smaller farmers in India, but to be redundant with much of the information already possessed by larger farmers.

Shingi and Mody (1976) found that larger farmers only watched a few of the televised programs before they were "turned off" by viewing agricultural information that they already knew. But smaller farmers eagerly watched the television series because the farm information that it contained was new to them. All farmers had unlimited access to viewing the programs on a community television set that was provided to each village by the government of India (Strategy I–3, dealing with access). Shingi and Mody (1976) measured the degree of agricultural knowledge before and after the television programs, by means of personal interviews. The gaps between the Ups and the Downs was narrowed by the television programs because of the ceiling effect: "By choosing program content that large farmers already understand, television producers can *close rather than widen* the communication effects gap" (emphasis in original). Shingi and Mody (1976) concluded that *"The communication effects gap is by no means inevitable*. It can be avoided if appropriate communication strategies are pursued in development efforts" (emphasis in original).

Summary

Consequences are the changes that occur to an individual or to a social system as a result of the adoption or rejection of an innovation. Although obviously important, the consequences of innovations have received inadequate attention by change agents and by diffusion researchers. Consequences have not been studied adequately because (1) change agencies have overemphasized adoption per se, assuming that the consequences will be positive; (2) the usual survey research methods may be inappropriate for investigating consequences; and (3) consequences are difficult to measure.

Consequences are classified as (1) desirable versus undesirable, (2) direct versus indirect, and (3) anticipated versus unanticipated. *Desirable consequences* are the functional effects of an innovation for an individual or for a social system. *Undesirable consequences* are the dysfunctional effects of an innovation to an individual or to a social system. It is often difficult to avoid value judgments when evaluating consequences as desirable or undesirable. Many innovations cause both positive and negative consequences, and it is thus erroneous to assume that the desirable impacts can be achieved without also experiencing the undesirable effects. We conclude that the effects of an innovation usually cannot be managed in a way that separates the desirable from the undesirable consequences (Generalization 11–1).

Direct consequences are the changes to an individual or a system that occur in immediate response to an innovation. *Indirect consequences* are the changes to an individual or a system that occur as a result of these direct consequences. They are consequences of consequences.

Anticipated consequences are changes brought on by an innovation that are recognized and intended by the members of a system. *Unanticipated consequences* are changes that are neither intended nor recognized by the members of a system.

The undesirable, indirect, and unanticipated consequences of an innovation usually go together, as do the desirable, direct, and anticipated consequences (Generalization 11–2). An illustration of this generalization is provided by the introduction of the steel ax among Australian aborigines, which caused many undesirable, indirect, and unanticipated consequences, including breakdown of the family structure, the emergence of prostitution, and misuse of the innovation itself. The case of the steel ax illustrates three intrinsic elements of an innovation: (1) *form*, the directly observable physical appearance and substance of an innovation, (2) *function*, the contribution made by the innovation to the way of life of individuals or to the social system, and (3) *meaning*, the subjective and frequently subconscious perception of the innovation by members of the social system. Change agents more easily anticipate the form and function of an innovation for their clients than its meaning (Generalization 11–3).

Stable equilibrium occurs when there is almost no change in the structure or functioning of a social system. *Dynamic equilibrium* occurs when the rate of change in a social system is commensurate with the system's ability to cope with it. *Disequilibrium* occurs when the rate of change is too rapid to permit the system to adjust. Change agents generally wish to achieve a rate of change that leads to dynamic equilibrium, and to avoid a state of disequilibrium.

One goal of diffusion programs is to raise the level of Good in a system; but a second dimension of consequences is whether the distribution of Good among the members of a system becomes more or less equal. The consequences of the diffusion of innovations usually widen the socioeconomic gap between the earlier- and later-adopting categories in a system (Generalization 11–4). Further, the consequences of the diffusion of innovations usually widen the socioeconomic gap between the audience segments previously high and low in socioeconomic status (Generalization 11–5).

A system's social structure partly determines the equality versus the inequality of an innovation's consequences (Generalization 11–6). When a system's structure is already very unequal, the consequences of an innovation (especially if it is a relatively high-cost innovation) will lead to even greater inequality in the form of wider socioeconomic gaps.

What strategies could be followed in order to narrow gaps? The answer depends on three main reasons why socioeconomic gaps ordinarily widen as a consequence of diffusion: (1) the Ups have greater access to information creating awareness about innovations, (2) they have greater access to innovation-evaluation information from peers, and (3) the Ups possess greater slack resources for adopting innovations than do the Downs. When special efforts are made by a diffusion agency, it is possible to narrow, or at least prevent the widening of, socioeconomic gaps in a social system (Generalization 11–7). In other words, widening gaps are not inevitable.

BIBLIOGRAPHY

This bibliography includes (1) all of the publications cited in the present book, and (2) a number of other diffusion publications, especially those that appeared in the past decade or so since my Third Edition. The present bibliography does not include all of the approximately 3,900 diffusion publications (75 percent empirical and 25 percent nonempirical) currently available, as such a complete bibliography would itself constitute a very large book. Most published work on the diffusion of innovations, however, is included either in the present bibliography or in my two previous books on diffusion (Rogers with Shoemaker, 1971, pp. 387–460; Rogers, 1983, pp. 414–439). Several nondiffusion publications that are cited in the present book may be identified in this bibliography by the fact that they do not end with letters (which indicate a diffusion research tradition).

Each of the diffusion publications that follows is coded (1) as to the diffusion research tradition of the author, based on his or her institutional affiliation at the time of publication (see the list of codes below), and (2) as to whether it is empirical (E) or nonempirical (N). Nonempirical diffusion publications include bibliographies, theoretical writings, and summaries of diffusion findings reported in other, empirical publications.

Author's Diffusion Tradition	Code for Tradition
Anthropology	A
Agricultural Economics	AE
Communication	C
Education	E
Early Sociology	ES
Geography	G
General Economics	GE

General Sociology   GS
Industrial Engineering   I
Marketing and Management   MR
Public Health and Medical Sociology   PH
Psychology   P
Public Administration and Political Science   PS
Rural Sociology   RS
Statistics   S
Others and Unknown   O

Ab-Della, Moktar M., Eric O. Holiberg, and Richard D. Warren (1981), "Adoption Behavior in Family Farm Systems: An Iowa Study," *Rural Sociology*, 46:42–61. RS(E)

Aberg, Leif, Greg Castillo, and Jay Goldberg (1976), "Restructuring of Transportation Patterns: A Study Centered about the Santa Monica Preferred (Diamond) Lane," Unpublished paper, Los Angeles, University of Southern California, Annenberg School for Communication. C(E)

Abernathy, William J., and K.B. Clark (1985), "Innovation: Mapping the Winds of Creative Destruction," *Research Policy*, 14:3–22. MR(E)

Abraham, S.C.S., and George Hayward (1984), "Understanding Discontinuance: Towards a More Realistic Model of Technological Innovation and Industrial Adoption in Britain," *Technovation*, 2:209–231. MR(E)

Abrahamson, Eric (1991), "Managerial Fads and Fashions: The Diffusion and Rejection of Innovations," *Academy of Management Review*, 16(3):586–612. MR(E)

Abu-Ismail, F. F. (1982), "Modeling the Dimensions of Innovation, Adoption, and Diffusion in Foreign Markets," *Management International Review*, 22:54–65. MR(N)

Acheson, James M., and Robert Reidman (1982), "Technical Innovation in the New England Fin-Fishing Industry: An Examination of the Downs and Mohr Hypothesis," *American Ethnologist*, 9(3):538–558. O(E)

Achilladelis, B., and others (1971), *Project Sappho: A Study of Success and Failure in Innovation*, Brighton, England, University of Sussex, Science Policy Research Unit, Report. O(E)

Adhikarya, Ronny, with Heimo Posametier (1987), *Motivating Farmers for Action: How Strategic Multi-Media Campaigns Can Help: Results and Experiences of the Bangladesh Rat Control Campaigns*, Eschborn, Germany, GTZ. C(E)

Aguirre, B. E., E. L. Quarantelli, and Jorge L. Mendoza (1988), "The Collective Behavior of Fads: The Characteristics, Effects, and Career of Streaking," *American Sociological Review*, 53:569–584. GS(E)

Akinola, Amos A. (1986), "An Application of the Bass Model in the Analysis of Diffusion of Cocoa-Spraying among Nigerian Cocoa Farmers," *Journal of Agricultural Economics*, 37(3):395–404. AE(E)

Alao, J. Ade (1981), "The Diffusion of Fishponds in Western State of Nigeria," in Bruce R. Crouch and Shankariah Chamala (eds.), *Extension Education and Rural Development*, Volume I, Chichester, England, Wiley. RS(E)

Albrecht, Terrance L., and Vickie A. Ropp (1984), "Communicating about Innovation in Networks of Three U.S. Organizations," *Journal of Communication*, 34:78–91. C(E)

Allen, Beth (1982), "Some Stochastic Processes of Inter-Dependent Demand and Technological Diffusion of an Innovation Exhibiting Externalities among Adopters," *International Economic Review*, 23:595–608. GS(E)

Allen, David (1983), "New Telecommunication Services: Network Externalities and Critical Mass," *Telecommunication Policy*, 12(3):257–271. GE(E)

Allen, Harley Earl (1956), *The Diffusion of Educational Practices in the Metropolitan School Study Council*, Ph.D. Thesis, New York, Columbia University, Teachers College. E(E)

Allen, R.C. (1983), "Collective Invention," *Journal of Economic Behavior and Organization*, 4:1–24. MR(E)

Amabile, Theresa M. (1988), "A Model of Creativity and Innovation in Organizations," in B. Staw, H. Angle, and L. Cummings (eds.), *Research in Organization Behavior*, Volume 10, Greenwich, CT, JAI Press. MR(E)

Anderson, Beverly, and others (1987), "State Strategies to Support Local School Improvement," *Knowledge*, 9(1):42–86. E(E)

Anderson, D.M., R.H. Needle, and S.R. Mosco (1986), "Diffusion of Innovations in Health Promotion: A Micro-Computer Enhanced Program for Children," *Family and Communication Health*, 9(2):27–36. PH(E)

Anderson, Geoffrey M., and Jonathan Lomas (1988), "Monitoring the Diffusion of a Technology: Coronary Artery Bypass Surgery in Ontario," *American Journal of Public Health*, 78(3):251–254. PH(E)

Anderson, James G., and Stephen J. Jay (1984), "The Diffusion of Computer Applications in Medical Settings," *Medical Information*, 9:251–254. PH(E)

——— (1985a), "Computers and Clinical Judgement: The Role of Physician Networks," *Social Science and Medicine*, 20(10):969–979. PH(E)

——— (1985b), "The Diffusion of Medical Technology: Social Network Analysis and Policy Research," *Sociological Quarterly*, 26:49–64. PH(E)

Anderson, James G., Stephen J. Jay, Harlan M. Schweer, and Marilyn M. Anderson (1986), "Physician Utilization of Computers in Medical Practice: Policy Implications Based on a Structural Model," *Social Science and Medicine*, 23(3):259–267. PH(E)

——— (1987), "The Diffusion of Computer Applications in Medical Practice," Paper presented at the Annual Sunbelt Social Network Conference, Clearwater Beach, Florida. PH(E)

Anderson, James G., Stephen J. Jay, Harlan M. Schweer, Marilyn M. Anderson, and David Kassing (1986), "Physician Communication Networks and the Adoption and Utilization of Computer Applications in Medicine," Paper presented at the Annual Sunbelt Social Network Conference, Santa Barbara, California. PH(E)

Andreasen, Per Buch, and Anker Brink Lund (1990), *Life-Cycles of Medical Technologies*, Frederiksberg, Denmark, Academic Publishing. PH(E)

Andrew, Chris O., and Jose Alwarez (1982), "Adoption of Agricultural Technology: Developments in Agro-Socio-Economic Thought," *Social and Economic Studies*, 31(9):170–189. AE(E)

Angle, Harold A. (1989), "Psychology and Organizational Invention," in Andrew H. Van de Ven, Harold A. Angle, and M. Scott Poole (eds.), *Research on the Management of Innovation: The Minnesota Studies*, Cambridge, MA, Ballinger/Harper & Row. MR(E)

Angle, Harold A., and Andrew H. Van de Ven (1989), "Suggestions for Managing the Innovation Journey," in Andrew H. Van de Ven, Harold A. Angle, and M. Scott Poole (eds.), *Research on the Management of Innovation: The Minnesota Studies*, Cambridge, MA, Ballinger/Harper & Row. MR(E)

Antonelli, Cristiano (1986), "The International Diffusion of New Information Technologies," *Research Policy*, 15:139–147. GE(E)

—— (1989), "The Diffusion of Information Technology and the Demand for Telecommunication Services," *Telecommunication Policy*, 9:255–264. GE(E)

—— (1991), *The Diffusion of Advanced Telecommunication in Developing Countries*, Paris, OECD. GE(E)

—— (1993), "Investment and Adoption in Advanced Telecommunications," *Journal of Economic Behavior and Organization*, 20:227–275. GE(E)

Arensberg, Conrad M., and Arthur H. Niehoff (1964), *Introducing Social Change*, Chicago, Aldine. A(N)

Arnould, Eric J. (1989), "Toward a Broadened Theory of Preference Formation and Diffusion of Innovations: Cases from Zinder Province, Niger Republic," *Journal of Consumer Research*, 16:239–267. MR(E)

Arthur, W. Brian, and David A. Lane (1991), *Information Constriction and Information Contagion*, Santa Fe, New Mexico, Santa Fe Institute, Economics Research Program, Working Paper. GE(N)

Arrow, Kenneth (1962), "The Economic Implications of Learning by Doing," *Review of Economic Studies*, 29:155–173. GE(N)

Asch, Susan M., and Charles Upton Lowe (1984), "The Consensus Development Program: Theory, Process, and Critique," *Knowledge*, 5(3):369–385. GS(N)

Ascoine, F.J., D.M. Kirkin, N.J. Wenzloff, T.A. Foley, and D.K. Kwok (1987), "Effects of Innovation Characteristics on Pharmacists' Use of Written Patient Medication Information," *Patient Education and Counseling*, 9(1):53–64. PH(E)

Ashby, Jacqueline A. (1982), "Technology and Ecology: Implications for Innovative Research in Peasant Agriculture," *Rural Sociology*, 47(2):234–250. RS(E)

—— (1983), "Armchair Agriculture or the Sociology of Agriculture? A Rejoinder to Gartrell," *Rural Sociology*, 48(4):667–669. RS(N)

Ashby, Jacqueline A., and E. Walter Coward, Jr. (1980), "Putting Agriculture Back into the Study of Farm Practice Innovation: Comment on Status, Knowledge, and Innovation," *Rural Sociology*, 45(1):520–523. RS(E)

Åstebro, Thomas (1989), "Intra-Firm Diffusion Patterns of Technological Change," Paper presented at the Conference on the Diffusion of Technologies and Social Behavior, Laxenburg, Austria. MR(E)

Atack, Jeremy, Fred Bateman, and Thomas Weiss (1980), "The Regional Diffusion and Adoption of the Steam Engine in American Manufacturing," *Journal of Economic History*, 40:281–308. O(E)

Attunell, Paul (1992), "Technology Diffusion and Organizational Learning: The Case of Business Computing," *Organization Science*, 3(1):1–19. GS(E)

Audirac, Ivonne, and Lionel J. Beaulieu (1986), "Microcomputers in Agriculture: A Proposed Model to Study Their Diffusion/Adoption," *Rural Sociology*, 51(1):60–77. RS(E)

Azcona, Sergio, Maria del Carmen, Elu de Lenero, Jorge Campos Cordero, and Alan Keller (1980), "Agent Characteristics and Productivity in the Mexican Rural Health Program," *Studies in Family Planning*, 11:247–254. PH(E)

Bach, Betsy Wackernagel (1989), "The Effect of Multiplex Relationships upon Innova-

Bibliography

on and Discontinuance of Motion Picture Attendence and Monochromatic Television: Further Tests of a Mathematical Model," Paper presented at the International ommunication Association, New Orleans. C(E)

ett, George A., Edward L. Fink, and Mary Beth Debus (1989), "A Mathematical Model of Academic Citation Age," *Communication Research*, 16(4):510–529. C(E)

ett, George A., and G. Siegel (1988), "The Diffusion of Computer-Assisted Legal Research Systems," *Journal of American Society for Information Sciences*, 9(4):224–234. C(E)

ett, Homer G. (1953), *Innovation: The Basis of Cultural Change*, New York, McGraw-Hill. A(E)

on, Allen (1968), "Bringing Society Back In: Survey Research and Macro-Methodology," *American Behavioral Scientist*, 12:1–9.

ch, Charles E. (1984), "Research on Disseminating and Implementing Health Education Programs in Schools," *School Health Research*, 54:57–66. PH(E)

sch, Charles E., J.D. Eveland, and Barry Portnoy (1986), "Diffusion Systems for Education and Learning about Health," *Family and Community Health*, 9(2):1–26. PH(E)

sch, Charles E., and E.M. Sliepcevich (1983), "Innovators, Innovations, and Implementations: A Framework for Curricular Research in Health Education," *Health Education*, 14(2):20–24. PH(E)

ss, Frank M. (1969), "A New Product Growth Model for Consumer Durables," *Management Science*, 13(5):215–227. MR(E)

—— (1980), "The Relationship Between Diffusion Rates, Experience Curves, and Demand Elasticities for Consumer Durable Technological Innovations," *Journal of Business*, 53:51–67. MR(E)

—— (1986a), "Diffusion Systems for Education and Learning about Health," *Family Community Health*, O.C:1–26. MR(N)

—— (1986b), "The Adoption of a Marketing Model: Comments and Observations," in Vijay Mahajan and Yoram Wind (eds.), *Innovation Diffusion of New Product Acceptance*, Cambridge, MA, Ballinger. MR(N)

attelle-Columbus Laboratories (1976), *Report of the President's Biomedical Research Panel: Analysis of Selected Biomedical Research Programs: Case Histories*, Columbus, Ohio, Battelle-Columbus Laboratories, Report to the U.S. Public Health Service. O(E)

Battista, Renaldo N. (1989), "Innovation and Diffusion of Health-Related Technologies: A Conceptual Framework," *International Journal of Technology Assessment in Health Care*, 5:227–248. PH(N)

Baumgarten, Steven A. (1974), "The Diffusion of Fashion Innovations among U. S. College Students," Paper presented at the ESOMAR Workshop Seminar on Fashions, Research, and Marketing, Milwaukee, University of Wisconsin. MR(E)

—— (1975), "The Innovative Communicator in the Diffusion Process," *Journal of Marketing Research*, 12:1–15. MR(E)

Bayer, Judy, and Nancy Melone (1989), "A Critique of Diffusion Theory as a Managerial Framework for Understanding Adoption of Software Engineering Innovations," *Journal of Systems and Softwares*, 9:161–166. MR(E)

Bayus, Bary L. (1987), "Forecasting Sales of New Contingent Products: An Application

tion Adoption: A Reconsideration of Rogers' Model," *Comm*
56:133–149. C(E)

Baer, Wally S., B. Johnson, and S. Merrow (1977), "Governme
strations of New Technologies," *Science*, 196:950–957. O(E)

Bagehot, Walter (1873), *Physics and Politics*, New York, Appleto

Bailey, Norman T.J. (1957), *The Mathematical Theory of Epidemi*
pp. 29–37, 155–159. PH(N)

Baker, Patti R. (1985), "Adoption of a Computer Software Catalog
ementary School," *School Library Media Quarterly*, 13:208–21

Balcer, Yves, and Steven A. Lippman (1984), "Technological Expec
of Improved Technology," *Journal of Economic Theory*, 34:292·

Bales, Richard W. (1983), "The Diffusion of Personal Computers,"
Buffalo, NY, Medaille College. C(E)

Bandura, Albert (1977), *Social Learning Theory*, Englewood Cliffs

———— (1986), *Social Foundations of Thought and Action*, Englewo
tice-Hall.

Bank, Adrianne, Nancy C. Snidman, and Marcella Pitts (1979), "Pers
tion, Linkage and Program Improvement," in Carolyn S. Cates
(eds.), *Dissemination and the Improvement of Practice: Cooperati
the School Improvement Process*, San Francisco, CA, Far West La

Banta, H. David (1980), "The Diffusion of Computer Tomography (C
United States," *International Journal of Health Services*, 10(2):251·

Banta, H. David, and others (1983), "Policy Implications of the Diffusi
Medical Technology," *Annals of American Academy of Political an*
468:165–181. GE(E)

Barabba, Vincent P. (1984), "Steel Axes for Stone Age Man," in Robert
Marketing in an Electronic Age, Boston, Harvard Business School P

Bar-Gal, Y. (1980), "Concept of Diffusion: Dimensions of Time and Sp
tive Agricultural Organizations in Non-Jewish Villages in Israel," *Middl
ies*, 16(10):236–245. U(E)

Bardini, Thierry (1994), "A Translation Analysis of the Green Revolutio
ence, Technology, and Human Values, 19(2):152–168. C(E)

Barker, D. (1977), "The Paracurve of Innovations: The Neglected Aftern
sion or a Wave Goodbye to an Idea," *Area*, 9:259–264. G(E)

Barker, James R. (1993), "Tightening the Iron Cage: Concertive Control in
ing Teams," *Administrative Science Quarterly*, 38:408–432. C(E)

Barker, James R., C. W. Melville, and Michael Pacanowsky (1993), "Self-Dir
at XEL: Changes in Communication during a Program of Cultural Tran
Journal of Applied Communication Research, 16:297–312. C(E)

Barley, S. (1986), "Technology as an Occasion for Structuring: Evidence fro
tions of CT Scanners and the Social Order of Radiology Departments,"
tive Science Quarterly, 31:78–108. MR(E)

Barnett, George A. (1988), "An Associational Model for the Diffusion of Con
vations," in George A. Barnett and Joel Woelfel (eds.), *Readings in the G
tem: Theory, Methods and Applications*, Dubuque, IA, Kendall/Hunt. C(E

Barnett, George A., Edward L. Fink, and Hsiu-Jung (Mindy) Chang (1988), " to the Compact Disc Market," *Journal of Product Innovation Management*, 4:243–255. MR(E)

—— (1988), "Accelerating the Durable Replacement Cycle with Marketing Mix Variables," *Journal of Product Innovation Management*, 5:216–226. MR(E)

Bayus, Bary L., Saman Hong, and Russel P. Labe, Jr. (1989), "Developing and Using Forecasting Models for Consumer Durables," *Journal of Product Innovation Management*, 6:5–19. MR(E)

Beal, George M., and Everett M. Rogers (1957), "Informational Sources in the Adoption Process of New Fabrics," *Journal of Home Economics*, 49:630–634. RS(E)

—— (1960), *The Adoption of Two Farm Practices in a Central Iowa Community*, Ames, Iowa Agricultural and Home Economics Experiment Station, Special Report 26, pp. 4, 6, 8, 10, 19. RS(E)

Beal, George M., Everett M. Rogers, and Joe M. Bohlen (1957), "Validity of the Concept of Stages in the Adoption Process," *Rural Sociology*, 22(2):166–168. RS(E)

Bearden, William O., Stephen E. Calcich, Richard Netemeyer, and Jesse E. Teel (1985), "An Exploratory Investigation of Consumer Innovativeness and Internal Influences," Paper presented at the Association for Consumer Research, Las Vegas. MR(E)

Becker, Daniel M., and others (1985), "Decision to Adopt New Medical Technology: A Case Study of Thrombolytic Therapy," *Social Science and Medicine*, 21:291–298. U(E)

Becker, Marshall H. (1970a), "Factors Affecting Diffusion of Innovations among Health Professional," *American Journal of Public Health*, 60:294–305. PH(E)

—— (1970b), "Sociometric Location and Innovativeness: Reformulation and Extension of the Diffusion Model," *American Sociological Review*, 35:262–282. PH(E)

Bee, E.R. (1988), "How to Improve Economic Development Advertising: Lessons from the Diffusion of Innovations," *Economic Development Review*, 6(2):47–52. U(N)

Begossi, Alpina, and Peter J. Richerson (1991), "The Diffusion of 'Lambreta': An Artificial Lure, at Buzios Island (Brazil)," *MAST*, 4(2):87–103. A(E)

Belasco, David Berton (1989), *Adoption of Community Water Systems: An Area Study in Three Villages in Muhafzat Kofr-Shaykh, Egypt*, Ph.D. Thesis, University of Denver. PS(E)

Benjamin, Gerald (1985), "The Diffusion of Executive Power in American State Constitutions: Tenure and Tenure Limitations," *Publius*, 15:71–84. PS(E)

Benvignati, A.M. (1982a), "Interfirm Adoption of Capital Goods Invention," *Review of Economics and Statistics*, 64:330–335. GE(E)

—— (1982b), "The Relationship Between the Origin and Diffusion of Industrial Innovation," *Economics*, 49:313–323. GE(E)

Berelson, Bernard, and Ronald Freedman (1964), "A Study in Fertility Control," *Scientific American*, 210(5):29–37. PH(E)

Berggren, Ulf (1985), "CT Scanning and Ultrasonography: A Comparison of Two Lines of Development and Dissemination," *Research Policy*, 14:213–223. MR(E)

Berman, Paul, and Edward W. Pauley (1975), *Federal Programs Supporting Educational Change, Volume 2: Factors Affecting Change Agent Projects*, Santa Monica, California, Rand Corporation, Report. E(E)

Berman, Paul, and Milbrey W. McLaughlin (1974), *Federal Programs Supporting Edu-*

cational Change, Volume 1: Model of Educational Change, Santa Monica, California, Rand Corporation, Report. E(E)

—————— (1975), *Federal Programs Supporting Educational Change, Volume 4: The Findings in Review*, Santa Monica, California, Rand Corporation, Report. E(E)

—————— (1978), *Federal Program Supporting Educational Change, Volume 8: Implementing and Sustaining Innovations*, Santa Monica, California, Rand Corporation. Report. E(E)

Berman, Paul, and others (1975), *Federal Program Supporting Educational Change, Volume 5: Executive Summary*, Santa Monica, California, Rand Corporation, Report. E(E)

—————— (1977), *Federal Programs Supporting Educational Change, Volume 7: Factors Affecting Implementation and Continuation*, Santa Monica, California, Rand Corporation, Report. E(E)

Bertrand, Jane T., Roberto Santiso, Stephen H. Linder, and Maria Antonieta Pienda (1987), "Evaluation of a Communication Program to Increase Adoption of Vasectomy in Guatemala," *Studies in Family Planning*, 18(6):361–370. PH(E)

Bhola, H.S. (1988), "The CLER Model of Innovation Diffusion, Planned Change, and Development: A Conceptual Update and Applications," *Knowledge in Society*, 4(1):55–56. E(N)

Bigoness, William T., and William D. Perreault, Jr. (1981), "A Conceptual Paradigm and Approach for the Study of Innovators," *Academy of Management Journal*, 24:68–82. MR(E)

Bingham, Richard D., Patricia K. Freeman, and Claire L. Felbinger (1981), "Toward an Understanding of Innovation Adoption: An Empirical Application of the Theoretical Contributions of Downs and Mohr," Milwaukee, University of Wisconsin, Report to the National Science Foundation. PS(E)

—————— (1984), "Innovation Adoption in an Urban Setting: An Application of Down's and Mohr's Methodological Prescriptions," *Knowledge*, 5(3):309–338. PS(E)

Bingham, Richard D., and John P. Frendreis (1978), "Innovation Characteristics and the Adoption of Zero-Base Budgeting: Agreement and Conflict in City Administration," Paper presented at the Midwest Political Science Association, Chicago. PS(E)

Bishop, Rowland, and C. Milton Coughenour (1964), *Discontinuance of Farm Innovations*, Columbus, Ohio State University, Department of Agricultural Economics and Rural Sociology, Mimeo Bulletin AE 361. RS(E)

Blakely, Craig, and others (1983), *Salient Processes in the Dissemination of Social Technologies*, East Lansing, Michigan State University, Report to the National Science Foundation. P(E)

—————— (1987), "The Fidelity-Adaptation Debate: Implications for the Implementation of Public Sector Social Programs," *American Journal of Community Psychology*, 15(3):253–268. P(E)

Blum, Abraham (1989), *What Can Be Learned from a Comparison of Two Agricultural Knowledge Systems? The Case of the Netherlands and Israel*, Jerusalem, Hebrew University of Jerusalem, Faculty of Agriculture, Research Report. RS(E)

Bohlin, Eric (1990), "Investment Appraisals and Diffusion of New Communications Technology: The Case of Swedish Telecom," Paper presented at the International Conference of the International Telecommunication Society, Venice. U(E)

Boist, M. (1987), "Convergence Revisited: The Codification and Diffusion of Knowledge in a British and Japanese Firm," *Journal of Management Studies*, 159–190. MR(E)

Bolton, William T. (1983), "Perceptual Factors that Influence the Adoption of Videotex Technology: Results of Channel 2000 Field Tests," *Journal of Broadcasting*, 27:141–153. C(E)

Boker, Fred (1987), "A Stochastic First-Purchase Diffusion Model: A Counting Process Approach," *Journal of Marketing Research*, 24:64–73. MR(E)

Bordenave, Juan Diaz (1976), "Communication of Agricultural Innovations in Latin America: The Need for New Models," *Communication Research*, 3(2):135–154. C(N)

Bose, Santi Priya (1964), "The Diffusion of a Farm Practice in Indian Villages," *Rural Sociology*, 29:53–66. RS(E)

Bouckaert, A., and X. Leroy (1985), "The Diffusion of a Vanguard Technique: The Case of Nuclear Medicine in Belgium," *Social Science and Medicine*, 21:1119–1224. U(E)

Bowers, Raymond V. (1937), "The Direction of Intra-Societal Diffusion," *American Sociological Review*, 2:826–836. ES(E)

―――― (1938), "Differential Intensity of Intra-Societal Diffusion," *American Sociological Review*, 3:21–31. ES(E)

Boyd, John P. (1980), "Three Orthogonal Models of Adoption of Agricultural Innovation," *Rural Sociology*, 45:309–324. RS(E)

Brancheau, James C., and James C. Wetherbe (1990), "The Adoption of Spreadsheet Software: Testing Innovation Diffusion Theory in the Context of End-User Computing," *Information Systems Research*, 1(2):115–143. MR(E)

Brenner, Donald J., and Robert A. Logan (1980), "Some Considerations in the Diffusion of Medical Technologies: Medical Information Systems," in Dan Nimmo (eds.), *Communication Yearbook 4*, New Brunswick, New Jersey, Transaction. C(E)

Bresnahan, Timothy P., and Paul A. David (1985), "The Diffusion of Automatic Teller Machines Across U. S. Banks," Paper presented at the International Conference on the Diffusion of Innovations, Venice, Italy. GE(E)

Bretschneider, Stuart I., and Barry Bozeman (1986), "Adaptive Diffusion Models for the Growth of Robotics in New York State Industry," *Technological Forecasting and Social Change*, 30:111–121. MR(E)

Bretschneider, Stuart I., and Vijay Mahajan (1980), "Adaptive Technological Substitution Models," *Technological Forecasting and Social Change*, 18:129–139. MR(E).

Brett, Judy L. Luckenbil (1989), "Organizational Integrative Mechanisms and Adoption of Innovations by Nurses," *Nursing Research*, 38(2):105–110. O(E)

Brewer, M. (1985), "Experimental Research and Social Policy: Must It Be Rigor Versus Relevance?" *Journal of Social Issues*, 41(4):159–176.

Broddason, Thorbjorn, Akiba A. Cohen, Walter Gantz, and Bradley S. Greenberg (1987), "News Diffusion of the Palme Assassination among Journalists in Iceland, Israel, and the U.S.," *European Journal of Communication*, 2:211–226. C(E)

Brown, Jacqueline Johnson, and Peter H. Reingen (1987), "Social Ties and Word-of-Mouth: Referral Behavior," *Journal of Consumer Research*, 14:350–362. MR(E)

Brown, Lawrence A. (1981), *Innovation Diffusion: A New Perspective*, New York, Methuen. G(N)

Brown, Lawrence A., and others (1979), "Innovation Diffusion and Development in a

Third World Setting: The Cooperative Movement in Sierra Leone," *Social Science Quarterly*, 60:249–268. G(E)

Browning, William C., and others (1984), "Diffusion of Innovations: Computer Technology in a Hospital Pharmacy," *American Journal of Hospital Pharmacy*, 41:2343–2347. U(E)

Bryson, J., and W. Roering (1989), "Mobilizing Innovation Efforts: The Case of Government Strategic Planning," in Andrew H. Van de Ven, Harold A. Angle, and M. Scott Poole (eds.), *Research on the Management of Innovation: The Minnesota Studies*, Cambridge, MA, Ballinger/Harper & Row. MR(E)

Buchner, Bradley J. (1988), "Some Control and the Diffusion of Modern Telecommunications Technologies: A Cross-National Study," *American Sociological Review*, 53:446–453. GS(E)

Bultena, Gordon L., and Eric O. Hoiberg (1983), "Factors Affecting Farmers' Adoption of Conservation Tillage," *Journal of Soil and Water Conservation*, 38(2):281–283. RS(E)

Burkhardt, Marlene E., and Daniel J. Brass (1990), "Changing Patterns of Change: The Effects of a Technology on Social Network Structure and Power," *Administrative Science Quarterly*, 35:104–127. MR(E)

Burstein, M.L. (1984), "Diffusion of Knowledge-Based Products: Application to Developing Economics," *Economic Inquiry*, 22:612–633. GE(E)

Burt, Ronald S. (1980), "Innovation as a Structural Interest: Rethinking the Impact of Network Position on Innovation Adoption," *Social Networks*, 2:327–355. GS(N)

———— (1987), "Social Contagion and Innovation: Cohesion Versus Structural Equivalence," *American Journal of Sociology*, 92:1287–1335. GS(E)

Buttel, Fred, and F.L. Swanson (1986), "Soil and Water Conservation: A Farm Structural and Public Policy Context," in S. Lovejoy and T. Napier (eds.), *Conserving Soil: Insights from Socio-Economic Research*, Ankeny, IA, Soil Conservation Society of America. RS(E)

Caffarella, Elizabeth A. (1982), "Predicting the Diffusability of Educational Innovations," *Educational Technology*, 22:16–18. E(E)

Caldeira, Gregory A. (1985), "Constitutional Change in America: Dynamics of Ratification under Article V," *Publius*, 15(4):29–49. PS(E)

Calogero, G. (1984), "La Diffusion de l'innovation et le Role des Participations de l'elat en Italie," *Annals of Public and Cooperative Economy*, 54:395–411. U(N)

Campbell, Bruce M. (1988), "The Diffusion of Vetches in Medieval England," *Economic History Review*, 41:193–208. O(E)

Cancian, Frank (1967), "Stratification and Risk-Taking: A Theory Tested on Agricultural Innovation," *American Sociological Review*, 32:912–927. A(E)

———— (1976a), "Who's to Blame?" *Psychology Today*, 8:99–104. A(E)

———— (1976b), "Reply to Morrison, Kumar, Rogers, and Fliegel," *American Sociology Review*, 41:919–923. A(E)

———— (1977), "The Innovator's Situation: Upper-Middle-Class Conservatism in Agricultural Communities," Irvine, University of California, School of Social Science, Working Paper 132. A(E)

———— (1979a), "A Useful Distinction between Risk and Uncertainity," Irvine, University of California, School of Social Science, Report, p. 73. A(N)

———— (1979b), *The Innovator's Situation: Upper-Middle-Class Conservatism in Agricultural Communities*, Stanford, California, Stanford University Press. A(E)

———— (1980), "Risk and Uncertanity in Agricultural Decision-Making," in Peggy F. Bartlett (ed.), *Agricultural Decision-Making*, New York, Academic Press. A(E)

———— (1981), "Community of Reference in Rural Stratification Research," *Rural Sociology*, 46:626–645. A(E)

Canon, Bradley C., and Lawrence Baum (1981), "Patterns of Adoption of Tort Law Innovations: An Application of Diffusion Theory to Judicial Doctrine," *American Political Science Review*, 75:975–987. PS(E)

Caplan, Nathan, and Stephen D. Nelson (1973), "On Being Useful: The Nature and Consequences of Psychological Research on Social Problems," *American Psychologist*, 28:199–211.

Capon, N. (1980), "International Diffusion of Corporate and Strategic Planning Practice," *Columbia Journal of World Business*, 15:5–13. MR(E)

Carboni, Silvana M. (1984), *The Adoption and Continued Use of Consumer Farm Technologies: A Test of a Diffusion Farm Structure Model*, Ph.D. Thesis, Columbus, Ohio State University. RS(E)

Carey, John, and Mitchell L. Moss (1985), "The Diffusion of New Telecommunication Technologies," *Telecommunication Policy*, 6:145–158. O(E)

Carlson, John E., and Don A. Dillman (1983), "Influence of Kinship Arrangements on Farmer Innovativeness," *Rural Sociology*, 48(2):183–200. RS(E)

———— (1988), "The Influence of Farmers' Mechanical Skill on the Development and Adoption of a New Agricultural Practice," *Rural Sociology*, 53(2):235–245. RS(E)

Carlson, Richard O. (1965), *Adoption of Educational Innovations*, Eugene, University of Oregon, Center for the Advanced Study of Educational Administration. E(E)

Carroci, Noreen M. (1985), "Diffusion of Information about Cyanide-Laced Tylenol," *Journalism Quarterly*, 62:630–633. C(E)

Carter, Thomas (1994), *The Process of Change: Tools for the Change Agent*, Anand, India, National Dairy Development Board, Report. O(N)

Chaffee, Steven H., and Connie Roser (1986), "Involvement and the Consistency of Knowledge, Attitudes, and Behaviors," in Charles Berger and Steven H. Chaffee (eds.), *Handbook of Communication Science*, Newbury Park, CA, Sage, pp. 817–846. C(E)

Chakrabarti, Alok K., and Juergen Hauschildt (1989), "The Division of Labor in Innovation Management," *R&D Management*, 19(2):161–169. MR(N)

Chamala, Shankariah, C. Milton Coughenour, and Ken J. Keith (1983), *Study of Conservation Cropping on the Darling Downs: A Basis for Extension Programming*, Queensland, Australia, University of Queensland, Report to the Department of Agriculture. RS(E)

Chamala, Shankariah, Ken J. Keith, and Petrina Quinn (1982), *Adoption of Commercial and Soil Conservation Innovations in Queensland: Information, Exposure, Attitudes, and Actions*, Queensland, Australia, University of Queensland, Report to the Department of Agriculture. RS(E)

Chang, H.J. (1990), *An Examination of the Diffusion of Innovations: A Mathematical Test of the Adoption and Disadoption Process*, Ph.D. Thesis, Buffalo, State University of New York at Buffalo. C(E)

Charters, W.W., Jr., and Roland S. Pellegrin (1972), "Barriers to the Innovation Process: Four Case Studies of Differentiated Staffing," *Educational Agricultural Quarterly*, 9:3–4. E(E)

Chatman, Elfreda A. (1986), "Diffusion Theory: A Review and Test of a Conceptual

Model in Information Diffusion," *Journal of the American Society for Information Science*, 37(6):377–386. O(E)

Cheney, George, Barbara L. Block, and Beth S. Gorden (1986), "Perceptions of Innovativeness and Communication about Innovations: A Study of Three Types of Service Organizations," *Communication Quarterly*, 34(3):213–230. MR(E)

Chowdhury, Tawfiq E. (1984), "Technological Diffusion in Agriculture: Theories and Evidence," *Bangladesh Development Studies*, 12:75–85. RS(E)

Clark, Gill (1984), *Innovation Diffusion: Contemporary Geographical Approaches*, Norwich, CT, Geo Books. G(E)

—— (1985), "Policy Diffusion and Program Scope: Research Directions," *Publius*, 15:61–70. PS(E)

Clark, Peter (1987), *Anglo American Innovation*, Berlin, Walter de Gruyter. MR(E)

Clark, Peter, and Neil Staunton (1989), *Innovation in Technology and Organization*, New York, Routledge. MR(E)

Clawson, David L., and Don R. Hoy (1987), "Nealtican, Mexico: A Peasant Community that Rejected the Green Revolution," *American Journal of Economics and Sociology*, 38:371–387. AE(E)

Cliff, A.D., P. Haggett, and R. Graham (1983), "Reconstitution of the Diffusion Process at Local Scales: Measles Epidemic in Iceland," *Journal of Historical Geography*, 9:29–46, 347–368. G(E)

Cliff, A.D., P. Haggett, J.K. Ord, and G. R. Versey (1981), *Spatial Diffusion: An Historical Geography of Epidemics in an Island Community*, New York, Cambridge University Press. G(E)

Cohn, S.F., and R.M. Turyn (1980), "The Structure of the Firm and the Adoption of Process Innovations," *IEEE Transactions on Engineering Management*, EM-27, 4:98–102. MR(E)

—— (1984), "Organizational Structure, Decision-Making Procedures, and the Adoption of Innovation," *IEEE Transaction on Engineering Management*, EM-31(4):154–161. MR(E)

Cohen, Wesley M., and Daniel A. Levinthel (1990), "Absorptive Capacity: A New Perspective on Learning and Innovation," *Administrative Science Quarterly*, 35:128–152. MR(E)

Coleman, James S. (1958), "Relational Analysis: The Study of Social Organizations with Survey Methods," *Human Organization*, 14:28–36.

Coleman, James S., Elihu Katz, and Herbert Menzel (1957), "The Diffusion of an Innovation Among Physicians," *Sociometry*, 20:253–270. PH(E)

—— (1959), "Social Processes in Physicians' Adoption of a New Drug," *Journal of Chronic Diseases*, 9:1–19. PH(E)

—— (1966), *Medical Innovation: A Diffusion Study*, New York, Bobbs-Merrill, pp. 25, 30–32, 52, 59, 79–92, 95–112, 119, 126. PH(E)

Comroe, Julius H., Jr. (1977), *Retrosprectoscope: Insights into Medical Discovery*, Menlo Park, CA, Von Gehr Press.

Coombs, Jeanne A., Jacob B. Shaersen, Everett M. Rogers, and Margaret E. Drolette (1981), "The Transfer of Preventive Health Technologies to Schools: A Focus on Implementation," *Social Science and Medicine*, 15:789–799. PH(E)

Cooper, Randolph B., and Robert W. Zmud (1990), "Information Technology Implementation Research: A Technological Diffusion Approach," *Management Science*, 36(2):123–139. MR(E)

Cooper, R.G. (1979), "The Dimensions of Industrial New Product Success and Failure," *Journal of Marketing*, 43:93–103. MR(E)

———— (1983), "A Process Model for Industrial New Product Development," *IEEE Transactions on Engineering Management*, EM-30(1):2–11. MR(E)

Cooper, R.G. (1988), "Predevelopment Activities Determine New Product Success," *Industrial Marketing Management*, 17:237–247. MR(E)

Cooper, R.G., and E.J. Kleinschmidt (1987), "Success Factors in Product Innovation," *Industrial Marketing Management*, 16:215–223. MR(E)

Copeland, Duncan G., and James L. McKenney (1988), "Airlines Reservations Systems: Lessons from History," *MIS Quarterly*, 353–370. MR(E)

Copp, James H. (1958), "Toward Generalization in Farm Practice Research," *Rural Sociology*, 23(2):104–111. RS(E)

Copp, James H., Maurice L. Sill, and Emory J. Brown (1958), "The Function of Information Sources in the Farm Practice Adoption Process," *Rural Sociology*, 23:70, 146–157. RS(E)

Corbet, Philip S. (1981), "Non-Entomological Impediments to the Adoption of Integrated Pest Management," *Protection Ecology*, 3:183–202. O(E)

Cosmas, Stephen C., and Jagdish N. Seth (1980), "Identification of Opinion Leaders Across Culture: An Assessment for the Use of Diffusion of Innovations and Ideas," *Journal of International Business Studies*, 11:66–73. MR(E)

Coughenour, C. Milton (1955), "The Problem of Reliability of Adoption Data in Survey Research," *Rural Sociology*, 30:184–203. RS(E)

Coughlan, Anne T., and Shlomo Kalish (1984), "Developing and Marketing New Products in Innovative Environments over Time: An Expository Survey," Working Paper, Rochester, NY, University of Rochester, Graduate School of Management. MR(E)

Cowan, Ruth Schwartz (1985), "How the Refrigerator Got Its Hum," in Donald Mackenzie and Judy Wajeman (eds.), *The Social Shaping of Technology: How The Refrigerator Got Its Hum*, Philadelphia, Open University Press, pp. 202–218. O(E)

Crane, Diana (1972), *Invisible Colleges*, University of Chicago Press, pp. 67, 74, 161, 188. GS(E)

Crouch, Bruce R. (1981), "Innovation and Farm Development: A Multidimensional Model," in Bruce R. Crouch and Shankariah Chamala (eds.), *Extension Education and Rural Development, Volume 1, International Experience in Communication and Innovation*, New York, Wiley. RS(E)

Crouch, Bruce R., and Graeme Payne (1984), "Value Orientations and the Adoption of Sheep Management Practices in the Arid Zone of Queensland," *Rural Sociologist*, 4:306–313. RS(E)

Curley, Kathleen F., and Lee L. Gremillion (1983), "The Role of the Champion in DSS Implementation," *Information and Management*, 6:203–209. MR(E)

Curry, Barbara K. (1992), *Instituting Enduring Innovations: Achieving Continuity of Change in Higher Education*, Washington, D.C., George Washington University, School of Education and Human Development, ASHE/ERIC Higher Education Report 7. E(E)

Czepiel, John A. (1975), "Patterns of Interorganizational Communications and the Diffusion of a Major Technological Innovation in a Competitive Industrial Community," *Academy of Management Journal*, 18(1):6–24. MR(E)

Daft, Richard L. (1982), "Bureaucratic Versus Non-Bureaucratic Structure and the Process of Innovation and Change," *Research in Sociology of Organizations*, 1:129–166. MR(E)

Damanpour, Fariborz (1987), "The Adoption of Technological, Administrative, and Ancillary Innovations: Impact of Organizational Factors," *Journal of Management*, 13(4):675–688. MR(E)

——— (1988), "Innovation Type, Radicalness, and the Adoption Process," *Communication Research*, 15(5):545–567. MR(E)

Damanpour, Fariborz, and William M. Evan (1984), "Organizational Innovation and Performance: The Problem of 'Organizational Lag'," *Administrative Science Quarterly*, 29:392–409. MR(E)

Daniels, Mark R., and Robert E. Darcy (1985), "As Time Goes By: The Arrested Diffusion of the Equal Rights Amendment," *Publius*, 15:51–60. PS(E)

Danko, William D., and James M. MacLachlan (1983), "Research to Accelerate the Diffusion of a New Innovation: The Case of Personal Computers," *Journal of Advertising Research*, 23(3):39–43. MR(E)

Danziger, James N. (1977), "Computers, Local Governments and the Litany to EDP," *Public Administration Review*, 37:28–37. PS(E)

D.A.R.E. America (1990), *D.A.R.E. Will Teach Over 4.5 Million Children Drug Resistance Skills in 1990*, Los Angeles, Brochure.

Dasgupta, Satadal (1989), *Diffusion of Agricultural Innovations in Village India*, New Delhi, Wiley Eastern. GS(N)

David, Paul A. (1986a), "Clio and the Economy of QWERTY," *American Economic Review*, 75(2):332–337. GE(E)

——— (1986b), "Technology Diffusion, Public Policy, and Industrial Competitiveness," in National Academy of Science (ed.), *The Positive Sum Strategy: Harnessing Technology for Economic Growth*, Washington, D.C., National Academy Press. GE(E)

David, Paul A., and Trond E. Olsen (1986), "Equilibrium Dynamics of Diffusion When Incremental Technological Innovations Are Forseen," Paper presented at the International Conference on the Diffusion of Innovations, Venice. GE(E)

Davies, S. (1979), *The Diffusion of Process Innovations*, New York, Cambridge University Press. G(N)

Davies, S. W. (1984), "Interfirm Diffusion of Process Innovations," *European Economic Review*, 12:299–378. G(E)

Davis, Fred D., Richard P. Bagozzi, and Paul R. Warshaw (1989), "User Acceptance of Computer Technology: A Comparison of Two Theoretical Models," *Management Science*, 35(8):982–1003. MR(E)

Day, Diana L. (1994), "Raising Radicals: Different Processes for Championing Innovative Corporate Ventures," *Organization Science*. MR(E)

Day, Ralph L., and Paul A. Herbig (1990), "How the Diffusion of Industrial Innovations Is Different from New Retail Products," *Industrial Marketing Management*, 19:261–266. MR(E)

de la Paz, Ponciano M. (1980), *Administrators in Land-Grant Colleges of Agriculture: An*

Analysis of Their Characteristics and Innovativeness, Ph.D. Thesis, Los Banos, California State Polytechnic University. E(E)

Dearing, James W. (1993), "Rethinking Technology Transfer," *International Journal of Technology Management*, 8:1–8. C(N)

Dearing, James W., and Gary Meyer (1994), "An Exploratory Tool for Predicting Adoption Decisions," *Science Communication*, 16(1):43–57. C(E)

Dearing, James W., Gary Meyer, and Jeff Kazmierczak (1994), "Portraying the New: Communication Between University Innovators and Potential Users," *Science Communication*, 16(1):11–42. C(E)

Dearing, James W., and Everett M. Rogers (in press), *Agenda-Setting*, Newbury Park, CA, Sage. C(E)

Deber, Raisa B., Gail G. Thompson, and Peggy Leatt (1988), "Technological Acquisition in Canada: Control in a Regulated Market," *International Journal of Technology Assessment in Health Care*, 4:185–206. PS(E)

DeFleur, Melvin (1987a), "The Growth and Decline of Research on the Diffusion of News, 1945–1985," *Communication Research*, 14(1):109–130. C(N)

—— (1987b), "Diffusing Information," *Society*, 25:72–81. C(E)

Dekluyver, Cornelis A. (1982), "A Comparative Analysis of the Bass and Weibull New Product Growth Models for Consumer Durables," *New Zealand Journal of Operations Research*, 10:99–130. MR(E)

Delberq, A., and John Pierce (1978), "Innovation in Professional Organizations," *Administration in Social Work*, 2:411–424. MR(E)

Derksen, Linda, and John Gartrell (1993), "The Social Context of Recycling," *American Sociological Review*, 58:434–442. GS(E)

Deutchmann, Paul J. (1963), "The Mass Media in an Underdeveloped Village," *Journalism Quarterly*, 40(1):27–35. C(E)

Deutschmann, Paul J., and Wayne A. Danielson (1960), "Diffusion of Knowledge of the Major News Story," *Journalism Quarterly*, 37:345–355. C(E)

Deutchmann, Paul J., and Orlando Fals Borda (1962a), *La Comunicacíon de las Ideas entre los Campesinos Colombianos*, Bogotá, Universidad Nacional de Colombia, Monografias Sociológicas 14. C(E)

—— (1962b), *Communication and Adoption Patterns in an Andean Village*, San José, Costa Rica, Programa Interamericano de Informacíon Popular, Report, p. 33. C(E)

Deutschmann, Paul J., and A. Eugene Havens (1965), "Discontinuances: A Relatively Uninvestigated Aspect of Diffusion," Unpublished Paper, Madison, University of Wisconsin, Department of Rural Sociology. C(E)

Dewar, Robert D., and Jane E. Dutton (1986), "The Adoption of Radical and Incremental Innovation: An Empirical Analysis," *Management Science*, 32(11):1422–1433. MR(E)

Dewees, Christopher M., and Glen R. Hawkes (1988), "Technical Innovation in the Pacific Coast Trawler Fishery: The Effects of Fishermen's Characteristics and Perceptions of Adoption Behavior," *Human Organization*, 47(3):224–234. O(E)

Dholakia, Rubi Roy (1984), "A Macromarketing Perspective on Social Marketing: The Case of Family Planning in India," *Journal of Macromarketing*, 4:53–61. MR(N)

Dickerson, Mary Dee, and James W. Gentry (1983), "Characteristics of Adopters and Non-Adopters of Home Computers," *Journal of Consumer Research*, 10:225–235. MR(E)

Dickmann, Andreas (1989), "Diffusion and Survival Models for the Process of Entry into Marriages," *Journal of Mathematical Sociology*, 14:31–44. GS(E)

Dill, David D., and Charles P. Friedman (1979), "An Analysis of a Framework for Research on Innovation and Change in Higher Education," *Review of Educational Research*, 49(3):411–435. E(N)

Dimit, Robert M. (1954), *Diffusion and Adoption of Approved Farm Practices in 11 Countries in Southwest Virginia*, Ph.D. Thesis, Ames, Iowa State University. RS(E)

Dixon, Robert (1980), "Hybrid Corn Revisited," *Econometrica*, 48(6):1451–1461. GE(E)

Dockner, Engelbert, and Steffen Jorgensen (1988a), "Optimal Advertising Policies for Diffusion Models of New Product Innovations in Monopolistic Situations," *Marketing Science*, 34(1):119–130. MR(E)

———— (1988b), "Optimal Pricing Strategies for New Products in Dynamic Oligopolies," *Marketing Science*, 7:315–334. MR(E)

Doctors, Samuel I. (1981), *Technological Transfer by State and Local Government*, Cambridge, O.G. & H. Publishers. MR(N)

Dodd, Stuart C. (1955), "Diffusion Is Predictable," *American Sociological Review*, 20:349–396. GS(E)

Dollar, David (1986), "Technological Innovation, Capital Mobility, and the Product Cycle in North-South Trade," *American Economic Review*, 76:177–190. GE(E)

Dorf, Richard C., and Kirby K.F. Worthington (1987), "Models for Commercialization of Technology from Universities and Research Laboratories," *Journal of Technology Transfer*, 12(1):1–8. MR(N)

Dornblaser, B.M., T. Lin, and Andrew H. Van de Ven (1989), "Innovation Outcomes, Learning, and Action Loops," in Andrew H. Van de Ven, H.A. Angel, and M. Scott Poole (eds.), *Research on the Management of Innovation: The Minnesota Studies*, New York, Ballinger/Harper & Row. MR(E)

Dosi, Giovanni (1990), "Finance, Innovation and Industrial Change," *Journal of Economic Behavior and Organization*, 13:299–319. GE(E)

Downs, George W., Jr., and Lawrence B. Mohr (1976), "Conceptual Issues in the Study of Innovations," *Administrative Science Quarterly*, 21:700–714. PS(E)

Drimmond, Michael F. (1987), "Economic Evaluation and the Rational Diffusion and Use of Health Technology," *Health Policy*, 7:309–324. U(E)

Duff, Robert W., and William T. Liu (1975), "The Significance of Heterophilous Structure in Communication Flows," *Philippine Quarterly of Culture and Society*, 3:159–175. PH(E)

Dumaine, Brian (December 5, 1993), "Payoff from the New Management," *Fortune*, 128:103–104, 108, 110. O(E)

Dunn, William N. (1981), "The Two-Communities Metaphor and Models of Knowledge Use: An Exploratory Case Survey," *Knowledge*, 1(4):515–536. PS(E)

Duric, D.A., and M.L. Phillips (1988), "Diffusion of an Innovation: Adoption of MRI," *Radiology Technology*, 59:239–241. U(E)

Dutton, William H. (1981), "The Rejection of an Innovation: The Political Environment of a Computer-Based Model," *Systems Objectives Solutions*, 1:179–201. C(E)

Dutton, William H., Everett M. Rogers, and Suk-Ho Jun (1987), "Diffusion and Social Impacts of Personal Computers," *Communication Research*, 14(2):219–250. C(N)

Dvorak, August, and others (1936), *Typewriting Behavior*, New York, American.

Easingwood, Christopher J. (1987), "Early Product Life-Cycle Forms for Infrequently Purchased Major Products," *International Journal of Research in Marketing*, 4(1):3–9. MR(E)

—— (1988), "Product Life-Cycle Patterns for New Industrial Products," *R&D Management*, 18(1):23–32. MR(E)

—— (1989), "An Analogical Approach to the Long-Term Forecasting of Major New Product Sales," *International Journal of Forecasting*, 5:69–82. MR(E)

Easingwood, Christopher J., Vijay Mahajan, and Eitan Muller (1981), "A Non-Symmetric Responding Logistic Model for Technological Substitution," *Technological Forecasting and Social Change*, 20:199–213. MR(E)

—— (1983), "A Nonuniform Influence Innovation Diffusion Model of New Product Acceptance," *Marketing Science*, 2(3):273–296. MR(E)

Ebadi, Yar M., and James M. Utterback (1984), "The Effects of Communication on Technological Innovation," *Management Science*, 30(5):572–585. MR(E)

Edquist, Charles, and Staffan Jacobsson (1983), *Flexible Automation: The Global Diffusion of New Technology in the Engineering Industry*, Oxford, Basil Blackwell. MR(E)

Eisenberg, Eric M. (1984), "Ambiguity as Strategy in Organizational Communication," *Communication Monographs*, 51:227–242. C(N)

—— (1990), "Jamming: Transcendence Through Organizing," *Communication Research*, 17(2):139–164. C(N)

Eliashberg, Jehoshua, and Rabikar Chatterjee (1986), "Stochastic Issues in Innovation Diffusion Models," in Vijay Mahajan and Yoram Wind (eds.), *Innovation Diffusion Models of New Product Acceptance*, Cambridge, MA: Ballinger. MR(E)

Eliashberg, Jehoshua, and Abel P. Jeuland (1986), "The Impact of Competitive Entry in a Developing Market upon Dynamic Pricing Strategies," *Marketing Science*, 5:20–36. MR(E)

Elkin, Stephen L. (1983), "Towards a Contextual Theory of Innovation," *Policy Sciences*, 15:367–387. PS(N)

Elliot, James Brian (1990), *HDTV: A Case Study of Early Adopters in the Diffusion of a New Technological Innovation*, M.A. Thesis, Waco, Texas, Baylor University. C(E)

Emrick, John A., and others (1977), *Evaluation of the National Diffusion Network, Volume 1: Findings and Recommendations*, Menlo Park, California, Stanford Research Institute, Report, pp. 116–119. E(E)

Ennett, Susan T., Nancy S. Tobler, Christopher L. Ringwalt, and Robert L. Flewelling (1994), "How Effective Is Drug Abuse Resistance Education? A Meta-Analysis of Project D.A.R.E. Outcome Evaluations," *American Journal of Public Health*, 84(9):1394–1401. PH(N)

Entwisle, Barbara, and John B. Casterline (1989), "Villages as Context for Contraceptive Behavior in Rural Egypt," *American Sociological Review*, 54:1019–1034. GS(E)

Ericksen, Eugene P., and others (1980), "The Cultivation of the Soil as a Moral Directive: Population Growth, Family Ties, and the Maintenance of Community among the Old Order Amish," *Rural Sociology*, 45:49–58. RS(E)

Ettlie, John E. (1980), "Adequacy of Stage Models for Decisions on Adoption of Innovation," *Psychological Reports*, 46:991–995. MR(N)

—— (1983), "Organizational Policy and Innovation Among Suppliers to the Food Processing Sector," *Academy of Management Journal*, 26:27–44. MR(E)

Ettlie, John E., and Robert D. O'Keefe (1982), "Innovative Attitudes, Values, and Intentions in Organizations," *Journal of Management Studies*, 19(2):163–182. MR(E)

Ettlie, John E., and D. B. Vellanga (1979), "Adoption Time Period for Some Transportation Innovations," *Management Science*, 26:1086–1094. MR(E)

Ettlie, John E., W.P. Bridges, and R.D. O'Keefe (1984), "Organization Strategy and Structural Differences for Radical vs. Incremental Innovation," *Management Science*, 30:682–695. MR(E)

Eulau, Heinz, and Jonathan W. Siegel (1981), "Social Network Analysis and Political Behavior: A Feasibility Study," *Western Political Quarterly*, 34(4):499–509. PS(E)

Evans, Patric T. (1988), "Designing Agroforestry Innovations to Increase Their Adoptability: A Case from Paraguay," *Journal of Rural Studies*, 4(1):45–85. U(E)

Eveland, J.D. (1979), "Issues in Using the Concept of 'Adoption of Innovation,'" Paper presented at the American Society for Public Administration, Baltimore. O(N)

——— (1986), "Diffusion, Technology Transfer and Implications: Thinking and Talking about Change," *Knowledge*, 8(2):303–322. O(N)

Eveland, J.D., and others (1977), *The Innovative Process in Public Organizations*, Ann Arbor, University of Michigan, Department of Journalism, Mimeo Report. C(E)

Fairweather, George W., David H. Sanders, and Louis G. Tornatzky (1974), *Creating Change in Mental Health Organizations*, New York, Pergamon Press. P(E)

Fals Borda, Orlando (1960), *Facts and Theory of Socio-Cultural Change in a Rural System*, Bogotá, Universidad Nacional de Colombia, Monographias Sociológicas 2 bis. RS(E)

Falcone, S. (1989), "Innovation in Public Organization," Unpublished Paper, Syracuse, New York, Syracuse University, Maxwell School of Citizenship and Public Affairs. PS(E)

Farrell, Joseph, and Garth Saloner (1985), "Standardization, Compatability, and Innovation," *Rand Journal of Economics*, 16(1):70–83. G(N)

Feder, Gershon (1980), "Farm Size, Risk Aversion, and the Adoption of New Technology under Uncertainty," *Oxford Economic Papers*, 32:263–283. GE(N)

——— (1982), "Adoption of Interrelated Agricultural Innovations: Complementarity and the Impacts of Risk, Scale, and Credit," *American Journal of Agricultural Economics*, 64(2):94–101. AE(E)

Feder, Gershon, and Gerald T. O'Mara (1981), "Farm Size and Diffusion of Green Revolution Technology," *Economic Development and Cultural Change*, 30:59–76. AE(E)

——— (1982), "On Information and Innovation Diffusion: A Bayesian Approach," *American Journal of Agricultural Economics*, 64:145–147. AE(E)

Feder, Gershon, and Roger Slade (1984), "The Acquisition of Information and the Adoption of New Technology," *American Journal of Agricultural Economics*, 66:312–320. AE(E)

——— (1985), "The Role of Public Policy in the Diffusion of Improved Agricultural Technology," *American Journal of Agricultural Economics*, 67:423–428. AE(E)

Feder, Gershon, Richard E. Just, and David Zilberman (1985), "Adoption of Agricultural Innovations in Developing Countries: A Survey," *Economic Development and Cultural Change*, 33:285–298. AE(E)

Feichtinger, Gustav (1982), "Optimal Pricing in a Diffusion Model with Concave Price-Dependent Market Potential," *Operations Research Letters*, 1:236–240. MR(E)

Feick, Lawrence F., and Linda L. Price (1987), "The Market Maven: A Diffuser of Marketplace Information," *Journal of Marketing*, 51:83–97. MR(E)

Fennell, Mary L. (1984), "Synergy, Influence, and Information in the Adoption of Administrative Innovations," *Academy of Management Journal*, 27(1):113–129. MR(E)

Fennell, Mary L., and Richard B. Warnecke (1988), *The Diffusion of Medical Innovations: An Applied Network Analysis*, New York, Plenum Press. PH(E)

Fenny, David (1985), "Neglected Issues in the Diffusion of Health Care Technologies: The Role of Skills and Learning," *International Journal of Technology Assessment in Health Care*, 1:686–692. PH(N)

Ferguson, John H. (1993), "NIH Consensus Conferences: Dissemination and Impact," *Annals of the New York Academy of Sciences*, 703:180–198. PH(N)

Fershtman, Chaim, Vijay Mahajan, and Etian Muller (1990), "Market Share and Pioneering Advantage: A Theoretical Approach," *Management Science*, 37:211–223. MR(E)

Festinger, Leon (1957), *A Theory of Cognitive Dissonance*, Stanford, CA, Stanford University Press.

Filder, Lori A., and J. David Johnson (1984), "Communication and Innovation Implementation," *Academy of Management Review*, 9(4):704–711. MR(E)

Filipick, J. (1983), "Diffusion Equation Model of Slightly Loaded M/M/I Queue," *Operation Research Letters*, 2:134–139. G(N)

Finkelstein, Stan N., and Dana L. Gilbert (1983), "Scientific Evidence and the Abandonment of Medical Technology: A Study of Eight Drugs," Working Paper, Cambridge, Massachusetts Institute of Technology, Sloan School of Management. MR(E)

Fischer, Claude S. (1978), "Urban-to-Rural Diffusion of Opinions in Contemporary America," *American Journal of Sociology*, 84:151–159. GS(E)

——— (1987), "The Revolution in Rural Telephony, 1900–1920," *Journal of Social History*, 21(1):5–26. GS(E)

Fischer, Claude S., and Glenn R. Carroll (1988), "Telephone and Automobile Diffusion in the United States, 1902–1937," *American Journal of Sociology*, 93:1153–1178. GS(E)

Fiske, Emmett Preston (1980), *The College and Its Constituency: Rural and Community Development at the University of California 1875–1895*, Ph.D. Thesis, University of California at Davis. AE(E)

Fliegel, Frederick C. (1993), *Diffusion Research in Rural Sociology: The Record and Prospects for the Future*, Westport, CT, Greenwood Press. RS(N)

Fliegel, Frederick C., and Joseph E. Kilvin (1966a), "Farmers' Perceptions of Farm Practice Attributes," *Rural Sociology*, 31:197–206. RS(E)

——— (1966b), "Attributes of Innovations as Factors in Diffusion," *American Journal of Sociology*, 72(3):235–248. RS(E)

Fliegel, Frederick C., Joseph E. Kivlin, and Gurmeet S. Sekhon (1968), "A Cross-National Comparison of Farmers' Perception of Innovation as Related to Adoption Behavior," *Rural Sociology*, 33:437–499. RS(E)

Flora, June A., with Darius Jatilus, Chris Jackson, and Stephen P. Fortmann (1993), "The Stanford Five-City Heart Disease Prevention Project," in Thomas E. Becker and Everett M. Rogers (eds.), *Organizational Aspects of Health Communication Campaigns: What Works?* Newbury Park, CA, Sage, pp. 101–128. C(E)

Fox, Karen F.A., and Philip Kotler (1980), "The Marketing of Social Causes: The First Ten Years," *Journal of Marketing*, 44:24–33. MR(E)

Foxall, Gordon R., and Christopher G. Haskins (1986), "Cognitive Style and Consumer Innovativeness," *European Journal of Marketing*, 20(3):63–80. MR(E)

Frambach, Ruud T. (1991), *The Diffusion of Innovation: The Influence of Supply-Side Factors*, Netherlands, Tilburg University, Department of Economics, Research Memorandum. MR(N)

—— (1993a), *De Adoptie en Diffusie van Innovaties in de Industriele Markt:Een Empirisch Onderzoek Naar de Verspreiding van Electronic Banking in Nederland*, Ph.D. Thesis, Brabant, Netherlands, Katholeika Universiteit Brabant. MR(E)

—— (1993b), "An Integrated Model of Organizational Adoption and Diffusion of Innovations," *European Journal of Marketing*, 27(5):22–41. MR(N)

Francis, David G., and Everett M. Rogers (1960), "Adoption of a Nonrecommended Innovation: The Grass Incubator," Paper presented at the Rural Sociological Society, University Park, Pennsylvania. RS(E)

Freedman, Ronald (1964), "Sample Surveys for Family Planning Research in Taiwan," *Public Opinion Quarterly*, 28:374–382. PH(E)

Freedman, Ronald, and John Y. Takeshita (1969), *Family Planning in Taiwan*, Princeton, NJ, Princeton University Press. PH(E)

Freedman, Ronald, and others (1964), "Fertility and Family Planning in Taiwan: A Case Study in Demographic Transition," *American Journal of Sociology*, 70:16–27. PH(E)

Freeman, Christopher (1982), *The Economics of Industrial Innovation*, Cambridge, MA, MIT Press. GE(E)

—— (1986), *The Economics of Industrial Innovation*, Cambridge, MA, MIT Press. GE(E)

—— (1988), *Diffusion: The Spread of New Innovation Technology and Finance*, Oxford, England, Basil Blackwell. GE(N)

Freeman, Christopher, and Luc Soete (1986), "Innovation Diffusion and Employment Policies," *Ricerche Economiche*, 40:836–854. GE(E)

Freeman, Patricia K. (1985), "Interstate Communication among State Legislators Regarding Energy Policy Innovation," *Publius*, 15:99–111. G(E)

Freiman, M.P. (1985), "The Rate of Adoption of New Procedures Among Physicians: The Impact of Speciality and Practice Characteristics," *Medical Care*, 23:939–945. U(E)

Frendreis, John P. (1983), "Innovation: A Practice in Search of a Theory, Or So What Does All This Research Mean, Anyway?" *Journal of Urban Affairs*, 5(2):109–123. RS(E)

Frey, R. Scott, and David M. Freeman (1981), "Stratification and Risk Taking in Pakistan: A Reply to Cancian," *Rural Sociology*, 46:645–651. RS(E)

Frey, R. Scott, and others (1979), "Cancian's 'Upper Middle Class Conservatism' Thesis: A Replication from Pakistan," *Rural Sociology*, 44:420–430. RS(E)

Friedkin, Noah (1980), "A Test of Structural Features of Granovetter's Strength of Weak Ties Theory," *Social Networks*, 2:411–422.

Friedland, William H., and Amy Barton (1975), *Destalking the Wily Tomato: A Case Study of Social Consequences in California Agricultural Research*, University of California at Santa Cruz, Research Monograph 15, p. 28. GS(E)

Friedland, William H., and others (1981), *Manufacturing Green Gold: Capital, Labor, and Technology in the Lettuce Industry*, New York, Cambridge University Press. GS(E)

Frost, Peter, Jr., and Carolyn P. Egri (1991), "The Political Process of Innovation," *Research in Organizational Behavior*, 13:229–295. MR(E)

Fulerton, Hugh (1989), "Rejoinder: Microeconomic Theory and Critical Mass," *Telecommunication Policy*, 13(2):167–168. C(N)

Fulton, Robert F., and Margaret A. Fulton (1984), "Diffusion and the Computer Age: A Modern Theory of Social Change," *Free Inquiry in Creative Sociology*, 12(2):219–223. GS(E)

Gantz, Walter (1983), "The Diffusion of News about the Attempted Reagan Assassination," *Journal of Communication*, 33:56–66. C(E)

Gantz, Walter, Michael Fitzmaurice, and Ed Fink (1991), "Assessing the Active Component of Information-Seeking," *Journalism Quarterly*, 63(4):630–637. C(E)

Gantz, Walter, Michael Fitzmaurice, and Euisun Yoo (1990), "Seat Belt Campaigns and Buckling Up: Do the Media Make a Difference?" *Health Communication*, 2(1):1–12. C(E)

Gantz, Walter, Kathy A. Krendl, and Susan R. Robertson (1986), "Diffusion of a Proximate News Event," *Journalism Quarterly*, 63:282–287. C(E)

Gantz, Walter, and Hiroshi Tokinoya (1987), "Diffusion of News about the Assassination of Olof Palme: A Trans-Continental, Two-City Comparison of the Process," *European Journal of Communication*, 2:197–210. C(E)

Gartrell, C. David (1983), "Commentary: The Social Ecology of Innovation: A Comment to Ashby," *Rural Sociology*, 48(4):661–666. RS(N)

Gartrell, C. David, and John W. Gartrell (1985), "Social Status and Agricultural Innovation: A Meta-Analysis," *Rural Sociology*, 50(1):38–50. RS(E)

Gartrell, John W. (1977), "Status Inequality and Innovation: The Green Revolution in Andhra Pradesh, India," *American Sociological Review*, 44:73–94. GS(E)

Gartrell, John W., and C. David Gartrell (1979), "Status, Knowledge, and Innovation," *Rural Sociology*, 44(1):73–94. RS(E)

Gartrell, John W., E.A. Wilkening, and H.A. Presser (1973), "Curvilinear and Linear Models Relating Status and Innovative Behavior: A Reassessment," *Rural Sociology*, 38:391–411. RS(E)

Gatignon, Hubert, Jehoshua Eliashberg, and Thomas S. Robertson (1989), "Modelling Multinational Diffusion Patterns: An Efficient Methodology," *Marketing Science*, 8(3):231–247. MR(E)

Gatingnon, Hubert, and Thomas S. Robertson (1985), "A Propositional Inventory for New Diffusion Research," *Journal of Consumer Research*, 11:849–867. MR(E)

——— (1989), "Technology Diffusion: An Empirical Test of Competitive Effects," *Journal of Marketing*, 53:35–49. MR(E)

——— (1991), "Diffusion of Innovations," in H.H. Kassarsian and Thomas S. Robertson (eds.), *Handbook of Consumer Theory and Research*, Englewood Cliffs, NJ, Prentice-Hall. MR(N)

Gatrell, Anthony C. (1984), "The Geometry of a Research Speciality: Spatial Diffusion Modeling," *Annals of the Association of American Geographers*, 74(3):437–453. G(E)

Geisler, Charles C., and Oscar B. Martinson (1982), "Social Structural Influences on the Adoption of Selected Land Use 'Innovations'" *Journal of Environmental Education*, 14:27–33. E(E)

Gerwin, Donald (1988), "A Theory of Innovation Process for Computer-Aided Manufacturing Technology," *IEEE Transactions on Engineering Management*, 35(2):90–100. MR(E)

Gibson, David V., and Everett M. Rogers (1994), *R&D Consortia on Trial*, Boston, Harvard Business School Press. MR(E)

Glaser, Edward M. (1981), "Durability of Innovations in Human Service Organizations," *Knowledge*, 3(2):167–185. P(E)

Glick, Henry R. (1992), *The Right to Die: Policy Innovation and Its Consequences*, New York, Columbia University Press. PS(E)

Globe, Samuel, and others (1973), *The Interactions of Science and Technology in the Innovative Process: Some Case Studies*, Columbus, Ohio, Battelle-Columbus Laboratories, Report to the National Science Foundation. O(E)

Gold, Bella (1981), "Technological Diffusion in Industry: Research Needs and Shortcomings," *Journal of Industrial Economics*, 29(3):247–269. GE(E)

Goldman, Keren D. (1992), *Perceptions of a Health Education Innovation as Predictors of Implementation: The March of Dimes Campaign for Healthier Babies*, Ph.D. Thesis, New York University. E(E)

Gore, A.P., and V.A. Lavraj (1987), "Innovation Diffusion in a Heterogeneous Population," *Technological Forecasting and Social Change*, 32:163–167. MR(E)

Gort, Michael, and Steven Klepper (1982), "Time Paths in the Diffusion of Product Innovations," *The Economic Journal*, 92:630–653. GE(E)

Gort, Michael, and Akira Konakayama (1982), "A Model of Diffusion in the Production of an Innovation," *American Economic Review*, 72:1111–1120. GE(E)

Gort, Michael, and Richard A. Wall (1986), "The Evolution of Technologies and Investment in Innovation," *Economic Journal*, 96:741–757. GE(N)

Goss, Kevin F. (1979), "Consequences of the Diffusion of Innovations," *Rural Sociology*, 44(4):754–772. RS(N)

Gotsch, Carl H. (1972), "Technical Change and the Distribution of Income in Rural Areas," *American Journal of Agricultural Economics*, 54:326–341. AE(E)

Gottlieb, N.H., L.E. Lloyd, and J.N. Bounds (1987), "The Adoption of Health Promotion Programs by State Agencies," *Public Personnel Management*, 16(3):235–242. PS(E)

Gow, James Iain (1989), "Diffusion of Administrative Innovations in Canadian Public Administrations," Paper presented at the Association of Canadian Studies in the United States, San Francisco. PS(E)

Granovetter, Mark S. (1973), "The Strength of Weak Ties," *American Journal of Sociology*, 78:1360–1380. GS(N)

——— (1978), "Threshold Models of Collective Behavior," *American Journal of Sociology*, 83:1420–1443. GS(N)

——— (1982), "The Strength of Weak Ties: A Network Theory Revisited," Paper presented at the International Communication Association, Acapulco.

——— (1982), "The Strength of Weak Ties: A Network Theory Revisited," in Peter Marsden (ed.), *Social Structure and Network Analysis*, Newbury Park, CA, Sage, pp. 105–130. GS(N)

——— (1985), "Economic Action and Social Structure: The Problem of Embeddedness," *American Journal of Sociology*, 91(3):481–510. GS(N)

Granovetter, Mark, and R. Soong (1983), "Threshold Models of Diffusion and Collective Behavior," *Journal of Mathematical Sociology*, 9:165–179. GS(N)

Granstrand, Ove (1986), "The Modelling of Buyer/Seller Diffusion Processes: A Novel Approach to Modelling Diffusion and Simple Evolution Structure," Paper presented at the Conference on Innovation Diffusion, Venice. MR(E)

Gray, Virginia (1973a), "Innovation in the States: A Diffusion Study," *American Political Science Review*, 67:1174–1185. PS(E)

——— (1973b), "Rejoinder to 'Comment' by Jack L. Walker," *American Political Science Review*, 4:1192–1193. PS(E)

Greasley, David (1982), "The Diffusion of Machine Cutting in the British Coal Industry, 1902–1938." *Explorations in Economic History*, 19:246–268. O(E)

Greenberg, Bradley S. (1964), "Diffusion of News About the Kennedy Assassination," *Public Opinion Quarterly*, 28:225–232; and in Bradley S. Greenberg and Edwin B. Parker (eds.) (1965), *The Kennedy Assassination and the American Public: Social Communication in Crisis*, Stanford, California, Stanford University Press. C(E)

Greenberg, Steve (1992), "Misunderstanding Black Popular Music in White America," in American Enterprise Institute (ed.), *The New Global Culture*, Washington, D.C. C(N)

Greer, Ann L. (1981), "Medical Technology: Assessment, Adoption, and Utilization," *Journal of Medical Systems*, 5:129–145. PH(E)

——— (1985), "Adoption of Medical Technology: The Hospital's Three Decision Systems," *International Journal of Technology Assessment in Health Care*, 1:669–690. PH(E)

——— (1988), "The State of the Art Versus the State of the Science: The Diffusion of New Medical Technologies into Practice," *International Journal of Technology Assessment in Health Care*, 4:5–26. PH(E)

Grieshop, James I., Frank G. Zalom, and Gene Miyao (1988), "Adoption and Diffusion of Integrated Pest Management Innovations in Agriculture," *Bulletin of the Entomological Society of America*, 34(2):77–78. O(E)

Griliches, Zvi (1957), "Hybrid Corn: An Exploration in the Economics of Technological Change," *Econometrica*, 25:501–522. AE(N)

Gronhaug, Kjell, and Geir Kaufmann (1988), *Innovation: A Cross-Disciplinary Perspective*, Oslo, Norwegian University Press. MR(N)

Gross, Neal C. (1942), *The Diffusion of a Culture Trait in Two Iowa Townships*, M.S. Thesis, Ames, Iowa State College, p. 57. RS(E)

Gupta, A.K., S.P. Raj, and J. Wilemon (1986), "A Model for Studying R&D Marketing Interface in the Product Innovation Process," *Journal of Marketing*, 50:7–17. MR(E)

Gurbaxani, Vijay (1990), "Diffusion in Computing Networks: The Case of BITNET," *Communications of the ACM*, 33(12):65–75. MR(E)

Haddock, Cynthia Carter, and James W. Begun (1988), "The Diffusion of Two Diagnostic Technologies Among Hospitals in New York State," *International Journal of Technology Assessment in Health Care*, 4:593–600. PS(E)

Hägerstand, Torsten (1952), *The Propogation of Innovation Waves*, Lund, Sweden, Lund Studies in Geography 4. G(E)

——— (1953), *Innovation of Loppet ur Korologisk Synpunkt* (Innovation Diffusion as a Spatial Process), Lund, Sweden, University of Lund, Department of Geography Bulletin 15; American edition, 1968, Chicago, University of Chicago Press. G(E)

Haining, Robert (1982), "Interaction Models and Spatial Diffusion Process," *Geographical Analysis*, 14(2):95–108. G(E)

—— (1983), "Spatial and Spatial-Temporal Interaction Models, and the Analysis of Patterns of Diffusion," *Transactions of the Institute of British Geographers*, 8:158–169. G(E)

Hall, Bradford (1991), "Relational and Content Differences Between Elites and Outsiders in Innovation Networks," *Human Communication Research*, 17:536–561. C(E)

Hamblin, Robert L., R.B. Jacobson, and J.L. Miller (1973), *A Mathematical Theory of Social Change*, New York, Wiley. GS(E)

Hamblin, Robert L., and others (1979), "Modeling Use Diffusion," *Social Forces*, 57:799–811. GS(E)

Haney, Roger D. (1993), "Agenda-Setting During the Persian Gulf Crisis," in Bradley S. Greenberg and Walter Gantz (eds.), *Desert Storm and the Mass Media*, Cresskill, NJ, Hampton Press, pp. 113–124. C(E)

Hannan, Timothy H., and John M. McDowell (1984a), "Market Concentration and the Diffusion of New Technology in the Banking Industry," *Review of Economics and Statistics*, 66:686–691. MR(E)

—— (1984b), "The Determinants of Technology Adoption: The Case of Banking Firms," *Rand Journal of Economics*, 15(3):328–335. MR(E)

Haraldsen, G., T. Broddason, E. Hedinsson, M.L. Kalkkinen, and Nordhal Svendsen (1987), "News Diffusion of the Assassination of a Neighbour," *European Journal of Communication*, 2:171–184. U(E)

Hardin, Garrett (1968), "The Tragedy of the Commons," *Science*, 162:1243–1248.

Harding, Joe, and others (1973), *Population Council Copper-T Study in Korea: Summary Report*, Berkeley, California, The 21C Corporation, Policy Research and Planning Group, pp. 10, 11, 210. A(E)

Hassinger, Edward (1959), "Stages in the Adoption Process," *Rural Sociology*, 24:52–53. RS(N)

Haugejorden, O. (1988), "Adoption of Fluoride-Based Caries Preventive Innovations in a Public Dental Service," *Community Dentistry and Oral Epidemiology*, 16:5–10. U(E)

Havelock, Ronald G. (1972), "The Role of Research Communities in National Problem Solving," Paper presented at the Institute of Electrical and Electronic Engineers. E(E)

—— (1974), "Locals Say Innovation Is Local: A National Survey of School Superintendents," in Stanford Temkin and Mary V. Brown (eds.), *What Do Research Findings Say about Getting Innovations into Schools: A Symposium*, Philadelphia, Research for Better Schools. E(E)

Havelock, Ronald G., and others (1969), *Planning for Innovation through Dissemination and Utilization of Knowledge*, Ann Arbor, University of Michigan, Institute for Social Research, Center for Research on the Utilization of Scientific Knowledge. E(N)

Havens, A. Eugene (1975), "Diffusion of New Seed Varieties and Its Consequences: A Colombian Case," in Raymond E. Dumett and Lawrence J. Brainard (eds.), *Problems of Rural Development: Case Studies and Multidisciplinary Perspective*, Leiden, Brill, pp. 94–111. RS(E)

Havens, A. Eugene, and William L. Flinn (1974), "Green Revolution Technology and Community Development: The Limits of Action Programs," *Economic Development and Cultural Change*, 23:469–481. RS(E)

Hawley, Florence (1946), "The Role of Pueblo Social Organization in the Dissemination of Catholicism," *American Anthropologist*, 48:407–415. A(E)

Haynes, K.E., and A.S. Fotheringham (1984), *Gravity and Spatial Interaction Models*, Newbury Park, CA, Sage. G(N)

Heany, E.F. (1983), "Degrees of Product Innovation," *Journal of Business Strategy*, 3:3–14. MR(E)

Heeler, Roger M., and Thomas P. Hustad (1980), "Problems in Predicting New Product Growth for Consumer Durables," *Management Science*, 26(10):1007–1020. MR(E)

Heirich, Max A., Victoria Cameron, John C. Erfurt, Andrea Foote, and Walt Gregg (1989), "Establishing Communication Networks for Health Promotion in Industrial Settings," *American Journal of Health Promotion*, 4(2):108–117. PH(E)

Henderson, Rebecca M., and Kim B. Clark (1990), "Architectural Innovation: The Reconfiguration of Existing Product Technologies and the Failure of Established Firms," *Administrative Science Quarterly*, 354(1):9–30. MR(E)

Hershey, Marjorie, and Darrell M. West (1984), "Senate Campaigners and the Pro-Life Challenge in 1980," *Micropolitics*, 3(4):547–589. PS(E)

Herzog, William A., J. David Stanfield, Gordon C. Whiting, and Lynne Svenning (1968), *Patterns of Diffusion in Rural Brazil*, East Lansing, Michigan State University, Department of Communication, Diffusion of Innovations Research Report 10, p. 72. C(E)

Hiemstra, G. (1982), "You Say You Want a Revolution? 'Information Technology' in Organizations," in Robert Bostrom (ed.), *Communication Yearbook 7*, Newbury Park, CA, Sage, pp. 802–827. C(E)

Hightower, James (1972), *Hard Tomatoes, Hard Times: The Failure of America's Land Grant Complex*, Cambridge, Massachusetts, Schenkman.

Higuchi, Yoichiro (1986), *Citrus Siam Adoption in a South Sumatran Rubber Small Holding Village: An Interdependent Approach*, Ph.D. Thesis, Australian National University, Research School of Pacific Studies. O(E)

Hillman, A.L., and J.S. Schwartz (1985), "The Adoption and Diffusion of CT and MRI in the United States: A Comparative Analysis," *Medical Care*, 23:1283–1294. U(E)

Hillman, Bruce J. (1986), "Government Health Policy and the Diffusion of New Medical Devices," *Health Services Research*, 21:681–711. O(E)

Hirsch, Paul M. (1986), "From Ambushes to Golden Parachutes: Corporate Takeovers as an Instance of Cultural Framing and Institutional Integration," *American Journal of Sociology*, 91(4):800–837. GS(E)

Hochbaum, Godfrey M. (1958), *Public Participation in Medical Screening Programs: A Socio-Psychological Study*, Washington D.C., U.S. Department of Health, Education, and Welfare, Public Health Service Publication 572. GS(E)

Hoffman, Eric, and Paul M. Roman (1984), "Information Diffusion in the Implementation of the Innovation Process," *Communication Research*, 11:117–140. C(E)

Holak, Susan L., Donald R. Lehmann, and Fareena Sultan (1987), "The Role of Expectations in the Adoption of Innovative Consumer Durables: Some Preliminary Evidence," *Journal of Retailing*, 63(3):243–259. MR(E)

Holden, Robert T. (1986), "The Contagiousness of Aircraft Hijacking," *American Journal of Sociology*, 91(4):874–904. GS(E).

Holland, Peter A. (1987), "Adopters and Innovators: Application of the Kirton Adoption-Innovation Inventory to Bank Employees," *Psychological Reports*, 60:263–270. P(E)

Holloway, Robert E. (1977), *Perceptions of an Innovation: Syracuse University's Project Advance*, Ph.D. Thesis, Syracuse, New York, Syracuse University. E(E)

Hölmov, P. G., and Karl-Eric Warneryd (1990), "Adoption and Use of Fax in Sweden," in M. Carnevale, M. Lucertini, and S. Nicosia (eds.), *Modeling the Innovation: Communications, Automation and Information Systems*, Amsterdam, Elsevier Science Publishers, pp. 95–108. MR(E)

Holmstrom, Bengt (1989), "Agency Cost and Innovation," *Journal of Economic Behavior and Organization*, 12:305–327. GE(N)

Holta, Risto (1989), *Multidimensional Diffusion of Innovation*, Helsinki, Finland, Helsinki School of Economics and Business Administration. MR(E)

Homer, Jack Bernard (1983), *A Dynamic Model for Analyzing the Emergence of New Medical Technologies*, Ph.D. Thesis, Boston, Massachusetts Institute of Technology, Department of Management. MR(E)

——— (1986), "An Extended Diffusion Model with Application to Evolving Medical Technologies," Los Angeles, University of Southern California, Institute for Safety and Systems Management. MR(E)

Hooks, Gregory M., Ted L. Napier, and Michael V. Carter (1983), "Correlates of Adoption Behaviors: The Case of Farm Technologies," *Rural Sociology*, 48:308–323. RS(E)

Horsky, Dan (1990), "A Diffusion Model Incorporating Product Benefits, Price, Income, and Information," *Marketing Science*, 9:(4):342–365. MR(E)

Horsky, Dan, and Leonard S. Simon (1983), "Advertising and the Diffusion of New Products," *Management Science*, 1:1–18. MR(E)

Hostetler, John A. (1980), *Amish Society*, Baltimore, MD, Johns Hopkins University Press.

——— (1987), "A New Look at the Old Order," *The Rural Sociologist*, 7:278–292.

Howell, Jane M., and Christopher A. Higgins (1990), "Champions of Technological Innovations," *Administrative Science Quarterly*, 35:317–341. MR(E)

Huberman, A. Michael, and Matthew B. Miles (1984), *Innovation Up Close: How School Improvement Works*, New York, Plenum. E(E)

Huberman, A. Michael, and David P. Crandall (1982), "People, Politics, and Practices: Examining the Chain of School Improvement," Volume IX: A Study of Dissemination Efforts Supporting School Improvement," Washington, D.C., U.S. Department of Education, Office of Planning, Budgeting, and Evaluation. E(E)

Huff, David L., James M. Lutz, and Rajendra Srivastava (1988), "A Geographical Analysis of the Innovativeness of States," *Economic Geography*, 64(2):137–146. G(E)

Hunt, R.J. (1983), "Community Characteristics, Opinion Leadership, and Fluoridation Outcome in Small Iowa Communities," *Journal of Public Health Dentistry*, 43:152–160. PH(E)

Huntington, Dale, Cheryl Lettenmaier, and Isaac Obeng-Quaidoo (1990), "User's Perspective of Counseling Training in Ghana: The 'Mystery Client' Trial," *Studies in Family Planning*, 21(3):171–177. PH(E)

Hurt, H. Thomas (1985), "The Measurement of Homophily, Optimal Heterophily, and Opinion Leadership in Diffusion Networks," Unpublished paper, Denton, North Texas State University, Department of Communication. C(E)

Hyman, Herbert H., and Paul B. Sheatsley (1974), "Some Reasons Why Information Campaigns Fail," *Public Opinion Quarterly*, 11:412–423.

Hyman, Michael R. (1988), "The Timeless Problem in the Application of Bass-Type New Product Growth Models to Durable Sales Forecasting," *Journal of Business Research*, 16(1):31–47. MR(E)

Illiot, James Brian (1990), *A Case Study of Early Adoptors in the Diffusion of a New Technological Innovation*, M.A. Thesis, Waco, TX, Baylor University. C(E)

Ireland, N., and P. Stoneman (1986), "Technological Diffusion, Expectations, and Welfare," *Oxford Economic Papers*, 38:283–304. U(E)

Isenson, Raymond S. (1969), "Project Hindsight: An Empirical Study of the Sources of Ideas Utilized in Operational Weapons System," in William Gruber and Donald G. Marquis (eds.), *Factors in the Transfer of Technology*, Cambridge, Massachusetts, MIT Press. U(E)

Jain, Dipak C., and Ram C. Rao (1989), "Effect of Price on the Demand for Durables: Modeling Estimation and Findings," *Journal of Business and Economic Statistics*, 39:57–69. MR(E)

Janz, N., and Marshall Becker (1984), "The Health Belief Model: A Decade Later," *Health Education Quarterly*, 11(1):1–47. PH(N)

Jarvis, L.S. (1981), "Predicting the Diffusion of Improved Pastures in Uruguay," *American Journal of Agricultural Economics*, 63:495–502. AE(E)

Jeffres, Leo W., and Rebecca Quarles (1984), "A Panel Study of News Diffusion," *Journalism Quarterly*, 60:722–724. C(E)

Jensen, Richard (1982), "Adoption and Diffusion of an Innovation of Uncertain Profitability," *Journal of Economic Theory*, 27:182–193. MR(E)

—— (1983), "Innovation Adoption and Diffusion: When There Are Competing Innovations," *Journal of Economic Theory*, 29:161–171. MR(E)

Johnson, Bonnie, and Ronald E. Rice (1987), *Managing Organizational Innovation: The Evolution from Word Processing to Office Information Systems*, New York, Columbia University Press. C(E)

Johnson, Harley E. (1971), "Diffusion of Strip Cropping in Southwestern Wisconsin," *Annals of the Association of American Geographers*, 61:671–683. G(E)

Johnson, J. David, and Hendrika Meischuke (1993), "A Comprehensive Model of Career-Related Information-Seeking Applied to Magazines," *Human Communication Research*, 19(3):343–367. C(E)

Johnson, Jeffrey C. (1986), "Social Networks and Innovation Adoption: A Look at Burt's Use of Structural Equivalence," *Social Networks*, 8:343–364. A(E)

Jorgensen, Steffen (1983), "Optimal Control of a Diffusion Model of New Product Acceptance with Price-Dependent Total Market Potential," *Optimal Control Applications and Methods*, 4:269–276. MR(E)

Joseph, A.E., and P.D. Keddie (1981), "Diffusion of Grain Corn Production through Southern Ontario, 1946–1971," *Canadian Geographer*, 25:333–349. G(E)

Kalish, Shlome (1985), "A New Product Adoption Model with Pricing, Advertising and Uncertainty," *Management Science*, 31(12):1569–85. MR(E)

Kalish, Shlome, and Gary L. Linen (1986a), "A Market Entry Timing Model for New Technologies," *Management Science*, 32(2):194–205. MR(E)

—— (1986b), "Applications of Innovation Diffusion Models in Marketing," in Vijay

Mahajan and Yoram Wind (eds.), *Innovation Diffusion Models of New Product Acceptance*, Cambridge, MA, Ballinger. MR(E)

Kalish, Shlome, and Subrata K. Sen (1986), "Diffusion Models and the Marketing Mix for Single Products," in Vijay Mahajan and Yoram Wind (eds.), *Innovation Diffusion Models of New Product Acceptance*, Cambridge, MA, Ballinger. MR(E)

Kalunzy, Arnold, Anna Schenk, and Thomas Ricketts (1986), "Cancer Prevention in the Workplace: An Organizational Innovation," *Health Promotion*, 3:293–299. PH(E)

Kamakura, Wagner A., and Siva K. Balasubramanian (1987), "Long-Term Forecasting with Innovation Diffusion Models: The Impact of Replacement Purchase," *Journal of Forecasting*, 6(1):1–19. MR(E)

——— (1988), "Long-Term View of the Diffusion of Durables: A Study of the Role of Price and Adoption Influence Processes via Tests of Nested Models," *International Journal of Research in Marketing*, 5:1–13. MR(E)

Kang, Nanjun, and Michael Chang (1990), "The Future of Theatrical Movies: From the Perspective of Diffusion Theory," Paper presented at the International Communication Association, Dublin. C(E)

Kanter, Rosabeth Moss (1983), *The Change Masters: Innovation and Entrepreneurship in the American Corporation*, New York, Simon and Schuster. MR(E)

——— (1988a), "When a Thousand Flowers Bloom: Structural, Collective, and Social Conditions for Innovation in Organizations," in B. M. Staw and L. L. Cummings (eds.), *Research in Organizational Behavior*, Volume 10, Greenwich, CT, JAI Press. MR(E)

——— (1988b), "Three Tiers for Innovation Research," *Communication Research*, 15(5):509–523. MR(E)

Kaplan, Abraham (1964), *The Conduct of Inquiry*, San Francisco, Chandler, p. 31.

Karatzas, I. (1984), "Gittins Indices in the Dynamic Allocation Problems for Diffusion Process," *Annals of Probability*, 12:173–192. G(N)

Karlson, Stephen H. (1986), "Adoption of Competing Innovations by United States Steel Producers," *Review of Economics and Statistics*, 15:415–422. GE(E)

Karmeshu, and R.K. Pathria (1980a), "Stochastic Evolution of a Nonlinear Model of Diffusion of Information," *Journal of Mathematical Sociology*, 7:59–71. MR(E)

——— (1980b), "Diffusion of Information in a Random Environment," *Journal of Mathematical Sociology*, 7:215–227. MR(E)

Katalanos, Nikki (1994), *When Yes Means No: Verbal and Non-Verbal Communication with Southeast Asian Refugees in the New Mexico Health Care System*, M.A. Thesis, Albuquerque, University of New Mexico. PH(E)

Katz, Elihu (1956), *Interpersonal Relations and Mass Communications: Studies in the Flow of Influence*, Ph.D. Thesis, New York, Columbia University. GS(E)

——— (1957), "The Two-Step Flow of Communication: An Up-to-Date Report on an Hypothesis," *Public Opinion Quarterly*, 21:61–78. GS(E)

——— (1961), "The Social Itinerary of Social Change: Two Studies on the Diffusion of Innovation," in Wilbur Schramm (ed.), *Studies of Innovation and of Communication to the Public*, Stanford, CA, Stanford University, Institute for Communication Research; and (1962), *Human Organization*, 20:70–82. GS(E)

——— (1962), "Notes on the Unit of Adoption in Diffusion Research," *Sociological Inquiry*, 32:3–9. GS(N)

Katz, Elihu, and Paul F. Lazarsfeld (1955), *Personal Influence: The Part Played by People in the Flow of Mass Communications*, New York, Free Press, pp. 16, 334.

Katz, Elihu, Martin L. Levin, and Herbert Hamilton (1963), "Traditions of Research on the Diffusion of Innovations," *American Sociological Review*, 28:237–253. GS(N)

Katz, Michael L., and Carl Shapiro (1985a) "Network Externalities, Competition, and Compatibility," *American Economic Review*, 75:424–440. GE(E)

—— (1985b) "Technology Adoption in the Presence of Network Externalities," *Journal of Political Economy*, 94(4):822–841. GE(N)

Katzman, M.T. (1980), "Municipal Bond Banking: The Diffusion of a Public-Finance Innovation," *National Tax Journal*, 33:149–160. U(E)

Kearns, Kelvin P. (1989), "Communication Networks among Municipal Administrators: Sharing Information about Computers in Local Governments," *Knowledge: Creation, Diffusion, Utilization*, 10(4):260–279. PS(E)

—— (1992), "Innovations in Local Governments: A Sociocognitive Network Approach," *Knowledge and Policy*, 5(2):45–67. PS(E)

Keller, Robert T., and Windford E. Holland (1983), "Communication and Innovators in Research and Development Organizations," *Academy of Management Journal*, 26(4):742–749. MR(E)

Kelley, Maryellen R., and Harvey Brooks (1991), "External Learning Opportunities and the Diffusion of Process Innovations to Small Firms," *Technological Forecasting and Social Change*, 39:103–125. MR(E)

Kennedy, Anita. (1983), "The Adoption and Diffusion of New Industrial Products: A Literature Review," *European Journal of Marketing*, 17:31–38. MR(N)

Kepplinger, Hans Mathias, Adam Levendel, Marino Livolsi, and Mallory Wober (1987), "More than Learning: The Diffusion of the News on the Assassination of Olof Palme in England, Germany, Italy, and Hungary," *European Journal of Communication*, 2:185–195. C(E)

Kervasdoué, Jean de (1981), "Institutions, Organizations, Medical Disciplines, and the Dissemination of Research Results," *Organization Studies*, 2(3):249–266. MR(E)

Kesner, D.M. (1981), "Diffusion of New Medical Information," *American Journal of Public Health*, 71:367–368. PH(E)

Khan, Safdar Ali (1989), *Channels of Communication in the Diffusion of Farm Forestry in Pakistan*, Ph.D. Thesis, Columbia, University of Missouri. RS(E)

Kikuchi, Masao, and Yujiro Hayami (1980), "Inducements to Institutional Innovations in an Agrarian Community," *Economic Development and Cultural Change*, 29:21–36. AE(E)

Kim, Joung-Im (1986), *The Strength of Weak Ties: A Conceptual Elaboration at the Dyad-Level*, Ph.D. Thesis, Stanford, CA, Stanford University. C(E)

Kim, Young-Mi, and others (1992), "Improving the Quality of Service Delivery in Nigeria," *Studies in Family Planning*, 23(2):118–127. PH(E)

Kimberly, John R. (1981), "Managerial Innovation," in William Starbuck and P. Nystrom (eds.), *Handbook of Organizational Design*, Volume 1, New York, Oxford University Press, pp. 84–104. MR(N)

Kimberly, John R., and Michael J. Evanisko (1981), "Organizational Innovation: The Influence of Individual, Organizational, and Contextual Factors on Hospital Adoption of Technological and Administrative Innovations," *Academy of Management Journal*, 24:689–713. MR(E)

Kimura, T., and T. Ohsone (1984), "A Diffusion Approximation for an M/G/M Queue with Group Arrivals," *Management Science*, 30:381–388. MR(E)

Kinsey, B.H., and Ahmed Iftikhar (1983), "Mechanical Innovations on Small African Farms," *International Labour Review*, 122:227–238. U(E)

Kirchhoff, Karin T. (1982), "A Diffusion Survey of Coronary Precautions," *Nursing Research*, 31(4):196–201. O(E)

Kivlin, Joseph E., and Frederick C. Fliegel (1967), "Orientations to Agriculture: A Factor Analysis of New Practices," *Rural Sociology*, 33:127–140. C(E)

Kiyokawa, Yukihoko (1984), "The Diffusion of New Technologies in the Japanese Sericulture Industry: The Case of the Hybrid Silkworm," *Hitotsubashi Journal of Economics*, 25:31–59. GE(E)

Klaiber, Susan E. (1986), *A Synthesis of the National Diffusion Network*, Hampton, NH, RMC Research Corporation, Research Report. E(E)

Klein, Josephine (1961), *Working with Groups: The Social Psychology of Discussion and Decision*, London, Hutchinson, p. 199.

Klingman, David (1980), "Temporal and Spatial Diffusion in the Comparative Analysis of Social Change," *American Political Science Review*, 74:123–137. PS(E)

Klonglan, Gerald E. (1962), *Message Sharpening in a Multi-Step Communication Situation*, M.S. Thesis, Ames, Iowa State University. RS(E)

———— (1963), *Role of a Free Sample Offer in the Adoption of Technological Innovation*, Ph.D. Thesis, Ames, Iowa State University. RS(E)

Klonglan, Gerald E., George M. Beal, Joe M. Bohlen, and E. Walter Coward, Jr. (1973), "Conceptualizing and Measuring the Diffusion of Innovations," *Sociologia Ruralis*, 27:36–47. RS(E)

Klonglan, Gerald E., and others (1960a), "The Role of Free Samples in the Adoption Process," Paper presented at the Midwest Sociological Society, St. Louis. RS(E)

Klonglan, Gerald E., and others (1960b), "Message Sharpening in a Multi-Step Communication Situation," Paper presented at the Rural Sociological Society, Northridge, California. RS(E)

Klovdahl, Alden S. (1985), "Social Networks and the Spread of Infectious Diseases: The AIDS Example," *Social Science Medicine*, 21(11):1203–1216. GS(E)

Knoke, David (1982), "The Spread of Municipal Reform: Temporal, Spatial, and Social Dynamics," *American Journal of Sociology*, 87:1314–1339. GS(E)

Kobrin, Stephen J. (1985), "Diffusion as an Explanation of Oil Nationalization or the Domino Effect Rides Again," *Journal of Conflict Resolution*, 29(3):3–32. MR(E)

Kohl, John W. (1966), *Adoption Stages and Perceptions of Characteristics of Educational Innovations*, Ed.D. Thesis, Eugene, University of Oregon, p. 68. E(E)

Kolbe, L.J., and D.C. Iverson (1981), "Implementing Comprehensive School Health Education: Educational Innovations and Social Change," *Health Education Quarterly*, pp. 57–80. PS(E)

Koontz, Virginia Landson (1976), *Determinants of Individuals' Levels of Knowledge, Attitudes Towards, and Decisions Regarding a Health Innovation in Maine*, Ph.D. Thesis, Ann Arbor, University of Michigan. PS(E)

Korsching, Peter F., Curtis W. Stofferhan, Peter J. Nowak, and Donald J. Wagner (1983), "Adopter Characteristics and Adoption Patterns of Minimum Tillage: Implications for Soil Conservation Programs," *Journal of Soil and Water Conservation*, 38(5):428–431. RS(E)

Kramer, Kenneth L., and James L. Perry (1989), "Innovation and Computing in the Public Sector," *Knowledge in Society*, 2:72–87. PS(E)

Kramer, Richard (1993), "The Policies of Information: A Study of the French Minitel System," in Jorge R. Schement and Brent D. Ruben (eds.), *Between Communication and Information*, Volume 4 of *Information and Behavior*, New Brunswick, NJ, Transaction, pp. 453–486. U(E)

Krassa, M.A. (1988), "Social Groups, Selective Perception, and Behavioral Contagion in Public Opinion," *Social Networks*, 10:109–136. O(E)

Kreiner, Peter Warren (1989), *The Diffusion of Major Process Technological Innovations: Toward A Structural Approach*, Ph.D. Thesis, Los Angeles, University of Southern California. MR(E)

Kroeber, A.L. (1937), "Diffusion," in Edwin R.A. Seligman and Alvin Johnson (eds.), *The Encyclopedia of Social Science, II*, New York, Macmillan, pp. 137–142. A(N)

Kuhn, Thomas S. (1970), *The Structure of Scientific Revolutions*, University of Chicago Press, p. viii. Originally published 1962.

Kunkel, John H. (1977), "The Behavioral Perspective of Social Dynamics," in Robert L. Hamblin and John H. Kunkel (eds.), *Behavioral Theory in Sociology*, New Brunswick, NJ, Transaction.

Labay, D.G., and T.C. Kinnear (1981), "Exploring the Consumer Decision Process in the Adoption of Solar Energy Systems," *Journal of Consumer Research*, 8:271–278. MR(E)

La Barbera, P.A. (1983), "The Diffusion of Trade Association Advertising Self-Regulation," *Journal of Marketing*, 47:58–67. MR(E)

Ladewig, Howard, John K. Thomas, and G. Mike McWhorter (1986), *Impact of Cotton Integrated Pest Management Program of the Texas Agricultural Extension Service: A Statement Assessment*, College Station, Texas A&M University System, Research Report. O(E)

Lal, V.B., Karmeshu, and S. Kaicker (1988), "Modeling Innovation Diffusion with Distributed Time Lag," *Technological Forecasting and Social Change*, 34:103–113. O(N)

LaMar, Ronald V. (1966), *In-Service Education Needs Related to Diffusion of an Innovation*, Ph.D. Thesis, Berkeley, University of California, p. 72. E(E)

Lambright, W. Henry (1980), "Decision-Making for Urban Technology," *Policy Sciences*, 11:329–341. PS(E)

Lambur, Michael T., Mark E. Whalon, and Frank A. Fear (1985), "Diffusion Theory and Integrated Pest Management: Illustrations from the Michigan Fruit IPM Program," *Bulletin of the Entomological Society of America*, 31:40–45. O(E)

Lame, Mark L. (1992), *A Study of the Diffusion of Integrated Pest Management in a Cotton-Growing Community*, Ph.D. Thesis, Tempe, Arizona State University. C(E)

Lancaster, G.A., and C.T. Taylor (1986), "The Diffusion of Innovations and Their Attributes: A Critical Review," *Quarterly Review of Marketing*, 11(4):13–20. MR(E)

Lancaster, G.A., and G. Wright (1983), "Forecasting the Future of Video Using a Diffusion Model," *European Journal of Marketing*, 17(2):70–79. MR(E)

Lane, Jeffrey, and David T. Hartgen (1989), "Factors Affecting the Adoption of Information Systems in State DOT's," Paper presented at the Transportation Research Board, Washington, D.C. G(E)

——— (1990), "Factors Affecting the Adoption of Information Systems in State DOT," Paper presented at the Transportation Research Board, Washington, D.C. G(E)

Langlois, Simon (1977), "Les Reseaux Personnels et la Diffusion des Informations sur les Emplois," *Researches Sociographiques*, 2:213–245. O(E)

Lansing, Stephen (1987), "Balinese 'Water Temples' and the Management of Irrigation," *American Anthropologist*, 89:326–341. A(E)

—— (1991), *Priests and Programmers: Engineering the Knowledge of Bali*, Princeton, NJ, Princeton University Press. A(E)

Lansky, P. (1983), "Inference for the Diffusion Models of Neuronal Activity," *Mathematical Bioscience*, 67:247–260. U(E)

Larsen, Judith K., and Everett M. Rogers (1984), "Consensus Development Conferences," *Knowledge*, 5:537–548. O(E)

Larsen, Judith K., and Rekha Agarwala-Rogers (1977), *Re-Invention of Innovation: A Study of Community Health Centers,* Palo Alto, California, American Institute for Research in the Behavioral Sciences, Report, p. 38. P(E)

Lavraj, U.A., and A.P. Gore (1990), "On Interpreting Probability Distribution Fitted to Times of First Adoption," *Technological Forecasting and Social Change*, 37(4):355–370. MR(E)

Lawless, Michael W. (1987), "Institutionalization of a Management Science Innovation in Police Departments," *Management Science*, 33(2):244–252. MR(E)

Lawrence, Kenneth D., and Michael Geurts (1984), "Converging Conflicting Forecasting Parameters in Forecasting Durable New Product Sale," *European Journal of Operational Research*, 16:42–47. MR(E)

Lawrence, Kenneth D., and William H. Lawton (1981), "Applications of Diffusion Models: Some Empirical Results," in Yorum Wind, Vijay Mahajan, and R.C. Cardozo (eds.), *New Product Forecasting*, Lexington, MA, Lexington, pp. 529–541. MR(E)

Lawton, Stephen B., and William H. Lawton (1979), "An Autocatalytic Model for the Diffusion of Educational Innovations," *Educational Administrative Quarterly*, 15(1):19–53. E(E)

Lazarsfeld, Paul F., and Herbert Menzel (1963), "Mass Media and Personal Influence," in Wilbur Schramm (ed.), *The Science of Human Communication*, New York, Basic Books, p. 96.

Lazarsfeld, Paul F., and Robert K. Merton (1964), "Friendship as Social Process: A Substantive and Methodological Analysis," in Monroe Berger and others (eds.), *Freedom and Control in Modern Society*, New York, Octagon, pp. 23, 63.

Lazarsfeld, Paul F., Bernard Berelson, and Hazel Gaudet (1944), *The People's Choice: How the Voter Makes Up His Mind in a Presidential Election*, New York, Duell, Sloan, and Pearce; reprinted 1948, 1968, New York, Columbia University Press, p. 157.

Lee, Jack C., and K.W. Loo (1987), "On a Family of Data-Based Transformed Models Useful in Forecasting Technological Substitutions," *Technological Forecasting and Social Change*, 31:61–78. O(E)

Lee, Robert H., and Donald M. Waldman (1985), "The Diffusion of Innovation in Hospitals: Some Econometric Considerations," *Journal of Health Economics*, 4:373–380. GE(E)

Leichter, Howard M. (1983), "The Patterns and Origins of Policy Diffusion: The Case of the Commonwealth," *Comparative Politics*, 1:223–233. PS(E)

Lenk, Peter J., and Ambar G. Rao (1990), "New Models from Old: Forecasting Product Adoption by Hierarchial Bayes Procedures," *Marketing Science*, 9(1):42–53. MR(E)

Leonard-Barton, Dorothy (1981), "Voluntary Simplicity Lifestyles and Energy Conservation," *Journal of Consumer Research*, 8:243–252. C(E)

———— (1983a), "Diffusing Innovations When the Users Are Not the Choosers: The Case of Dentists," Working Paper, Cambridge, Massachusetts Institute of Technology, Sloan School of Management. MR(E)

———— (1983b), "Introducing Production Innovations into an Organization: Structured Methods for Producing Computer Software," Cambridge, Massachusetts Institute of Technology, Sloan School of Management, Research Report 103. MR(E)

———— (1984), "Implementing Changes in Production Methods: The Case of Structured Computer Software Methodologies," Working Paper, Boston, Harvard University, Graduate School of Business Administration. MR(E)

———— (1985), "Experts as Negative Opinion Leaders in the Diffusion of a Technological Innovation," *Journal of Consumer Research*, 11:914–926. MR(E)

———— (1987), "The Case for Integrative Innovation: An Expert System at Digital," *Sloan Management Review*, 29(1):7–19. MR(E)

———— (1988a), "Implementation as Mutual Adoption of Technology and Organization," *Research Policy*, 17:251–267. MR(E)

———— (1988b), "Implementation and Characteristics of Organizational Innovation: Limits and Opportunities for Managerial Strategies," *Communication Research*, 15(5):603–631. MR(E)

Leonard-Barton, Dorothy, and Isabelle Deschampss (1988), "Managerial Influence in the Implementation of New Technology," *Management Science*, 34(10):1252–1262. MR(E)

Leonard-Barton, Dorothy, and William A. Kraus (1985), "Implementing New Technology," *Harvard Business Review*, 63(6):102–110. MR(E)

Leonard-Barton, Dorothy, and Everett M. Rogers (1980), "Voluntary Simplicity: Precursor or Fad?" Paper presented at the American Association for the Advancement of Science, San Francisco. C(E)

Lester, James P., Ann O'M. Bowman, Malcolm L. Goggin, and Laurence J. O'Toole Jr. (1987), "Future Directions for Research in Implementation," *Policy Studies Review*, 7(1):200–216. PS(N)

Lessley, Bradley J. (1980), *The Dvorak Keyboard*, Salem, OR, Dvorak International Federation Report.

Leuthold, Frank O. (1965), *Communication and Diffusion of Improved Farm Practices in Two Northern Saskatchewan Communities*, Saskatoon, Saskatchewan, Centre for Community Studies, Mimeo Report. RS(E)

———— (1967), *Discontinuance of Improved Farm Innovations by Wisconsin Farm Operators*, Ph.D. Thesis, Madison, University of Wisconsin, p. 106. RS(E)

Levin, Sharon G., and others (1985), "Intermarket Differences in the Early Diffusion of an Innovation," *Southern Economic Journal*, 51: 672–680. U(E)

———— (1987), "A Dynamic Analysis of the Adoption of a New Technology: The Case of Optical Scanners," *Review of Economics and Statistics*, 69:12–17. U(E)

Levine, A. (1980), *Why Innovation Fails*, Albany, NY, State University Press. E(E)

Lewit, Eugene M. (1986), "The Diffusion of Surgical Technology: Who's on First," *Journal of Health Economics*, 5:99–102. U(E)

Liander, Karl, and Thomas Åstebro (1989), *Factors Affecting the Intra-Firm Diffusion of Electronic Mail Systems*, Gotenberg, Sweden, Chalmers University of Technology, Department of Industrial Management and Economics, Report 89:1. MR(E)

Lieberman, Marvin B. (1987), "The Learning Curve, Diffusion, and Competitive Strategy," *Strategic Management Journal*, 8:441–452. MR(N)

Lievrouw, Leah A., and Janice T. Pope (1994), "Contemporary Art as Aesthetic Innovation: Applying the Diffusion Model to the Art World," *Knowledge*, 15(4):373–395. C(E)

Light, Alfred B. (1978), "Intergovernmental Sources of Innovation in State Administration," *American Political Quarterly*, 10:147–166. PS(E)

Lilien, G.L., and E. Yoon (1990), "The Timing of Competitive Market Entry: An Exploratory Study of New Industrial Products," *Management Science*, 36(5):568–585. MR(E)

Lilien, G.L., and S. Yoon (1989), "Determinants of New Industrial Product Performance: A Strategic Re-Examination of the Empirical Literature," *IEEE Transactions on Engineering Management*, 36(1):3–10. MR(E)

Lin, Nan, and others (1981), "Social Resources and Strength of Ties: Structural Factors in Occupational Status Attainment," *American Sociological Review*, 46:393–405. GS(E)

Linder, Stephen H., and B. Guy Peters (1987), "Relativism, Contingency, and the Definition of Success in Implementing Research," *Policy Studies Review*, 7(1):116–127. PS(N)

Linquist, K., and J. Mauriel (1989), "Depth and Breadth in Innovation Implementation: The Case of School-Based Management," in Andrew H. Van de Ven, H.A. Angle, and M. Scott Poole (eds.), *Research on the Management of Innovation: The Minnesota Studies*, New York, Ballinger/Harper & Row. MR(E)

Linton, Ralph (1936), *The Study of Man*, New York, Appleton-Century-Crofts, pp. 324–336. A(N)

Linton, Ralph, and Abram Kardiner (1952), "The Change from Dry to Wet Rice Cultivation in Tanala-Bertsileo," in Guy E. Swanson and others (eds.), *Readings in Social Psychology*, New York, Henry Holt, pp. 222–231. A(E)

Lippit, Mary E., J.P. Miller, and Jerry Halamaj (1980), "Patterns of Use and Correlates of Adoption of an Electronic Mail System," Proceedings of the American Institute of Decision Sciences. MR(E)

Lipton, Jack P., and Alan M. Hershaft (1985), "On the Widespread Acceptance of Dubious Medical Findings," *Journal of Health and Social Behavior*, 26:336–351. P(E)

Liu, William T., and Robert W. Duff (1972), "The Strength of Weak Ties," *Public Opinion Quarterly*, 36:361–366. GS(E)

Lockeretz, William, Georgia Shearer, and Daniel H. Kohl (1981), "Organic Farming in the Corn Belt," *Science*, 211:540–548. U(E)

Lockeretz, William, and Sarah Wernick (1980), "Commercial Organic Farming in the Corn Belt in Comparison to Conventional Practices," *Rural Sociology*, 45(4):708–722. U(E)

Lockwood, R.C. (1987), "Diffusion and Adoption of New Technology at the Farm Level," *Canadian Journal of Agricultural Economics*, 34:147–150. AE(E)

Lomas, Jonathan (1991), "Words without Action? The Production, Dissemination, and Impact of Consensus Recommendations," *Annual Review of Public Health*, 12:41–65. PH(N)

Longo, Rose Mary Juliano (1990), "Information Transfer and the Adoption of Agricultural Innovations," *Journal of the American Society for Information Science*, 41(1):1–9. C(E)

Lovejoy, Stephen B., and F. Dale Parent (1981), "Social Aspects of a Nonpoint Source Water Pollution Abatement Program: A Panel Study of the Black Creek Project," West Lafayette, Purdue University, Department of Agricultural Economics, Indiana Agricultural Experiment Station Bulletin 350. RS(E)

—— (1982), "Conservation Behavior: A Look at the Explanatory Power of the Traditional Adoption-Diffusion Model," Paper presented at the Rural Sociological Society, San Francisco. RS(E)

Loveless, Ronald Dale (1983), *The S.W.A.T. Innovation: The Diffusion of Special Weapons and Tactics Units in Michigan Police Departments*, M.A. Thesis, Ypsilanti, Eastern Michigan University, GS(E)

Lowe, Charles U. (1980), "The Consensus Development Programme: Technology Assessment at the National Institute of Health," *British Medical Journal*, 153–158. O(E)

—— (1981), *Biomedical Discoveries Adopted by Industry for Purposes Other than Health Services*, Washington, D.C., National Institute of Health, Office of Medical Applications of Research, Report. O(E)

Lucas, Anelissa (1983), "Public Policy Diffusion Research: Integrating an Analytic Paradigm," *Knowledge*, 4(3):379–408. U(E)

Lundvall, Bengt-Ake (1985), *Product Innovation and User-Producer Interaction*, Aaiborg, Denmark, Aaiborg University, Research Report 31. MR(E)

Luthra, Rashmi (1994), "A Case of Problematic Diffusion: The Use of Sex Determination Techniques in India," *Knowledge*, 15(3):259–272. C(E)

Lutz, James M. (1986a), "The Spatial and Temporal Diffusion of Selected Licensing Laws in the United States," *Political Geography Quarterly*, 5:141–159. PS(E)

—— (1986b), "Regional Leadership Patterns in the Diffusion of Public Policies," *American Political Quarterly*, 15:387–398. PS(E)

Lynn, Leonard (1981), "New Data on the Diffusion of the Basic Oxygen Furnace in the U.S. and Japan," *Journal of Industrial Economics*, 2:123–136. GE(E)

Machiavelli, Niccolo (1961), *The Prince*, translated by George Bull, Baltimore, Penguin Books. Originally published 1513.

Magill, Kathleen P., and Everett M. Rogers (1981), "Federally Sponsored Demonstrations of Technological Innovations," *Knowledge*, 3(1):23–42. C(E)

Magill, Kathleen P., Thomas E. Shanks, and Everett M. Rogers (1980), *The Innovation Process for Three Mass Transportation Innovations: Vanpooling, Auto-Restricted Zones, and Priority Highway Lanes for High Occupancy Vehicles*, Stanford, Stanford University, Institute for Communication Research, Report to the Urban Mass Transportation Administration. C(E)

Mahajan, Vijay, Stuart I. Bretschneider, and John W. Bradford (1980), "Feedback Approaches to Modeling Structural Shifts in Market Response," *Journal of Marketing*, 44:71–80. MR(E)

Mahajan, Vijay, Charlotte H. Mason, and V. Sriniwasan (1986), "An Evaluation of Estimation Procedures for New Product Diffusion Models," in Vijay Mahajan and Yoram Wind (eds.), *Innovation Diffusion Models of New Product Acceptance*, Cambridge, MA, Ballinger. MR(E)

Mahajan, Vijay, and Eitan Muller (1979), "Innovation Diffusion and New Product Growth Models in Marketing," *Journal of Marketing*, 43:55–68. MR(E)

—— (1986a), "Advertising Pulsing Policies for Generating Awareness for New Products," *Marketing Science*, 5(2):89–106. MR(E)

———— (1986b), "Determination of Adopter Categories Using Innovation Diffusion Models," Unpublished paper, Dallas, Southern Methodist University, School of Business. MR(E)

Mahajan, Vijay, Eitan Muller, and Frank M. Bass (1990), "New Product Diffusion Models in Marketing: A Review and Directions for Research," *Journal of Marketing*, 54:1–26. MR(N)

Mahajan, Vijay, Eitan Muller, and Roger A. Kerin (1984), "Introduction Strategy for New Products with Positive and Negative Word-of-Mouth," *Management Science*, 30(12):1389–1404. MR(E)

Mahajan, Vijay, Eitan Muller, and Subhash Sharma (1984), "An Empirical Comparison of Awareness Forecasting Models of New Product Acceptance," *Marketing Science*, 3(3):179–197. MR(E)

Mahajan, Vijay, Eitan Muller, and Rajendra K. Shrivastava (1990), "Determination of Adoptor Categories by Using Innovation Diffusion Models," *Journal of Marketing Research*, 27:37–50. MR(E)

Mahajan, Vijay, and Robert A. Peterson (1978), "Innovation Diffusion in a Dynamic Potential Adopter Population," *Management Science*, 24(15):1589–1597. MR(E)

———— (1979), "Integrating Time and Space in Technological Substitution Models," *Technological Forecasting and Social Change*, 14(8):231–241. MR(E)

———— (1982), "Erratum to Innovation Diffusion in a Dynamic Potential Population," *Management Science*, 28(9):1087. MR(E)

———— (1985), *Models for Innovation Diffusion*, Newbury Park, CA, Sage. MR(E)

Mahajan, Vijay, Robert A. Peterson, and Subhash Sharma (1986), "Simple Algebraic Estimation Procedures for Innovation Diffusion Models of New Product Acceptance," *Technological Forecasting and Social Change*, 30(12):331–346. MR(E)

Mahajan, Vijay, Subhash Sharma, and Richard A. Bettis (1988), "The Adoption of the M-Form Organizational Structure: A Test of the Imitation Hypothesis," *Management Science*, 34(12):188–201. MR(E)

Mahajan, Vijay, and Yoram Wind (eds.)(1986), *Innovation Diffusion Models of New Product Acceptance*, Cambridge, MA, Ballinger. MR(N)

Maidique, Modesto A. (1980), "Entrepreneurs, Champions, and Technological Innovation," *Sloan Management Review*, 21(2):59–76. MR(E)

Maidique, Modesto, and B. J. Zirger (1984), "A Study of Success and Failure in Product Innovation: The Case of the U.S. Electronics Industry," *IEEE Transactions on Engineering Management*, EM-31(4):192–203. MR(E)

Mamer, J.W., and K.F. McCardle (1987), "Uncertainty, Competition, and the Adoption of New Technology," *Management Science*, 33:161–177. MR(E)

Manross, George, and Ronald E. Rice (1986a), "Don't Hang Up: Organizational Diffusion of Intelligent Telephones," *Information and Management*, 10:161–175. C(E)

———— (1986b), "Innovation Diffusion Models of New Acceptance: A Reexamination," in Vijay Mahajan and Yoram Wind (eds.), *Innovation Diffusion Models of New Product Acceptance*," Cambridge, MA, Ballinger. C(E)

———— (1988), "New Product Forecasting Models: Directions for Research and Implementation," *International Journal of Forecasting*, 4(3):341–358. C(E)

March, James G. (1981), "Footnotes to Organizational Change," *Administrative Science Quarterly*, 26:563–577.

Marcus, Alan S., and Raymond A. Bauer (1964), "Yes: There Are Generalized Opinion Leaders," *Public Opinion Quarterly*, 28:628–652. GS(N)

Markus, Alfred A. (1988), "Implementing Externally Induced Innovations: A Comparison of Rule-Bound and Autonomous Approaches," *Academy of Management Journal*, 31(2):235–256. MR(E)

Markus, A., and M. Weber (1989), "Externally Induced Innovation," in Andrew H. Van de Ven, H. A. Angle, and M. Scott Poole (eds.), *Research on the Management of Innovation: The Minnesota Studies*, New York, Ballinger/Harper & Row. MR(E)

Markus, M. Lynne (1987), "Toward a 'Critical Mass' Theory of Interactive Media: Universal Access, Interdependence and Diffusion," *Communication Research*, 14:491–511. MR(N)

———(1990), "Toward a 'Critical Mass' Theory of Interactive Media," in Janet Fulk and Charles Steinfield (eds.), *Organizations and Communication Technology*, Newbury Park, CA, Sage, pp. 194–218. MR(N)

Marsden, Peter V., and Joel Podolny (1990), "Dynamic Analysis of Network Diffusion Processes," in Jerver Wessie and Hank Flap (eds.), *Social Networks Through Time*, Utrecht, The Netherlands, ISOR, pp. 197–214. GS(E)

Marsh, Colin J. (1984), "Implementation of Curriculum Innovations in Australian Schools, " *Knowledge*, 6(1):37–58. E(E)

Marshall, Joanne Gard (1989a), "Characteristics of Early Adoptors of End-User Online Searching in the Health Profession," *Bulletin of Medical Library Association*, 77(1):48–55. O(E)

——— (1989b), "End-User Training: Does It Make a Difference?" *Medical Reference Services Quarterly*, 8(3):15–25. O(E)

——— (1990), "Diffusion of Innovation Theory and End-User Searching," *Library and Information Science Research*, 12(1):55–69. O(E)

Mason, Robert, Larry Boersma, and G. David Faulkenberry (1988), "The Use of Open and Closed Questions to Identify Holders of Crystallized Attitudes: The Case of Adoption of Erosion-Control Practices among Farmers," *Rural Sociology*, 53(1):96–109. RS(E)

Mason, Robert G. (1962), "An Ordinal Scale for Measuring the Adoption Process," in Wilbur Schramm (ed.), *Studies of Innovation and Communication to the Public*, Stanford, CA, Stanford University, Institute for Communication Research. C(E)

Mass, William (1985), "Technological Change and Industrial Relations: The Diffusion of Automatic Weaving in the United States and Britain," *Journal of Economic History*, 45:458–460. O(E)

Mattingly, P. F. (1984), "Disadoption of Milk Cows by Farmers in Illinois: 1930–1978," *Professional Geographer*, 36:40–51. G(E)

Mayer, Michael E., William B. Gudykunst, and Bruce D. Merrill (1986), *Diffusion of Information about the Shuttle Explosion*, Department of Communication, Arizona State University, Tempe, Research Report. C(E)

Mayer, Michael E., William B. Gudykunst, Norman K. Perrill, and Bruce D. Merrill (1990), "A Comparison of Competing Models of the News Diffusion Process," *Western Journal of Speech Communication*, 54:113–123. C(E)

McAdam, Doug (1986), "Recruitment to High-Risk Activism: The Case of Freedom Summer," *American Journal of Sociology*, 92(1):64–90. GS(E)

McAdam, Doug, and Ronnelle Paulsen (1993), "Specifying the Relationship between Social Ties and Activism," *American Journal of Sociology*, 99(3):640–667. GS(E)

McAnany, Emile G. (1984), "The Diffusion of Innovation: Why Does It Endure?" *Critical Studies in Mass Communication*, 1(4):439–442. C(N)

McCardle, K.F. (1985), "Information Acquisition and the Adoption of New Technology," *Management Science*, 31:1372–1389. MR(E)

McCombie, J.S. (1982), "How Important Is the Spatial Diffusion of Innovation in Explaining Regional Growth Rate Disparities?" *Urban Studies*, 19:377–382. G(E)

McGuire, William J. (1989), "Theoretical Foundations of Campaigns," in Ronald E. Rice and Charles K. Atkin (eds.), *Public Communication Campaigns*, Second Edition, Newbury Park, CA, Sage, pp. 43–65.

McIntyre, Shelby H. (1985), "Perspective: Market Adoption as a Process in the Product Life Cycle of Radical Innovations and High Technology Products," *Journal of Production Innovation Management*, 5:140–149. MR(N)

McKeague, I.W. (1984), "Estimation for Diffusion Processes under Misspecified Models," *Journal of Applied Probability*, 21:511–520. S(E)

McKee, Neill (1991), *Social Mobilization and Social Marketing in Developing Countries: Lessons for Communicators*, Penang, Malaysia, Southbound. C(N)

McKinley, John B. (1981), "From 'Promising Report' to 'Standard Procedure': Seven Stages in the Career of a Medical Innovation," *Milbank Memorial Fund Quarterly/Health and Society*, 59(3):374–411. PH(N)

McKinney, Martha M., Janet M. Barnsley, and Arnold D. Kaluzny (1992), "Organizing for Cancer Control: The Diffusion of a Dynamic Innovation in a Community Cancer Network," *International Journal of Technology Assessment in Health Care*, 8(2):268–288. PH(E)

McLeroy, K. R., K. McCann, D. Smith, and R. Goodman (1986), "The Role of Summer Institutes in the Diffusion of Comprehensive School Health," *Family and Community Health*, 12(3):26–39. E(E)

Meade, Nigel (1984), "The Use of Growth Curves in Forecasting Market Development: A Review and Appraisal," *Journal of Forecasting*, 3:429–451. MR(E)

——— (1985), "Forecasting Using Growth Curves: An Adaptive Approach," *Journal of the Operational Research Society*, 36(12):1103–1115. MR(E)

Meir, A. (1980a), "The Diffusion of Industry Adoption by Kibbutz Rural Settlements in Israel," *Journal of Developing Areas*, 14:539–552. U(E)

——— (1980b), "Innovation Diffusion and Regional Economic Development: The Spatial Diffusion of Automobiles in Ohio," *Regional Studies*, 15:11–122. G(E)

Melkote, Srinivas Rajagopal (1984a), *The Biases in Extension Communication: Revealing the Comprehension Gap: An Examination of the World Bank Sponsored T & V Extension System in Andhra Pradesh State, India*, Ph.D. Thesis, University of Iowa. C(E)

——— (1984b), "Communication Constraints to Adoption of Agricultural Innovations: An Investigation of Message Biases," *Journal of Communication Inquiry*, 8(1):59–70. C(N)

——— (1988), "Communication Constraints in Extension Communication Strategies," *Knowledge in Society*, 1(2):42–56. C(E)

——— (1989a), "Revealing Communication Constraints in Extension Communication Strategies," *Knowledge in Society*, 1(2):42–57. C(E)

————— (1989b), "Effectiveness of Development-Radio Programming among Poor Farmers: A Case Study," *Gazette*, 43:17–30. C(E)

Mendell, Stefanie, and Daniel M. Ennis (1985), "Looking at Innovation Strategies," *Research Management*, 28:33–40. O(N)

Mendelsohn, Harold (1973), "Some Reasons Why Information Campaigns Can Succeed," *Public Opinion Quarterly*, 39:50–61. C(E)

Menzel, Herbert (1957), "Public and Private Conformity under Different Conditions of Acceptance in the Group," *Journal of Abnormal and Social Psychology*, 55:398–402. PH(E)

————— (1959), *Social Determinants of Physicians' Reaction to Innovation in Medical Practice*, Ph.D. Thesis, Madison, University of Wisconsin. PH(E)

————— (1960), "Innovation, Integration, and Marginality: A Survey of Physicians," *American Sociological Review*, 25(5):704–713. PH(E)

Menzel, Herbert, James S. Coleman, and Elihu Katz (1959), "Dimensions of Being 'Modern' in Medical Practice," *Journal of Chronic Diseases*, 9(1):20–40. PH(E)

Menzel, Herbert, and Elihu Katz (1955), "Social Relations and Innovation in the Medical Profession: The Epidemiology of a New Drug," *Public Opinion Quarterly*, 19:337–353. PH(E)

Merton, Robert K. (1968), *Social Theory and Social Structure*, New York, Free Press. Originally published 1949.

Mesak, H.I, and W.M. Mikhail (1988), "Prelaunch Sales Forecasting of a New Industrial Product," *Omega*, 16(1):41–51. MR(E)

Metcalfe, J.S. (1981), "Impulses and Diffusion in the Study of Technical Change," *Futures*, 13(5):347–359. G(E)

Meyer, Alan D., and James B. Goes (1988), "Organizational Assimilation of Innovations: A Multilevel Contextual Analysis," *Academy of Management Journal*, 31(4):897–923. MR(E)

Mezias, Stephen J. (1990), "An Institutional Model of Organizational Practice: Financial Reporting at the *Fortune* 200," *Administrative Science Quarterly*, 35:431–457. MR(E)

Michaelson, Alaina G. (1993), "The Development of a Scientific Speciality as Diffusion through Social Relations: The Case of Role Analysis," *Social Networks*, 15:217–236. P(E)

Miles, Mathew B. (ed.) (1964), *Innovation in Education*, New York, Columbia University, Teachers College. E(N)

Miller, Danny, and Peter H. Fricsen (1982), "Innovation in Conservative and Entrepreneurial Firms: Two Models of Strategic Momentum," *Strategic Management Journal*, 3:1–25. MR(E)

Mintzberg, Henry, Duru Raisinghani, and André Théôrét (1976), "The Structure of 'Unstructured' Decision Processes," *Administrative Science Quarterly*, 21:246–275. MR(N)

Modis, T, and A. Debecker (1988), "Innovation in the Computer Industry," *Technological Forecasting and Social Change*, 33:267–278. O(E)

Mogee, Mary Ellen (1987), "Indicators of the Diffusion of Innovations for Science Indicators: Implications Drawn from the Diffusion Literature," Paper prepared for the National Science Foundation. U(E)

Mohr, Lawrence B. (1966), *Determinants of Innovation in Organizations*, Ph.D. Thesis, Ann Arbor, University of Michigan. PS(E)

———— (1969), "Determinants of Innovation in Organizations," *American Political Science Review*, 63:111–126. PS(E)

———— (1978), "Process Theory and Variance Theory in Innovation Research," in Michael Radnor and others (eds.), *The Diffusion of Innovations: An Assessment*, Evanston, Illinois, Northwestern University, Center for Interdisciplinary Study of Science and Technology, Report to the National Science Foundation. PS(E)

———— (1982), *Explaining Organizational Behavior: The Limits and Possibilities of Theory and Research*, San Francisco, Jossey-Bass. PS(N)

Monahan, Jennifer L., and Mary Ann Scheirer (1988), "The Role of Linking Agents in the Diffusion of Health Promotion Programs," *Health Education Quarterly*, 15(4):417–433. PH(E)

Moore, Gary C., and Izak Benbasat (1990), "An Examination of the Adoption of Information Technology by End-Users: A Diffusion of Innovations Perspective," Vancouver, Canada, University of British Columbia, Department of Commerce and Business Administration, Working Paper 90-MIS-012. MR(E)

———— (1991), "Development of an Instrument to Measure the Perceived Characteristics of Adopting an Information Technology Innovation," *Information System Research*, 11:192–220. MR(E)

Moore, Roger A. (1983), "Overcoming Barriers to the Adoption of High Technology in Industrial Markets," *Business Quarterly Review of Marketing*, 24:13–20. MR(E)

Moriarty, Rowland T., Jr., and Robert E. Spekman (1984), "An Empirical Investigation of the Information Sources Used During the Industrial Buying Process," *Journal of Marketing Research*, 21:137–147. MR(E)

Morrill, Richard L. (1985), "The Diffusion of the Use of Tractors Again," *Geographical Analysis*, 17(1):88–94. G(E)

Morrill, Richard L., and J. Angulo (1981), "Multivariate Analysis of School Attendance in the Introduction of Variola Minor into the Household," *Social Sciences and Medicine*, 15:479–487. G(E)

Morrill, Richard L., Gary L. Gale, and Grant Ian Thrall (1988), *Spatial Diffusion*, Newbury Park, CA, Sage. G(N)

Morrison, Denton E., Krishna Kumar, Everett M. Rogers, and Frederick C. Fliegel (1976), "Stratification and Risk Taking: A Further Negative Replication of Cancian's Theory," *American Sociological Review*, 41(5):912–918. RS(E)

Mort, Paul R. (1953), "Educational Adaptability," *The School Executive*, 71:1–23, 199–200. E(E)

Mosteller, Frederick (1981), "Innovation and Evaluation," *Science*, 211:881–886. S(N)

Mowery, David C. (1983), "Economic Theory and Government Technology Policy," *Policy Sciences*, 16:27–43. GE(N)

Murray, Stephen O., and others (1981), "Strong Ties and Job Information," *Sociology of Work and Occupations*, 8:119–136. GS(E)

Musmann, Klaus, and William H. Kennedy (1989), *Diffusion of Innovations: A Select Bibliography*, New York, Greenwood Press. O(N)

Myers, Summer (1978), *The Demonstration Project as a Procedure for Accelerating the Application of New Technology*, Washington, D.C., Institute of Public Administration, Report. O(N)

Mytinger, Robert E. (1968), *Innovation in Local Health Services: A Study of the Adoption of New Programs by Local Health Departments with Particular Reference to New Health Practices,* Washington, D.C., U.S. Department of Health Education and Welfare, Public Health Service, Division of Medical Care Administration, p. 7. PH(E)

Nader, Ralph (1965), *Unsafe at Any Speed,* New York, Grossman.

Napier, Ted L., Cameron S. Thraen, Akia Gore, and W. Richard Gore (1984), "Factors Affecting Adoption of Conventional and Conservation Tillage Practices in Ohio," *Journal of Social and Water Conservation,* 39:205–209. RS(E)

Nariman, Heidi Noel (1993), *Soap Operas for Social Change: Toward a Methodology for Entertainment-Education Television,* Westport, CT, Praeger.

Narsimhan, Chakravarthi (1989), "Incorporating Consumer Price Expectations in Diffusion Models," *Marketing Science,* 8(4):343–357. MR(E)

Nasbeth, L., and G.F. Ray (1984), *The Diffusion of Mature Technologies,* New York, Cambridge University Press. U(E)

Ndiaye, Serigne, and Andrew J. Sofranko (1988), "Importance of Labor in Adoption of a Modern Farm Input," *Rural Sociology,* 53(4):421–432. RS(E)

Niehoff, Arthur (1964), "Theravada Buddhism: A Vehicle for Technical Change," *Human Organization,* 23:108–112. A(E)

——— (1966), *A Casebook of Social Change,* Chicago, Aldine. A(N)

Nooteboom, Bart (1984), "Innovation, Life Cycle and the Share of Independents: Cases from Retailing," *International Small Business Journal,* 3(1):21–33. MR(E)

——— (1989), "Diffusion, Uncertainity, and Firm Size," *International Journal of Research in Marketing,* 6:109–128. MR(E)

Nord, W.R., and S. Tucker (1987), *Implementing Routine and Radical Innovations,* Lexington, MA, Heath. MR(E)

Norton, John A., and Frank M. Bass (1987), "A Diffusion Theory Model of Adoption and Substitution for Successive Generations of High Technology Products," *Management Science,* 33(9):1069–1086. MR(E)

Nowak, Peter J. (1982), "Application of an Adoption-Diffusion Model to Resource Conservation: A Supporting View," Paper presented at the Rural Sociological Society, San Francisco. RS(N)

——— (1983a), "Adoption and Diffusion of Soil and Water Practices," *Rural Sociologist,* 3(2):1–9. RS(N)

——— (1983b), "Obstacles to Adoption of Conservation Tillage: Effectively Promoting the Use of Conservation Tillage Requires a Look at the Adoption Process Through the Eyes of the Farmer," *Journal of Soil and Water Conservation,* 38(3):162–165. RS(E)

——— (1987), "The Adoption of Agricultural Conservation Technologies: Economic and Diffusion Explanations," *Rural Sociology,* 52(1):208–220. RS(E)

Nowak, Peter J., and Peter F. Korsching (1983), "Social and Institutional Factors Affecting the Adoption and Maintenance of Agricultural BMPs," in F. Schaller and G. Bailey (eds.), *Agricultural Management and Water Quality,* Ames, Iowa State University Press. RS(E)

Noyce, Robert N., and Marcian E. Hoff, Jr. (1981), "A History of Microprocessor Development at Intel," *IEEE Micro,* 7:8–21.

Nyre, G.F. (1985), "Drug Abuse Resistance Education (Project D.A.R.E.) in Elementary Schools: Police as Teachers," in L.H. Berkovitz and J. Selinger (eds.), *Expanding Mental Health Interventions in Schools,* Los Angeles, CA, Kendall/Hunt. E(E)

Olshavsky, Richard W. (1980), "Time and the Rate of Adoption of Innovations," *Journal of Consumer Research*, 6(3):425–428. MR(E)

Olson, Jerome, and Seungmook Choi (1985), "A Product Diffusion Model Incorporating Repeat Purchases," *Technological Forecasting and Social Change*, 27:385–397. MR(E)

Olson, Mancur H. (1965), *The Logic of Collective Action: Public Goods and the Theory of Groups*, Cambridge, MA, Harvard University Press.

Opake, K. Dua (1987), "The Role of Agricultural Extension in the Adoption of Innovations by Cocoa Growers in Ghana," *Rural Sociology*, 42:72–82. RS(E)

Oren, Shmuel S., and Rick G. Schwartz (1988), "Diffusion of New Products in Risk-Sensitive Markets," *Journal of Forecasting*, 7:273–287. MR(E)

Orlandi, Mario A. (1986), "The Diffusion and Adoption of Worksite Health Promotion Innovations: An Analysis of Barriers," *Preventive Medicine*, 15:522–536. PH(E).

Orlandi, Mario A., C. Landers, R. Weston, and N. Haley (1991), "Diffusion of Health Promotion Innovations," in Karen Glanz, F.M. Lewis, and B.K. Rimer (eds.), *Health Behavior and Health Education: Theory, Research, and Practice*, San Francisco, Jossey-Bass, pp. 288–313. PH(E)

Orlikowski, Wanda J. (1992), "The Duality of Technology: Rethinking the Concept of Technology in Organization," *Organization Science*, 3(3):398–428. MR(N)

Paddock, W.C. (1992), "Our Last Chance to Win the War on Hunger," *Advances in Plant Pathology*, 8:197–222.

Pake, George E. (October, 1985), "Research at Xerox PARC: A Founder's Assessment," *IEEE Spectrum*, 62–75.

Palumbo, Dennis J. (1987), "Implementation: What Have We Learned and Still Need to Know," *Policy Studies Review*, 7(1):91–102. PS(N)

Papa, Michael J. (1990), "Communication Network Patterns and Employee Performance with New Technology," *Communication Research*, 17(3):344–368. C(E)

Parcel, Glenn S., and others (1989), "Translating Theory into Practice: Intervention Strategies for the Diffusion of a Health Promotion Innovation," *Family and Community Health*, 12(3):1–13. PH(E)

Parcel, Guy S., and others (1989), "The Diffusion of School-Based Tobacco Use Prevention Programs: Project Description and Baseline Data," *Health Education Research*, 4(1):111–124. PH(E)

Parcel, Guy S., Cheryl L. Perry, and Wendell C. Taylor (1990), "Beyond Demonstration: Diffusion of Health Promotion Innovations," in Neil Bracht (ed.), *Health Promotion at the Community Level*, Newbury Park, CA, Sage, pp. 229–251. PH(E)

Parkinson, Robert (1972), "The Dvorak Simplified Keyboard: Forty Years of Frustration," *Computers and Automation*, 21:1–8.

Pavalko, Eliza K. (1989), "State Timing of Policy Adoption: Workmen's Compensation in the United States, 1909–1929," *American Journal of Sociology*, 95(3):595–615. GS(E)

Peay, Marilyn Y., and Edmond R. Peay (1988), "The Role of Commercial Sources in the Adoption of a New Drug," *Social Science and Medicine*, 26:1183–1189. U(E)

Pelto, Pertti J. (1973), *The Snowmobile Revolution: Technology and Social Change in the Arctic*, Menlo Park, CA, Cummings, p. 192. A(E)

Pelto, Pertti J., and Ludger Müller-Wille (1972), "The Snowmobile Revolution: Technology and Social Change in the Arctic," in H. Russell Bernard and Pertti Pelto (eds.), *Technology and Social Change*, New York, Macmillan. A(E)

Pelto, Pertti J., and others (1969), "The Snowmobile Revolution in Lapland," *Journal of the Finno-Ugrian Society*, 69:1–42. A(E)

Pelz, Donald C. (1981), *Use of Information in Innovating Processes by Local Governments*, Ann Arbor, University of Michigan, Center for Research on Utilization of Scientific Knowledge, Research Report. P(E)

—— (1983a), "Quantitative Case Histories of Urban Innovations: Are There Innovative Stages?" *IEEE Transactions on Engineering Management*, EM-30, 2:60–67. P(E)

—— (1983b), "Use of Information Channels in Urban Innovations," *Knowledge*, 5(1):3–25. P(E)

—— (1985), "Innovation Complexity and the Sequence of Innovating Stages," *Knowledge: Creation, Diffusion, and Utilization*, 6(3):261–291. P(E)

Pelz, Donald C., and Fred C. Munson (1982), "Originality Level and the Innovation Process in Organizations," *Human Systems Management*, 3:173–187. P(E)

Pemberton, H. Earl (1936a), "The Curve of Culture Diffusion Rate," *American Sociological Review*, 1:547–556. ES(E)

—— (1936b), "Culture-Diffusion Gradients," *American Journal of Sociology*, 42:226–233. ES(E)

—— (1937), "The Effect of a Social Crisis on the Curve of Diffusion," *American Sociological Review*, 1:547–556. ES(E)

—— (1938), "The Spatial Order of Culture Diffusion," *Sociology and Social Research*, 246–251. ES(E)

Pennings, Johannes, and Arend Buitendam (1987), *New Technology as Organizational Innovation*, Cambridge, MA, Ballinger. MR(E)

Pennings, Johannes M., and Farid Harianto (1990), "The Diffusion of Technological Innovation in the Commercial Banking Industry," Philadelphia, University of Pennsylvania, Wharton School, Research Paper. MR(E)

Perez, Carlota (1983), "Structural Change and Assimilation of New Technologies in the Economic and Social Systems," *Futures*, 15(4):357–375. GE(N)

Perry, James L., and James N. Danziger (1980), "The Adoptability of Innovations: An Empirical Assessment of Computer Applications in Local Governments," *Administration & Society*, 11(4): 460–492. MR(E)

Perry, James L., and Kenneth L. Kraemer (1979), *Technological Innovation in American Local Governments: The Case of Computing*, New York, Pergamon Press. PS(E)

Perry, Seymour (1984), "Diffusion of New Technologies: Rational and Irrational," *Journal of Health Care Technology*, 1(2):73–88. PH(N)

Perry, Tekla S., and Paul Wallich (October 1985), "Inside the PARC: The Information Architects," *IEEE Spectrum*, 62–75.

Peterson, Robert A., and Vijay Mahajan (1978), "Multi-Product Growth Models," in Jagdish Sheth (ed.), *Research Marketing*, Greenwich, CT, JAI Press, pp. 201–231. MR(E)

Petrini, Frank, and others (1968), *The Information Problem of an Agricultural College*, Uppsala, Sweden, Nordisk Jordbrukforkning 50. RS(E)

Petty, Gary R., Richard M. Perloff, and Kimberly A. Neundorf with Barry Pollick (1986), "Feeling and Learning about a Critical Event: The Shuttle Explodes," Paper presented to the Association for Education in Journalism and Mass Communication, Norman, Oklahoma. C(E)

Phillips, M.L., and D.A. Duric (1985), "Diffusion of an Innovation: Adoption of CT Scanners," *Radiologic Technology*, 57:137–140. U(E)

Piotrow, Phyllis T., and others (1990), "Mass Media Family Planning Promotion in Three Nigerian Cities," *Studies in Family Planning*, 21(5):265–274. PH(E)

Pitcher, Brian L., Robert L. Hamblin, and Jerry L.L. Miller (1978), "The Diffusion of Collective Violence," *American Sociological Review*, 43:23–25. GS(E)

Placek, Paul J. (1975), "Welfare Workers as Family Planning Change Agents and the Perennial Problem of Heterophily with Welfare Clients," *Applied Behavioral Science*, 2:298–316. MS(E)

Pool, Ithiel de Sola, and Manfred Kochen (1981), "Contacts and Influence," *Social Network* 1(1981):5–51. PS(E)

Poole, Marshall Scott, and Andrew H. Van de Ven (1989), "Toward a General Theory of Innovation Process," in Andrew H. Van de Ven, H.A. Angle, and M. Scott Poole (eds.), *Research on the Management of Innovation: The Minnesota Studies*, New York, Ballinger/Harper & Row. C(E)

Pope, Alexander (1711), *An Essay on Criticism*, Part II.

Portony, B., D.M. Anderson, and M.P. Eriksen (1986), "Application of Diffusion Theory to Health Promotion Research," *Family and Community Health*, 12(3):63–71. PH(E)

Prahl, Ralph, Gerald Marwell, and Pamela E. Oliver (1991), "Reach and Selectivity as Strategies of Recruitment for Collective Action: A Theory of the Critical Mass," *Journal of Mathematical Sociology*, 16(2):137–164. GS(N)

Pratt, Stephen R., and David L. Rogers (1986), "Correlates of the Adoption of Land Use Controls," *Rural Sociology*, 51(3):354–362. RS(E)

Pred, Allan (1981), "Power, Everyday Practice and the Discipline of Human Geography," in Torsten Hägerstand (ed.), *Space and Time Geography*, Berlings, Lund. G(A)

Preston, Murray A., Tom Baranowski, and John C. Higginbotham (1988), *Orchestrating the Points of Community Intervention: Enhancing the Diffusion Process*, Department of Preventive Medicine and Community Health, University of Texas, Research Report. PH(N)

Price, Derek J. de Solla (1963), *Little Science, Big Science*, New York, Columbia University Press.

Price, Linda L., Lawrence F. Feik, and Daniel C. Smith (1985), "A Re-Examination of Communication Channel Usage by Adoptor Categories," Paper presented at the Association for Consumer Research, Las Vegas. MR(E)

Prochaska, James O., Carlo C. DiClemente, and John C. Norcross (1992), "In Search of How People Change: Applications to Addictive Behaviors," *American Psychologist*, 47(9):1102–1114. P(E)

Prontius, Steven K. (1983), "The Communication Process of Adoption: Agriculture in Thailand," *Journal of Developing Areas*, 18:93–118. U(E)

Prottas, Jeffrey (1984), "The Impacts of Innovation: Technological Change in a Mass Transit Authority," *Administration and Society*, 16(1):117–135. PS(E)

Puro, Marsha, Peter J. Bergerson, and Steven Puro (1985), "An Analysis of Judicial Diffusion: Adoption of the Missouri Plan in the American States," *Publius*, 15:85–97. PS(E)

Puska, P., and others (1986), "Use of Lay Opinion Leaders to Promote Diffusion of Health

Innovations in a Community Programme: Lessons Learned from the North Karelia Project," *Bulletin of the World Health Organization*, 64(3):437–446. PH(E)

Quarles, Rebecca, L.W. Jeffres, C.I. Sanchez, and K. Neuwirth (1983), "News Diffusion of Assassination Attempts on President Reagan and Pope John Paul II," *Journal of Broadcasting*, 27:387–394. C(E)

Quirmbach, Herman C. (1986), "The Diffusion of New Technology and the Market for an Innovation," *Rand Journal of Economics*, 17(1):33–47. GE(N)

Rabin, Robert A., and Stephen D. Sugarman (eds.)(1993), *Smoking Policy: Law, Politics, and Culture*, New York, Oxford University Press. O(E)

Rabino, S. (1983), "Influencing the Adoption of an Innovation," *Industrial Marketing Management*, 12:233–241. MR(E)

Rahim, S.A. (1961), *The Diffusion and Adoption of Agricultural Practices: A Study in a Village in East Pakistan*, Comilla, East Pakistan, Pakistan Academy for Village Development. C(E)

——— (1965), *Communication and Personal Experience in an East Pakistan Village*, Comilla, East Pakistan, Pakistan Academy for Village Development. C(E)

Rajagopal, Srinivas (1981), "The Utility of Diffusion Research to the Third World: A Boon or Bane?" *Media Asia*, 8(1):12–17. C(N)

Randles, F. (1983), "On the Diffusion of Computer Terminals in an Established Engineering Environment," *Management Science*, 29(4):465–476. MR(E)

Randolfi, E.A. (1986), *The Diffusion of Curriculum Innovations in Higher Education: A Course in Microcomputer Applications for Health Educators*, Ph.D. Thesis, Eugene, University of Oregon. E(E)

Rao, Amber G., and Masataka Yamada (1988), "Forecasting with a Repeat Purchase Diffusion Model," *Management Science*, 34(6):734–752. MR(E)

Rao, G. Appa, Everett M. Rogers, and S.N. Singh (1980), "Interpersonal Relations in the Diffusion of an Innovation in Two Indian Villages," *Indian Journal of Extension Education*, 16(1&2):19–24. RS(E)

Rao, Ram C., and Frank M. Bass (1985), "Competition, Strategy, and Price Dynamics: A Theoretical and Empirical Investigation," *Journal of Marketing Research*, 22(8):283–296. MR(E)

Rao, Sanjay-Kumar (1985), "An Empirical Comparison of Sales Forecasting Models," *Journal of Product Innovation Management*, 2(12):232–242. MR(E)

Rasmussen, Wayne D. (1968), "Advances in American Agriculture: The Mechanical Tomato Harvester as a Case Study," *Technology and Culture*, 9:531–543.

Ray, George F. (1988), "The Diffusion of Innovations: An Update," *National Institute Economic Review*, 126:51–56. GE(N)

Regan, Joey (1987), "Classifying Adopters and Using Political Activity, Media Use and Demographic Variables," *Telematics and Informatics*, 4(1):3–16. C(E)

Reinarman, Craig (1988), "The Social Construction of an Alcohol Problem: The Case of Mothers Against Drunken Drivers and Social Control in the 1980s," *Theory and Society*, 17:91–120. U(E)

Reinganum, Jennifer F. (1981a), "Market Structure and the Diffusion of New Technology," *Bell Journal of Economics*, 12:618–624. GE(N)

——— (1981b), "On the Diffusion of New Technology: A Game Theoretic Approach," *Review of the Economic Studies*, 47:395–405. GE(N)

────── (1983), "Technology Adoption Under Imperfect Information," *Bell Journal of Economics*, 14:57–69. GE(N)

────── (1985), "Innovation and Industry Evolution," *Quarterly Journal of Economics*, 100:81–99. GE(N)

Repetto, Robert (1969), "India: A Case Study of the Madras Vasectomy Program," *Studies in Family Planning*, 31:8–16. GE(E)

────── (1985), *Paying the Price: Pesticide Subsidies in Developing Countries*, Washington, D.C., World Resources Institute Report, p. 3. GE(E)

Rice, Ronald E., and George Manross (1986), "The Role of Job Category in the Diffusion of an Information Technology: The Case of the Intelligent Telephone," in Margaret McLaughlin (ed.), *Communication Yearbook*, Volume 10, Newbury Park, CA, Sage. C(E)

────── (1987), "The Case of the Intelligent Telephone: The Relationship of Job Category to the Adoption of an Organizational Communication Technology," in Margaret McLaughlin (ed.), *Communication Yearbook*, Volume 11, Newbury Park, CA, Sage. C(E)

Rice, Ronald E., and Everett M. Rogers (1980), "Re-Invention in the Innovation Process," *Knowledge*, 1:499–514. C(E)

Richins, Marsha L. (1983), "Negative Word-of-Mouth by Dissatisfied Consumers: A Pilot Study," *Journal of Marketing*, 47:68–78. MR(E)

Ricketts, T.C., and Arnold D. Kaluzny (1986), "Innovation within Innovation: A Paradox for Cancer Control Research," *Family and Community Health*, 12(3):54–62. PH(E)

Riffe, Daniel, and James Glen Stovall (1987), "Diffusion of News of the Shuttle Disaster: What Role for Emotional Response?" *Journalism Quarterly*, 64:551–556. C(E)

Roberts-Gray, Cynthia (1985), "Managing the Implementation of Innovations," *Education and Program Planning*, 8:261–269. O(E)

Robertson, Thomas S. (1971), *Innovative Behavior and Communication*, New York, Holt, Rinehart and Winston. MR(E)

Robertson, Thomas S., and Hubert Gatignon (1987), "The Diffusion of High Technology Innovations: A Marketing Perspective," in Johannes Pennings and Arend Buitendam (eds.), *New Technology as Organizational Innovation*, Cambridge, MA, Ballinger, pp. 179–196. MR(E)

Robertson, Thomas S., and Yoram Wind (1980), "Organizational Psychographics and Innovativeness," *Journal of Consumer Research*, 7:24–31. MR(E)

Robinson, W.T. (1990), "Product Innovation and Start-Up Business Market Share Performance," *Management Science*, 36(10):1279–1289. MR(E)

Rogers, Everett M. (1958), "Categorizing the Adopters of Agricultural Practices," *Rural Sociology*, 23(4):346–354. RS(E)

────── (1961), *Characteristics of Agricultural Innovators and Other Adopter Categories*, Wooster, Ohio Agricultural Experiment Station Research Bulletin 882. RS(E)

────── (1962), *Diffusion of Innovation*, New York, Free Press, pp. x, 173–174, 276. RS(N)

────── (1973), *Communication Strategies for Family Planning*, New York, Free Press pp. 130, 157–174, 215–217, 237, 295–296, 378, 408. C(N)

────── (1976), "Communication and Development: The Passing of the Dominant Paradigm," *Communication Research*, 3:121–148. C(N)

────── (1978), "New Product Adoption and Diffusion," in Robert Ferber (ed.), *Selected*

Aspects of Consumer Behavior: A Summary from the Perspective of Different Disciplines, Washington D.C., U.S. Government Printing Office. C(N)

——— (1981), "Diffusion of Innovation: An Overview," in Edward B. Roberts, and others (eds.), *Biomedical Innovation*, Cambridge, M.I.T. Press. C(E)

——— (1982a), "Information Exchange and Technological Innovation," in Devendra Sahal (ed.), *The Transfer and Utilization of Technical Knowledge*, Lexington, MA, Lexington Books. C(N)

——— (1982b), *Introduction to Diffusion Science: An Interdisciplinary Cross-Cultural Approach Through Communication Sciences to the Study of the Diffusion of Innovations*, Translated by Yoshiyasu Uno, Tokyo, Japan, Sangyo Noritsu Press. C(N)

——— (1983), *Diffusion of Innovations*, Third Edition, New York, Free Press, p. 232. C(N)

——— (1985), "The Diffusion of Home Computers among Households in Silicon Valley," *Marriage and Family Review*, 8:89–101. C(E)

——— (1986a), "Models of Knowledge Transfer: Critical Perspectives," in George M. Beal, Wimal Dissanayake, and Sumiye Konoshima (eds.), *Knowledge Generation, Exchange, and Utilization*, Boulder, CO, Westview Press, pp. 37–60. C(N)

——— (1986b), *Communication Technology: The New Media in Society*, New York, Free Press. C(N)

——— (1987), "Progress, Problems, and Prospects for Network Research: Investigating Relationships in the Age of Electronic Communication Technologies," *Social Networks*, 9:285–310. C(N)

——— (1988a), "The Intellectual Foundation and History of the Agricultural Extension Model," *Knowledge*, 9:410–510. C(N)

——— (1988b), "Information Technologies: How Organizations Are Changing," in Gerald M. Goldhaber and George A. Barnett (eds.), *Handbook of Organizational Communication*, Norwood, NJ, Ablex, pp. 437–452. C(N)

——— (1990a), "The R&D/Marketing Interface in the Technological Innovation Process," in Massoud M. Saghafi and Ashok K. Gupta (eds.), *Advances in Telecommunications Management, Volume 1, Managing the R&D/Marketing Interface for Product Success: The Telecommunication Focus*, Greenwich, CT, JAI Press, pp. 5–14 C(N)

——— (1990b), "The 'Critical Mass' in the Diffusion of Interactive Technologies," in M. Carnevale, M. Lucertini, and S. Nicosia (eds.), *Modeling the Innovation: Communication, Automation, and Information Systems*, Amsterdam, Elsevier, pp. 79–94. C(N)

——— (1991a), "Rise of the Classical Diffusion Model," *Current Contents*, 13(15):16. C(N)

——— (1991b), "The 'Critical Mass' in the Diffusion of Interactive Technologies in Organizations," in Kenneth L. Kraemer, James I. Cash, Jr., and Jay F. Nunmaker, Jr. (eds.), *The Information System Research Challenges: Survey Research Methods*, Boston, Harvard Business School Press, pp. 245–263. C(N)

——— (1992), "Communication Campaigns to Change Health-Related Lifestyles," *Supplement Hygine*, 11(2):29–34. C(N)

——— (1993a), "Diffusion and the Re-Invention of Project D.A.R.E," in Thomas E. Backer and Everett M. Rogers (eds.), *Organizational Aspects of Health Communication Campaigns: What Works?* Newbury Park, CA, Sage, pp. 139–162. C(E)

———(1993b), "The Diffusion of Innovations Model," in Ian Masser and Harlan J. Onsrud (eds.), *Diffusion and Use of Geography Information Technology*, Dordrecht, The Netherlands, Kluwer Academic Publishers. C(N)

———(1994), *A History of Communication Study: A Biographical Approach*, New York, Free Press.

Rogers, Everett M., and Rekha Agarwala-Rogers (1976), *Communication in Organizations*, New York, Free Press, p. 26. C(N)

Rogers, Everett M., Joseph R. Ascroft, and Niels G. Röling (1970), *Diffusion of Innovations in Brazil, Nigeria, and India*, East Lansing, Michigan State University, Department of Communication, Diffusion of Innovations Research Report 24, pp. 6–12. C(E)

Rogers, Everett M., and Thiery Bardini (1994), "Personal Computing Technology Flows from SRI to Xerox to Apple: Funneling the Future," Unpublished Paper, Los Angeles, University of Southern California, Annenberg School for Communication. C(E)

Rogers, Everett M., and Pi-Chao Chen (1980), "Diffusion of Health and Birth Planning Innovations in the People's Republic of China," in George I. Lythscott and others (eds.), *Report of the Chinese Rural Health Delegation*, Washington, D.C., U.S. Department of Health and Human Services, Foggarty Center for International Health, Report. C(E)

Rogers, Everett M., Hugh Daley, and Thomas Wu (1980), *The Diffusion of Personal Computers*, Stanford, CA, Stanford University, Institute for Communication Research, Report. C(E)

Rogers, Everett M., and James W. Dearing (1988), "Agenda-Setting Research: Where Has It Been, Where Is It Going?" in James Anderson (ed.), *Communication Yearbook 11*, Newbury Park, CA, Sage. C(N)

Rogers, Everett M., J.D. Eveland, and Alden Bean (1982), *Extending the Agricultural Extension Model*, Stanford, CA, Stanford University, Institute for Communication Research, Report. C(N)

Rogers, Everett M., J.D. Eveland, and Constanie Klepper (1977), *The Innovation Process in Public Organizations: Some Elements of a Preliminary Model*, Ann Arbor, University of Michigan, Department of Journalism, Report to the National Science Foundation. C(E)

Rogers, Everett M., and D. Lawrence Kincaid (1981), *Communication Networks: Toward a New Paradigm for Research*, New York, Free Press. C(E)

Rogers, Everett M., and Judith K. Larsen (1984), *Silicon Valley Fever: Growth of High-Technology Culture*, New York, Basic Books.

Rogers, Everett M., and Dorothy Leonard-Barton (1978), "Testing Social Theories in Marketing Settings," *American Behavioral Scientist*, 21:479–500. C(N)

Rogers, Everett M., and Udai Pareek (1982), *Acceptability of Fertility Regulating Mechanism: A Synthesis of Research Literature*, Stanford, California, Stanford University, Institute of Communication Research, Report to the World Health Organization. C(N)

Rogers, Everett M., and L. Edna Rogers (1961), "A Methodological Analysis of Adoption Scales," *Rural Sociology*, 26(4):325–336. RS(E)

Rogers, Everett M., with F. Floyd Shoemaker (1971), *Communication of Innovations: A Cross-Cultural Approach*, New York, Free Press, p. 46–47, 78–79, 257. C(E)

Rogers, Everett M., and J. Douglas Storey (1988), "Communication Campaigns," in

Charles R. Berger and Steven H. Chaffee (eds.), *Handbook of Communication Science*, Newbury Park, CA, Sage, pp. 621, 817–846. C(N)

Rogers, Everett M., with Lynne Svenning (1969), *Modernization Among Peasants: The Impact of Communication*, New York, Holt, Rinehart and Winston, p. 230–231, 300. C(E)

Rogers, Everett M., and Johannes C. van Es (1964), *Opinion Leadership in Traditional and Modern Colombian Peasant Communities*, East Lansing, Michigan State University, Department of Communication, Diffusion of Innovations Research Report 2. C(E)

Rohlfs, J. (1974), "A Theory of Interdependent Demand for a Communication Service," *Bell Journal of Economics and Management Science*, 5:16–37. O(N)

Röling, Niels (1981), "Alternative Approaches in Extension," in Gwyen E. Jones and M. Roll (eds.), *Progress in Rural Extension and Community Development*, Chichester, England, Wiley. RS(N)

―――― (1985), "Extension Science: Increasingly Preoccupied with Knowledge System," *Sociologia Ruralis*, 25(3/4):269–290. RS(N)

Röling, Niels, and others (1976), "The Diffusion of Innovations and the Issue of Equity in Rural Development," *Communication Research*, 3:155–170. C(E)

Rollo, F. David (1984), "The Role of Hospitals and Physicians in Technology Diffusion," *Journal of Health Care Technology*, 2:121–132. PH(N)

Rosengren, Karl Eric (1987a), "Introduction to a Special Issue on News Diffusion," *European Journal of Communication*, 2:135–142. C(N)

Rosengren, Karl Eric (1987b), "The Comparative Study of News Diffusion," *European Journal of Communication*, 2:227–255. C(E)

Rosenstock, Irwin M. (1966), "Why People Use Health Services," *Milbank Memorial Fund Quarterly*, 44(2):94–127. PH(E)

Rosenstock, Irwin M., V. Strecher, and Marshall Becker (1988), "Social Learning Theory and the Health Belief Model," *Health Education Quarterly*, 15 (2):175–183. PH(N)

Ross, Donald H. (1958), *Administration for Adaptability*, New York, Metropolitan School Study Council. E(E)

Rota, Josep (1986), "Patterns and Correlates of News Diffusion in Mexico City," Paper presented at Speech Communication Association, Chicago. C(E)

Rothwell, Roy (1984), "The Role of Small Firms in the Emergence of New Technologies," *Omega*, 12(1):19–29. MR(E)

Ruttan, Vernon W., and Yujiro Hayami (1984), "Toward a Theory of Induced Institutional Innovation," *Journal of Development Studies*, 203–223. AE(N)

Ryan, Bryce (1948), "A Study in Technological Diffusion," *Rural Sociology*, 13:273–285. RS(E)

Ryan, Bryce, and Neal C. Gross (1943), "The Diffusion of Hybrid Seed Corn in Two Iowa Communities," *Rural Sociology*, 8:15–24. RS(E)

―――― (1950), *Acceptance and Diffusion of Hybrid Corn Seed in Two Iowa Communities*, Ames, Iowa Agricultural Experiment Station, Research Bulletin 372, pp. 665–666, 679. RS(E)

Sadowsky, Donald, and Carol Kunzel (1986), "Acquisition of Knowledge about an Innovation in Patient Management: Impact of Dentists' Attitudes and Orientations," *Knowledge*, 7(3):291–302. PH(E)

Sahel, Devendra (1981), *Patterns of Technological Innovation*, Reading, Massachusetts, Addison-Wesley. GE(N)

Sampford, Karen Ann (1984), "Coronary Intensive Care for Cardiac Infarction: A Case Study of the Diffusion of High Technology in the Australian Hospital Sector," *Prometheus*, 2(1):73–92. GE(E)

Saren, M.A. (1984), "A Classification and Review of Models of the Intra-Firm Innovation Process," *R&D Management*, 14(1):11–24. MR(N)

Saunders, C., and J. Jones (1989), "Temporal Sequences in Information Acquisition for Decision-Making: A Focus on Source and Medium," *Academy of Management Review*, 15(1):29–46. MR(E)

Savage, Robert L. (1985a), "Diffusion Research Traditions and the Spread of Policy Innovation in a Federal System," *Publius*, 15:1–27. PS(E)

——— (1985b), "When a Policy's Time Has Come: Cases of Rapid Policy Diffusion, 1983–1984," *Publius*, 15:111–125. PS(E)

Scannel, J.G., and others (1971), "Optimal Resources for Cardiac Surgery," *Circulation*, 221–236. U(E)

Scheirer, M.A. (1987), "The Adoption and Implementation of Fluoride Mouthrinse Program: Descriptive Results from School Districts," *Journal of Public Health Dentistry*, 47:98–107. O(E)

Schelling, Thomas C. (1978), *Micromotives and Macrobehavior*, New York, Norton, pp. 13, 89, 94.

Schmittlein, David C., and Vijay Mahajan (1982), "Maximum Likelihood Estimation for an Innovation Diffusion Model of New Product Acceptance," *Marketing Science*, 1(1):57–78. MR(E)

Schmittlein, David C., and K. Ramanathan (1981), "Binomial Innovation Diffusion Models with Dynamic Potential Adoptor Population," *Technological Forecasting and Social Change*, 20:63–87. MR(E)

——— (1982), "Polynomial Diffusion Models," *Technological Forecasting and Social Change*, 21:301–323. MR(E)

Schmitz, Andrew, and David Seckler (1970), "Merchanized Agriculture and Social Welfare: The Case of the Tomato Harvester," *American Journal of Agricultural Economics*, 52:569–577. AE(E)

Schön, Donald A. (1963), "Champions for Radical New Inventions," *Harvard Business Review*, 41:77–86. MR(E)

——— (1967), *Technology and Change: The New Heraclitus*, New York, Delacorte Press.

Schroeder, R.G. (1989), "The Development of Innovation Ideas," in Andrew H. Van de Ven, H.A. Angle, and M. Scott Poole (eds.), *Research on the Management of Innovation: The Minnesota Studies*, New York, Ballinger/Harper & Row. MR(E)

Schroeder, R.G., Andrew H. Van de Ven, G.D. Scudder, and D. Polley (1986), "Managing Innovation and Change Processes: Findings from the Minnesota Innovation Research Program," *Agribusiness Management*, 2(40):501–523. MR(E)

Schumpeter, Joseph A. (1950), *Capitalism, Socialism, and Democracy*, New York, Harper and Row. GE(N)

Schwalbe, Ted (1976), "A Study in Public Policy: The Santa Monica Freeway Diamond Lane Experiment," Unpublished paper, Los Angeles, University of Southern California, Annenberg School for Communication. C(E)

Scott, Richard (1990), "Innovation in Medical Care Organizations: A Synthetic Review," *Medical Care Review*, 47(2):165–192. GS(N)

Seekins, Tom, and Stephen B. Fawcett (1984), "Planned Diffusion of Social Technologies for Community Groups," in S.C. Palne, G.T. Bellamy, and B. Wilcox (eds.), *Human Services that Work: From Innovation to Standard Practice*, Baltimore, Carl H. Brooks. O(E)

Shannon, Claude E., and Warren Weaver (1949), *The Mathematical Theory of Communication*, Urbana, University of Illinois Press.

Sharif, M.N., and K. Ramnathan (1981), "Binomial Innovation Diffusion Models with Dynamic Potential Adoptor Population," *Technological Forecasting and Social Change*, 20:63–87. IE(E)

——— (1982), "Polynomial Innovation Diffusion Models," *Technological Forecasting and Social Change*, 21:301–323. IE(E)

Sharp, Lauriston (1952), "Steel Axes for Stone Age Australians," in Edward H. Spicer (ed.), *Human Problems in Technological Change*, New York, Russell Sage Foundation, pp. 69–72. A(E)

Shaw, Robin N., and Anna Bodi (1986), "Diffusion of Product Code Scanning Systems," *Industrial Marketing Management*, 15:225–235. MR(E)

Sheff, David (1993), *Game Over: How Nintendo Zapped an American Industry, Captured Your Dollars, and Enslaved Your Children*, New York, Random House. O(E)

Shiller, Robert J., and John Pound (1989), "Survey Evidence of Diffusion of Interest and Information among Investors," *Journal of Economic Behavior and Organization*, 12:47–66. GE(N)

Shingi, Prakash M. (1981), "Agriculture Technology and the Issue of Unequal Distribution of Rewards: An Indian Case Study," *Rural Sociology*, 46:430–445. RS(E)

Shingi, Prakash M., and Bella Mody (1976), "The Communication Effects Gap: A Field Experiment on Television and Agricultural Ignorance in India," *Communication Research*, 3:171–193. MR(E)

Shorett, Jean Elizabeth (1986), *Residential Energy Conservation: A Threshold Model*, Ph.D. Thesis, Ann Arbor, University of Michigan. O(E)

Shrave, S.R., J.P. Lecaczky, and D.P. Gaver (1984), "Optimal Consumptions for Diffusion with Absorbing and Reflecting Barriers," *SIAM Journal of Control and Optimization*, 22:55–75. U(E)

Sigelman, Lee, Philip W. Roeder, and Carol K. Sigelman (1981), "Social Service Innovations in the American States: Deinstitutionalization of the Mentally Retarded," *Social Science Quarterly*, 62(3):503–515. PS(E)

Silk, Alvin, and M. Kalwen (1982), "Measuring Influence in Organizational Purchase Decisions," *Journal of Marketing Research*, 19:165–181. MR(E)

Sill, Maurice L. (1958), *Personal, Situational, and Communicational Factors Associated with the Farm Practice Adoption Process*, Ph.D. Thesis, University Park, Pennsylvania State University. RS(E)

Silver, Steven D. (1984), "A Simple Mathematical Theory of Innovative Behavior: A Comment," *Journal of Consumer Research*, 10(3):441–444. MR(E)

Silverman, Leslie J., and Wilfrid C. Bailey (1961), *Trends in the Adoption of Recommended Farm Practices*, State College, Mississippi Agricultural Experiment Station Bulletin 617. RS(E)

Simmel, Georg (1964), *The Sociology of Georg Simmel*, translated by Kurt H. Wolf, New York, Free Press, pp. 404–405. Originally published in 1908. GS(N)

Simonds, Kenneth (1986), "Marketing as Innovation: The Eighth Paradigm," *Journal of Management Studies*, 23(5):479–499. MR(N)

Simon, Herman, and Karl-Heinz Sebastan (1987), "Diffusion and Advertising: The German Telephone Campaign," *Management Science*, 33(4):451–466. MR(E)

Skiadas, Christos (1985), "Two Generalized Rational Models for Forecasting Innovation Diffusion," *Technological Forecasting and Social Change*, 27:39–61. MR(E)

———— (1986), "Innovation Diffusion Models Expressing Asymmetry and/or Positively or Negatively Influencing Forces," *Technological Forecasting and Social Change*, 30(12):313–330. MR(E)

Sloan, Frank, and others (1986), "Diffusion of Surgical Technology: An Exploratory Study," *Journal of Health Economics*, 5:31–61. U(E)

Smith, Ann Crowley, and Delbert A. Taebel (1985), "Administrative Innovation in Municipal Government," *International Journal of Public Administration*, 7(2):149–177. PS(E)

Smith, Douglas K., and Robert C. Alexander (1988), *Fumbling the Future: How Xerox Invented, and Then Ignored, the First Personal Computer*, New York, Morrow.

Soete, Luc (1985), "International Diffusion of Technology, Industrial Development and Technological Leapfrogging," *World Development*, 13(3):409–422. MR(E)

Soete, Luc, and Roy Turner (1984), "Technological Diffusion and the Rate of Technological Change," *Economic Journal*, 94:612–623. MR(E)

Sommers, David G., and Ted L. Napier (1993), "Comparison of Amish and Non-Amish Farmers: A Diffusion/Farm-Structure Perspective," *Rural Sociology*, 58(1):130–145. RS(E)

Sommers, R. (1980), "The Adoption of Nuclear Power Generation," *Journal of Economics*, 11(1):283–291. GE(E)

Sonis, Michael (1986), "Unified Theory of Innovation Diffusion, Dynamic Choice of Alternatives, Ecological Dynamics and Urban/Regional Growth and Decline," *Ricerche Economiche*, 40:696–723. MR(E)

Soumerai, Stephen B., and Jerry Avorn (1990), "Principles of Educational Outreach ('Academic Detailing') to Improve Clinical Decision Making," *Journal of American Medical Association*, 263(4):549–556. O(N)

Sounder, William E., and M.A. Quaddus (1982), "A Decision Modeling Approach to Forecasting the Diffusion of Long-Wall Mining Technologies," *Technological Forecasting and Social Change*, 21:1–14. MR(E)

Sparkes, Vernone M., and NamJun Kang (1986), "Public Reactions to Cable Television: Time in the Diffusion Process," *Journal of Broadcasting and Electronic Media*, 30(2):213–229. C(E)

Spence, A. Michael (1981), "The Learning Curve and Competition," *Bell Journal of Economics*, 12:49–70. GE(N)

Spicer, Edward H. (ed.)(1952), *Human Problems in Technological Change*, New York, Russell Sage Foundation. A(E)

Sriniwasan, V., and Charlotte H. Mason (1986), "Nonlinear Least Squares Estimation of New Product Diffusion Models," *Marketing Science*, 5(2):169–178. MR(E)

Srivastava, Rajendra K., Vijay Mahajan, Sridhar N. Ramaswami, and Joseph Cherian (1985), "A Multi-Attribute Diffusion Model for Forecasting the Adoption of Investment Alternatives for Consumers," *Technological Forecasting and Social Change*, 28:325–333. MR(E)

Star, Shirley A., and H.G. Hughes (1950), "Report on an Education Campaign: The Cincinnati Plan for the United Nations," *American Journal of Sociology*, 55:389–400.

Steckler, A., and others (1986), "The Importance of School District Policies in the Disseminations of Tobacco Use Curricula in North California Schools," *Family and Communication Health*, 12(3):14–25. PH(E)

Steinberg, Earl P., Jane E. Sisk, and Katherine E. Locke (1985a), "X-Ray CT and Magnetic Resonance Imagers: Diffusion Patterns and Policy Issues," *New England Journal of Medicine*, 313(14):859–864. O(E)

——— (1985b), "The Diffusion of Magnetic Resonance Imagers in the United States and Worldwide," *International Journal of Technology Assessment in Health Care*, 1:499–514. PH(E)

Stevens, Robert E., William E. Warren, and Rinne T. Martin (1989), "Nonadoptors of Automatic Teller Machines," *Akron Business and Economic Review*, 20(3):55–63. MR(E)

Stewart, Charles T., Jr. (1987), "Technology Transfer vs. Diffusion: A Conceptual Clarification," *Journal of Technology Transfer*, 12(1):71–78. GE(N)

Stofferahn, Curtis W., and Peter K. Korsching (1980), *Communication, Diffusion, and Adoption of Innovations: A Bibliographical Update*, Monticello, Illinois, Vance Bibliographies. RS(N)

Stolz, Stephanie B. (1981), "Adoption of Innovation from Applied Behavioral Research: 'Does Anybody Care?'" *Journal of Applied Behavior Analysis*, 14:491–505. PH(E)

Stone, John T. (1952), *How Country Agricultural Agents Teach*, East Lansing, Michigan State University, Agricultural Extension Service, Mimeo Bulletin. RS(E)

Stoneman, Paul (1981), "Intra-Firm Diffusion, Bayesian Learning and Profitability," *Economic Journal*, 91(6):375–388. GE(E)

——— (1985), "Technological Diffusion: The Viewpoint of Economic Theory," *Ricerche Economiche*, 40:585–606. GE(E)

Stoneman, Paul, and N. J. Ireland (1982), "The Role of Supply Factors in the Diffusion of New Process Technology," *Economic Journal*, 93(2):66–78. GE(E)

Strang, David (1990), "From Dependency to Sovereignty: An Event History Analysis of Decolonization 1870–1987," *American Sociological Review*, 55:846–860. GE(E)

——— (1991), "Adding Social Structures to Diffusion Models: An Event History Framework," *Sociological Methods and Research*, 19:324–353. GS(E)

Strang, David, and John W. Meyer (1993), "Institutional Conditions for Diffusion," *Theory and Society*, 22:487–511. GS(N)

Strang, David, and Nancy Brandon Tuma (1993), "Spatial and Temporal Heterogeneity in Diffusion," *American Journal of Sociology*, 99(3):614–619. GS(E)

Strock, D.W., and S.R.S. Varadham (1979), *Multidimension Diffusion Processes*, Berlin, Springer. G(E)

Sultan, Fareena, John U. Farley, and Donald R. Lehmann (1990), "A Meta-Analysis of Diffusion Models," *Journal of Marketing Research*, 37:70–77. MR(E)

Summers, Gene F. (1983), *Technology and Social Change in Rural Areas: A Festschrift for Eugene A. Wilkening*, Boulder, Westview Press. RS(N)

Takeshita, John Y. (1964), "Taiwan: The Taichung Program of Prepregnancy Health," *Studies in Family Planning*, 4:10–12. PH(E)

―――― (1966), "Lessons Learned from Family Planning Studies in Taiwan and Korea," in Bernard Berelson and others (eds.), *Family Planning and Population Programs*, University of Chicago Press. PH(E)

Takeshita, John, and others (1964), "A Study of Effectiveness of the Prepregnancy Health Program in Taiwan," *Eugenics Quarterly*, 2:222–233. PH(E)

Talaysum, Adil T. (1985), "Understanding the Diffusion Process for Technology-Intensive Products," *Research Management*, 28:22–26. MR(E)

Tanny, S.M., and N.A. Derzko (1988), "Innovation and Imitators in Innovation Diffusion Modeling," *Journal of Forecasting*, 7(4):225–234. MR(E)

Tarde, Gabriel (1903), *The Laws of Imitation*, translated by Elsie Clews Parsons, New York, Holt; reprinted 1969, University of Chicago Press, pp. 4, 27, 64, 140, 178, 221. GS(E)

Taylor, James A. (1982), *People, Policies, and Practices: Examining the Chain of School Improvement*, Volume 7, Massachusetts, The Network. C(E)

Teece, David J. (1980), "The Diffusion of an Administrative Innovation," *Management Science*, 26(5):464–470. MR(E)

―――― (1986), "Profiting from Technological Innovation: Implications for Integration, Collaboration, Licensing and Public Policy," *Research Policy*, 15:285–305. MR(E)

Teisberg, E.O. (1992), "McCaw Cellular Communications, Inc. in 1990," *Harvard Business Review*, 53:127–133. MR(E)

Teotia, A.P.S., and P.S. Raju (1986), "Forecasting the Market Penetration of New Technologies Using a Combination of Economic Cost and Diffusion Models," *Journal of Product Innovation Management*, 3(12):225–237. MR(E)

Tetzeli, Rick (December 27, 1993), "Videogames: Serious Fun," *Fortune*, 128:110–116. O(E)

―――― (March 7, 1994), "The Internet and Your Business," *Fortune*, 129:86–96. O(E)

Thayer, William R., and W.C. Wolf, Jr. (1988), "The Generalizability of Selected Knowledge Diffusion/Utilization Know-How," *Knowledge*, 5(4):447–467. E(E)

Thomas, John K., Howard Ladewig, and William Alex McIntosh (1990), "The Adoption of Integrated Pest Management Practices among Texas Cotton Growers," *Rural Sociology*, 55(3):395–410. RS(E)

Thomas, Robert J. (1985), "Estimating Market Growth for New Products: An Analogical Diffusion Model Approach," *Journal of Product Innovation Management*, 2(3):45–55. MR(E)

Thomas, W.I., and Florian Znaniecki (1927), *The Polish Peasant in Europe and America*, New York, Knopf, p. 81.

Thompson, Gerald L., and Jinn-Tsair Teng (1984), "Optimal Pricing and Advertising Policies for New Product Oligopoly Models," *Marketing Science*, 3:146–168. MR(E)

Thompson, James D. (1967), *Organization in Action*, New York, McGraw-Hill.

Tichenor, Philip J., and others (1970), "Mass Media Flow and Differential Growth in Knowledge," *Public Opinion Quarterly*, 34:159–170.

Tigert, Douglas, and Behrooz Farivar (1981), "The Bass New Product Growth Model: A

Sensitivity Analysis for a High Technology Product," *Journal of Marketing*, 45:81–90. MR(E)

Tolbert, Pamela S., and Lynne G. Zucken (1983), "Institutional Sources of Change in the Formal Structure of Organizations: The Diffusion of Civil Services Practices," *Administrative Science Quarterly*, 28:22–39. GS(E)

Tornatzky, Louis G., and Katherine J. Klein (1981), *Innovation Characteristics and Innovation Adoption-Implementation: A Meta-Analysis of Findings*, Washington, D.C., National Science Foundation, Division of Industrial Science and Technological Innovation, p. 5. P(N)

Tornatzky, Louis G., and Katherine J. Klein (1982), "Innovation Characteristics and Adoption-Implementation: A Meta-Analysis of Findings," *IEEE Transactions on Engineering Management*, EM-29(1):28–45. P(N)

Tornatzky, Louis G., and Michele Fleischer (1990), *The Process of Technological Innovation*, Lexington, MA, Lexington Books. P(N)

Tornatzky, Louis, G., Esther O. Fergus, Joseph W. Avellar, and George W. Fairweather (1980), *Innovation and Social Process: A National Experiment in Implementing Social Technology*, NY, Pergamon Press. P(N)

Tushman, M.L., and Philip Anderson (1986), "Technological Discontinuties and Organizational Environments," *Administrative Science Quarterly*, 31:439–465. MR(E)

Tushman, M.L., and R.R. Nelson (1990), "Introduction: Technology, Organizations, and Innovation," *Administrative Science Quarterly*, 35(1):1–8. MR(N)

Tyre, Marcie J., and Oscar Hauptman (1992), "Effectiveness of Organizational Responses to Technological Change in the Production Process," *Organization Science*, 3(3):301–319. MR(E)

Tyre, Marcie J., and Wanda J. Orlikowski (1994), "Windows of Opportunity: Temporal Patterns of Technological Adaptation in Organizations," *Organization Science*, 5(1):98–118. MR(E)

Unwin, Tim (1988), "The Propagation of Agrarian Change in North-West Portugal," *Journal of Rural Studies*, 4(3):223–238. G(E)

Urban, Glen L., and Eric Von Hippel (1988), "Lead User Analysis for the Development of New Industrial Products," *Management Science*, 74(5):569–582. MR(E)

Uttal, Bo (September 5, 1983), "The Lab that Ran Away from Xerox," *Fortune*, pp. 67.

Valente, Thomas W. (1991), *Thresholds and the Critical Mass in Mathematical Models of the Diffusion of Innovation*, Ph.D. Thesis, Los Angeles, University of Southern California. C(E)

—— (1993), "Diffusion of Innovation and Policy Decision-Making," *Journal of Communication*, 43(1):30–41. C(E)

—— (1994), *Network Models of the Diffusion of Innovations*, Creskill, NJ, Hampton Press. C(E)

Valente, Thomas W., and Everett M. Rogers (1995), "The Origins and Development of the Diffusion of Innovations: Paradigm as an Example of Scientific Growth," *Science Communication*, 1. C(N)

Van den Ban, A.W. (1963), *Hoe Vinden Nieuee Landbouwmethodeningand* (How a New Practice Is Introduced), *Landbouwvoorlichting*, 20:227–239. RS(E)

Van de Ven, Andrew H. (1980), "Problem Solving, Planning, and Innovation. Part II: Speculations for Theory and Practice," *Human Relations*, 33(11):775–779. MR(E)

——— (1986), "Central Problems in the Management of Innovation," *Management Science*, 32(5):590–607. MR(E)

——— (1990), "The Process of Adopting Innovations in Organizations: Three Cases of Hospital Innovations," in B. Guile, E. Laumann, and D. Gerald Nadler (eds.), *Designing for Technical Change*, Washington, D.C., National Academy Press. MR(E)

——— (1991), "Managing Processes of Organizational Innovation," in George P. Huber (ed.), *Organizational Change, Redesign, and Performance*, New York, Oxford University Press. MR(E)

Van de Ven, Andrew H., and Harold L. Angle (1989), "Suggestions for Managing the Innovation Journey," Minneapolis, University of Minnesota, Carlson School of Management, Advance Management Practices Paper 9. MR(N)

Van de Ven, Andrew H., H.A. Angle, and M. Scott Poole (eds.) (1989), *Research on the Management of Innovation: The Minnesota Studies*, New York, Ballinger/Harper & Row. MR(E)

Van de Ven, Andrew H., and Everett M. Rogers (1988), "Innovations and Organizations: Critical Perspectives," *Communication Research*, 15(5):632–651. MR(N)

Van de Ven, Andrew H., S. Venkatraman, R. Garud, and D. Polley (1989), "Process of New Business Creation in Different Organizational Settings," in Andrew H. Van de Ven, H.A. Angle, and M. Scott Poole (eds.), *Research on the Management of Innovation: The Minnesota Studies*, New York, Ballinger/Harper & Row. MR(E)

Van de Ven, Andrew H., and Y. Chu (1989), "A Psychometric Assessment of the Minnesota Innovation Survey," in Andrew H. Van de Ven, H.A. Angle, and M. Scott Poole (eds.), *Research on the Management of Innovation: The Minnesota Studies*, New York, Ballinger/Harper & Row. MR(E)

Van Es, J.C. (1982), "The Adoption/Diffusion Tradition Applied to Resource Conservation: Inappropriate Use of Existing Knowledge," Paper presented at the Rural Sociological Society, San Francisco. RS(E)

Van Es, J.C., and Theodore Tsoukalas (1987), "Kinship Arrangements and Innovativeness: A Comparison of Palouse and Prairie Findings," *Rural Sociology*, 52(3):389–397. RS(E)

Venkatraman, Meera P., and Linda L. Price (1989), "Differentiating Between Cognitive and Sensory Innovativeness: Concepts, Measurements, and Implications," Cambridge, MIT, Sloan School of Management, Working Paper 89-08. MR(E)

Von Hippel, Eric (1976), "The Dominant Role of Users in the Scientific Instrument Innovation Process," *Research Policy*, 5(3):212–239. MR(E)

——— (1982), "Get New Products," *Harvard Business Review*, 60:117–122. MR(E)

——— (1988), *The Sources of Innovation*, NY, Oxford University Press, p. 4. MR(E)

——— (1990), "Task Partitioning: An Innovation Process Variable," *Research Policy*, 19:407–418. MR(N)

Von Hippel, Eric, and Stan N. Finkelstein (1978), "Product Designs Which Encourage—or Discourage—Related Innovation by Users: An Analysis of Innovation in Automated Clinical Chemistry Analyzer," Cambridge, Massachusetts Institute of Technology, Sloan School of Management, Working Paper WP 1011-78. MR(E)

——— (1979), "Analysis of Innovation in Automated Clinical Chemistry Analyzers," *Science and Public Policy*, 6:24–37. MR(E)

Voss, Chris A. (1985), "The Need for a Field Study of Implementation of Innovations," *Journal of Product Innovation Management*, 4:266–271. MR(E)

—— (1988), "Implementation: A Key Issue in Manufacturing Technology: The Need for a Field of Study," *Research Policy*, 17:55–63. MR(N)

Wagener, Donald J., and others (1981), "Cancian's 'Upper-Middle Class Conservatism' Thesis: An Application to Noncommercial Agricultural Innovations," Paper presented at the Rural Sociological Society, Guelph, Canada. RS(E)

Walker, Jack L. (1966), "The Diffusion of Innovations Among the American States," *American Political Science Review*, 63:880–899. PS(E)

—— (1971), "Innovation in State Policies," in Herbert Jacob and Kenneth N. Vines (eds.), *Politics in the American States: A Comparative Analysis*, Boston, Little Brown, pp. 358, 381. PS(E)

—— (1973), "Comment: Problems in Research on the Diffusion of Policy Innovations," *American Political Science Review*, 67:1186–1191. PS(N)

—— (1976), "Setting the Agenda in the U.S. Senate: A Theory of Problem Selection," Ann Arbor, University of Michigan, Institute of Public Policy Studies, Discussion Paper 94, pp. 26–32. PS(N)

—— (1977), "Setting the Agenda in the U.S. Senate: A Theory of Problem Selection," *British Journal of Political Science*, 7:423–445. PS(N)

Walker, Thomas S., and K.G. Kshirsagar (1985), "The Village Impact of Machine Threshing and Implications for Technology Development in the Semi-Arid Tropics of Peninsular India," *Journal of Development Studies*, 21:215–231. U(E)

Walling, Victor C., Jr. (1984), *VALS and Innovations*, Menlo Park, CA, SRI International, Values and Lifestyles Program, CA. C(E)

Warner, Kenneth E. (1974), "The Need for Some Innovative Concepts of Innovation: An Examination of Research on the Diffusion of Innovations," *Policy Sciences*, 5:433–451. MS(E)

Wearing, C.H. (1988), "Evaluating the IPM Implementation Process," *Annual Review of Entomology*, 33:17–38. O(E)

Weaver-Larisgy, Ruth Ann, and Barbara Sweeny (1984), "Communication During Assassination Attempts: Diffusion of Information in Attacks on President Reagan and the Pope," *Southern Speech Communication Journal*, 49:258–276. C(E)

Webber, M.J., and A.E. Joseph (1978), "Spatial Diffusion Processes 1: A Model and an Approximation Method," *Environment and Planning A*, 10:651–665. G(E)

Webber, M.J., and A.E. Joseph (1979), "Spatial Diffusion Processes 2: Numerical Analysis," *Environment and Planning A*, 11:335–347. G(E)

Weber, Max (1958), *The Protestant Ethic and the Spirit of Capitalism*, New York, Scribner's, pp. 180–181 .

Weibull, Lennart, Rutger Lindahl, and Karl Eric Rosengreen (1987), "News Diffusion in Sweden: The Role of the Media," *European Journal of Communication*, 2:143–170. C(E)

Weimann, Gabriel (1982), "On the Importance of Marginality: One More Step Into the Two-Step Flow of Communication," *American Sociological Review*, 47:764–773. GS(E)

Weimer, D.L. (1980), "Federal Intervention in the Process of Innovation in Local Public Agencies: A Focus on Organizational Incentives," *Public Policy*, 28(1):93–116. PS(E)

Weinstein, Jay, and John R. McIntyre (1986), "Multinational Corporations and the Diffusion of World Standards: A Theoretical Exploration," *Studies in Comparative International Development*, 21:51–54. GS(E)

Weiss, Andrew R., and Philip H. Birnbaum (1989), "Technological Infrastructure and the Implementation of Technological Strategies," *Management Science*, 35(8):1013–1025. GE(E)

Welch, Susan, and Kay Thompson (1980), "The Impact of Federal Incentives on State Innovation," *American Journal of Political Science*, 24(4):715–729. PS(E)

Wellin, Edward (1955), "Water Boiling in a Peruvian Town," in Benjamin D. Paul (ed.), *Health, Culture and Community*, New York, Russell Sage Foundation. A(E)

West, Patrick C. (1983), "Collective Adoption of Natural Resource Practices in Developing Nations," *Rural Sociology*, 48(1):44–59. RS(E)

Westermarck, Harri (1987), "An Evaluation of the Extensionists' Rate of Symbolic Adoption of Profitable and Non-Profitable Innovations in Four Nordic Countries," *Acta Agriculture Scandinavia*, 37:207–250. RS(E)

Whiteside, T. (1972), *The Investigation of Ralph Nader: General Motors vs. One Determined Man*, New York, Arbor House.

Whyte, William H. Jr. (1954), "The Web of Word of Mouth," *Fortune*, 50:140–143, 204–212.

Wiebe, Gerhard D. (1952), "Merchandising Commodities and Citizenship on Television," *Public Opinion Quarterly*, 15:679–691.

Wildemuth, Barbara M. (1992), "An Empirically Grounded Model of the Adoption of Intellectual Technologies," *Journal of the American Society for Information Science*, 43(3):210–224. O(E)

Wilkening, Eugene A. (1952), *Acceptance of Improved Farm Practices in Three Coastal Plains Counties*, Raleigh, North Carolina Agricultural Experiment Station Bulletin 98. RS(E)

——— (1958), "Joint Decision-Making in Farm Families as a Function of Status and Role," *American Sociological Review*, 23(2):187–192. RS(E)

Wilkening, Eugene A., and others (1969), "Stratification and Innovative Behavior: A Reexamination of Cancian's Curvilinear Hypothesis," Paper presented at the Rural Sociological Society, San Francisco. RS(E)

Williams, Frederick R., Ronald E. Rice, and Everett M. Rogers (1988), *Research Methods and the New Media*, New York, Free Press. C(N)

Wind, Yoram, and others (1982), "Industrial Product Diffusion by Market Segment," *Industrial Marketing Management*, 11:1–8. MR(E)

Winer, Russell S. (1985), "A Price Vector Model of Demand for Consumer Durables: Preliminary Developments," *Marketing Science*, 4:74–90. MR(E)

Winett, R.A. (1986), "Diffusion from a Behavioral Systems Perspective," in R.A. Winett (ed.), *Information and Behavior: Systems of Influence*, Hillsdale, NJ, Erlbaum. U(N)

Wissler, Clark (1914), "The Influence of the Horse in the Development of Plains Culture," *American Anthropologist*, 16:1–25. A(E)

——— (1923), *Man and Culture*, New York, Thomas Y. Crowell, p. 111–129. A(E)

Wolf, W.C., Jr. (1981), "Selected Knowledge Diffusion/Utilization Know-How," *Knowledge*, 2(3):331–340. E(N)

Wozniak, Gregory D. (1984), "The Adoption of Interrelated Innovations: A Human Capital Approach," *Review of Economics and Statistics*, 66:70–79. GE(E)

Wulf, Kathleen M. (1987), "A Study of the Implementation of the D.A.R.E. Program in Law Enforcement Agencies," Paper presented to the Crime Prevention Advisory Council, University of Southern California, School of Education, Los Angeles, CA. E(E)

Zaltman, Gerald, Robert Duncan, and Jonny Holbek (1973), *Innovations and Organizations*, New York, Wiley and Sons. MR(E)

Zhou, Xueguang (1993), "Occupational Power, State Capacities, and Diffusion of Licensing in the American States, 1890 to 1950," *American Sociological Review*, 58:536–552. GS(E)

Zirger, B.J., and M.A. Maidique (1990), "A Model of New Product Development: An Empirical Test," *Management Science*, 36(7):867–883. MR(E)

Zmud, Robert W. (1984), "An Examination of 'Push-Pull' Theory Applied to Process Innovation in Knowledge Work," *Management Science*, 30(6):727–738. MR(E)

NAME INDEX

SUBJECT INDEX

509

ABOUT THE AUTHOR

Everett M. Rogers is professor and chair of the Department of Communication & Journalism at the University of New Mexico. A past president of the International Communications Association, he is the author of *A History of Communication Study* (Free Press, 1994), *Communication Technology* (Free Press, 1986), and several other widely acclaimed books and articles on communication and innovation.